TALES AND SKETCHES
Volume 1: 1831–1842

E. E. Coleman
1873

TALES

OF THE

GROTESQUE AND ARABESQUE.

BY EDGAR A. POE.

Seltsamen tochter Jovis
Seinem schosskinde
Der *Phantasie.*
GOETHE.

IN TWO VOLUMES.

VOL. I.

PHILADELPHIA:
LEA AND BLANCHARD.
1840.

Edgar Allan Poe

TALES AND SKETCHES

Volume 1: 1831–1842

EDITED BY

THOMAS OLLIVE MABBOTT

with the assistance of Eleanor D. Kewer
and Maureen C. Mabbott

UNIVERSITY OF ILLINOIS PRESS

Urbana and Chicago

Previously published as *Collected Works of Edgar Allan Poe,*
volume 2: *Tales and Sketches, 1831–1842*

Library of Congress Cataloging-in-Publication Data
Poe, Edgar Allan, 1809–1849.
[Selections. 2000]
Tales and sketches / Edgar Allan Poe ;
edited by Thomas Ollive Mabbott with the assistance of
Eleanor D. Kewer and Maureen C. Mabbott. — 1st Illinois pbk.
p.   cm.
Originally published as v. 2–3 of: Collected works of Edgar Allan Poe.
Cambridge, Mass. : Belknap Press of Harvard University Press, 1978.
Includes bibliographical references and index.
Contents: v. 1. 1831–1842 — v. 2. 1843-1849.
ISBN 0-252-06922-6 (v. 1 : alk. paper)
ISBN 0-252-06923-4 (v. 2 : alk. paper)
1. Fantasy literature, American. I. Mabbott, Thomas Ollive, 1898–1968.
II. Kewer, Eleanor D. III. Mabbott, Maureen Cobb.
IV. Poe, Edgar Allan, 1809–1849. Works. 1969. V. Title.
PS2612.M33   2000
813'.3—dc21   00-039217

P 5 4 3 2 1

ACKNOWLEDGMENTS

In completing Volumes II and III of the *Collected Works of Edgar Allan Poe* the assisting editors have tried to keep faithfully to the task to which they were assigned — the preparation of Mr. Mabbott's typescript for the press, in the way he would have wished it done. In his edition of Poe's *Works* he emphasizes sources and records rather than his own opinions. This emphasis has made it possible to complete his work on the *Tales* by verifying and fleshing out references, and by following closely his leads. In addition, Poe scholarship since his death in 1968 has been studied with his views for this edition in mind, and some new references have been added. During the more than fifty years of his work on Poe, Mr. Mabbott reserved some of the results of that work for his edition. Therefore, while credit has been given to authors presenting material he did not have, it has not been feasible to recognize those who have independently discovered and published material already in his notes.

As in Volume I, help on particular points is usually acknowledged in the appropriate notes, but a number of individuals and institutions must be mentioned for their general helpfulness and guidance throughout the work. First among these are Clarence Gohdes and Rollo G. Silver, specifically named by Mr. Mabbott as "guardians of the Poe." That they have been. All during the work they have given counsel and encouragement.

Burton R. Pollin, collaborating editor with Mr. Mabbott for the remaining volumes of this edition, has given of his time and shared his wide knowledge of Poe scholarship. We particularly thank him for his careful reading of the proofs of the two volumes of *Tales and Sketches.*

Throughout his work Mr. Mabbott often expressed his appreciation of libraries and librarians. The latter, he felt, had a special understanding and sympathy with his emphasis on facts in the study of his author. The continuity of their interest and helpfulness has been one of the greatest resources in continuing his work. Thus it is

ACKNOWLEDGMENTS

with a warm sense of appreciation and gratitude that our thanks go to Lola L. Szladits of the Henry W. and Albert A. Berg Collection, Maud Cole of the Rare Book Division, and Paul R. Rugen in the Manuscript Division, of the New York Public Library; James Gregory of the New-York Historical Society; Herbert Cahoon of the Pierpont Morgan Library; Howell J. Heaney of the Free Library of Philadelphia; Alexander P. Clark at Princeton University; John H. Stanley of Brown University, and Carey S. Bliss at the Henry E. Huntington Library and Art Gallery. The kindness of June Moll, formerly librarian of the Miriam Lutcher Stark Library at the University of Texas, has been continued by F. W. Roberts of the Humanities Research Center Library of that University. Marcus A. McCorison of the American Antiquarian Society, W. H. Bond of the Houghton Library, Harvard University, and Randolph Church formerly of the Virginia State Library, have all been helpful for these volumes as for the first.

We acknowledge with appreciation the help we have received from Evelyn A. Hanley, Craig B. Brush, John E. Reilly, and Benjamin Franklin Fisher IV. We thank George E. Hatvary who assisted on this edition from 1965 to 1968 when some of these tales were being prepared; and David K. Jackson for reading the proofs of Volume III. We are especially grateful to the Reverend Dom Anselm Strittmatter, O.S.B. (of St. Anselm's Abbey, Washington, D.C.), long Mr. Mabbott's friend, to whom we have turned for help with classical references.

Michael Papantonio of the Seven Gables Bookshop has never failed to respond helpfully when called upon; again, these volumes, like the first, are indebted to H. Bradley Martin for his generous permission to use materials from his fine collection of Poeana.

We wish to thank our friends at the University of Iowa: for general support and help in many ways, Willard L. Boyd, President, Leslie W. Dunlap, Dean of Library Administration, and Frank Paluka, in charge of Special Collections, including the Thomas Ollive Mabbott Poe Collection; for checking the list of variants for Poe's tale "Ligeia," O. M. Brack, formerly in charge, and his staff at the Iowa Center for Textual Studies.

Patricia Edwards Clyne has assisted the work on this edition

ACKNOWLEDGMENTS

from the time Mr. Mabbott began to prepare Volume I for the press. A student of his, trained by him, she has been unflagging in her dedication to the task of helping to make the result of his lifelong research available in print.

Eleanor D. Kewer
Maureen C. Mabbott
October 1977

CONTENTS
Volume I

CONTENTS

CONTENTS

Volume II

TALES: 1843–1844

TALES: 1844–1845

CONTENTS

TALES: 1845–1846

TALES: 1847–1849

SOURCES OF TEXTS COLLATED

ILLUSTRATIONS

VOLUME I

VOLUME II

ILLUSTRATIONS

INTRODUCTION

I. POE AND HIS TALES

Poe's tales are his chief contribution to the literature of the world. They are — like "The Raven," which is a tale in verse — eminently translatable, and they are known in practically every major language. That Poe himself cared more for his lyric poems than for even his imaginative prose there is no doubt. His preface to *The Raven and Other Poems* (1845) suggests that he was disturbed because the tales were written "with an eye to the paltry compensations, or the more paltry commendations, of mankind." Yet in the preface to the *Tales of the Grotesque and Arabesque* (1840) he had written, "I cannot conscientiously claim indulgence on the score of hasty effort . . . These brief compositions are . . . the results of matured purpose and very careful elaboration." How meticulously he worked over his stories is known to every reader who looks through the variants collected in James A. Harrison's *Complete Works of Edgar Allan Poe* (1902) or in this edition. At the end of his career Poe seems to have regarded many of the tales as finished, and the revisions made in his last years are relatively few; but I suspect that some stories would have been further polished had time been given the author. He came to value his stories more highly, too, and in the summer of 1849 he told his young friend Susan Archer Talley that he thought he had done all he could in verse, but perhaps not yet in prose.

We first hear of Poe as a writer of prose stories in 1826, while at the University of Virginia. Little is known of them save what is given below in the discussion of "Gaffy." We hear of no prose stories as having been written at West Point, but before the end of 1831 several short stories had been composed, and at least five were submitted in a prize contest of the Philadelphia *Saturday Courier.* Although none received a prize, five tales were printed anonymously in the *Courier,* beginning in January 1832. In the summer of 1832

INTRODUCTION

Poe was in touch with Lambert A. Wilmer, who in the *Baltimore Saturday Visiter* of August 4, 1832, mentioned reading some manuscript tales by him. Wilmer gave no titles, and it is probable that Poe first conceived the scheme of his Folio Club in 1833. Eleven stories were done, he intimated, when the surviving introduction was finished. He submitted some — how many pieces must remain uncertain — to the *Visiter* contest, whose terminal date was October 1, 1833. One of the "Tales of the Folio Club" won the prize; the "MS. Found in a Bottle" appeared in the issue of October 19, and from that day Poe was never again to be obscure.

The opening up in 1835 of the *Southern Literary Messenger* as a channel of publication made it possible for him to gain a national reputation, and, as editor, to give his older stories and some specially written for the *Messenger* wide circulation. Although it was his criticisms rather than his tales that attracted attention and increased the sales of the magazine, he had now found his métier in the short story. He wrote for periodicals primarily; he wrote perhaps more when the editorial chairs of the *Messenger, Burton's,* and *Graham's* called for a monthly feature, but he wrote steadily for the annuals and magazines. Every year saw at least one new tale and sometimes several. As with the poems, although the style varied, the author's powers never flagged, and his finest things are distributed proportionately over the years.

STYLE AND MANNER

Poe's early stories are marked by extravagant and magnificent over-elaboration, and by a mixture of the serious and ludicrous suggestive of Byron's *Don Juan* and the younger Disraeli's *Vivian Grey.* At first he consciously wrote "in the manners of" other writers as he had in his poems, and just as did Robert Louis Stevenson later on. In "The Folio Club" he named some of his models plainly and others by implication. Yet he was not a slavish imitator, and even at the beginning was striking out for himself. The comic and the serious came to be separated, and the style became less elaborate. The extremely ornate Arabesque manner may derive from Bulwer and De Quincey, but it is something far less discursive, and more magnificent. Irving may be felt in places; the "Man of the Crowd" is Dickens. Others whose influence can be discerned include the obscure Miss Mercer and the forgotten Joseph C. Neal.

In mid-career, Poe's individuality powerfully asserted itself; witness "The Fall of the House of Usher" and "Ligeia." "William Wilson" was admittedly derived from a suggestion of Irving's, but is not too much like him. About 1841, after the *Tales of the Grotesque and Arabesque* had been collected, there appeared in Poe's stories a tendency toward simplicity, which he had belittled before* — and this tendency increased with every year. Ornament was not eschewed, but, in accordance with Corinna's advice to Pindar, it was now sown not by the sack, but by the handful. In his last years Poe wrote plain, straightforward, functional prose.

PRINCIPLES OF COMPOSITION

In the tales "the evident and most prominent aim of Mr. Poe is originality, either of idea, or the combination of ideas."† "I prefer commencing," he said, "with the consideration of an *effect*. Keeping originality *always* in view . . ."‡ This, I believe, was consciously his first principle. The originality of Poe's tales can hardly be overestimated. The "individuality and strangeness of his stories give them an enigmatic quality that is not readily analyzed . . . his work cannot be reduced to the materials he started from and the hints he used." His stories involve "situations like those in the derivative Gothic fiction . . . popular in *Blackwood's* and other magazines in the 1830's . . . Precise borrowings exist . . . but Poe chose to borrow some things and not others, and his stories have had lasting success, whereas his presumed models have not. These are the very considerations that lend point to source-research."§

*In a letter to Thomas W. White, April 30, 1835, Poe had written: "Nobody is more aware than I am that simplicity is the cant of the day — but take my word for it no one cares any thing about simplicity in their hearts. Believe me also, in spite of what people say to the contrary, that there is nothing easier in the world than to be extremely simple."

†The quotation is from a review of "Poe's Tales" in the *Aristidean* for October 1845, which must have been written by Dr. Thomas Dunn English after discussions with Poe, for it includes information that could only have come from Poe himself.

‡"The Philosophy of Composition," *Graham's Magazine*, April 1846, p. 163.

§Patrick F. Quinn, *The French Face of Edgar Poe* (1957), p. 219, quoted here, and on pages 607 and 661, by permission of Southern Illinois University Press, Carbondale, Illinois.

INTRODUCTION

The second principle was variety: he wrote to T. W. White, in his letter of April 30, 1835, "I propose to furnish you every month with a Tale . . . no two of these Tales will have the slightest resemblance one to the other in matter or manner." In a letter to Charles Anthon, written probably in late October 1844, he said, "Variety has been one of my chief aims." Devotion to these principles remained constant throughout his career. He did, of course, use some ideas more than once, but the combinations are always novel for him. Observe how varied are the five stories that involve ratiocination: Dupin investigates a strange crime, a real murder, and the theft of a letter, which involves only a misdemeanor; in "Thou Art the Man" a villain is caught who aimed to avoid suspicion; in "The Gold-Bug" a puzzle is solved. Of course, Poe is most usually thought of as one who treats of dangerous adventures, and probes the darkest corners of the human soul,* yet "Three Sundays in a Week" is a simple story of young love; "Eleonora" tells of devotion, forgiveness, and happy marriage; and from "The Domain of Arnheim" all strong emotion is excluded. But he does not forego originality even in these. All have singular settings.

A third principle, that of unity, "became a cardinal doctrine of [Poe's] critical theory," said A. H. Quinn,† remarking on Poe's mention, as early as 1836, of "what is rightly termed by Schlegel, 'the *unity or totality of interest*'."‡ Some six months later§ Poe declared that "unity of effect . . . is indispensable in the 'brief article'"; and six years later* he set forth what has been called his definition of the short story, formulated in the course of his own practice:

A skilful literary artist has constructed a tale. If wise, he has not fashioned his thoughts to accommodate his incidents; but having conceived, with deliberate care, a certain unique or single *effect* to be wrought out, he then invents such incidents — he then combines such events as may best aid him in establishing

---

*Edwin Fussell well said that Poe made a "restless patrol along the lines between the senses, between waking and sleep, between sanity and insanity . . . between the organic and the inorganic, between life and death" (*Frontier: American Literature and the American West*, 1965, pp. 173–174).
†Arthur Hobson Quinn, *Edgar Allan Poe: A Critical Biography* (1941), p. 244.
‡See Poe's review of Mrs. Sigourney's *Zinzendorf and Other Poems* (*SLM*, January 1836).
§Reviewing *Watkins Tottle and Other Sketches . . . By Boz* (*SLM*, June 1836).
*Reviewing Hawthorne's *Twice-Told Tales* in *Graham's Magazine* for May 1842.

this preconceived effect. If his very initial sentence tend not to the outbringing of this effect, then he has failed in his first step. In the whole composition there should be no word written, of which the tendency, direct or indirect, is not to the one pre-established design. And by such means, with such care and skill, a picture is at last painted which leaves in the mind of him who contemplates it with a kindred art, a sense of the fullest satisfaction. The idea of the tale has been presented unblemished, because undisturbed; and this is an end unattainable by the novel.

My friend Floyd Stovall, commenting on Poe's "major contribution to the development of the short story as a literary type," summarized much in one sentence: "His own special creation was the story having but one main character and one main incident and producing in the mind of the reader a single impression or effect."†

IMAGINATION, FANCY, FANTASY, AND HUMOR

As he grew older, Poe formed a definite theory about imagination, fancy, fantasy, and humor. His essay on N. P. Willis in the *Broadway Journal,* January 18, 1845,‡ should be read, but a brief synopsis may be given here. Poe rejects the notion of Coleridge that "Fancy combines — Imagination creates." Nothing at all creates, he says, save the thoughts of God. We may imagine a griffin, but "it is no more than a collation of known limbs — features — qualities." He further declares that:

Imagination, Fancy, Fantasy, and Humor, have in common the elements, Combination and Novelty. The Imagination is the artist of the four. From novel arrangements of old forms . . . it selects only such as are harmonious: — the result, of course, is *beauty* . . . [but] when in addition to the element of novelty, there is introduced . . . *unexpectedness* . . . the result then appertains to the Fancy . . . Carrying its errors into excess . . . Fancy is at length found impinging upon the province of *Fantasy.* The votaries of this latter delight . . . in the *avoidance* of proportion.

With this statement few will quarrel, but Poe goes on:

When . . . Fantasy seeks . . . incongruous or antagonistical elements . . . we laugh outright in recognizing Humor . . . but when either Fancy or Humor is expressed to gain an end . . . it becomes, also, pure Wit or Sarcasm, just as the purpose is well-intended or malevolent.

†See the illuminating introduction to Mr. Stovall's edition of *The Poems of Edgar Allan Poe* (1965) at page xxxiii.
‡"American Prose Writers No. 2: N. P. Willis."

INTRODUCTION

Poe's ideas concerning imagination, fancy, and fantasy are accepted by many critics; with his notions of humor few will agree. C. F. Briggs wrote that he had "an inconceivably extravagant idea of his capacities as a humorist."§ He thought combination of elements that do not belong together produced a comic effect, and so aimed at low comedy, farce, and burlesque. Brander Matthews said that "Poe had humor but not good humor"; there is little or no high comedy. In satire Poe does sometimes excel, but the makers of textbooks have tended to select only "Lionizing" from that department. To my mind the best comic piece is "The Literary Life of Thingum Bob, Esq.," but it requires for appreciation a considerable knowledge of the world of magazine publishing in the 1830's and 1840's — something few readers of our day can be expected to acquire.

MATERIALS AND TECHNIQUES

Poe said many times that the writer of stories should invent or select incidents to combine for a preconceived desired effect* Although this procedure may not have been thought out philosophically before he observed his own practice, it describes that practice in his later years. He selected far more than he invented, but it is in the mastery of combination that his genius is most strikingly exemplified.

Primarily Poe used things he found in print. Most common, probably, were accounts of incidents and events he believed to be factual. Secondly, he used obviously fictional stories. A good example of a combination of materials may be found in "The Oblong Box," where a recent crime is combined with a dramatic scene in a Byronic poem by Rufus Dawes. Occasionally Poe took up a challenge and wrote an answer to a story by somebody else, as in "MS. Found in a Bottle," or worked out completely a narrative left in some way unfinished by another, as in "A Descent into the Maelström." On a few occasions the inspiration came from pictures; "Morning on the Wissahiccon" was written to accompany an illustration; a painting by a friend was the inspiration for "The Oval Portrait."

§Briggs to Lowell, October 13, 1845, quoted by G. E. Woodberry, *Life of Edgar Allan Poe* (1909), II, 147.

*For two instances, see Poe's definition of the short story, quoted above, and "The Philosophy of Composition," in *Graham's Magazine*, April 1846.

POE AND HIS TALES

A few tales are founded on personal experiences, as is "Landor's Cottage." Poe said he based "Ligeia" on a dream, although that story has literary sources too. It is said that he also talked about writing up a delirious vision he had in his last summer,† but inspiration from drugs is not supported by any evidence at all. Of the storytellers that he may have heard, little is known. In the Old South, children frequented the kitchen and listened to stories told by the servants; there, one assumes, the poet heard talk of premature burials. Yet little even probably comes from a Negro source, unless the eyeless devil of "Bon-Bon" be related to a voodoo divinity. Poe had at least one friend who may have been a source of ideas. This was a minor magazinist and newspaper editor named Jesse E. Dow. On a letter from Poe to F. W. Thomas, May 4, 1845, Thomas wrote: "It was delightful to hear the two talk together, and to see how Poe would start at some of Dow's STRANGE notions as Poe called them."

Something may be added on Poe's choice of material, and methods of handling the sensational as well as the impossible. The letter he wrote T. W. White on April 30, 1835 contains a better expression of his purpose when he wrote his early tales than we have anywhere else. White had complained that "Berenice" was too horrible. Poe (who later eliminated several repulsive paragraphs) agreed, but he went on:

The history of all Magazines shows plainly that those which have attained celebrity were indebted for it to articles *similar in nature — to Berenice* ... in what does this nature consist? In the ludicrous heightened into the grotesque: the fearful coloured into the horrible: the witty exaggerated into the burlesque: the singular wrought out into the strange and mystical ... But whether the articles of which I speak are, or are not in bad taste is little to the purpose. To be appreciated you must be *read,* and these things are invariably sought after with avidity. They are, if you will take notice, the articles which find their way into other periodicals, and into the papers, and in this manner, taking hold upon the public mind they augment the reputation of the source where they originated ... To be sure originality is an essential in these things — great attention must be paid to style, and much labour spent in their composition, or they will degenerate into the tu[r]gid or the absurd.

Many of Poe's stories relate events that we do not believe could happen. He discussed treatment of "deviations from nature" in his

---

†See John R. Thompson's lecture, *The Genius and Character of Edgar Allan Poe,* privately printed from his manuscript by J. H. Whitty and J. H. Rindfleish, 1929.

review (*SLM*, September 1836) of Dr. Robert Montgomery Bird's anonymous novel, *Sheppard Lee*. One method pointed out "is the treating of the whole narrative in a jocular manner throughout . . . or the solution of the various absurdities by means of a dream, or something similar." But, he said, he preferred a "second general method." It consists, said he:

in a variety of points — principally in avoiding . . . *directness* of expression . . . and thus leaving much to the imagination — in writing as if the author were firmly impressed with the truth, yet astonished at the immensity of the wonders he relates, and for which, professedly, he neither claims nor anticipates credence — in minuteness of detail, especially upon points which have no immediate bearing upon the general story . . . in short, by making use of the infinity of arts which give verisimilitude to a narration — and by leaving the result as a wonder not to be accounted for . . . The reader . . . perceives and falls in with the writer's humor, and suffers himself to be borne on thereby. On the other hand what difficulty, or inconvenience, or danger can there be in leaving us uninformed of the important facts that a certain hero *did not* actually discover the elixir vitae, *could not* really make himself invisible, and *was not* either a ghost in good earnest, or a bonâ fide Wandering Jew?

He used two and perhaps all three of the themes just mentioned in his favorite tale of "Ligeia." Important as the passage quoted obviously is, critics have given it scant attention.‡ It certainly tells us what Poe's early ideal was for a kind of story of which his mastery is acknowledged.

Verisimilitude — semblance of accuracy — Poe sought with the zeal of a Daniel Defoe. He was factual about places, dates, costumes, and scenery. (This is not true of "The Bargain Lost," which is very early, but the "nonsense" disappeared when it was rewritten as "Bon-Bon.") From about 1835, Poe often made slight concessions to extremely matter-of-fact readers — in suggesting that hallucination resulting from delirium, true insanity, or the use of opium§ might account for the wonders. After 1843, he practically abandoned what could not be credible to his readers. The two stories about Mesmeric wonders are not real exceptions — Poe's readers were ready to believe them, and many did.

‡The review of *Sheppard Lee* was reprinted by Griswold in *Works* (1850), III, 261, and is in every subsequent collected edition, but major commentators seem to ignore its importance as self-revelation.

§Poe's characters use opium only when they tell a tall tale. See the comments on "Ligeia" for heroic efforts of the matter-of-fact school to explain away a ghost, invisibility, and the elixir of life — the very things Poe discussed in reviewing Dr. Bird.

POE AND HIS TALES

Like Molière, Poe "took his own where he found it." He adopted plots with Shakespearean nonchalance. He was skillful at the misapplication of quotations.* Something absurd may be made to serve a serious purpose — witness the end of "The Oblong Box." And a pregnant expression of Bacon's can be made to create beauty in "Ligeia" and grotesquerie in "The Man that was Used Up." One should read "How to Write a Blackwood Article" for Poe's satirical account of his own method; he laughed rarely, but he could laugh at himself. What is remarkable is the freedom with which he treated his materials, skillfully combining discrete and various elements to obtain the result desired. As Floyd Stovall said in a clear-headed little paper,† he was at all times a conscious artist. He has too carelessly been called a hoaxer in some tales when he was using selected materials with an artist's design for effect.

FOREIGN INFLUENCES

It has been widely stated that Poe was under the influence of German writers, and numerous scholars have found a fascinating exercise in tracking down his supposed borrowings, especially in the works of E. T. A. Hoffmann. Yet when Poe declared in his preface to the *Tales of the Grotesque and Arabesque* that only one of his first twenty-five stories was Germanic, he was telling the truth — or something very like it. Poe's German was self-taught, a bilingual book by Sarah Austin was his primer,‡ and there is no evidence that he progressed beyond it. He could find and copy out a passage from Humboldt's *Kosmos,* of which an English version was before him, and probably could have read a simple German text by the aid of a dictionary, but that he ever read three consecutive pages of German is to be doubted.§ The German analogues brought forward turn out usually to be less close than something else that can be cited. There is one exception: "Loss of Breath" owes its primary idea to

---

*See "Marginalia," no. 78, *Democratic Review,* December 1844.

†"Poe as a Conscious Artist," by Floyd Stovall, in *College English,* March 1963.

‡*Characteristics of Goethe: from the German of Falk von Müller* [et al.], S. Austin (London 1833), 3 vols.

§Poe's knowledge of French was greater, although he took liberties with his quotations and was frequently incorrect. He had also some knowledge of Italian, having studied that language as well as French with a German professor at the University of Virginia.

INTRODUCTION

Peter Schlehmiel's loss of his shadow, mentioned in all versions of Poe's tale. But Chamisso's story of Peter Schlehmiel was very popular in translations. Any borrowings from German authors must be through translations to be credited.

Poe's characters are sometimes inspired by real people, sometimes by those in books. He has a close relation to a great many of them, something almost every critic has discussed. But they are more independent of the sources than are his plots and incidents. The character who most obviously resembles Poe, William Wilson, has Poe's own birthday and school but, although we are assured in the vaguest terms of his many vices, only his unamiable custom of cheating at cards is given much attention, something which we may be sure a consistent loser like Poe had not practiced.

Even where the author puts much of himself into one of his characters, such as William Wilson, the person does not greatly resemble Poe. Vincent Buranelli well said, "Poe is not Roderick Usher, but the creator of Roderick Usher." The acute critic N. Bryllion Fagin observed aptly in *The Histrionic Mr. Poe* (1949) that the poet did not live in his protagonists, but acted them, as an actor plays a role. Although we observe these people's deeds, and sometimes know their innermost hearts, we have not met them, nor shall we meet them. If we knew them as possible friends, we should suffer with them. Forbearance in this respect is part of Poe's artistic mastery.

There are some apparent exceptions. Dupin is everything Poe wished to be, and in some measure was; we think of him, especially in his alter ego, Sherlock Holmes, as a man we know and like. Ellison of "The Domain of Arnheim" has in him, as Poe assured Mrs. Whitman, "much of my soul." To many, the Duc de L'Omelette is a sympathetic character. But these three are happy and successful.

Some of the women come vividly before us. Morella and Ligeia are prodigies of learning and of affection, able to instruct and inspire the men to whom they are devoted. Clearly they are what the poet longed to find and had not found in life. There is indeed something of Poe's wife, as he wished she might have been, in "Eleonora"; but only Kate, of "Three Sundays in a Week," is really much like Virginia Clemm. Annie (Mrs. Richmond) is mentioned in "Landor's Cottage."

POE'S REVISIONS

Poe constantly revised his stories, sometimes rewriting them completely. The most completely changed of all is "Bon-Bon," which differs so much from its prototype, "The Bargain Lost," that it is hard to say if they be one story or two. "Loss of Breath" was originally short, then much lengthened, and finally shortened. "The Landscape Garden" is so greatly expanded into "The Domain of Arnheim" that Griswold (and Harrison) presented it as two stories — as do I. Fairly extensive additions were made to "Mesmeric Revelation" and "Diddling." Much shortened are "Berenice" and "The Oval Portrait." In some cases, notably "The Spectacles" and "The Imp of the Perverse," there are versions written at almost the same time which differ so much in phraseology that one suspects the author rewrote them from memory. In most cases, however, a printed text was sent with manuscript changes to the printer of the next appearance, then sometimes corrected a little further in proof.

Poe's skill and taste in revision have been much discussed; a dissenting correspondent wittily writes that greater taste might have been shown in suppressing some of the poorest things — "King Pest," for example, deserves no such meticulous care as it received from its fond parent. Yet "Ligeia" was much revised and improved; and "The Masque of the Red Death" and others were pruned with a masterly hand. The purposes of revision vary. Errors are corrected, mottoes added — a nonexistent title is removed from Usher's library. Cadences are improved. More pertinent allusions replace less happy references, and witty phrasing supplants occasional flatness. In a very few cases plot is clarified.

USE OF ALLEGORY

It remains to speak of Poe's attitude to and use of allegory in his tales. This is a fertile and provocative field for psychological and interpretative criticism, but only to be touched on briefly in this edition. Poe's own comments are best known from his review of Hawthorne's tales in *Godey's Lady's Book* for November 1847, in which he says, "In defence of allegory . . . there is scarcely one respectable word to be said." He believes "it must always interfere with that unity of effect which to the artist, is worth all the allegory in the world." However, he does allow it a place and says it is available where "the suggested meaning runs through the obvious one in a *very* profound undercurrent so as never to show itself unless *called* to the surface." No one supposes that Poe's tales do not have an undercurrent of meaning, and Richard Wilbur's *House of Poe* brilliantly sets forth a modern poet's response to what he believes is "accessible allegorical meaning" in Poe's work.*

Finally, as Killis Campbell and others have emphasized, it is well recognized now that Poe as an artist was not "out of space, out of time." He was a representative American of his day. The results of years of research by many scholars, collected in this edition of his Works, are evidence of Edgar Poe's supreme ability to absorb and transform the "news" of his own time, of his own place. This ability was the rock base of the originality that created his tales, no matter what strangeness they may explore.

II. PLAN OF THIS EDITION

CRITERIA FOR SELECTION

It might be possible to show from Poe's own remarks in his critical writings that he thought a tale *ought to be* what we now usually call a short story. But he was not rigidly consistent in classifying his own works, and he estimated their number in 1844 and 1845 in a way that makes me conclude with Woodberry that Poe counted as tales what others might call essays.* Hence I have established a category of "Tales and Sketches," and include in it shorter prose articles by Poe in which there is an element of fic-

---

*Library of Congress Anniversary Lecture, May 4, 1959. Reprinted in *The Recognition of Edgar Allan Poe,* ed. Eric W. Carlson (1966), pp. 255–277.

*Woodberry, *Life* (1909) II, 405. Poe called "Mesmeric Revelation" a "tale" in a letter of May 28, 1844, to Lowell; an "article" in a letter to George Bush, January 4, 1845; and an "essay" in a letter to Griswold, February 24, 1845.

tional narration.† The principle governing my decisions is a desire to include all the articles that involve narration. Extreme brevity does not lead to exclusion. I have included nine definitely new pieces, over Harrison's collection, most of them short. They include, however, Poe's latest and unfinished story, "The Light-House."‡

The canon of Poe's imaginative prose is not hard to establish. Practically everything collected here is either his acknowledged work, or established by incontrovertible evidence. Two or three sketches are accepted with slight reservations, but only one, the strange story called "A Dream" (1831), can be classed as of highly doubtful authorship, and even this one cannot be firmly dismissed. It may be added that we have no reason to think any tale composed by Poe in maturity has been lost.

SOURCES OF THE TEXTS

(For details see Sources Collated, at the end of Volume III)

The sources for the texts of Poe's short fiction are of several kinds. In addition to nine complete manuscripts and three fragments that survive, there are authorized first printings in monthly magazines, weeklies, daily newspapers, and gift books known as annuals. There are also reprints authorized by Poe which show revisions. No proofsheets survive.

Three collections of the shorter fiction were issued during the lifetime of the writer. They are: (1) *Tales of the Grotesque and Arabesque* (Philadelphia, 1840), issued late in 1839 in two volumes containing twenty-five stories; (2) *The Prose Romances* (Philadelphia, 1843), of which only the first number, containing "The Murders in the Rue Morgue" and "The Man that was Used Up," appeared; and (3) *Tales* (New York, 1845). This last is a selection of a dozen stories made by E. A. Duyckinck.

---

†For the purposes of presentation, it is convenient to group together the longer stories in Volume IV of this edition. *The Narrative of Arthur Gordon Pym* (1838) is of book length; "The Journal of Julius Rodman" (1840) was meant to be, as was, apparently, "Hans Pfaall" (1835) at first. The pieces are closely akin in manner, although the two earlier involve the impossible while the other does not.

‡Besides "The Light-House," the new pieces are "A Dream," "Instinct vs Reason," "Cabs," "Moving Chapters," "Desultory Notes on Cats," "The Swiss Bell-Ringers," "Theatrical Rats," and "A Reviewer Reviewed." I also include a number of pieces collected by Harrison but placed elsewhere than among the tales.

INTRODUCTION

In addition, we have copies of several volumes in which Poe made manuscript changes, usually with a view to future reprintings:

The first of these is called PHANTASY-PIECES. It originally consisted of the two-volume set, *Tales of the Grotesque and Arabesque*, for which Poe made a new title page and table of contents in manuscript and in which he indicated numerous emendations, some of them abortive. Only the first volume survives; it was found in Poe's trunk after his death. The second volume has disappeared. I suspect that it was broken up and used as copy by Griswold's printers, and was the source of the *Works* texts of "Metzengerstein" and "Hans Pfaall." There is another copy of *Tales of the Grotesque and Arabesque*, given by Poe to the Misses Pedder, in which the author added a manuscript footnote.

Of the *Tales* (1845) there is the celebrated J. Lorimer Graham copy (bound up with *The Raven and Other Poems*), with penciled manuscript revisions. Poe kept the book with him, even in his final summer, and hence the changes can hardly be dated individually, since all were not necessarily made at one time.

Manuscript changes were also made in what is known as the Bishop Hurst copy of *Eureka* (1848).

There are two bound files of periodicals containing Poe's manuscript alterations. One is the Duane set of the *Southern Literary Messenger* with a few changes, meant as printer's copy for the collected edition of 1840. The other file, the *Broadway Journal*, was given by Poe to Mrs. Helen Whitman, with numerous markings in pencil. Most of them are acknowledgments of his authorship of unsigned articles, but they include a few important verbal revisions.

Finally, there is the Rufus W. Griswold edition of the *Works of the Late Edgar Allan Poe* (1850 and 1856). The versions there are usually to be accepted. Careful study of the variants shows that Griswold had for some tales obviously superior readings, improvements that must have come from Poe. For these it may be assumed that Griswold had clippings with revisions in Poe's hand.§ Even when Griswold's edition shows but one or two changes, the pre-

§There is preserved an example of Poe's correcting in this way one of his printed pieces. See "Poe's Revision of Marginalia," in *Ex Libris* (January 1940), a quarterly leaflet issued by the friends of the library, The Johns Hopkins University.

sumption is in their favor, and when the last periodical text is verbally the same as Griswold's, nothing is gained by insisting on a return to the former. Hence, although the merits of each text are considered individually, Griswold's *Works of . . . Edgar Allan Poe* (Volumes I and II, 1850; and Volume IV, 1856) is accepted for the majority. But some of Poe's latest changes were not included in Griswold's texts. He did not use the J. Lorimer Graham copy of *Tales* (1845), undoubtedly because he did not receive it until after he had sent an uncorrected copy of the book to the printer. Neither did he have access to the file of the *Broadway Journal* Poe gave Mrs. Whitman in 1848. Our texts have incorporated these changes.

ARRANGEMENT

The tales in Volumes II and III are arranged chronologically. The precise order in which Poe wrote them cannot be completely determined; but the approximate date of the original version, as well as the exact date of the earliest publication, is now known for all the stories except one. The exception is "Why the Little French-man Wears His Hand in a Sling," which presumably first appeared between 1837 and 1839 in a periodical not yet discovered. The advantages of arrangement by date are very great to any serious student. He cannot fail to see development, for both Poe's method and his style changed markedly with the years, as did his opinions.

The order of the present edition differs to some extent from Harrison's because of the discoveries made since his great work appeared in 1902. More than fifty additional texts are collated here; by far the largest number are manuscripts and early printings. At one time or another I have seen all the printed originals described, and every manuscript known to be extant.

DISCUSSION

The discussion of the individual tales follows the plan set forth in my Preface to the edition in Volume I. The most pertinent passages are restated here:

The introductory note to each item gives the history of composition and an account of Poe's major sources if they are certainly known or plausibly suggested. The history of publication and the list of texts which follows include mention of all authorized versions of the item now known. In the case of articles which neither Poe nor his literary executor collected, record is made of first publication in periodicals and of first inclusion in books.

Purely aesthetic criticism is deliberately kept to a minimum. It is usually confined to pointing out the merits of widely recognized masterpieces and to evaluation of pieces less well known. Something is said of the estimates of his work (not always favorable) that stem from Poe himself, but very little of his vast influence on his contemporaries and on those who have come after him. Mention is made, however, of all known reprints in America and in Britain before 1850, and of translations made on the Continent during Poe's lifetime.

In the notes I give, as far as I can, the sources of Poe's direct and indirect quotations, and explanations of his references and allusions, that may not be clear to a reader of today. Cruces are discussed, but record is usually omitted of views outmoded in the light of present knowledge and of explanations withdrawn or abandoned by their proponents.

Credit for their discoveries is given to my predecessors, I hope with some thoroughness. I am also indebted to my students and friends for unprinted suggestions given to me directly, which I have tried to acknowledge and for which I express my sincere thanks.

VARIANT READINGS

My policy is of extreme respect for the text. I correct nothing verbal in Poe's texts except obvious misprints. Fashions in spelling changed while Poe was writing and some of his forms look curious to our eyes, but spellings of his time have been allowed to stand, and, if they deserve it, receive comment in my notes.

In a few cases it has seemed desirable to reprint *in toto* the earliest version of a tale as well as the final text.

All verbal variants in the authorized texts are recorded, but only such variations in accidentals as seem of any significance. Differences in spelling, if the forms used were generally accepted in Poe's day, are not recorded, but typographical errors in all texts have been listed among the variants.

Changes in italicization are recorded.

Punctuation variants are not recorded, with the following exceptions:

1. Poe's manuscript changes in the J. Lorimer Graham copy of *Tales* (1845) are recorded.

2. Complete punctuation changes of the seven texts of "Ligeia" are recorded, as an example of Poe's work in revising his tales.

3. Poe's manuscript changes in the punctuation of PHANTASY-PIECES are summarized but not recorded, with the exception of those in "Ligeia," as mentioned above.*

4. Differences in paragraphing are not recorded, except in the case of surviving manuscripts, and in "Ligeia."

5. Hyphenations in the manuscripts are recorded if they differ from the printed texts. Only in the manuscripts can one be sure that the word compounds originated with Poe.

The following kinds of emendation have been made:

French. Verbally Poe's French is allowed to stand, but errors in accents and spelling are corrected — from other texts, if possible; if not, editorially. The incorrect forms in Poe's texts are recorded in the variants.

Greek. Errors in spelling are corrected, but accents are used only if they appear in the original.

Punctuation. In some texts emendations in punctuation seem required. Actual errors are corrected, generally from first printings, but editorially if necessary. The errors are recorded in the variants.

Two kinds of changes have been made silently. (1) Hyphenations within a particular tale have been made consistent according to the form apparently favored by Poe. (2) In the case of texts from the *Broadway Journal,* there are a number of occasions when, in order to fill out a line to the right-hand margin, the printer inserted a dash after the period following a sentence. A few of these dashes were carried over to Griswold's edition of the *Works,* where they

---

*The punctuation changes in PHANTASY-PIECES are particularly interesting, however, because we are certain that Poe made them. For this reason these changes have been summarized and the summary placed under the list of texts of each tale. In the twelve tales involved, 1832–1839, Poe was most concerned with his use of dashes, industriously eliminating a large number in favor of commas and semicolons. In 1848 he was accusing printers of doing this, to the vexation of the writer. See "Marginalia," number 197, *Graham's Magazine,* February 1848, p. 130.

often fall in the middle of a line. All these "printer's dashes" have been silently eliminated. They have nothing to do with Poe's punctuation, although Harrison and other editors have reproduced them in their texts from the *Broadway Journal*.

ABBREVIATIONS

AL   *American Literature*
DAB   *Dictionary of American Biography*
DNB   *Dictionary of National Biography*
MLN   *Modern Language Notes*
OED   *Oxford English Dictionary*
PMLA   *Publications of the Modern Language Association*
SLM   *Southern Literary Messenger*

EARLIEST IMAGINATIVE PROSE
PROSE
1826-1831

EARLIEST IMAGINATIVE PROSE
1826–1831

Of Poe's 'prentice work as a writer of fiction a little is known. We have a single account of stories written in 1826 at the University, including a description of a tale that Poe destroyed. There is a short story printed in 1831 that has been ascribed to his pen, tentatively, but for reason of some weight. In addition we have two small fragments, of which Poe certainly composed one or at least rewrote it; the other may or may not be in his hand.

These four items are here grouped together. They certainly antedate the tales Poe gave to the world with his name. In those the author usually held himself to certain standards, especially one of correctness — an avoidance of "allusions contrary to fact" unless essential to the plot. The author of "A Dream" did not adhere to this standard, but neither did Poe live up to it when he composed two of the very earliest tales now acknowledged — "The Bargain Lost" and "A Decided Loss."

[GAFFY]

During his stay at the University of Virginia, 1826–27, Poe tried his hand at composing tales in prose. The only account of them is that of Poe's fellow student Thomas Goode Tucker, as recorded by Douglass Sherley, published in the *Virginia University Magazine,* April 1880, and quoted in James A. Harrison's *Complete Works of Edgar Allan Poe* (1902), I, 42. More than fifty years elapsed between the events and publication of any record of them, but Tucker's story of a cheerful tale is basically unsuspect. Pruned of some literary flourishes, it reads:

Poe showed his warm appreciation and high respect for his friend Tucker by reading to him the early productions of his youth, — productions that his critical hand afterwards destroyed, thinking them unfit for publication. Sometimes . . . he would call in a few of his friends and read...to them...They were mostly stories characterized by...weirdness of style....

On one occasion Poe read a story of great length to some of his friends who, in a spirit of jest, spoke lightly of its merits, and jokingly told him that his hero's name, "Gaffy," occurred too often...Before his friends could prevent him, he had flung every sheet into a blazing fire, and thus was lost a story of more than ordinary parts which, unlike most of his stories, was intensely amusing, entirely free from his usual sombre coloring...He was for a long time afterwards called by those in his particular circle "Gaffy" Poe, a name he never altogether relished.

William Peterfield Trent in his unfinished and unpublished manuscript life of Poe observed that the description of the weirdness of many of these early stories might well be the result of perusal of Poe's published productions. But this objection hardly can apply to Tucker's recollection of the amusing story of Gaffy — an account of a cheerful story by Poe is not likely to be from imperfect memory or imagination. Although the title of the story is not specifically given, the nickname of its protagonist (which means "talkative") is adopted here.

[AN OLD ENGLISH TALE]

One of Poe's early footnotes deserves collection here. We now know that his quotations from memory were sometimes extraordinarily free; for example, his mottoes for "William Wilson" and "The Gold-Bug" bear only the slightest resemblance to their "originals." It is quite likely that they were composed by Poe himself. The language of the quotation in Poe's note on "Al Aaraaf," II, 124, definitely resembles the Chattertonian jargon in the wholly imagined story of *The Mad Tryst* in "The Fall of the House of Usher" and may be "quoted" for a similar creation. See *Al Aaraaf, Tamerlane and Minor Poems* (1829), page 31; *Poems* (1831), page 101; and *The Raven and Other Poems* (1845), pages 67–68. The two earlier versions show slight misprints; but there are no author's changes in the final text here reprinted:

I met with this idea in an old English tale, which I am now unable to obtain and quote from memory: — "The verie essence and, as it were, springe-heade and origine of all musiche is the verie pleasaunte sounde which the trees of the forest do make when they growe."

A DREAM

[SUMMER AND WINTER]

The following is on a single leaf, which an old-time bookseller said was written by Poe as a child (Yale List,* number 6). The many changes and corrections clearly show it is the composition of its writer. It is now printed by permission of the Richard Gimbel Collection of the Free Library of Philadelphia.

How chang'd the scene — but now the Summer reign'd, her varied tints prevail'd throughout triumphant. Here where the beauteous rosebud sat a briar frowns — the woodbine too hath lost her suit of brilliant green — the leafless grove is silent, desolate! No songster cheers with merry note the passing hour. The hum of Bees is hush'd and all around proclaims, that Winter is at hand — how clear.

The style is reminiscent of Macpherson's Ossianic poems, praised by Poe in his introductory "Letter to — —" in his *Poems* of 1831; lines 17, 20, and 22 of Poe's own poem, "The Coliseum," echo part of the second sentence. The prose fragment, if Poe's, must be dated very early. In the absence of a complete history of the manuscript, judgment on its authenticity as a product of Poe's pen must be suspended, but I see nothing in the handwriting that seems to me impossible for Poe.

A DREAM

"A Dream" was first noticed by Killis Campbell in *Modern Language Notes,* May 1917. He once remarked to me that it was the only tale he had found in his wide reading of early periodicals that he suspected might be Poe's work. I too have read much in the old periodicals, and have found nothing else that impresses me so strongly as being possibly Poe's as this tale. Dearth of comment from other students means little; no text of "A Dream" has been easily accessible until now. The piece is signed "P." and marked as an original contribution in the Philadelphia *Saturday Evening Post* of August 13, 1831, which was then edited by Poe's friend

*" 'Quoth the Raven': an exhibition of the works of Edgar Allan Poe," etc., *The Yale University Library Gazette,* April 1959.

Lambert A. Wilmer. In *The Mind of Poe* (1933), page 210, Campbell observed that the story is "in mood and diction . . . not unlike . . . the more gruesome of Poe's early tales."

The tale was timely, for there had been an eclipse on February 12, 1831. The story of the Crucifixion and the earthquake, eclipse, and breaking of tombs that followed it is based on St. Matthew 27:45–53, but in the Pharisee's dream some changes are made from the Bible narrative.

Strong arguments could be brought against Poe's authorship as an experienced writer of fiction; but these are all weakened when the piece, if assumed to be his, is examined (as it must be) as one of his earliest efforts in prose. The strongest objection of all, Poe's failure to collect the story, is to be met by the theory that he had not preserved a copy. The use of "incorrect" references is paralleled in the very early story "A Decided Loss." Poe's later avoidance of a dream setting (except in the comic "Angel of the Odd" and "Some Words With a Mummy") may have been the result of this experiment. The use of a New Testament theme, unusual for Poe, means little, since "A Dream" is entirely reverent, and Poe was deeply interested in Biblical antiquities. Under the circumstances, I feel a text of the story should be presented, with a caveat, as tentatively assigned to Poe.

The story is now first reprinted from the only text, that in the *Saturday Evening Post*, August 13, 1831. The form "eminated" in the fourth paragraph was probably tolerated at the time.

A DREAM

A few evenings since, I laid myself down for my night's repose. It has been a custom with me, for years past, to peruse a portion of the scriptures before I close my eyes in the slumbers of night. I did so in the present instance. By chance, I fell upon the spot where inspiration has recorded the dying agonies of the God of Nature.[1] Thoughts of these, and the scenes which followed his giving up the ghost, pursued me as I slept.

There is certainly something mysterious and incomprehensible in the manner in which the wild vagaries of the imagination often arrange themselves; but the solution of this belongs to the physiologist rather than the reckless "dreamer."

It seemed that I was some Pharisee, returning from the scene of death. I had assisted in driving the sharpest nails through the palms of Him who hung on the cross, a spectacle of the bitterest woe that mortality ever felt. I could hear the groan that ran through his soul, as the rough iron grated on the bones when I drove it through. I retired a few steps from the place of execution, and turned around to look at my bitterest enemy. The Nazarene was not yet dead: the life lingered in the mantle of clay, as if it shuddered to walk alone through the valley of death. I thought I could see the cold damp that settles on the brow of the dying, now standing in large drops on his. I could see each muscle quiver: — The eye, that began to lose its lustre in the hollow stare of the corpse. I could hear the low gurgle in his throat. — A moment, — and the chain of existence was broken, and a link dropped into eternity.

I turned away, and wandered listlessly on, till I came to the centre of Jerusalem. At a short distance rose the lofty turrets of the Temple; its golden roof reflected rays as bright as the source from which they eminated. A feeling of conscious pride stole over me, as I looked over the broad fields and lofty mountains which surrounded this pride of the eastern world. On my right rose Mount Olivet, covered with shrubbery and vineyards; beyond that, and bounding the skirts of mortal vision, appeared mountains piled on mountains; on the left were the lovely plains of Judea; and I thought it was a bright picture of human existence, as I saw the little brook Cedron[2] speeding its way through the meadows, to the distant lake. I could hear the gay song of the beauteous maiden, as she gleaned in the distant harvest-field; and, mingling with the echoes of the mountain, was heard the shrill whistle of the shepherd's pipe, as he called the wandering lamb to its fold. A perfect loveliness had thrown itself over animated nature.

But, "a change soon came o'er the spirit of my dream;"[3] I felt a sudden coldness creeping over me. I instinctively turned towards the sun, and saw a hand slowly drawing a mantle of crape over it. I looked for stars; but each one had ceased to twinkle; for the same hand had enveloped them in the badge of mourning. The silver light of the moon did not dawn on the sluggish waves of the Dead Sea, as they sang the hoarse requiem of the cities of the Plain;[4] but she hid her face, as if shuddering to look on what was doing on the earth. I heard a muttered groan, as the spirit of darkness spread his pinions over an astonished world.

Unutterable despair now seized me. I could feel the flood of life slowly rolling back to its fountain, as the fearful thought stole over me, that the day of retribution had come.

Suddenly, I stood before the temple. The veil, which had hid its secrets from unhallowed gaze, was now rent. I looked for a moment: the priest was standing by the altar, offering up the expiatory sacrifice. The fire, which was to kindle the mangled limbs of the victim, gleamed for a moment, on the distant walls, and then 'twas lost in utter darkness. He turned around, to rekindle it from the living fire of the candlestick; but that, too, was gone. — 'Twas still as the sepulchre.

I turned, and rushed into the street. The street was vacant. No sound broke the stillness, except the yell of the wild dog, who revelled on the half-burnt corpse in the Valley of Hinnom.[5] I saw a light stream from a distant window, and made my way towards it. I looked in at the open door. A widow was preparing the last morsel she could glean, for her dying babe. She had kindled a little fire; and I saw with what utter hopelessness of heart she beheld the flame sink away, like her own dying hopes.

Darkness covered the universe. Nature mourned, for its parent had died. The earth had enrobed herself in the habiliments of sorrow, and the heavens were clothed in the sables of mourning. I now roamed in restlessness, and heeded not whither I went. At once there appeared a light in the east. A column of light shot athwart the gloom, like the light-shot gleams on the darkness of the midnight of the pit, and illumined the sober murkiness that surrounded me. There was an opening in the vast arch of heaven's broad expanse. With wondering eyes, I turned towards it.

Far into the wilderness of space, and at a distance that can only be meted by a "line running parallel with eternity,"[6] but still awfully plain and distinct, appeared the same person whom I had clothed with the mock purple of royalty. He was now garmented in the robe of the King of kings. He sat on his throne; but 'twas not one of whiteness. There was mourning in heaven; for, as each angel knelt before him, I saw that the wreath of immortal amaranth which was wont to circle his brow, was changed for one of cypress.

I turned to see whither I had wandered. I had come to the burial ground of the monarch of Israel. I gazed with trembling, as I saw the clods which covered the mouldering bones of some tyrant begin to move. I looked at where the last monarch had been laid, in all the splendour and pageantry of death, and the sculptured monument began to tremble. Soon it was overturned, and from it issued the tenant of the grave.[7] 'Twas a hideous, unearthly form, such as Dante, in his wildest flights of terrified fancy, ne'er conjured up. I could not move, for terror had tied up volition. It approached me. I saw the grave-worm twining itself amongst the matted locks which in part covered the rotten scull. The bones creaked on each other as they moved on the hinges, for its flesh was gone. I listened to their horrid music, as this parody on poor mortality stalked along. He came up to me; and, as he passed, he breathed the cold damps of the lonely, narrow house directly in my face. The chasm in the heavens closed; and, with a convulsive shudder, I awoke.

NOTES

1. See "Pinakidia," number 59 *(SLM,* August 1836, p. 577) — references are to the original sequence of items in the *Southern Literary Messenger* for August 1836 (2:573–582) — for Poe's account of a letter in the Suidas Lexicon *(s.v.* "Dionysius Areopagita"), referring to a total eclipse at noon in the year of the Crucifixion, which caused Dionysius to say, "Either the author of nature suffers, or he sympathizes with some who do."

2. See "Pinakidia," number 17 (p. 575), for a comment on Kedron as meaning darkness, from Hebrew *kiddar,* black, rather than Greek, *kedrōn,* of cedars. Compare a footnote on p. 313 of Frederic Shoberl's translation (Philadelphia, 1813) of Chateaubriand's *Itinéraire de Paris à Jerusalem* — a source of references in several of Poe's poems of this period as well as some of his tales (see "A Tale of Jerusalem," n. 12).

3. The quotation is from Byron's "The Dream," III, 1, a favorite with Poe but also with his contemporaries.

4. For Poe's interest in the Dead Sea, see my notes on his poem "The City in

the Sea," which in an early version, "The Doomed City," was included in his *Poems* (1831) .

5. A valley lying to the west and south of the old city of Jerusalem. See notes on "Morella," below.

6. The quotation, "a line running parallel with eternity," has not yet been traced.

7. St. Matthew 27:52–53 says, "And the graves were opened; and many bodies of the saints which slept arose, and came out of the graves after his resurrection, and went into the holy city, and appeared unto many." The last king of Israel can hardly, however, be called a saint. He was Hoshea ("Deliverance") who reigned 730–722 B.C. after he rebelled against Pekah ("Vision of God") and slew him. Shalmaneser, King of Assyria, discovering that Hoshea was conspiring with the King of Egypt, "shut him up, and bound him in prison." See II Kings 15:30–31, and 17:1–23.

TALES OF THE FOLIO CLUB
1831-1835

TALES OF THE FOLIO CLUB

"Tales of the Folio Club" is a title Poe gave in 1833 to a proposed collection of his early stories. The collection as he originally described it was never published, although several optimistic references to it as forthcoming appeared after the initial suggestion. A number of the tales he planned to include were composed before the end of 1831. He sent several of them to the newly founded *Saturday Courier* of Philadelphia, which on June 4, 1831, had carried the announcement that "as soon as proper arrangements can be effected, a premium of one hundred dollars will be awarded for the best American tale." Rules for the contest were published in July, setting December 1 as the deadline for the submission of manuscripts. Poe submitted several, but the prize went to Delia Bacon for "Love's Martyr." In announcing the award on December 31, however, the *Courier* remarked: "Many of the other Tales offered for the Premium, are distinguished by great merit"; and in the course of the year 1832 it published five of Poe's stories anonymously. These early texts were identified by Killis Campbell in 1916, and published in facsimile by John Grier Varner in 1933.*

Meanwhile, in the *Baltimore Saturday Visiter* of August 4, 1832 there was an editorial note, perhaps written by Lambert A. Wilmer, which indicates that Poe had composed a number of stories by that time:

Mr. Edgar A. Poe, has favoured us with the perusal of some manuscript tales written by him. If we were merely to say that we had *read* them, it would be a compliment, for manuscript of this kind are very seldom read by anyone but the author. But we may further say that we have read these tales every syllable, with the greatest pleasure, and for originality, richness of imagery and purity of the style, few American authors in our opinion have produced anything su-

* See Killis Campbell, "New Notes on Poe's Early Years," *The Dial*, February 17, 1916, and J. G. Varner, *Edgar Allan Poe and the Philadelphia Saturday Courier* (Charlottesville, 1933).

perior. With Mr. Poe's permission we may hereafter lay one or two of the tales before our readers.†

By May 4, 1833, Poe had formulated a plan for a volume to be called "Eleven Tales of the Arabesque," which he described in a letter to Joseph T. and Edwin Buckingham, editors of the *New England Magazine*, sending "Epimanes" as a sample. The Messrs. Buckingham offered no encouragement, but within a few weeks it came from another source. On June 15, the *Baltimore Saturday Visiter* announced a competition with a prize of fifty dollars for the best tale and twenty-five dollars for the best poem submitted before October 1. Poe sent in a poem — "The Coliseum" — and a manuscript volume, "The Tales of the Folio Club," containing six stories very neatly written in small, print-like characters. On October 12, the *Visiter* announced the awards and on October 19 published the prizewinners: John H. Hewitt's poem, "The Song of the Wind," submitted under a pseudonym, and Poe's story, "MS. Found in a Bottle." Poe's poem was published the following week. Through this competition Poe first attracted attention as a writer of fiction. John P. Kennedy, one of the judges, became much interested in him, and suggested that he send his collection of tales to the Philadelphia publishers Carey & Lea. Carey felt that the volume would not be profitable, but he arranged the sale of at least one of the stories to an annual.

"The Tales of the Folio Club" never appeared as an independent volume. A revival of the scheme was mentioned in the *Southern Literary Messenger* for August 1835, with the number of tales being given as sixteen. On September 2 of the following year, in a letter trying to interest the Philadelphia publisher Harrison Hall in the project, Poe said there were seventeen tales, "originally written to illustrate a larger work, 'On the Imaginative Faculties.'" Hall was not sufficiently interested, however, and the first collection of Poe's stories — *Tales of the Grotesque and Arabesque* (dated 1840) — did not appear until late in 1839.

The introduction Poe composed for the collection of tales he envisioned in 1833 was first published by Harrison in 1902. It is

† Quoted by Arthur H. Quinn, in *Edgar Allan Poe* (1941), pp. 194–195.

given here in what seems to be its proper place in chronological order of composition, following the first eleven tales below.

METZENGERSTEIN

Publication of Poe's world-famous tales began auspiciously, when "Metzengerstein" was printed in the Philadelphia *Saturday Courier* of January 14, 1832, a few days before his twenty-third birthday. It may justly be called a masterpiece, though a minor one, for it shows Poe as already a master of a craft in which his genius was to be supreme. "Metzengerstein" was not perfect, and Poe was to improve it markedly by fairly extensive revision. Yet even in the earliest version can be seen the distinguishing merits of Poe's best work — unity of tone and expression, maintenance of suspense, and a stirring climax.

The author regarded the tale as Germanic, and the subtitle of the second publication calls it "A tale in imitation of the German." (It may be recalled that as part of the Holy Roman Empire, Hungary was considered Germanic, and indeed, the population was of mixed ethnic origin.) It has been well said by Edd Winfield Parks in *Edgar Allan Poe as Literary Critic* (1964), page 24, that "Metzengerstein . . . started as an imitation of the Gothic romances but . . . gathered such momentum that it became a powerful allegory, with evil leading to its own self-destruction." A. H. Quinn in *Edgar Allan Poe* (1941), pages 192–193 — a fine discussion — says it is "no mere burlesque," but "a powerful story of evil passions in a young man's soul" and remarks on the superiority of Poe's "use of the Gothic material" to "Walpole's absurd treatment." The tale is hardly a burlesque at all, unless in reverse, but Poe and his early readers may have found the characters' names funny.*

Poe's sources were not all Germanic, any more than the idea of transmigration of souls — which he used in "Morella," "Ligeia," "A Tale of the Ragged Mountains," "The Black Cat," and perhaps in

* See Lucille King, "Notes on Poe's Sources," *Studies in English*, no. 10 (University of Texas Bulletin, No. 3026, July 8, 1930), p. 129. She seems to have been the first to comment on the relation of Poe to Walpole's story.

"Eleonora" — is peculiarly Hungarian. His paramount source for "Metzengerstein" is a New England ghost story told by an American poet, "The Buccaneer" by Richard Henry Dana the elder, published in *The Buccaneer, and Other Poems* (1827) and once extremely well known. R. W. Griswold gave a text of it in *Poets and Poetry of America* (1842), page 65, calling it "a story in which [Dana] has depicted with singular power the stronger and darker passions... based on a tradition of a murder committed on an island on the coast of New England." No notice seems to have been taken of Poe's use of Dana's legend until I pointed it out in *Selected Poetry and Prose of Edgar Allan Poe,* Modern Library (1951), page 414.

In Dana's poem, Matthew Lee, a pirate posing as a merchant, takes on board his ship a young Spanish widow with her retinue and her "white steed." He murders most of his passengers, tries to rape the lady — who escapes by jumping into the sea — throws the horse in, burns the ship near shore to conceal his crimes, and returns to his home with the remnant of his wicked crew, all well stored with gold. On the anniversary of his success, as he holds a feast, a blazing hulk is seen at sea from which swims a horse who makes for the pirate. Lee is impelled to ride the horse to a cliff, whence he can see the phantom ship disappear. A year later, although there is no celebration, the visit of the horse is repeated and the wicked Lee is warned by the spirit horse that he will come "Once more — and then a dreadful way!/And thou must go with me!" On the third anniversary, the wreck goes down and the spectre-horse comes slowly up from the sea, by his "fix'd eye" holding Lee, who mounts and is carried into the ocean, never to be seen again.

Poe's second cardinal source is in Horace Walpole's *Castle of Otranto* (1764). It was edited in 1811 by Sir Walter Scott, with an important Introduction to which Poe may have owed as much as to Walpole's story. In that story we have, besides much typical of all Gothic romances, several things that are peculiarly similar to some Poe used in "Metzengerstein." There is a mysterious prophecy about an event that will put an end to the castle and the house of the wicked Manfred. An ancestral picture — that of a former rightful owner of the castle — "comes alive." This ghost assumes gigan-

METZENGERSTEIN

tic size. The young hero of Walpole's story is named Frederic. He is not the son of Manfred and his wife Hippolita, but the latter is saintly like the mother of Metzengerstein.

A third probable source for the story (briefly noticed by Woodberry in the Stedman and Woodberry edition of Poe's *Works*, 1895, IV, 295) is in a book of which we know Poe was fond, Benjamin Disraeli's *Vivian Grey* (1826). In the third chapter of the sixth book we read the story of the mediatized Prince of Little Lilliput at his castle. He has an equestrian portrait of an ancestor painted by Lucas Cranach, of which Vivian says, "The horse seems quite living, and its fierce rider actually frowns upon us." The Prince feels that the rider frowns upon *him,* because for a large sum of money he has given up his sovereign rights over a tiny principality and is now subordinate to a more successful neighbor, the Grand-Duke of Reisenburg, descended from servants of the nobleman in the portrait. The Prince's son, a young boy, expresses his hatred for Reisenburg. Disraeli also says that the mediatized princes "seldom frequent the Courts of their sovereigns, and scarcely condescend to notice the attentions of their fellow nobility . . . at their solitary forest castles."

"Metzengerstein" was one of the stories Poe submitted to the Philadelphia *Saturday Courier* in the contest advertised in June 1831. Since the closing date for entries was December 1, the tale must have been completed before that time. Although "Love's Martyr" by Delia Bacon was given the award, "Metzengerstein" was published in the *Courier* only one week later than the prize-winner. It was the first of Poe's acknowledged tales to be printed, but there is no reason to suppose it the first to be written. Indeed, I believe that "The Bargain Lost" — much inferior — preceded it, because there Poe used allusions which are not essential to the plot, a practice he avoided in the four other very early stories and eliminated in rewriting "The Bargain Lost" as "Bon-Bon."

TEXTS

(A) Philadelphia *Saturday Courier,* January 14, 1832, pp. 9–24; *(B) Southern Literary Messenger,* January 1836 (2:97–100): *(C)* Duane copy of the last with manuscript revisions (1839); *(D) Tales of the Grotesque and Arabesque* (1840), II, 151–165; *(E) Works* (1850), I, 475–483. PHANTASY-PIECES, title only.

For this edition we print Griswold's much improved final form *(E)*. It was, I suspect, based on Poe's revision in the second volume of PHANTASY-PIECES, the disappearance of which may be accounted for by its use as printer's copy by Griswold in 1849. Only the abortive title of the tale is preserved, in the table of contents in the first volume.

The earliest text *(A)* was mechanically reproduced by John Grier Varner in *Edgar Allan Poe and the Philadelphia Saturday Courier* (1933). Poe revised "Metzengerstein" skilfully, making many stylistic changes in 1836 for the *Southern Literary Messenger*. He also, at some time after 1840, wisely removed some unnecessary material on the death of the protagonist's mother. For Poe's spelling "stupified," see Introduction.

METZENGERSTEIN. [*E*]

Pestis eram vivus — moriens tua mors ero.

Martin Luther.[1]

Horror and fatality have been stalking abroad in all ages. Why then give a date to the story I have to tell?[a] Let it suffice to say, that at the period of which I speak, there existed, in the interior of Hungary, a settled although hidden belief in the doctrines of the Metempsychosis. Of the doctrines themselves — that is, of their falsity, or of[b] their probability — I say nothing. I assert, however, that much of our incredulity (as La Bruyère[c] says[d] of all our unhappiness) *"vient de ne pouvoir être[e] seuls."**[f] [2]

But there were some points in the Hungarian superstition[h] [3] which were fast verging to absurdity. They — the Hungarians — differed very[i] essentially from their[j] Eastern authorities. For ex-

---

* Mercier, in *"L'an deux mille quatre cents quarante,"* seriously maintains the doctrines of Metempsychosis, and I.[g] D'Israeli says that "no system is so simple and so little repugnant to the understanding." Colonel Ethan Allen, the "Green Mountain Boy," is also said to have been a serious metempsychosist.

Title: Metzengerstein. A Tale in Imitation of the German. *(B, C);* The Horse-Shade (PHANTASY-PIECES)
a   tell? I will not. Besides I have other reasons for concealment. *(A);* tell? Besides I have other reasons for concealment. *(B) changed in C*
b   *Omitted (A)*
c   Bruyere *(A, B, C, D, E)*
d   observes *(A)*

e   *etre (A, B, C, D, E)*
f   *Footnote omitted (A, B, C, D) Poe follows D'Israeli in using* cents *for* cent *in Mercier's title*
g   J. *(E) misprint*
h   superstition (the Roman term was religio,) *(A)*
i   *Omitted (A)*
j   the *(A)*

ample. *"The soul,"*[k] said the former — I give the words of an acute and intelligent Parisian — *"ne demeure*[l] *qu'un seule*[m] *fois dans un corps sensible: au reste —* [n]*un cheval, un chien, un homme même,*[o] *n'est que la ressemblance*[n] *peu tangible de ces animaux."*[4]

The families of Berlifitzing[5] and Metzengerstein had been at variance for centuries. Never before were two houses so illustrious, mutually embittered by hostility so deadly.[p] The origin of this enmity seems to be found in the words of an ancient prophecy — "A lofty name shall have a fearful fall when, as[q] the rider over his horse, the mortality of Metzengerstein shall triumph over the immortality of Berlifitzing."

To be sure the words themselves had little or no meaning. But more trivial causes have given rise — and that no long while ago — to consequences equally eventful. Besides, the estates, which were contiguous, had long exercised a rival influence in the affairs of a busy government. Moreover, near neighbors are seldom friends; and the inhabitants[r] of the Castle Berlifitzing might look, from their lofty buttresses, into the very windows of the Palace[s] [t]Metzengerstein. Least[t] of all had[u] the more than feudal magnificence,[v] thus discovered, a tendency[w] to allay the irritable feelings of the less ancient and less wealthy Berlifitzings. What wonder, then, that the words, however silly, of that prediction, should have succeeded in setting and keeping at variance two families already predisposed to quarrel by every instigation of hereditary jealousy? [x]The prophecy seemed to imply — if it implied anything —[x] a final triumph on the part of the already more powerful house; and was[y] of course

---

k   "The soul," *(A)*
l   *demure (E) misprint, corrected from A, B, C, D*
m   *quun seul (A); qu'un seul (B, C, D, E)*
n . . . n   *ce quon croit d'etre un cheval — un chien — un homme — n'est que le resemblance (A)*
o   *meme, (E) accent added from B, C, D*
p   *After this:* Indeed, at the era of this history, it was remarked [observed *B, C, D*] by an old crone of haggard, and sinister appearance, that fire and water might sooner mingle than a Berlifitzing clasp the hand of a Metzengerstein. *(A, B, C, D)*
q   like *(A, B, C, D)*
r   inmates *(A)*
s   Chateau *(A, B, C, D)*
t . . . t   Metzengerstein: and least *(A)*
u   was *(A, B, C, D)*
v   magnificence *(E) comma added by editor*
w   a tendency/calculated *(A, B, C, D)*
x . . . x   The words of the prophecy implied, if they implied any thing, *(A)*
y   were *(A)*

remembered with the more bitter animosity by[z] the weaker and less influential.

Wilhelm, Count Berlifitzing, although[a] loftily descended, was, at the epoch of this narrative, an infirm and doting old man, remarkable for nothing but an inordinate and inveterate personal antipathy to the family of his rival, and so passionate a love of horses, and of hunting, that neither bodily infirmity,[b] great age, nor mental incapacity, prevented his daily participation in the dangers of the chase.[c]

Frederick, Baron Metzengerstein, was, on the other hand, not yet of age. His father, the Minister G——, died young. His mother, the Lady Mary, followed him quickly.[d] Frederick was, at that time, in his eighteenth[e] year. In a city, eighteen[f] years are no long [g]period: but[g] in a wilderness — in so magnificent a wilderness as that old principality, [h]the pendulum vibrates with a[h] deeper meaning.[i]

From some peculiar circumstances attending the administration of his father, the young Baron, at the decease of the former, entered immediately upon his vast possessions. Such estates [j]were seldom held before[j] by a nobleman of Hungary. His castles were without

---

z   on the side of *(A, B, C, D)*
a   although honourably and *(A, B, C, D)*
b   decrepitude, *(A)*
c   chace. *(A) misprint*
d   him quickly./quickly after. *(A, B, C, D)*
e   fifteenth *(A, B, C, D)*
f   fifteen *(A, B, C, D)*
g . . . g   period — a child may be still a child in his third lustrum. But *(A, B, C, D)*
h . . . h   fifteen years have a far *(A, B, C, D)*
i   *After this A, B, C and D have the following material, here reproduced from A:*
The beautiful Lady Mary! — how could she die? — and of consumption! But it is a path I have prayed to follow. I would wish all I love to perish of that gentle disease. How glorious! to depart in the hey-day of the young blood — the heart all passion — the imagination all fire — amid the remembrances of happier days — in the fall of the year, and so be buried up forever in the gorgeous, autumnal leaves. Thus died the Lady Mary. The young Baron Frederick stood, without a living relative, by the coffin of his dead mother. He laid [placed *(B, C, D)*] his hand upon her placid forehead. No shudder came over his delicate frame — no sigh from his gentle [flinty *(B, C, D)*] bosom — no curl upon his kingly lip. Heartless, self-willed, and impetuous from his childhood, he had arrived at [reached *(B, C, D)*] the age of which I speak, through a career of unfeeling, wanton, and reckless dissipation, and a barrier had long since arisen in the channel of all holy thoughts, and gentle recollections.
j . . . j   were, never before, held *(A)*

^knumber. The^k chief in point of splendor and extent was the "Palace^l Metzengerstein." The boundary line of his dominions was never clearly defined; but his principal park embraced a circuit of fifty^m miles.

Upon the succession of a proprietor so young, with a character so well known, to a fortune so unparalleled, little speculation was afloat in regard to his probable course of conduct. And, indeed, for the space of three days, the behaviour of the heir out-heroded Herod,[6] and fairly surpassed the expectations of his most enthusiastic admirers. Shameful debaucheries — flagrant treacheries — unheard-of atrocities[7] — gave his trembling vassals quickly to understand that no servile submission on their part — no punctilios of conscience on his own — were thenceforward to prove any securityⁿ against the remorseless^o fangs of a petty Caligula.[8] On the night of the fourth day, the stables of the Castle Berlifitzing were discovered to be on fire; and the ^punanimous opinion of the neighborhood^p added^q the crime of the incendiary to the already hideous^r list of the Baron's misdemeanors and enormities.

But during the tumult occasioned by this occurrence, the young nobleman himself sat,^s apparently buried in meditation, in a vast and desolate upper apartment of the^t family palace of Metzengerstein. The rich although faded tapestry hangings which swung gloomily upon the walls, represented the ^ushadowy and majestic^u forms of a thousand illustrious ancestors. *Here,*^v rich-ermined priests, and pontifical dignitaries, familiarly seated with the autocrat and the sovereign, put a veto on the wishes of a^w temporal king, or restrained with the fiat of papal supremacy the rebellious sceptre of the Arch-enemy. *There,*^x the dark, tall statures of the Princes Metzengerstein — their muscular war-coursers plunging over the ^ycarcasses of fallen foes^y — startled the steadiest^z nerves with their

---

k . . . k   number — of these, the *(A, B, C, D)*
l   Chateau *(A, B, C, D)*
m   one hundred and fifty *(A)*
n   protection *(A)*
o   bloodthirsty and remorseless *(A);* remorseless and bloody *(B, C, D)*
p . . . p   neighbourhood unanimously *(A)*
q   instantaneously added *(B, C, D)*
r   frightful *(A)*

s   himself sat,/himself, sat *(E)* *repunctuated from B, C, D*
t   his *(A)*
u . . . u   majestic, and shadowy *(A)*
v   *Here,*/Here *(A)*
w   some *(A)*
x   *There,*/Here *(A)*
y . . . y   carcass of a fallen foe *(A, B, C, D)*
z   firmest *(A)*

vigorous expression: and *here,* again,[a] the voluptuous and swan-like figures of the dames of days gone by, floated away in the mazes of an unreal dance to the strains of imaginary melody.

But as the Baron listened, or affected to listen, to the gradually[b] increasing uproar in the stables of[c] Berlifitzing — or perhaps [d]pondered upon some more novel,[d] some more decided act of audacity — his eyes [e]were turned unwittingly[e] to the figure of an enormous, and unnaturally colored horse, represented in the tapestry as belonging to a Saracen ancestor of the family of his rival. The horse itself, in the fore-ground of the design, stood motionless and statue-like — while, farther back, its discomfited rider perished by the dagger of a Metzengerstein.

[f]On Frederick's lip arose a fiendish expression,[f] as he became aware of the direction which[g] his glance had,[h] without his consciousness, assumed. Yet[i] he did not remove it. On the contrary, [j]he could by no means account for the[k] overwhelming anxiety which appeared falling like a pall[l] upon his senses. It was with difficulty that he reconciled his dreamy and incoherent feelings with the certainty of being awake. The longer he gazed, the more absorbing became the spell — the more impossible did it appear that he could ever withdraw his glance from the fascination of that tapestry.[j] But the tumult without becoming suddenly more violent, with a compulsory[m] exertion he diverted his attention to the glare of ruddy light thrown full by the flaming stables upon the windows of the apartment.

The action, however,[n] was but momentary; his gaze returned mechanically to the wall. To his extreme horror and astonishment,[o]

---

a   *here,* again,/here, *(A)*
b   rapidly *(A)*
c   of the Castle *(A)*
d . . . d   pondered, like Nero, upon *(A)*
e . . . e   were unwittingly rivetted *(A);*
became rivetted *(B, C, D)*
f . . . f   There was a fiendish expression
on the lip of the young Frederick, *(A)*
g   *Omitted (B, C, D)*
h   had, thus, *(A)*
i   But *(A)*
j . . . j   the longer he gazed, the more
impossible did it appear that he might
ever withdraw his vision from the
fascination of that tapestry. It was with

difficulty that he could reconcile his
dreamy and incoherent feelings, with
the certainty of being awake. He could,
by no means, account for the singular,
intense, and overwhelming anxiety
which appeared falling, like a shroud,
upon his senses. *(A)*
k   the singular, intense and *(B)*
changed in C
l   shroud *(B, C, D)*
m   kind of compulsory, and desperate
(A, B, C, D)
n   action, however,/action *(A)*
o   surprise, *(A)*

the head of the gigantic steed had, in the meantime, altered its position. The neck of the animal, before arched, as if in compassion, over the prostrate body of its lord, was now extended, at full length, in the direction of the Baron. The eyes, before invisible, now wore an energetic and human expression, while they gleamed with a fiery and unusual red; and the distended lips of the apparently enraged horse left in full view his sepulchral[p] and disgusting teeth.

Stupified with terror, the young nobleman tottered to the door. As he threw it open, a flash of red light, streaming far into the chamber, flung his shadow with a clear[q] outline against the quivering tapestry; and he shuddered to perceive[r] that shadow — as he [s]staggered awhile[s] upon the threshold — assuming the exact position, and precisely filling up the contour, of the relentless and triumphant murderer of the Saracen Berlifitzing.

[t]To lighten the depression[t] of his spirits, the Baron hurried into the open air. At the principal gate of the palace[u] he encountered three equerries. With much difficulty, and at the imminent[v] peril of their lives, they were restraining the[w] convulsive plunges of a gigantic and fiery-colored horse.

[x]"Whose horse?[x] Where did you get him?" demanded the youth, in a querulous and husky tone,[y] as he became instantly aware that the mysterious steed in the tapestried chamber was the very counterpart of the furious animal before his eyes.

"He is your own property, sire," replied one of the equerries, "at least he is claimed by no other owner. We caught him[z] flying, all smoking and foaming with rage, from the burning stables of the Castle Berlifitzing. Supposing him to have belonged to the old Count's stud of foreign horses, we led him back as an estray. But the grooms there disclaim any title to the creature; which is strange,[a] since he bears evident marks of having made[b] a narrow escape from the flames."

---

p   gigantic *(D)*
q   clear, decided *(A)*
r   pereeve *(A) misprint*
s . . . s   staggered, for a moment, *(A)*
t . . . t   With the view of lightening the oppression *(A)*
u   Chateau *(A, B, C, D)*

v   imininent *(A) misprint*
w   the unnatural, and *(A, B, C, D)*
x . . . x   "Whose horse is that? *(A)*
y   tone of voice, *(A, B, C, D)*
z   him, just now, *(A)*
a   singular, *(A)*
b   having made *omitted (A)*

"The letters W. V. B. are also[c] branded very distinctly on[d] his forehead,"[9] interrupted a second equerry; [e]"I supposed them, of course,[e] to be the initials of Wilhelm[f] Von [g]Berlifitzing — but all at the castle are positive in denying any knowledge of the horse."[g]

"Extremely singular!" said the young Baron, with a musing air, and[h] apparently unconscious of the meaning of his words. "He is, as you say, a remarkable horse — a prodigious horse! although, as you very justly observe, of a suspicious and untractable character; let him be mine, however," he added,[i] after a pause, "perhaps a rider like Frederick of Metzengerstein, may tame even the devil from the stables of Berlifitzing."

"You are[j] mistaken, my lord; the horse, as I think we mentioned, is *not* from the stables of the Count. If such had been[k] the case, we know our duty better than to bring him into[l] the presence of a noble of your family."[m]

"True!" observed the Baron, drily; and at that instant a page of the bed-chamber came from the palace[n] with a heightened color, and a[o] precipitate step. He whispered into his master's ear an account of the[p] sudden disappearance of a small portion of the tapestry, in an apartment which he designated; entering, at the same time, into particulars of a minute and circumstantial character; but from the low tone of voice in which these latter were communicated, nothing escaped to gratify the excited curiosity of the equerries.

The young Frederick,[q] during the conference, seemed agitated by a variety of emotions. He soon, however, recovered his composure, and an expression of determined malignancy settled upon his countenance, as he gave peremptory orders that [r]the apartment in question[r] should be immediately locked up, and the key placed[s] in his own possession.

"Have you heard of the unhappy death of the old[t] hunter Ber-

---

c are also/are, moreover, *(A)*	l in *(A)*
d upon *(A)*	m name." *(A)*
e . . . e "We, at first, supposed them *(A)*	n Chateau *(A, B, C, D)*
f William *(A)*	o *Omitted (A, B, C, D)*
g . . . g Berlifitzing." *(A)*	p the miraculous, and *(A, B, C, D)*
h *Omitted (A)*	q Frederick, however, *(A)*
i added he, *(A)*	r . . . r a certain chamber *(A, B, C, D)*
j appear to be *(A)*	s placed, forthwith, *(A)*
k had been/were *(A, B, C, D)*	t *Omitted (A)*

lifitzing?" said one of his vassals to the Baron, as, after the departure[u] of the page, the huge[v] steed which that nobleman had adopted as his own, plunged and curveted, with redoubled[w] fury, down the long avenue which extended from the palace[x] to the stables of Metzengerstein.

"No!" said the Baron, turning abruptly towards the speaker, "dead! say you?"

"[y]It is indeed true, my lord; and, to the[z] noble of your name, will be, I imagine, no unwelcome intelligence."[y]

A rapid smile[a] shot over the[b] countenance of the listener. "How died he?"

"In his rash[c] exertions to rescue a favorite portion of his hunting stud, he has himself perished miserably in the flames."

"I—n—d—e—e—d—!" ejaculated the Baron, as if slowly and deliberately impressed with the truth of some exciting idea.

"Indeed;" repeated the vassal.

"Shocking!" said the youth, calmly, and turned quietly[d] into the palace.[e]

From this date a marked alteration took place in the outward demeanor of the dissolute young Baron Frederick Von[f] Metzengerstein. Indeed, [g]his behaviour[g] disappointed every expectation, and proved little in accordance with the views of many a manœuvring mamma; while his habits and manners, still less than formerly, offered anything congenial with those of the neighboring aristocracy. [h]He was never to be seen[h] beyond the limits of his own [i]domain, and, in this wide and social world, was utterly companionless — unless,[i] indeed, that unnatural, impetuous, and fiery-colored

---

u   affair *(A)*
v   huge and mysterious *(A, B, C, D)*
w   redoubled, and supernatural *(A, B, C, D)*
x   Chateau *(A, B, C, D)*
y . . . y   "It is true, my lord, and is no unwelcome intelligence, I imagine, to a noble of your family?" *(A)*
z   the/a *(B, C, D)*
a   smile, of a peculiar and unintelligible meaning, *(A, B, C, D)*
b   the beautiful *(A, B, C, D)*

c   great *(A)*
d   turned quietly/returned *(A)*
e   Chateau. *(A, B, C, D)*
f   Frederick Von/Frederick, of *(A)*
g . . . g   the behaviour of the heir *(A)*
h . . . h   He was seldom to be seen at all; never *(A)*
i . . . i   domain. There are few, in this social world, who are utterly companionless, yet so seemed he; unless, *(A)*

horse, which he henceforward[j] continually bestrode, had any mysterious right to the title of his friend.

Numerous invitations on the part of the neighborhood for a long time, however, periodically came[k] in. "[l]Will the Baron honor our festivals with his presence?" [m]"Will the Baron join us in a hunting of the boar?"[m] — "Metzengerstein[n] does not hunt;" "Metzengerstein[o] will not attend," were the haughty and laconic answers.

These repeated insults were not to be endured by an imperious nobility. Such invitations became less cordial — less frequent — in time they ceased altogether. The widow of the unfortunate Count Berlifitzing was even heard to express a hope "that the Baron might be at home when he did not wish[p] to be at home, since he disdained the company of his equals; and ride when he did not wish to ride, since he preferred the society of a horse." This to be sure was a very silly explosion of hereditary pique; and merely proved how singularly unmeaning our sayings are apt to become, when we desire to be unusually energetic.

The charitable, nevertheless, attributed the alteration in the conduct of the young nobleman to the natural sorrow of a son for the untimely loss of his parents; — forgetting, however, his atrocious and reckless behaviour during the short period immediately succeeding that bereavement. Some there were, indeed, who suggested a too haughty idea of self-consequence and dignity. Others again (among whom may be mentioned the family physician) did not hesitate in speaking of morbid melancholy, and hereditary ill-health; while dark hints, of a more equivocal nature, were current among the multitude.

Indeed, the Baron's perverse attachment to his lately-acquired charger — an attachment which seemed to attain new strength from every fresh example of the animal's[q] ferocious and demon-like propensities — at length became, in the eyes of all reasonable men, a hideous and unnatural fervor. In the glare of noon — at the dead hour of night — in sickness or in health[10] — in calm or in tempest

---

j thenceforward *(A)*	m . . . m *Omitted (A)*
k periodically came/continually flocked *(A)*	n "Baron Frederick *(A)*
	o Baron Frederick *(A)*
l *After this:* Will the Baron attend our excursions? *(A)*	p choose *(A)*
	q brute's *(A)*

— [r] the young Metzengerstein seemed riveted to the saddle of that colossal horse, whose intractable[s] audacities so well accorded with [t]his own spirit.[t]

There were circumstances, moreover, which, coupled with late events, gave an unearthly and portentous character to the mania of the rider, and to[u] the capabilities of the steed. The space passed over in a single leap had been accurately measured, and was found to exceed by an [v]astounding difference,[v] the wildest expectations of the most imaginative.[w] The Baron, besides, had no particular *name*[x] for the animal, although all the rest in[y] his[z] collection were distinguished by characteristic appellations.[11] His[a] stable, too,[b] was appointed at a distance from the rest;[c] and with regard to grooming and other necessary offices, none but the owner in person had[d] ventured to officiate, or even to enter the enclosure of that horse's[e] particular stall. It was also to be observed, that although the three grooms, who had caught the steed[f] as he fled from the conflagration at Berlifitzing, had succeeded in arresting his course, by means of a chain-bridle and noose — yet no one of the three could with any certainty affirm that he had, during that dangerous struggle, or at any period thereafter, actually placed his hand upon the body of the beast. [g]Instances of peculiar intelligence in the demeanor of a noble and high-spirited horse[h] are not to be supposed capable of exciting unreasonable attention,[i] but there were certain circumstances which intruded themselves per force upon the most skeptical and phlegmatic; and it is said there were times when the[j]

---

r   tempest — /tempest, in moonlight or in shadow, *(A, B, C, D)*
s   untractable *(A)*
t . . . t   the spirit of his own. *(A, B, C, D)*
u   Omitted *(A)*
v . . . v   incalculable distance, *(A)*
w   imaginative; while the red lightning, itself, was declared to have been outridden in many a long-continued, and impetuous career. *(A)*
x   name *(A)*
y   of *(A)*
z   his extensive *(A, B, C, D)*

a   Its *(A)*
b   stable, too,/stable *(A)*
c   rest;/others, *(A)*
d   had ever *(A)*
e   Omitted *(A, B, C, D)*
f   horse, *(A, B, C, D)*
g . . . g   *These sentences are omitted in A*
h   steed *(B, C, D)*
i   attention — especially among men who, daily trained to the labors of the chase, might appear well acquainted with the sagacity of a horse — *(B, C, D)*
j   this singular and mysterious *(B) changed in C*

animal caused the gaping crowd who stood around to recoil in[k] horror from the deep and impressive meaning of his terrible stamp — times when the young Metzengerstein turned pale and shrunk away from the rapid and searching expression of his earnest[l] and human-looking eye.[g]

Among all the retinue of the Baron, however, none were found to doubt the ardor of that extraordinary affection which existed on the part of the young nobleman for the fiery qualities of his horse; at least, none but an insignificant and misshapen little page, whose deformities were in every body's way, and whose opinions were of the least possible importance. He (if his ideas are worth mentioning at all,) had the effrontery to assert that his master never vaulted into the saddle, without an unaccountable and almost imperceptible shudder; and that, upon his return from every [m]long-continued and[m] habitual ride,[n] an expression of triumphant malignity distorted every muscle in his countenance.

[o]One tempestuous night, Metzengerstein, awaking from heavy[p] slumber, descended like a maniac from his chamber,[o] and, mounting in hot[q] haste, bounded away into the mazes of the forest. An occurrence so common attracted no particular attention, but his return was looked for with intense anxiety on the part of his domestics, when, after some hours'[r] absence, the stupendous and magnificent battlements of the Palace[s] Metzengerstein, were discovered crackling and rocking to their very foundation, under the influence of a dense and livid mass of ungovernable fire.

As the flames, when first seen, had already made so terrible a progress that all efforts to save any portion of the building were evidently futile, the astonished neighborhood stood idly around in silent, if not[t] apathetic wonder. But a new and fearful object soon

---

k   in silent (B, C, D)
l   intense (B) changed in C
m . . . m   Omitted (A)
n   ride, during which his panting and bleeding brute was never known to pause in his impetuosity, although he, himself, evinced no appearance of exhaustion, yet (A)
o . . . o   These ominous circumstances portended in the opinion of all people, some awful, and impending calamity. Accordingly one tempestuous night, the Baron descended, like a maniac, from his bed-chamber, (A)
p   a heavy and oppressive (B, C, D)
q   great (A, B, C, D)
r   hours (A); hour's (B, C, D)
s   Chateau (B, C, D)
t   if not/and (A, B, C, D)

riveted the attention of the multitude, and proved [u]how much more intense is the excitement wrought in the feelings of a crowd by the contemplation of human agony, than that brought about by[u] the most appalling spectacles of inanimate matter.

Up the long avenue of aged oaks which led from the forest to the main entrance of the Palace[v] Metzengerstein, a steed, bearing an unbonneted and disordered rider, was seen leaping with an impetuosity which outstripped the very Demon of the Tempest.[w] [12]

The career of the horseman was indisputably, on his own part, uncontrollable. The agony of his countenance, the convulsive struggle[x] of his frame, gave evidence of superhuman exertion: but no sound, save a solitary shriek, escaped from his lacerated lips, which were bitten through and through in the intensity of terror. One instant, and the clattering of hoofs resounded sharply and shrilly above the roaring of the flames and the shrieking of the winds — another, and, clearing at a single plunge the gate-way and the moat, the [y]steed bounded far up the tottering staircases of the palace, and, with its rider, disappeared amid the whirlwind of chaotic fire.[y] [13]

The fury of the tempest[z] immediately died away, and a dead calm sullenly[a] succeeded. A white flame still enveloped the building like a shroud, and, streaming far away into the quiet atmosphere, shot forth a glare of preternatural light; while a cloud of[b] smoke settled heavily over the [c]battlements in the distinct colossal figure of — *a horse.*[c] [d]

---

u . . . u   the vast superiority of excitement which the sight of human agony exercises in the feelings of a crowd, above *(A)*
v   Chateau *(A, B, C, D)*
w   tempest, and called forth from every beholder an ejaculation of "Azrael!" *(A);* Tempest, and extorted from every stupified beholder the ejaculation — "horrible!" *(B, C, D)*
x   struggling *(A)*
y . . . y   animal bounded, with its rider, far up the tottering staircase of the palace, and was lost in the whirlwind of hissing, and chaotic fire. *(A)*
z   storm *(A)*
a   suddenly *(A)*
b   of wreathing *(A)*
c . . . c   battlements, and slowly, but distinctly assumed the appearance of a motionless and colossal horse.
   Frederick, Baron Metzengerstein, was the last of a long line of princes. His family name is no longer to be found among the Hungarian aristocracy. *(A)*
d   a horse *not italicized (B, C, D)*

NOTES

(Notes 3 and 12 pertain only to the early text, *A*. See the variants.)

Title: The name is apparently not historical, and is of uncertain meaning. In German *Metz* (plural *Metzen*) is meal (flour), and the name of a city; and *Ger* is a spear, but *Metzger* is a butcher. *Stein* is stone. Poe may have thought the name meant Butcherstone or Stonespear of Metz.

1. The motto is part of a hexameter, addressed by Martin Luther to the Pope, meaning, "Living I have been your plague, dying I shall be your death." Where Poe read it is uncertain; Luther said it more than once. Professor Francis A. Christie referred me to a letter of February 27, 1537 to Melancthon, in De Wette's edition of *Luthers Briefe*, V, 58.

2. "... comes of being unable to be alone," from Jean de la Bruyère (1645–1696), *Les Caractères*, section 99, "De l'homme," used also in the motto of Poe's "Man of the Crowd." The footnote was first published in *Works* (1850); its first sentence repeats "Pinakidia," no. 90, from the *Southern Literary Messenger*, August 1836, p. 578, which in turn was taken from the chapter "Metempsychosis" in *Curiosities of Literature* by Isaac D'Israeli (1776–1848). The primary source is Louis-Sebastien Mercier's *L'An 2440* (1770), chapter XIX, "Le Temple." Ethan Allen's precise idea I do not find in his *Reason, the Only Oracle of Man* (1784), but I have met with a legend that he said he might live again in his great white horse.

3. *(A)* Poe remarks again on the meaning of *religio* in Classical Latin in "The Purloined Letter," and in "Marginalia," number 176 (*Graham's*, November 1846, p. 246).

4. The acute Parisian remains unidentified. He said the soul "dwells but once in a material body — for the rest — a horse, a dog, even a human being — it is only an intangible phantom of those creatures."

5. The name Berlifitzing is apparently invented; it may mean something like Little Son of a Bear.

6. The expression to "out-Herod Herod" from *Hamlet*, III, ii, 16, is a favorite of Poe, who uses it in "William Wilson" and "The Masque of the Red Death."

7. Some Hungarian nobles were notoriously cruel. Countess Elizabeth Bathori, who lived until 1614, compelled young peasant women to dance in the icy courtyard of her castle, wearing nothing but their boots. Some of her exploits were less picturesque, and more horrible.

8. The youthful emperor Caligula (Gaius Caesar), like Metzengerstein, was probably mad, and loved horses. He once expressed a wish to make his favorite racehorse a consul, according to Suetonius, "Gaius," Chapter 55.

9. The brand on the forehead recalls the mark of Cain (Genesis 4:15).

10. "In sickness and in health" is from the wedding ceremony in the Book of Common Prayer.

11. Metzengerstein knew the horse was Wilhelm von Berlifitzing, and dared use no other name. Compare the idea in "Morella."

12. *(A)* Azrael, the Mahometan angel of death, is also mentioned in *Politian*, IX, 4, in "Ligeia," and in "Mesmeric Revelation"; "the Archangel Death" is mentioned in early versions of "King Pest."

13. Such evil beings as the horse and his rider could be destroyed only by fire. See Quinn, *Poe*, p. 193, on the suggested allegory of the bad man so enthralled by evil that he cannot part from it.

THE DUC DE L'OMELETTE

This is one of the few stories involving humor in which Poe seems to me to be wholly successful. Of all the *Tales of the Grotesque and Arabesque,* it most harmoniously blends the two elements of decoration and grotesquerie; and there is an element of adventure — one hopes the Duke may escape, for he is a bold and daring fellow, whom we know and tend to like better than most of Poe's heroes.

"Beat the devil" is a proverbial expression for something practically incredible, but there are many stories in folklore and literature of people who did it. Pride, and not goodness of heart, makes the Devil keep his word literally, and avoid actions beneath his dignity such as cheating at cards or taking advantage of a drunken man, as in "The Bargain Lost" and "Bon-Bon." Other stories of Lucifer playing cards are to be found.* For the plot of "The Duc de L'Omelette" Poe accepts the notion that "the devil studies complexions. He cannot read our thoughts."† (In "The Bargain Lost" and "Bon-Bon" he *can* read minds.)

Poe's important sources are traced in detail in the notes following the text of the story below. The physiognomical ideas of Le Brun, and Montfleury's death from violent action on the stage,

---

* See "Legends of Glamis Castle" by Jessie A. Middleton in *A Grey Ghost Book* (1915), pp. 167ff.

† Pierre Crespet, *Deux Livres de la hayne de Sathan* (Paris, 1590), as quoted in [Robert] *Southey's Common-place Book* (4 vols., 1849–51), III, 409. See also Daniel Defoe's *History of the Devil* (1726), part II, ch. III, paragraph 2: "Whether the Devil knows our thoughts or not? . . . I deny that he knows anything of our thoughts, except of those which he puts us upon thinking" (quoted from an edition issued in Durham in 1822).

come from Isaac D'Israeli's *Curiosities of Literature.* The fatal effects of an ortolan and other details were suggested by his son Benjamin Disraeli's novel *The Young Duke* and a burlesquing review of that novel in the *Westminster Review,* October 1831, may have influenced Poe even more.‡ The infernal palace may owe something to William Beckford's *Vathek* (1786, often reprinted), but there is general agreement on the magnificence of Lucifer's residence, which Milton called Pandemonium.

Poe's story was presumably written in 1831 and sent almost at once to the *Saturday Courier.* It was considerably revised for publication in the *Southern Literary Messenger* in 1836, but touched only very lightly thereafter. In the *Messenger* it was ascribed to Edgar A. Poe; in the *Broadway Journal* it was signed "Littleton Barry," the first time Poe used the signature appended also to the *Broadway Journal* versions of "Loss of Breath," "King Pest," "Mystification," and "Why the Little Frenchman Wears His Hand in a Sling." (See note 41 on "Loss of Breath.")

TEXTS

(A) Philadelphia *Saturday Courier,* March 3, 1832; *(B)* Southern Literary *Messenger,* February 1836 (2:150–151); *(C)* Tales of the Grotesque and Arabesque (1840), I, 105–110; *(D)* PHANTASY-PIECES (manuscript revisions of the last, 1842); *(E)* Broadway Journal, October 11, 1845 (2:206–208); *(F)* Works (1850), II, 347–350.

Griswold's text *(F),* showing one new reading, is followed in this edition.

The earliest text *(A)* was mechanically reproduced by John Grier Varner in *Edgar Allan Poe and the Philadelphia Saturday Courier* (1933), pp. 25–31. The French words are not accented, and the punctuation, capitalization and paragraphing are quite different from later texts. Poe's principal changes were made for the *Southern Literary Messenger* in 1836. In PHANTASY-PIECES there are seven punctuation changes, all of which eliminate dashes.

Reprints

The *Baltimore Minerva,* March 10, 1832, and the *Albany Literary Gazette,* March 24, 1832, both from the *Saturday Courier;* English and American editions of *Bentley's Miscellany,* October 1840, from *Tales of the Grotesque and Arabesque,* without acknowledgment.

‡ See Ruth Leigh Hudson, "Poe and Disraeli," *American Literature,* January 1937, and David Hirsch, "Another Source for Poe's 'The Duc De L'Omelette,'" in the same periodical for January 1967. See also Mabbott I, 324, where it is pointed out that the impulse to write "The Conqueror Worm" may have come from a review.

THE DUC DE L'OMELETTE

THE DUC DE L'OMELETTE. [*F*]

And stepped at once into a cooler clime. —— Cowper.[a]

Keats fell by a criticism.[1] Who was it died of *"The Andro-mache?"**[b] Ignoble souls! — De L'Omelette perished of an orto-lan.[3] *L'histoire en est brève.* Assist me, Spirit of[f] Apicius![4]

A golden cage bore the [g]little winged[g] wanderer, enamored, melting, indolent, to the *Chaussée D'Antin,*[5] from its home in far Peru. From its queenly possessor La Bellissima, to the Duc De L'Omelette, six peers of the empire conveyed the happy bird.[h] [6]

That night the Duc[i] was to sup alone. In the privacy of his bureau he reclined languidly on that ottoman for which he sacri-ficed his loyalty in outbidding his king, — the notorious ottoman of Cadêt.[7]

He buries[j] his face in the pillow. The clock strikes![k] Unable to restrain his feelings his Grace swallows[l] an olive.[8] [m]At this mo-ment the door gently[m] opens to the sound of soft music, and lo![n] the most delicate of birds is before the most enamored of men! [o]But what inexpressible dismay now overshadows the countenance of the Duc? —— *"Horreur! — chien! — Baptiste! — l'oiseau! ah, bon*

---

* Montfleury. The author of the *Parnasse Réformé* makes him speak in Hades: — *"L'homme donc qui voudrait savoir ce dont Je suis mort, qu'il[c] ne demande pas [d]s'il fut de fièvre[d] ou de podagre ou d'autre chose, mais qu'il entende que ce fut de 'l'Andromache.' "*[e] [2]

Title: The Duke de L'Omelette *(A)*
a *Ascription omitted (A)*
b *Footnote omitted (A); in B, C, D it reads* Montfleury. The author of the *Parnasse Reformé* makes him express himself in the shades. "The man then who would know of what I died, let him not ask if it were of the fever, the dropsy, or the gout; but let him know that it was of The Andromache." *In E the note is as in the final text except that it has* thus speak *instead of* speak
c *qui'l (E, F)*
d ... d *si'l fût de fievre (E, F)*

e 'L' Andromache' " *(E);* 'I' Andromache' " *(F) misprint*
f Spirit of *omitted (A)*
g ... g luxurious little *(A)*
h bird. It was "All for Love." *(A, B, C, D)*
i Duke *(A) here and hereafter in all except two cases*
j buried *(A)*
k struck. *(A)*
l swallowed *(A)*
m ... m The door *(A)*
n and lo!/and *(A)*
o ... o — horror! — dog! — Baptiste! — l'oiseau — *(A)*

Dieu![o] *cet oiseau modeste que tu as déshabillé*[p] *de ses plumes, et que tu as servi sans papier!"*[9] It is superfluous to say more: — the Duc expired in a paroxysm of disgust. * * * * *

"Ha! ha! ha!" said his Grace on the third day after his decease.

"He! he! he!" replied the Devil faintly, drawing[q] himself up with an air of *hauteur.*

"Why, surely you are not serious," retorted De [r]L'Omelette. "I have sinned — *c'est vrai* — but, my good sir, consider! — you have no actual intention of[r] putting such — such — barbarous threats into execution."

"No *what?*" said his majesty[s] — "come, sir, strip!"

"Strip, indeed! — very pretty i' faith![t] — no, sir, I shall *not* strip. Who are you, pray, that I, Duc De L'Omelette, Prince de Foie-Gras,[u] just come of age, author of the 'Mazurkiad,'[10] and Member of the Academy, should divest myself at your bidding of the sweetest pantaloons ever made by Bourdon,[v] the daintiest *robe-de-chambre* ever put together by Rombêrt[11] — [w]to say nothing of[w] the taking my hair out of paper — [x]not to mention the trouble I should have in drawing off my gloves?"[x]

"Who am I? — ah, true! I am Baal-Zebub, Prince of the Fly.[12] I took thee, just now, from [y]a rose-wood coffin inlaid with ivory. Thou wast[y] curiously scented, and labelled as per invoice. Belial sent thee, — my Inspector of Cemeteries. The pantaloons, which thou sayest were made by Bourdon,[z] are an excellent pair of linen drawers, and thy *robe-de-chambre* is a shroud of no scanty dimensions."

"Sir!" replied the Duc,[a] "I am not to be insulted with impunity! — Sir! I shall take the earliest opportunity of avenging this insult! — Sir! you shall hear from me! In the meantime *au revoir!*" — and the Duc was bowing himself out of the Satanic presence, when he was interrupted and brought back by a gentleman in

---

p *deshabille (A); deshabillé (B, C, D, E, F)*
q *and drawing (A)*
r . . . r *l'Omelette — 'you have no bona fide intentions of — of — (A)*
s *said his majesty omitted (A)*
t i' *faith!/'faith! (A)*
u *Fois-Gras, (A)*

v *Stultz, (A)*
w . . . w *not to mention (A)*
x . . . x *and all to gratify your blood-thirsty propensities!" (A)*
y . . . y *an inlaid coffin, (A)*
z *Stultz, (A)*
a *replied the Duc, omitted (A)*

waiting. Hereupon[b] his Grace rubbed his eyes, yawned, shrugged his shoulders, [c]reflected. Having[c] become satisfied of his identity, he[d] took a bird's eye view of his whereabouts.[e]

The apartment was superb. Even[f] De L'Omelette pronounced it *bien comme il faut.* It was not [g]its length nor its breadth,[g] — but its height — ah, that was appalling! — There was no ceiling — certainly none — but a dense whirling mass of fiery-colored clouds. His Grace's brain reeled as he glanced upwards. [h]From above, hung[h] a chain of an unknown blood-red metal[13] — its upper end lost, like [i]the city of Boston,[i] *parmi les nues.*[14] From its nether extremity swung[j] a large[k] cresset. The Duc knew it to be a ruby; but [l]from it there poured[l] a light so intense, so still, so terrible, Persia never worshipped such — Gheber never imagined such — Mussulman never dreamed of such when, drugged with opium, he has tottered to a bed of poppies, his back to the flowers,[m] and his face to the God Apollo.[15] The Duc muttered[n] a slight oath, decidedly approbatory.

The corners of the room were rounded into niches. — Three of these were filled with statues of gigantic proportions. Their beauty was Grecian, their deformity Egyptian, their *tout ensemble* French.[o] In the fourth niche the statue was veiled; it was *not* colossal. But then[p] there was a taper ankle, a sandalled foot. De L'Omelette pressed[q] his hand upon his heart, closed his eyes, raised them, and caught his Satanic Majesty — in a blush.

But the paintings! — Kupris![r] Astarte! Astoreth! — a thousand and the same![16] And Rafaelle has beheld them! Yes, Rafaelle has been here; for did he not paint the——? and was he not consequently damned?[17] The paintings! — the paintings! O luxury! O love! — who, gazing on those forbidden beauties, shall have eyes for the

---

b Upon this *(A)*

c . . . c reflected: and having *(A)*

d *Omitted (A)*

e whereabout. *(A)*

f *Omitted (A)*

g . . . g very long, nor very broad, *(A, B, C, D)*

h . . . h There was *(A)*

i . . . i Col — e, *(A);* C —, *(B, C);* Carlyle, *(D)*

j hung *(A, B, C, D)*

k huge *(A)*

l . . . l there poured from it *(A)*

m earth, *(A)*

n murmured *(A)*

o French. His grace could not understand them, and said 'Bah!' *(A)*

p But then/Then *(A)*

q laid *(A, B, C, D)*

r Rupris! *(A) misprint*

dainty devices of the golden frames that [s]besprinkled,[t] like stars, the hyacinth[18] and the porphyry walls?[s]

[u]But the[v] Duc's heart is fainting within him. He[w] is not, however,[x] as you suppose, dizzy with magnificence, nor drunk with the ecstatic breath of those innumerable censers. *C'est vrai que de toutes ces choses il a [y]pensé beaucoup[y] — mais!*[19] The Duc De L'Omelette is terror-stricken;[z] for, through the lurid vista which a single uncurtained window is affording, lo! gleams the most ghastly of all fires!

Le pauvre Duc! [a]He could not help imagining[a] that the glorious, the voluptuous, the never-dying [b]melodies which pervaded that[b] hall, as they passed filtered and transmuted through the alchemy of [c]the enchanted window-panes,[c] were the wailings and the howlings of the hopeless and the damned![20] And there, too! — there! — upon[d] that ottoman! — who could *he* be? — he, the *petit-maître*[e] — no, the Deity — who sat as if carved in marble, *et qui sourit,* with his pale countenance, *si amèrement?*[f] [21]

Mais il faut [g]agir,[22] — that is to say, a[g] Frenchman never faints outright. Besides, his Grace hated a scene — De L'Omelette is[h] himself again.[23] There were some foils upon[i] a table — some points also. The Duc had studied under B———; *il avait tué ses six hommes.*[24] Now, then, *il peut s'échapper.*[j] [25] [k]He measures two points, and, with a grace inimitable, offers his Majesty the choice.[k] *Horreur!* his Majesty does not fence!

Mais il joue![l] — how happy a[l] thought![m] — but his Grace had

---

s . . . s lie imbedded, and asleep in those swelling walls of eider-down? *(A, B, C, D) except that B, C, D have* against *instead of* in

t besprinkle, *(E)*

u *Before this A has another paragraph:* But the lofty, narrow windows of stained glass, and porphyry! — how many! — how magnificent! — And the curtains! — ah! that aerial silk! — the vapour-like floating of that gorgeous drapery!

v But the/The *(A)*

w No — oh, no. He *(A)*

x *Omitted (A)*

y . . . y *fait un memorandum (A)*

z horror-stricken — *(A)*

a . . . a Could he have imagined *(A)*

b . . . b symphonies of that melodious *(A)*

c . . . c that enchanted glass, *(A)*

d on *(A)*

e *petit-maitre (all texts)*

f *amerement? (A, B, C, D); amérement? (E, F)*

g . . . g *agir. A (A)*

h *Omitted (A)*

i on *(A)*

j *Accent added in D*

k . . . k *Omitted (A)*

l . . . l What a *(A);* — what a happy *(B, C) changed in D*

always[m] an excellent memory. He had[n] dipped in the *"Diable"* of the Abbé Gualtier. Therein it[o] is said *"que le Diable n'ose pas refuser un*[p] *jeu d'écarté."*[26]

[q]But the chances — the chances![q] True — desperate; [r]but scarcely[s] more desperate than the Duc.[r] Besides, was he not in the secret? — had he not skimmed over Père Le Brun?[t] — [27]was he not a member of the Club Vingt-un?[u] *"Si je perds,"* said he, *"je serai deux fois perdu* — I shall be doubly damned — *voilà*[v] *tout!* (Here his Grace[w] shrugged his shoulders.) [x]*Si je gagne, je reviendrai à mes ortolans*[x] — *que les cartes soient préparées!"*[28]

His Grace was all care, all attention — his Majesty all confidence. A spectator would have thought of Francis and Charles.[29] His Grace[y] thought of his game. His Majesty did not think; he shuffled. [z]The Duc cut.[z]

The cards are dealt. The trump is turned[a] — it is — it is — the king! No — it was the queen. His Majesty cursed her masculine habiliments. De L'Omelette placed[b] his hand upon his heart.

They play. The Duc counts. The hand is out. His Majesty counts heavily, smiles, and is taking[c] wine. The Duc slips a card.

"C'est à vous à faire,"[30] said his Majesty, cutting. His Grace bowed, dealt, and arose from the table *en présentant*[d] *le Roi.*[31]

His Majesty looked chagrined.

Had Alexander[e] not been Alexander, he would have been Diogenes;[32] and the Duc assured his [f]antagonist in taking leave,[f] *"que s'il*[g] [h]*n'eût pas été*[h] *De L'Omelette il n'aurait point d'objection d'être le Diable."*[i] [33]

---

m . . . m   His grace has *(A)*
n   He had/Have you *(A)*
o   Therein it/It *(A)*
p   *Omitted (A)*
q . . . q   But the chances! *(A)*
r . . . r   But not more than himself. *(A)*
s   not *(B, C, D)*
t   Le Brun?/La Chaise? *(A)*
u   Club Vingt-un?/Academy? *(A)*
v   *voila (all texts)*
w   his Grace/the duke *(A)*
x . . . x   *Eh bien! si Je gagne! (A);* Si Je gagne Je serai libre *(B, C, D)*

y   His grace/De l'Omelette *(A)*
z . . . z   His grace *coupa. (A);* The Duc coupa. *(B)*
a   turned slowly *mais avec un air de fierte.* The corner appears *(A)*
b   laid *(A, B, C, D)*
c   is taking/has taken *(A)*
d   *presentant (all texts)*
e   the drunkard *(A)*
f . . . f   majesty *en partant, (A)*
g   sit *(A) misprint*
h . . . h   *n'etait pas (A, B, C, D)*
i   *Signed* Littleton Barry *(E)*

TALES OF THE FOLIO CLUB

NOTES

Motto: William Cowper, *The Task*, I, 337.

1. John Keats was commonly supposed to have died of a broken heart after a savage attack (by John Wilson Croker) in the *Quarterly Review* for April 1818.

2. Poe took his footnote straight from Isaac D'Israeli's article on "Tragic Actors" in the *Curiosities of Literature*. D'Israeli says: "Montfleury, a French player ... died of the violent efforts he made in representing Orestes in the Andromache of Racine. The author of the *Parnasse Reformé* makes him thus express himself in the shades — 'A thousand times have I been obliged to force myself to represent more passions than Le Brun ever painted or conceived ... and consequently to strain all the parts of my body to render my gestures fitter to accompany these different impressions. The man then who would know of what I died, let him not ask if it were of the fever, the dropsy, or the gout; but let him know that it was of *the Andromache!*' " The *Parnasse Reformé* is by Gabriel Guéret (1641–1688) — the passage translated may be found in the edition of 1668, at pp. 74–75. In earlier versions of his tale *(B, C, D)* Poe used D'Israeli's English; in later, French of his own. He repeated the anecdote in "Marginalia," number 135 (*Godey's*, September 1845, p. 120).

3. The ortolan is a European bunting, a small bird of the family that includes also finches and sparrows. Trapped during the autumn migration, fattened, and cooked at an open fire, the birds sizzle in their own fat. A bird is picked up in the fingers and the breast eaten whole as a mouthful. To avoid soiling the diner's fingers, the bird's legs are wrapped in paper. The ortolan is considered the most delicate of all French birds in flavor. In *The Young Duke* by Benjamin Disraeli (published anonymously in 1831), in the tenth chapter of the first book, a character says: "O, doff then, thy waistcoat of vine leaves, pretty rover, and show me that bosom more delicious even than woman's! What gushes of rapture! What a flavor! How peculiar! Even, how sacred! Heaven at once sends both manna and quails. Another little wanderer! Pray follow my example! Allow me. All paradise opens! Let me die eating ortolans to the sound of soft music!" This passage, as David Hirsch pointed out, was one of those quoted in the *Westminster Review*.

4. There are a number of references in classical literature to M. Gavius Apicius, an epicure of the time of the Emperor Tiberius. It is said that, finding his fortune depleted so that he could no longer indulge in the most expensive dishes, he killed himself (Seneca, *Dialogues*, xii.10.8–11). A cookbook in Latin entitled *Apicius,* circulated several centuries later, has been sometimes attributed to him, but was probably by one Caelius.

5. The Chaussée d'Antin was a fashionable street in Paris. It was mentioned in Lady Sydney Morgan's popular *Book of the Boudoir* (New York, 1829).

6. The canceled reference here is to John Dryden's tragedy *All for Love.*

7. The Ottoman of Cadêt has not been satisfactorily explained.

8. This is quite obviously a satire on N. P. Willis, who in 1829 had ridiculed Poe's poem "Fairy-Land" but in later years became Poe's good friend. In 1829, at twenty-three, Willis established the *American Monthly Magazine* of Boston. He

THE DUC DE L'OMELETTE

there struck a pose that horrified his more sober-minded critics. He pretended to write at a rosewood desk in a sanctum with crimson curtains, to have a French valet, and always to have fresh blossoms of japonica. He asked his readers to imagine themselves on a *dormeuse,* with a bottle of Rudesheimer and a plate of olives at hand. See Kenneth L. Daughrity's "Poe's Quiz on Willis," *American Literature,* March 1933, and his sketch of Willis in the *Dictionary of American Biography.*

9. "Horror! — dog! — Baptist! — the bird — oh, good God, that modest bird you have stripped of her feathers, and served without paper!"

10. Dozens of poems with titles ending in "-iad" appeared in the eighteenth century and later. The Duke's presumably concerned the mazurka, a round dance of Polish origin.

11. My correspondent, Mlle. Madeline Delpierre, found mention in Paris directories of a tailor named Bourdon, at 7, Boulevard St. Denis, from 1831 to 1836. Authorities at the London Museum say George Stultz in 1809 established a business at 10, Clifford Street, off Bond Street, continued there by himself and successors until 1915. No tailor Rombêrt has yet been identified.

12. Baal-Zebub (Prince of Flies) and Belial are more fully annotated in note 23 to "A Tale of Jerusalem," below. It is not certain that Belial (Shame) was considered a god or even a person by the ancients, but Milton made him a leading lieutenant of Satan in *Paradise Lost.*

·13. The blood-red metal comes from the lost Atlantis, as described in Plato's *Critias,* 114 E. It is called in Latin *orichalcum,* a word used for the yellow brass of Roman Imperial coinage.

14. "Among the clouds." This expression is used to describe Mount Atlas by Pomponius Mela, *De Situ Orbis,* III, 10. In the first version *(A)* of Poe's tale it was Coleridge that was thus lost; Carlyle was named in 1842; reference to the City of Boston was introduced in the *Broadway Journal* version of October 11, 1845 — a few days prior to Poe's unfortunate appearance before the Boston Lyceum.

15. The ancient Persians worshipped fire, as do their modern descendants, the Parsees of Bombay. Ghebers is the name given them by Mahometans. There is an allusion to Persian sun worship in "The Visionary." Although spoken of in a playful vein, the light "so intense, so still, so terrible," depending from a chain that is lost in the clouds, would seem to echo Poe's source for "A dome, by linkéd light, etc." in "Al Aaraaf," which he found in Pope's version of the *Iliad:*

> Let down our golden everlasting chain,
> Whose strong embrace holds Heaven and Earth and Main.

See the comment on "linkéd light" in "Al Aaraaf" (Mabbott I, 121, n. 20).

16. Kupris, Lady of Cyprus, where she had a great temple, is a Greek name for Aphrodite, with whom the Phoenician goddess Astarte is identified. The meaning here of Astoreth is the same, although in the Bible the name is a general plural: "We have forsaken the Lord, and have served Baalim and Ashtaroth": see I Samuel 12:10.

17. The joke about Raphael Sanzio has not been fully explained.

18. Hyacinth is here the costly stone called jacinth in Revelation 21:20. The canceled reference to "aerial silk" may be compared with the *gaze aërienne* of "The Spectacles," below.

19. "It is true he thought a great deal of all these things — but!"

20. Compare the shrieks of the victims of the bull of Phalaris, which is mentioned in "Loss of Breath" and "The System of Doctor Tarr and Professor Fether," below.

21. "And who smiled so bitterly."

22. "But something must be done."

23. "Richard is himself again" is from an addition by Colley Cibber to the fifth act of Richard III. There is another allusion to this expression in Poe's letter to F. W. Thomas, September 8, 1844.

24. "He'd killed his six men."

25. "He might escape."

26. "But he does play cards!" The abbé Louis-Édouard-Camille Gaultier (1746–1818) sought to teach languages and geography through games. His *Cours complet de jeux instructifs* was published in 1807, but no such title as *Diable* is recorded to his credit in the Catalogue of the Bibliothèque Nationale. The book was probably invented by Poe as a means of pointing out "that the Devil dares not refuse a game of cards."

27. Charles Le Brun (1619–1690) was a French painter and designer of great influence in the period of Louis XIV. He was the author, among other works, of *Conference sur l'expression des differents caracteres des passions* (Paris, 1667). A translation called *A Method to Learn to Design the Passions* was issued in London in 1734. Poe's reference in a canceled passage to Père La Chaise (the confessor of Louis XIV, for whom the great Parisian cemetery is named) seems to have been a mere slip of the pen or the memory.

28. "If I lose, I'll be doubly damned; if I win, I return to my ortolans; let the cards be made ready."

29. Poe has in mind here an old story, thus told by Francis Bacon, *Apophthegms,* number 200 (90), Spedding edition: "Bresquet, jester to Francis the first of France, did keep a calendar of fools, wherewith he did use to make the king sport, telling him ever the reason why he put one into his calendar. When Charles the fifth, emperor, upon confidence of the noble nature of Francis, passed through France, for the appeasing of the rebellion of Gaunt, Bresquet put him into his calendar. The king asked him the cause. He answered 'Because you having suffered at the hands of Charles the greatest bitterness . . . he would trust his person into your hands.' 'Why, Bresquet,' said the king, 'what wilt thou say, if thou seest him pass in as great safety?' . . . Saith Bresquet, 'Why then I will put him out, and put in you.'"

30. "It's your play."

31. "Laying down the king."

A TALE OF JERUSALEM

32. Alexander the Great visited Diogenes of Sinope in his tub (a great grain or oil jar) at Athens, and asked if he could do him any favor. "Get out of my sunlight," said the Cynic; and Alexander remarked that were he anyone but Alexander, he would like to be Diogenes. This story comes from Diogenes Laërtius' *Lives of the Philosophers,* VI, "Diogenes of Sinope," vi, and was also used by Poe in a review of a life of Washington (*SLM,* December 1835), in a notice of J. F. Cooper's *Precaution* in *Burton's* for August 1839, and in "Diddling." Alexander was a notoriously hard drinker, which explains the reading of the first version.

33. "Had he not been De L'Omelette, he'd have had no objection to being the devil."

A TALE OF JERUSALEM

Another of the tales submitted in 1831 to the *Saturday Courier,* this story is a harmless buffoonery upon a very old theme. The attitude of Jews toward swine has frequently seemed amusing to those who do not share it. Poe made the most of a historical incident in which some ancient Romans played a clever trick upon the defenders of Jerusalem. Its cleverness lay in the fact that the legalistic Romans, who preferred to respect all divinities, including those of their enemies, avoided impiety, since for them a boar was a highly acceptable sacrificial victim; a boar, a ram and a bull were offered in the great purification ceremony called Suovetaurilia.

The Biblical injunctions against pigs are usually thought of chiefly as dietary laws, but in Deuteronomy 14:8 we read: "The swine . . . is unclean unto you: ye shall not eat of their flesh, nor touch their dead carcase." Clearly the prohibition concerns more than what may be eaten, and involves ceremonial conduct.

Poe's source was pointed out by James Southall Wilson in the *American Mercury,* October 1931, as a novel by Horatio Smith, *Zillah, a Tale of the Holy City* (1828), from which Poe took his plot, most of his allusions, and the high-flown language of his characters. The novel is overlong, but enjoyable even now. Its scene is laid about 37 B.C., when Herod the Great, aided by Mark Antony, overthrew King Aristobulus. The heroine, Zillah, is the daughter of the Sagan, or Deputy High Priest, who, like the other Jewish characters, quote the Bible on every possible occasion. Poe used the

King James Bible directly to some extent in the story, but a very rare spelling (see note 34 below) confirms *Zillah* as his principal source.

The incident central to Poe's story is related in *Zillah* (I, 219) by the heroine's aged nurse, who, recalling the siege of Jerusalem in 65 B.C. by Pompey, says:

> When the Holy City was besieged, not many years agone, they let down in a basket, every day, over the walls, so much money as would buy lambs for the daily sacrifices, which lambs they drew up again in the same basket. But an Israelite, who spoke Greek, having acquainted the besiegers that so long as sacrifices were offered, the city could not be taken, the profane villains popped a hog in the basket instead of the usual victim, and from that time we have been accustomed to curse every one that could speak Greek.

The ancient source is in the Talmud, *Soteh,* fol. 49, col. 2; (see *Hebraic Literature: Translations from the Talmud, Midrashim and Kabbala,* with an introduction by Maurice H. Harris, copyright 1901, pp. 203–204).

As Poe later sketched the members of the Folio Club, the narrator of "A Tale of Jerusalem" was obviously to be "Mr. Chronologos Chronology, who admired Horace Smith." Poe shared that admiration and in *Graham's Magazine* for August 1841, reviewing a later novel, *The Moneyed Man,* called Smith "perhaps, the most erudite of all the English novelists, and unquestionably one of the best in every respect." It should be observed that "A Tale of Jerusalem" is not a burlesque of Poe's original, but a story told in the manner of Horace Smith.* If there be satire, it is on writers who think any story connected with Bible times must be edifying. In "A Tale of Jerusalem," as in "Four Beasts in One," we see that absurdity is as much of the past as of the present.

There is a translation of Poe's tale into modern Hebrew by Ben-Zion Yedidiah in a recent anthology, *Gaheleth-Ha-Esh* (Tel-Aviv, 1950; the title of the book means "Burning Coal").

---

* Smith, baptized Horatio, was almost always called Horace. Poe availed himself in other places of the erudition displayed in *Zillah.* See the notes on "Loss of Breath" and "The Assignation" below. "Pinakidia," number 83 *(SLM,* August 1836, p. 578) also draws upon *Zillah.* [For a full treatment of the role of Horace Smith in Poe's works, see Burton R. Pollin, "Figs, Bells, Poe and Horace Smith," *Poe Newsletter,* June 1970.]

A TALE OF JERUSALEM

TEXTS

(A) Philadelphia *Saturday Courier,* June 9, 1832; *(B) Southern Literary Messenger,* April 1836 (2:313–314); *(C) Tales of the Grotesque and Arabesque* (1840), II, 97–103; *(D) Broadway Journal,* September 20, 1845 (2:166–167); *(E) Works* (1850), II, 306–310. PHANTASY-PIECES, title only.

The *Broadway Journal* version *(D)* is followed. Griswold introduces three verbal misprints and has several punctuation omissions. The earliest text *(A)* was mechanically reproduced by John Grier Varner in *Edgar Allan Poe and the Philadelphia Saturday Courier* (1933), pp. 32–37. The few italicized words were first introduced in the *Southern Literary Messenger (B)* with the exception of the last phrase in the tale. This was first so emphasized in the *Broadway Journal (D).*

A TALE OF JERUSALEM. [*D*]

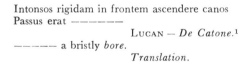

Intonsos rigidam in frontem ascendere canos
Passus erat —————
                    LUCAN — *De Catone.*[1]
————— a bristly *bore.*
                    Translation.

"Let us hurry to the walls," said Abel-Phittim[a] to Buzi-Ben-Levi and Simeon the Pharisee,[2] on the tenth day of the month Thammuz, in the year of the world three thousand nine hundred and forty-one[3] — "let us hasten to the ramparts adjoining the gate[b] of Benjamin, which is in the city of David,[4] and overlooking the camp of the uncircumcised; for it is the last hour of the fourth watch, being sunrise; and the idolaters, in fulfilment of the promise of Pompey, should be awaiting[c] us with the lambs for the sacrifices."[5]

Simeon, Abel-Phittim, and Buzi-Ben-Levi were the Gizbarim, or sub-collectors of the offering,[6] in the holy city of Jerusalem.[d]

"Verily," replied the Pharisee, "let us hasten: for this generosity in the heathen is unwonted; and fickle-mindedness has ever been an attribute of[e] the worshippers of Baal."

"That they are fickle-minded and treacherous is as true as the Pentateuch,"[7] said Buzi-Ben-Levi, "but that is only towards the

---

Title: A Pig Tale *(Table of Contents,*
PHANTASY-PIECES*)*
Motto: Intonsos *(A, B, C, D, E)*
misprint
a Abel-Shittim *throughout (A, B)*
b gates *(E) misprint*

c waiting for *(A)*
d Jerusalem — more correctly
Jeruschalaim, which signifies, being
interpreted, "the possession of the
inheritance of peace." *(A)*
e to *(A)*

people of Adonai.[8] When was it ever known that the Ammonites proved wanting to their own interests?[f] Methinks it is no great stretch of generosity to allow us lambs for the altar of the Lord, receiving in lieu thereof thirty silver shekels per head!"

"Thou forgettest, however, Ben-Levi," replied[g] Abel-Phittim, "that the Roman Pompey, who is now impiously besieging the city of the Most High, has no assurity[h] that we apply not the lambs thus purchased for the altar, to the sustenance of the body, rather than of the spirit."

"Now, by[i] the five corners of my beard,"[9] shouted the Pharisee, who belonged to the sect called The Dashers (that little knot of saints whose manner of *dashing* and lacerating the feet against[j] the pavement was long a thorn and a reproach to less zealous devotees — a stumbling-block to less gifted perambulators)[10] — "by the five corners of that beard which as a priest I am forbidden to shave! — have we lived to see the day when a blaspheming and idolatrous [k]upstart of Rome[k] shall accuse us of appropriating to the appetites of the flesh the most holy and consecrated elements? [l]Have we lived to see the day when"——[l]

"Let us not question the motives of the Philistine," interrupted Abel-Phittim,[m] "for to-day we profit for the first time by his avarice or by[n] his generosity; but rather let us hurry to the ramparts, lest offerings should be wanting for that altar whose fire the [o]rains of heaven[o] cannot extinguish,[p] and whose pillars[q] of smoke [r]no tempest can[r] turn aside."[11]

That part of the city to which our worthy Gizbarim now hastened, and which bore the name of its architect King David, was esteemed the most strongly fortified district of Jerusalem; being situated upon[s] the steep and lofty hill of Zion.[12] Here a broad, deep, circumvallatory trench, hewn from the solid rock, was defended by a wall of great strength erected upon its inner edge. This

---

f   interest? *(A, B, C)*
g   said *(A)*
h   assurance *(A)*
i   Now, by/By *(A)*
j   upon *(A)*
k...k   Roman upstart *(A)*
l...l   Have we –" *(A)*

m   Abel-Phittem, *(E)*
n   Omitted *(A)*
o...o   rain *(A)*
p   put out, *(A)*
q   pillar *(A)*
r...r   the winds cannot *(A)*
s   on *(A)*

wall was adorned,[t] at regular interspaces, by square towers of white marble; the lowest sixty, and[u] the highest one hundred and twenty cubits in height. But, in the vicinity of the gate of Benjamin, the wall arose by no means[v] from the margin of the fosse. On the contrary, between the level of the ditch and the basement of the rampart, sprang up[w] a perpendicular cliff of two hundred and fifty cubits; forming part of the precipitous Mount Moriah.[13] So that when Simeon and his associates arrived on the summit of the tower called Adoni-Bezek[14] — the loftiest[x] of all the turrets around[y] about Jerusalem, and the usual place of conference with the besieging army — they looked down upon the camp of the enemy from an eminence excelling, by many feet, that of the Pyramid of Cheops, and, by several, that of the Temple of Belus.[15]

"Verily," sighed the Pharisee, as he peered dizzily over the precipice, "the uncircumcised are as the sands by the sea-shore — as the locusts in the wilderness![16] The[z] valley of The King hath become the valley[a] of Adommin."[17]

"And yet," added Ben-Levi, "thou canst not point me out a Philistine — no, not [b]one — from Aleph to Tau — from the wilderness to the battlements — [b]who seemeth any bigger than the letter Jod!"[18]

"Lower away the basket with the shekels of silver!" here[c] shouted a Roman soldier in a hoarse, rough voice, which appeared[d] to issue from the regions of Pluto — "lower away the basket with the[e] accursed coin which it has[f] broken the jaw of a noble Roman to pronounce! Is it thus you[g] evince your gratitude to our master Pompeius, who, in his condescension, has thought fit[h] to listen to your idolatrous importunities? The god Phœbus, who is a true god,[i] has been charioted for an hour[19] — and were you not to be[j] on the ramparts[k] by sunrise? Ædepol![20] do you think that we,

---

t beautified, *(A)*	battlements — from Aleph to Tau, *(A)*
u *Omitted (A, B, C)*	c *Omitted (A)*
v means *immediately (A, no italics*	d seemed *(A)*
B, C)	e that *(A, B, C)*
w sprang up/arose *(A)*	f it has/hath *(A)*
x highest *(A)*	g that you *(A)*
y round *(A)*	h proper *(A)*
z And the *(A)*	i god, and no barbarian, *(A)*
a vally *(E) misprint*	j have been *(A, B)*
b . . . b from the forest to the	k walls *(A)*

the conquerors of the world, have nothing better to do than stand[1] waiting by the walls of every kennel, to traffic with the[m] dogs of the earth? Lower away! I say — and see that your trumpery be [n]bright in color, and just in weight!"[n]

"El Elohim!"[21] ejaculated the Pharisee, as the discordant tones of the centurion rattled up the crags of the precipice, and fainted away against the temple — "El Elohim! — *who* is the God Phœbus? — *whom* doth the blasphemer invoke? Thou, Buzi-Ben-Levi! who art read in the laws of the Gentiles, and hast sojourned among them[o] who dabble with the Teraphim![22] — is it Nergal of whom the idolator[p] speaketh? — or Ashimah? — or Nibhaz? — or Tartak? — or Adramalech? — or Anamalech? — or Succoth-Benith?[q] — or Dagon? — or Belial? — or Baal-Perith? — or Baal-Peor? — or Baal-Zebub?"[23]

"Verily it is neither — but beware how thou lettest the rope slip too rapidly through thy fingers; for should the wicker-work chance to hang on the projection of yonder crag, there will be a woful outpouring of the holy things of the sanctuary."[r]

By the assistance of some rudely constructed machinery, the heavily laden basket was now [s]carefully lowered[s] down among the multitude; and, from the giddy pinnacle, the Romans were seen gathering[t] confusedly round[u] it; but owing to the vast height and the prevalence of a fog,[v] no distinct view of their operations could be obtained.

Half an[w] hour had already elapsed.

"We shall be too late," sighed[x] the Pharisee, as at the expiration of this period, he looked over into the abyss — "we shall be too late! we shall be turned out of office by the Katholim."[24]

"No more," responded Abel-Phittim, "no more[y] shall we feast upon the fat of the land [25] — no longer shall our beards be odorous

---

l   to stand *(A)*
m   *Omitted (A)*
n . . . n   just in weight, and bright in color." *(A)*
o   those *(A)*
p   idolater *(A, B, E)*
q   Succoth-Benoth? *(A, B, C)*
r   santuary." *(E) misprint*

s . . . s   lowered carefully *(A, B, C)*
t   crowding *(A, B, C)*
u   around *(A, B, C)*
v   fog, (which is unusual at Jerusalem,) *(A)*
w   Half an/A half *(A, B, C)*
x   said *(A)*
y   no more *omitted (A)*

with frankincense — our loins girded up with fine linen from the Temple."

"Raca!"[26] swore Ben-Levi, "Raca! do they mean to defraud us of the purchase money? or, Holy Moses! are they weighing the shekels of the tabernacle?"

"They have given the signal at last," cried[z] the Pharisee, [a]"they have given the signal at last! — pull[a] away, Abel-Phittim! — and thou, Buzi-Ben-Levi, pull away! — for verily the Philistines have [b]either still hold upon[b] the basket, or the Lord hath softened their hearts to place therein a beast of good weight!" And the Gizbarim pulled away, while their burthen swung heavily upwards through the still[c] increasing mist.

* * * * * * * * * *

"Booshoh [d]he!"[27] — as, at[d] the conclusion of an hour, some object [e]at the extremity of the rope became indistinctly visible — "Booshoh he!" was the exclamation which burst from the lips of Ben-Levi.[e]

"Booshoh[f] he! — for shame![28] — it is a ram from the thickets of Engedi, and as rugged as the valley of Jehoshaphat!"[g] [29]

"It is a firstling of the flock,"[30] said Abel-Phittim, "I know him by the bleating of his lips, and the innocent folding of his limbs. His eyes are more beautiful than the jewels of the Pectoral,[31] and his flesh is like the honey of Hebron."[32]

"It is a fatted calf from the pastures of Bashan,"[33] said the Pharisee, "the heathen have dealt wonderfully with us! — let us raise up our voices in a psalm! — let us give thanks on the shawm and on the psaltery — on the harp and on[h] the huggab — on the cythern and on the sackbut!"[34]

It was not until the basket had arrived within a few feet of the Gizbarim, that a low grunt betrayed to their perception a *hog* of no common size.

"Now El Emanu!" slowly, and with upturned eyes ejaculated the trio, as, [i]letting go[i] their hold, the emancipated porker tum-

---

z   roared *(A, B)*
a...a   "Pull *(A)*
b...b   still hold of *(A)*
c   *Omitted (A)*
d...d   he!" said Ben-Levi, as at *(A)*
e...e   became indistinctly visible at

the extremity of the rope — *(A)*
f   "Vah! Climah *(A)*
g   Jehosaphat *(B, C, D, E)*, *corrected from A*
h   *Omitted (A)*
i...i   releasing *(A)*

bled[j] headlong among the Philistines, "El Emanu! — God be with us! — *it is the unutterable flesh!*"[k] [35]

NOTES

Title: The running title of Smith's novel is *Zillah, a Tale of Jerusalem.*

1. Poe altered the passage about Cato from Lucan's *Pharsalia,* II, 375–376, putting "ascendere" for "descendere." The original means "he let his uncut gray hair hang down over his stern forehead"; Poe says "his hair stood on end." At least one Victorian editor, not seeing the joke, *corrected* the passage.

2. Abel-Shittim (in the first two texts, changed *pudoris causa* in later versions) means grove of acacia trees, and is the name of a place in the plain of Moab, mentioned in Numbers 33:49. Buzi, derived from Buz, contempt, was, according to Ezekiel 1:3, the name of the prophet's father; Poe's Buzi, son of Levi, is a Levite, as is a leading character in *Zillah*. Simeon, or Shimeon, means a hearkening; a man of the name is in Ezra 10:31 and another in Luke 2:25.

3. Thammuz is the tenth month of the Hebrew year; the tenth day does not seem to be significant. *Anno mundi* 3941 was 65–64 B.C. Poe uses this system of dating again in "Epimanes."

4. *Zillah,* IV, 276: "They passed out by the gate Benjamin, at the northeast corner of the city," based on Jeremiah 38:7. "The city of David" — frequently used for Jerusalem — for a long time referred specifically to the ancient quarter where David established his capital.

5. Exodus 29:38f.: "Now this is that which thou shalt offer upon the altar; two lambs of the first year, day by day continually . . . one . . . in the morning, and the other . . . at even."

6. *Zillah,* I, 44: "three Gizbarin, or sub-collectors of the offerings." Poe uses the correct plural form, *Gizbarim*.

7. "As true as the Pentateuch" is in *Zillah,* I, 17; Poe quotes it also in his review of Lambert A. Wilmer's *Quacks of Helicon* in *Graham's Magazine* for August 1841.

8. Adonai (translated Lord) is the word pronounced when the form written JHVH and printed "Jehovah" is spoken by pious Jews.

9. A footnote in *Zillah,* I, 103, reads: "The Jews reckoned five corners of their beards — one on either cheek, one on either lip, and one below on the chin, — all of which a priest was forbidden to shave." This rule is based on Leviticus 21:5.

---

j   fell *(A)*
k   *After this is another paragraph*
"Let me no longer" — said the
Pharisee, "let me no longer be called
Simeon, which signifieth 'he who listens,'
but Boanerges, 'the son of thunder.' "
(A); "Let me no longer," said the

Pharisee, wrapping his cloak around
him and departing within the city —
"let me no longer be called Simeon,
which signifieth 'he who listens' — but
rather Boanerges, 'the Son of
Thunder.' " *(B, C)*

10. *Zillah*, IV, 144: "The Dashing Pharisee, so called, because he crawled along apart and in humility, the heel of one foot touching the great toe of the other, and neither foot being lifted from the ground, so that his toes were dashed against the stones." See II Corinthians 12:7, for "a thorn in the flesh"; and Leviticus 19:14, for "a stumbling block."

11. A footnote in *Zillah*, I, 195, reads: "It is maintained by the Talmudists, that the rains never put out the fire of the altar, nor did the wind ever prevail over its pillar of smoke." The Talmudists had Exodus 13:21 in mind.

12. See Psalms 2:6, "Yet have I set my king upon my holy hill of Zion." The story of David's capture of the site is told in II Samuel 5:6–9. Some of Poe's descriptions may have come from Chateaubriand's *Itinéraire de Paris à Jérusalem* in F. Shoberl's translation, *Travels in Greece, Palestine, Egypt, and Barbary* (Philadelphia, 1813) – a source of material in "Al Aaraaf" and others of his early poems.

13. Mount Moriah, "chosen of God," site of the Temple, is referred to vividly in *Zillah*, I, 3.

14. *Zillah*, IV, 112: "Adoni-bezek, the lightning of the Lord." The name was that of a king of Bezek, taken captive to Jerusalem during the conquest of Canaan, for whom see Judges 1:5–7.

15. The Great Pyramid of Cheops (Khufu) is over 480 feet high. The temple of Belus at Babylon is also notable among ancient monuments – "some writers ... make the whole one mile in height." ("Pinakidia," no. 141, *SLM*, August 1836, p. 580).

16. Genesis 22:17, "The sand which is upon the sea shore." St. Matthew 3:3–4: "one crying in the wilderness ... his meat was locusts and wild honey."

17. Joshua 15:7, "the going up to Adummim" – according to the *Jewish Encyclopedia*, the steep road from the plain of Jericho to the hilly country around Jerusalem. It formed part of the boundary of the land of the tribe of Judah and its name – translated "The Red" – referred to the color of the road.

18. In *Zillah*, II, 156, reference is made to "all the letters from Aleph to Tau," the first and last letters of the Hebrew alphabet; in *Zillah*, I, 14, a little boy is said to be "no bigger than the letter Jod" – the smallest letter, a jot.

19. The sun had been up for an hour.

20. A contracted Latin oath, "by Pollux" (cited from Terence), used by a Roman character in *Zillah*, II, 56.

21. *Zillah*, II, 38: "El Elohim!" he exclaimed – "these Romans beat us in every way...." El Elohim (cognate with Arabic Allah) means "the Gods," but is used with singular meaning in the Hebrew text of Genesis.

22. *Zillah*, I, 79, refers to Teraphim, idols mentioned in Judges 17:5 and Hosea 3:4.

23. The first seven in the list of the gods of the heathen come from II Kings 17:30–31; the rest from *Zillah*, II, 109. Nergal was a god of the men of Cuth. Ashimah was a god of the men of Hameth, mentioned by Poe also in "Four Beasts

in One." Nibhaz and Tartak were gods of the Avites. To Adrammelech and Anammelech the Sepharvites burnt their children. Succoth-benoth, worshipped at Babylon, is described as a goddess in *Zillah*, II, 109. She is to be identified with Ishtar (Venus). Dagon, half man and half fish in form, was a sea divinity of the Philistines, mentioned several times in the Bible, and, of course, in *Zillah*. Belial is a word for worthlessness, and wicked men are called "sons of Belial"; it is doubtful if Belial was worshipped as a person, but he is regarded as one in *Paradise Lost,* in *Zillah,* II, 41, and Poe's "Duc de L'Omelette." Baal-Perith, more usually called Baal-berith, was worshipped by the Israelites in Shechem after Gideon's death, according to Judges 8:33 and 9:4. Baal-peor was worshipped by the Moabites; see Numbers 25:3. Baal-zebub, "Prince of Flies," a god of Ekron, is mentioned in II Kings 1:2f. He is Satan's second in command in *Paradise Lost,* and is also mentioned in "The Duc de l'Omelette," and "Loss of Breath."

24. Poe has in mind *Zillah*, I, 43: "the two Katholikin, or overseers of the Treasury were comparing their accounts together." Katholim is modern Hebrew for Catholics.

25. Genesis 45:18, "ye shall eat the fat of the land."

26. *Zillah,* II, 117, "Raca! ... the fools!" The word is mentioned as offensive in St. Matthew 5:22.

27. "Booshoh he! Shame upon you!" is used in *Zillah*, II, 194.

28. "Vah! Climah he!" used in the first version obviously means something like the last Hebrew phrase. *Zillah,* II, 163: "Vah! Booshoh he!" and I, 17: "Climah he! shame, shame!" Hebraists consulted think it should be "U-Climah," meaning "and disgrace."

29. *Zillah,* I, 185: "as a stag is entangled by night in the thickets of Engaddi." David once dwelt in the wilderness of Engedi, which means "of the kid," according to I Samuel 24:1. Jehoshaphat ("God is judge") was the name of a good king of Judah. In *Zillah,* I, 3, as in Poe's story, it is merely a geographical name, sometimes applied to the valley of the Kedron without regard to the prophecies about it in Joel 3:2.

30. Genesis 4:4, "Abel ... brought of the firstlings of his flock."

31. The twelve jewels of the pectoral of the High Priest are listed in Exodus 28:15ff. In *Zillah,* II, 161, we find "no pontifical breastplate ... ever boasted so bright, so fiery a gem."

32. *Zillah,* I, 202: "Here is the rich honey of Hebron...." The place is in the south of Canaan.

33. *Zillah,* II, 40: "meat, not comparable to that which was produced from the pastures of Bashan" (compare Psalm 22:12, "strong bulls of Bashan"). The name means "sandy soil" and is that of one of the ancient divisions of Palestine east of the Jordan, an area proverbial for its fertility.

34. The musical instruments are all named in *Zillah,* I, 31, 148 or 210, and most of them in Daniel 3:5. The shawm is named in the prayer-book version of

Psalm 98:6 (the King James version translates it "cornet"). The huggab appears in *Zillah,* I, 210: "Their companions played on the huggab, or Hebrew organ — a rude instrument, resembling Pan's pipe"; the word — usually transliterated *ugab* — is in the Hebrew of Psalm 150:4, it is translated "pipe" in the Book of Common Prayer, "organ" in the King James version. Cythern (in *Zillah,* I, 31) denotes a stringed instrument sometimes referred to the lyre family (Greek *kithara*), sometimes to the zither family. Daniel 3:5, in the King James version, lists the dulcimer.

35. *Zillah,* III, 281: "El emanu! God be with us!" In *Zillah,* III, 51, at a feast given by Mark Antony, a wild boar is brought in and the heroine's father exclaims, "El Elohim! — it is the unutterable flesh."

"Boanerges . . . son of thunder" in the early version echoes St. Mark 3:17: "And James the son of Zebedee and John the brother of James . . . he surnamed them Boanerges, which is, The sons of thunder."

A DECIDED LOSS and
LOSS OF BREATH

The story — or stories, for it is hard to say if there be one, two, or three — cannot be called a success. "A Decided Loss," the first form, was one of the five tales Poe submitted for the contest announced by the Philadélphia *Saturday Courier* in June 1831. He labored over his satire "of the extravagancies of Blackwood" (he called it that in a letter to J. P. Kennedy, February 11, 1836) with a zeal worthy of a better cause. He greatly expanded it into "Loss of Breath" in 1833 for the Tales of the Folio Club, and this expanded version was published in the *Southern Literary Messenger* and in *Tales of the Grotesque and Arabesque.* Sometime after 1840, he cut it down, reducing its bulk by nearly one third. One feels today that the sensational fictions of the British magazinists were incapable of exaggeration. Poe did better in "How to Write a Blackwood Article" when he ridiculed the methods of the authors.

Critics have said little about any of the versions. Quinn (*Poe,* p. 194) found in the first some "interest on account of . . . references to contemporary literature." George E. Woodberry (*The Life of Edgar Allan Poe,* 1909, I, 130) saw especially in the longest form "a parody on the inane jargon (as it was then thought) of German metaphysics." Actually Poe, in a footnote in *Tales of the Grotesque and Arabesque,* pointed out that he had in mind Friedrich Wilhelm Joseph von Schelling's transcendentalism.

The first and final forms of the tale are presented here, with the material excised after 1840 included as an appendix.

One of Poe's sources was undoubtedly Adelbert von Chamisso's *Peter Schlemihl* (1814) — a very popular work, widely translated. Its hero is mentioned in all versions of Poe's tale. Haldeen Braddy calls attention to a source in Voltaire's *Candide* (1759), where Dr. Pangloss was unskillfully hanged, and revived when a surgeon who bought his body began to dissect it *(Glorious Incense,* 1953, pp. 32, 44; *Candide,* chapters 6 and 28). At least one commentator thought Poe was satirizing his own preoccupation with premature burials (Walter F. Taylor in *Sewanee Review,* July-September, 1934).

The unnamed scene of the story is Philadelphia, where the mail robber mentioned — a real person — was convicted.

TEXTS

A Decided Loss

(A) Philadelphia *Saturday Courier,* November 10, 1832, facsimiled by John Grier Varner in *Edgar Allan Poe and the Philadelphia Saturday Courier* (1933), pp. 38–49.

The sole authorized version *(A)* is followed without emendation.

Loss of Breath

(A) Southern Literary Messenger, September 1835 (1:735–740); *(B)* Duane copy of the last, with changes in manuscript, 1839; *(C) Tales of the Grotesque and Arabesque* (1840), II, 123–149; *(D) Broadway Journal,* January 3, 1846 (2:397–401); *(E) Works* (1856), IV, 302–314. PHANTASY-PIECES, title only.

Griswold's version *(E),* which shows slight changes from that of the *Broadway Journal (D),* is given. The twenty-six paragraphs dropped in 1845 and replaced by six are given at the end from *Tales of the Grotesque and Arabesque (C).*

Poe signed this tale "Littleton Barry" in the *Broadway Journal.*

A DECIDED LOSS.

Oh! breathe not, &c.
Moore's Melodies.[1]

'Thou wretch! — thou vixen! — thou shrew!' said I to my wife on the morning after the wedding — 'thou witch! — thou whippersnapper! — thou sink of iniquity! — thou fiery-faced quintessence of all that is abominable! — thou — thou' ——; here standing upon tiptoe, seizing her by the throat, and placing my mouth close to her ear, I was preparing to launch forth a new and most unequivocal epithet of opprobrium, which could not fail, if uttered, to convince her of her insignificance, when, to my extreme horror and astonishment, I discovered that I had lost my breath.

The phrases 'I have lost my breath,' 'I am quite out of breath,' &c., are often enough repeated in common conversation: but it never entered my imagination that such an accident could (the sufferer surviving) bona fide, and actually, occur. It was shocking. Imagine my consternation. I was, indeed, very peculiarly situated. But my good Genius never entirely deserts me. In my most ungovernable furies I still retain a sense of propriety, and 'le chemin des passions me conduit' (as it did Rousseau) 'a la philosophie veritable.'[2] Although I could not, at first, precisely ascertain to what degree the occurrence had affected me, yet I unhesitatingly determined to conceal the matter at all events from my wife until experience should assure me of the extent of my unheard-of calamity. The imminent danger of discovery brightened every faculty of my soul, and, with a facility peculiar to the desperate, I put in execution a design conceived with the rapidity of lightning. Altering my countenance in a moment from its bepuffed and distorted appearance (I was in a terrible passion) to an expression of the most arch and coquettish benignity, I gave my wife a kiss on one cheek, and a pat on the other, and without saying one word (Furies I could not!) deliberately shuffled myself out of the room, leaving her as much in love with my fund of good humour (O blasphemy!) as in admiration of my exquisite drollery, and fine theatrical talent.

Behold me then safely shut up in my own boudoir, a fearful instance of the evil consequences attending upon irascibility — alive with the qualifications of the dead — dead with the propensities of the living — an anomaly on the face of the earth — very calm, yet breathless. Yes, breathless! I am serious in asserting that my breath was entirely gone. I could not have stirred with it a feather if my life had been at issue, or sullied the polish upon the surface of a mirror. Hard fate! yet there was some alleviation to the first overwhelming paroxysm of my sorrow. I found upon trial that the powers of utterance (which, upon my inability to proceed in the conversation with my wife, I then concluded to be totally destroyed) were, in fact, only partially impeded; and I discovered that had I, at the interesting crisis aforesaid, dropped my voice to a singularly deep guttural, (oh the devil!) I might still have continued to her the communication of my sentiments. For this pitch of voice (the guttural) depends, I find, not upon the current of the breath, but upon a certain spasmodic action of the muscles of the throat — thus the race of frogs, &c.; see Hippocrates in his dissertation.[3]

Throwing myself upon a settee, I remained for some time buried in thought. My reflections, be sure, were of no consolatory description. A thousand vague and lachrymatory fancies took possession of my spirit. I had heard of Peter Schlemil, but I did not believe in him until now.[4] I had heard of compacts with the devil, and would gladly have accepted his assistance, but knew not in what manner to proceed, having studied very little of *diablerie*. Then the phantom suicide flitted across my imagination, but it is a trait in the perversity of human nature to reject the obvious, and the ready for the far-distant and equivocal; and, with one foot in the grave, I shuddered at self-murder as the most flagrant of enormities. Then through a single broken pane of glass, the four winds of the Heaven all poured into the apartment — and, like the Mulciberian bellows,[5] roared loudly the huge sea-coal fire — and the tabby cat purred lustily upon the rug — and the fat water-dog wheezed strenuously under the table — all taking much merit to themselves for the hideous strength of their lungs, and obviously deriding my own pulmonary incapacity. Oppressed with a tumult of vague hopes and fears, I, at length, heard my wife's step descending the stair-case. Being now assured of her absence, with a palpitating heart I returned to the scene of my disaster. Carefully locking the door on the inside, I commenced a vigorous search. It was probable, I thought, that, concealed in some closet or drawer, or lurking in some obscure corner, might be found the lost object of my desires. It might have a vapoury — it might even have a tangible form. Most philosophers upon many points of philosophy, are still very unphilosophical. Anaxagoras, however, maintained that snow was black.[6] I have since discovered this to be the fact. Wm. Godwin, too, says, somewhere in his Mandeville, that invisible things (a case more in point) are the only realities.[7] I would have the world pause before accusing such asseverations of an undue quantum of absurdity. My exertions, however, proved fruitless. Drawer after drawer, closet after closet, corner after corner, were scrutinized to no purpose. Several false teeth, an eye, two pair of hips,[8] and a bundle of billet-doux, from a neighbour to my wife, were the contemptible reward of my industry and perseverance. At one time, indeed, I thought myself sure of my prize; having, in rummaging a dressing-case, accidentally demolished a bottle of (I had a remarkably sweet breath) Hewitt's 'Seraphic, and highly-scented double extract of Heaven, or Oil of Archangels,'[9] which, as an agreeable perfume, I here take the liberty of recommending. With a heavy heart, I repaired again to my boudoir, there to ponder upon some method of eluding my wife's sagacity, until I could make arrangements prior to my leaving the country — for to this I had already made up my mind. In a foreign climate, being unknown, I might, with more probability of success, endeavour to conceal my unhappy bereavement — a bereavement calculated, even more than beggary, to estrange the affections of the multitude, and to draw down upon the wretch the well-merited indignation of the virtuous and the happy. To sharpen my invention, I took down a prize poem on ————,[10] and reading half an hour, found myself fuddled. Jumping up in despair, I hit upon an expedient, and immediately set about carrying it into execution. Being naturally quick, I committed to memory the entire tragedies of Metamora and Miantinimoh.[11] I had the acuteness to recollect that in the accentuation of these dramas, the tones of voice in which I found myself deficient, were totally unnecessary, and that the deepest guttural should reign monotonously throughout. Having, therefore, practised by the borders of a large, and well-frequented marsh, I found myself, in a few hours, as well qualified to quiz the Aborigines as their original representative himself. Thus armed at all points, I determined to make my wife believe that I was suddenly seized with a passion for the stage. In this I succeeded to a miracle; and to every question or suggestion, felt myself at liberty to reply, in my most sepulchral tones, with a passage from the tragedies, folding my arms, working my knees, shuffling my feet, looking asquint, and showing my teeth, with the energy of the most accomplished and popular performer. To be sure they talked of confining me in a straight jacket — but, good God! they never suspected me of having lost my breath. Having thus, at length, put my affairs in order, and affixed a codicil to my will, in which, after many charitable legacies, I bequeathed to my wife my fine quarto copy of Calbrinachus[12] in Dianam, I took my seat, one frosty night, in the mail stage for ———,[13] giving it to be understood among my acquaintance, that business in Europe, of the last importance, rendered indispensable my immediate personal attendance. The coach was crammed to repletion; but, from the darkness of the night, the features of my companions could not be distinguished. Without making any effectual resistance, I suffered myself to be ensconced between two ambiguous bipeds, while a third, requesting pardon for the liberty which he was about to take, threw himself at full length upon my carcase, and falling asleep in an instant, drowned all my guttural ejaculations for relief, in a snore which would put thy roarings to the blush, thou bell-metal bull of Phalaris![14] Happily the state of my respiratory faculties rendered suffocation an accident entirely out of the question.

The day broke at length, and my persecutor, arising and adjusting his shirt-collar, thanked me in a very friendly manner for my civility. Perceiving that I remained without motion, and made him no reply, (all my limbs were dislocated, and my head twisted on one side) his apprehensions began to be excited, and, arousing the rest of the passengers, he communicated, in a very decided manner, his opinion that a corpse had been palmed upon them during the night, for a living and responsible fellow traveller — here giving me a thump on the right eye by way of evidencing the truth of his assertion. One after another (there were fifteen in all) now gave me a pull by the ear; and a young practitioner having applied a pocket-mirror to my mouth, and found me without breath, the suggestion of my tormentor was pronounced to be a true bill; and, stopping the coach, the whole assembly declared their determination to proceed, for the present, no farther with any such carcases; and, for the future, to endure tamely no such impositions. As we were at this time passing through the village of ——, I was accordingly thrown out of the coach at the sign of the Three Crows, without meeting with any farther accident except the breaking of my thighs under the left hind wheel of the vehicle; and I must do the driver the justice to acknowledge that he did not forget to throw after me my largest trunk, which alighting on my head, fractured my scull in a manner at once interesting and extraordinary. The landlord of the Three Crows, who is a hospitable man, finding that my trunk contained sufficient to indemnify him for any trifling expenditure, sent forthwith for an undertaker, and made every preparation for a reputable burial. I was laid out very decently in a garret, and afforded every convenience suitable to my funeral estate. The landlady accommodated me with a pair of her own stockings, and her husband having fastened my hands, and tied up my jaws with a pocket-handkerchief, bolted the door on the outside as he took his departure, leaving me alone to silence and to meditation.

Having, by this time, recovered, in a measure, from the stunning sensation of my bruises, I found, to my infinite delight, that I could have spoken had not my jaws been tied up by the pocket-handkerchief. Consoling myself with this reflection I was mentally repeating a few verses of the ——,[15] as is my custom, before resigning myself to sleep, when two cats of a greedy and vituperative disposition entering at a hole in the wall, leapt up simultaneously with a flourish a la Catalani,[16] and alighting opposite one another on my countenance, betook themselves to unseemly, and indecorous controversy for the paltry consideration of my nose.

But as the loss of his ears proved the means by which the Persian Mige-Gush ascended the empire of Cyrus,[17] so the loss of a few ounces of my visage was the salvation of my body. Aroused by the pain, and burning with indignation, I burst, at a single effort, the fastenings, and the bandage, and starting majestically upon my feet, opened the lattice, and to the extreme terror and disappointment of the belligerents, precipitated myself in triumph from the window.

The mail-robber W——,[18] to whom I bear a singular resemblance, was, at this moment, passing through the village, on his way to execution at ———. His great infirmity, and long continued ill-health had obtained him the privilege of remaining unmanacled; and, habited in his gallows costume, he lay at full length in the bottom of the hangman's cart, (which happened to be under the windows of the Three Crows at the moment of my precipitation) without any other guard than the driver, who was asleep, and two recruits of the — Regiment of Infantry, who were drunk. As ill-luck would have it I alit upon my feet within the cart. W——, who is an acute fellow, perceiving his opportunity, immediately leaped up, slipped out at the back of the vehicle, and turning down an alley was out of sight in an instant. The recruits aroused by the bustle, and not precisely comprehending the transaction, saw nevertheless a figure, the exact counterfeit of the felon, standing upright before their eyes, and were of opinion that the rascal, meaning W——, was after making his escape. Having communicated this idea to one another, they took each a dram, and then felled me with the butt end of their muskets. It was not long before the cart arrived at the place of execution. It was of course useless for me to say a word in my defence. Hanged, I must be — there could be no doubt of it, and I resigned myself to my fate with a mingled feeling of astonishment and tranquillity. The hangman adjusted the noose about my neck, and as, through the stupefying effects of my wounds, I was unable to make myself heard at so great a distance from the ground, it was reported in the newspapers of the following day that I died in my obstinacy like a wicked, and bloody-minded cut-throat as I was, stubbornly refusing to make any confession — a monster of mankind — an awful warning to all little children, and (so ran the Gazette) a duodecimo compendium of all horrible atrocities. The Editors were wrong — at least in the most important particular — I did not die. Upon the falling of the drop, I felt, as may be imagined no other inconvenience than was occasioned by the shock. To be sure my neck was chafed by the rope, and there was a violent determination of blood to the brain — but I stood in no danger of suffocation. I had, however, sufficient presence of mind to counterfeit the most extraordinary convulsions, and here my talents for grimace stood me in great service. Several gentleman fainted away, and three ladies were carried home in hysterics. The celebrated Pinxit, too, availed himself of the opportunity to retouch, from a sketch taken on the spot, his admirable painting of the "Marsyas flayed alive."[19]

But the most courageous spirit — the toughest constitution must at length yield to an obstinate run of ill luck, as the proudest cities have been humbled by the pertinacity of an enemy. Salmanezer, as we have it in the holy writings, lay three years before Samaria — yet it fell. Sardanapalus (see Diodorus) maintained himself seven years in Nineveh to no purpose. Troy fell at the end of the 2d lustrum, and Psammitticus (as Aristœus declares upon his honor as a gentleman) was admitted into Azoth after it had valourously sustained a siege for the 5th part of a century.[20] After half an hour's performance (as long as I thought necessary) I became motionless, and shortly afterwards, being cut down, was delivered to a practising physician with a bill and receipt for five and twenty dollars. He took me to his apartment forthwith, and commenced operations immediately. Having deprived me of both my ears, he discovered signs of animation. He therefore rang the bell, and told the servant to call in a neighbouring apothecary with whom he might consult in the emergency. However, in case of my proving to be alive, he first made an incision into my stomach, and, being naturally of a benevolent disposition, removed several of my viscera for private examination. The apothecary confirmed his suspicion with regard to my existence, and this suspicion I endeavoured to strengthen; kicking and plunging with all my might, and making the most furious contortions, the hangman's cap which still covered my face rendering any attempt at explanation out of the question. All this was, however, attributed to the effect of the new Galvanic Battery, which the apothecary, upon learning my situation, had brought with him, and from the moment of his entrance to that of my decease, which took place a few minutes afterwards, had never ceased to apply with the most unremitting assiduity.[21]

NOTES

1. The motto is the opening of "Oh! breathe not his name" in the *Irish Melodies* of Thomas Moore (1779–1852).

2. J. J. Rousseau (1712–1778), *Julie, ou la Nouvelle Héloïse*, part II, letter iii, paragraph 2: "The road of the passions has led me to true philosophy."

3. Hippocrates is reported to have believed that diseases were caused by air given off by undigested food.

4. Peter Schlemihl, hero of the romance of that name by Adelbert von Chamisso, gave his shadow in exchange for the services of the devil for twenty-four years. He fled abroad and in time escaped from his bad bargain by forcing the Prince of Darkness to perform only good deeds.

5. See Homer's *Iliad*, XVIII, 474, and Vergil's *Aeneid,* VIII, 416ff., for the bellows in the workshop of Hephaestus/Vulcan (called Mulciber).

6. Anaxagoras really said there must be blackness in snow which turned into dark water; but Pierre Bayle in his *Dictionaire* (first edition, Amsterdam, 1696) accused him of saying snow was black, and the canard has been often repeated. "Il disait que la neige est noire" appears under the Anaxagoras entry in the Beuchot edition (Paris, 1820), II, 21, and was used by Poe three times — here, in "Tennyson vs. Longfellow," *Alexander's Weekly Messenger,* February 12, 1840, and in his review of *Barnaby Rudge* in *Graham's Magazine* for February 1842.

7. See William Godwin, *Mandeville* (1817), vol. III, ch. iii, par. 8.

8. Compare "The Man That Was Used Up" and "The Spectacles" on artificial aids to beauty.

9. Hair tonics often had high-sounding names, and the reference is probably to B. R. Hewitt, whose drugstore was on Passyunk Road above Carpenter in Philadelphia, but reference to John H. Hewitt, the Baltimore poet and editor, who had been contemptuous of "Al Aaraaf," is suggested by Quinn (*Poe*, p. 194).

10. The allusion here was omitted in later versions, but compare note 15 below, and "Loss of Breath" at note 15.

11. *Metamora* by John Augustus Stone (1800–1834) was first played by Edwin Forrest at the Park, New York, December 15, 1829, and in Philadelphia at the Arch Street Theatre, January 22, 1830. The hero is King Philip of Pokanoket, son of Massasoit. No complete text survives, but see Richard Moody, *Edwin Forrest* (1960), pp. 94f., and an article on the play in *American Literature,* November 1962. Forrest was an actor of great vigor and power. *Miantinomoh, or the Wept of Wish-ton-Wish,* a play founded on Cooper's novel, was presented at the Bowery Theatre, New York, November 12, 1830. See the *New York American* of that date.

12. Probably a misreading of Poe's manuscript; Callimachus' Hymn to Artemis praises the goddess as patron of the Amazons; this bequest to a wife was not a compliment. The reference was omitted in "Loss of Breath."

13. The city meant is clearly Philadelphia.

14. Phalaris, tyrant of Agrigentum, about 510 B.C. had a huge hollow brazen bull into which an offender was put, and a fire lit beneath. The victim's cries

simulated the roarings of a bull. Poe refers to this also in "The System of Doctor Tarr and Professor Fether."

15.   See note 10 above, and "Loss of Breath," below, at note 15.

16.   Angélique Catalani (1782–1849) was a great, though not faultless, opera singer; a pun on her name is intended.

17.   The Persian Magian later referred to as the Pseudo-Smerdis had lost his ears (instead of his head) for a serious offense under Cyrus; he thus lived to usurp the throne after the murder of Cyrus' elder son Smerdis by order of his brother Cambyses. See Isaac Taylor's translation, *Herodotus* (London, 1829), pp. 201–202, 217–229, esp. 222–223.

18.   The mail robber was George Wilson. His accomplice, James Porter, was hanged on July 2, 1830, at Philadelphia. Wilson was reprieved and imprisoned. His ultimate pardon and release were recorded in the *Saturday Evening Post,* January 16, 1841.

19.   Pinxit means "he painted." Marsyas was a Phrygian Satyr punished by Apollo for presumption in challenging the god to a contest in flute-playing. "The Flaying of Marsyas" is the subject of a painting by Raphael. See Benjamin Disraeli, *Vivian Grey* (1827), vol. IV, bk. vii, chap. ii, p. 323, for a reference to a piece of sculpture that may be "of the flayer of Marsyas."

20.   For the siege of Samaria, see II Kings 17:3–6; of Nineveh, Diodorus Siculus, II, 27; and of Troy, the *Odyssey.* Aristaeus of Proconnesus, a half-fabulous poet (Herodotus, *Histories,* IV, 13–16), is said to have been a source of Herodotus, whose account of the siege of Azoth by Psammetichus I in the seventh century B.C. (*Histories,* II, 157), does not credit him specifically.

21.   Compare accounts of experiments with the Galvanic battery in "The Premature Burial" and "Some Words With a Mummy."

LOSS OF BREATH. [*E*]

A TALE NEITHER IN NOR OUT OF "BLACKWOOD"

O breathe not, &c. — MOORE'S MELODIES.[1]

The most notorious ill-fortune must, in[a] the end, yield to the untiring courage of philosophy — as the most stubborn city to the ceaseless vigilance of an enemy. Salmanezer, as we have it in the holy writings, lay three years[b] before Samaria; yet it fell. Sardanapalus — see Diodorus — maintained himself seven in Nineveh; but to no purpose. Troy expired at the close of the second lustrum; and Azoth, as Aristæus declares upon his honor as a gentleman, opened

---

Title: Loss of Breath. A Tale a la   *from A, B, C, D*
Blackwood. *(A, B);* Loss of Breath *(C)*   b   year *(C)*
a   must, in/must in *(E) comma added*

at last her gates to Psammitticus, after having barred them for the fifth part of a century.   *   *   *[2]

"Thou wretch! — thou vixen! — thou shrew!" said I to my wife on the morning after our wedding, "thou witch! — thou hag! — thou whipper-snapper! — thou sink of iniquity! — thou fiery-faced quintessence of all that is abominable! — thou — thou —" here standing upon tiptoe, seizing her by the throat, and placing my mouth close to her ear, I was preparing to launch forth a new and more decided epithet of opprobrium, which should not fail, if ejaculated, to convince her of her insignificance, when, to my extreme horror and astonishment, I discovered that *I had lost my breath.*

The phrases "I am out of breath," "I have lost my breath," &c., are often enough repeated in common conversation; but it had never occurred to me that the terrible accident of which I speak could *bona fide*[c] and actually happen! Imagine — that is if you have a fanciful turn — imagine, I say, my wonder — my consternation — my despair!

There is a good genius, however, which has never[d] entirely deserted me. In my most ungovernable moods I still retain a sense of propriety, *et le chemin des passions me conduit* — as [e]Lord Edouard in the "Julie"[e] says it did him — *à la philosophie véritable.*[f] [3]

Although I could not at first precisely ascertain to what degree the occurrence had affected me, I [g]determined at all events to conceal[g] the matter from my wife, until further[h] experience should discover to me the extent of this my unheard of calamity. Altering my countenance, therefore, in a moment, from its bepuffed and distorted appearance, to an expression of arch and coquettish[i] benignity, I gave my lady a pat on the one cheek, and a kiss on the other, and without saying one syllable, (Furies! I could not), left her astonished at my drollery, as I pirouetted out of the room in a *Pas de Zéphyr.*[j] [4]

Behold me then safely ensconced in my private *boudoir*, a fear-

---

c   *bonâ fide (A, B, C, D)*
d   never, at any time, *(A, B, C)*
e . . . e   Rousseau *(A, B, C)*
f   *Accent added editorially*
g . . . g   unhesitatingly determined to

conceal at all events *(A, B, C)*
h   farther *(A, B, C, D)*
i   coqeuttish *(E) misprint*
j   *Accent added editorially*

ful instance of the ill consequences attending upon irascibility —
alive, with the qualifications of the dead — dead, with the propensities of the living — an anomaly[k] on the face of the earth —
being very calm, yet breathless.

Yes! breathless. I am serious in asserting that my breath was
entirely gone. I could not have stirred with it a feather if my life
had been at issue, or sullied[l] even the delicacy of a mirror. Hard
fate! — yet there was some alleviation to the first overwhelming
paroxysm of my sorrow. I found, upon trial, that the powers of
utterance which, upon my inability to proceed in the conversation
with my wife, I then concluded to be totally destroyed, were in fact
only partially impeded, and I discovered that had I at that interesting crisis, dropped my voice to a singularly deep guttural, I
might still have continued to her the communication of my sentiments; this pitch of voice (the guttural) depending,[m] I find, not
upon the current of the breath, but upon a certain spasmodic action of the muscles of the throat.

Throwing myself upon a chair, I remained for some time absorbed in meditation. My reflections, be sure, were of no consolatory kind. A thousand vague and lachrymatory fancies took
possession of my soul — and even the idea of[n] suicide flitted across
my brain; but it is a trait in the perversity of human nature to reject the obvious and the ready, for the far-distant and equivocal.
Thus I shuddered at self-murder as the most decided of atrocities
while the tabby cat purred strenuously[o] upon the rug, and the very
water-dog wheezed assiduously under the table; each taking to itself much merit for the strength of its lungs, and all obviously done
in derision of my own pulmonary incapacity.

Oppressed with a tumult of vague hopes and fears, I at length
heard the footsteps[p] of my wife descending the staircase. Being now
assured of her absence, I returned with a palpitating heart to the
scene of my disaster.

Carefully locking the door on the inside, I commenced a vigorous search. It was possible, I thought that, concealed in some

---

k   anomoly (E) misprint
l   suilied (D) misprint
m   depening, (D) misprint

n   idea of/phantom (A, B, C)
o   strenously (D) misprint
p   footstep (A, B, C)

obscure corner, or lurking in some closet or drawer, might be found the lost object of my inquiry. It might have a vapory — it might even have a tangible form. Most philosophers, upon many points of philosophy, are still very unphilosophical. William Godwin, however, says in his "Mandeville," that "invisible things are the only qrealities,"[5] and thisq all will allow, is a case in point. I would have the judicious reader pause before accusing such asseverations of an undue quantum of absurdity. Anaxagoras, it will be remembered, maintained that snow is rblack,[6] and thisr I have since found to be the case.

Long and earnestly did I continue the investigation: but the contemptible reward of my industry and perseverance proved to be only a set of false teeth, two pair of hips, an eye,[7] and a bundle of *billets-doux*s from Mr. Windenough to my wife. I might as well here observe that this confirmation of my lady's partiality for Mr. W. occasioned me little uneasiness. That Mrs. Lackobreatht should admire anything so dissimilar to myself was a natural and necessary evil. I am, it is well known, of a robust and corpulent appearance, and at the same time somewhat diminutive in stature. What wonder then that the lath-like tenuity of my acquaintance, and his altitude, which has grown into a proverb, should have met with all due estimation in the eyes of Mrs. Lackobreath.u But to return.

My exertions, as I have before said, proved fruitless. Closet after closet — drawer after drawer — corner after corner — were scrutinized to no purpose. At one time, however, I thought myself sure of my prize, having, inv rummaging a dressing-case, accidentally demolished a bottle wof Grandjean's[8] Oil of Archangelsw — which, as an agreeable perfume, I here take the liberty of recommending.

With a heavy heart I returned to my *boudoir* — there to ponder upon some method of eluding my wife's penetration, until I could

---

q . . . q   realities." This, *(A, B, C)*
r . . . r   black. This *(A, B, C)*
s   *billet-doux (A, B, C)*; billetts-doux
(D, E)
t   Lacko'breath *(A, B) throughout;*
Lack-o'Breath *(C) throughout*
u   *After this* It is by logic similar to this that true philosophy is enabled

to set misfortune at defiance. *(A, B, C)*
v   having, in/having in *(E) comma added from A, B, C, D*
w . . . w   (I had a remarkably sweet breath) of Hewitt's "Seraphic and Highly-Scented Extract of Heaven or Oil of Archangels" *(A, B, C)*

make arrangements prior to my leaving the country, for to this I had already made up my mind. In a foreign climate, being unknown, I might, with some probability of success, endeavor to conceal my unhappy calamity — a calamity calculated, even more than beggary, to estrange the affections of the multitude, and to draw down upon the wretch the well-merited indignation of the virtuous and the happy. I was not long in hesitation. Being naturally quick, I committed to memory the entire ˣtragedy of "Metamora."ˣ I had the good fortune to recollect that in the accentuation of this drama,ʸ or at least of such portion of itᶻ as is allotted to the hero,ᵃ the tones of voice in which I found myself deficient were altogether unnecessary, and that the deep guttural was expected to reign monotonously throughout.⁹

I practised for some time by the borders of a well frequented marsh; — herein, however, having no reference to a similar proceeding of Demosthenes,¹⁰ but from a design peculiarly and conscientiously my own. Thus armed at all points, I determined to make my wife believe that I was suddenly smitten with a passion for the stage. In this, I succeeded to a miracle; and to every question or suggestion found myself at liberty to reply in my most froglike and sepulchral tones with some passage from the tragedyᵇ — any portion of which, as I soon took great pleasure in observing, would apply equally well to any particular subject. It is not to be supposed, however, that in the delivery of such passages I was found at all deficient in the looking asquint — the showing my teeth — the working my knees — the shuffling my feet — or in any of those unmentionable graces which are now justly considered the characteristics of a popular performer.¹¹ To be sure they spoke of confining me in a straight-jacket — but, good God! they never suspected me of having lost my breath.

Having at length put my affairs in order, I took my seat very early one morning in the mail stage for ———, giving it to be understood, among my acquaintances, that business of the last im-

---

x . . . x   tragedies of —, and —. *(A, B, C)*   z   them *(A, B, C)*
y   this drama,/these dramas, *(A, B, C)*   a   the hero,/their heroes, *(A, B, C)*
     b   tragedies *(A, B, C)*

portance required my immediate personal ^cattendance in that city.^c

The coach was crammed to repletion; but in the uncertain twilight the features of my companions could not be distinguished. Without making any effectual resistance, I suffered myself to be placed between two gentlemen of colossal dimensions; while a third, of a size larger, requesting pardon for the liberty he was about to take, threw himself upon my body at full length, and falling asleep in an instant, drowned all my guttural ejaculations for relief, in a snore which would have put to^d blush the roarings of ^ethe bull of Phalaris.^{e 12} Happily the state of my respiratory faculties rendered suffocation an accident entirely out of the question.

As, however, the day broke more distinctly in our approach to the outskirts of the city, my tormentor arising and adjusting his shirt-collar, thanked me in a very friendly manner for my civility. Seeing that I remained motionless, (all my limbs were dislocated and my head twisted on one side,) his apprehensions began to be excited; and arousing the rest of the passengers, he communicated in a very decided manner, his opinion that a dead man had been palmed upon them during the night for a living^f and responsible fellow-traveller; here giving me a thump on the right eye, by way of demonstrating^g the truth of his suggestion.

Hereupon^h all, one after another, (there were nine in company), believed it their duty to pull me by the ear. A young practising physician, too, having applied a pocket-mirror to my mouth, and found me without breath, the assertion of my persecutor was pronounced a true bill; and the whole party expressed aⁱ determination to endure tamely no such impositions for the future, and to proceed no farther with any such carcasses for the present.

I was here, accordingly, thrown out at the sign of the "Crow," (by which tavern the coach happened to be passing,) without meeting with any farther accident than the breaking of both my arms, under the left hind wheel of the vehicle. I must besides do the driver the justice to state that he did not forget to throw after me the largest of my trunks, which, unfortunately falling on my head,

---

c...c attendance. (A) changed in B
d to the (A, B, C)
e...e a Phalarian bull. (A, B, C)
f living bonâ fide (A) changed in B

g evidencing (A, B, C)
h Thereupon (A, B, C)
i their (A, B, C)

fractured my skull in a manner at once interesting and extraordinary.

The landlord of the "Crow," who is a hospitable man, finding that my trunk contained sufficient to indemnify him for any little trouble he might take in my behalf, sent forthwith for a surgeon of his acquaintance, and delivered me to his care with a bill and receipt for ten[j] dollars.

The purchaser took me to his apartments and commenced operations immediately. [k]Having cut off my ears, however,[k] he discovered signs of animation. He now rang the bell, and sent for a neighboring apothecary with whom to consult in the emergency. In case[l] of his suspicions with regard to my existence proving ultimately correct, he, in the meantime, made an incision in my stomach, and removed several of my viscera for private dissection.

The apothecary had an idea that I was actually dead. This idea I endeavored to confute, kicking and plunging with all my might, and making the most furious contortions — for the operations of the surgeon had, in a measure, restored me to the possession of my faculties. All, however, was attributed to the effects of a new galvanic battery,[13] wherewith the apothecary, who is really a man of information, performed several curious experiments, in which, from my personal share in their fulfilment, I could not help feeling deeply interested. It was a source of mortification to me nevertheless, that although I made several attempts at conversation, my powers of speech were so entirely in abeyance, that I could not even open my mouth; much less then make reply to some ingenious but fanciful theories of which, under other circumstances, my minute acquaintance with the Hippocratian pathology[14] would have afforded me a ready confutation.

Not being able to arrive at a conclusion, the practitioners remanded me for farther[m] examination. I was taken up into a garret; and the surgeon's lady having accommodated me with drawers and stockings, the surgeon himself fastened my hands, and tied up my jaws with a pocket handkerchief — then bolted the door on the out-

---

j   five-and-twenty (A, B, C)
k . . . k   Having, however, cut off my ears, (A, B, C)

l   case, however, (A, B, C)
m   further (A, B, C)

side as he hurried to his dinner, leaving me alone to silence and to meditation.

I now discovered to my extreme delight that I could have spoken had not my mouth been tied up by the pocket handkerchief. Consoling myself with this reflection, I was mentally repeating some passages of [n]the "Omnipresence of the Deity,"[n] as is my custom before resigning myself to sleep,[15] when two cats, of a greedy and vituperative turn, entering at a hole in the wall, leaped up with a flourish *à*[o] *la Catalani,*[16] and alighting opposite one another on my visage, betook themselves to[p] indecorous contention for the paltry consideration of my nose.

But, as the loss of his ears proved the means of elevating to the throne of Cyrus, the Magian or Mige-Gush of Persia, and as the cutting off his nose gave Zopyrus possession of Babylon,[17] so the loss of a few ounces of my countenance proved the salvation of my body. Aroused by the pain, and burning with indignation, I burst, at a single effort, the fastenings and the bandage. Stalking across the room I cast a glance of contempt at the[q] belligerents,[r] and throwing open the sash to their extreme horror and disappointment, precipitated myself, very dexterously, from the window.

The mail-robber W———,[18] to whom I bore a singular resemblance, was at this moment passing from the city jail to the scaffold erected for his execution in the suburbs. His extreme infirmity, and long continued ill health, had obtained him the privilege of remaining unmanacled; and habited in his gallows costume — one[s] very similar to my own — he lay at full length in the bottom of the hangman's cart (which happened to be under the windows of the surgeon at the moment of my precipitation) without any other guard than the driver who was asleep, and two recruits of the sixth infantry, who were drunk.

As ill-luck would have it, I alit upon my feet within the vehicle. W———, who was an acute fellow, perceived his opportunity. Leaping up immediately, he bolted out behind, and turning down an alley, was out of sight in the twinkling of an eye.[19] The recruits,

---

n . . . n the ——————, *(A, B, C)*
o *Accent added from A, B, C, D*
p to unseemly and *(A, B, C)*
q the feline *(B)*
r belligerants, *(E) misprint*
s a dress *(A, B, C)*

aroused by the bustle, could not exactly comprehend the merits of the transaction. Seeing, however, a man, the precise counterpart of the felon, standing upright in the cart before their eyes, they were of opinion that the rascal (meaning W———) was after making his escape, (so they expressed themselves,) and, having communicated this opinion to one another, they took each a dram, and then knocked me down with the butt-ends of their muskets.

It was not long ere we arrived at the[t] place of destination. Of course nothing could be said in my defence. Hanging was my inevitable fate. I resigned myself thereto with a feeling half stupid, half acrimonious. Being little of a cynic, I had all the sentiments of a dog.[20] The hangman, however, adjusted the noose about my neck. The drop fell.[u]

I forbear[v] to depict my sensations upon the [w]gallows; although here, undoubtedly, I could speak to the point, and it is a topic upon which nothing has been well said. In fact, to[w] write upon such a theme it is necessary to have been hanged.[21] Every author should confine himself to matters of experience. Thus Mark Antony composed[x] a treatise upon getting drunk.[y] [22]

[z]I may just mention, however, that die I did not. My body *was,* but I had no breath *to be* suspended; and but for the knot under my left ear (which had the feel of a military stock) I dare say that I should have experienced very little inconvenience. As for the jerk given to my neck upon the falling of the drop, it merely proved a corrective to the twist afforded me by the fat gentleman in the coach.

For good reasons, however, I did my best to give the crowd the worth of their trouble. My convulsions were said to be extraordinary. My spasms it would have been difficult to beat. The populace

---

t   our *(B)*
u   *After this* My convulsions were said to be extraordinary. Several gentlemen swooned, and some ladies were carried home in hysterics. Pinxit, too, availed himself of the opportunity to retouch, from a sketch taken upon the spot, his admirable painting of the "Marsyas flayed alive." *(A, B, C);* be *is changed illegibly in B*
v   will endeavor *(A, B, C)*

w . . . w   gallows. To *(A, B, C)*
x   wrote *(A, B, C)*
y   getting drunk./drunkenness. *(A, B, C)*
z . . . z   [*These six paragraphs were substituted in D and E for twenty-six paragraphs in A, B, and C. Because of the length of the passage it is presented separately, after the conclusion of the final version of the tale.*]

encored. Several gentlemen swooned; and a multitude of ladies were carried home in hysterics. Pinxit availed himself of the opportunity to retouch, from a sketch taken upon the spot, his admirable painting of the "Marsyas flayed alive."[23]

When I had afforded sufficient amusement, it was thought proper to remove my body from the gallows; — this the more especially as the real culprit had in the meantime been retaken and recognized; a fact which I was so unlucky as not to know.

Much sympathy was, of course,[a] exercised in my behalf, and as no one made claim to my corpse, it was ordered that I should be interred in a public vault.

Here, after due interval, I was deposited. The sexton departed, and I was left alone. A line of Marston's "Malcontent" —

Death's a good fellow and keeps open house — [24]

struck me at that moment as a palpable lie.

I knocked off, however, the lid of my coffin, and stepped out. The place was dreadfully dreary and damp, and I became troubled with *ennui.* By way of amusement, I felt my way among the numerous coffins ranged in order around. I lifted them down, one by one, and breaking open their lids, busied myself in speculations about the mortality within.[z]

"This," I soliloquized,[b] tumbling over a carcass,[25] puffy, bloated, and rotund — "this has been, no doubt, in every sense of the word, an unhappy — an unfortunate man. It has been his terrible lot not to walk, but to waddle — to pass through life not like a human being, but like an elephant — not like a man, but like a rhinoceros.

"His attempts at getting on have been mere abortions, and his circumgyratory proceedings a palpable failure. Taking a step forward, it has been his misfortune to take two towards[c] the right, and three towards[d] the left. His studies have been confined to the poetry[e] of Crabbe.[26] He can have had no idea of the wonder[f] of

---

a course *(E) comma added from D*
b reflected, *(A, B, C)*
c toward *(D)*
d toward *(D)*
e Philosophy *(A, B)*
f wonders *(A, B, C, D)*

a *pirouette*. To him a *pas de papillon* has been an abstract conception. He has never ascended the summit of a hill. He has never viewed from any steeple the glories of a metropolis.[27] Heat has been his mortal enemy. In the dog-days his days have been the days of a dog. Therein, he has dreamed of flames and suffocation — of mountains upon mountains — of Pelion upon Ossa.[28] He was short of breath — to say all in a word, he was short of breath. He thought it extravagant to play upon wind instruments. He was the inventor of self-moving fans, wind-sails, and ventilators. He patronized Du Pont the bellows-maker,[29] and died miserably in attempting to smoke a cigar. His was a case in which I feel a[g] deep interest — a lot in which I sincerely sympathize.

"But here," — said I — "here" — and I dragged spitefully from its receptacle a gaunt,[h] tall, and peculiar-looking form, whose remarkable appearance struck me with a sense of unwelcome familiarity — "here[i] is a wretch entitled to no earthly commiseration." Thus saying, in order to obtain a more distinct view of my subject, I applied my thumb and fore-finger to its[j] nose, and causing it[k] to assume a sitting position upon the ground, held it[l] thus, at the length of my arm, while I continued my soliloquy.

—"Entitled," I repeated, "to no earthly commiseration. Who indeed would think of compassionating a shadow? Besides, has he not had his full share of the blessings of mortality? He was the originator of tall monuments — shot-towers — lightning-rods — lombardy poplars. His treatise upon "Shades and Shadows" has immortalized him. [m]He edited with distinguished ability the last edition of "South on the Bones."[m] [30] He went early to college and studied pneumatics. He then came home, talked eternally, and played upon the French-horn. He patronized the bag-pipes. Captain Barclay, who walked against Time, would not walk against *him*.[31] Windham and Allbreath[32] were his favorite writers [n]— his favorite artist, Phiz[n].[33] He died gloriously while inhaling gas — *levique*

---

g   *Omitted (A, B, C)*
h   guant, *(D) misprint*
i   "here," said I — "here *(A, B, C)*
j   his *(A, B, C)*

k   him *(A, B, C)*
l   him *(A, B, C)*
m . . . m   *Omitted (A, B, C)*
n . . . n   *Omitted (A, B, C)*

flatu corrumpitur,[o] like the *fama pudicitiæ* in Hieronymus.*[34]
He was indubitably a "———

"How *can* you? — how — *can* — you?" — interrupted the object
of my animadversions, gasping for breath, and tearing off, with a
desperate exertion, the bandage around its[s] jaws — "how *can* you,
Mr. Lackobreath, be so infernally cruel as to pinch me in that
manner by the nose? Did you not see how they had fastened up my
mouth — and you *must* know — if you know anything — how vast
a[t] superfluity of breath I have to dispose of! If you do *not* know,
however, sit down and you shall see. — In my situation it is really
a great relief to be able to open one's mouth — to be able to expatiate — to be able to communicate with a person like yourself, who
do not think yourself called upon at every period to interrupt the
thread of a gentleman's discourse. — Interruptions are annoying
and should undoubtedly be abolished — don't you think so? — no
reply, I beg you, — one person is enough to be speaking at a time.
— I shall be done by-and-by, and then you may begin. — How the
devil, sir, did you get into this place? — not a word I beseech you —
been here some time myself — terrible accident! — heard of it, I
suppose — awful calamity! — walking under your windows — some
short while ago — about the time you were stage-struck — horrible
occurrence! — heard of "catching one's breath," eh? — hold your
tongue I tell you! — I caught somebody else's! — had always too
much of my own — met Blab at the corner of the street — wouldn't
give me a chance for a word — couldn't get in a syllable edgeways —
attacked, consequently, with epilepsis — Blab made his escape —
damn all fools! — they took me up for dead, and put me in this
place — pretty doings all of them! — heard all you said about me —
every word a lie — horrible! — wonderful! — outrageous! — hideous!

* *Tenera res in feminis fama*[p] *pudicitiæ, et quasi flos pulcherrimus, cito ad
levem marcescit*[q] *auram, levique flatu corrumpitur,*[r] *maxime, &c.* — Hieronymus ad
Salvinam.

o *corrupitur, (D); corrupitor, (E)*
   corrected from A, B, C
p *famas (E) corrected from A, B, C, D*
q *marcessit (A, B, C, D, E) corrected
   editorially*
r *corrupitur, (D, E) corrected from
   A, B, C*
s his *(A, B, C)*
t how vast a/what a vast *(A, B, C)*

— incomprehensible! — et cetera — et cetera — et cetera — et cetera —" ___35

It is impossible to conceive my astonishment at so unexpected a discourse; or the[u] joy with which I became gradually convinced that the breath so fortunately caught by the gentleman (whom I soon recognized as my neighbor Windenough) was, in fact, the identical expiration mislaid by myself in the conversation with my wife. Time, place, and circumstance[v] rendered it a matter beyond question. I did not, however, immediately release my hold upon Mr. W.'s proboscis — not at least during the long period in which the inventor of lombardy-poplars continued to favor me with his explanations.

In this respect I was actuated by that habitual prudence which has ever been my predominating trait. I reflected that many difficulties might still lie in the path of my preservation which only[w] extreme exertion on my part would be[x] able to surmount. Many persons, I considered, are prone to estimate commodities in their possession — however valueless to the then proprietor — however troublesome, or distressing — in direct[y] ratio with the advantages to be derived by others from their attainment, or by themselves from their abandonment. Might not this be the case with Mr. Windenough? In displaying anxiety for the breath of which he was at present so willing to get rid, might I not lay myself open to the exactions of his avarice? There are scoundrels in this world, I remembered with a sigh, who will not scruple to take unfair opportunities with even a next door neighbor, and (this remark is from Epictetus)[36] it is precisely at that time when men are most anxious to throw off the burden of their own calamities that they feel the least desirous of relieving them in others.

Upon considerations similar to these, and still retaining my grasp upon the nose of Mr. W., I accordingly thought proper to model my reply.

"Monster!" I began in a tone of the deepest indignation, "monster; and double-winded idiot! — dost *thou* whom,[z] for thine

---

u   the extravagant *(A, B, C)*
v   incidental circumstances *(A, B, C)*
w   *Omitted (A, B)*
x   be alone *(A, B)*

y   precise *(A, B, C)*
z   *thou* whom,/*thou*, whom *(E)*
    repunctuated from A, B, C, D

iniquities, it has pleased heaven to accurse with a two-fold respiration — dost *thou,* I say, presume to address me in the familiar language of an old acquaintance? — "I lie," forsooth! and "hold my tongue," to be sure! — pretty conversation,[a] indeed, to a gentleman with a single breath! — all this, too, when I have it in my power to relieve the calamity under which thou dost so justly suffer — to curtail the superfluities of thine unhappy respiration."

Like Brutus, I paused for a reply —[37] with which, like a tornado, Mr. Windenough immediately overwhelmed me. Protestation followed upon protestation, and apology upon apology. There were no terms with which he was unwilling to comply, and there were none of which I failed to take the fullest advantage.

Preliminaries being at length arranged, my acquaintance delivered me the respiration; for which (having carefully examined it) I gave him afterwards a receipt.

I am aware that by many I shall be held to blame for speaking; in a manner so cursory, of a transaction so impalpable. It will be thought that I should have entered more minutely into the details of an occurrence by which — and this[b] is very true — much new light might be thrown upon a highly interesting branch of physical philosophy.

To all this I am sorry that I cannot reply. A hint is the only answer which I am permitted to make. There were *circumstances* — but I think it much safer upon consideration to say as little as possible about an affair so delicate — *so delicate,* I repeat, and[c] at the[d] time involving the interests of a third party whose sulphurous[e] resentment I have not the least desire, at this moment, of incurring.[38]

We were not long after this necessary arrangement in effecting an escape from the dungeons of the sepulchre. The united strength of our resuscitated voices was soon sufficiently[f] apparent. Scissors, the Whig Editor, republished a treatise upon "the nature and origin of subterranean noises." A reply — rejoinder — confutation

---

a   conversation *(E) comma added from A, B, C, D*
b   all this *(A, B, C)*
c   and and *(E) misprint*
d   the same *(A, B, C, D)*
e   *Omitted (A, B, C)*
f   efficiently *(A, B, C)*

— and justification — followed in the columns of [g]a Democratic[g] Gazette. It was not until the opening of the vault to decide the controversy, that the appearance of Mr. Windenough and myself proved both parties to have been decidedly in the wrong.

I cannot conclude these details of some very singular passages in a life at all times sufficiently eventful, without again recalling to the attention of the reader the merits of that indiscriminate philosophy which is a sure and ready shield against those shafts of calamity which can neither be[h] seen, felt, nor fully understood. It was in the spirit of this wisdom that, among the Ancient Hebrews, it was believed the gates of Heaven would be inevitably opened to that sinner, or saint, who, with good lungs and implicit confidence, should vociferate the word *"Amen!"*[39] It was in the spirit of this wisdom that, when a great plague raged at Athens, and every means had been in vain attempted for its removal, Epimenides, as Laertius relates in his second book of[i] that philosopher, advised the erection of a shrine and temple[j] "to the proper God."[40]

LYTTLETON BARRY.[k] [41]

NOTES

(In these notes the reader is referred to notes on "A Decided Loss" [DL]; only references and allusions not already treated there are discussed here.)

1. DL n. 1.   2. DL n. 20.   3. DL n. 2.

4. A *pas-de-Zéphyr* is also mentioned in "The Devil in the Belfry"; here, the ostensible reference to a ballet step affords a pun.

5. DL n. 7.   6. DL n. 6.   7. DL n. 8.

8. Auguste Grandjean, "hair comp.," 1 Barclay" Street, is in the New York Directory, 1844; and there is an allusion to a hair tonic of his in "The Angel of the Odd." Compare DL at n. 9.

9. DL n. 11.

10. For Demosthenes' practicing on the beach, see Quintilian, *Institutes,* XI, iii, 53.

11. Edwin Forrest was one of the most popular performers of his day.

g . . . g an ultra *(A, B, C)*
h neither be/be neither *(A, B, C)*
i of the life of *(A, B, C)*
j temple *to prostekonti Theo (A)*

changed in B
k *Only the last two versions have Poe's pseudonymous signature:* Littleton Barry. *(D);* Lyttleton Barry. *(E)*

Adrian Joline *(Meditations of an Autograph Collector,* 1902, p. 45) remembered seeing and hearing him many years before: "I certainly *heard* him ... His stalwart personality was somewhat impressive, although not altogether fascinating, and he stalked about, howled, and made many, strange, loud sounds."

12. DL n. 14.   13. DL n. 21.   14. DL n. 3.

15. A very dull but wide-selling poem (1828) by Robert Montgomery. John Neal called Montgomery "a rhyming popinjay" in the *Yankee,* December 1829, the issue in which he published a letter from Poe and made kindly mention of "Al Aaraaf" and "Tamerlane." Poe showed his dislike of Robert Montgomery (and his brother James) in "The Angel of the Odd" and expressed it in "Marginalia" numbers 19 and 83 *(Democratic Review,* November 1844, p. 487, and December 1844, p. 586). See also "Never Bet the Devil Your Head," at n. 20.

16. DL n. 16.

17. DL n. 17, and for Zopyrus see Herodotus, *Histories,* III, 153–160.

18. DL n. 18.

19. For "twinkling of an eye," see I Corinthians 15:52.

20. The philosophers are said to have been called cynics, from the Greek word for dog, because of their sneering, aggressive behavior.

21. Charles Lamb's essay "On the Inconveniences of Being Hanged" recounts the adventures of a man reprieved, and cut down alive.

22. Horace Smith in *Zillah* (1828), III, 40, has Mark Antony say, "as to toping ... I have had long ... practice, and I have ... written a treatise upon drunkenness." This was probably Poe's source. Antony's *De Ebrietate Sua* is mentioned in Pliny's *Natural History,* XIV, 28.

23. DL n. 19.

24. The verse is not from John Marston's *Malcontent,* but inaccurately from his *Antonio and Mellida,* Part 1, Act III, Scene ii, lines 194, 195.

25. There are similar repulsive passages in "King Pest."

26. The poetry of George Crabbe is chosen merely because crabs do not walk forward.

27. For viewing a city from a steeple see "How to Write a Blackwood Article."

28. The Giants, warring against the gods, tried to pile Mount Pelion on Mount Ossa to reach the summit of Olympus (Homer, *Odyssey,* XI, 315; Vergil, *Georgics,* I, 281).

29. Du Pont as a bellows-maker has not been found.

30. *South on the Bones* is the cover title of some American reprints of *A Short Description of the Bones* (1825) by John Flint South, M.D.

31. Captain Robert Barclay-Allardyce, a Scot, walked a thousand miles in as many hours in 1809. See *DNB.*

LOSS OF BREATH: EXCISED MATTER

32. A "Life and Speeches" of William Windham (1750–1810), British states-man, was reviewed in the *American Quarterly Review* for September 1833. I can find no writer named Allbreath.

33. Phiz was the *nom de plume* of Hablot Knight Browne (1815–1882), the English illustrator, especially noted for his association with Dickens.

34. The Latin appears in St. Jerome's seventy-ninth letter to Salvina; see *Sancti Eusebii Hieronymi stridonensis presbyteri opera omnia* (Paris, 1842), vol. I, column 730, and Migne's *Patrologia Latina*. It means, "A reputation for modesty among women is a delicate thing, and as if a most beautiful flower, as soon as it is exposed to the light air, is greatly damaged by a slight breeze."

35. The speaker's "stream of consciousness" remarks, first published in 1835, are earlier than those of this kind in *Pickwick Papers* (April 1836–November 1837). Mr. Blab obviously liked to talk himself.

36. The reference is to fragment 122 of Epictetus, given in Upton's edition (1741), I, 781. It is translated by T. W. Higginson, "In prosperity it is very easy to find a friend; in adversity, nothing is so difficult." Some modern editors reject the passage.

37. Shakespeare's *Julius Caesar,* III, ii, 37.

38. There is a hint of something sinister here. The third party was pre-sumably an acquaintance of Peter Schlemihl, and of the Duc de L'Omelette!

39. Smith, *Zillah,* I, 151: "The Jews having imbibed the strange notion, that the gates of Heaven would be opened to him who answered *Amen* with all his might, the . . . multitude chanted this word." See the *Jewish Encyclopedia,* s.v. Amen, on rabbinical sources.

40. The Greek inscription was *to prostekonti theo,* meaning "to the proper divinity." The record comes from Diogenes Laertius, *Lives,* I, "Epimenides," 3. Poe perhaps took it from a commentary on Acts 17:23.

41. The signature is probably a combination of two pseudonyms. "Barry Cornwall" was that of the songwriter Bryan Waller Proctor whom Poe men-tioned a number of times. John P. Kennedy signed "Mary Littleton" to his novel *Horse-Shoe Robinson.* And I agree with Killis Campbell (*MLN,* March 1913) that it shows the influence of Thackeray's *Barry Lyndon* which ran serially in *Fraser's Mazazine* in 1844. In the *Broadway Journal* Poe signed "Littleton Barry" to five tales: "The Duc de L'Omelette," "King Pest," "Mystification," and "Why the Little Frenchman Wears His Hand in a Sling," as well as to "Loss of Breath," but the last named is the only one to carry a signature in Griswold's edition, where it is spelled Lyttleton Barry.

APPENDIX

TWENTY-SIX PARAGRAPHS (A, B, C) REPLACED BY SIX IN D AND E

Die I certainly did not. The sudden jerk given to my neck upon the falling of the drop, merely proved a corrective to the unfortunate twist afforded me by the gentleman in the coach. Although my body certainly *was,* I had, alas! no breath *to be* suspended; and but for the chafing[a] of the rope, the pressure of the knot under my ear, and the rapid determination of blood to the brain, I[b] should, I dare say, have experienced very little inconvenience.

The latter feeling, however, grew momently[c] more painful. I heard my heart beating with violence — the veins in my hands and wrists swelled nearly to bursting — my temples throbbed tempestuously — and I felt that my eyes were starting from their sockets. Yet when I say that in spite of all this my sensations were not absolutely intolerable, I will not be believed.

There were noises in my ears — first like the tolling of huge bells — then like the beating of a thousand drums — then, lastly, like the low, sullen murmurs of the sea. But these noises were very far from disagreeable.

Although, too, the powers of my mind were confused and distorted, yet I was — strange to say! — well aware of such confusion and distortion. I could, with unerring promptitude determine at will in what particulars my sensations were correct — and in what particulars I wandered from the path. I could even feel with accuracy *how far* — to *what very point,* such wanderings had misguided me, but still without the power of correcting my deviations. I took besides, at the same time, a wild delight in analyzing my conceptions.*

Memory, which, of all other faculties, should have first taken its departure, seemed on the contrary to have been endowed with quadrupled power. Each incident of my past life flitted before me like a shadow. There was not a brick in the building where I was born — not a dog-leaf in the primer I had thumbed over when a child — not a tree in the forest where I hunted when a boy — not a street in the cities I had traversed when a man — that I did not at that time most palpably behold. I could repeat to myself entire lines, passages,[d] chapters, books, from the studies of my earlier days; and while, I dare say, the crowd around me were blind with horror, or aghast with awe, I was alternately with Æschylus, a demi-god, or with Aristophanes, a frog.[1]

*   *   *   *   *   *   *   *

A dreamy delight now took hold upon my spirit, and I imagined that I had been eating opium, or feasting upon the hashish of the old assassins.[2] But glimpses of pure, unadulterated reason — during which I was still buoyed up by the hope of finally escaping that death which hovered like a vulture above me — were still caught occasionally by my soul.

By some unusual pressure of the rope against my face, a portion of the cap was chafed away, and I found to my astonishment that my powers of vision were not altogether destroyed. A sea of waving heads rolled around me. In the intensity of my delight I eyed them with feelings of the deepest commiseration, and blessed, as I looked upon the haggard assembly, the superior benignity of *my* proper stars.

I now reasoned, rapidly I believe — profoundly I am sure — upon principles of common law — propriety of that law especially, for which I hung — absurdities

---

* The general reader will, I dare say, recognise, in these *sensations* of Mr. Lack-o'Breath, much of the absurd *metaphysicianism* of the redoubted Schelling. [Poe's note]

---

a	shaking (A) *changed in B*	c	momentarily *(A, B)*
b	*Omitted (A, B)*	d	passages, names, acts, *(A, B)*

in political economy which till then I had never been able to acknowledge —
dogmas in the old Aristotelians now generally denied, but not the less intrinsically
true — detestable school formulæ in Bourdon, in Garnier, in Lacroix —[3] synonymes in Crabbe —[4] lunar-lunatic theories in St. Pierre —[5] falsities in the Pelham
novels — beauties in Vivian Grey — more than beauties in Vivian Grey — profundity in Vivian Grey — genius in Vivian Grey — everything in Vivian Grey.[6]

Then came like a flood, Coleridge, Kant, Fitche, and Pantheism —[7] then like
a deluge, the Academie, Pergola, La Scala, San Carlo, Paul, Albert, Noblet,
Ronzi Vestris, Fanny Bias, and Taglioni.[8]

*　　*　　*　　*　　*　　*　　*　　*

A rapid change was now taking place in my sensations. The last shadows of
connection flitted away from my meditations. A storm — a tempest of ideas, vast,
novel, and soul-stirring, bore my spirit like a feather afar off. Confusion crowded
upon confusion like a wave upon a wave. In a very short time Schelling himself
would have been satisfied with my entire loss of self-identity.[9] The crowd became
a mass of mere abstraction.

About this period I became aware of a heavy fall and shock — but, although
the concussion jarred throughout my frame, I had not the slightest idea of its
having been sustained in my own proper person; and thought of it as of an incident peculiar to some other existence — an idiosyncrasy belonging to some other
Ens.[10]

It was at this moment — as I afterwards discovered — that having been suspended for the full term of execution, it was thought proper to remove my body
from the gallows — this the more especially as the real culprit had now been
retaken and recognised.

Much sympathy was now exercised in my behalf — and as no one in the city
appeared to identify my body, it was ordered that I should be interred in the
public sepulchre early in the following morning. I lay, in the meantime, without
sign[e] of life — although from the moment, I suppose, when the rope was loosened
from my neck, a dim consciousness of my situation oppressed me like the nightmare.

I was laid out in a chamber sufficiently small, and very much encumbered
with furniture — yet to me it appeared of a size to contain the universe. I have
never before or since, in body or in mind, suffered half so much agony as from
that single idea. Strange! that the simple conception of abstract magnitude —
of infinity — should have been accompanied with pain. Yet so it was. "With how
vast a difference," said I, "in life and in death — in time and in eternity — here and
hereafter, shall our merest sensations be imbodied!"

The day died away, and I was aware that it was growing dark — yet the same
terrible conceit still overwhelmed me. Nor was it confined to the boundaries of
the apartment — it extended, although in a more definite manner, to all objects,
and, perhaps I will not be understood in saying that it extended also to all *sentiments*. My fingers as they lay cold, clammy, stiff, and pressing helplessly one
against another, were, in my imagination, swelled to a size according with the
proportions of the Antœus.[11] Every portion of my frame betook of their enor-

---

e　signs *(A, B)*

mity. The pieces of money — I well remember — which being placed upon my eyelids, failed to keep them effectually closed, seemed huge, interminable chariot-wheels of the Olympia, or of the Sun.[12]

Yet it is very singular that I experienced no sense of weight — of gravity. On the contrary I was put to much inconvenience by that buoyancy — that tantalizing *difficulty of keeping down,* which is felt by the swimmer in deep water. Amid the tumult of my terrors I laughed with a hearty internal laugh to think what incongruity there would be — could I arise and walk — between the elasticity of my motion, and the mountain of my form.

* * * * * * * *

The night came — and with it a new crowd of horrors. The consciousness of my approaching interment began to assume new distinctness, and consistency — yet never for one moment did I imagine *that I was not actually dead.*

"This then" — I mentally ejaculated — "this darkness which is palpable, and oppresses with a sense of suffocation — this — this — is indeed *death.* This is death — this is death the terrible — death the holy. This is the death undergone by Regulus — and equally by Seneca.[13] Thus — thus, too, shall I always remain — always — always remain. Reason is folly, and philosophy a lie. No one will know my sensations, my horror — my despair. Yet will men still persist in reasoning, and philosophizing, and making themselves fools. There is, I find, no hereafter but this. This — this — this — is the only eternity! — and what, O Baalzebub![14] — *what* an eternity! — to *lie* in this vast — this awful void — a hideous, vague, and unmeaning anomaly — motionless, yet wishing for motion — powerless, yet longing for power — forever, forever, and forever!"

But the morning broke at length — and with its misty and gloomy dawn arrived in triple horror the paraphernalia of the grave. Then — and not till then — was I fully sensible of the fearful fate hanging over me. The phantasms of the night had faded away with its shadows, and the actual terrors of the yawning tomb left me no heart for the bug-bear speculations of transcendentalism.

I have before mentioned that my eyes were but imperfectly closed — yet as I could not move them in any degree, those objects alone which crossed the direct line of vision were within the sphere of my comprehension. But across that line of vision spectral and stealthy figures were continually flitting, like the ghosts of Banquo.[15] They were making hurried preparations for my interment. First came the coffin which they placed quietly by my side. Then the undertaker with attendants and a screw-driver. Then a stout man whom I could distinctly see and who took hold of my feet — while one whom I could only feel lifted me by the head and shoulders. Together they placed me in the coffin, and drawing the shroud up over my face proceeded to fasten down the lid. One of the screws, missing its proper direction, was screwed by the carelessness of the undertaker deep — deep — down into my shoulder. A convulsive shudder ran throughout my frame. With what horror, with what sickening of heart did I reflect that one minute sooner a similar manifestation of life, would, in all probability, have prevented my inhumation. But alas! it was now too late, and hope died away within my bosom as I felt myself lifted upon the shoulders of men — carried down the stairway — and thrust within the hearse.

LOSS OF BREATH: EXCISED MATTER

During the brief passage to the cemetery my sensations, which for some time had been lethargic and dull, assumed, all at once, a degree of intense and unnatural vivacity for which I can in no manner account. I could distinctly hear the rustling[f] of the plumes — the whispers of the attendants — the solemn breathings of the horses of death. Confined as I was in that narrow and strict embrace, I could feel the quicker or slower movement of the procession — the restlessness of the driver — the windings of the road as it led us to the right or to the left. I could distinguish the peculiar odor of the coffin — the sharp acid smell of the steel screws. I could see the texture of the shroud as it lay close against my face; and was even conscious of the rapid variations in light and shade which the flapping to and fro of the sable hangings occasioned within the body of the vehicle.

In a short time, however, we arrived at the place of sepulture,[g] and I felt myself deposited within the tomb. The entrance was secured — they departed — and I was left alone. A line of Marston's "Malcontent,"

"Death's a good fellow and keeps open house,"

struck me at that moment as a palpable lie. Sullenly I lay at length, the quick among the dead — *Anacharsis inter Scythas.*[16]

From what I overheard early in the morning, I was led to believe that the occasions when the vault was made use of were of very rare occurrence. It was probable that many months might elapse before the doors of the tomb would be again unbarred — and even should I survive until that period, what means could I have more than at present, of making known my situation or of escaping from the coffin? I resigned myself, therefore, with much tranquillity to my fate, and fell, after many hours, into a deep and deathlike sleep.

How long I remained thus is to me a mystery. When I awoke my limbs were no longer cramped with the cramp of death — I was no longer without the power of motion. A very slight exertion was sufficient to force off the lid of my prison — for the dampness of the atmosphere had already occasioned decay in the woodwork around the screws.

My steps as I groped around the sides of my habitation were, however, feeble and uncertain, and I felt all the gnawings of hunger with the pains of intolerable thirst. Yet, as time passed away, it is strange that I experienced little uneasiness from these scourges of the earth, in comparisons with the more terrible visitations of the fiend *Ennui.* Stranger still were the resources by which I endeavored to banish him from my presence.

The sepulchre was large and subdivided into many compartments, and I busied myself in examining the peculiarities of their construction. I determined the length and breadth of my abode. I counted and recounted the stones of the masonry. But there were other methods by which I endeavored to lighten the tedium of my hours. Feeling my way among the numerous coffins ranged in order around, I lifted them down, one by one, and breaking open their lids, busied myself in speculations about the mortality within.

---

f   restling (C) *misprint, corrected from*   g   sculpture *(A, B) misprint*
A, B

TALES OF THE FOLIO CLUB

NOTES ON THE PARAGRAPHS REMOVED IN 1845

1. The references are to the *Prometheus Vinctus* of Aeschylus, and the *Ranae* of Aristophanes.

2. Hashish, the hallucinatory drug made from hemp and employed by the sect of the Assassins, appears in "Pinakidia," number 24 (*SLM* August 1836, p. 575).

3. Louis-Pierre-Marie Bourdon, Jean-Guillaume Garnier, and Silvestre-François Lacroix were contemporary French mathematicians.

4. George Crabb (1778–1851) compiled *English Synonymes Explained* (London, 1816).

5. Jacques-Henri Bernardin de St. Pierre (the author of *Paul et Virginie*) in his *Études de la Nature* (1784), a generally admirable work, announced his belief that the moon does *not* affect the tides, which caused some readers to think him insane. (Poe quoted Henry Hunter's translation — *Studies of Nature,* first published in London in 1796 — in notes to lines 68 and 70 of "Al Aaraaf," part I.)

6. *Pelham* (1828) is by Edward Bulwer (later Bulwer-Lytton); *Vivian Grey* (1826–27) is by Benjamin Disraeli. Both authors were early favorites of Poe.

7. Coleridge, Kant, and Johann Gottlieb Fichte were transcendental philosophers; Poe always misspells the last name.

8. The Académie de Musique is the Paris Opera; the Pergola that at Florence; La Scala at Milan; San Carlo at Naples. The other names are those of famous dancers and singers. Both lists are in Book VII, chapter VII of *Vivian Grey*.

9. Compare "the doctrines of *Identity* as urged by Schelling" in "Morella" at n. 4.

10. An Ens is an existence.

11. Antaeus was a giant, son of Ge (the Earth), and was regarded as invincible, because when he touched his mother, his strength was renewed. Hercules slew him by lifting him in the air and strangling him. He is also mentioned in Poe's review of J. F. Cooper's *Sketches of Switzerland* (*SLM,* October 1836).

12. For the burning chariot wheels of the Olympic games see Horace, *Odes,* I, i, 3–6.

13. Marcus Atilius Regulus, captured by the Carthaginians and sent back to Rome to urge a humiliating peace, urged the Romans to continue the war and returned to Carthage to die willingly for his country. See Horace, *Odes,* III, v, for the story. Annaeus Seneca the Younger, who had been Nero's tutor, killed himself at the command of his former pupil. See Tacitus, *Annals,* XV, lx—lxiv.

14. Baalzebub, the Lord of Flies, was a Palestinian divinity, made Satan's lieutenant in *Paradise Lost,* and mentioned in "The Duc de L'Omelette" at n. 12.

15. See *Macbeth,* III, iv, *passim.*

16. Anacharsis the Scythian, alone of his countrymen, came to Greece to study philosophy. The phrase "Anacharsis among the Scythians" is proverbial for the only one of a kind.

THE BARGAIN LOST and BON-BON

The fifth of Poe's tales printed in the *Saturday Courier,* "The Bargain Lost," is of special interest to the student of his methods as a storyteller. It was an experiment in a peculiar form of extravaganza, which the author obviously did not think quite successful, for he rewrote it almost completely before its appearance as "Bon-Bon" some two and a half years later. The differences between "The Bargain Lost" and "Bon-Bon" are so great that it might be desirable to treat them as two distinct entities, but there is a great deal that the two stories have in common.

"The Bargain Lost" is a mere anecdote of how a comic philosopher defeats a visitor from the nether regions because "the Prince of Darkness is a gentleman." That he is interested in eating souls may be suggested by the thirty-fourth canto of Dante's *Inferno,* but Poe is thought to have had in mind specifically something in the section of the "Reformation of Hell" in William Elliot's translation of *The Visions of Quevedo.* There one reads: "Lucifer is very fond of this meal, and the expression 'may the devil swallow me,' which tailors often use, is not inappropriate; for he does swallow many."*

The author's manner in "The Bargain Lost" is unusual for him in one respect. Although Poe thought all wholly inappropriate combinations comic, in this early tale he used far more made-up nonsensicalities than was his practice later. Some of them are not essential to the plot, and were removed when Poe recast the story as "Bon-Bon." Because of these inartistic errors, I incline to think "The Bargain Lost" was composed earlier than the other stories printed in the *Saturday Courier.*

Its successor, "Bon-Bon," published in the *Southern Literary Messenger* for August 1835, is one of Poe's best comic stories. Vin-

* The satirical *Sueños* ("Visions") of Francisco Quevedo y Villegas were translated into English as early as 1640. The quotation above from Elliot's translation is on p. 176 of an edition printed in Philadelphia in 1831. I saw a copy in which someone had written the word "Poe" and marked a few passages in pencil; it was owned by Roger G. Lewis in New York about 1925. I have seen no other copy of this particular edition.

cent Buranelli remarks, "Whether Poe was really capable of writing farces for the stage is debatable. He certainly was capable . . . of writing farces for the magazines," and instances "Bon-Bon." In fact, the story has been played on the stage, with dialogue "word for word" from Poe, in New York.†

In expanding and recasting "The Bargain Lost," Poe changed his Italian philosopher into a Frenchman who is both a philosopher and a cook. This probably was suggested by a remark of Baron Bielfeld (1717–1770) concerning gourmets who consider a chef a divine mortal and argue, by rather plausible reasoning, that his art is more useful and demands as much intellect and sagacity as Metaphysics.‡

Poe's revised story won admiration at once. In the *Southern Literary Messenger,* May 1836, J. N. McJilton of Baltimore, a friend and correspondent of Poe, had a tale of diablerie called "The Hall of Incholese" in which he wrote: "Incholese was a foreigner . . . and many a Venetian hated him, . . . the inimitable Pierre Bon-Bon himself had not more sworn enemies."

TEXTS

The Bargain Lost

(A) Philadelphia *Saturday Courier,* December 1, 1832, facsimiled by John Grier Varner in *Edgar Allan Poe and the Philadelphia Saturday Courier* (1933), pp. 50–63.

The text of the *Courier* is followed without emendation. Thus the spellings "Bossarion," "escrutoire," and "cobler" are retained, and the double quotation marks obviously required at the opening of the 24th paragraph are not supplied. The facsimile in Varner's book is the first appearance in book form.

† See Buranelli, *Edgar Allan Poe* (1961), p. 42. Buranelli also quotes John P. Kennedy's advice to Poe in a letter of September 19, 1835, that Poe try to write "farces after the manner of the French Vaudevilles." The playlet, by William Barstow, was given a special benefit performance at the Little Theatre, Sunday evening, February 29, 1920. Mr. F. C. McCarthy had the title role, the playwright the part of the devil. See Mary E. Phillips, *Edgar Allan Poe the Man* (1926), I, 428.

‡ Jacob Friedrich, freiherr von Bielfeld, *Les Premiers Traits de l'erudition universelle, ou analyse abregée de toutes les sciences, des beaux-arts et des belles-lettres* (3 vols., Leide [Leyden], S. & J. Luchtmans, 1767), Book II, chapter xvi, section 10: "gourmets . . . qui estiment qu'un *Cuisinier est un mortal divin;* et qui soutiennent par des raisonnemens assez plausibles, mais spécieux, que son art est plus utile, et qu'il exige autant d'esprit et de sagacité que la Métaphysique."

THE BARGAIN LOST

Bon-Bon

(A) Southern Literary Messenger, August 1835 (1:693–698); *(B)* Duane copy of last with manuscript changes (1839); *(C) Tales of the Grotesque and Arabesque* (1840), I, 127–151; *(D)* PHANTASY-PIECES, copy of last with manuscript changes (1842); *(E) Broadway Journal,* April 19, 1845 (1:243–247); *(F) Works* (1850), II, 479–495.

The text is based on Griswold's *(F)* which shows auctorial changes. The *Broadway Journal (E)* follows most of the revisions made by Poe in PHANTASY-PIECES *(D)* and independently adds many others. Among the 57 punctuation changes made in PHANTASY-PIECES, 28 dashes are eliminated and semi-colons or commas substituted. Some changes are abortive, and some are as badly scrawled as those in "King Pest."

The French spelling and accents in "Bon-Bon" are corrected, a few from other texts, others editorially. Spelling and accents of each text are recorded in the variants.

Reprint

Spirit of the Times (Philadelphia), July 22, continued July 23, 1845, from the *Broadway Journal,* where it was not signed.

THE BARGAIN LOST

> The heathen philosopher, when he had a mind to eat a grape, would open his lips when he put it into his mouth, meaning thereby that grapes were made to eat and lips to open. — *As You Like It.*[1]

At Venice, in the year ———— ,[2] in the street ———— , lived Pedro Garcia, a metaphysician. — With regard to date and residence, circumstances of a private and sacred nature forbid me to be more explicit. In all mental qualifications our hero was gigantic. Moreover, in bodily circumference, he had no cause of complaint; but, in right ascension, four feet five was the philosopher's ne plus ultra.

Now Pedro was descended from a noble Florentine family;[3] yet it was with little concern that, in certain boilings of the pot revolutionary, (during which, saith Machiavelli, the scum always comes uppermost)[4] he beheld his large estates silently slipping through his fingers. Indeed, from his earliest youth, had Pedro

Garcia been addicted to the most desperate abstrusities. He had studied at Padua, at Milan, at Gottingen. It is he — but let this go no farther — it is he to whom Kant is mainly indebted for his metaphysics. I have MSS. in my possession sufficient to establish what I say.

The doctrines of our friend were not very generally understood, although by no means difficult of comprehension. He was not, it is true, a Platonist — nor strictly an Aristotelian — nor did he, with Leibnitz, reconcile things irreconcileable. He was, emphatically, a Pedronist. He was Ionic and Italic. He reasoned a priori and a posteriori. His ideas were innate, or otherwise. He believed in George of Trebizond, he believed in Bossarion. Of his other propensities little is recorded. It is said that he preferred Catullus to Homer, and Sauterne to Medoc.

Yet even this comprehensive philosophy proved an insufficient protection against the shafts of calumny and malice. At Venice wicked men were not wanting to hint that the doctrines of certain people evinced neither the purity of the Academy nor the depth of the Lyceum.

*   *   *   *   *   *

The great bell of St. Mark's had already sounded midnight, yet our hero was not in bed. He sat, alone, in the little chamber, his study, redeemed from the filth and bustle of the day. I hold minute attention to trifles unworthy the dignity of serious narrative; otherwise I might here, following the example of the novelist, dilate upon the subject of habiliment, and other mere matters of the outward man. I might say that the hair of our patrician was worn short, combed smoothly over his forehead, and surmounted with a violet-coloured, conical cap with tassels — that his green fustian jerkin was not after the fashion of those worn by the nobility of Venice at that day — that the sleeves were more deeply slashed than the reigning costume permitted — that the slashes were faced — not, as usual in that barbarous period, with parti-coloured silk, but with the beautiful red leather of Morocco — that his stiletto was a specimen piece of workmanship from the factory of Pan Ispan, of Damascus, attaghan-maker to the Effendi[5] — that his slippers were of a bright purple, curiously filagreed, and might have been made in Japan, but for the exquisite pointing of the toes, and the fact that Baptista, the Spanish cobler on the Rialto, opined to the contrary — that his breeches were of the white, satin-like cloth called 'celeste' — that his sky-blue cloak, or wrapper, resembling, in form, the anomaly, ycleped, a morning-gown, floated, like a mist, upon his shoulders, richly bestudded with crimson and yellow patches — and that his tout ensemble gave rise to the remarkable words of Benevenuta, the improvisatrice, to wit: — "That the paroquet, upon a certain cathedral, resembled nothing so much as Pedro, the metaphysician."[6] All this and more — had I been a novelist — might I have detailed. But, thanks to St. Urfino,[7] whatever I am, *that* am I not. Therefore upon all these subjects I say 'mum.'

The chamber in which sat our hero was of singular beauty. The floor was covered with a mat (for it was the summer season) of the most brilliant and glossy pale yellow, formed from the rare and valuable reeds of Siam.[8] All around from the ceiling fell tapestry-hangings of the richest crimson velvet. The ceiling, itself, was of brown and highly-polished oak, vaulted, carved, and fretted, until all its innumerable angles were rounded into a dense mass of shadow, from whose gloomy depth, by a slender golden chain with very long links, swung a fantastic Arabesque lamp of solid silver.[9] A black, heavy, and curiously-pannelled door, opening inwardly, was closed, after the fashion of that day, with a chased brazen bar; while a single, huge, bowed, and trelliced window glared out upon the waters of the Adriatic.

The minor furniture of the room consisted, principally, of a profusion of elegantly-bound and illuminated books scattered here and there in classical disorder, on the tables, on the floor, and on two or three luxurious settees, having every appearance of the ottomans of Mahomet.[10]

It was a dark and stormy night. The rain fell in cataracts; and drowsy citizens started, from dreams of the deluge, to gaze upon the boisterous sea, which foamed and bellowed for admittance into the proud towers and marble palaces. Who would have thought of passions so fierce in that calm water that slumbers all day long? At a slight alabaster stand, trembling beneath the ponderous tomes which it supported, sat the hero of our story.

He heeded not the clanging of the half extinguished lamp, as it rattled overhead in the currents of air; and the roar of the waters he heard not. A voluminous MSS., intended for publication on the morrow, was receiving the last touches of its author. I am sorry that our record has extracted nothing from this valuable work, which has, undoubtedly, perished in some ecclesiastical intrigue. Its title, however, I find to be "A complete exposition of things not to be exposed;" and its motto a line from Pulci, thus happily translated by a modern satirist: —

> Brethren, I come from lands afar
> To show you all what fools you are.[11]

As the storm grew stronger and more terrible, Pedro, totally absorbed in his occupation, could not perceive that, while his left palm rested upon a volume in sable binding, the blue lightning fluttered among its leaves with most portentous velocity.

"I am in no hurry, Signor Pedro," whispered a soft voice in the apartment.

"The devil!" ejaculated our hero, starting from his seat, upsetting the alabaster stand, and looking around him in astonishment.

"Very true!" calmly replied the voice.

"Very true! — What is very true? — How came you here?" vociferated the metaphysician, as his eye fell upon a man with singularly thin features, who lay, at full length, upon an ottoman in a corner of the chamber.

"I was saying," continued the figure, without replying to Pedro's interrogatories, "I was saying that I am in no hurry — that the business upon which I took the liberty of calling is of minor importance — that I can wait until you have finished your Exposition."

"My Exposition! How do *you* know I am writing an Exposition? Good God!"

"Hush!" replied the figure in a shrill undertone; and, arising from the settee, he made a step towards our hero, while the arabesque lamp suddenly ceased its convulsive swinging and became motionless.

The philosopher's amazement did not prevent a narrow scrutiny of the stranger's dress and appearance. The outlines of a figure much above the common standard were blurred and rendered indefinite by the huge folds of a black Roman toga. Above his left ear he carried, after the fashion of a modern scribe, an instrument resembling the stylus of the ancients; and, from his left arm, depended a crimson bag of a material totally unknown to our hero, being luminous. There was another article of habiliment equally a mystery to the patrician. The toga, being left open at the throat, displayed the neatly folded cravat and starched shirt-collar of 1832. All these things excited little of Pedro's attention; for his antiquarian eye had fallen upon the *sandals* of the intruder, and he recognised therein the exact pattern of those worn before the flood, as given, with minute accuracy, in the Ptolemaiad of the Rabbi Vathek.[12]

I find, upon looking over certain archives in Venice, that "Garcia, the metaphysician, was an exceedingly little, yet pugnacious man." Accordingly, when his visitor drew a chair close by the huge bowed window that looked out upon the sea, our hero silently followed his example.

"A clever book that of yours, Pedro," said the stranger, tapping our friend, knowingly, upon the shoulder.

Pedro stared.

"It is a work after my own heart," continued the former, "I suppose you knew Confucius."[13]

Our hero's amazement redoubled.

A sad set of fools now-a-days *I* tell you. Philosophy is a mere trumpery. O, nous estin autos, as some one very justly observed, meaning 'auyos.'[14] But, to tell the truth, it was very little better at any time. The fact is, Garcia," here the stranger's voice dropped to a whisper, "men know nothing about these matters. *Your* doctrines, however, come nearer to the point than any with which I am acquainted. I *like* your doctrines, Signor Pedro, and have come a long way to tell you so."

The philosopher's eyes sparkled, and he fumbled, in great haste, among the rubbish on the floor, for his overthrown MSS. Having found it, he took, from an ivory escrutoire, a flask of the delightful wine of Sauterne, and placing them, with the sable-bound volume, on the alabaster stand, wheeled it before the visitor, and re-seated himself at his elbow.

Here, if the reader should wish to know why our hero troubled himself to place upon the stand any thing so ominous as that book in sable binding, I reply that Pedro Garcia was, by no means, a fool; no man ever accused him of being a fool. He had, accordingly, very soon arrived at the conclusion that his knowing friend was neither more nor less than his August and Satanic Majesty. Now, although persons of greater height have been frightened at less serious circumstances, and although under certain dispensations of Providence (such as the visitation of a spider, a rat, or a physician) Pedro did not always evince the philosopher, yet fear of the devil never once entered his imagination. — To tell the truth, he was rather gratified, than otherwise, at a visit from a gentleman whom he so highly respected. He flattered himself with spending an agreeable hour; and it was with the air of being 'up to snuff' that he accommodated his visitor with a volume best suited to his acquirements and literary taste.

"But I *must* say," continued the stranger, without noticing Pedro's arrangements, "I must say that, upon some points, you are wrong, my friend, wrong; totally *out,* as that rogue Sanconiathon used to say — ha! ha! ha! — *poor* Sanconiathon!"[15]

"Pray, sir, how old — may — you — call yourself?" inquired the metaphysician, with a cut of his eye.

"Old? Sir? Eh? Oh! a mere trifle. As I was saying, you have certain very *outre* notions in that book of yours. Now, what do you mean by all that humbug about the soul? Pray, sir, what is the soul?"

"The soul," replied Pedro, referring to his MSS., "is undoubtedly —"

"No, sir!"

"Indubitably —"

"No, sir!"

"Evidently —"

"No, sir!"

"And beyond all question —"

"No, sir! — the soul is no such thing."

"Then what *is* it?"

"That is neither here nor there, Signor Pedro," replied the stranger, musing, "I have tasted — that is I mean I have known some very bad souls and some pretty good ones."

Here the stranger licked his lips; and having, unconsciously, let fall his hand upon the sable volume, was seized with a violent fit of sneezing upon which our hero, reaching his common-place book, inserted the follow memorandum: —

N. B. — *Divorum inferorum cachinnatio sternutamentis mortalium verisimillima est.*[16]

The stranger continued. "There was the soul of Cratinus — passable! Aristophanes — racy! Plato — exquisite! Not *your* Plato, but Plato the comic poet — your Plato would have turned the stomach of Cerberus — faugh! Then — let me see — there were Catullus, and Naso, and Plautus, and Quinty — *dear* Quinty, as I called him when he sung a 'seculare' for my amusement, while I toasted him good-humouredly on a fork. But they want flavour, these Romans, one fat Greek is worth a dozen of them, and, besides, will *keep,* which cannot be said of a Quirite. — Terence, however, was an exception — firm as an Esquimaux, and juicy as a German — the very recollection of the dog makes my mouth water. — Let us taste your Sauterne."

Our hero had, by this time, made up his mind to the '*nil admirari,*' and merely filled his visitor's glass. He was, however, conscious of a strange sound in the chamber, like the wagging of a tail, but of this he took no notice, simply kicking the large water-dog that lay asleep under his chair, and requesting him to be quiet. — The stranger proceeded.

"But, if I *have* a penchant, Signor Pedro, if I *have* a penchant, it is for a philosopher. Yet let me tell you, sir, it is not every dev—— I mean every gentleman who knows how to *choose* a philosopher. Long ones are *not* good, and the best, if not very carefully shelled, are apt to be a little rancid on account of the gall.

"Shelled?"

"I mean taken out of the body."

"What do you think of a physician?"

"*Don't* mention them," here the stranger retched violently, "ugh! I never tried but one, that rascal — (ugh!) — Hippocrates. Smelt of asafœtida — (ugh! ugh!) — took particular pains with the villain too — caught a wretched cold washing him in the Styx — and, after all, he gave me the cholera morbus."

"The wretch! the abortion of a pill box!" ejaculated Pedro, dropping a tear, and, reaching another bottle of Sauterne, he swallowed three bumpers in rapid succession. The stranger followed his example.

"After all, Signor Pedro," said he, "if a dev —— if a gentleman wishes to live, he must have more talents than one or two, and, with us, a fat face is an evidence of diplomacy."

"How so?"

"Why we are, sometimes, exceedingly pushed for provisions. You ought to know that, in a climate so sultry as mine, it is frequently impossible to keep a soul alive for more than two or three hours; and after death, unless pickled immediately, (and a pickled spirit is *not* good) they will smell — you understand — eh? Putrefaction is always to be apprehended when the spirits are consigned to us in the usual way."

"Good God! how do you manage?"

Here the Arabesque lamp commenced swinging with redoubled violence, and the stranger half started from his seat; however, with a slight sigh, he recovered his composure; merely saying to our hero, in a low tone: — "I tell you what, Pedro Garcia, once for all, we must have no more swearing."

Pedro swallowed another bumper, and his visitor continued.

"Why there are *several* ways of managing. — The most of us starve. Some put up with the pickle. For my part, I purchase my spirits *vivente corpore,* in which case I find they keep very well."

"But the body, my dear sir, the body!" vociferated the philosopher, for the wine had gotten a little into his head. Here he reached another bottle of Sauterne.

"The body! — well, what of the body? oh! ah! I perceive — why the body is not *all* affected by the transaction. I have made innumerable purchases of the kind in my day, and the parties never experience any inconvenience. There was Cain, and Nimrod, and Nero, and Caligula, and Dionysius, and Pisistratus, and — and the Jew — [17] and — and a thousand others, all very good men in their way, who never knew what a soul was during the latter part of their lives. Yet these men adorned society. Why is n't there V——, now? — whom you know as well as I — is he not in full possession of his faculties, mental and corporeal? Who writes a keener epigram? Who reasons more wittily? Who ——— but I have his agreement in my pocket book." Thus saying, he drew, from the luminous bag, a book with clasps of cornelian, and, from the book, a bundle of papers, upon some of which Pedro caught a glimpse of the letters MACHIA, MAZA, RICHEL, and the words DOMITIAN and ELIZABETH. From these papers he selected a narrow slip of parchment, and, from it, read aloud the following words: —

In consideration of certain mental endowments, which it would be unnecessary to specify, and in farther consideration of the sum of one thousand Louis d'or, I, being aged one year and one month, do, hereby, from this date, make over, to the bearer of this bond, all my right, title, and appurtenance in the shadow called 'my soul.'

Done at Paris, this _____ day of _____ , in the year of our Lord _____ , FRANCOIS MARIE AROUET.[18]

"A clever fellow that," resumed the stranger, "but he was wrong about the shadow — the soul a shadow! — no such nonsense, Signor Pedro. — Only think of a fricaseed shadow!"

"Only think of a fricaseed s — h — a — d — o — w!" echoed our hero, whose faculties were becoming gloriously illuminated, "now, damme," continued he, "Mr. — humph! — damme! (hiccup) if *I* would have been such a nincompoop. *My* soul, Mr. — humph! — yes, sir, my soul."

"Your soul, Signor Pedro?"

"Yes, sir, *my* soul is — is — is — no shadow, damme!"

"I should be sorry to suppose, Signor Pedro — "

"Yes, sir, *my* soul is peculiarly calculated for — for — a stew, damme!"

"Ha!"

"A ragout — "

"Eh?"

"A fricasee — "

"Ah!"

"Or (hiccup) a cotelette — and I'll let you have it a bargain."

"Could n't think of such a thing," said the stranger, calmly, at the same time arising from his seat.

Pedro stared.

"Am supplied at present — "

"Eh?"

"Have no cash on hand — "

"What?"

"Very ungentlemanly in me — "

"Humph!"

"To take advantage of — "

"Sir!"

"Your peculiar situation."

Here the stranger bowed and withdrew, in what manner our philosopher could not exactly ascertain; but, in a well concerted effort to discharge a bottle at the scoundrel, the slender chain was severed that hung from the ceiling, and the metaphysician prostrated by the downfall of the lamp.

NOTES

(Since "Bon-Bon" is annotated a few pages below, these notes pertain only to the material that Poe later abandoned or changed essentially.)

1. The motto is from *As You Like It*, V, i, 36f., a passage Poe copied in his two-page manuscript of selections from Shakespeare, written about 1830, now owned by the Poe Foundation and housed in the Virginia State Library at Richmond.

2. Venice is the scene of another of Poe's early stories, "The Visionary." "The Bargain Lost" must be set in the eighteenth century, since near the end of the story Voltaire is referred to as if still alive.

3. Pedro Garcia is a rather plebeian name, and actually Spanish—hardly appropriate for a nobleman of Florence.

4. The remark ascribed to Machiavelli has not been verified.

5. Pan Ispan's name seems to be part Greek and part Persian, from Ispahan.

He made curved Turkish swords of the best Damascus steel. Effendi was at first a Turkish title of high rank, and Poe may have taken it to be generic for nobleman, but in his day the word already meant little more than Esquire, or Monsieur.

6. Poe presumably saw the paroquet at Irvine, in Scotland, as a boy; he referred to it in the poem "Romance" of 1829, line 5 (see Mabbott I, 128).

7. In the *Courier* the saint's name was printed from broken types; Urfino seems to be more probable than Urtino, but no saint of either name is recorded.

8. "Reeds of Siam" means bamboo.

9. This is one of the more beautiful of Poe's hanging lamps. (See "The Duc de L'Omelette," n. 15).

10. The ottomans of Mahomet may be those of the prophet of Islam, or of a Turkish Sultan. Some joke may have escaped commentators here. Compare the ottoman of Cadêt in "The Duc de L'Omelette."

11. No line clearly the basis of the pithy couplet has been found in Pulci's well-known *Morgante Maggiore;* it may be Poe's own invention. See *New York Times Book Review,* October 8, 1967 for query.

12. Vathek was the name of a real caliph—the hero of the romance of the name by William Beckford with which Poe was undoubtedly familiar. That a Hebrew scholar should bear the name is most improbable, and no such *Ptolemaiad* is recorded, but the Egyptian king, Ptolemy II, did commission a translation of the Old Testament into Greek (The Septuagint)—and so might be praised by learned Jews.

13. This seems to be Poe's only reference to the great Chinese philosopher Confucius.

14. The Greek joke is told in a different and more elaborate form in "Bon-Bon" (at note 20), which enables me to explain what is found in "The Bargain Lost." Poe wrote the five words in Greek letters which happen to be so similar to our letters that the printer took them to be such, but mistook the rough breathing on the first word for an apostrophe, and a gamma for *y.* "Ho nous estin autos" means "The mind is itself," and a change to "augos" makes it mean "The mind is a light."

15. Sanchuniathon, reputed author of a treatise on the ancient Phoenician religion (including Baal-worship) may have lived before the siege of Troy. His work is known to scholars only through fragments translated by Philo Byblos and quoted by Eusebius. Long held to be fabulous, he was referred to humorously in chapter 14 of Goldsmith's *Vicar of Wakefield,* but twentieth-century archeological discoveries at Ras Shamra in northern Syria confirm much of his information.

16. The Latin means "The laughter of infernal powers is very like the sneezing of mortals."

17. The Jew was probably Herod the Great. Note that he, the Roman Emperor Domitian (81–96 A.D.), and Cardinal Richelieu were dropped from the list of wicked but successful people in "Bon-Bon."

18. The compact is signed with the real name of Voltaire.

BON-BON. [*F*]

Quand un bon vin meuble mon estomac,
Je suis plus savant que Balzac —
Plus sage que Pibrac;
Mon bras seul faisant l'attaque
De la nation Cosaque,
La mettroit au sac:
De Charon je passerois le lac,
En dormant dans son bac;
J'irois au fier Eac,
Sans que mon cœur fît tic ni tac,
Présenter du tabac.

French Vaudeville.

THAT Pierre Bon-Bon was a *restaurateur* of uncommon qualifications, no man who, during the reign of ——— , frequented the
little Câfé[a] in the cul-de-sac[b] Le Febvre at Rouen, will, I imagine,
feel himself at liberty to dispute. That Pierre Bon-Bon[c] was, in an
equal degree, skilled in the philosophy of that period is, I presume,
still more especially undeniable. His *pâtés[d] à la fois*[1] were beyond
doubt immaculate; but what pen can do justice to his essays *sur la
Nature* — his thoughts *sur l'Ame* — his observations *sur l'Esprit?*
If his *omelettes* — if his *fricandeaux* were inestimable, what *littéra-
teur*[e] of that day would not have given twice as much for an *"Idée
de Bon-Bon"* as for all the trash of all the *"Idées"* of all the rest of
the *savants?* Bon-Bon had ransacked libraries which no other man
had ransacked — had read more than any other would have entertained a notion of reading — had understood more than any other
would have conceived the possibility of understanding; and although, while he flourished, there were not wanting some authors
at Rouen to assert "that his *dicta* evinced neither the purity of the
Academy, nor the depth of the Lyceum" —[2] although, mark me,
his doctrines were by no means very generally comprehended, still
it did not follow that they were difficult of comprehension. It was,

---

Title: Bon-Bon — A Tale. *(A, B)*
Motto: "Notre Gulliver" — dit le Lord
Bolingbroke — "a de telles fables." —
Voltaire. *(A) canceled in B; C and D
have neither motto nor introductory
verse. Spelling and punctuation of
F (which is identical with E) have been*

changed to conform to the source.
a Câfé *(A, B, C, D, E, F)*
b Cal-de-sac *(A, B) misprint*
c Pierre Bon-Bon/he *(D)*
d *Patés (A) throughout; patés (B, C,
D, E, F) throughout*
e *literateur (A)*

I think, on account of their[f] self-evidency that many persons were led to consider them abstruse. It is to Bon-Bon — but let this go no farther — it is to Bon-Bon that Kant himself is mainly indebted for his metaphysics. The former was indeed not[g] a Platonist, nor strictly speaking an Aristotelian — nor did he, like the modern Leibnitz, waste those precious hours which might be employed in the invention of a *fricassée*,[h] or, *facili gradu*,[i] the analysis of a sensation, in frivolous attempts at reconciling the obstinate oils and waters of ethical discussion.[3] Not at all. Bon-Bon was Ionic — Bon-Bon was equally Italic.[4] He reasoned *à priori* — He reasoned also *à posteriori*. His ideas were innate — or otherwise. He believed in George of Trebizond — He believed in Bessarion.[j] Bon-Bon was emphatically a — Bon-Bonist.[5]

I have spoken of the philosopher in his capacity of *restaurateur*. I would not, however, have any friend of mine imagine that, in fulfilling his hereditary duties in that line, our hero wanted a proper estimation of their dignity and importance. Far from it. It was impossible to say in which branch of his[k] profession he took the greater pride. In his opinion the powers of the intellect[l] held intimate connection with the capabilities of the stomach. [m]I am not sure, indeed, that he greatly disagreed with the Chinese, who hold that the soul lies in the abdomen.[6] The Greeks at all events were right, he thought, who employed the same word for the mind and the diaphragm.*[m] By this I do not mean to insinuate a charge of gluttony, or indeed any other serious charge to the prejudice of the metaphysician. If Pierre Bon-Bon had his failings — and what great man has not a thousand? — if Pierre Bon-Bon, I say, had his failings, they were failings of very little importance — faults indeed which, in other tempers, have often been looked upon rather in the light of virtues. As regards one of these foibles, I should not even[n] have mentioned it in this history but for the remarkable prominency — the extreme *alto rilievo*[o] — in which it jutted out

* Φρενes.

---

f   their entire *(A, B, C, D)*
g   indeed not/not indeed *(A, B, C, D)*
h   *fricasée, (E, F)*
i   *gradú, (E, F)*
j   Bossarion. *(A, B, C, D, E, F)*
misprint, corrected editorially

k   his duplicate *(A, B, C, D)*
l   mind *(A, B, C, D)*
m . . . m   *Omitted (A, B, C, D)*
n   *Omitted (A, B, C, D)*
o   *relievo (A, B, C, D, E F) corrected editorially*

from the plane of his general disposition. — He[p] could never let slip an opportunity of making a bargain.

Not that he[q] was avaricious — no. It was by no means necessary to the satisfaction of the philosopher, that the bargain should be to his own proper advantage. Provided a trade could be effected — a trade of any kind, upon any terms, or under any circumstances — a triumphant smile was seen for many days thereafter to enlighten his countenance, and a knowing wink of the eye to give evidence of his sagacity.

At any epoch it would not be very wonderful if a humor so peculiar as the one I have just mentioned, should elicit attention and remark. At the epoch of our narrative, had this peculiarity *not* attracted observation, there would have been room for wonder indeed. It was soon reported that, upon all occasions of the kind, the smile of Bon-Bon was wont to differ widely from the down-right grin with which he[r] would laugh at his own jokes, or welcome an acquaintance. Hints were thrown out of an exciting nature; stories were told of perilous bargains made in a hurry and repented of at leisure; and instances were adduced of unaccountable capacities, vague longings, and unnatural inclinations implanted by the author of all evil for wise purposes of his own.

The philosopher had other weaknesses — but they are scarcely worthy our serious examination. For example, there are few men of extraordinary profundity who are found wanting in an inclination for the bottle. Whether this inclination be an exciting cause, or rather a valid proof, of such profundity, it is a nice thing[s] to say. Bon-Bon, as far as I can learn, did not think the subject adapted to minute investigation; — nor do I. Yet in the indulgence of a propensity so truly classical, it is not to be supposed that the *restaurateur* would lose sight of that intuitive discrimination which was wont to characterize, at one and the same time, his *essais* and his *omelettes*. [t]In his seclusions the Vin de Bourgogne has its allotted hour, and there were appropriate moments for the Côtes du Rhone.[t]

---

p   Bon-Bon *(A, B)*
q   Bon-Bon *(A, B)*
r   that Restaurateur *(A, B);* that *restaurateur (C, D)*

s   a nice thing/impossible *(A, B, C, D)*
t . . . t   *This sentence is placed after the two that now follow it in A, B, C, transposed in D*

With him Sauterne was to Médoc[u] what Catullus was to Homer.[7] He would sport with a syllogism in sipping St. Péray,[v] but unravel an argument over Clos de Vougeot, and upset a theory in a torrent of Chambertin. Well had it been if the same quick sense of propriety had attended him in the peddling propensity to which I have formerly alluded — but this was by no means the case. Indeed, to say the truth, *that* trait of mind in the philosophic Bon-Bon *did* begin at length to assume a character of strange intensity and mysticism, and[w] appeared deeply tinctured with the[x] *diablerie* of his favorite German studies.

To enter the little *Café*[y] in the *Cul-de-Sac* Le Febvre[z] was, at the period of our tale, to enter the *sanctum*[a] of a man of genius. Bon-Bon was a man of genius. There was not a *sous-cuisinier* in Rouen, who could not have told you that Bon-Bon was a man of genius. His very cat knew it, and forebore to whisk her tail in the presence of the man of genius. His large water-dog was acquainted with the fact, and upon the approach of his master, betrayed his sense of inferiority by a sanctity of deportment, a debasement of the ears, and a dropping of the lower jaw not altogether unworthy of a dog. It is, however, true that much of this habitual respect might have been attributed to the personal appearance of the metaphysician. A distinguished exterior will, I am constrained to say, have its weight even with a beast; and I am willing to allow much in the outward man of the *restaurateur* calculated to impress the imagination of the quadruped. There is a peculiar majesty about the atmosphere of the little great — if I may be permitted so equivocal an expression — which mere physical bulk alone will be found at all times inefficient in creating. If, however, Bon-Bon was barely three feet in height, and if his head was diminutively small, still it was impossible to behold the rotundity of his stomach without a sense of magnificence nearly bordering upon the sublime. In its size both dogs and men must have seen a type of his acquirements — in its immensity a fitting habitation for his immortal soul.

---

u   Medoc *(A, B, C, D, E, F)*
v   Peray, *(A, B, C, D, E, F)*
w   and, however singular it may seem, *(A, B, C, D)*

x   the grotesque *(A, B, C, D)*
y   *Câfé (E); Câfe (F)*
z   Febre *(F) misprint*
a   sanctum *(A, B, C, D) here and below*

TALES OF THE FOLIO CLUB

I might here — if it so pleased me — dilate upon the matter of habiliment, and other mere circumstances of the external meta-physician. I might hint that the hair of our hero was worn short, combed smoothly over his forehead, and surmounted by a conical-shaped white flannel cap and tassels — that his pea-green jerkin was not after the fashion of those worn by the common class of *restaura-teurs* at that day — that the sleeves were something fuller than the reigning costume permitted — that the cuffs were turned up, not as usual in that barbarous period, with cloth of the same quality and color as the garment, but faced in a more fanciful manner with the particolored velvet of Genoa[8] — that his slippers were of a bright purple, curiously filagreed, and might have been manufactured in Japan, but for the exquisite pointing of the toes, and the brilliant tints of the binding and embroidery — that his breeches were of the yellow satin-like material called *aimable* — that his sky-blue cloak, resembling in form a dressing-wrapper, and richly bestudded all over with crimson devices, floated cavalierly upon his shoulders like a mist of the morning — and that his *tout ensemble* gave rise to the remarkable words of Benevenuta, the Improvisatrice of Florence,[9] "that it was difficult to say whether Pierre Bon-Bon was indeed a bird of Paradise, or the rather a very Paradise of perfection."[b] — I might, I say, expatiate upon all these points if I pleased; — but I for-bear: — merely personal details may be left to historical novelists; — they are beneath the moral dignity of matter-of-fact.[b]

I have said that "to enter the *Café*[c] in the *Cul-de-Sac* Le Febvre was to enter the *sanctum* of a man of genius" — but then it was only the man of genius who could duly estimate the merits of the *sanc-tum*. A sign, consisting of a vast folio, swung before the entrance. On one side of the volume was painted a bottle; on the reverse a *pâté.*[d] On the back were visible in large letters *Œuvres*[e] *de Bon-Bon.* Thus was delicately shadowed forth the two-fold occupation of the proprietor.

Upon stepping over the threshold, the whole interior of the building presented itself to view. A long, low-pitched room, of an-tique construction, was indeed all the accommodation afforded by

b...b *Omitted (A, B, C, D)*
c *Câfé (E, F)*
d *paté. (A, B, C, D); pate. (E, F)*
e the words *Æuvres (A, B, C, D)*

the *Café.*[f] In a corner of the apartment stood the bed of the meta-physician. An array of curtains, together with a canopy *à la Grec-que,*[g] gave it an air at once classic and comfortable. In the corner diagonally opposite, appeared, in direct family[h] communion, the properties of the kitchen and the *bibliothèque.*[i] A dish of polemics stood peacefully upon the dresser. Here lay an oven-full of the latest ethics — there a kettle of duodecimo *mélanges.* Volumes of German morality were hand and glove with the gridiron — a toasting fork might be discovered by the side of Eusebius — [10] Plato reclined at his ease in the frying pan — and contemporary[j] manuscripts were filed away upon the spit.

In other respects the *Café*[k] *de Bon-Bon* might be said to differ little from the [l]usual *restaurants*[l] of the period.[11] A large[m] fire-place yawned opposite the door. On the right of the fire-place an open cupboard displayed a formidable array of labelled bottles.[n] [12]

It was here, about twelve o'clock one night, during the severe winter of ———, that Pierre Bon-Bon, after having listened for some time to the comments of his neighbors upon his singular propensity — that Pierre Bon-Bon, I say, having turned them all out of his house, locked the door upon them with [o]an oath,[o] and betook himself in no very pacific mood to the comforts of a leather-bottomed arm-chair, and a fire of blazing faggots.

It was one of those terrific nights which are only met with once or twice during a century. [p]It snowed fiercely,[p] and the house[q] tottered to its[r] centre with the floods of wind that, rushing through the

---

f   *Café* in the *Cul-de-Sac* Le Febvre. *(A) changed in B; Càfe. (E, F)*
g   *Greque, (A, B, C, D, E, F) misprint, corrected editorially*
h   and friendly *(A, B, C, D)*
i   *bibliothéque. (A, B, C, D); accent omitted (E, F)*
j   cotemporary *(A, B)*
k   *Càfe (E, F)*
l . . . l   *Cafés (A, B, C, D)*
m   gigantic *(A, B, C, D)*
n   *After this:* There Mousseux, Chambertin, St. George, Richbourg, Bordeaux, Margaux, Haubrion, Leonville, Medoc, Sauterne, Bârac, Preignac, Grave, Lafitte, and St. Peray contended with many other names of

lesser celebrity for the honor of being quaffed. From the ceiling, suspended by a chain of very long slender links, swung a fantastic iron lamp, throwing a hazy light over the room, and relieving in some measure the placidity of the scene. *(A, B, C, D except that* of very . . . links *is canceled in B and omitted in C, D)*
o . . . o   *a sacre Dieu, (A, B, C);* a sacré, *(D)*
p . . . p   The snow drifted down bodily in enormous masses, *(A, B, C) changed in D*
q   *Café* de Bon-Bon *(A, B, C, D)*
r   its very *(A, B, C, D)*

crannies of[s] the wall, and pouring impetuously down the chimney, shook awfully the curtains of the philosopher's bed, and disorganized the economy of his pâté-pans[t] and papers. The huge folio sign that swung without, exposed to the fury of the tempest, creaked ominously, and gave out a moaning sound from its[u] stanchions of solid oak.

[v]It was in no placid temper, I say, that[v] the metaphysician drew up his chair to its customary station by the hearth. Many circumstances of a perplexing nature had occurred during the day, to disturb the serenity of his meditations. In attempting *des œufs*[w] *à la Princesse,* he had unfortunately perpetrated an *omelette*[x] *à la Reine;*[13] the discovery of a principle in ethics had been frustrated by the overturning of a stew; and last, not least, he had been thwarted in one of those admirable bargains which he at all times took such especial delight in bringing to a successful termination. But in the chafing of his mind at these unaccountable vicissitudes, there did not fail to be mingled some[y] degree of that nervous anxiety which the fury of a boisterous night is so well calculated to produce. Whistling to his more immediate vicinity the large black water-dog we have spoken of before, and settling himself uneasily in his chair, he could not help casting a wary and unquiet eye towards those distant recesses of the apartment whose inexorable shadows not even the red fire-light itself could more than partially succeed in overcoming. Having completed a scrutiny whose exact purpose was perhaps unintelligible to himself, he[z] drew close[a] to his seat a small table covered with books and papers, and soon became absorbed in the task of re-touching a voluminous manuscript, intended for publication on the morrow.

[b]He had been thus occupied for some minutes, when[b] "I am in no hurry, Monsieur Bon-Bon," suddenly[c] whispered a whining voice in the apartment.

---

s   in *(A, B, C, D, E)*
t   paté-pans *(A, B, C, D, E);* patépans *(F)*
u   it *(E) misprint*
v . . . v   I have said that it was in no very placid temper *(A, B, C, D)*
w   *Des Æufs (A) changed to lower case* in *B*
x   *omelete (E, F)*
y   a *(A) changed in B*
z   Bon-Bon *(A) changed in B*
a   closer *(A, B, C, D)*
b . . . b   *Omitted (A, B, C) added in D*
c   *Omitted (A, B, C) added in D*

"The devil!" ejaculated our hero, starting to his feet, overturning the table at his side, and staring around him in astonishment.

"Very true," calmly replied the voice.

"Very true! — what is very true? — how came you here?" vociferated the metaphysician, as his eye fell upon something which lay stretched at full-length upon the bed.

"I was saying," said the intruder, without attending to the[d] interrogatories, "I was saying, that I am not at all pushed for time — that the business upon which I took the liberty of calling, is of no pressing importance — in short, that I can very well wait until you have finished your Exposition."

"My Exposition! — there now! — how do *you* know? — how came *you* to understand that I was writing an Exposition — good God!"

"Hush!" replied the figure, in a shrill under tone; and, arising quickly from the bed, he made a single step towards our hero, while [e]an iron lamp that depended[e] overhead swung convulsively back from his approach.

The philosopher's amazement did not prevent a narrow scrutiny of the stranger's dress and appearance. The outlines of his[f] figure, exceedingly lean, but much above the common height, were rendered minutely distinct by means of a faded suit of black cloth which fitted tight to the skin, but was otherwise cut very much in the style of a century ago. These garments had evidently been intended[g] for a much shorter person than their present owner. His ankles and wrists were left naked for several inches. In his shoes, however, a pair of very brilliant buckles gave the lie to the extreme poverty implied by the other portions of his dress. His head was bare, and entirely bald, with the exception of the hinder-part, from which depended a *queue* of considerable length. A pair of green spectacles, with side glasses, protected his eyes from the influence of the light, and at the same time prevented our hero from ascertaining either their color or their conformation. About the entire person there was no evidence of a shirt; but a white cravat,

---

d   Bon-Bon's *(A);* his *(B)*
e . . . e   the iron lamp *(A, B, C, D)*

f   a *(A, B, C, D, E)*
g   intended *a priori (A) changed in B*

of filthy appearance, was tied with extreme precision around the throat, and the ends, hanging down formally side by side, gave (although I dare say unintentionally) the idea of an ecclesiastic. Indeed, many other points both in his appearance and demeanor might have very well sustained a conception of that nature. Over his left ear, he carried, after the fashion of a modern clerk, an instrument resembling the *stylus* of the ancients. In a breast-pocket of his coat appeared conspicuously a small black volume fastened with clasps of steel. This book, whether accidentally or not, was so turned outwardly from the person as to discover the words *"Rituel Catholique"* in white letters upon the back. His entire physiognomy was interestingly saturnine — even cadaverously pale. The forehead was lofty, and deeply furrowed with the ridges of contemplation. The corners of the mouth were drawn down into an expression of the most submissive humility. There was also a clasping of the hands, as he stepped towards our hero — a deep sigh — and altogether a look of such utter sanctity as could not have failed to be unequivocally[h] prepossessing.[14] Every shadow of anger faded from the countenance of the metaphysician, as, having completed a satisfactory survey of his visiter's person, he shook him cordially by the hand, and conducted him to a seat.

There would however be a radical error in attributing this instantaneous transition of feeling in the philosopher, to any one of those causes which might naturally be supposed to have had an influence. Indeed, Pierre Bon-Bon, from what I have been able to understand of his disposition, was of all men the least likely to be imposed upon by any speciousness of exterior deportment. It was impossible that so accurate an observer of men and things should have failed to discover, upon the moment, the real character of the personage who had thus intruded upon his hospitality. To say no more, the conformation of his visiter's feet was sufficiently remarkable [i]— he maintained lightly upon his head an inordinately tall hat[i] — there was a tremulous swelling about[j] the hinder part of his breeches — and the vibration of his coat tail was a palpable fact. Judge, then, with what feelings of satisfaction our hero found him-

---

h   *Canceled (D)*   j   in *(A, B, C, D)*
i . . . i   *Omitted (A, B, C, D)*

self thrown thus at once into the society of a[k] person for whom he had at all times entertained the most[l] unqualified respect. He was, however, too much of the diplomatist to let escape him any intimation of his suspicions[m] in regard to the true state of affairs. It was not his cue to appear at all conscious of the high honor he thus unexpectedly enjoyed; but, by leading his guest into conversation, to elicit some important ethical ideas, which might, in obtaining a place in his contemplated publication, enlighten the human race, and at the same time immortalize himself — ideas which, I should have added, his visiter's great age, and well-known proficiency in the science of morals, might very well have enabled him to afford.

Actuated by these enlightened views, our hero bade the gentleman sit down, while he himself took occasion to throw some faggots upon the fire, and place upon the now re-established table some bottles of[n] *Mousseux.* Having quickly completed these operations, he drew his chair *vis-à-vis* to his companion's, and waited until the latter[o] should open the conversation. But, plans even the most skilfully matured[p] are often thwarted in the outset of their application — and the *restaurateur* found himself *nonplussed*[q] by the very first words of his visiter's speech.

"I see you know me, Bon-Bon," said he: "ha! ha! ha! — he! he! he! — hi! hi! hi! — ho! ho! ho! — hu! hu! hu!" — and the devil, dropping at once the sanctity of his demeanor, opened to its fullest extent a mouth from ear to ear, so as to display a set of jagged and fang-like teeth, and throwing back his head, laughed long, loudly,[r] wickedly, and uproariously, while the black dog, crouching down upon his haunches, joined lustily in the chorus, and the tabby cat, flying off at a tangent, stood up on end, and shrieked in the farthest corner of the apartment.

Not so the philosopher: he was too much a man of the world either to laugh like the dog, or by shrieks to betray the indecorous

---

k   of a/of a — of a *(A, B, C, D)*
l   the most/such *(A, B, C, D)*
m   suspicions, or rather — I should say — his certainty *(A, B, C, D)*
n   of the powerful *Vin de (A, B, C, D)*

o   the latter/he *(A, B, C, D)*
p   matured, *(F) comma deleted to follow A, B, C, D, E*
q   entirely *nonplused (A, B, C, D)*
r   loud, *(A, B, C, D)*

trepidation of the cat. It must be confessed,[s] he felt a little astonishment to see the white letters which formed the words *"Rituel Catholique"* on the book in his guest's pocket, momently,[t] changing both their color and their import, and in a few seconds, in place of the original title, the words, *"Registre[u] des Condamnés"* blaze forth in characters of red.[15] This startling circumstance, when Bon-Bon replied to his visiter's remark, imparted to his manner an air of embarrassment which [v]probably might not otherwise have been observed.[v]

"Why, sir," said the philosopher, "why, sir, to speak sincerely — I believe you are — upon my word — the d———dest — that is to say, I think — I imagine — I *have* some faint — some *very* faint idea — of the remarkable honor —— "

"Oh! — ah! — yes! — very well!" interrupted his Majesty; "say no more — I see how it is." And hereupon, taking off his green spectacles, he wiped the glasses carefully with the sleeve of his coat, and deposited them in his pocket.

If Bon-Bon had been astonished at the incident of the book, his amazement was now much[w] increased[x] by the spectacle which here presented itself to view. In raising his eyes, with a strong feeling of curiosity to ascertain the color of his guest's, he found them by no means black, as he had anticipated — nor gray, as might have been imagined — nor yet hazel nor blue — nor indeed yellow nor red — nor purple — nor white — nor green — nor any other color in the heavens above, or in the earth beneath, or in the waters under the earth.[16] In short, Pierre Bon-Bon not only saw plainly that his Majesty had no eyes whatsoever, but could discover no indications of their having existed at any previous period — for the space where eyes should naturally have been, was, I am constrained to say, simply a dead level of[y] flesh.[17]

It was not in the nature of the metaphysician to forbear making some inquiry into the sources of so strange a phenomenon;

---

s   confessed, however, that *(A, B, C, D)*
t   momently,/momentarily *(A, B)*
u   Regitre *(A, B, C, D); Régitre (E, F)*
corrected editorially
v . . . v   might not probably have

otherwise been observable. *(A, B, C, D)*
w   now much/now *(A) changed in B*
x   increased to an intolerable degree
(A) changed in B
y   of cadaverous *(A, B, C, D)*

and[z] the reply of his Majesty was at once prompt, dignified, and satisfactory.

"Eyes! my dear Bon-Bon — eyes! did you say? — oh! — ah! — I perceive! The ridiculous prints, eh, which are in circulation, have given you a false idea of my personal appearance? Eyes! — true. Eyes, Pierre Bon-Bon, are very well in their proper place — *that,* you would say, is the head? — right — the head of a worm. To *you* likewise these optics are indispensable — yet I will convince you that my vision is more penetrating than your own. There is a [a]cat, I see,[a] in the corner — a pretty cat — look at her — observe her well. Now, Bon-Bon, do you behold the thoughts — the thoughts, I say — the ideas — the reflections — [b]which are being engendered[b] in her pericranium? There it is, now — you do not! She is thinking we admire [c]the length of her tail and[c] the profundity of her mind. She has just concluded that I am the most distinguished of ecclesiastics, and that you are the most superficial[d] of metaphysicians. Thus you see I am not altogether blind; but to one of my profession, the eyes you speak of would be merely an incumbrance, liable at any time to be put out by a toasting iron or a pitchfork. To you, I allow, these optical affairs[e] are indispensable. Endeavor, Bon-Bon, to use them well; — *my* vision is the soul."[18]

Hereupon the guest helped himself to the wine upon the table, and pouring out a bumper for Bon-Bon, requested him to drink it without scruple, and make himself perfectly at home.

"A clever book that of yours, Pierre," resumed his Majesty, tapping our friend knowingly upon the shoulder, as the latter put[f] down his glass after a thorough compliance with [g]his visiter's[g] injunction. "A clever book that of yours, upon my honor. It's a work after my own heart. Your arrangement of the[h] matter, I think, however, might be improved, and many of your notions remind me of Aristotle. That philosopher was one of my most intimate acquaintances. I liked him as much for his terrible ill temper, as for his happy knack at making a blunder. There is only one solid truth in

---

z   and to his surprise *(A, B, C, D)*
a . . . a   cat, I see *(E);* cat I see *(F) punctuated from A, B, C, D*
b . . . b   engendering *(A, B, C, D)*
c . . . c   *Omitted (A, B, C, D)*

d   superfluous *(A, B, C, D, E)*
e   optical affairs/optics *(A, B, C, D)*
f   set *(A, B)*
g . . . g   this *(A) changed in B*
h   *Omitted (A, B, C, D, E)*

all that he has written, and for that I gave him the hint out of pure compassion for his absurdity. I suppose, Pierre Bon-Bon, you very well know to what divine moral truth I am alluding?"

"Cannot say that I —— "

"Indeed! — why it was I who[i] told Aristotle, that, by sneezing, men expelled superfluous ideas through the proboscis."[19]

"Which is — hiccup! — undoubtedly the case," said the metaphysician, while he poured out for himself another bumper of Mousseux, and offered his snuff-box to the fingers of his visiter.

"There was Plato, too," continued his Majesty, modestly declining the snuff-box and the[j] compliment it implied[k] — "there was Plato, too, for whom I, at one time, felt all the affection of a friend. You knew Plato, Bon-Bon? — ah, no, I beg a thousand pardons. He met me at Athens, one day, in the Parthenon, and told me he was distressed for an idea. I bade him write down that $o\ \nu o \upsilon \varsigma$ $\epsilon \sigma \tau \iota \nu$.[l] He said that he would do so, and went home, while I stepped over to the pyramids. But my conscience smote me for [m]having uttered a truth, even to aid a friend,[m] and hastening back to Athens, I arrived behind the philosopher's chair as he was inditing the '$\alpha \upsilon \lambda o \varsigma$.' Giving the lamma a fillip with my finger, I turned it upside down. So the sentence now reads '$o\ \nu o \upsilon \varsigma\ \epsilon \sigma \tau \iota \nu\ \alpha \upsilon \gamma o \varsigma$,' and is, you[n] perceive, the fundamental doctrine in[o] his metaphysics."[20]

"Were you ever at Rome?" asked the *restaurateur,* as he finished his second bottle of Mousseux, and drew from the closet a larger supply of[p] Chambertin.

"But once, Monsieur Bon-Bon, but once. There was a time," said the devil, as if reciting some passage from a book — "there [q]was a time when occurred[q] an anarchy of five years, during which the republic, bereft of all its officers, had no magistracy besides the tribunes of the people, and these were not legally vested with any

---

i it was I who/I *(A, B, C, D)*
j *Canceled (D)*
k it implied *omitted (A, B, C, D)*
l [*Poe transliterated the Greek words thus:* o nous estin augos; augos; o nous estin aulos *in A. He put them in Greek letters in the Duane copy B which was followed in C. In D, which later texts followed, he changed three Greek* words *and interchanged* gamma *and* lambda *and permitted the latter to be spelled* lamma; *see note.*]
m . . . m the lie, *(A, B, C) changed in D*
n as you *(D)*
o of *(A, B, C, D)*
p of Vin de *(A, B, C, D)*
q . . . q was *(A) changed in B*

degree of executive power — at that time, Monsieur Bon-Bon — at that time *only* I was in Rome, and I have no earthly acquaintance, consequently,[r] with any of its philosophy." * [21]

"What do you think of[t] — what do you think of — hiccup! — Epicurus?"

"What do I think of *whom?*" said the devil, in astonishment; "you cannot surely mean to find any fault with Epicurus! What do I think of Epicurus! Do you mean me, sir? — *I* am Epicurus! I am the same[u] philosopher who wrote each of the three hundred treatises commemorated by Diogenes Laertes."[v] [22]

"That's a lie!" said the metaphysician, for the wine had gotten a little into his head.

"Very well! — very well, sir! — very well, indeed, sir!" said his [w]Majesty, apparently much flattered.[w]

"That's a lie!" repeated the *restaurateur,* dogmatically, "that's a — hiccup! — a[x] lie!"

"Well, well, have it your own way!" said the devil, pacifically; and Bon-Bon, having beaten his Majesty at an argument, thought it his duty to conclude a second bottle of Chambertin.

"As I was saying," resumed the visiter, "as I was observing a little while ago, there are some very *outré*[y] notions in that book of yours, Monsieur Bon-Bon. What, for instance, do you mean by all that humbug about the soul? Pray, sir, what *is* the soul?"[23]

"The — hiccup! — soul," replied the metaphysician, referring to his MS., "is undoubtedly —— "

"No, sir!"

"Indubitably —— "

"No, sir!"

"Indisputably —— "

"No, sir!"

---

* Ils ecrivaient sur la Philosophie, *(Cicero, Lucretius, Seneca)* mais c'etait la Philosophie Grecque. — *Condorcet.*[s]

---

r   therefore, *(D)*
s   *Poe's French. See note. Unaccented in any text except that A, B, C, D, E have* Grécque.
t   of Epicurus *(A, B, C, D)*
u   *Canceled (D)*

v   It's sure [?] it's a fact. *added in a scrawling hand (D)*
w . . . w   majesty. *(A, B, C, D)*
x   *Omitted (A, B, C, D)*
y   *outre (E, F)*

"Evidently —— "

"No, sir!"

"Incontrovertibly —— "

"No, sir!"

"Hiccup! —— "

"No, sir!"

"And beyond all question, a —— "

"No, sir, the soul is no such thing!" (Here, the [z]philosopher, looking daggers, took occasion to make an end, upon the spot, of[z] his third bottle of Chambertin.)

"Then — hiccup! — pray, sir — what — what is it?"

"That is neither here nor there, Monsieur Bon-Bon," replied his Majesty, musingly. "I have tasted — that is to say, I have known some very bad souls, and some too — pretty good ones."[24] Here he smacked[a] his lips, and, having unconsciously let fall his hand upon the volume in his pocket, was seized with a violent fit of sneezing.

He[b] continued:

"There was the soul of Cratinus — passable: Aristophanes — racy: Plato — exquisite — not *your* Plato, but Plato the comic poet: your Plato would have turned the stomach of Cerberus — faugh! Then let me see! there were Nævius,[c] and Andronicus, and Plautus, and Terentius. Then there were Lucilius, and Catullus, and Naso, and Quintus[d] Flaccus, — dear Quinty! as I called him when he sung a *seculare* for my [e]amusement, while I toasted him, in pure good humor, on a fork.[e] But they want *flavor* these Romans.[25] One fat Greek is worth a dozen of them, and besides will *keep*, which cannot be said of a Quirite.[26] — Let us taste your Sauterne."

Bon-Bon had by this time made up his mind to the *nil admirari*,[27] and endeavored to hand down the bottles in question. He was, however, conscious of a strange sound in the room like the wagging of a tail. Of this, although extremely indecent in his Majesty, the philosopher took no notice: — simply kicking the

---

z . . . z philosopher finished *(A, B, C)*; philosopher, being in high dudgeon, finished *(D)*; *comma after* philosopher *in text above added editorially*
a he smacked/the devil licked *(A, B, C, D)*

b His majesty *(A, B, C) changed in D*
c Noevius, *(A, B, C, D, E, F) misprint, corrected editorially*
d Quintius *(A, B, C, D, E, F) misprint, corrected editorially*
e . . . e amusement — *(D)*

dog,[f] and requesting him to be quiet. The visiter continued:

"I found that Horace tasted very much like Aristotle; — you know I am fond of variety. Terentius I could not have told from Menander. Naso, to my astonishment, was Nicander in disguise. Virgilius had a strong twang of Theocritus. Martial put me much in mind of Archilochus — and Titus Livius[g] was positively Polybius and none other."[28]

"Hiccup!" here replied Bon-Bon, and his Majesty proceeded:

"But if I *have* a *penchant,* Monsieur Bon-Bon — if I *have* a *penchant*, it is for a philosopher. Yet, let me tell you, sir, it is not every dev — I mean it is not every gentleman, who knows how to *choose* a philosopher. Long ones are *not* good; and the best, if not carefully shelled, are apt to be a little rancid on account of the gall."

"Shelled!!"

"I mean, taken out of the carcass."

"What do you think of a — hiccup! — physician?"

"Don't mention them![h] — ugh! ugh!" (Here his Majesty retched violently.) "I never tasted but one — that rascal Hippocrates! — smelt of asafœtida — ugh! ugh! ugh! — caught a wretched cold washing him in the Styx — and after all he gave me the cholera morbus."

"The — hiccup! — wretch!" ejaculated Bon-Bon, "the — hiccup! — abortion of a pill-box!" — and the philosopher dropped a tear.

"After all," continued the visiter, "after all, if a dev — if a gentleman wishes to *live,* he must have more talents than one or two; and with us a fat face is an evidence of diplomacy."

"How so?"

"Why we are sometimes exceedingly pushed for provisions. You must know that, in a climate so sultry as mine, it is frequently impossible to keep a spirit alive for more than two or three hours; and after death, unless pickled immediately, (and a pickled spirit is *not* good,) they will — smell — you understand, eh? Putrefaction is always to be apprehended when the souls[i] are consigned to us in the usual way."

"Hiccup! — hiccup! — good God! how *do* you manage?"

---

f   black water dog *(A, B, C, D)*   h   one! *(D)*
g   Livy *(A, B, C, D)*   i   spirits *(A, B, C, D)*

Here the iron lamp commenced swinging with redoubled violence, and the devil half started from his seat; — however, with a slight sigh, he recovered his composure, merely saying to our hero in a low tone, "I tell you what, Pierre Bon-Bon, we *must* have no more swearing."[j]

The host[k] swallowed another bumper, [l]by way of denoting thorough[m] comprehension and acquiescence,[l] and the[n] visiter continued:

"Why, there are *several* ways of managing. The most of us starve: some put up with the pickle: for my part I purchase my spirits *vivente corpore,* in which case I find they keep very well."

"But the body! — hiccup! — the body!!!"[o]

"The body, the body — well, what of the body? — oh! ah! I perceive. Why, sir, the body is not *at all* affected by the transaction. I have made innumerable purchases of the kind in my day, and the parties never experienced any inconvenience. There were Cain and Nimrod, and Nero, and Caligula, and Dionysius, and Pisistratus,[29] and — and a thousand others, who never knew what it was to have a soul during the latter part of their lives; yet, sir, these men adorned society. Why is n't there A——, now, whom you know as well as I? Is *he* not in possession of all his faculties, mental and corporeal? Who writes a keener epigram? Who reasons more wittily? Who —— but, stay! I have his agreement in my pocket-book."

Thus saying, he produced a red leather wallet, and took from it a number of papers. Upon some of these Bon-Bon caught a glimpse of the letters *Machi — Maza — Robesp —* with[p] the words [q]*Caligula, George,*[q] *Elizabeth.*[30] His Majesty selected a narrow slip of parchment, and from it read aloud the following words:

"In consideration of certain mental endowments which it is unnecessary to specify, and in farther consideration of one thousand louis d'or, I, being aged one year and one month, do hereby make over to the bearer of this agreement all my right, title, and appur-

---

j   swearing. Will you mind that, eh? —
will you?" *(D)*
k   The host/Bon-Bon *(A, B, C, D)*
l...l   *Omitted (A, B, C) changed in D*
m   *Omitted (D)*
n   his *(A, B, C, D)*

o   *After this:* — vociferated the
philosopher, as he finished a bottle of
Sauterne. *(A, B, C, D)*
p   *Robesp —* with/RICH..... , and
(A, B, C, D)
q...q   CALIGULA and *(A, B, C, D)*

BON-BON

tenance in the shadow called my soul." (Signed) A . . . . .*[31] (Here his Majesty repeated a name which I do not feel myself justified[s] in indicating more unequivocally.)

"A clever fellow that,"[t] resumed he; "but like you, Monsieur Bon-Bon, he was mistaken about the soul. The soul a shadow, truly![u] The soul a shadow! Ha! ha! ha! — he! he! he! — hu! hu! hu! Only think of a fricasséed shadow!"[32]

"*Only* think — hiccup! — of a [v]fricasséed shadow!"[v] exclaimed[w] our hero, whose faculties were becoming much[x] illuminated by the profundity of his Majesty's discourse.

"Only think of a — hiccup! — fricasséed shadow!! Now, damme! — hiccup! — humph! If *I* would have been such a — hiccup! — nincompoop. *My* soul, Mr. — humph!"

"*Your* soul, Monsieur Bon-Bon?"

"Yes, sir — hiccup! — *my* soul is" —

"What, sir?"[y]

"*No* shadow, damme!"

"Did you[z] mean to say" —

"Yes, sir, *my* soul is — hiccup! — humph! — yes, sir."

"Did not intend to assert" —

"*My* soul is — hiccup! — peculiarly qualified for — hiccup! — a" —

"What, sir?"

"Stew."

"Ha!"

"Soufflée."

"Eh?"

"Fricassée."

"Indeed!"

"Ragoût[a] and[b] fricandeau — and see here,[c] my good fellow![d] I'll

*Quære — Arouet?[r]

r Quære — Arouet? — *Editor. (A, B);* Quære — Arouet? *(C, D)*
s justifiable *(A, B, C, D)*
t that,"/that A. . . . ." *(A, B, C, D)*
u truly! — no such nonsense, Monsieur Bon-Bon. *(A, B, C, D)*
v . . . v f-r-i-c-a-s-s-e-e-d s-h-a-d-o-w! !" *(A) changed in B*

w echoed *(A, B, C, D)*
x gloriously *(A, B, C, D)*
y sir!" *(A) changed in B*
z not *(A, B, C, D)*
a Ragout *(all texts)*
b or *(A, B, C, D)*
c see here, *omitted (A) added in B*
d my good fellow! *omitted (A, B, C, D)*

let you have it — hiccup! — a bargain." ᵉHere the philosopher slapped his Majesty upon the back.ᵉ

"Couldn't think of such a thing," said the latterᶠ calmly, at the same time risingᵍ from his seat. The metaphysician stared.

"Am supplied at present," said his Majesty.

"Hic-cup! — e-h?" said the philosopher.

"Have no funds on hand."

"What?"

"Besides, very unhandsomeʰ in me" —

"Sir!"

"To take advantage of" —

"Hic-cup!"

"Your present ⁱdisgusting and ungentlemanlyⁱ situation."

Here the visiterʲ bowed and withdrew — in what mannerᵏ could not precisely be ascertainedˡ — but in a well-concerted effort to discharge a bottle at "the villain," the slender chain was severed that depended from the ceiling, and the metaphysician prostrated by the downfall of the lamp.³³

NOTES

Motto: This may be translated, "When a good wine fills my stomach, I am more learned than Balzac, wiser than Pibrac; my lone arm attacking the Cossack nation would plunder it; I would cross Charon's lake sleeping in his bark; would go to proud Aeacus, without my heart going pit-a-pat, to offer him some snuff." Poe found it in Bielfeld's *Érudition Universelle* (Book II, chap. vii, section 29) in the discussion of Versification, and included it in his "Pinakidia," number 154 (*SLM,* August 1836, p. 581). Balzac is Jean-Louis Guez de Balzac (1597–1654), master of French prose style. Guy du Faur, Seigneur de Pibrac (1529–1584), was a French jurist of great influence who composed moral verses and was a friend of Ronsard. Aeacus, a legendary king of Aegina, was one of the judges in Hades, whither souls were ferried by Charon. Poe's earlier motto, used in text *A* (SLM, August 1835), was from Voltaire's *La Bible enfin expliquée,* 1776; Beuchot edition (1829), XLIX, 259. It means, "Lord Bolingbroke said, 'Our Gulliver has such fables.' "

e . . . e *Omitted (A, B, C, D)*
f the latter/his majesty *(A, B, C, D)*
g arising *(A, B, C, D)*
h ungentlemanly *(A, B, C) changed in D*

i . . . i *Omitted (A, B, C);*
ungentlemanly and disgusting *(D)*
j the visiter/his majesty *(A, B, C, D)*
k manner the philosopher *(A, B, C, D)*
l be ascertained/ascertain *(A, B, C, D)*

BON-BON

1. *Pâtés à la fois,* literally "pâtés at the time."

2. The Academy is the school of Plato, the Lyceum that of Aristotle.

3. Poe often ridiculed Kant, but usually wrote of Leibnitz with respect.

4. The Ionic school included the earlier Greek philosophers; Thales, Anaximander, and Heraclitus hailed from Ionia, and Heraclitus studied there. The Italic or Eleatic school (from Elea in Southern Italy) included Parmenides, who held that "the All is One."

5. George of Trebizond in 1464 wrote a comparison of Plato and Aristotle, which in 1469 brought a severe reply *In Calumniatorem Platonis* from Jean Bessarion, also a native of Trebizond. To agree with both was a remarkable feat, but Bon-Bon's creator may have recalled that Bielfeld, in *L'Érudition Universelle* (Book I, chapter xxxviii, section 21), said that the true philosopher is a man who has philosophy in himself—who reasons, reflects, seeks for himself the cause of everything, and has courage enough to find it, without embarrassing himself with a system.

6. The Chinese placing the intellect in the abdomen is mentioned again in "Marginalia," number 285 (*SLM,* July 1849, p. 416).

7. Like his predecessor Pedro, Bon-Bon preferred light and pleasing poetry and wine to the weighty and salubrious. Sauterne is sweet, Médoc therapeutic, like the amorous Catullus and the sublime Homer. The healthful quality of Médoc is used ironically in "The Cask of Amontillado."

8. Genoa velvet is mentioned in *Politian,* VIII, 52, and in "Landor's Cottage."

9. Benevenuta, "well come upon," is an appropriate name for a composer of impromptu verses.

10. Eusebius, who became Bishop of Caesarea about 313 A.D., is called the father of ecclesiastical history.

11. The first dining room to be known as a restaurant was opened in Paris in 1765 by one Boulanger.

12. In the canceled passage, compare the list of wines in "Lionizing" at n. 19. [See also "Poe's Wine List," by L. Moffitt Cecil, *Poe Studies,* December 1972.]

13. "À la Princesse" involves asparagus tips, rich cream sauce, and truffles—"À la Reine," purée of chicken with sauce suprême, made of butter, flour, chicken bouillon, eggs and cream, to which are sometimes added truffles, mushrooms and ripe olives. The joke is solely on the names.

14. Maxwell Morton in *A Builder of the Beautiful,* p. 39f., points out a description of the devil in Dr. Robert Macnish's "Metempsychosis" in *Blackwood's* for May 1826. There he sneezes "finickly," and is described as a little, meagre, brown-faced, elderly "person with a 'hooked nose' and long well-powdered queue." He wore a surtout of "snuff-color" and "black small clothes buckled at the knee," and "tortoise-shell spectacles" with glasses of unusual dimensions. He has a large snuff-box, and carries a pen behind his right ear "after the manner of the counting-house" and has a manuscript book. He "whines" and talks of great

philosophers of the past. Morton cites other material from tales by Macnish, but far less strikingly like "Bon-Bon." See also "The Devil in the Belfry," especially at n. 4.

15. Compare the changing letters on a cliff in "Silence — a Fable." There is a parallel in Beckford's *Vathek*.

16. See Exodus 20:4: "any thing that is in heaven above, or that is in the earth beneath, or that is in the water under the earth."

17. There is a voodoo war and blood divinity named Shango who is eyeless, and of whom Poe may have heard from Negroes. If so, this is his only clear use of such stories.

18. Poe allows the devil to read minds here, but not in "The Duc de L'Omelette."

19. What Aristotle, *Problemata*, xxxiii, 9, said was that "Sneezing comes from . . . the head . . . the seat of reasoning." Poe refers to this again in one of the early paragraphs in *Eureka*.

20. Poe has in mind an old story to be found in Richard Griffith's *Koran* (often ascribed to Lawrence Sterne), III, 152: "Even so late as near the beginning of the sixteenth century, a certain priest, having met with this passage in some Greek author, *ho nous estin aülos, mens humana immaterialis est,* and finding, in his Lexicon, that aulós signified a flute or pipe, brought no less than fifteen arguments, in an academic exercise, to prove the human soul to be a whistle."

By changing a lambda to gamma the word becomes *augos*, morning light. "The mind is a light" is not one of Plato's doctrines. Poe's form "lamma" is not Greek, but I forbear emendation as it is in a joke. Compare "The Bargain Lost," n. 14.

21. Rome was in chaos in 86–82 B.C. between the death of Marius and the return of Sulla. Poe's footnote is from Condorcet's *Esquisse d'un tableau historique,* Epoque V. It can be found in the edition of O'Connor and Arago (Paris, 1847), VI, 94; there was a complete edition of Condorcet's works in 1804. The French here, however, is Poe's.

22. On the voluminous works of Epicurus see Diogenes Laertius, *Lives,* X, 17.

23. See Aristotle *De Anima,* II, 1–4, for complex definitions of the soul. He talks of nutritive soul, and Poe makes it nutritious.

24. See introductory remarks on William Elliot's translation of *The Visions of Quevedo,* above.

25. Cratinus at least once defeated Aristophanes. Almost nothing survives of Plato comicus. Naevius is a very early Roman poet and playwright. Livius Andronicus, who translated Homer's *Odyssey,* flourished in the third century B.C. Terentius Afer we call Terence. C. Lucilius (180–102 B.C.) seems to have been the first writer of satires. Catullus, the lyrist of Verona, has by some been thought the wanderer of Poe's "To Helen." Naso is Ovid. Quintus Horatius Flaccus, in 53 B.C., composed the *Secular Ode* for Rome's 700th birthday; we judge from his *Satire,* II, vi, 37, that he disliked the familiar use of his first name by mere acquaintances; the vocative form is "Quinte."

26. A Quirite is a Roman citizen not in military service.

27. *Nil admirari,* meaning "be astonished at nothing," is from Horace, *Epistolae,* I, vi, 1.

28. Horace's *Ars Poetica* versifies much from Aristotle's *Poetics.* Terence owed much to Menander, more of whose comedy is now known than in Poe's day. Julius Caesar called Terence half a Menander. Nicander, a grammarian and physician, wrote on beasts and poisons in the second century before our era, and may have influenced Ovid. Vergil's *Eclogues* imitate the pastoral poems of Theocritus of Syracuse. Martial (first century A.D.) wrote biting epigrams; the savage verses of Archilochus (seventh century B.C.) are said to have driven a woman who rejected his suit to suicide. Polybius (204–122 B.C.) was a source for the historical writings of T. Patavinus Livius whom we call Livy, and the French, Tite Live.

29. Poe's collection is of successful but wicked people. Nimrod, King of Babylon, a great-grandson of Noah, is merely called "a mighty hunter before the Lord" in Genesis 10:9, but he has a traditional reputation for slaughter and cruelty, based on commentaries on Micah 7:2. Caligula, a madman, was Roman Emperor 37–41 A.D. He is also mentioned in "Metzengerstein." Dionysius was a tyrant of Syracuse; Pisistratus of Athens. The latter is undeserving of this condemnation.

30. Machiavelli, Mazarin, and Robespierre are patent; Elizabeth I perhaps joins the bad company because of having had Mary Queen of Scots put to death; George must be the Fourth, whom Poe disliked. Rich[ard III] was omitted from the final version of the story.

31. See "The Bargain Lost" at n. 18.

32. Compare *The Visions of Quevedo,* p. 146: "the Persian [souls] fricasseed with gravy de demon."

33. The "iron lamp that depended overhead" had, we recall, "swung convulsively back" from the Devil's first approach.

EPIMANES (FOUR BEASTS IN ONE)

This tale, entitled "Epimanes" in its early versions, is amusing when its background is understood. Poe's combination of stories about the freaks of a mad ancient monarch and the caricatures of a nineteenth-century king of France is a happy one; the result is one of the best of the tales of the grotesque. The cardinal idea is the baseness of the ancient mob — shared by its modern counterpart. The author here tolerated anachronisms, but he carefully chose appropriately characteristic elements.

The fable is invented only in the principal incident, for the ancient king was certainly capable of the behavior described. Some of his extravagant frolics recorded by the historians are almost as incredible as Poe's tale. Antiochus IV, surnamed Epiphanes ("illustrious"), was nicknamed Epimanes, "madman," during his lifetime. He reigned as monarch of the Seleucid Kingdom of Syria, 175–163 B.C., and figures largely in both books of Maccabees and in Josephus. He had been brought up as a hostage in Rome, and admired everything Roman, as he came to hate everything Jewish. Having his subjects sing a Latin song, though anachronistic, is not out of character, for he dressed some of his soldiers as Roman legionaries. The hymn in his own honor, intentionally bathetic, in Poe's original version contained the line, "Who is God but Epiphanes?" Poe revised it at some sacrifice of point, since Antiochus was regarded as divine by himself and by his subjects.

A magnificent procession celebrating Antiochus' opulence and power is described by Athenaeus (V, 194–195), who subsequently describes an even more magnificent demonstration produced earlier by Ptolemy Philadelphus (pp. 196–204). No mention is made of a large aggregation of wild animals in Antiochus' procession, but in Ptolemy's there were many, including *kamelopardalis*, a giraffe. In Poe's day also there were associations of giraffes and royalty. About 1827 two of the animals came from Mohammed Ali, Pasha of Egypt, as gifts to the kings of England and France respectively, and occasioned Thomas Hood's "Ode to the Cameleopard." George IV kept his giraffe at Brighton. The animal at the Jardin des Plantes inspired the couturiers of Paris to design gloves and ribbons of imitation giraffe skin. (See Miche Wynants, *The Giraffe of King Charles X*, 1961, pp. 49–54). The animal, a female, was seen by 600,000 visitors before the end of 1827, called the Year of the Giraffe in France. The popularity of the beast led to cartoons of which Poe presumably had heard and which he may have seen. In the *Southern Literary Messenger* for July 1835 (1:620), in "My First Night in a Watchhouse," Pertinax Placid (Edward Vernon Sparhawk) wrote of these French caricatures: "I remember a series of prints representing Charles X and his ministers. . . . The king was personated by the *Giraffe*. . . . The Fox played Prince Polignac; the Wolf, Count Peyronnet . . . to indicate the cunning and rapacity of those ministers. The accuracy of the likenesses . . . was remarkable." (This note is by courtesy of David K. Jackson.) A satirical print in the Parisian weekly *La Caricature,* February 28, 1833, aimed at the succeeding regime, represents a carnival procession in which the second and most striking figure is a man walking on stilts and wearing a "hobby-horse" costume that makes him appear to be riding giraffe-back.

On May 4, 1833, Poe sent to Joseph T. and Edwin Buckingham for their *New England Magazine* a manuscript of his story in a letter describing a projected series "under the title of 'Eleven Tales of the Arabesque' " but it was not accepted. Many months later Poe expressed his further disappointment in a letter to John P. Kennedy, September 11, 1835, when the tale was not chosen for *The Gift for 1836.*

TEXTS

(A) Manuscript in a letter of May 4, 1833; *(B) Southern Literary Messenger,* March 1836 (2:235–238); *(C) Tales of the Grotesque and Arabesque* (1840), II, 5–17; *(D) Broadway Journal,* December 6, 1845 (2:333–335); *(E) Works* (1850), II, 465–472. PHANTASY-PIECES, title only.

Griswold's text *(E)* is followed, as it shows one superior reading.

The manuscript was long in the hands of John Stieler, an old-time collector, who returned to his native Germany. See T. R. Ybarra in the *New York Times,* September 14, 1924. It is now owned by Mr. H. Bradley Martin.

The manuscript consists of three sheets, quarto. The letter, on the first page, is in script, and carries the signature of Edgar Allan Poe. The tale portion, beginning below the letter, is printed in a very small hand, and has an extraordinary number of dashes, decoratively done with shorter and longer wavy lines. Forty-one of these dashes were eliminated for the printing in the *Southern Literary Messenger* (B). For the most part commas and periods were substituted. The paragraphing of the manuscript is followed in the printed texts except for two instances, recorded in the variants. The line of asterisks is in the manuscript.

FOUR BEASTS IN ONE;   [*E*]

THE HOMO-CAMELEOPARD.

> Chacun a ses vertus.
> *Crébillon's Xerxes.*

Antiochus Epiphanes is very generally looked upon as the Gog of the prophet Ezekiel. This honor is, however, more properly at-

---

Title: Epimanes (*A, B, C*); The Homocameleopard (PHANTASY-PIECES)

Motto: *Crébillon's accent omitted (A, B, C)*

tributable to Cambyses, the[a] son of Cyrus.[1] And, indeed, the character of the Syrian monarch[b] does by no means stand in need of any adventitious[c] embellishment.[2] His accession to the throne, or rather his usurpation of the sovereignty, a hundred and seventy-one years before the coming of Christ;[3] his attempt to plunder the temple of Diana at Ephesus;[4] his implacable hostility to the Jews; his pollution of the Holy of Holies;[5] and his miserable death at Taba,[6] after a tumultuous reign of eleven years, are circumstances of a prominent kind, and therefore more generally[d] noticed by the historians of his time, than the impious, dastardly, cruel, silly and whimsical achievements[e] which make[f] up the sum total of his private life and reputation.

*   *   *   *   *   *   *   *   *

Let us suppose, gentle reader, that it is now the year of the world three thousand eight hundred and thirty,[7] and let us, for a few minutes, imagine ourselves at that most grotesque habitation of man, the remarkable city of Antioch. To be sure there were, in Syria and other countries, sixteen cities of that appellation,[g] besides the one to which I more particularly allude. But [h]ours is that[h] which went by the name[i] of Antiochia Epidaphne, from its vicinity to the little village of[j] Daphne, where stood a temple to that divinity. It[k] was built (although about this matter there is some dispute) by Seleucus Nicanor, the first king of the country after Alexander the Great,[l] in memory of his father Antiochus, and[m] became immediately the residence of the Syrian monarchy. In the flourishing times of the Roman Empire, it was the ordinary station of the prefect of the eastern provinces; and many of the emperors of the queen [n]city, (among whom may be mentioned especially,[o] Verus and Valens,)[n] spent here the greater part of their time. But I perceive we have arrived at the city itself. Let us ascend this battle-

---

a *Omitted (A)*
b king *(A)*
c extraneous *(A)*
d particularly *(A)*
e achievments *(D) misprint*
f made *(A)*
g name *(A, B, C)*
h ... h I mean that Antioch *(A)*
i title *(A)*
j *Omitted (A, B)*
k The city *(A)*
l great. He erected it *(A)*
m and it *(A)*
n ... n city — among whom Verus and Valens may be mentioned — *(A)*
o most especially, *(B, C)*

ment, and throw our eyes[p] upon the town and neighboring country.[8]

"What broad and rapid river [q]is that which forces its way, with innumerable falls, through the mountainous wilderness, and finally[q] through the wilderness of buildings?"

[r]That is the Orontes, and it is[r] the only water in[s] sight, [t]with the exception of the[t] Mediterranean, which stretches like a broad[u] mirror, about twelve miles off to the southward. Every one has seen[v] the Mediterranean; but let me tell you, there are few who have had a peep at Antioch. By few, I mean, few who, like you and me,[w] have had, at the same time, the advantages of a modern education. Therefore cease to regard that sea, and give your whole attention to the mass of houses that lie beneath us. You will remember that it is now the year of the world three thousand eight hundred and thirty. Were it later — for example, were it[x] the year of our Lord eighteen hundred and forty-five,[y] we should be deprived of this extraordinary spectacle. In the nineteenth century Antioch is — that [z]is to say,[z] Antioch *will be* — in a lamentable state of decay. It will have been, by that time, totally destroyed, at three different periods, by three successive earthquakes. Indeed, to say the truth, what little of its former self may then remain, will be found[a] in so desolate and ruinous a state that the patriarch [b]shall have removed[b] his residence to Damascus.[9] This is well. I see you profit by my advice, and are making the most of your time in inspecting the [c]premises — in

> ——— satisfying your eyes
> With the memorials and the things of fame
> That most renown this city. ——[10]

I beg pardon; I had forgotten that Shakespeare will not flourish

---

p   eyes around *(A, B, C)*
q . . . q   do I see forcing its passage *(A)*
r . . . r   The Orontes. It is *(A);* That is the Orontes, and *(B, C)*
s   within *(A)*
t . . . t   save only the blue *(A)*
u   *Omitted (A)*
v   beheld *(A, B, C)*
w   I, *(B, C)*

x   it unfortunately *(A, B, C)*
y   thirty three, *(A);* thirty-six, *(B);* thirty-nine, *(C)*
z . . . z   is, I should say, *(A);* is, *(B, C)*
a   *Omitted (A)*
b . . . b   will have removed *(A, C);* will remove *(B)*
c . . . c   premises. Does *(A)*

for[d] seventeen hundred and fifty years to come. But does[c] not the appearance of Epidaphne justify me in calling it *grotesque?*

"It is well fortified; and[e] in this respect is[f] as much indebted to nature as to art."

Very true.

"There are[g] a prodigious number of stately palaces."

There are.[h]

"And the numerous[i] temples, sumptuous and magnificent, may bear[j] comparison with the most lauded of antiquity."

All this I must acknowledge. Still there is an infinity of mud huts, and abominable[k] hovels. We cannot help perceiving abundance of filth in every kennel, and, were it not for the overpowering fumes of idolatrous incense, I have no doubt we should find a most[l] intolerable stench. Did you ever behold streets so insufferably narrow, or houses so miraculously tall? What a gloom their shadows cast upon the ground! It is well the swinging lamps in those endless colonnades are kept burning throughout the day; we should otherwise have the darkness of Egypt in the time of her desolation.[11]

"It is [m]certainly a strange[m] place! What is the meaning of yonder singular building? See! it towers above all[n] others, and lies to the eastward of what I take to be the royal palace!"

That is the new Temple of the Sun, who is adored in Syria under the title[o] of Elah Gabalah. Hereafter a very notorious Roman Emperor will institute this worship in Rome, and thence derive a cognomen, Heliogabalus. I dare say you would like to take a[p] peep at the divinity of the temple. You need not look up[q] at the heavens; his Sunship is not there — at least not the Sunship[r] adored by the Syrians. *That* deity will be found in the interior of yonder building. He is worshipped under the figure of a large stone pillar terminating at the summit in a cone or *pyramid,* whereby is denoted Fire.[12]

---

d for nearly *(B, C)*
e being *(A)*
f *Omitted (A)*
g is *(A)*
h is. *(A)*
i innumerable *(A)*
j challenge a *(A)*
k *Omitted (A)*

l a most/an *(A)*
m...m a most wild-looking and whimsical *(A)*
n all the *(A, B)*
o name *(A)*
p to take a/a *(A, B, C)*
q upwards *(A)*
r one *(A)*

FOUR BEASTS IN ONE

"Hark! — behold! — who *can* those ridiculous beings be, half naked, with their faces painted, shouting and gesticulating to the rabble?"

Some few are mountebanks. Others more particularly belong to the race of philosophers. The greatest portion, however — those especially who belabor the populace with clubs — are the principal courtiers of the palace, executing, as in duty bound, some laudable comicality of the king's.

"But[s] what have we here? Heavens! the town is swarming with wild beasts! [t]How terrible a[t] spectacle! — [u]how dangerous a[u] peculiarity!"

Terrible, if you please; but not in the least degree dangerous. Each animal, if you will take the pains to observe, is following, very quietly, in the wake of its master. Some few, to be sure, are led with a rope about the neck, but these are chiefly the lesser or[v] timid species. The lion, the tiger, and the leopard are entirely without restraint. They have been trained without difficulty to their present profession, and attend upon their respective owners in the capacity of *valets-de-chambre*.[w] It is true, there are occasions when Nature asserts her violated dominion; — but then the devouring of a man-at-arms,[x] or the throttling of a[y] consecrated bull, [z]is a circumstance[z] of too little moment to be more than hinted at in Epidaphne.

"But what extraordinary tumult do I hear? Surely this is a loud noise even for Antioch! It argues some commotion of unusual interest."

Yes — undoubtedly. The king has ordered some novel[a] spectacle — some gladiatorial[b] exhibition at the Hippodrome — or perhaps the massacre of the Scythian prisoners — or the conflagration of his new palace — or the tearing down of a handsome temple — or, indeed, a bonfire of a few Jews. The uproar increases. Shouts of laughter ascend the skies. The air becomes dissonant with wind

---

s   But again! *(A)*
t . . . t   What a terrible *(A, B)*
u . . . u   what a dangerous *(A, B)*
v   or more *(A, B, C)*
w   *men-at-arms. (A)*

x   freeman, *(A)*
y   a courtezan or a *(A)*
z . . . z   are circumstances *(A, B, C)*
a   favourite *(A)*
b   *Omitted (A)*

instruments, and horrible with the clamor of a million throats. Let us descend, for the love of fun, and see what is going on! This way — be careful! Here we are in the principal street, which is called the street of Timarchus.[c] The sea of people is coming this way, and we shall find a difficulty in stemming the tide. They are pouring through the alley of Heraclides,[13] which leads directly from the palace — therefore the king is most probably among the rioters. Yes — I hear the shouts of the herald proclaiming his approach in the pompous phraseology of the East. We shall have a glimpse of his person as he passes by the temple of Ashimah.[14] Let us ensconce ourselves in the vestibule of the sanctuary; he will be here anon. In the meantime let us survey this image. What is it? Oh, it is the god Ashimah in proper person. You perceive, however, that he is neither a [d]lamb, nor a goat,[d] nor a satyr; neither has he much[e] resemblance to the Pan of the Arcadians. Yet all these appearances have been given — I beg pardon — *will* be given — by the learned of future ages, to the [f]Ashimah of the Syrians.[f] Put on your spectacles, and tell me what it is. What is it?

"Bless me! it is an ape!"

True — a baboon; but by no means the less a deity. His name is a derivation of the Greek *Simia*[g] — what[h] great fools are antiquarians! [i]But see! — see! — yonder scampers a ragged little urchin. Where is he going? What is he bawling about? What does he say? [j]Oh! he[k] says the king is coming in triumph; that he is dressed in state;[l] that he has just finished putting to death, with his own hand, a thousand chained Israelitish prisoners! For this exploit the ragamuffin is lauding him to the skies! Hark! here comes[m] a troop of a similar description.[n] They have made a Latin hymn upon the valor of the king, and are singing it as they go:

> Mille, mille, mille,
> Mille, mille, mille,

---

c Timarchus after one of the catamites of the king. *(A)*
d ... d goat, nor a lamb, *(A)*
e any *(A)*
f ... f Syrian Ashimah. *(A)*
g *In Greek letters (A)*
h and *(A)*
i *New paragraph (A)*
j *New paragraph (A)*
k Oh! he/He *(A)*
l state — and *(A, B, C)*
m come *(A, B)*
n kind — *(A)*

FOUR BEASTS IN ONE

Decollavimus, unus homo!
Mille, mille, mille, mille, decollavimus!
Mille, mille, mille!
Vivat qui mille mille occidit!
Tantum vini habet nemo
Quantum sanguinis effudit!*⁰

Which may be thus paraphrased:

A thousand, a thousand, a thousand,
A thousand, a thousand, a thousand,
We, with one warrior, have slain!
A thousand, a thousand, a thousand, a thousand,
Sing a thousand over again!
Soho! — let us sing
Long life to our king,
Who knocked over a thousand so fine![15]
Soho! — let us roar,
He has given us more
Red gallons of gore
Than all Syria can furnish of wine!

"Do you hear that flourish of trumpets?"

Yes — the king is coming! See! the people are aghast with admiration, and lift up their eyes to the heavens in reverence![16] He comes! — he is coming! — there he is!

"Who? — where? — the king? — I[r] do not behold him; — cannot say that I perceive him."

Then you must be blind.

"Very possible. Still I see nothing but a tumultuous mob of idiots and madmen, who are busy in prostrating themselves before a gigantic cameleopard,[s] and endeavoring to obtain a kiss of the animal's hoofs. See! the beast has very justly kicked one of the rabble over — and another — and another — and another. Indeed, I cannot help admiring the animal for the excellent[t] use he is making of his feet."

---

* Flavius Vopiscus[p] says, that the hymn[q] here introduced, was sung by the rabble upon the occasion of Aurelian, in the Sarmatic war, having slain with his own hand, nine hundred and fifty of the enemy.

---

o *Footnote omitted (A)*
p Vopsicus *(D);* Vospicus *(E) misprint*
corrected from B, C
q hymn which is *(B, C)*

r *Omitted (B, C, D)*
s camelopard *throughout (C)*
t dexterous *(A)*

Rabble, indeed! — why these are the noble and free citizens of Epidaphne! Beast, did you say? — take care that[u] you are not overheard. Do you not perceive that the animal has the visage of a man? Why, my dear sir, that cameleopard is no other than Antiochus Epiphanes — Antiochus the Illustrious, King of Syria, and the most potent of all[v] the autocrats of the East! It is true, that he is entitled, at times, Antiochus Epimanes — Antiochus the madman — but that is because all people have not the[w] capacity to appreciate his merits. It is also certain that he is at present ensconced in the hide of a beast, and is doing his best to play the part of a cameleopard; but [x]this is done[x] for the better sustaining his dignity as king. Besides, the monarch is óf[y] gigantic stature, and the dress is therefore neither unbecoming nor over large. We may, however, presume he [z]would not have adopted it but for[z] some occasion of especial state. Such, you will allow, is the massacre of a thousand Jews. With [a]how superior a[a] dignity the monarch perambulates on[b] all fours! His tail, you[c] perceive, is held aloft by his two principal concubines, Ellinë and Argelaïs;[17] and his whole appearance would be infinitely prepossessing,[d] were it not for the protuberance[d'] of his eyes, which will certainly start out of his head, and the queer color of his face, which has become nondescript from the quantity of wine[e] he has swallowed. Let us follow him[f] to the hippodrome, whither he is proceeding, and listen to the song of triumph which he is commencing:

> Who is king but Epiphanes?
>   Say — do you know?
> Who is king[g] but Epiphanes?
>   Bravo! — bravo![h]
> There is none but Epiphanes,
>   No — there is none:
> So tear down the temples,
>   And put out the sun![i] [18]

---

u   *Omitted (A)*
v   *Omitted (A, B, C)*
w   *Omitted (A)*
x . . . x   *that is (A)*
y   *of a (A, B, C)*
z . . . z   *wears it upon (A)*
a . . . a   *a how supreme a (A); what a superior (B)*
b   *upon (A, B, C)*

c   *you will (A)*
d   *prepossessing, (D) misprint*
d'   *protruberance (D, E) misprint*
e   *wine which (A)*
f   *Omitted (A, B, C)*
g   *God (A)*
h   *Line 4 Say do you know? (A)*
i   *Lines 1–4 repeated after line 8 (B, C)*

FOUR BEASTS IN ONE

Well and strenuously sung! The populace are hailing him "Prince of Poets," as well as "Glory of the East," "Delight of the Universe," and "most remarkable of Cameleopards." They have *encored* his effusion, and — do you hear? — he is singing it over[j] again. When he arrives at the hippodrome, he will be crowned with the poetic wreath, in anticipation of [k]his victory at the approaching Olympics.[k]

"But, good Jupiter! what is the matter in the crowd behind us?"

Behind us, did you say? — oh! ah! — I perceive. My friend, it is well that[l] you spoke in time. Let us get into a place of safety as soon as possible. Here! — let us conceal ourselves in the arch of this aqueduct, and I will inform you presently of the origin of the[m] commotion. It has turned out as I have been anticipating. The singular appearance of the cameleopard with the head of a man, has, it seems, given offence to the notions of propriety entertained in general, by the wild animals domesticated in the city. A mutiny has been the result; and, as is usual upon such occasions, all human efforts will be [n]of no avail[n] in quelling the mob. Several of the Syrians[o] have already been devoured; but the general voice of the four-footed patriots seems to be for eating up the cameleopard. "The Prince of Poets," therefore, is upon[p] his hinder legs,[q] running for his life. His courtiers have[r] left him in the lurch, and his concubines have [s]followed so excellent an example.[s] "Delight of the Universe," thou art[t] in a sad predicament! "Glory of the East," thou art in danger of mastication! [u]Therefore never regard so piteously thy tail; it will undoubtedly[u] be draggled in the mud, and for this there is no help. Look not behind thee, then, at its unavoidable degradation; but take courage, ply thy legs with vigor, and scud for the hippodrome![v] Remember that thou art Antiochus Epiphanes, Antiochus the Illustrious! — also "Prince of Poets,"

---

j   *Omitted (A)*
k . . . k   the time when he shall obtain it at Olympia. *(A)*
l   *Omitted (A)*
m   this *(A, B, C)*
n . . . n   ineffectual *(A)*
o   Epidaphnians *(A)*
p   on *(A)*
q   legs, and *(A, B, C, D)*

r   have have *(E) misprint, corrected from A, B, C, D*
s . . . s   let go their hold upon his tail. *(A);* let fall his tail. *(B, C)*
t   art now *(A)*
u . . . u   Thy tail will *(A)*
v   *After this:* Remember that the beasts are at thy heels! *(A, B)*

"Glory of the East," "Delight of the Universe," and "most Remarkable of Cameleopards!" Heavens! what a power of speed thou art displaying! What a capacity for leg-bail thou art developing! Run, Prince! — Bravo, Epiphanes! — Well done,[w] Cameleopard! — Glorious Antiochus! He runs! — he leaps![x] — he flies! Like an arrow[y] from a catapult he approaches the hippodrome! He leaps! — he shrieks! — he is there! [z]This is well; for[z] hadst thou, "Glory of the East," been half a second longer in [a]reaching the gates of[a] the Amphitheatre, there is not a bear's cub in Epidaphne that[b] would not have had a nibble at thy carcass. Let us be off — let us take our departure! — for we shall find our delicate modern ears unable to endure the vast uproar which is about to commence in celebration of the king's escape! Listen! it has already commenced. See! — the whole town is topsy-turvy.

"Surely this is the most populous city of the East! What a wilderness of people! what a jumble of all ranks and ages! what a multiplicity of sects and nations! what a variety of costumes! what a Babel of languages! what a screaming of beasts! what a tinkling of instruments! what a parcel of philosophers!"[c]

Come let us be off!

"Stay a moment! I see a vast hubbub in the hippodrome; what is the meaning of it I beseech you!"

"That? — oh nothing! The noble and free citizens of Epidaphne[d] being, as they declare, well satisfied of the faith, valor, wisdom, and divinity of their king, and having, moreover, been eye-witnesses[e] of his late superhuman agility, do think it no more than their duty to invest his brows (in addition to the poetic crown) with the wreath of victory in the[f] foot-race — a wreath which[g] it is evident he *must* obtain at the celebration of the next [h]Olympiad, and which, therefore, they now give him in advance.[h] [19]

---

w Well done,/hurrah! *(A)*
x moves *(A);* moves! *(B, C)*
y an arrow/a shell *(A, B, C)*
z ... z Ah! *(A)*
a ... a arriving at *(A)*
b who *(A, B, C)*
c philosophers! what a swarm of children! — what a deal of women! —

what a devil of a noise!' *(A)*
d Antioch *(A)*
e witnesses *(A)*
f the *stadium* or *(A)*
g which is esteemed the most honourable of all, and which *(A)*
h ... h Olympiad. *(A, B)*

FOUR BEASTS IN ONE

NOTES

Title: The four beasts may be taken to be man, camel, lion, and pard (a panther); they are combined in one make-believe man-giraffe. "Cameleopard" is an erroneous spelling, according to the OED, although it has been widely used. The word is properly "camelopard," through the Latin from the Greek *kamelos* and *pardalis,* for the beast having the neck and legs of the camel with the spots of the panther, or pard. Apparently the publishers of Poe's *Tales of the Grotesque and Arabesque* "corrected" the spelling followed in the earlier texts, but Poe restored it – perhaps with a punning intent – in his projected PHANTASY-PIECES.

Motto: "Everyone has his good qualities" is in Prosper Jolyot de Crébillon's *Xerxes* (1714), IV, ii, 4.

1. For Gog see Ezekiel, chapters 38 and 39. Cambyses, who reigned over the Persian Empire from 529 to 522 B.C., was "utterly deranged" according to Isaac Taylor's translation of Herodotus (London, 1829), p. 206.

2. Poe's summary of Antiochus' career generally accords with most brief accounts, such as John Lemprière's in his *Classical Dictionary* (first American edition, 1809) and Charles Anthon's in his revised and augmented sixth American edition (1827) of Lemprière.

3. Poe accepts 4 B.C. as the date of the Nativity – and 4004 B.C. as that of the creation of the world – as do the chronologies in Lemprière and Anthon's Lemprière. This method of dating *anno mundi* is also used in "A Tale of Jerusalem."

4. Major reference works fail to mention the famous temple at Ephesus as the one Antiochus sought to plunder; ancient sources (Polybius, Maccabees) give the temple of Diana at Elymais in Persia or Persepolis. Poe seems to have slipped here.

5. The inner sanctuary of the Temple in Jerusalem.

6. Poe follows the report in Polybius 31:9, but other ancient sources and modern scholars differ. See the footnote on p. 185 of Volume VII of the Loeb edition of Josephus, edited by Ralph Marcus.

7. 175 B.C., see note 3 above.

8. Antioch in Syria – Antioch Epidaphne, Antioch on the Orontes – was for some six centuries one of the most important cities of the ancient world, outranked only by Alexandria and Rome. Poe's allusions are for the most part founded on accepted history. (For details concerning Antioch, Daphne, and their surroundings, see Glanville Downey, *A History of Antioch and Syria,* 1961, and *Ancient Antioch,* 1963, both published by Princeton University Press.) Poe errs in limiting the number of destructive earthquakes to three, and along with the English editions through 1879 and the earliest American editions of Lemprière (under "Antiochia") in giving the founder's surname as Nicanor. The error was corrected by Anthon in his 1827 edition of Lemprière. The founder was Seleucus Nicator (Victorious), one of Alexander's generals, whose name is given correctly by Lemprière in the article on Seleucus himself. Poe's parenthetical "although about this matter there is some dispute" is worth noting.

9. In the course of the Middle Ages, Antioch was superseded by Damascus as the great city of Syria.

10. *Twelfth Night,* III, iii, 22–24.

11. See Exodus 10:21 for the darkness of Egypt.

12. Ela Gabal (God of the Mountain) was the name of the Sun as worshipped in a sacred stone (a baetyl) at the city of Emesa (modern Homs). The hereditary high priests, who claimed descent from Alexander the Great, included a youth named Varius Avitus who, as Roman Emperor, A.D. 218–222, assumed the name of his famous predecessor, Marcus Aurelius Antoninus. He believed himself a theophany of his divinity, was called Elagabalus, and tried to extend his cult to Rome. The form Heliogabalus is often mistakenly used, even by ancient writers, thinking the first element connected with Greek Helios, the Sun. It is actually Semitic and cognate to Elohim and Allah. "Elah Gabalah" is probably inappropriate to Antioch. There are references to the Emperor in Poe's "William Wilson" and "Mellonta Tauta."

13. Timarchus and his brother Heracleides were worthies of the time of Antiochus IV; they were responsible for building a council chamber for him at Miletus. See Downey, *Ancient Antioch,* p. 58, and the Pauly-Wissowa *Realencyclopedia* under the second name.

14. Ashimah, or Ashima, was a god of the men of Hamath (modern Hamah), mentioned in 2 Kings 17:30. Poe refers to him also in "A Tale of Jerusalem." In the manuscript Poe wrote *Simia* in Greek letters, undoubtedly parodying etymologies in the scholarly works he makes fun of. Indeed, the article "Ashima" in William Smith's Bible Dictionary, if it hadn't been published years after Poe's story, might well have served as Poe's model, even to the list of "resemblances." A genuine connection between the Greek and Semitic names is unlikely, however.

15. The Latin verses are from Salmasius' edition of the *Scriptores Historiae Augustae,* "Divus Aurelianus," chapter six. See my fuller annotation of these and of Poe's paraphrase in the volume of Poems (Mabbott I, 218–219).

16. See Deuteronomy 4:19; "lift up thine eyes unto heaven" is in a passage forbidding the worship of all things save the Lord.

17. Ellinë and Argelaïs seem to be possible Grecian names, although I have not found any record of women who had them. The diaereses have been added by the editor.

18. See my fuller notes cited in note 15, above. The changes from the earliest version were obviously made to avoid shocking the pious.

19. The Ancient Roman custom of giving honors in advance may be recalled.

MS. FOUND IN A BOTTLE

This story is a masterpiece in the literal sense of the word. By winning a prize contest it set its author on the way to lasting fame. Messrs. Charles F. Cloud and William L. Pouder publishers of the *Baltimore Saturday Visiter,* in the issue of June 15, 1833, announced premiums of "50 dollars for the best Tale and 25 dollars for the best poem, not exceeding one hundred lines." Poe submitted his poem "The Coliseum" and six stories from the projected collection he now called "Tales of the Folio Club." Two judges, John Pendleton Kennedy and Dr. James Henry Miller, met with the third, John H. B. Latrobe, early in October at his home, 11 West Mulberry Street, Baltimore, and unanimously awarded the prize for the best tale to Poe.* The award was announced in the *Visiter* of October 12, 1833.

The story was printed in the next week's paper, with the comment: "The following is the Tale to which the Premium of Fifty Dollars has been awarded by the Committee. It will be found highly graphic in its style of Composition."

Poe obtained some immediate publicity away from home;† and most important of all, the story brought Poe to the attention of John P. Kennedy,‡ who was to remain a friend while Poe lived, and who gave invaluable impetus to the young author's career by putting him in touch with Thomas W. White in Richmond. Poe became an early contributor to White's *Southern Literary Messenger,* and at twenty-six its editor.

Poe's story combines several themes. One is the notion of Captain John Cleves Symmes, who believed the earth was hollow, open at both of the poles, and capable of habitation within. With James McBride, Symmes published *Symmes' Theory of Concentric Spheres* (Cincinnati, 1826). He had first propounded his ideas in 1818, and a story, *Symzonia,* by "Captain Adam Seaborn" (perhaps Symmes himself), appeared in 1820, and was reprinted in facsimile

* Rumor may have spread that there was really no contest, since nothing else of any merit was submitted. To still any gossip, Henry B. Hirst stated in a footnote to his sketch of Poe in the *Philadelphia Saturday Museum* of March 4, 1843, that Timothy Shay Arthur had entered a story. Hence, Poe did compete with at least one author whose work would not have been discreditable to the paper.

† A reprint in the Newburyport *People's Advocate* of October 26, 1833 is known.

‡ Poe also was to receive the friendship of Dr. Miller (1788–1853). Phillips, *Poe the Man,* I, 468, mentions letters from Poe to the physician or to his niece, which have not been published. Latrobe's reminiscences of the poet are notoriously inaccurate. See John Ward Ostrom, *The Letters of Edgar Allan Poe* (1948), p. 571, "Check List," numbers 99 and 100.

with an introduction by J. O. Bailey in 1965. Symmes' monument in Hamilton, Ohio, with a figure of the pierced globe, is famous.§

The second theme is that of the Flying Dutchman. Sir Walter Scott says in a note to *Rokeby* (1813) II, xi, 25:

> This is . . . a well-known nautical superstition concerning a fantastic vessel, called by sailors the Flying Dutchman, and supposed to be seen about the latitude of the Cape of Good Hope. She is distinguished from earthly vessels by bearing a press of sail when all others are unable, from stress of weather, to show an inch of canvas. The cause of her wandering is not altogether certain; but the general account is that she was originally a vessel loaded with great wealth, on board of which some horrid act . . . had been committed; that the plague broke out among the wicked crew . . . and that they sailed in vain . . . excluded from every harbor for fear of the contagion which was devouring them; and that, as a punishment of their crimes, the apparition of the ship still continues to haunt those seas in which the catastrophe took place, and is considered by the mariners as the worst of all possible omens.

In *Burton's Gentleman's Magazine,* June 1839, is a review of *The Phantom Ship* by Captain Marryat. This I now believe was one of Poe's first contributions to the magazine. The reviewer says: "The old legend of the Flying Dutchman is one possessing all the rich *materiel* which a vigorous imagination could desire."

A story that probably aroused Poe's immediate interest in the theme of the ghostly ship was found by Professor John C. Guilds, Jr. It is "A Picture of the Sea" by William Gilmore Simms, published in the Charleston *Southern Literary Gazette,* December 1828, when Poe was in the army and stationed at Fort Moultrie. It is practically unthinkable that he did not see a local magazine of this kind at the time.*

The parallels between the beginnings of Poe's story and that of Simms are striking enough. The narrator of the Simms story is a ship passenger who professes disbelief in superstition. A sudden furious storm strikes after the sea takes on a mysterious foreboding

§ See J. O. Bailey's *Pilgrims Through Space and Time* (*1947*), pages 40–41, and for Symmes, J. W. Peck in *Ohio Archaeological and Historical Publications,* 18:28–42 (1909). Poe had his Hans Pfaall report seeing one of the holes, and again used the idea in *Arthur Gordon Pym* (1838).

* See London *Notes and Queries,* October 1956. Professor Guilds kindly sent me a photocopy of the now extremely rare original, of which there is an exemplar in the A.S. Salley Collection in the Library of the University of South Carolina.

MS. FOUND IN A BOTTLE

appearance. The captain rebukes the narrator and some other passengers who play cards at such a time, and thinks this may provoke a visit from the Flying Dutchman who frequents the German Ocean (North Sea) where the ship is sailing. Mountainous seas begin to overwhelm it. Then appears a large and majestic vessel under full sail — and passes over the narrator's ship, which begins to sink. One of his fellow passengers clings to a spar, which the narrator also seizes; finding it insufficient for both, he strangles his companion, but both sink. The conclusion does not parallel Poe's tale, for Simms's narrator finds himself in the presence of "the most bewitching of the fairy race," kisses her, receives "a violent blow of her fist," and wakes up in church!

Poe has his hero actually get on board the ghostly ship and send an account of his fatal adventure to the world by putting his message in a bottle. Poe employed this simple device again in "Mellonta Tauta," and in a less significant way in "The Balloon Hoax."

Floyd Stovall in *University of Texas Studies in Literature* (1930) sought for parallels to "The Rhyme of the Ancient Mariner." Poe could hardly have written about a ghostly ship involved in a shipwreck without thinking of Coleridge's unforgettable old sailor; and the suggestion of an association of the Flying Dutchman with the South Pole may have come from it. But it is rather a minor contributory source than a major one. Ice and albatross in Antarctic regions are factual, as are phosphorescent waters in tropical and semitropical seas.†

It has been suspected that an anonymous story called "MSS Found in a Drawer" in the *Saturday Visiter* of November 30, 1833 might be a burlesque of Poe's tale, but this is not the case, although it may be remotely inspired by Poe's narrative. Miss Margaret C.

† [Another source has been suggested by Burton Pollin. In 1829, four years before writing "MS. Found in a Bottle," Poe had made footnote references to Bernardin de St. Pierre in "Al Aaraaf" (Mabbott I, 102, 117); in 1835 in the long canceled passage in "Loss of Breath" (at n. 5) he spoke of the "lunar-lunatic theories of St. Pierre." Professor Pollin believes that Poe would have been stimulated by Bernardin's discussion of ocean currents and that he drew upon him also for other details, using Henry Hunter's translation, *Studies of Nature,* in the first edition (1797). See Pollin, "Poe's Use of Material from Bernardin de Saint-Pierre's *Etudes,*" in *Romance Notes,* Spring 1971.]

Kelley, secretary of the late William H. Koester, kindly sent me a typewritten copy of the piece. The narrator tells how he was, with two other men, in a small boat run down by a larger craft. Both of his companions were lost, but the hero became delirious, and his wild laughter was heard by several Negroes having a picnic on the nearby shore, who rescued him.

Poe's story was presumably composed in 1832; had it been submitted in the Philadelphia *Saturday Courier* contest in 1831, it would almost certainly have been published in that periodical during the following year. Miss Leslie paid Poe twenty dollars for this tale,‡ but her decision to reprint it in *The Gift for 1836,* instead of one of the unpublished tales he had offered her, surprised and disappointed Poe, as he wrote to John P. Kennedy on September 11, 1835.

TEXTS

(A) Baltimore Saturday Visiter, October 19, 1833; *(B) The Gift: A Christmas and New Year's Present for 1836* (1835), pp. 67–87; *(C) Southern Literary Messenger,* December 1835 (2:33–37); *(D) Tales of the Grotesque and Arabesque* (1840) I, 111–126; *(E)* PHANTASY-PIECES (copy of last with manuscript changes, 1842); *(F) Broadway Journal,* October 11, 1845 (2:203–206); *(G) Works* (1850) I, 150–160.

Griswold had a version with additional material – hence his text *(G)* is followed. It may be noted here that the text of *Works* (1850) is free of many of the typographical errors that marred later issues.

The file of the *Visiter (A)* I examined personally in 1918 when it was still owned by Miss Elizabeth Seip. It was later in the collection of William H. Koester, and is now at the University of Texas. The preface of *The Gift (B)* is dated October 1835. Of the seventeen punctuation changes in PHANTASY-PIECES ten were adopted in the later texts. Eight of these substitute semi-colons for dashes. All texts use the first line of asterisks; only *F* and *G* use the others—obviously marking breaks in the narrative, and varying in position and number at the convenience of the printer.

Reprints

The People's Advocate (Newburyport, Mass.), October 26, 1833, from the *Baltimore Saturday Visiter; Richmond Semi-Weekly Examiner,* October 19, 1849, from *Tales of the Grotesque and Arabesque* (1840).

‡ See Kennedy's statement made in 1851 and recorded in a letter of William Hand Browne to John H. Ingram, June 22, 1893 (Ingram List, number 395, and Phillips, I, 468).

MS. FOUND IN A BOTTLE

MS. FOUND IN A BOTTLE. [G]

Qui n'a plus qu'un moment à vivre
N'a plus rien à dissimuler.   *Quinault — Atys.*

Of my country and of my family I have little to say. Ill usage
and length of years have driven me from the one, and estranged
me from the other. Hereditary wealth afforded me an education of
no common order, and a contemplative turn of mind enabled me
to methodise the stores which early study very diligently garnered
up. Beyond all things, the works of the German moralists gave me
great delight; not from any ill-advised admiration of their eloquent
madness, but from the ease with which my habits of rigid thought
enabled me to detect their falsities. I have often been reproached
with the aridity of my genius; a deficiency of imagination has been
imputed to me as a crime; and the Pyrrhonism[1] of my opinions has
at all times rendered me notorious. Indeed, a strong relish for physical philosophy has, I fear, tinctured my mind with a very common
error of this age — I mean the habit of referring occurrences, even
the least susceptible of such reference, to the principles of that
science. Upon the whole, no person could be less liable than myself
to be led away from the severe precincts of truth by the *ignes fatui*[2]
of superstition. I have thought proper to premise thus much, lest
the incredible tale I have to tell should be considered rather the
raving[a] of a crude imagination, than the positive experience of a
mind to which the reveries of fancy have been a dead letter and
a nullity.

After many years spent in foreign travel, I sailed in the year
18 — , from the port of Batavia,[3] in the rich and populous island of
Java, on a voyage to the Archipelago of the Sunda islands. I went as
passenger — having no other inducement than a kind of nervous
restlessness which haunted me as[b] a fiend.

Our vessel was a beautiful ship of about four hundred tons,

Title: Manuscript Found in a Bottle
(B) and Table of Contents *of*
PHANTASY-PIECES
Motto: A wet sheet and a flowing sea.
CUNNINGHAM. *(A, B, C); no motto in D*

and E; the French motto first appeared
in F — accents are added to our text
from F
a   ravings *(A, B, C)*
b   like *(A, B, C, D) changed in E*

copper-fastened, and built at Bombay of Malabar teak. She was freighted with cotton-wool and oil, from the Lachadive islands.[4] We had also on board coir, jaggeree, ghee,[5] cocoa-nuts, and a few cases of opium. The stowage was clumsily done, and the vessel consequently crank.[6]

We got under way with a mere breath of wind, and for many days stood along the eastern coast of Java, without any other incident to beguile the monotony of our course than the occasional meeting with some of the small grabs[7] of the Archipelago to which we were bound.

One evening, leaning over the taffrail, I observed a very singular, isolated cloud, to the N. W. It was remarkable, as well for[c] its color, as from its being the first we had seen since our departure from Batavia. I watched it attentively until sunset, when it spread all at once to the eastward and westward, girting in the horizon with a narrow strip of vapor, and looking like a long line of low beach. My notice was soon afterwards attracted by the dusky-red appearance of the moon, and the peculiar character of the sea. The latter was undergoing a rapid change, and the water seemed more than usually transparent. Although I could distinctly see the bottom, yet, heaving the lead, I found the ship in fifteen fathoms. The air now became intolerably hot, and was loaded with spiral exhalations similar to those arising from heated iron. As night came on, every breath of wind died away, and a more entire calm it is impossible to conceive. The flame of a candle burned upon the poop without the least perceptible motion, and a long hair, held between the finger and thumb, hung without the possibility of detecting a vibration. However, as the captain said he could perceive no indication of danger, and as we were drifting in bodily to shore, he ordered the sails to be furled, and the anchor let go. No watch was set, and the crew, consisting principally of Malays, stretched themselves deliberately upon deck. I went below — not without a full presentiment of evil. Indeed, every appearance warranted me in apprehending a Simoon.[d] [8] I told the captain my fears; but he paid no attention to what I said, and left me[e] without deign-

---

c   as for *(A)*; from *(B)*   E, F)
d   Simoom *throughout (A, B, C, D,*   e   left me/went below *(A, B)*

ing to give[f] a reply. My uneasiness, however, prevented me from sleeping, and about midnight I went upon deck. As I placed my foot upon the upper step of the companion-ladder, I was startled by[g] a loud, humming noise, like that occasioned by the rapid revolution of a mill-wheel, and before I could ascertain its meaning, I found the ship quivering to its centre. In the next instant, a wilderness of foam hurled us upon our beam-ends, and, rushing over us fore and aft, swept the entire decks from stem to stern.

The extreme fury of the blast proved, in a great measure, the salvation of the ship. Although completely water-logged, yet, as[h] her masts had gone by the board, she rose, after a minute, heavily from the sea, and, staggering awhile beneath the immense pressure of the tempest, finally righted.

By what miracle I escaped destruction, it is impossible[i] to say. Stunned by the shock of the water, I found myself, upon recovery, jammed in between the stern-post and rudder. With great difficulty I gained my feet, and looking dizzily around, was at first struck with the idea of our being among breakers; so terrific, [j]beyond the wildest imagination,[j] was the whirlpool of mountainous[k] and foaming ocean within which we were[l] ingulfed. After a while, I heard the voice of an old Swede, who had shipped with us at the moment of our leaving port. I hallooed to him with all my strength, and presently he came reeling aft. We soon discovered that we were the sole survivors of the accident. All on deck, with the exception of ourselves, had been swept overboard; the[m] captain and mates must have perished as they slept, for the cabins were deluged with water. Without assistance, we could expect to do little for the security of the ship, and our exertions were at first paralyzed by the momentary expectation of going down. Our cable had, of course, parted like pack-thread, at the first breath of the hurricane, or we should have been instantaneously overwhelmed. We scudded with frightful velocity before the sea, and the water made clear breaches over us. The frame-work of our stern was shattered excessively, and, in

---

f give me *(A, B)*
g with *(A, B, C, D, E)*
h as all *(A, B, C, D, E)*
i impossible for me *(A)*

j . . . j *Canceled (E)*
k mountains *(A)*
l are *(A)*
m and the *(A, B, C, D, E)*

almost every respect, we had received considerable injury; but to our extreme[n] joy we found the pumps unchoked, and that we had [o]made no great shifting of our ballast.[o] The main fury of the blast[p] had already blown over, and we apprehended little danger from the violence of the wind; but we looked forward to its total cessation with dismay; well believing, that,[q] in our shattered condition, we should inevitably perish in the tremendous swell which would ensue. But this very just apprehension seemed by no means likely to be soon verified. For five entire days and nights — during which our only subsistence was a small quantity of jaggeree, procured with great difficulty from the forecastle — the hulk flew at a rate defying computation, before rapidly succeeding flaws of wind, which, without equalling the first violence of the Simoon, were still more terrific than any tempest I had before encountered. Our course for the first four days was, with trifling variations, S. E. and by S.; and we must have run down the coast of New Holland.[9] On the fifth day the cold became extreme, although the wind had hauled round a point more to the northward. The sun arose with a sickly yellow lustre, and clambered a very few degrees above the horizon — emitting no decisive light. There were no clouds[r] apparent, yet the wind was upon the increase, and blew with a fitful and unsteady fury. About noon, as nearly as we could guess, our attention was again arrested by the appearance of the sun. It gave out[s] no light, properly so called, but a dull and sullen glow [t]without reflection, as if all its rays were polarized.[t] Just before sinking within the turgid[u] sea, its central fires suddenly went out, as if hurriedly extinguished by some unaccountable power. It was a dim, silver-like rim, alone, as it rushed down the unfathomable ocean.

We waited in vain for the [v]arrival of the[v] sixth day — that day to me has not[w] arrived — to the Swede,[x] never did arrive. Thenceforward we were enshrouded in pitchy darkness, so that we could not have seen an object at twenty paces from the ship. Eternal

---

n *Canceled (E)*
o...o no great difficulty in keeping free. *(A, B, C)*
p Simoom *(A, B, C, D, E)*
q that,/that *(A, G) comma added from C, D, E, F*
r clouds whatever *(A, B, C, D, E)*

s gave out/emitted *(A, B)*
t...t unaccompanied by any ray. *(A, B, C, D, E)*
u furgid *(A) misprint*
v...v *Omitted (B)*
w not yet *(A, B, C)*
x the Swede,/him, *(A, B, C)*

night continued to envelop us, all unrelieved by the phosphoric sea-brilliancy to which we had been accustomed in the tropics. We observed too, that, although the tempest continued to rage with unabated violence, there was no longer to be discovered the usual appearance of surf, or foam, which had hitherto attended us. All around were[y] horror, and[z] thick gloom, and a black sweltering desert of ebony. Superstitious[a] terror crept by degrees into the spirit of the old Swede, and my own soul was wrapped up[b] in silent wonder. We neglected all care of the ship, as worse than useless, and securing ourselves, as well as possible, to the stump of the mizen-mast, looked out bitterly into the world of ocean. We had no means of calculating time, nor could we form any guess of our situation. We were, however, well aware of having made farther to the southward than any previous navigators,[10] and felt great[c] amazement at not meeting with the usual impediments of ice. In the meantime every moment threatened to be our last — every mountainous billow hurried to overwhelm us. The swell surpassed anything I had imagined possible, and that we were not instantly buried is a miracle. My companion spoke of the lightness of our cargo, and reminded me of the excellent qualities of our ship; but I could not help feeling the utter hopelessness of hope itself, and prepared myself gloomily for that death which I thought nothing could defer beyond an hour, as, with every knot of way the ship made, the swelling of the black stupendous seas became more dismally appalling. At times we gasped for breath at an elevation beyond the albatross — at times became dizzy with the velocity of our descent into some watery hell, where the air grew stagnant, and no sound disturbed the slumbers of the kraken.[11]

We were at the bottom of one of these abysses, when a quick scream from my companion broke fearfully upon the night. "See! see!" cried he, shrieking in my ears, "Almighty God! see! see!" As he spoke, I became aware of a dull, sullen glare of red[d] light which streamed[e] down the sides of the vast chasm where we lay, and threw a fitful brilliancy upon our deck. Casting my eyes upwards, I be-

---

y   us was (A, B); was (C, D, E)
z   and a (B)
a   Superstition's (A)
b   wrapped up/wrapt (B)

c   extreme (A, B, C, D, E)
d   Omitted (A, B, C)
e   rolled, as it were, (A, B, C)

held a spectacle which froze the current of my blood. At a terrific height directly above us, and upon the very verge of the precipitous descent, hovered a gigantic ship, of perhaps[f] four thousand tons. Although upreared upon the summit of a wave[g] more than a hundred[h] times her own altitude, her apparent size still exceeded that of any ship of the line or East Indiaman in existence. Her huge hull was of a deep dingy black, unrelieved by any of the customary carvings of a ship. A single row of brass cannon protruded from her open ports, and dashed[i] from their polished surfaces the fires of innumerable battle-lanterns, which swung to and fro about her rigging. But what mainly inspired us with horror and astonishment, was that she bore up under a press of sail in the very teeth of that supernatural sea, and of that ungovernable hurricane. When we first discovered her, her[j] bows were alone to be seen, as she rose[k] slowly from the [l]dim and horrible[l] gulf beyond her. For a moment of intense terror she paused upon the giddy pinnacle, as if in contemplation of her own sublimity, then trembled and tottered, and — came down.

At this instant, I know[m] not what sudden self-possession came over my spirit. Staggering as far aft as I could,[12] I awaited fearlessly the ruin that was to overwhelm. Our own[n] vessel was at length ceasing from her struggles, and sinking with her head to the sea. The shock of the descending mass struck her, consequently, in that portion of her frame which was already under water, and the inevitable result was to hurl me, with irresistible violence, upon the rigging of the stranger.[13]

As I fell, the ship hove in stays, and went about; and to the confusion ensuing I attributed my escape from the notice of the crew. With little difficulty I made my way, unperceived, to the main hatchway, which was partially open, and soon found an opportunity of secreting myself in the hold. Why I did so I can hardly tell. An[o] indefinite sense of awe, which at first sight of the naviga-

---

f   nearly *(A, B, C, D, E)*
g   wave of *(A, B, C, D, E)*
h   a hundred/a million *(A, B)*; fifty (E)
i   dashed off *(A, B, C, D, E)*
j   her stupendous *(A, B, C, D, E)*
k   rose up, like a demon of the deep,

(A, B, C, D, E)
l...l   everlasting *(A, B)*
m   knew *(A)*
n   *Omitted (B)*
o   A nameless and *(A, B, C, D, E)*

tors of the ship had taken hold of my mind, was perhaps the principle of my concealment. I was unwilling to trust myself with a race of people who had offered, to the cursory glance I had taken, so many points of vague novelty, doubt, and apprehension. I therefore thought proper to contrive a hiding-place in the hold. This I did by removing a small portion of the shifting-boards, in such a manner as to afford me a convenient retreat between the huge timbers of the ship.

I had scarcely completed my work, when a footstep in the hold forced me to make use of it. A man passed by my place of concealment with a feeble and unsteady gait. I could not see his face, but had an opportunity of observing his general appearance. There was about it an evidence of great age and infirmity. His knees tottered beneath a load of years, and his entire frame quivered under the burthen. He muttered to himself, in a low broken tone, some words of a language which I could not understand, and groped in a corner among a pile of singular-looking instruments, and decayed charts of navigation. His manner was a wild mixture of the peevishness of second childhood and the solemn dignity of a God. He at length went on deck, and I saw him no more.

*   *   *   *   *

A feeling, for which I have no name,[14] has taken possession of my soul — a sensation which will admit of no analysis, to which the lessons of by-gone time are inadequate, and for which I fear futurity itself will offer me no key. To a mind constituted like my own, the latter consideration is an evil. I shall never — I know that I shall never — be satisfied with regard to the nature of my conceptions. Yet it is not wonderful that these conceptions are indefinite, since they have their origin in sources so utterly novel. A new sense — a new entity is added to my soul.

*   *   *   *   *

It is long since I first trod the deck of this terrible ship, and the rays of my destiny are, I think, gathering to a focus. Incomprehensible men! Wrapped up in meditations of a kind which I cannot divine, they pass me by unnoticed.[15] Concealment is utter folly on my part, for the people *will not* see. It was but just now that I passed directly before the eyes of the mate; it was no long while ago that I ventured into the captain's own private cabin, and took thence the materials with which I write, and have written. I shall from time to time continue this journal. It is true that I may not find an opportunity of transmitting it to the world, but I will not fail to make the endeavor. At the last moment I will enclose the MS. in a bottle, and cast it within the sea.

*   *   *   *   *

An incident has occurred which has given me new room for meditation. Are such things the operation[p] of ungoverned chance? I had ventured upon deck and[q] thrown myself down, without attracting any notice, among a pile of ratlin-stuff and old sails, in the bottom of the yawl. While musing upon the singularity of my fate, I unwittingly daubed with a tar-brush the edges of a neatly-folded studding-sail which lay near me on a barrel. The studding-sail is now bent upon the ship, and the thoughtless touches of the brush are spread out into the word DISCOVERY.   *   *   *

I have made many observations lately upon the structure of the vessel. Although well armed, she is not, I think, a ship of war. Her rigging, build, and general equipment, all negative a supposition of this[r] kind. What she *is not,* I can easily perceive; what she *is,* I fear it is impossible to say. I know not how it is, but in scrutinizing her strange model and singular cast of spars, her huge size and overgrown suits of canvass, her severely simple bow and antiquated stern, there will occasionally flash across my mind a sensation of familiar things, and there is always mixed up with such [s]indistinct shadows[s] of recollection, an unaccountable memory of old foreign chronicles and ages long ago.[16]   *   *   *   *   *

I have been looking at the timbers of the ship. She is built of a material to which I am a stranger. There is a peculiar character about the wood which strikes me as rendering it unfit for the purpose to which it has been applied. I mean its extreme *porousness,*[t] considered independently of the worm-eaten condition which is a consequence of navigation in these seas, and apart from the rottenness attendant upon age. It will appear perhaps an observation somewhat over-curious, but this wood would have[u] every character-

---

p   operations *(A, B, C, D, E)*
q   and had *(B)*
r   the *(A, B)*

s ... s   shadows, as it were, *(A, B, C)*
t   *porousnses,* (F) *misprint*

istic of Spanish oak, ^vif Spanish oak were distended by any unnatural means.^v

In reading the above sentence, a curious apothegm of an old
weather-beaten Dutch navigator comes full upon my recollection.
"It is as sure," he was wont to say, when any doubt was entertained of his veracity, "as sure as there is a sea where the ship itself
will grow in bulk like the living body of the seaman."[17]

*   *   *   *   *

About an hour ago, I made bold to thrust myself among a
group of the crew. They paid me no manner of attention, and, although I stood in the very midst of them all, seemed utterly unconscious of my presence. Like the one I had at^w first seen in the
hold, they all bore about them the marks of a hoary old age. Their
knees trembled with infirmity; their shoulders were bent double
with decrepitude; their shrivelled skins rattled in the wind; their
voices were low, tremulous, and broken; their eyes glistened with
the rheum of years; and their gray hairs streamed terribly in the
tempest. Around them, on every part of the deck, lay scattered
mathematical instruments of the most quaint and obsolete construction.   *   *   *   *   *

I mentioned, some time ago, the bending of a studding-sail.
From that period, the ship, being thrown dead off the wind, has
continued^x her terrific course due south, with every rag of canvass
packed upon her, from her trucks to her lower studding-sail booms,
and rolling every moment her top-gallant yard-arms into the most
appalling hell of water which it can enter into the mind of man to
imagine. I have just left the deck, where I find it impossible to
maintain a footing, although the crew seem to experience little inconvenience. It appears to me a miracle of miracles that our enor-
mous bulk^y is not swallowed^z up at once and for ever. We are surely
doomed to hover continually upon the brink of eternity, without
taking a final plunge into the abyss. From billows a thousand times
more stupendous than any I have ever seen, we glide away with

---

u   would have/has *(A, B, C, D) changed*
in E
v . . . v *if Spanish oak were distended*
or swelled by any unnatural means. (A,
B, C, D) changed in E

w   *Omitted (B)*
x   held *(A, B, C, D, E)*
y   hulk *(A, B)*
z   buried *(A, B, C, D, E)*

the facility of the arrowy sea-gull; and the colossal waters rear their heads above us like demons of the deep, but like demons confined to simple threats, and forbidden to destroy. I am led to attribute these frequent escapes[a] to the only natural cause which can account for such effect. I must suppose the ship to be within the influence of some strong current, or impetuous under-tow.   *   *   *

I have seen the captain face to face, and[b] in his own cabin — but, as I expected, he paid me no attention. Although in his appearance there is,[c] to a casual observer, nothing which might bespeak him more or less than man, still, a feeling of irrepressible reverence and awe mingled with the sensation of wonder with which I regarded him. In stature, he is nearly my own height; that is,[d] about five feet eight inches.[18] He is of a well-knit and compact frame of body, neither robust nor remarkable[e] otherwise. But it is the singularity of the expression which reigns upon the face — it is the intense, the wonderful, the thrilling evidence of old age,[19] so utter, so extreme, which [f]excites within my spirit a sense — a sentiment ineffable.[f] His forehead, although little wrinkled, seems to bear upon it the stamp of a myriad of years. His gray hairs are records of the past, and his grayer eyes are sybils[g] [20] of the future. The cabin floor was thickly strewn with strange, iron-clasped folios, and mouldering instruments of science, and obsolete long-forgotten charts. His head was bowed down upon his hands, and he pored, with a fiery, unquiet eye,[21] over a paper which I took to be a commission, and which, at all events, bore the signature of a monarch. He muttered to himself — as did the first seaman whom I saw in the hold — some low peevish syllables of a foreign tongue; and although the speaker was close at my elbow,[h] his voice seemed to reach my ears from the distance of a mile.   *   *   *   *   *

The ship and all in it are imbued with the spirit of Eld.[22] The crew glide to and fro like the ghosts of buried centuries; their eyes

---

a   escapes from imminent and deadly peril *(A, B)*
b   face, and/face *(B)*
c   was, *(A, B)*
d   is, I mean, *(A, B)*

e   remarkably *(A, B, C, D, E, F)*
f . . . f   strikes upon my soul with the shock of a Galvanic battery. *(A, B, C)*
g   Sybils *(A, C, F);* Sibyls *(B)*
h   elbow, yet *(A, B, C, D, E)*

have an eager and uneasy meaning; and when their figures[i] fall athwart my path in the wild glare of the battle-lanterns,[j] [23] I feel as I have never felt before, although I have been all my life a dealer in antiquities, and have imbibed the shadows of fallen columns at Balbec, and Tadmor, and Persepolis, until my very soul has become a ruin.[24]   *   *   *   *   *

When I look around me, I feel ashamed of my former apprehensions. If I trembled at the blast which has hitherto attended us, shall I not stand aghast at a warring of wind and ocean, to convey any[k] idea of which, the words tornado and simoon are trivial and ineffective? All in the immediate vicinity of the ship is[l] the blackness of eternal night, and a chaos of foamless water; but, about a league on either side of us, may be seen, indistinctly and at intervals, stupendous ramparts of ice, towering away into the desolate sky, and looking like the walls of the universe.   *   *

As I imagined, the ship proves to be in a current — if that appellation can properly be given to a tide which, howling and shrieking by the white ice, thunders on to the southward with a velocity like the headlong lashing of a cataract.   *   *   *

To conceive the horror of my sensations is, I presume, utterly impossible; yet a curiosity to penetrate the mysteries of these awful regions, predominates even over my despair, and will reconcile me to the most hideous aspect of death.[25] It is[m] evident that we are hurrying onwards to some exciting knowledge — some never-to-be-imparted secret, whose attainment is destruction. Perhaps this current leads us to the southern pole itself.[26] It must be confessed that a supposition apparently so wild has every probability in its favor.

   *   *   *   *   *

The crew pace the deck with unquiet and tremulous step; but there is upon their countenances an expression more of the eagerness of hope than of the apathy of despair.

In the meantime the wind is still in our poop, and, as we carry a crowd of canvass, the ship is at times lifted bodily from out the

---

i   fingers (G) *misprint, corrected from all other texts*
j   battle-latterns, (C, D, E) *misprint*
k   an (B)

l   ship is/ship, is (G) *corrected from all other texts*
m   it (G) *misprint*

sea! Oh, horror upon horror! — the ice opens suddenly to the right, and to the left, and we are whirling dizzily, in immense concentric circles, ⁿround and roundⁿ the borders of a gigantic amphitheatre, the summit of whose walls is lost in the darkness and the distance. But little time will be left me to ponder upon my destiny! The circles rapidly grow small — we are plunging madly within the grasp of the whirlpool — and amid a roaring, and bellowing, and thundering° of ocean and of tempest, the ship is quivering — oh God! and —— going down!

ᵖ*Note.* — The "MS. Found in a Bottle," was originally published in 1831; and it was not until many years afterwards that I became acquainted with the maps of Mercator, in which the ocean is represented as rushing, by four mouths, into the (northern) Polar Gulf, to be absorbed into the bowels of the earth; the Pole itself being represented by a black rock, towering to a prodigious height.ᵖ ²⁷

NOTES

Motto: "He who has but a moment to live, has no longer anything to dissemble" is from *Atys,* I, vi, 15–16, by Philippe Quinault (1635–1688). The earlier motto is the opening line of a lyric by Allan Cunningham (1784–1842) first published in 1825.

1. Pyrrho of Elis (about 360–270 B.C.) was an extreme skeptic who held that there is as much to be said for as against any opinion, that reason and the senses are untrustworthy, and that when we are convinced that we know nothing we cease to care. Hence pyrrhonism has come to mean absolute skepticism, or universal doubt. "Pyrro" is the name of the narrator in the first version of Poe's "Eleonora."

2. *Ignes fatui* are will-o'-the-wisps.

3. Batavia may be chosen as ill-omened; the town was completely destroyed by earthquake and flood in 1699.

4. The Laccadive Islands are a coral group two hundred miles west of the Malabar coast of India, in the Arabian Sea.

5. Coir is the prepared fiber of the husks of coconuts, used to make mats and ropes; jaggery is a coarse sugar made from the sap of palms, or from coconuts; ghee is clarified butter made from buffalo milk.

6. Crank means unstable, liable to capsize.

7. Grabs are light-draft coasting vessels with two or three masts, used in the East Indies.

---

n ... n round and round and
round *(B)*

o shrieking *(A, B, C, D, E)*

p ... p *Omitted in all earlier texts*

MS. FOUND IN A BOTTLE

8. The Simoon (or Simoom) is properly a hot wind sweeping over the African desert, across the Mediterranean to Italy, mentioned also in "Al Aaraaf," II, 165; in the 1831 version of "Tamerlane," line 180; and in a canceled passage in "Silence – a Fable," but the word is here used in the general sense of a tropical storm.

9. New Holland is an old name of Australia.

10. Compare Coleridge, "The Ancient Mariner," lines 105–106, "We were the first that ever burst/Into that silent sea."

11. The mythical Kraken, largest sea-monster in the world, was believed in by Scandinavian sailors even in Poe's day. See A. deCapell Brooke, *Travels Through Sweden (London,* 1823), p. 188. It is sometimes pictured as a huge squid or octopus, large enough to seize a ship in its tentacles and sink it.

12. The action may need clarification; the narrator has now unfastened himself from the stump of the mast.

13. A passenger actually was saved in this way in the collision of the *Andrea Doria* and the *Stockholm* in 1957.

14. Compare "The Lake" *(F)*, lines 15–16, "A feeling not the jewelled mine/Could teach or bribe me to define."

15. Compare "Ill-fated and mysterious man – bewildered in the brilliancy of thine own imagination," from the opening of "The Assignation."

16. Compare "Old unhappy far off things/And battles long ago," from Wordsworth's "Solitary Reaper."

17. The source (if there be one) for the navigator's remark is not known. It may well have been heard by Poe in some sailor's yarn.

18. Poe was of the same height as the narrator.

19. See "Ligeia" for "the glances of unusually aged people."

20. Sibyls are prophetesses noted for longevity.

21. Compare "I gazed with unquiet eye," from "Ligeia" at n. 13.

22. Compare "The Coliseum," line 10: "Vastness! and Age! and Memories of Eld!"

23. Compare *Arthur Gordon Pym,* chapter VIII: "the dim light of a kind of battle-lantern."

24. Compare "Al Aaraaf," II, 36–37 (Mabbott, I, 107):

> Friezes from Tadmor and Persepolis –
> From Balbec, and the stilly, clear abyss
> Of beautiful Gomorrah!

and "The Coliseum," lines 8–9, "so drink within/My very soul thy grandeur, gloom, and glory!"

25. Poe is saying that the human response to the extremities of danger and

despair is not resignation but the keenest mental activity. The protagonists in "A Descent into the Maelström (see at note 16), and "The Pit and the Pendulum" (see at note 17) respond in the same way.

26. Here Poe obviously had the hollow earth theory of Symmes in mind, as he did later on in "Hans Pfaall" and *Arthur Gordon Pym*.

27. The disclaimer of a debt to Mercator was omitted in all earlier texts. Gerhard Kremer (1512–1594), who called himself Gerardus Mercator, was the greatest cartographer of his time. He first published his projection in 1568; it showed the North Pole as a high black rock, *rupes nigra et altissima*, says Sidney Kaplan in the introduction to his edition of *Arthur Gordon Pym* (1960), p. xiv.

The wrong date of publication, 1831 instead of 1833, is typical of Poe's inaccuracy in such matters.

THE VISIONARY (THE ASSIGNATION)

In "The Visionary" — its first title is better than "The Assignation" — we have the most romantic story Poe ever wrote. A discerning critic well said that it is "such a mixture of bitter and sweet that it clings to one's memory like a ballad. The characters are sharply and consistently drawn, motives clear and convincing the more incredible the action grows."*

The protagonist is obviously modeled on Lord Byron, as must have been apparent to Poe's contemporaries and to later readers deeply interested in the poets and poetry of his period. How close the resemblance is has been ably studied.† The heroine is a combination of the two women Byron believed he really loved, Mary Chaworth and the Contessa Guiccioli. Like Byron the hero is an English nobleman and he writes a poem echoing lines addressed by Byron to his first love. (See the notes on "To One in Paradise" in this edition, Mabbott, I, 215–216.) He resides in magnificence in Venice, he becomes the lover of the very young wife of a much older Italian nobleman.

Poe took a leading incident of his story from the twenty-third

* New York *Critic,* January 2, 1886, quoted by Miss Phillips, I, 469.
† See Roy P. Basler, in *American Literature,* May 1937, and Richard P. Benton in *Nineteenth Century Fiction,* September 1963. Poe, of course, knew Thomas Moore's life of Byron.

chapter of Oliver Goldsmith's *Vicar of Wakefield* (1766), as was pointed out by Jeanie Begg Dixon.‡ "Matilda was married . . . to a Neapolitan nobleman . . . and found herself a widow and a mother at the age of fifteen. As she stood one day caressing her infant son in the open window of an apartment which hung over the river Volturna, the child with a sudden spring leaped from her arms into the flood below and disappeared in a moment."

Poe took nothing essential from his other sources. He may have owed a little to Mrs. Ann Radcliffe, whom he mentions in "The Oval Portrait," but resemblances to her *Mysteries of Udolpho* (1794) are commonplaces of romantic stories.§ Attempts to show Poe's debt to a story by E. T. A. Hoffmann are chimerical. The story is "Doge and Dogaressa" which has the same setting (Venice), and involves a liaison between a lady and a young man who saves her *husband* from drowning. It seems to me that the two stories are not much alike, but this "source," which was first suggested by Palmer Cobb in 1908, was received with respect by Killis Campbell, *Mind of Poe,* page 171, and Quinn, *Edgar Allan Poe,* page 214, where references are given.*

Poe seems to have been pleased, in general, with his story. It is the first in which he treats his favorite theme, the death of a beautiful lady, so highly praised as poetic in "The Philosophy of Composition." It is specifically stated in the *Southern Literary Messenger,* August 1835, that "The Visionary" had been submitted in the *Baltimore Visiter* contest in 1833. The unsigned publication in *The Lady's Book* — Godey had not yet added his name to the title — was Poe's first contribution to a national monthly magazine. The poet at West Point had been a friend of the son of its editress, Mrs. Sarah Josepha Hale.

‡ London *N & Q,* November 12, 1932. The incident is often omitted from abridged editions of *The Vicar.*

§ Celia Whitt in the University of Texas *Studies in English* (1937), 17:124f., points out several "parallels," of which the name of the husband Montoni and the anonymity of the lover alone are of interest. Poe is using such conventional material that his story has been thought a burlesque by Edward Davidson, *Poe, a Critical Study* (1957), passim, but notions that Poe would have put so lovely a poem as "To One in Paradise" into a burlesque, or have considered the death of a beautiful woman comic, I cannot accept.

* For the improbability that Poe had seen Hoffman's story in 1833, see Woodberry, *Life* (1909), I, 133.

TEXTS

(A) The Lady's Book for January 1834 (8:40–43); *Southern Literary Messenger*, July 1835 (1:637–640); *(C)* Duane copy of the last, with manuscript changes, 1839; *(D) Tales of the Grotesque and Arabesque* (1840), II, 193–211; *(E) Broadway Journal*, June 7, 1845 (1:357–360); *(F) Works* (1850), I, 370–381. PHANTASY-PIECES (1842), title only.

The latest text *(F)* is given here. When Poe refurbished the story for publication in the *Southern Literary Messenger (B)*, he substituted the moving lines of Henry King for the German mottoes, and struck out the two introductory paragraphs. He also combined a number of the short paragraphs, changed the heroine's name from Bianca to Aphrodite, inserted rows of asterisks to mark breaks in the narrative, and made a number of minor changes in wording.

Reprint

Bentley's Miscellany (English and American editions, December 1840) from *Tales of the Grotesque and Arabesque*, without acknowledgment.

THE ASSIGNATION. [*F*]

Stay for me there! I will not fail
To meet thee in that hollow vale.
[*Exequy on the death of his wife, by Henry King, Bishop of Chichester.*]

Ill-fated and mysterious man! — bewildered in the brilliancy of thine own imagination, and fallen in the flames of thine own youth![1] Again in fancy I behold thee! Once more thy form hath

---

Title: The Visionary. *(A, D);* The Visionary — A Tale. *(B, C); changed in* PHANTASY-PIECES
Motto and initial paragraphs of A:

Ich habe gelebt, und geliebet.
— *Schiller's Wallenstein.*
I have lived, and I have loved.

Und sterbich denn, so sterbich doch
Durch sie — durch sie. — *Goethe.*

And if I die, at least I die
With her — *with* her.

There is a name — a sound — which, above all other music, vibrates upon my ear with a delicious, yet wild and solemn melody. Devoutly admired by the few who read, and by the very few who think, it is a name not as yet, indeed, blazoned in the escutcheon of immortality; but there, nevertheless, heralded in characters of the Tyrian fire hereafter to be rendered legible by the breath of centuries.

It is a name, moreover, which for reasons intrinsically of no weight, yet in fact conclusive, I am determined to conceal. Nor will I, by a fictitious appellation, dishonour the memory of that great dead whose life was so little understood, and the received account of whose melancholy end is a tissue of malevolent blasphemies. I am not of that class of writers who, making some euphonous cognomen the key-stone to the arch of their narrations, can no more conclude without the one than the architect without the other.

risen before me! — not — oh not as thou art[a] — in the cold valley and shadow — but as thou *shouldst be* — squandering away a life of magnificent meditation in that city of dim visions, thine own Venice — which is a star-beloved Elysium[b] of the sea, and the wide windows of whose Palladian[c] palaces[d] [2] look down with a deep[e] and bitter meaning upon the secrets of her silent waters. Yes! I repeat it — as thou *shouldst be.*[f] There are surely other worlds than this — other thoughts than the thoughts of the multitude —[g] other speculations than the speculations of the sophist. Who then shall call thy conduct into question? who blame thee for thy visionary hours, or denounce[h] those occupations as[i] a wasting away of life, which were but the overflowings of thine everlasting energies?

It was at Venice, beneath the covered archway there called the *Ponte di Sospiri,*[j] that I met[k] for the third or fourth time the person of whom I speak. It is[l] with a confused recollection that I bring[m] to mind the circumstances of that meeting. Yet I remember — ah! how should I forget? — the deep midnight, the Bridge of Sighs, the beauty of woman, and the Genius[n] of [o]Romance that[o] stalked up and down the narrow canal.

It was a night of unusual gloom. The great clock of the Piazza had sounded the fifth hour of the Italian evening. The square of the Campanile lay silent and deserted, and the lights in the old Ducal Palace were dying fast away. I was returning home from the Piazzetta,[p] by way of the Grand Canal. But as my gondola arrived opposite the mouth of the canal San Marco, a female voice from its recesses broke[q] suddenly upon the night, in one wild, hysterical, and long continued shriek. Startled at the sound, I sprang upon my feet: while the[r] gondolier, letting slip his single[s] oar, lost it in

---

a   *art (A)*

b   city *(A)*

c   Paladian *(A)*

d   palaces, gleaming with the fires of midnight revelry, *(A)*

e   sad *(A)*

f   should'st be. *(A)*

g   multitude — I would almost venture to say *(A)*

h   declare *(A)*

i   *Omitted (A)*

j   "Ponte di Sospiri," *(A)*

k   I met/met me *(A)*

l   is, however, *(A)*

m   recall *(A)*

n   Demon *(A)*; demon *(B, C, D)*

o . . . o   Romance who *(A)*; romance, who *(B, C, D)*

p   Piazzetta, *(B, C, D, E, F) corrected from A*

q   burst *(A)*

r   my *(A)*

s   *Omitted (A)*

the pitchy darkness beyond a chance of recovery, and we were 'consequently left to the guidance' of the current which here sets from the greater into the smaller channel. Like some huge ᵘand sable-feathered condor,³ we were slowly driftingᵘ down towards the Bridge of Sighs, when a thousand flambeaux flashing from the windows, and down the staircases of the Ducal Palace, turned all at once thatᵛ deep gloom intoʷ a lividˣ and preternaturalʸ day.

A child, slipping from the arms of its own mother, had fallen from an upper window of the lofty structure into the deep and dim canal. The quiet waters had closed placidly over their victim; and, although my own gondola was the only one in sight, many a stout swimmer, already in the stream, was seeking in vain upon the surface, the treasure ᶻwhich was to be found, alas! only withinᶻ the abyss. Upon the broad black marble flagstones at the entrance of the palace, and a few steps above the water, stood a figure which none who then saw can ᵃhave ever sinceᵃ forgotten. It was the Marchesa Aphrodite⁴ —ᵇ the adoration of all Venice — the gayest of the ᶜgay — the most lovely where all were beautiful — but stillᶜ the young wife of the old and intriguing Mentoni,⁵ and the motherᵈ of that fair child, her first and only one, who now, deep beneath the murkyᵉ water, was thinking in bitterness of heart upon her sweetᶠ caresses, and exhausting its little life in struggles to call upon her name.

She stood alone. Her small, bare and silvery feet gleamed in the black mirror of marble beneath her.ᵍ Her ʰhair, not as yet more than halfʰ loosened for the night from its ball-room array, clustered, amid a shower of diamonds, round and round her classical head, in curls like those ofⁱ the young hyacinth.⁶ A snowy-white and gauze-like drapery seemed to be nearly the sole covering to her delicate form; but the mid-summer and midnight air was hot,

---

t . . . t left at the mercy *(A)*
u . . . u bird of sable plumage, we were drifting slowly *(A)*
v the *(A)*
w to *(B, C)*
x ghastly *(A)*
y supernatural *(A, B, C, D)*
z . . . z which, alas! was only to be found in *(A)*

a . . . a ever since have *(A)*
b Bianca, *(A)*
c . . . c gay;" but, alas! *(A)*
d mother — the mother *(A)*
e *Omitted (A)*
f gentle *(A)*
g beneath her./beneath. *(A)*
h . . . h hair partly *(A)*
i like those of/like *(A, B, C, D)*

sullen, and still, and no motion[j] in the[k] statue-like form itself, stirred even the folds of that raiment of very vapor which hung around it as the heavy marble hangs around the[l] Niobe.[7] [m]Yet — strange to say! — her[m] large lustrous eyes were not turned[n] downwards upon that[o] grave wherein[p] her brightest[q] hope lay buried — but riveted[r] in a widely different direction! The prison of the Old Republic[s] is, I think, the stateliest[t] building in all Venice — but how could[u] that lady gaze so fixedly upon it, when [v]beneath her lay stifling her own[w] child?[v] Yon dark, gloomy niche, too,[x] yawns right opposite her chamber window — what, then, *could* there[y] be in its shadows — in its [z]architecture — in its ivy-wreathed and solemn cornices — that[z] the Marchesa di Mentoni had not wondered at a thousand times before? Nonsense! — Who does not remember that, at such a time as this, the eye, like a shattered mirror, multiplies[a] the images of its sorrow,[8] and sees in innumerable[b] far off places, the wo which is close at hand?

Many steps above the Marchesa, and within the arch of the water-gate, stood, in full dress, the Satyr-like figure of Mentoni himself. He was occasionally occupied in thrumming a guitar, and seemed *ennuyé*[c] to the very death, as at intervals he gave directions for the recovery of his child. Stupified and aghast,[d] I had myself[e] no power to move from the upright position I had assumed upon first hearing the shriek, and must have presented to the eyes of the agitated group a spectral and ominous appearance, as with[f] pale countenance and rigid limbs, I floated[g] down among them in that funereal[h] gondola.

---

j   motion — no shadow of motion *(A, B, C, D)*
k   that *(A, B, C)*
l   the weeping *(A)*
m . . . m Her *(A)*
n   however bent *(A)*
o   upon that/to the *(A)*
p   where *(A)*
q   dearest *(A)*
r   rivetted — ah! strange to say! *(A)*
s   Old Republic/city *(A)*
t   fairest *(A)*
u   *could (A)*
v . . . v her only child lay stifling at her feet? *(A)*
w   only *(B, C, D, E)*
x   niche, too/niche *(A)*
y   *could* there/could there possibly *(A)*
z . . . z architecture, that *(A)*
a   multiples *(F) misprint*
b   a million *(A)*
c   ennuied *(A, B, C, D); ennuye (F)*
d   bewildered, *(A)*
e   had myself/had *(A)*
f   with my *(A)*
g   drifted *(A)*
h   funeral *(A)*

All efforts proved[i] in vain. Many of the most energetic in the search were relaxing their exertions,[j] and yielding to a gloomy sorrow. There seemed but little hope for the child; [k](how much less than for the mother!)[k] but now, from the [l]interior of that dark niche[l] which has been already[m] mentioned as forming a[n] part of the Old Republican prison, and[o] as fronting the lattice of the Marchesa, a figure,[p] muffled in a cloak, stepped out within reach of the light, and, pausing a moment upon the verge of the giddy descent,[q] plunged headlong into the canal. As, in an instant afterwards, he stood with the still living and breathing child within his grasp, upon the marble flagstones by the side of the Marchesa, his cloak, heavy with the drenching[r] water, became unfastened, and, falling in folds about his feet, discovered to the wonder-stricken spectators the graceful person of a very young man, with [s]the sound of[s] whose name the greater part of Europe was then ringing.

No word spoke the deliverer.[t] But the Marchesa! She will now receive her child — she will press it to her heart — she will cling to its little form, and smother it with her caresses. Alas! *another's*[u] arms have taken it [v]from the stranger — *another's* arms have taken it[v] away, and borne it afar off, unnoticed, into the palace! And the Marchesa! [w]Her lip — her beautiful lip trembles: tears are gathering in[w] her eyes — those eyes which, like Pliny's[x] acanthus, are "soft and almost liquid."[9] [y]Yes! tears are gathering in those eyes — and see! the[y] entire woman thrills throughout the soul, and the statue has started into life! The pallor of the marble countenance, the swelling of the marble bosom, the very purity of the marble feet, we behold[z] suddenly flushed over with a tide of ungovernable crimson; and a slight shudder quivers about her deli-

---

i were *(A)*	r *Omitted (A)*
j endeavors, *(A)*	s . . . s *Omitted (A)*
k . . . k *Omitted (B, C, D)*	t stranger. *(A)*
l . . . l dark niche *(A)*	u another's *(A)*
m before *(A)*	v . . . v *Omitted (A)*
n *Omitted (A)*	w . . . w a tear is gathering into *(A)*
o *Omitted (A)*	x Pliny's own *(A, B, C, D)*
p figure *(A, E, F) comma added from*	y . . . y Her lip — her beautiful lip
B, C, D	trembles; the *(A)*
q height, *(A)*	z we behold/is *(A)*

cate[a] frame, [b]as a gentle air[b] at Napoli about the rich silver[c] lilies in the grass.

Why *should* that lady blush! To this demand there is no answer — except that, having left, in the eager[d] haste and terror of a mother's heart, the privacy of her own *boudoir*,[e] she has neglected to enthral her tiny[f] feet in their[g] slippers, and utterly forgotten to throw over her Venetian[h] shoulders that drapery which is their due. What other possible reason[i] could there have been for her so blushing? — for the glance of those wild[j] appealing eyes? for the unusual tumult of that throbbing bosom? — for the convulsive pressure of that trembling [k]hand? — that hand[k] which fell, as Mentoni turned into the palace, accidentally, upon the hand of the [l]stranger. What reason could there have been for the low[l] — the singularly low tone of those unmeaning words which the lady [m]uttered hurriedly in bidding him adieu?[m] "Thou hast conquered," she said, or the murmurs of the water deceived me; "thou hast conquered — one hour after [n]sunrise — we shall meet — so let[n] it be!"

*   *   *   *   *

The tumult had subsided, the lights had died away within the palace,[o] and the stranger, whom I now recognised, stood alone upon the flags. He shook with inconceivable agitation, and his eye glanced around in search of a gondola. I could not do[p] less than offer him the service of my own; [q]and he accepted the[q] civility. [r]Having obtained an oar[r] at the water-gate, [s]we proceeded[s] together to his residence, while[t] he rapidly recovered his self-possession, and spoke of our former slight acquaintance in terms of great apparent cordiality.

a   her delicate/the entire *(A)*
b ... b   like a soft wind *(A)*
c   *Omitted (A)*
d   *Omitted (A)*
e   bureau, *(A)*
f   *Omitted (A)*
g   their tiny *(A)*
h   Venitian *(A, B, C, D, E)*
i   cause *(A)*
j   large *(A)*
k ... k   hand *(A)*

l ... l   stranger? — or for the low *(A)*
m ... m   uttered, and departed? *(A)*
n ... n   sun-rise — let *(A)*
o   Piazzo, *(A)*
p   not do/do no *(A)*
q ...q   in a hurried manner he accepted my *(A)*
r ... r   An oar was obtained *(A)*
s ... s   and as we passed *(A)*
t   *Omitted (A)*

TALES OF THE FOLIO CLUB

There are some subjects upon which I take pleasure in being minute. The person of the stranger — let me call him by this[u] title, who to all the world was still a stranger — the person of the stranger is one of these subjects. In height he might have been below rather than above the medium size: although there were moments of intense passion when his frame actually *expanded* and belied the assertion. The light, almost slender symmetry of his figure, promised more of that ready activity which he evinced at the Bridge of Sighs, than of that Herculean strength which he has been known to wield without an effort, upon occasions of more dangerous emergency. With the mouth and chin of a [v]deity — singular, wild, full, liquid eyes,[v] whose shadows varied from pure hazel to intense and brilliant jet — and a profusion of curling,[w] black hair, from which a [x]forehead of unusual breadth[x] gleamed forth at intervals all light and ivory — his were features than which I have seen none more classically regular, except, perhaps, the marble ones of the Emperor Commodus.[10] Yet his countenance was, nevertheless, one of those which all men have seen at some period of their lives, and have never afterwards seen again. It had no peculiar[y] — it had[z] no [a]settled predominant expression[a] to be fastened upon the memory; a countenance seen and instantly forgotten — but forgotten with a vague[b] and never-ceasing desire of recalling it to mind. Not that the spirit of each rapid passion failed, at any time, to throw its own distinct image upon the mirror of that face — but that the mirror, mirror-like, retained no vestige of the passion, when the passion had departed.

Upon leaving[c] him on the night of our adventure, he solicited [d]me, in what I thought[d] an urgent manner, to call upon him *very*[e] early the next morning. Shortly after sunrise, I found myself accordingly at his Palazzo, one of those huge structures[f] of gloomy,

u that *(A)*
v . . . v deity — a nose like those delicate creations of the mind to be found only in the medallions of the Hebrew, full [liquid *B, C*] eyes, *(A, B, C)*
w glossy *(A)*
x . . . x rather low than otherwise, *(A, B, C, D)*
y peculiar — I wish to be perfectly

understood *(A, B, C, D)*
z it had *omitted (A)*
a . . . a *Italicized (B, C, D)*
b vague, intense, *(A)*
c parting from *(A)*
d . . . d me in *(A)*
e very *(A)*
f piles *(A, B, C, D)*

yet fantastic pomp,[g] which tower above the waters of the [h]Grand Canal in the vicinity of the Rialto.[h] I was shown up a broad winding staircase of mosaics, into an apartment whose unparalleled splendor burst through the opening door with an actual glare, making me blind[i] and dizzy with luxuriousness.

I knew my acquaintance to be wealthy. Report had spoken of his possessions in terms which I had even ventured to call terms of ridiculous exaggeration. But as I gazed about me, I could not[j] bring myself to believe that the wealth of any subject in Europe could have supplied the princely[k] magnificence which burned and blazed around.

Although, as I say, the sun had arisen,[l] yet the room was still brilliantly lighted [m]up. I judge[m] from this circumstance, as well as from an air of[n] exhaustion in the countenance of my friend, that he had not retired to bed during the whole of the preceding night. In the architecture and embellishments of the chamber, the evident design had been[o] to dazzle and astound. Little attention had been paid to the *decora* of what is technically called *keeping*,[p] or to the proprieties of nationality. The eye wandered from object to object, and rested upon none — neither the *grotesques*[q] of the Greek painters, nor the sculptures of the best Italian days, nor the huge carvings of untutored Egypt. Rich draperies in every part of the room trembled to the vibration[r] of low, melancholy music, whose [s]origin was not to be discovered.[s] The senses were oppressed by mingled and conflicting perfumes, reeking up from strange convolute[t] censers, [u]together with multitudinous flaring and flickering tongues of emerald and violet fire.[u] The rays of the newly risen[v] sun poured in upon the whole, through windows[w] formed each of

g   grandeur *(A, B, C, D)*
h . . . h   Great Canal. *(A)*
i   sick *(A, B, C, D)*
j   with difficulty *(A)*
k   far more than imperial *(A, B, C, D)*
l   risen, *(A)*
m . . . m   up, and I judged *(A)*
n   of apparent *(A)*
o   had been/was *(A)*
p   "keeping," *(A)*
q   "Grotesques" *(A)*
r   vibrations *(A, B, C)*
s . . . s   unseen origin undoubtedly lay

in the recesses of the crimson [red coral *A*] trellice-work which tapestried the ceiling. *(A, B, C, D)*
t   Arabesque *(A, B, C)*
u . . . u   which seemed actually endued with a monstrous vitality as their particoloured fires writhed up and down, and around about their extravagant proportions. *(A, B, C, D)*
v   newly risen/rising *(A)*
w   windows, *(F) comma deleted to follow A, B, C, D, E*

a single[x] pane of crimson-tinted [y]glass. Glancing[y] to and fro, in a thousand reflections, from curtains which rolled from their cornices like cataracts[z] of molten silver, [a]the beams of natural glory[a] mingled at length fitfully with the artificial light, and lay weltering [b]in subdued masses[b] upon a carpet of rich, liquid-looking cloth of Chili[c] gold.[d] [11]

"Ha! ha! [e]ha! — ha! ha![e] ha!" — laughed the proprietor, motioning[f] me to a [g]seat as I entered the room,[g] and throwing himself back at full-length[h] upon an ottoman. "[i]I see," said he, perceiving that[i] I could not immediately reconcile myself to the *bienséance*[j] of so singular a [k]welcome — "I see you are astonished[k] at my apartment — at[l] my statues — my pictures — my originality of conception in [m]architecture and[m] upholstery! absolutely drunk, eh,[n] with my magnificence? But[o] pardon me, my dear sir, [p](here his tone of voice dropped to the very spirit of cordiality,) pardon me[q] for my uncharitable laughter. You appeared so *utterly* astonished. Besides, some things are so completely ludicrous, that a man *must* laugh, or die. To die laughing, must be the most glorious of all glorious deaths! Sir Thomas More — a very fine man was Sir Thomas More — Sir Thomas More died laughing, you remember.[12] [r]Also in the *Absurdities* of Ravisius Textor,[13] there[r] is a long list of characters who came to the same magnificent end.[s] Do[p] you know,

---

x   single huge *(A)*
y ... y   glass, and glancing *(A)*
z   streams *(A)*
a ... a   *Omitted (A)*
b ... b   and subdued *(A)*
c   *Omitted (A)*
d   *After this a new paragraph:* Here then had the hand of genius been at work. — A wilderness — a chaos of beauty was before me; a sense of dreamy and incoherent grandeur took possession of my soul, and I remained speechless. *(A, in a new paragraph);* Here then had the hand of genius been at work. A chaos — a wilderness of beauty lay before me. A sense of dreamy and incoherent grandeur took possession of my soul, and I remained within the doorway speechless. *(B, C, D, not a new paragraph)*
e ... e   *Omitted (A)*

f   pointing *(A)*
g ... g   seat, *(A, B, C, D)*
h   at full-length *omitted (A)*
i ... i   There was, I thought, a tincture of bitterness in the laugh, and *(A)*
j   *bienseance (A, B, C, D, F) accent added from E*
k ... k   welcome. *new paragraph* "Ha! ha! ha! — ha! ha! ha!" continued he. "I see you are surprised, *(A)*
l   *Omitted (A)*
m ... m   architecture — in *(A)*
n   drunk, eh,/drunk *(A)*
o   But/Ha! ha! ha! *(A)*
p ... p   pardon me — I must laugh or die — perhaps both," continued he, after a pause. "Do *(A)*
q   me, my dear sir, *(B, C, D)*
r ... r   Also there *(B, C, D)*
s   end, in the Absurdities of Ravisius Textor. *(B, C, D)*

however," continued[t] he, musingly, "that at Sparta (which is now Palæochori,) at Sparta, I say, to the west of the citadel, among [u]a chaos of scarcely[u] visible ruins, is a kind of *socle*,[v] upon which are still legible[w] the letters ΛΑΣΜ. They [x]are undoubtedly[x] part of ΓΕΛΑΣΜΑ .[y] [z]Now, at Sparta were a thousand temples and shrines to a thousand different divinities. How exceedingly strange that the altar of Laughter should have survived all the others![14] But in the present instance," he resumed, with a singular alteration of voice and [a]manner, "I[a] have no right to be merry at your expense. You might well have been amazed. Europe cannot produce anything so fine as this, my little regal cabinet.[15] My other apartments are by no means of the same order — mere *ultras* of fashionable insipidity.[z] This is better than fashion — is it not? Yet this has but to be seen to become the rage — that is,[b] with those who could afford it at the cost[c] of their entire patrimony. I[d] have [e]guarded, however,[e] against any such [f]profanation. With one[f] exception, you are the only human being besides [g]myself and my *valet*,[g] who has [h]been admitted within the mysteries of these imperial precincts, since they have been bedizzened as you see!"[h]

I bowed in acknowledgment — for the [i]overpowering sense of splendor and perfume, and music, together with the unexpected eccentricity of his address and manner, prevented me from expressing,[i] in words, my appreciation of what I might have construed into a compliment.

---

t   said *(A)*
u . . . u   the scarce *(A)*
v   socle, *(A)*
w   visible *(A)*
x . . . x   are, I verily believe, *(A)*
y   *The two Greek words are corrected from A, B, C*
z . . . z   How many divinities had altars at Sparta, and how strange that that of Laughter should be found alone surviving! But just now, to be sure, I have no right to be surprized at your astonishment. Europe — the world, cannot rival this my regal cabinet. My other apartments, however, are mere matters of fact — ultras of fashionable insipidity. *(A)*
a . . . a   manner — in the present

instance I *(B, C, D)*
b   is to say, *(A)*
c   expense *(A)*
d   But I *(A)*
e . . . e   guarded *(A)*
f . . . f   profanation, with one exception" — (here the pallor of death rapidly overspread his countenance, and as rapidly spread away) — "with one *(A)*
g . . . g   myself, *(A, B, C, D)*
h . . . h   ever set foot within its imperial precincts." *(A)*; been admitted within the mysteries of these imperial precincts." *(B, C, D)*
i . . . i   unexpected eccentricity of his address and manner, had filled me with amazement, and I could not express *(A)*

"Here," he resumed,[j] arising and leaning on[k] my arm as he sauntered around the apartment, "here are paintings [l]from the Greeks[l] to Cimabue,[16] and from Cimabue to the present hour. Many are chosen, as you see, with little deference to the opinions of Virtu.[m] [n]They are all, however, fitting tapestry for a chamber such as this.[n] Here, too, are some *chefs d'œuvre*[o] of the unknown great; and here,[p] unfinished designs by men, celebrated in their day, whose very names the perspicacity of the academies has left to silence and to me.[17] What think you," said he, turning abruptly[q] as he spoke — "what think you of this Madonna della Pietà?"[r]

"It is Guido's own!" I said, with all the enthusiasm of my nature, for I had been poring intently over its surpassing loveliness. "It is Guido's own! — how *could* you have obtained it?[18] she is undoubtedly in painting what the Venus is in sculpture."

"Ha!" said he, thoughtfully, "the Venus[19] — the beautiful Venus? — [s]the Venus of the Medici?[t] — she of [u]the diminutive head and[u] the gilded hair?[v] Part of the left arm (here his voice dropped so as to be heard with difficulty,)[s] and all the right, are restorations; and in the coquetry of that right arm lies, I think, the quintessence of all[w] affectation. [x]Give *me* the Canova![x] [20] The [y]Apollo, too, is a copy[21] — there can be no doubt of it — blind fool that I am, who cannot behold the boasted inspiration of the Apollo! I cannot help — pity me! — I cannot help preferring the Antinous.[22] Was it not Socrates who said that the statuary found his statue in the block

---

j   he resumed,/said he, *(A)*
k   upon *(A)*
l . . . l   of all ages, from the Greek painters *(A)*
m   Vertu. *(A); Virtû. (B, C, D, E)*
n . . . n   *Omitted (A)*
o   *chef-dœuvres (A); chéf d'œuvres (B, C, D, E); chef d'oeuvres (F)*
p   there, *(A)*
q   *Omitted (A)*
r   Pieta?" *(A, F); Pietà?" (B, C, D, E)*
s . . . s   the Venus of Venuses! — the Venus de Medicis! — the work of Cleomenes, the son of the Athenian! as much as it is the work of mine own hands! — part of the left arm, *(A)*
t   Medicis? *(B, C)*

u . . . u   *Omitted (B, C, D)*
v   hair? — the work of Cleomenes, the son of the Athenian? *(B) changed in C*
w   *Omitted (A)*
x . . . x   *Omitted (A)*
y . . . y   Apollo too! — you spoke of Apollo! — it is a copy; there can be no reasonable doubt of it. Sir, I will not bow to falsity, although begrimed with age — there is *no* inspiration in the boasted Apollo, and the Antinous is worth a dozen of it. After all, there is much in the saying of Socrates — 'that the statuary found his statue in the block of marble.' Michel Angelo was not *(A)*

of marble?[23] Then Michæl Angelo was by no means[y] original in his couplet —

'Non ha l'ottimo artista alcun[z] concetto
Che un marmo solo in se non circonscriva.' "[a] [24]

It has been, or should be remarked, that, in the manner of the true gentleman, we are always aware of a difference from the bearing of the vulgar, without being[b] at once precisely able[c] to determine in what such difference consists. Allowing the remark to have applied in its full force to the outward demeanor of my acquaintance,[d] I felt it, on that eventful morning, still more fully applicable to his moral temperament and character. Nor can[e] I better define that peculiarity of spirit which seemed to place him so essentially apart from all other human beings, than by calling it a *habit*[f] of intense and continual thought, pervading even his most trivial actions — intruding upon his moments of dalliance — and interweaving itself with[g] his very flashes of merriment — like[h] adders which writhe from out the eyes of the grinning masks in the cornices around the temples of Persepolis.[i] [25]

I could not help, however, repeatedly observing, through the mingled tone of levity and solemnity with which he rapidly descanted upon[j] matters of little importance, a certain air of trepidation — [k]a degree of nervous *unction*[l] in action and in speech — an unquiet excitability of manner which appeared to me at all times unaccountable, and upon some occasions[k] even filled me with alarm. Frequently, too,[m] pausing in the middle of a sentence whose commencement he had apparently forgotten, he seemed to be listening in the deepest attention, as if either in momentary[n] expectation of a visiter, or to sounds which must have had existence in his[o] imagination alone.[26]

---

z   aleun *(A)*
a   circunscriva *(A, B, C, D, E, F)*
misprint
b   being able *(A)*
c   *Omitted (A)*
d   friend, *(A)*
e   could *(A)*
f   habit *(A)*
g   into *(A)*
h   like the *(A)*

i   Cybele. *(A)*
j   on *(A)*
k . . . k   a nervous inquietude of manner, which appeared to me unaccountable, and at times *(A)*
l   *intensity (B, C)*
m   Frequently, too,/Frequently *(A)*
n   *Omitted (A)*
o   *Omitted (A)*

TALES OF THE FOLIO CLUB

It was during one of these[p] reveries or pauses of apparent[q] abstraction, that, in turning over a page of [r]the poet and scholar[r] Politian's beautiful tragedy, "The Orfeo," [s](the first native Italian tragedy,)[s] which lay near me upon an ottoman, I discovered[t] a passage underlined in pencil. It was[u] a passage [v]towards the end[v] of the third act — a passage of the most[w] heart-stirring excitement[x] — a passage which, [y]although tainted with[y] impurity, no man shall[z] read without a [a]thrill of novel emotion — no woman[a] without a sigh.[27] The whole page was blotted with fresh tears; and, upon the opposite interleaf, were the following [b]English[c] lines, written[b] in a hand so very different from the peculiar[d] characters of my acquaintance, that I had some[e] difficulty in recognising it as his own: —[28]

> Thou wast that all to me, love,
> For which my soul did pine —
> A green isle in the sea, love,
> A fountain and a shrine,
> All wreathed [f]with fairy fruits and[f] flowers;
> And [g]all the flowers[g] were mine.
>
> [h]Ah, dream too bright to[h] last!
> [i]Ah, starry Hope, that didst arise[i]
> But to be overcast!
> A voice from out the Future cries,
> "Onward!" — but[j] o'er the Past
> (Dim gulf!) my spirit hovering lies,
> Mute — motionless — aghast!
>
> For alas! alas! with me
> [k]The light of life[k] is o'er.
> "No more — no more — no more,"
> (Such language holds the solemn[l] sea

---

p these apparent *(A)*
q *Omitted (A)*
r...r *Omitted (A)*
s...s *Omitted (A)*
t found *(A)*
u is *(A)*
v...v near the conclusion *(A)*
w of the most/of *(A)*
x pathos *(A)*
y...y divested of its *(A)*
z could *(A)*
a...a thrill — no maiden *(A)*
b...b lines written, as I now write them, in English; but *(A)*

c *Omitted (B, C, D)*
d peculiar and bold *(A)*
e *Omitted (A)*
f...f round with wild *(A);* around about with *(B, C, D)*
g...g the flowers — they all *(B, C, D)*
h...h But the dream — it could not *(A, B, C, D)*
i...i Young Hope! thou did'st arise *(A);* And the star of Hope did rise *(B, C, D)*
j while *(A, B, C, D)*
k...k Ambition — all — *(A, B, C, D)*
l breaking *(A)*

THE ASSIGNATION

To the sands upon the shore,)
Shall bloom the thunder-blasted tree,
Or the stricken eagle soar!

Now[m] all my hours are trances;
And all my nightly dreams
Are where the[n] dark eye glances,
And where thy footstep gleams,
In what ethereal[o] dances,
By what[p] Italian streams.

Alas! for that accursed time
They bore thee o'er the billow,
From Love[q] to titled age and crime,
And an unholy pillow! —
From me,[r] and from our misty clime.
Where weeps the silver willow!

That these lines were written in English — a language with which I [s]had not believed[s] their author acquainted — afforded me little matter for surprise. I was too well aware of the extent[t] of his acquirements, [u]and of the singular[u] pleasure he took in conceal-ing[v] them from observation,[w] to be astonished at any similar dis-covery; [x]but the place of date, I must confess, occasioned me no little amazement.[x] It had been originally[y] written *London*,[z] and afterwards carefully overscored — [a]not, however,[a] so effectually as to conceal the word from a scrutinizing eye. [b]I say, this occasioned me no little amazement; for I well remember that, in a former conver-sation with my friend, I particularly inquired if he had at any

---

m   And *(A, B, C, D)*
n   thy *(A)*
o   etherial *(A)*
p   far *(A)*
q   me — *(A)*
r   Love, *(A)*
s . . . s   did not believe *(A)*
t   variety *(A)*
u . . . u   as well as the strange *(A)*
v   hiding *(A)*
w   the world, *(A)*
x . . . x   But I must confess that the date of the M.S. appeared to me singular. *(A)*
y   *Omitted (A)*
z   "London," *(A)*
a . . . a   although not *(A);* but not,

however, *(B, C, D)*
b . . . b   I repeat that this appeared to me singular — for I well remembered having asked him if he had ever met with, some person — I think, the Marchesa di Mentoni, who resided in England some years before her marriage — if he had, at any time, met with her in London; and his answer led me to understand that he had never visited Great Britain. I must here add that I have more than once heard, but, of course, never gave credit to a report involving so much improbability — that the person of whom I write, was not only by birth, but in education an Englishman. *(A)*

· 1 6 3 ·

time met in London the Marchesa di Mentoni, (who for some years previous to her marriage had resided in that city,) when his answer, if I mistake not, gave me to understand that he had never visited the metropolis of Great Britain. I might as well here mention, that I have more than once heard, (without, of course, giving credit to a report involving so many improbabilities,) that the person of whom I speak[c] was not only by birth, but in education, an *Englishman.*[b]

*   *   *   *   *   *

"There is one painting," said he, [d]without being aware of my notice of the tragedy[d] — "there is still one painting which you have not seen." And throwing aside a drapery, he discovered a full-length portrait of the Marchesa Aphrodite.[f]

Human art could have done no more in the[g] delineation of her superhuman beauty. The same ethereal[h] figure which stood before me the preceding night upon the steps of the Ducal Palace, stood before me once again. But in the expression of the[i] countenance, which was beaming all over with smiles, there still lurked [k](incomprehensible anomaly!) that fitful stain[k] of melancholy which [l]will ever be found[l] inseparable from the perfection of the beautiful.[m] Her right arm lay[n] folded over[o] her [p]bosom. With her[p] left she pointed downward[q] to a curiously fashioned vase.[29] One small, fairy foot, alone visible, barely touched the earth; and, scarcely discernible in the brilliant atmosphere which seemed to encircle and enshrine her loveliness, floated a pair of the most[r] delicately imagined wings.[s] My glance fell[t] from the painting to the figure of my friend, and the vigorous[u] words of Chapman's *Bussy D'Ambois,*[v] quivered instinctively upon my lips:

---

c   speak *(F) comma deleted to follow B, C, D, E*
d . . . d   turning to me with evident emotion, as I replaced the volume upon the Ottoman *(A)*
e   *Omitted (A)*
f   di Mentoni. *(A)*
g   the accurate *(A)*
h   sylph-like *(A)*
i   her *(A)*
j . . . j   *Omitted (A)*
k . . . k   that incomprehensible strain *(A)*
l . . . l   is, I do believe, *(A)*

m   *After this:* On a scroll which lay at her feet were these words — "I am waiting but for thee." *(A)*
n   was *(A)*
o   across *(A)*
p . . . p   bosom, and with the *(A)*
q   downwards *(A, B, C, D)*
r   the most *omitted (A)*
s   silvery wings. *(A)*
t   My glance fell/I glanced *(A)*
u   powerful *(A)*
v   Bussy D'Ambois, *(A)*

THE ASSIGNATION

"He is^w up
There^x like a Roman statue! He^y will stand
'Till Death hath made him^z marble!"^{30}

"Come," he said at length, ^{a}turning towards a table of richly enamelled and massive silver,^{a} upon which were ^{b}a few goblets fantastically stained,^{b} together with two large Etruscan vases, ^{c}fashioned in the same extraordinary model as that in the foreground of the portrait, and filled with what I supposed to be Johannisberger.^{c} ^{31} "Come," he said, abruptly, "let us drink! It is early — but let us drink. It is *indeed*^{d} early," he continued, musingly,^{e} as a cherub with a heavy golden hammer made the apartment^f ring with the first hour after sunrise: "it is *indeed* early — but what matters it? let us drink! Let us pour out^g an offering to yon^h solemn sun which the gaudy^i lamps and censers are ^{j}so eager to subdue!"^{j} And,^{k} having made me pledge him in a bumper, he swallowed in rapid succession several goblets of the wine.

"To dream," ^{l}he continued,^{l} resuming the tone of his desultory conversation, as he held up to the rich light of a censer one of the magnificent vases — "to dream has been the business of my life.^{m} I have therefore framed^n for myself, as you see, a bower of dreams. In^o the heart of Venice could I have erected a better? You behold around you, it is true, a medley of architectural embellishments. The chastity of Ionia is offended by antediluvian devices, and the sphynxes of Egypt are outstretched^p upon carpets^q of gold. Yet the effect is incongruous to the timid alone. Proprieties of place, and^r especially of time, are the bugbears which terrify mankind from

---

w   I am *(A)*
x   Here *(A)*
y   I *(A)*
z   me *(A)*
a . . . a   approaching a table of massy silver, *(A)*
b . . . b   some beautifully dyed and enamelled goblets, *(A)*
c . . . c   filled with what I took to be Vin de Barac, and fashioned in the same extraordinary model as the vase in the foreground of the portrait. *(A) B and C are like F but have* Johannisberger./Vin de Barac.
d   indeed *(A)*

e   *Omitted (A);* thoughtfully *(B, C, D)*
f   chamber *(A)*
g   out, like true Persians, *(A)*
h   that *(A);* the *(B, C, D)*
i   *Omitted (A)*
j . . . j   struggling to overpower." *(A)*
k   And,/Here *(A)*
l . . . l   continued he, *(A)*
m   life, and *(A)*
n   decked out *(A)*
o   Here, in *(A)*
p   stretching *(A, B, C, D)*
q   cloth *(A)*
r   *Omitted (A)*

the contemplation of the magnificent. Once I was myself a decorist; but that sublimation of folly has palled upon my soul. All this is now the fitter for my purpose. Like these arabesque censers, my spirit is writhing in fire, and the[s] delirium of this scene is fashioning me for the wilder visions of that land of real dreams whither I am now[t] rapidly departing." [u]He here paused abruptly, bent his head to his bosom, and seemed to listen to a sound which I could not hear. At length, erecting his frame, he looked upwards, and ejaculated the lines of the Bishop of Chichester:

> *"Stay for me there! I will not fail*
> *To meet thee in that hollow vale."*[u]

[v]In the next instant, confessing[v] the power of the wine, he[w] threw himself at full-length upon an ottoman.[x]

A quick step was now heard upon the staircase, and a loud knock at the door rapidly succeeded. I was hastening[y] to anticipate a second disturbance, when a page of [z]Mentoni's household[z] burst into the room, and[a] faltered [b]out, in a voice choking with emotion the[b] incoherent words, [c]"My mistress! — my mistress! — Poisoned! — poisoned! Oh, beautiful — oh, beautiful Aphrodite!"[c]

Bewildered, I flew to the ottoman, and endeavored to arouse the sleeper[d] to a sense of the startling intelligence. [e]But his limbs were rigid — his lips were livid — his lately beaming eyes were riveted in *death*.[e] I staggered back towards the table — my hand fell upon a cracked and blackened goblet — and a consciousness of the entire and terrible truth flashed suddenly over my soul.[32]

NOTES

Motto: *(A)* The first of the two German mottoes of the earliest version is not from Schiller but from Adelbert von Chamisso, *Frauen Liebe und Leben*

---

s   the whirling *(A)*
t   *Omitted (A)*
u . . . u   *Omitted (A, B, C, D)*
v . . . v   Thus saying, he confessed *(A, B, C, D)*
w   and *(A, B, C, D)*
x   an ottoman./a *chaise-longue. (A)*
y   was hastening/hurried *(A)*
z . . . z   the Marchesa di Mentoni *(A)*

a   and, in a voice choking with emotion, *(A)*
b . . . b   out the *(A)*
c . . . c   "my mistress! — Bianca! — poison! horrible! horrible!" *(A)*
d   the sleeper/him *(A)*
e . . . e   but his lips were livid — his form was rigid — his beautiful eyes were rivetted in death. *(A)*

THE ASSIGNATION

(1830), VIII, 7. The second is from Goethe's ballad "Das Veilchen," lines 19–20. The poem was quoted in full by George Bancroft, with a translation, in his "Life and Genius of Goethe" in the *North American Review* (October 1824). The same two lines were misquoted and humorously misascribed to Schiller by Poe in "How to Write a Blackwood Article." In both uses he adapts the translation to his own purposes.

(F) Poe doubtless knew "The Exequy" of Henry King (1592–1669) through some anthology; he quotes lines 89–90 here, and cites another passage in his "Reply to Outis" in 1845.

1. Compare *Measure for Measure*, II, iii, 11, "Who falling in the flames of her own youth" — a passage quoted in Poe's early manuscript of selected lines from Shakespeare (see "The Bargain Lost," n. 1). The reading "flames" is an emendation that goes back to Sir William Davenant, and is supported by *All's Well That Ends Well*, IV, ii, 5–6, although it was not adopted by Kittredge. See also Byron, *Childe Harold*, III, lxxviii, 1–3,

> His love was passion's essence, as a tree
> On fire by lightning; with ethereal flame
> Kindled he was, and blasted.

2. Andrea Palladio (1518–1580), Italian architect, had great influence in Poe's America.

3. Compare "Romance," line 11, "eternal Condor years," and "The Conqueror Worm," lines 15–16, "Flapping from out their Condor wings/Invisible Wo!"

4. Aphrodite is a name sometimes borne by modern Greek women. It is the name of the heroine of *The Young Duke* (1831) by Benjamin Disraeli. The name Bianca in the earliest version is appropriate for the lady's purity.

5. "Intriguing" meant "plotting" in Poe's day, and Mentoni's name suggests lying.

6. The comparison of curly hair to the florets of the hyacinth can be traced back to Homer (*Odyssey*, VI, 231). Poe used the allusion in "To Helen" (see Mabbott, I, 166, 170) and again in "Ligeia," below.

7. The Niobe is a celebrated group at Florence, thought to be a copy of an original by Praxiteles or Scopas.

8. Compare Byron, *Childe Harold*, III, xxxiii, 1–3,

> Even as a broken mirror, which the glass
> In every fragment multiplies; and makes
> A thousand images of one that was.

9. See Horace Smith, *Zillah* (1828), III, 220, "what Pliny calls the soft and almost liquid Acanthus." Pliny the Younger, *Epistolae*, V, vi, 16, calls the acanthus *mollis et paene dixerim, liquidus*.

10. The Emperor Commodus, like his mother Faustina II, wife of Marcus Aurelius, was very beautiful in form and features. For an explanation of Hebrew medallions, mentioned in the first version *(A)*, see note 6 on "Ligeia," to which Poe transferred the allusion.

11. Compare the palace of "The Masque of the Red Death." The "cloth of Chili gold" is probably from the province of Chihli in China.

12. See William Roper, *The Mirrour of Vertue in Worldly Greatnes; or the life of Sir Thomas More* (Paris, 1626), near the end: Sir Thomas "turned . . . a cheerful countenance, and said . . . my neck is very short, take heed, therefore, thou strikest not awry, for saving of thyne honesty." There was a sketch of Sir (now St.) Thomas More in *The Lady's Book* for November 1833.

13. Poe refers to a chapter (II, lxxxvii) "De gaudio et risu mortuis" in the *Theatrum Poetarum . . . sive Officina Io. Ravisii Textoris* (Paris, 1520). The work is a handbook of classical lore by Jean Tixtier, Seigneur de Ravisy, who died in 1524. Poe must have used a source that called Ravisius' writings "absurdities" and from it mistakenly took the word for a title.

14. Plutarch *(Parallel Lives)* records of Lycurgus that Sosibius said he dedicated a little statue of Laughter at Sparta. The remains of its pedestal are not now known, but, as Alfred G. Engstrom pointed out *(MLN,* November 1954) Chateaubriand thought he had found it. The word socle is in both his *Itinéraire* (1811) and Poe's probable source, the translation by Shoberl (Philadelphia, 1813), p. 117, but in neither is it italicized.

15. There were and still are important works of art in the palazzo Byron occupied in Venice. Poe's hero's collection, described in the next few paragraphs, was impossible, since it included what were already national treasures. But it is significant that Poe, who had seen few great pictures or sculptures, perceived that the best works of art can be grouped together harmoniously, without regard to schools.

16. Giovanni Cimabue (1240–1302) was the Florentine "reviver of painting."

17. The unknown painters are described in a phrase reminiscent of Gray's *Elegy,* line 4, "And leaves the world to darkness and to me," also echoed in "The Coliseum," line 32.

18. This Madonna is a masterpiece of Guido Reni (1575–1642) now in the Gallery of his native Bologna. It is very large, over ten by twenty feet. Poe probably knew it from an engraving, and may have been unaware of its size.

19. The Venus de Medici is said in the epigraph on the pedestal to be by "Cleomenes son of Apollodorus the Athenian" (a name Poe gave in the first and second version). This inscription is now thought to be a Renaissance forgery. See also "Ligeia," on Cleomenes.

20. Antonio Canova's Venus (1805) is really a nude portrait of Pauline Bonaparte, riding on a lion's back. For a contemporary opinion, see Byron's observation in *Childe Harold,* IV, lv, 9, "Such as the great of yore, Canova is today."

21. The Apollo Belvidere is meant; it is surely a Roman copy. Many people think the statue looks like Lord Byron.

22. Antinoüs, the favorite of Hadrian, was given divine honors in the Hellenic parts of the Empire and commemorated by statues and coins. Canova, among others, used him as a subject.

23. According to Diogenes Laertius in his second book of *Lives,* "Socrates," section XVI: "[Socrates] often said that he wondered at those who made stone statues, when he saw how careful they were that the stone should be like the man it was intended to represent, but how careless they were of themselves, as to guarding against being like the stone."

24. Michelangelo's Sonnet is numbered xv in J. A. Symonds' translation. "The best of artists does not have a concept, that the marble block does not circumscribe." Poe mentions this in a letter of August 18, 1844 to Lowell, and in "Marginalia," number 79 (*Democratic Review,* December 1844, p. 586).

25. On Persepolis compare "Al Aaraaf," II, 36, and Poe's note (Mabbott I, 107, 121).

26. Compare "hearkening to imaginary sounds/And phantom voices" in *Politian,* VI, 23f., and "listening to some imaginary sound" in "The Fall of the House of Usher."

27. For the passage in the *Orfeo,* II, 19–26, see Mabbott I, 212–213. In Poe's day Angelo Poliziano's poem was divided into acts. Poe hardly had the tragedy before him, for it contains nothing to blush about.

28. Poe himself had two or more styles of handwriting. The "English lines" are one of his most often reprinted poems, best known under the title, "To One in Paradise." In the separately printed versions the fifth stanza is omitted. The poem is closely related to lines Byron wrote out for Mary Chaworth; for further annotation see Mabbott I, 211–216.

29. In the earliest version the Marchesa has a scroll at her feet. Compare the earliest version of "To Helen," where Psyche holds a scroll.

30. *Bussy D'Ambois,* V, iv, 96–98, reads:

> ...I am up.
> Here, like a Roman statue I will stand
> Till death hath made me marble.

Poe gave the quotation more correctly in the first version of his tale.

31. Johannisberger, a favorite in Poe's stories, is one of the finest of all Rhine wines. In early versions he names Vin de Barac (properly Barsac), a wine also named in "Lionizing" and "William Wilson."

32. Medieval Venetian glass was supposed to break if filled with poison.

LIONIZING

"Lionizing" is often considered the best of Poe's humorous stories, the only one of them selected by Evert A. Duyckinck for inclusion among the stories he chose for the 1845 *Tales.* Poe revised it with great skill and care, and it is amusing even today; the fun can be appreciated on its own account, without knowledge of the background of the satire. The piece is obviously a quiz on N. P. Willis, and is also a parody on a story by Bulwer.

Willis went abroad in 1831, and sent home to the *New York Mirror* a series of newsletters, known when collected in book form as *Pencillings by the Way*. He got into a duel, happily bloodless, with the novelist Captain Marryat. More important to him was the friendship of Lady Blessington. That once world-renowned widow wrote books and edited annuals, to one of which even Tennyson contributed. Now she is remembered chiefly for her salons in London. Believing that some ladies, disapproving of her supposed liaison with Count D'Orsay, would not come to her parties, she invited gentlemen only. Through her Willis met most of the English literati.

Woodberry (*Edgar Allan Poe*, 1885, p. 85, and *Life*, I, 130) pointed out a leading source of part of Poe's story in Bulwer's "Too Handsome for Anything," one of the "other pieces" in Bulwer's book, *Conversations with an Ambitious Student in Ill Health, with Other Pieces* (New York: J. & J. Harper, 1832), pp. 189ff.

A most beautiful creature was Mr. Ferdinand Fitzroy! Such eyes — such hair — such teeth — such a figure — such manners, too, — and such an irresistible way of tying his neckcloth! ... [But his schoolmaster said] ... "he is a great deal too handsome ever to be a scholar."

[It is proposed to] let him go to the bar ... The Lord Chancellor ... said ... "no, no, that will never do! — Send him into the army" ... So they bought Mr. Ferdinand Fitzroy a cornetcy ... They sent him to riding-school, and every body laughed at him.

"He is a d — d ass!" said Cornet Horsephiz, who was very ugly; "A horrid puppy!" said Lieutenant St. Squintem, who was still uglier; "If he does not ride better, he will disgrace the regiment!" said Captain Rivalhate, who was very good-looking; "If he does not ride better, we will cut him!" said Colonel Everdrill, who was a wonderful martinet ...

And Mr. Ferdinand Fitzroy was accordingly cut.

Our hero was a youth of susceptibility — he quitted the — Regiment, and challenged the Colonel. The Colonel was killed!

"What a terrible blackguard is Mr. Ferdinand Fitzroy!" said the Colonel's relations.

"Very true!" said the world.

The parents were in despair! ... They borrowed some thousands from the uncle, and bought his beautiful nephew a seat in Parliament ...

LIONIZING

He rose to speak.

"What a handsome fellow!" whispered one member.

"Ah, a coxcomb!" said another . . .

Discouraged by his reception, Mr. Ferdinand Fitzroy grew a little embarrassed.

"Poor devil!" said the civilest of the set . . . "By Jove he is going to speak again — this will never do; we must cough him down!"

And Mr. Ferdinand Fitzroy was accordingly coughed down.

Our hero was now seven or eight-and-twenty, handsomer than ever, and the adoration of all the young ladies at Almack's.

The rest of the story — Ferdinand's vain efforts to marry an heiress, disinheritance by his uncle, and final imprisonment for debt — was not used by Poe.

There is a good deal of humorous literature about noses. Poe undoubtedly knew "Slawkenbergius' Tale" in *Tristram Shandy* by Laurence Sterne, and also most probably knew Robert Macnish's "Man With the Nose" in *Blackwood's Magazine* for August 1826.* Since Poe's tale was one of the Folio Club stories and probably one of the group of eleven he mentioned when he sent "Epimanes" to the Buckinghams in May 1833, I think it unlikely that it owed anything to a once famous *jeu d'esprit* by James Gates Percival — "Lecture Extraordinary Upon Nosology," satirizing a phrenologist named Barber — which was first published in the New Haven *Daily Herald,* August 17, 1833.†

Poe commented on the general meaning of his story several times. In one unsigned review of the number of the *Southern Literary Messenger* that contained it he said, "Lionizing . . . is an admirable piece of burlesque which displays much reading, a lively humor, and an ability to afford amusement or instruction"; and in another puff he remarked, "It is an extravaganza . . . and gives evidence of high powers of fancy and humor."‡ To J. P. Kennedy he wrote on February 11, 1836 that it was a satire "properly speak-

---

* See Maxwell Morton, *A Builder of the Beautiful* (1928), p. 39. [For later discussion see Richard P. Benton, "Poe's 'Lionizing'; A Quiz on Willis and Lady Blessington," *Studies in Short Fiction,* Spring 1968, and G. R. Thompson, "On the Nose. . ." with Benton's reply, *ibid.,* Fall 1968.]

† Reprinted by Julius H. Ward in *Life and Letters of . . . Percival* (1866), pp. 408–411.

‡ *Baltimore Republican,* June 13 and 15, respectively.

ing — at least so meant — ... of the rage for Lions and the facility of becoming one."

"The Successful Novel!!" by F. (Theodore S. Fay), in the *New-York Mirror,* April 9, 1836, is a burlesque of "Lionizing." Whether Poe's story had any influence on *Nasology or Hints towards the Classification of Noses* by Eden Warwick, published by Bentley in London in 1848 (and noticed in the New York *Literary World,* August 26 of that year) I have not ascertained.

TEXTS

(A) Southern Literary Messenger, May 1835 (1:515–516); *(B) Tales of the Grotesque and Arabesque* (1840), I, 19–25; *(C)* PHANTASY-PIECES (copy of the last with manuscript changes, 1842); *(D) Broadway Journal,* March 15, 1845 (1:164–166); *(E) Tales* (1845), pp. 58–63; *(F) Works* (1850), II, 392–397.

The earliest version *(A)* and the latest authorized *(E)* are printed in full.

Poe made a number of verbal changes in his text for the *Tales of the Grotesque and Arabesque,* added a few more for the proposed PHANTASY-PIECES, revised the tale considerably for publication in the *Broadway Journal,* and made still further changes for the slim volume of *Tales* issued later in 1845.

Variants of the second and third versions are recorded against the first, variants of the fourth against the fifth. Griswold's *(F)* was merely reprinted from the *Tales* without change. Of the six punctuation changes made in PHANTASY-PIECES, three were adopted in later printings.

LION-IZING. A TALE. [A]

———— all people went
Upon their ten toes in wild wonderment.
Bishop Hall's Satires.

I am — that is to say, I *was,* a great man. But I am neither the author of Junius, nor the man in the mask — for my name is Thomas[a] Smith, and I was born somewhere in the city of Fum-Fudge. The first action of my life was the taking hold of my nose with both hands. My mother saw this and called me a genius. My father wept for joy, and bought me a treatise on Nosology. Before I was breeched I had not only mastered the treatise, but had col-

---

Title: Lionizing (B, C)   a John (C)

lected into a common-place book all that is said on the subject, by Pliny, Aristotle, Alexander Ross, Minutius Felix, Hermanus Pictorius, Del Rio, Villarêt, Bartholinus, and Sir Thomas Browne.[b]

I now began to feel my way in the science, and soon came to understand, that, provided a man had a nose sufficiently big, he might, by merely following it, arrive at a Lionship. But my attention was not confined to theories alone. Every morning I took a dram or two, and gave my proboscis a couple of pulls. When I came of age my father [c]sent for me to[c] his study.

'My son' — said he —[d] 'what is the chief end of your existence?'

'Father' — I said — 'it is the study of Nosology.'

'And what, Thomas'[e] — he continued — 'is Nosology?'[f]

'Sir' — I replied — 'it is the Science of Noses.'

'And can you tell me' — he asked — 'what is the meaning of a nose?'

'A nose, my father' — said I — 'has been variously defined, by about a thousand different authors.[g] It is now noon, or thereabouts. We shall therefore[h] have time enough to get through with them all by[i] midnight. To [j]commence: —[j] The nose, according to Bartholinus, is that protuberance, that bump, that excrescence, that' ———

'That will do Thomas'[k] — said [l]my father.[l] 'I am positively[m] thunderstruck at the extent of your information — I am,[n] upon my soul. Come here! (and he took me by the arm.) Your education may[o] be considered as finished, and it is high time[p] you should scuffle for yourself — so — so — so (here he kicked me down stairs and out of the door,) so get out of my house, and God bless you!'

As I felt within me the divine *afflatus,* I considered this accident rather fortunate than otherwise, and determined to follow my nose.

---

b   The authors here named have all really treated, at some length, of the nose. *Footnote added (C)*
c . . . c   asked me, one day, if I would step into *(B, C)*
d   he —/he, when we got there, *(B);* he, when we were seated, *(C)*
e   John" *(C)*
f   nosology?" *(B) Changed back to upper case in C*
g   authors. (here I pulled out my watch). *(B);* authors. (Here I pulled out my watch). *(C)*
h   *Omitted (B, C)*
i   before *(B, C)*
j . . . j   commence, then. *(B, C)*
k   John" *(C)*
l . . . l   the old gentleman. *(B, C)*
m   *Omitted (B, C)*
n   am positively — *(B, C)*
o   may now *(B, C)*
p   time that *(B, C)*

So I gave it a pull or two, and wrote a pamphlet on Nosology. [q]All Fum-Fudge was in an uproar.

'Wonderful genius!' — said the Quarterly.

'Superb physiologist!' — said the New Monthly.

'Fine writer!' — said the Edinburg.[r]

'Great man!' — said Blackwood.

'*Who* can he be?' — said Mrs. Bas-Bleu.

'*What* can he be?' — said big Miss Bas-Bleu.

'*Where* can he be?' — said little Miss Bas-Bleu.

But I paid them no manner of attention, and walked into the shop of an artist.

The Duchess of Bless-my-soul was sitting for her portrait. The Marchioness of So-and-so was holding the Duchess's poodle. The Earl of This-and-that was flirting with her salts, and His Royal Highness of Touch-me-not was standing behind her chair. I merely walked towards the artist, and held up my proboscis.

'O beautiful!' — sighed the [s]Duchess of Bless-my-soul.[s]

'O pretty!' — lisped the [t]Marchioness of So-and-so.[t]

'Horrible!'[u] — groaned the [v]Earl of This-and-that.[v]

'Abominable!'[w] — growled his [x]Highness of Touch-me-not.[x]

'What will you take for it?' — said the artist.

'A thousand pounds' — said I, sitting down.

'A thousand pounds?' — he inquired, turning the nose to the light.

'Precisely' — said I.

'Beautiful!' — said he, looking at the nose.

'A thousand pounds' — said I, twisting it to one side.

'Admirable!' — said he.

'A thousand pounds' — said I.

'You shall have them' — said he — 'what a piece of Virtû!'[y] So he paid me the money, and made a sketch of my nose. I took rooms in Jermyn street, sent his[z] Majesty the ninety-ninth edition

---

q   *New paragraph (C)*
r   Edinburgh. *(B, C)*
s . . . s   Duchess. *(B, C)*
t . . . t   Marchioness. *(B, C)*
u   "O horrible!" *(B, C)*

v . . . v   *Earl. (B, C)*
w   "O abominable!" *(B, C)*
x . . . x   Royal Highness. *(B, C)*
y   virtu!" *(B, C)*
z   her *(B, C)*

of the Nosology with a portrait of the author,[a] and his Royal Highness of Touch-me-not invited me to dinner.

We were all Lions and *Recherchés*.

There was a Grand Turk from Stamboul. He said that the angels were horses, cocks, and bulls — that somebody in the sixth heaven had seventy thousand heads and seventy thousand tongues — and that the earth was held up by a sky-blue cow with[b] four hundred horns.

There was Sir Positive Paradox. He said that all fools were philosophers, and[c] all philosophers were fools.

There was a writer on Ethics. He talked of Fire, Unity, and Atoms — Bi-part, and Pre-existent soul — Affinity and Discord — primitive Intelligence and Homoomeria.

There was Theologos Theology. He talked of Eusebius and Arianus — Heresy and the Council of Nice — Consubstantialism, Homousios, and Homouioisios.

There was Fricassée from the Rocher de Cancale. He mentioned Latour, Markbrunnen and Mareschino — Muriton of red tongue, and Cauliflowers with Velouté sauce — veal *à la* St. Menehoult, Marinade *à la* St. Florentin, and orange jellies *en mosaiques*.[d]

There was Signor Tintontintino from Florence. He spoke of Cimabue,[e] Arpino, Carpaccio, and Argostino — the gloom of Caravaggio — the amenity of Albano — the golden glories of Titian — the frows of Rubens, and the waggeries of Jan Steen.

There was the great Geologist Feltzpar. He talked of [f]Hornblende, Mica-slate, Quartz, Schist, Schorl, and Pudding-stone.[f]

There was the President of the Fum-Fudge University. He said that the moon was called Bendis in Thrace, Bubastis in Egypt, Dian in Rome, and Artemis in Greece.

There was Delphinus Polyglot.[g] He told us what had become of the eighty-three lost tragedies of Æschylus — of the fifty-four orations of Isæus — of the three hundred and ninety-one speeches

---

a author's nose, *(B, C)*
b cow with/cow, having *(B, C)*
c and that *(C)*
d *mosäiques (C)*
e Cimabué, *(B, C)*
f . . . f internal fires and tertiary formations; of aeriforms, fluidiforms, and solidiforms; of quartz and marl; of schist and schorl; of gypsum, hornblende, mica-slate, and pudding-stone. *(B, C)*
g Polyglott *(B, C)*

of Lysias — of the hundred and eighty treatises of Theophrastus — of the eighth book of the Conic Sections of Apollonius — of Pindar's Hymns and Dithyrambics, and the five and forty Tragedies of Homer Junior.

There was a modern Platonist. He quoted Porphyry, Iamblichus, Plotinus, Proclus, Hierocles, Maximus, Tyrius,[h] and Syrianus.

There was a human-perfectibility man. He quoted Turgot, Price, Priestly, Condorcet, De Staël,[i] and the "Ambitious Student in rather ill[j] health."

There was myself. I talked[k] of Pictorius, Del Rio, Alexander Ross, Minutius Felix, Bartholinus, Sir Thos. Browne, and the Science of Noses.

'Marvellous clever man!' — said his Highness.

'Superb!' — said the[l] guests: and the next morning her Grace of Bless-my-soul paid me a visit.

'Will you go to Almacks,[m] pretty creature?' she said.[n]

'Certainly'[o] — said I. 'Nose and all?' — she asked.

'Positively'[p] — I replied.

'Here then is a [q]card' — she said — 'shall[q] I say you will[r] be there?'

'Dear Duchess! with all my heart.'

'Pshaw! no — but with all your nose?'

'Every bit of it, my life,'[s] — said I. So I gave it a pull or two, and found myself at Almacks.[t] The rooms were crowded to suffocation.

'He is coming!' — said somebody on the stair case.

'He is coming!' — said somebody farther[u] up.

'He is coming!' — said somebody farther[v] still.

'He is come!' — said the Duchess — 'he is come, the little love!'

---

h Maximus, Tyrius,/Maximus Tyrius, (B, C)
i De Stael (B, C)
j rather ill/Ill (B, C)
k spoke (B, C)
l his (B, C)
m Almack's, (B, C)
n said, chucking me under the chin. (B, C)
o "Upon honor," (B, C)
p "As I live," (B, C)
q...q card, my life, shall (B); card, my life; shall (C)
r will (B, C)
s love," (B, C)
t Almack's, (B, C)
u further (B, C)
v further (B, C)

And she caught me by both hands, and looked me in the nose.

'Ah joli!ʷ — said Mademoiselle Pas Seul.

'Dios guarda!' — said Don Stiletto.

'Diavolo!' — said Count Capricornuto.

'Tousand Teufel!' — said Baron Bludenuff.ˣ

'Tweedle-dee ——— tweedle-dee ——— tweedle-dum!' said the orchestra.

'Ah joli! — Dios guarda! — Diavolo! — and Tousand Teufel!' repeated Mademoiselle Pas Seul, Don Stiletto, Count Capricornuto, and Baron Bludenuff. Itʸ was too bad — it was not to be borne. I grew angry.

'Sir!' — said I to the Baron — 'you are a baboon.'

'Sir!' — replied he,ᶻ after a pause, ——— 'Donner andᵃ Blitzen!'

ᵇThis was sufficient.ᶜ The next morning I shot off his nose at six o'clock, and then called upon my friends.

'Bête!' — said the first.

'Fool!' — said the second.

'Ninny!' — said the third.

'Dolt!' — said the fourth.

'Noodle!' — said the fifth.

'Ass!' — said the sixth.

'Be off!' — said the seventh.

At all this I felt mortified, andᵈ called upon my father.

'Father' — I said — 'what is the chief end of my existence!'ᵉ

'My son' — he replied — 'it is still the study of Nosology. But in hitting the Baron's nose you have overshot your mark. You have a fine nose it is true, but then Bludenuff has none. You are d —— d, and he has became the Lion of the day. In Fum-Fudge great is a Lion with aᶠ proboscis, but ᵍgreater by far is a Lion withᵍ no proboscis at all.'

---

w 'Ah joli!/"Ah joli!" (B, C)
x Bludennuff. (B, C) Here and later
y This applause — it was obstreperous;
was not *the thing;* it (B, C)
z replied he,/he replied (B, C)
a und (B, C)
b *No paragraph (B); changed back to
paragraph (C)*

c sufficient. We exchanged cards.
(B, C)
d and so (B, C)
e existence?" (B, C)
f a big (B, C)
g . . . g he should not even attempt a
rivalry with a lion who has (C)

LIONIZING.   [*E*]

> ———— all people went
> Upon their ten toes in wild wonderment.
>
> *Bishop Hall's Satires.*[1]

I am — that is to say I *was* — a great man; but I am neither the author of Junius nor the man in the mask; for my name, I believe, is Robert Jones, and I was born somewhere in the city of Fum-Fudge.[2]

The first action of my life was the taking hold of my nose with both hands. My mother saw this and called me a genius: — my father wept for joy and presented me with a treatise on Nosology.[3] This I mastered before I was breeched.

I now began to feel my way in the science, and soon came to understand that, provided a man had a nose sufficiently conspicuous, he might, by merely following it, arrive at a Lionship. But my attention was not confined to theories alone. Every morning I gave my proboscis a couple of pulls and swallowed a half dozen of drams.

When I came of age my father asked me, one day, if I would step with him into his study.

"My son," said he, when we were seated, "what is the chief end of your existence?"[4]

"My father," I answered, "it is the study of Nosology."

"And what, Robert," he inquired, "is Nosology?"

"Sir," I said, "it is the Science of Noses."

"And can you tell me," he demanded, "what is the meaning of a nose?"

"A nose, my father," I replied, greatly softened, "has been variously defined by about a thousand different authors." [Here I pulled out my watch.]ᵃ "It is now noon or thereabouts — we shall have time enough to get through with them all before midnight. To commence then: — The nose, according to Bartholinus, is that protuberance — that bump — that excrescence — that ——"

"Will do, Robert," interrupted the good old gentleman. "I am

Title: Some Passages in the Life of a   a *The square brackets throughout the*
Lion (D)   *tale are Poe's.*

thunderstruck at the extent of your information — I am positively — upon my soul." [Here he closed his eyes and placed his hand upon his heart.] "Come here!" [Here he took me by the arm.] "Your education may now be considered as finished — it is high time you should scuffle for yourself — and you cannot do a better thing than merely follow your nose — so — so — so — " [Here he kicked me down stairs and out of the door.]ᵇ — "so get out of my house, and God bless you!"

As I felt within me the divine *afflatus,* I considered this accident rather fortunate than otherwise. I resolved to be guided by the paternal advice. I determined to follow my nose. I gave it a pull or two upon the spot, and wrote a pamphlet on Nosology forthwith.

All Fum-Fudge was in an uproar.

"Wonderful genius!" said the Quarterly.

"Superb physiologist!" said the Westminster.

"Clever fellow!" said the Foreign.

"Fine writer!" said the Edinburgh.

"Profound thinker!" said the Dublin.

"Great man!" said Bentley.

"Divine soul!" said Fraser.

"One of us!" said Blackwood.⁵

"Who can he be?" said Mrs. Bas-Bleu.⁶

"What can he be?" said big Miss Bas-Bleu.

"Where can he be?" said little Miss Bas-Bleu. — But I paid these people no attention whatever — I just stepped into the shop of an artist.

The Duchess of Bless-my-Soul⁷ was sitting for her portrait; the Marquis of So-and-So was holding the Duchess' poodle; the Earl of This-and-That was flirting with her salts; and his Royal Highness of Touch-me-Not was leaning upon the back of her chair.

I approached the artist and turned up my nose.

"Oh, beautiful!" sighed her Grace.

"Oh my!" lisped the Marquis.

"Oh, shocking!" groaned the Earl.

"Oh, abominable!" growled his Royal Highness.

"What will you take for it?" asked the artist.

b   door] *(E, F,) Period added from D*

"For his *nose!*" shouted her Grace.

"A thousand pounds," said I, sitting down.

"A thousand pounds?" inquired the artist, musingly.

"A thousand pounds," said I.

ᶜ"Beautiful!" said he, entranced.

"A thousand pounds," said I.ᶜ

"Do you warrant it?" he asked, turning the nose to the light.

"I do," said I, blowing it well.

"It is *quite* original?" he inquired,ᵈ touching it with reverence.

"Humph!" said I, twisting it to one side.

"Has *no* copy been taken?" he demanded, surveying it through a microscope.

"None," said I, turning it up.

"Admirable!" he ejaculated, thrown quite off his guard by the beauty of the manœuvre.

"A thousand pounds," said I.

"A *thousand* pounds?" said he.

"Precisely," said I.

"A thousand *pounds?*" said he.

"Just so," said I.

"You shall have them," said he. "What a piece of *virtu!*"[8] So he drew me a check upon the spot, and took a sketch of my nose. I engaged rooms in Jermyn street,[9] and sent her Majesty[10] the ninety-ninth edition of the "Nosology," with a portrait of the proboscis. — That sad little rake, the Prince of Wales,[11] invited me to dinner.

We were all lions and *recherchés.*[12]

There was a modern Platonist. He quoted Porphyry, Iamblicus, Plotinus, Proclus, Hierocles, Maximus Tyrius, and Syrianus.[13]

There was a human-perfectibility man. He quoted Turgot,ᵉ Price, Priestley,ᶠ Condorcet,ᵍ De Staël,ʰ and the "Ambitious Student in Ill Health."[14]

There was Sir Positive Paradox. He observed that all fools were philosophers, and that all philosophers were fools.[15]

---

c . . . c   *Omitted (D)*
d   he inquired,/inquired he, *(D)*
e   Turgôt, *(E, F) corrected from D*
f   Priestly, *(D, E, F) corrected*

editorially
g   Condorcêt *(E, F) corrected from D*
h   Stäel, *(D, E, F)*

LIONIZING

There was Æstheticus Ethix. He spoke of fire, unity, and atoms; bi-part and pre-existent soul; affinity and discord; primitive intelligence and homöomeria.[16]

There was Theologos Theology. He talked of Eusebius and Arianus; heresy and the Council of Nice; Puseyism and consubstantialism; Homousios and Homouioisios.[17]

There was Fricassée from the Rocher de Cancale. He mentioned Muriton of red tongue; cauliflowers with *velouté* sauce; veal *à la* St. Menehoult; marinade *à la* St. Florentin; and orange jellies *en mosaïques*.[i][18]

There was Bibulus O'Bumper. He touched upon Latour and Markbrünnen; upon Mousseux and Chambertin; upon Richbourg and St. George; upon Haubrion, Leonville, and Medoc; upon Barac and Preignac; upon Grâve, [j]upon Sauterne, upon Lafitte,[j] and upon St. Peray. He shook his head at Clos de Vougeot, and told, with his eyes shut, the difference between Sherry and Amontillado.[19]

There was Signor Tintontintino from Florence. He discoursed of Cimabue,[k] Arpino, Carpaccio, and Argostino — of the gloom of Caravaggio, of the amenity of Albano, of the colors of Titian, of the frows of Rubens, and of the waggeries of Jan Steen.[20]

There was the President of the Fum-Fudge University. He was of opinion that the moon was called Bendis in Thrace, Bubastis in Egypt, Dian in Rome, and Artemis in Greece.[21]

There was a Grand Turk from Stamboul. He could not help thinking that the angels were horses, cocks, and bulls; that somebody in the sixth heaven had seventy thousand heads; and that the earth was supported by a sky-blue cow with an incalculable number of green horns.[22]

There was Delphinus Polyglott. He told us what had become of the eighty-three lost tragedies of Æschylus; of the fifty-four orations of Isæus; of the three hundred and ninety-one speeches of Lysias; of the hundred and eighty treatises of Theophrastus; of the

---

i *mosaïques (D, E, F) accent corrected editorially*
j . . . j *Omitted (D)*

k Cimababué, (D) *misprint;* Cimabué (E, F)

eighth book of the conic sections of Apollonius; of Pindar's hymns and dithyrambics; and of the five and forty tragedies of Homer Junior.[23]

There was Ferdinand Fitz-Fossillus Feltspar. He informed us all about internal fires and tertiary formations; about aëriforms, fluidiforms, and solidiforms; about quartz and marl; about schist and schorl; about gypsum and trap; about talc and calc; about blende and horn-blende; about mica-slate and pudding-stone; about cyanite and lepidolite; about hæmatite and tremolite; about antimony and calcedony; about manganese and whatever you please.[24]

There was myself. I spoke of myself; — of myself, of myself, of myself; — of Nosology, of my pamphlet, and of myself. I turned up my nose, and I[l] spoke of myself.

"Marvellous clever man!" said the Prince.

"Superb!" said his guests: — and next morning her Grace of Bless-my-Soul paid me a visit.

"Will you go to Almack's,[m] [25] pretty creature?" she said, tapping me under the chin.

"Upon honor," said I.

"Nose and all?" she asked.

"As I live," I replied.

"Here then is a card, my life. Shall I say you *will* be there?"

"Dear Duchess, with all my heart."

"Pshaw, no! — but with all your nose?"

"Every bit of it, my love," said I: — so I gave it a twist or two, and found myself at Almack's.

The rooms were crowded to suffocation.

"He is coming!" said somebody on the staircase.

"He is coming!" said somebody farther up.

"He is coming!" said somebody farther still.

"He is come!" exclaimed the Duchess. "He is come, the little love!" — and, seizing me firmly by both hands, she kissed me thrice upon the nose.

A marked sensation immediately ensued.

"*Diavolo!*" cried Count Capricornutti.

---

l *Omitted (D)*　　　　　　　　m Almacks *(D) here and later*

LIONIZING

[n]"*Dios guarda!*" muttered Don Stiletto.[n]

"*Mille tonnerres!*" ejaculated the Prince de Grenouille.

"*Tousand teufel!*" growled the Elector of Bluddennuff.

It[o] was not to be borne. I grew angry. I turned short upon Bluddennuff.

"Sir!" said I to him,[p] "you are a baboon."

"Sir," he replied, after a pause, "*Donner und Blitzen!*"

This was all that could be desired. We exchanged cards. At Chalk-Farm,[26] the next morning, I shot off his nose — and then called upon my friends.

"*Bête!*" said the first.

"Fool!" said the second.

"Dolt!" said the third.

"Ass!" said the fourth.

"Ninny!" said the fifth.

"Noodle!" said the sixth.

"Be off!" said the seventh.

At all this I felt mortified, and so called upon my father.

"Father," I asked,[q] "what is the chief end of my existence?"

"My son," he replied, "it is still the study of Nosology; but in [r]hitting the Elector upon the[r] nose you have overshot your mark. You have a fine nose, it is true; but then Bluddennuff has none. You are damned, and he has become the hero of the day. I grant you that in Fum-Fudge the greatness of a lion is in proportion to the size of his proboscis — but, good heavens! there is no competing with a lion who has no proboscis at all."

NOTES

(The following notes apply to both versions, but they are presented in a sequence keyed to the later text.)

1. The motto is misquoted from Bishop Joseph Hall's *Satires* (1597), II, iii, 19–20: "Genus and Species long since barefoote went/Upon their ten-toes in wilde wanderment."

2. "Junius" was the author of a famous series of political letters in the

---

n . . . n *Omitted (D)*	q said, *(D)*
o This *(D)*	r . . . r shooting off the Elector's *(D)*
p to him *omitted (D)*	

TALES OF THE FOLIO CLUB

London *Public Advertiser,* 1769–1772; the Man in the Iron Mask (referred to again in "The Man That Was Used Up") was a political prisoner in France, well known to readers of romance. The identity of neither person is surely known even now, although Junius was probably Sir Philip Francis. The name of the city may owe something to a name in Benjamin Disraeli's *Vivian Grey* — Mr. Foaming Fudge — or to Thomas Moore's popular book *The Fudge Family in Paris* (1818); see note 21 below.

3. Nosology is properly the science of diseases; Poe makes a pun, as if it were the science of noses; the jest was apparently not original.

The authors mentioned in the early versions *(A, B, C),* as Poe remarked in PHANTASY-PIECES *(C),* all seem to have written about noses: Pliny the Elder wrote on the subject in *Natural History,* XI, 59, and elsewhere. Aristotle discussed snub noses in *Problemata,* XXXIII, 18. Alexander Ross, Master of Southampton Grammar School and an opponent of Sir Thomas Browne, wrote on anatomy. Minucius Felix, the early Christian apologist, has a passage in his *Octavius,* XXXVIII, 2, about smelling flowers. Hermanus Pictorius I believe is an error — perhaps due to a missing comma — for Paulus Hermannus, an eighteenth-century Dutch botanist, and Georg Pictorius, a sixteenth- century writer on medicine. Martin-Antoine Del Rio (1551–1608) was a Jesuit and bitter critic of the views of Heinrich Cornelius Agrippa; his voluminous works seem to be unindexed, but I think we can take his interest in noses on faith. Foulques de Villaret was a Grand Master (1307–1319) of the Order of the Hospitallers of St. John of Jerusalem and died in 1327. He does not seem to fit here. Casparus Bartholinus, one of a family of Scandinavian scholars and physicians, published *De olfactus organo* in 1679 and *De respiratione animalium* in 1700.

4. An echo of the Westminster Shorter Catechism, which begins, "What is the chief end of man?"

5. Poe lists the leading British reviews of the time.

6. The Bas-Bleu, or Bluestocking, family appears also in "The Man That Was Used Up."

7. The Duchess of Bless-my-soul is transparent for Lady Blessington; N. P. Willis mentions her portrait by Sir Thomas Lawrence, and an "unfavorable likeness" in the *Book of Beauty* (a London annual, edited in 1833 by Letitia E. Landon and from 1834 by Lady Blessington herself). Poe has in mind the following from Willis, chapter CXVI of *Pencillings by the Way,* reprinted in his *Prose Works* (1845), p. 182, describing a salon of the Countess of Blessington:

> A German prince, with a star at his breast, trying with all his might, but, from his embarrassed look, quite unsuccessfully, to comprehend the drift of the argument; the Duke de Richelieu, whom I had seen at the court of France, the inheritor of nothing but the name of his great ancestor, a dandy and a fool, making no attempt to listen; a famous traveller, just returned from Constantinople; and the splendid person of Count D'Orsay in a careless attitude upon the ottoman, completed the *cordon.*

8. Compare "The Visionary," and "The Assignation" near note 16: "with little deference to the opinions of Virtu."

9.   Jermyn Street, in a fashionable part of London where there are many clubs, is noted particularly for the distinguished men who have had lodgings there. (Newton, Berkeley, Gray, and Scott are mentioned in Muir's Blue Guide.)

10.   "His Majesty" in the first version becomes "Her Majesty" in the versions published after the accession of Queen Victoria on the death of William IV, June 20, 1837.

11.   The Prince of Wales was added in 1845; nobody had the title from 1820 when George IV became king until 1842 when Albert Edward, later Edward VII, received the title at less than two years of age. Poe may have had the former in mind, though he was neither sad nor little.

12.   The same guests appear in all versions, except for Bibulus O'Bumper, who is not mentioned in *A, B,* and *C.* The order of the list in the later versions is followed in the notes below.

13.   At a Blessington soiree, described by Willis in *Pencillings,* chapter cxxi, *Prose Works,* p. 190, Benjamin Disraeli discussed Platonism and told how Thomas Taylor, a modern Platonist, was turned out of his lodgings in London when he sacrificed a bull to Jupiter in his back parlor. Reference was also made to the Alexandrian Platonists, discussed in *Vivian Grey.* The following is from the sixth chapter of the first book of that novel: "Father! I wish to make myself master of the latter Platonists. I want Plotinus, and Porphyry, and Iamblichus, and Syrianus, and Maximus Tyrius, and Proclus, and Hierocles, and Sallustius, and Damascius." They flourished between circa 150 B.C. and A.D. 485.

14.   All the believers in human perfectibility are named again in "The Landscape Garden" and "The Domain of Arnheim," save the "Ambitious Student." Bulwer's series of "Conversations . . ." appeared in the London *New Monthly Magazine* in 1831 and 1832 before being reprinted by the Harpers in book form. All the perfectionists are well known, save perhaps Richard Price (1723-1791), an English moralist and preacher.

15.   For the "paradox" see also the "Purloined Letter," where the Chief of Police thinks "All fools are poets . . . and . . . all poets are fools."

16.   The "bi-part soul" figures in "William Wilson" and "The Fall of the House of Usher," and is mentioned in "The Murders in the Rue Morgue"; homoeomery is the doctrine that elementary substances are composed of parts each similar to the whole.

17.   Eusebius, Bishop of Nicomedia, died in 342; Arius, founder of Arianism, thought Christ less than the Father, something condemned at the Council of Nice (Nicaea in Bithynia) in 325, when the Nicene Creed was framed. Puseyism (in later versions) is a reference to Edward Bouverie Pusey (1800-1882), who led the high-church party of Anglicans; Poe thought poorly of him; see "Marginalia," number 3, *Democratic Review,* November 1844, p. 485 ("the great tweedle-dee tweedle-dum paroxysm – the uproar about Pusey"), and "Desultory Notes on Cats," below.

The usual English forms of the Greek words are homoousian (of the same essence) and homoiousian (of like essence). They refer to abstruse arguments concerning the nature of Christ: whether the same as that of the Father, or merely similar to His. The Constantinopolitan mob is said to have rioted about these disputes.

18. The Rocher de Cancale is a great rock in Brittany. It gave its name to a Parisian restaurant, of which N. P. Willis said, in chapter xiv of *Pencillings by the Way*, that it was "now the first eating-house in Paris, yet they only excel in fish." See Willis' *Prose Works* (1845), p. 23.

Some of the dishes mentioned reappear in "How to Write a Blackwood Article" and "The System of Doctor Tarr and Professor Fether." All except marinade *à la* St. Florentin are described in the *Larousse Gastronomique* (New York, 1961).

19. The wine list (not in the early versions) resembles one in early versions of "Bon-Bon." Many of the items in Poe's list are not accurate, but it seems unwise to tamper with it. [For a recent discussion, see "Poe's Wine List," by L. Moffitt Cecil, *Poe Studies*, December 1972.]

20. The names of the artists are all well enough known to be found in a good biographical dictionary. An Italian and Flemish art collection in Benjamin Disraeli's *The Young Duke* (Book II, chapter xiii) contains "Rubens' satyrs and Albano's boys." I take "frows" to mean "fraus." By "Argostino" Poe meant Agostino dalle Prospettive, a Bolognese who flourished in 1525; the spelling was correct in the first version of the story. The realistic Dutch painter Jan Steen (1626–1679) is mentioned in Poe's review of Longfellow in *Graham's* for April! 1842: "If truth is the highest aim of . . . painting . . . Jan Steen was a greater artist than Angelo." In a review of Charles James Lever's *Charles O'Malley, the Irish Dragoon, By Harry Lorrequer* in the same magazine for March 1842, Poe said, "For one Angelo there are five hundred Jan Steens."

21. For the President's information see B. Disraeli's *Vivian Grey*, Bk. iii, chapter vi: "Queen of Night! in whatever name thou most delightest! Or Bendis, as they hail thee in rugged Thrace; or Bubastis, as they howled to thee in mysterious Egypt; or Dian, as they sacrificed to thee in gorgeous Rome; or Artemis, as they sighed to thee on the bright plains of ever glorious Greece." Observe the caution of the academic character, whose opinion nobody could dispute. [See a further gloss on this paragraph with reference to Moore's *Fudge Family in Paris* and his *The Epicurean* (1827) in B. Pollin's "Light on 'Shadow' and Other Pieces by Poe; . . . " *Emerson Society Quarterly*, Third Quarter, 1972.]

22. These extravagant Mahometan legends are referred to again in "The Thousand-and-Second Tale of Scheherazade."

23. Delphinus Polyglott takes his first name from the Delphin edition of the Latin classics prepared by order of Louis XIV "For the Use of the Dauphin." With the exception of Homer Junior's lost works all of the lost Greek books are mentioned in "Some Ancient Greek Authors" in the *Southern Literary Messenger*, April 1836. The article is signed "P." and has been assigned to Poe; but like Campbell (*Mind of Poe*, p. 215) I think the author was probably Lucian Minor. Whether Poe and Minor relied on a common source is not determined. The forty-five tragedies of Homer Junior not in the *Southern Literary Messenger* list are mentioned in Anthon's Lemprière, p. 357, col. 2, as well as in the 1806 London edition of Lemprière.

24. The geological collection was expanded from earlier versions. Ferdinand's given names echo Bulwer's character Ferdinand Fitzroy, mentioned above.

25. Admission was only by ticket to Almack's Balls held in the Assembly Rooms opened in 1765 by William Almack in King Street, St. James's, and inherited by his niece, Mrs. Willis, in 1781. The rooms are mentioned factually in "The Balloon Hoax."

26. Chalk Farm was a well-known duelling place north of Regents' Park. There Moore met Jeffrey in a bloodless encounter celebrated by Byron in "English Bards and Scotch Reviewers." Poe again satirized the duello in "Mystification."

SHADOW—A PARABLE

This very brief tale is one of the finest of all Poe's productions and, with its companion piece, "Silence — A Fable," has had great influence on later writers, especially in France. Woodberry remarked:

Shadow ... is at once the most noble and most artistic expression of Poe's imagination during the first period of his career, and ... is alone distinguished by the even flow and delicacy of transition that belong to his best prose style. The elements in this rhapsody of gloom are simple and massive, the accessories in perfect keeping; the ... emotion ... is just sustained at its initial pitch until the ... emergence of the shadow from the black draperies of the chamber ... *

The style recalls the King James Bible, as do the styles of Bulwer and De Quincey (whom Poe seems to have had in mind when writing "Silence") — and if the reader is reminded of Macpherson's "Ossian" or of Coleridge's unfinished "Wanderings of Cain," he need not doubt that Poe was acquainted with both.

The story may be easily understood by the unlearned but the historical setting is surprisingly correct. The action takes place in the twilight of Greco-Roman civilization in Egypt, where even older cultures had flourished and were no more. The scene is appropriately laid in the city of Ptolemais, where the Sun casts no shadow at noon during the summer solstice; what better city could have been chosen for the ever-present Shadow, Death, than that in which the Sun himself casts none? The idea of speaking with many

* *Edgar Allan Poe* (1885), p. 82; *Life* (1909), I, 127.

voices is as old as the *Odyssey*. The names of the characters are both significant. Oinos means One.† Zoilus is the name of an Alexandrian — a critic who found faults in Homer — but his name is connected with *zoë,* meaning life. The whole story may be likened to a richly embroidered robe; the sources from which Poe took details are discussed in the notes below.‡

Although it has not been proved that "Shadow" was one of the original eleven tales in the series described by Poe in May 1833, its kinship to "Silence" ("Siope") leads me to place it here, just ahead of "Silence," which seems without question to have been the final tale in Poe's little manuscript volume.

TEXTS

(A) Southern Literary Messenger, September 1835 (1:762–763); *(B)* Duane copy of last with one manuscript change, 1839; *(C) Tales of the Grotesque and Arabesque* (1840), I, 153–156; *(D)* PHANTASY-PIECES, manuscript revision of last, 1842; *(E) Broadway Journal,* May 31, 1845 (1:341–342); *(F) Works* (1850), II, 292–294.

Griswold's text *(F)* showing one verbal change is followed.

SHADOW. — A PARABLE.   [*F*]

Yea! though I walk through the valley of the *Shadow: — Psalm of David*

Ye who read are still among the living;[a] but I who write shall have long since gone my way into the region of shadows. For indeed

---

† The word is rare in ancient texts, being confined almost entirely to the ace of dice, but as it is the cognate of Latin *unus,* and English *one,* it is much discussed by scholars. (See Liddell and Scott, *Greek-English Lexicon,* 1968 edition.) Poe was interested in words for unity; compare his "Colloquy of Monos and Una," and the motto of "Morella." The word for wine is also *oinos* in Greek, but that was originally *woinos;* it has lost the initial digamma. A reference to wine would be pointless here, as would be one to Oenus, King of Calydon.

[‡ Burton Pollin argues convincingly that Thomas Moore's *The Epicurean* (1827) was a significant influence on this tale. See his paper in *Emerson Society Quarterly,* Third Quarter, 1972.]

Title: Shadow. A Fable — By – *(A)*	a living, *(A, B, C)*; living: *(F) comma*
By *canceled in B;* Shadow. A Fable *(C,*	*changed to semicolon in D, followed by*
D); Shadow — A <Fable> Parable *(in*	E *where at first glance it looks like a*
table of contents of D)	*colon. In this text it is changed back to*
Motto: This first appears in D	*semicolon to follow D and E*

strange things shall happen, and[b] secret things be known, and many centuries shall pass away, ere these memorials be seen of men. And, when seen, there will be some to disbelieve, and some to doubt, and yet a few who will find much to ponder upon in the characters here graven with a stylus of iron.[1]

The year had been a year of terror, and of feelings more intense than terror for which there is no name upon the earth. For many prodigies and signs had taken place, and far and wide, over sea and land, the black wings of the Pestilence were spread abroad.[2] To those, nevertheless, cunning in the stars, it was not unknown that the heavens wore an aspect of ill; and to me, the Greek Oinos, among others, it was evident that now had arrived the alternation of that seven hundred and ninety-fourth year when, at the entrance of Aries, the planet Jupiter is conjoined with the red ring of the terrible Saturnus.[3] The peculiar spirit of the skies, if I mistake not greatly, made itself manifest, not only in the physical orb of the earth, but in the souls, imaginations, and meditations of mankind.

Over some flasks of the red Chian wine,[4] within the walls of a noble hall, in a dim city [c]called Ptolemais,[c] we sat, at night, a company of seven. And to our chamber there was no entrance save by a lofty door of brass: and the door was fashioned by the artisan Corinnos,[5] and, being of rare workmanship, was fastened from within. Black draperies, likewise, in the gloomy room, shut out from our view the moon, the lurid stars, and the peopleless streets — but the boding and the memory of Evil, they would not be so excluded. There were things around us and about of which I can render no distinct account — things material and [d]spiritual — heaviness[d] in the atmosphere — a sense of suffocation — anxiety — and, above all, that terrible state of existence which the nervous experience when the senses are keenly living and awake, and meanwhile the powers of thought lie dormant. A dead weight hung upon us. It hung upon our limbs — upon the household furniture — upon the goblets from which we drank; and all things were depressed, and borne down thereby — all things save only the flames of the seven

---

b   and many *(A, B)*
c . . . c   by the melancholy sea, *(A, B)*
d . . . d   spiritual. Heaviness *(A, C)*

The punctuation was changed in B and again in D to the present reading.

iron lamps which illumined our revel.[6] Uprearing themselves in tall slender lines of light, they thus remained burning all pallid and motionless; and in the mirror which their lustre formed upon the round table of ebony at which we sat, each of us there assembled beheld the pallor of his own countenance, and the unquiet glare in the downcast eyes of his companions. Yet we laughed and were merry in our proper way — which was hysterical; and sang the songs of Anacreon — which are madness;[7] and drank deeply — although the purple wine reminded us of blood. For there was yet another tenant of our chamber in the person of young Zoilus. Dead, and at full length he lay, enshrouded; — the genius and the demon of the scene. Alas! he bore no portion in our mirth, save that his countenance, distorted with the plague, and his eyes in which Death had but half extinguished the fire of the pestilence, seemed to take such interest in our merriment as the dead may haply[e] take in the merriment of those who are to die. But although I, Oinos, felt that the eyes of the departed were upon me, still I forced myself not to perceive the bitterness of their expression, and, gazing down steadily into the depths of the ebony mirror, sang with a loud and sonorous voice the songs of the son of Teios.[8] But gradually my songs they ceased, and their echoes, rolling afar off among the sable draperies of the chamber, became weak, and un-distinguishable,[f] and so faded[g] away. And lo! from among those sable draperies where the sounds of the song departed, there came forth a dark and undefined shadow — a shadow such as the moon, when low in heaven, might fashion from the figure of a man: but it was the shadow neither of man, nor of God, nor of any familiar thing. And,[h] quivering awhile among the draperies of the room, it at length rested in full view upon the surface of the door of brass. But the shadow was vague, and formless, and indefinite,[i] and was the shadow neither of man nor[j] God — neither God of Greece, nor God of Chaldæa, nor any Egyptian God. And the shadow rested upon the brazen doorway, and under the arch of the entablature of the door, and moved not, nor spoke any word, but there became

---

e   may haply/may (A) changed in B
f   indistinguishable, (A, B, C, D)
g   fainted (A, B, C, D)
h   And (A, C, D, F) comma added in

B, followed in E, restored here.
i   indefinitive, (A, B, C, D)
j   nor of (E)

stationary and remained. And the door whereupon the shadow rested was, if I remember aright, over against the feet of the young Zoilus enshrouded. But we, the seven there assembled, having seen the shadow as it came out from among the draperies, dared not steadily behold it, but cast down our eyes, and gazed continually into the depths of the mirror of ebony. And at length I, Oinos, speaking some low words, demanded of the shadow its dwelling and its appellation. And the shadow answered, "I am SHADOW, and my dwelling is near to the Catacombs of Ptolemais, and hard by those dim plains of Helusion[9] which border upon the foul Charonian canal." And then did we, the seven, start from our seats in horror, and stand trembling, and shuddering, and aghast: for the tones in the voice of the shadow were not the tones of any one being, but of a multitude of beings,[10] and, varying in their cadences from syllable to syllable, fell duskily upon our ears in the well remembered and familiar accents of many[k] thousand departed friends.

NOTES

Motto: Poe, as is pointed out in my notes on the poem "Eldorado" (Mabbott, I, 464–465), knew of the two interpretations of Psalm 23:4. The Hebrew expression rendered as "shadow of death" in the Septuagint (the Greek translation made at Alexandria) some scholars think means merely "shadow."

1. The phrase "be seen of men" is from St. Matthew 6:5. A stylus or pen of iron is mentioned in Jeremiah 17:1, and in Job 19:24. Poe planned to call his projected magazine *The Stylus*.

2. The Plague first appeared at the port of Pelusium in the Nile Delta during the reign of Justinian, A.D. 542, as Gibbon relates in chapter xliii of the *Decline and Fall of the Roman Empire* — a chapter from which Poe quoted in "Marginalia," Number 29 (*Democratic Review*, November 1844, p. 489).

3. Astrologers regard a conjunction of Jupiter and Saturn as a warning of change; in the sign of the Ram, great violence and misfortune are predicted. Its occurrence there once in 794 years is mentioned in the section, "Les Mathématiques," in Poe's favorite little encyclopedia, Bielfeld, Book I, chapter xlix, section 78.

4. Wine of the Greek island of Chios is praised in Pliny's *Natural History*, XIV, 9. Several ancient cities were named Ptolemais; Poe may have had in mind

k   a *(A, B)*

Ptolemais Theron on the Red Sea, where, Pliny said (II, lxxv, 183; VI, xxxiii, 171), for ninety days in midsummer the sun at noon cast no shadow.

5. The name of a legendary poet who lived at the time of the Trojan War. No artist of the name is recorded. Corinthian brass, however, had gold and silver in it, and Poe may have thought there was some connection between Corinnos and Corinth.

6. For the lamps see *Paradise Lost*, XII, 255f., "Sev'n Lamps as in a Zodiac representing/The Heav'nly fires." See also Josephus, *Jewish Antiquities,* III, vi, 7.

7. Compare Poe's "Introduction" in his *Poems* (1831), lines 21–22, "Anacreon rhymes/Were almost passionate sometimes" (Mabbott I, 157).

8. Anacreon was born about 550 B.C. at Teos, a seaport of Ionia. The name of his father is not known, but the poet was obviously a son of Teios — a man of Teos. He is referred to as "the Teian" in "Morella."

9. Elysium. Poe took his description of the canal from Jacob Bryant's *New System . . . of Antient Mythology* (Third Edition, 1807), I, 34: "The Elysian plain, near the Catacombs in Egypt, stood upon the foul Charonian canal." For Elysium, compare "Eleonora" at n. 20; for the canal, Pliny, VI, xxxiii, 165–166.

10. According to the *Odyssey,* IV, 277–279, Helen of Troy could speak with the voices of the wives of many Greek heroes.

SIOPE (SILENCE)

First published with the title "Siope — A Fable," this companion piece to "Shadow" is generally regarded as another masterpiece of poetic prose. It is, however, the most cryptic of Poe's tales, and has baffled editors of his day, and many modern commentators. But, when one compares it with "Sonnet — Silence," and considers the clue in the early motto from "Al Aaraaf," one need not find the meaning beyond all conjecture.

Man clings to the rock of reality, however terrible; the true silence, cessation of being, terrifies even a brave man.* "It is the Demon of the Imagination's interpretation of the Universe. . . . The setting is a valley called Desolation, full of activity. A dignified man sadly contemplates the tumult of Life about him. Then the

---

* This interpretation is close to that of A. H. Quinn, expressed to me in conversation. The quoted words following are Professor Rae Blanchard's, written in 1923, but now first printed.

SILENCE

valley is called Silence, a type of death, which terrifies the man."

The principal source is pointed out by A. H. Quinn *(Poe,* p. 215) as a story by Bulwer in the London *New Monthly,* May 1830 — a story Poe named as a good sensational magazine article in a letter of April 30, 1835 to T. W. White and later praised in a review of Bulwer's *Rienzi* in the *Southern Literary Messenger* for February 1836. Bulwer's tale, "Monos and Daimonos, A Legend," is a rambling story of a youth brought up by a father who abjured all society to live on a rock in a rocky waste. The greatest luxury of the young Monos was solitude. After his father's death, having attained his majority and his estate, he left England and went "into the enormous woods of Africa, where human step never trod" — woods peopled by "the wandering lion, or the wild ostrich, or that huge serpent." To quote a typical passage: "There, too, as beneath the heavy and dense shade I couched in the scorching noon, I heard the trampling as of an army, and the crash and fall of the strong trees, and beheld through the matted boughs the behemoth pass on its terrible way, with its eyes burning as a sun, and its white teeth arched and glistening in the rabid jaw, as pillars of spar glitter in a cavern."

Deciding to return home, Monos sails on a ship where, to his distress, one man persistently cleaves to him. Says Monos, "I longed ... to strangle him when he addressed me! ... would have ... hurled him into the sea to the sharks, which lynx-eyed and eager jawed, swam night and day around our ship."

The ship sinks, all are drowned save Monos and his tormentor, who joins him in a cavern. Monos runs away, but in vain. He murders his companion, whose ghost continues to haunt him, unseen by others.

Here is much that Poe took — Africa, the rock, solitude, caverns, the demon, the wild beasts, even sentences almost verbatim, like "As the Lord liveth, I believe the tale that I shall tell you will have sufficient claim on your attention." So much indeed — but Poe's genius has transformed the overwrought grandiloquence of his source into something rich and strange.

The story was one of the eleven Tales of the Folio Club, as the single leaf of its manuscript, formerly accompanying the introduction, shows (see "The Folio Club," below). Hence, it was probably in existence before May 4, 1833, and may have been one of the stories in which John P. Kennedy tried to interest the publishers Carey and Lea. It is clear that it was to be told by the protagonist who described the Club's members.

On Sepetmber 11, 1835, Poe wrote John P. Kennedy he could not understand why *The Gift* had not used "Epimanes" or "Siope."

In 1837 plans were made for a *Baltimore Book* for the Christmas and New Year's trade, on the plan of the previously issued *Boston Book, New York Book,* and *Philadelphia Book.* Poe wrote on February 28 to W. H. Carpenter, J. S. Norris, and James Brown that he would be glad to send something for their gift book, if April 1, 1837 would be in time, and suggesting "the theme should be left to my own choice." The book, edited by Carpenter and T. S. Arthur, appeared late in 1837, containing "Siope."

Years later in a letter cited by Woodberry, Poe's friend N. C. Brooks claimed to have saved "Siope" from the wastebasket, but his memory was probably of a later submission, in 1838 or 1839, while he was editor of Fairfield's *North American Quarterly* and its short-lived successor, the *American Museum of Science, Literature and the Arts.*†

TEXTS

(A) Manuscript fragment, about 1832, facsimiled by John W. Robertson, *Commentary on the Bibliography of Edgar A. Poe* (1934), II, 114–115; *(B) Baltimore Book* (1838), pp. 79–85; *(C) Tales of the Grotesque and Arabesque* (1840), II, 19–24; *(D) Broadway Journal,* September 6, 1845 (2:135–136); *(E) Works* (1850), II, 295–298. PHANTASY-PIECES, title only.

Griswold's version *(E)* is followed. It shows one presumably auctorial change.

The manuscript *(A)* was the last leaf of the codex, of which the first leaf carried the text of "The Folio Club." I saw them both together, lent for exhibition at Richmond in 1922, by the Griswold family, but the fragment of "Silence" was not given to Harvard with its companion piece. The manuscript fragment is one of the holdings of the Poe Foundation and is housed in the State Library, at Richmond, Virginia.

† See Woodberry, *Poe* (1885), pp. 54, 109, and *Life* (1909), I, 198, where the date of first publication is given incorrectly.

SILENCE

SILENCE — A FABLE. [E]

'Ενδουσιν δ' ορεων κορυφαι τε καὶ φάραγγες
Πρώονές τε καὶ χαράδραι.   ALCMAN.
The mountain pinnacles slumber; valleys, crags and caves *are silent.*

"Listen to *me*," said the Demon, as he placed his hand upon my head.[a] "The region of which I speak is a dreary region in Libya, by the borders of the river Zäire.[1] And there is no quiet there, nor silence.

"The waters of the river have a saffron and sickly hue; and they flow not onward[b] to the sea, but palpitate forever and forever beneath the red eye of the sun with a tumultuous and convulsive motion. For many miles on either side of the river's oozy bed is a pale desert of gigantic water-lilies. They sigh one unto the other in that solitude, and stretch towards the heaven their long and[c] ghastly necks, and nod to and fro their everlasting heads.[2] And there is an indistinct murmur which cometh out from among them like the rushing of subterrene water. And they sigh one unto the other.

"But there is a boundary to their realm — the boundary of the dark, horrible, lofty forest. There, like the waves about the Hebrides, the low underwood is agitated continually. But there is no wind throughout the heaven. And the tall primeval trees rock eternally hither and thither with a crashing and mighty sound. And from their high summits, one by one, drop everlasting dews. And at the roots strange poisonous flowers lie writhing in perturbed slumber. And overhead, with a rustling and loud noise, the gray clouds rush westwardly forever, until they roll, a cataract, over

---

Title: Siope. A Fable. [In the manner of the Psychological Autobiographists] *Square brackets are Poe's (B, C) The first part of the manuscript A is lost but in a letter of September 11, 1835, Poe called the tale* Siope.
Motto:
Ours is a world of words: Quiet we call *Silence* — which is the merest word of all.
     Al Aaraaf. (B)
The Greek words of Alcman appear first in C; the English was added in D.
a   *After this B and C have:* "There is a spot upon this accursed earth which thou hast never yet beheld. And if by any chance thou *hast* beheld it, it must have been in one of those vigorous dreams which come like the Simoom [Simoon *(C)*] upon the brain of the sleeper who hath lain down to sleep among the forbidden sunbeams — among the sunbeams, I say, which slide from off the solemn columns of the melancholy temples in the wilderness. [*The paragraph continues with* The region etc.]
b   onwards *(B, C, D)*
c   Omitted *(B, C)*

the fiery wall of the horizon.[3] But there is no wind throughout the heaven. And by the shores of the river Zäire there is neither quiet nor silence.

"It was night, and the rain fell; and, falling, it was rain, but, having fallen, it was blood.[4] And I stood in the morass among the tall lilies, and the rain fell upon my head — and the lilies sighed one unto the other in the solemnity of their desolation.

"And, all at once, the moon arose through the thin ghastly mist, and was crimson in color. And mine eyes fell upon a huge gray rock which stood by the shore of the river, and was lighted[d] [5] by the light of the moon. And the rock was gray, and ghastly, and tall, — and the rock was gray. Upon its front were characters engraven in the stone; and I walked through the morass of water-lilies, until I came close unto the shore, that I might read the characters upon the stone. But I could not decypher them.[e] And I was going back into the morass, when the moon shone with a fuller red, and I turned and looked again upon the rock, and upon the characters; — and the characters were DESOLATION.

"And I looked upwards, and there stood a man upon the summit of the rock; and I hid myself among the water-lilies that I might discover the actions of the man. And the man was tall and stately in form, and was wrapped up from his shoulders to his feet in the toga of old Rome. And the outlines of his figure were indistinct — but his features were the features of a deity; for the mantle of the night, and of the mist, and of the moon, and of the dew, had left uncovered the features of his face. And his brow was lofty with thought, and his eye wild with care; and, in the few furrows upon his cheek I read the fables of sorrow, and weariness, and disgust with mankind, and a longing after solitude.[f] [6]

"And the man sat[g] upon the rock, and leaned his head upon his hand, and looked out upon the desolation.[7] He looked down into the low unquiet shrubbery, and up into the tall primeval trees,[h]

---

d   litten *(B, C)*
e   the characters. *(B, C)*
f   *After this:* And the moon shone upon his face, and upon the features of his face, and oh! they were more beautiful than the airy dreams which

hovered about the souls of the daughters of Delos! *(B)*
g   sat down *(B, C)*
h   forest, *(A) The first word of the manuscript fragment preserved*

and up higher at the rustling heaven, and into the crimson moon. And I lay close within shelter of the lilies, and[i] observed the actions of the man. And the man trembled in the solitude; — but the night waned, and he sat upon the rock.

"And the man turned his attention from the heaven, and looked out upon the dreary river Zäire, and upon the yellow ghastly waters, and upon the pale legions of the water-lilies. And the man listened to the sighs of the water-lilies, and to[j] the murmur that came up from among them. And I lay close within my covert and[k] observed the actions of the man. And the man trembled in the solitude; — but the night waned and he sat upon the rock.

"Then I went down into the recesses of the morass, and waded afar[l] in among the wilderness of the lilies, and called unto the hippopotami which dwelt among the fens in the recesses of the morass. And the hippopotami heard my call, and came, with the behemoth,[8] unto the foot of the rock, and roared loudly and fearfully beneath the moon. And I lay close within my covert and observed the actions of the man. And the man trembled in the solitude; — but the night waned and he sat upon the rock.

"Then I cursed the [m]elements with the curse of tumult; and[m] a frightful tempest gathered in the heaven[n] where, before, there had been no wind. And the heaven became livid with the violence of the tempest — and the rain beat upon the head of the man — and the floods of the river came down — and the river was tormented into foam — and the water-lilies shrieked within their beds — and the forest[o] crumbled before the wind — and the [p]thunder rolled[p] — and the lightning[q] fell — and the rock rocked to its foundation. And I lay close within my covert and[r] observed the actions of the man. And the man trembled in[s] the solitude; — but the night waned and he sat upon the rock.

"Then I grew angry and cursed, with [t]the curse of *silence*,[t] the

---

i   and I *(A)*
j   of *(B)*
k   and I *(A)*
l   far *(A)*
m . . . m   elements, and *(A)*
n   heaven, *(E) comma deleted to follow A, B, C, D*

o   trees *(A)*
p . . . p   lightning flashed *(A)*
q   thunder *(A)*
r   and I *(A)*
s   within *(A)*
t . . . t   a silent curse *(A); the curse of silence, (B)*

river, and the lilies, and the wind, and the forest, and the heaven, and the thunder, and the sighs of the water-lilies. And they became accursed, and *were still*. And the moon ceased to totter up^u its pathway to^v heaven[9] — and the thunder died away — and the lightning did not flash — and the clouds hung motionless — and the waters sunk to their level and remained — and the trees ceased to rock — and the water-lilies sighed no more — and the murmur was heard no longer from among them, nor any shadow of sound throughout the vast illimitable desert. And I looked upon the characters of the rock, and they were changed; — and the characters were SILENCE.[10]

"And mine eyes fell upon the countenance of the man, and his countenance was wan with terror. ^{w}And, hurriedly, he^w raised his head from his hand, and stood forth upon the rock and listened. But there was no voice throughout the vast illimitable desert, and the characters upon the rock were SILENCE. And the man shuddered, and turned his face away, and fled afar off, ^{x}in haste, so that I beheld^x him no more."

*   *   *   *   *

Now there are fine tales in the volumes of the Magi — in the iron-bound, melancholy volumes of the Magi.[11] Therein, I say, are glorious histories of the Heaven, and of the Earth, and of the mighty sea[12] — and of the Genii[13] that overruled the sea, and the earth, and the lofty heaven. There was much lore too in the sayings which were said by the Sybils;[14] and holy, holy things were heard of old by the dim leaves that trembled around Dodona[15] — but, as Allah liveth, that fable which the demon told me as he sat by my side in the shadow of the tomb,^{y} [16] I hold to be the most wonderful of all! And as the Demon made an end of his story, he fell back within the cavity of the tomb and laughed. And I^z could not laugh with the Demon, and he cursed me because I could not laugh. And the lynx[17] which dwelleth ^{a}forever in^a the tomb, came

---

<table>
<tr><td>u</td><td>in (A, B, C)</td><td></td><td>(B, C)</td></tr>
<tr><td>v</td><td>up the (A, B, C)</td><td>y</td><td>old tomb at Balbec, (A)</td></tr>
<tr><td>w...w</td><td>And he (A)</td><td>z</td><td>I tried, but (A)</td></tr>
<tr><td>x...x</td><td>and I saw (A); and I beheld</td><td>a...a</td><td>in the cavern by (A)</td></tr>
</table>

out therefrom,[b] and lay[c] down at the feet of the Demon, and[d] looked at him steadily in the face.[18]

NOTES

Headnote in B and C: The Psychological Autobiographists are Bulwer and De Quincey.

Motto: The motto in *B* was from Poe's own "Al Aaraaf," I, 126–127. The present motto, introduced in *C,* is from a famous fragment of Alcman, quoted by Apollonius in his *Homeric Lexicon* s.v. *knōdalon;* see Loeb Classics *Lyra Graeca,* I, 76 (No. 36).

1.   Libya was used by the ancient Greeks to designate the whole continent of Africa, according to Pliny's *Natural History,* V, 1. Zäire is the old Portuguese name for the Congo.

In the canceled passage *(B, C),* the Simoom (or simoon) is a hot wind from the Sahara, mentioned also in Poe's "Al Aaraaf," II, 165, in the 1831 version of "Tamerlane," in "MS. Found in a Bottle," and in "Berenicë." Compare also Byron, "The Dream," IV, 2–4,

> The Boy was sprung to manhood: in the wilds
> Of fiery climes he made himself a home,
> And his Soul drank their sunbeams.

2.   Several of Poe's poems contain references to waving or "lolling" lilies. See "Irenë" (1831), "The Valley of Unrest" (*B,* 1836), and "Dream-Land" (1844). Poe may have in mind *Nelumbo lutea,* the long-stemmed yellow water lily, found in profusion by early botanical explorers in rivers and lakes from New Jersey to Florida. See William Bartram, *Travels* (Philadelphia, 1791), p. 327 of Mark Van Doren's edition (1928).

3.   Compare "The Valley Nis" (1831), lines 33–42,

> One by one from the tree top
> There the eternal dews do drop —
> There the vague and dreamy trees
> Do roll like seas in northern breeze
> Around the stormy Hebrides —
> There the gorgeous clouds do fly,
> Rustling everlastingly,
> Through the terror-stricken sky,
> Rolling like a waterfall
> O'er the horizon's fiery wall.

Compare also *Arthur Gordon Pym,* Chapter XXV, "The range of vapor . . . had arisen prodigiously in the horizon . . . a limitless cataract, rolling silently into the sea from some . . . rampart in the heaven."

4.   Red rain undoubtedly occurs in nature. There is a reference to the phenomenon in "A Chapter on Science and Art" in *Burton's Gentleman's Magazine,* April 1840, p. 194.

---

b   from his lair, *(A)*
c   lying *(A)*

d   *Omitted (A)*

5. With the canceled "litten" compare "red-litten windows" in early texts of "The Haunted Palace," line 42.

6. The reference in the canceled passage to "the dreams of the daughters of Delos" alludes to a passage in "A Manuscript Found in a Madhouse" by Bulwer. Poe later placed his phrase in "Ligeia" and retained it there; see a fuller discussion in note 3 on that story, below.

7. Pliny, in the chapter cited in note 1 above, says that many Romans of high rank boasted of having penetrated into Africa as far as Mount Atlas. Some readers will think of Gaius Marius amidst the ruins of Carthage, a type of desolation.

8. The behemoth is mentioned in Job 40:15–24, and is usually thought to be the hippopotamus. Poe obviously was one of those who think the animal was the elephant. Compare Bishop Reginald Heber, *Poetical Works* (Philadelphia, 1841), p. 292.

9. Compare "Israfel," the second stanza, "Tottering above ... /The enamoured Moon"; and "To Helen Whitman," lines 4–5, "A full-orbed moon ... / Sought a precipitate pathway up through heaven."

10. Characters inscribed on a cliff change in Beckford's *Vathek,* as do those on the cover of the Devil's book in Poe's "Bon-Bon."

11. The Magi, priests among the Persians, were famed for mystical lore.

12. Compare Exodus 20:4, quoted in "Bon-Bon," n. 16.

13. Some Genii, or Jinns, fabled Eastern spirits of power, are good and some are bad.

14. Sibyls were prophetesses among the Greeks and Romans.

15. At Dodona in Epirus, the priest and priestess at the grove of Zeus interpreted the sounds of the leaves oracularly. Poe refers to this also in the introduction to his "Marginalia."

16. (See the canceled phrase.) There are references to Balbec in "Al Aaraaf," II, 37, and in "MS. Found in a Bottle."

17. The lynx was sacred to Apollo, hence a symbol of prophecy.

18. Compare "I grew wearied, and ... gazed at him steadfastly in the face," in the last paragraph of Poe's "Man of the Crowd."

THE FOLIO CLUB

Poe composed this piece as an introduction for a collection of his stories as planned in 1833 (see p. 13, above). How many "manuscript tales" he had allowed Lambert A. Wilmer to read, and praise in the *Baltimore Saturday Visiter* of August 4, 1832, is not recorded. On May 4, 1833, Poe sent a manuscript of "Epimanes" embodied in a letter to Joseph T. and Edwin Buckingham, in which he said:

> It is one of a number of similar pieces which I have contemplated publishing under the title of "Eleven Tales of the Arabesque." They are supposed to be read at table by the eleven members of a literary club, and are followed by the remarks of the company upon each. These remarks are intended as a burlesque upon criticism. In the whole, originality more than any thing else has been attempted.

This certainly describes Poe's plans on May 4 but not necessarily what he had actually finished. The burlesque criticisms never appeared — and I suspect were never written. The Boston publishers showed no interest in any of Poe's tales. Since we know that his little manuscript volume was what the judges of the *Saturday Visiter* contest had before them, we may consider the final date for entry in that contest, October 1, 1833, as a *terminus ante quem* for completion of that manuscript.

The imaginary club was modeled, as Dr. John C. French pointed out *(Maryland Historical Magazine,* June 1937), on two actual organizations of which Poe must have known. There had been a literary group in Annapolis in the eighteenth century called The Tuesday Club — and Poe's club met on Tuesday. There was from 1816 to 1825 (and perhaps later) a Delphian Club, to which John Neal and Poe's acquaintance William Gwynn belonged. Its members adopted odd pseudonyms; Neal used his when he published his poem *The Battle of Niagara* in 1818 as by Jehu O'Cataract.

It now seems to me possible to identify the eleven stories, and to assign each with confidence to its appropriate narrator.* Five stories had appeared in the Philadelphia *Saturday Courier* in 1832, namely those now called "Metzengerstein," "The Duc de L'Omelette," "A Tale of Jerusalem," "Loss of Breath" and "Bon-Bon." Three more were published, or submitted for publication,

---

* Poe scholars have enjoyed indulging in this pastime. See my discussion in the *Sewanee Review* for April 1928 — I have since changed three of the ascriptions I made then; see also the important article by James Southall Wilson in the *American Mercury,* October 1931; and Quinn, *Poe,* pp. 745–746. I take into account our knowledge that "A Descent into the Maelström" was not among the eleven.

in 1833: "MS. Found in a Bottle," "The Visionary" ("The Assignation"), and "Epimanes" ("Four Beasts in One"). The single leaf of
manuscript that formerly accompanied "The Folio Club" is of the
conclusion of "Silence." In the *Southern Literary Messenger,*
August 1835 (1:716), it is stated that "Lionizing" was one of the
stories. The eleventh must be "Shadow."

No text of "The Folio Club" was printed until 1902.

LATER PLANS FOR THE FOLIO CLUB

Poe's failure to find a publisher for his little volume in 1833
did not discourage him completely. In the *Southern Literary
Messenger,* August 1835 (1:716), a notice by E. V. Sparhawk appeared: "The *Tales of the Folio Club* are sixteen in all, and we
believe it is the author's intention to publish them in the autumn."

On September 2, 1836, Poe wrote Harrison Hall, a publisher,
about the tales:

> I have prepared them for republication, in book form, in the following man-
> ner. I imagine a company of 17 persons who call themselves the Folio Club. They
> meet once a month at the house of one of the members, and, at a late dinner,
> each member reads aloud a short prose tale of his own composition. The votes are
> taken in regard to the merits of each tale. The author of the worst tale, for the
> month, forfeits the dinner and wine at the next meeting. The author of the best,
> is President at the next meeting. The seventeen tales which appeared in the
> Messenger are supposed to be narrated by the seventeen members at one of these
> monthly meetings. As soon as each tale is read — the other sixteen members
> criticise it in turn — and these criticisms are intended as a burlesque upon criticism
> generally. The author of the tale adjudged to be the worst demurs from the gen-
> eral judgment, seizes the seventeen MSS upon the table, and, rushing from the
> house, determines to appeal, by printing the whole, from the decision of the
> Club, to that of the public.

In this letter, first printed in the *Sewanee Review,* April 1928,
Poe went on to tell Hall that the critical remarks would "make one
fourth of the whole," and that the book would run to 300 pages. In
view of Poe's habit of anticipating accomplishments, it is very
doubtful that the criticisms were ever written, and some of the six
new tales may also have been merely planned. Four new stories
were in print before September 1836, namely: "Berenicë," "Mor-

ella," "Hans Phaall,"† and "King Pest." No two others can be identified with confidence. Wilson and Quinn, both cited above, suggest "Mystification," which was the first printed after Poe left the *Southern Literary Messenger*. Wilson, and William Bittner in *Poe* (1962), page 290, suggest "Why the Little Frenchman," of which no first printing in a periodical has been found. Neither of those stories seems to me earlier than 1837.

TEXTS

(A) Manuscript, 1833, now in the Harvard College Library; (B) *Complete Works*, ed. James A. Harrison (1902), II, xxxvi–xxxix.

The original manuscript (A), presented to Harvard by the Griswold family, is followed. It is written on both sides of a single leaf in a small printlike hand, with two small auctorial cancelations (indicated in our text by enclosure in angle brackets). Harrison's text (B) is merely the first publication.

THE FOLIO CLUB [A]

There is a Machiavelian plot
Though every nare olfact it not.
                              BUTLER

The Folio Club is, I am sorry to say, a mere Junto of *Dunderheadism*. I think too the members are quite as ill-looking as they are stupid. I also believe it their settled intention to abolish Literature, subvert the Press, and overturn the Government of Nouns and Pronouns. These are my private opinions which I now take the liberty of making public.

Yet when, about a week ago, I first became one of this diabolical association, no person could have entertained for it more profound sentiments of admiration and respect. Why my feelings in this matter have undergone a change will ᵃappear, very obviously,ᵃ in the sequel. In the meantime I shall vindicate my own character, and the dignity of Letters.

I find, upon reference to the records, that the Folio Club was organized as such on the —— day of —— in the year ——. I like to

---

† To be included in Volume IV of this edition.

Motto: nare/hare (B)   a . . . a appear very obviously (B)

begin with the beginning,[1] and have a partiality for dates. A clause in the Constitution then adopted forbade the members to be otherwise than erudite and witty: and the avowed objects of the Confederation were 'the instruction of society, and the amusement of themselves.' For the latter purpose a meeting is held monthly at the house of some one of the association,[b] when each individual is expected to come prepared with a 'Short Prose Tale' of his own composition. Each article thus produced is read by its <respective>[c] author to the company assembled over a glass of wine at <a very late>[d] dinner. Much rivalry will of course ensue — more particularly[e] as the writer of the 'Best Thing' is appointed President of the Club *pro tem:*, an office endowed with many dignities and little expence, and which endures until its occupant is dispossessed by a superior *morceau*. The father of the Tale held, on the contrary, to be the least meritorious, is bound to furnish the dinner and wine at the next similar meeting of the Society. This is found an excellent method of occasionally supplying the body with a new member, in the place of some unfortunate who, forfeiting two or three entertainments in succession, will naturally decline, at the same time, the 'supreme honour' and the association. The number of the Club is limited to eleven. For this there are many good reasons which it is unnecessary to mention, but which will of course suggest themselves to every person of reflection. One of them, however, is that on the first of April, in the year three hundred and fifty before the Deluge, there are said to have been just eleven spots upon the sun. It will be seen that, in giving these rapid outlines of the Society, I have so far restrained my indignation as to speak with unusual candour and liberality. The *exposé* which it is my intention to make will be sufficiently effected by a mere detail of the Club's proceedings on the evening of Tuesday last, when I made my *debût*[f] as a member of that body, having been only chosen in place of the Honourable Augustus Scratchaway, resigned.

At five P.M. I went by appointment to the house of Mr. Rouge-et-Noir who admires Lady Morgan, and whose Tale was con-

---

b   Association, *(B)*   very late] *B*
c   *Canceled in the manuscript*   e   particularly, *(B)*
d   *Canceled in the manuscript* [at a   f   *début (B)*

demned at the previous monthly meeting. I found the company already assembled in the dining-room, and must confess that the brilliancy of the fire, the comfortable appearance of the apartment, and the excellent equipments of the table, as well as a due confidence in my own abilities, contributed to inspire me, for the time, with many pleasant meditations. I was welcomed with great show of cordiality, and dined with much self-congratulation at becoming one of so wise a Society.

The members,[g] generally, were most remarkable men. There was, first of all, Mr. Snap, the President, who is a very lank man with a hawk nose, and was formerly in the service of the Down-East Review.

Then there was Mr. Convolvulus Gondola, a young gentleman who had travelled a good deal.

Then there was De Rerum Naturâ, Esqr., who wore a very singular pair of green spectacles.

Then there was a very little man in a black coat with very black eyes.

Then there was Mr. Solomon Seadrift who had every appearance of a fish.

Then there was Mr. Horribile Dictû,[h] with white eyelashes, who had graduated at Gottingen.[i]

Then there was Mr. Blackwood Blackwood who had written certain articles for foreign Magazines.[j]

Then there was the host, Mr. Rouge-et-Noir, who admired Lady Morgan.

Then there was a stout gentleman who admired Sir Walter Scott.

Then there was Chronologos Chronology who admired Horace Smith, and had a very big nose which had been in Asia Minor.[2]

Upon the removal of the cloth Mr. Snap said to me 'I believe there is little need of my giving you any information, Sir, in regard to the regulations of our Club. I think you know we intend to instruct society, and amuse ourselves. To night[k] however we propose

---

g   *Comma omitted (B)*
h   Dictu, *(B)*
i   Göttingen. *(B)*

j   magazines. *(B)*
k   To-night *(B)*

doing the latter solely, and shall call upon you in turn to contribute your quota. In the meantime I will commence operations.' Here Mr. Snap, having pushed the bottle, produced a M.S.[1] and read as follows.

NOTES

Motto: This is from Samuel Butler's *Hudibras*, I, i, 741–742.

1. Compare "the folly of not beginning at the beginning — of neglecting the giant Moulineau's advice to his friend Ram" in "Marginalia," number 191 (*Graham's,* January 1848, p. 191). Poe earlier referred to the same advice in his review of L. A. Wilmer's *Quacks of Helicon,* in *Graham's* for August 1841. In the story of Count Anthony Hamilton, "Le Bélier" (*Œuvres,* Paris, 1812, II, 153), the giant Moulineau says, *"Bélier, mon ami...Si tu voulois commencer par le commencement tu me ferois plaisir."*

2. Mr. Snap's tale is "Lionizing." Dr. John C. French identified Mr. Snap with John Neal, whose names are likewise monosyllabic, and who wrote severe criticisms of N. P. Willis, the person satirized in the story. Neal disapproved of duels; had written a novel, *The Down Easters;* and had edited a magazine called *The Yankee.* Poe has another character called Snap in "The Business Man."

Convolvulus Gondola appropriately told the Venetian story of "The Visionary," later called "The Assignation." Miss Helen Convolvulus is a character in Bulwer's "Too Handsome for Anything."

De Rerum Natura, named for the philosophical poem of Lucretius, told of the philosopher, "Bon-Bon." In "A Few Words on Etiquette," in *Godey's Lady's Book* for August 1846, Poe says green spectacles are for students of theology.

The little man in black is a good person to discuss "Shadow."

To Mr. Solomon Seadrift may be assigned "MS. Found in a Bottle."

Horribile Dictu had been at Göttingen, and hence told of the Germanic nobles of Transylvania in "Metzengerstein." The Latin quotation means "Horrible to tell," and is a commonplace traced to Florus, *Epitome,* I, xvi, 12. Poe also used the phrase in "The Murders in the Rue Morgue."

Mr. Blackwood Blackwood obviously told "Loss of Breath," which in the *Southern Literary Messenger* of September 1835 was subtitled "A Tale a la Blackwood."

Mr. Rouge-et-Noir, whose name is that of a game, surely told of "The Duc de L'Omelette," a story of a French gambler. The Irish Lady Sydney Morgan wrote a book on France, received with great praise and blame by critics of different political bias. Like the Duc she resided in the Chaussée d'Antin, as N. P. Willis tells us in the twentieth chapter of his *Pencillings by the Way,* first printed in the *New-York Mirror,* June 30, 1832. See his *Prose Works* (1845), p. 32.

---

1 M.S./M. S. (B)

BERENICE

The stout gentleman who admired Scott presumably told "Epimanes," a historical story, for no other tale is appropriate to him.

Chronologos Chronology, who admired Horace Smith, must have written "A Tale of Jerusalem" which is founded on Smith's *Zillah* (1828). In it is a reference to an ancient date by the system of "years of the world," which placed the creation in 4004 B.C.

To the narrator, who is silent about his own name, "Siope," now called "Silence," is appropriately assigned, since it is "in the manner of the Psychological Autobiographists," Bulwer and Thomas DeQuincey. The position of the manuscript fragment of "Silence" with relation to that of "The Folio Club" suggests that "Silence" may have been the last of the collection. An observation in a review — probably by Poe — of *Legends of a Log Cabin, by a Western Man,* in the *Southern Literary Messenger* for December 1835 may be significant. "The *Minute Men* is the last of the series, and from its being told by the author himself, is, we suppose, considered by him the best."

BERENICE

This is one of Poe's best known stories. Critics have received it variously, but almost no selection omits it. The magnificence of its style is undeniable. Yet even in its present form, from which four unpleasant paragraphs of the earlier versions were wisely omitted by the author, many readers find the tale too repulsive by far.

Soon after its publication in the *Southern Literary Messenger* for March 1835, Poe, on April 30, wrote apologetically to the editor, T. W. White, who had apparently received complaints:

The subject is far too horrible. . . . The Tale originated in a bet that I could produce nothing effective on a subject so singular, provided I treated it seriously. . . . I allow that it approaches the very verge of bad-taste — but I will not sin quite so egregiously again.

The basis of the challenge pretty surely was a scandal in Baltimore about the "robbing of graves for the sake of obtaining human teeth" for dentists. An account of it in the *Baltimore Saturday Visiter* of February 23, 1833 was discovered by Lucille King.*

---

* See *Studies in English,* no. 10 (University of Texas Bulletin, 1930), p. 135, and Campbell's *Mind of Poe,* p. 167. [See also Roger Forclaz, "A Source for 'Berenice' and a Note on Poe's Reading," *Poe Newsletter,* October 1968. "The Visionary" which appeared in *The Casket* for 1832 is pointed out as a possible source.]

TALES OF THE FOLIO CLUB

The zealous searchers for Poe's personality in his characters have seized upon this story. Psychiatrists assure me the fascination of teeth might be a sign of necrophilism. What is forgotten is that all the ladies with whom Poe was (or fancied himself) in love were in normal health when he became interested in them.

The names of the characters are significant. Egeus is the name of Hermia's father in *Midsummer Night's Dream,* who failed to understand love. Berenicë was the wife of King Ptolemy III Euergetes of Egypt. She cut off her hair in fulfillment of a vow for her husband's safe return from battle, and hung it in a temple — whence, according to the court astronomer, the gods took it and placed it in the heavens as the constellation Coma Berenices. The event has inspired several poets. Callimachus wrote a poem on the subject at the time. The Greek version is preserved only in fragments; but there is a complete Latin version by Catullus, remotely a source of Pope's *Rape of the Lock.*

Since no appropriate narrator for "Berenicë" appears in the introduction to *Tales of the Folio Club,* it seems unlikely that the tale was one of the eleven Poe alluded to in his letter to the Buckinghams, May 4, 1833. Hence the date of its composition may be assumed to be any time between the spring of 1833 and early 1835, when it was sent to White.

TEXTS

(A) Southern Literary Messenger, March 1835 (1:333-336); *(B)* Duane copy of last with manuscript changes, 1839; *(C) Tales of the Grotesque and Arabesque* (1840), II, 167-181; *(D) Broadway Journal,* April 5, 1845 (1:217-219); *(E) Works* (1850), I, 437-445. PHANTASY-PIECES, title only.

Griswold's text *(E)* is followed. Poe made seven verbal changes in the Duane *Messenger (B),* presumably as "copy" for the printers of *C,* but more changes were made in proof. PHANTASY-PIECES in the table of contents gave a new and abortive title, but the actual changes are lost with the second volume of the set. For the *Broadway Journal (D)* changes in phraseology and punctuation were fairly extensive and included the deletion of four gruesome paragraphs. The asterisked divisions occur in all texts.

Reprint
The Spirit of the Times (Philadelphia), April 11, 1845, from the *Broadway Journal.*

BERENICE

BERENICE. [*E*]

Dicebant mihi sodales, si sepulchrum amicæ visitarem, curas meas aliquantulum fore levatas. — *Ebn Zaiat.*[1]

Misery is manifold. The wretchedness of earth is multiform. Overreaching the wide horizon as[a] the rainbow, its hues are as various as the hues of that arch — as distinct too, yet as intimately blended. Overreaching the wide horizon as[b] the rainbow! How is it that from beauty I have derived a type of unloveliness? — from the covenant of peace,[2] a simile of sorrow? But[c] as, in ethics, evil is a consequence of good, so, in fact, out of joy is sorrow born. Either the memory of past bliss is the anguish of to-day, or the agonies which *are*[d] have their origin in the ecstasies[e] which *might have been*.[f]

My baptismal name is Egæus; that of my family I will not mention. Yet there are no towers in the land more time-honored than my gloomy, gray, hereditary halls. Our line has been called a race of visionaries; and in many striking particulars — in the character of the family mansion — in the frescos of the chief saloon — in the tapestries of the dormitories — in the chiselling of some buttresses in the armory — but more especially in the gallery of antique paintings — in the fashion of the library chamber — and, lastly, in the very peculiar nature of the library's contents — there is more than sufficient evidence to warrant the belief.

The recollections[g] of my earliest years are connected with that chamber, and with its volumes — of which latter I will say no more. Here died my mother. Herein was I born. But it is mere idleness to say that I had not lived before — that the soul has no previous existence.[3] You deny it? — let us not argue the matter. Convinced myself, I seek not to convince. There is, however, a remembrance

---

Title: Berenice — A Tale *(A, B);* The Teeth (PHANTASY-PIECES)
Motto: Omitted *(A, B, C)*
a like *(A, B, C)*
b like *(A, B, C)*
c But thus is it. And *(A) changed in B*
d *are, (A, B, E) comma deleted to follow C, D*

e ecstacies *(E) misprint*
f *After this:* I have a tale to tell in its own essence rife with horror — I would suppress it were it not a record more of feelings than of facts. *(A, B, C)*
g recollection *(D, E) misprint, corrected from A, B, C*

of aerial forms — of spiritual and meaning eyes — of sounds, musical yet sad; a remembrance which will not be excluded; a memory like a shadow — vague, variable, indefinite, unsteady; and like a shadow, too, in the impossibility of my getting rid of it while the sunlight of my reason shall exist.

In that chamber was I born. Thus awaking[h] from the long night of what seemed, but was not, nonentity, at once into the very regions of fairy land — into a palace of imagination — into the wild dominions of monastic thought and erudition — it is not singular that I gazed around me with a startled and ardent eye — that I loitered away my boyhood in books, and dissipated my youth in revery; but it *is* singular, that as years rolled away, and the noon of manhood found me still in the mansion of my fathers — it *is* wondeful what stagnation there fell upon the springs of my life — wonderful how total an inversion took place in the character of my [i]commonest thought.[i] The realities of the world affected me as visions, and as visions only, while the wild ideas of the land of dreams became, in turn, not the material of my every-day existence, but in very deed that existence utterly and solely in itself.

*　　*　　*　　*　　*

Berenicë and I were cousins, and we grew up together in my paternal halls. Yet differently we grew — I, ill of health, and buried in gloom — she, agile, graceful, and overflowing with energy; hers,[j] the ramble on the hill-side — mine, the studies of the cloister; I, living within my own heart, and addicted, body and soul, to the most intense and painful meditation — she, roaming carelessly through life, with no thought of the shadows in her path, or the silent flight of the raven-winged hours. Berenicë! — I call upon her name — Berenicë! — and from the gray ruins of memory a thousand tumultuous recollections are startled at the sound! Ah, vividly is her image before me now, as in the early days of her lightheartedness and joy! Oh, gorgeous yet fantastic beauty! Oh, sylph amid the shrubberies of Arnheim![4] Oh, Naiad among its[k] fountains! And then — then all is mystery and terror, and a tale which

---

h awaking, as it were, *(A) changed in B*
i...i common thoughts. *(A, B, C)*

j her's, *(E) misprint, corrected from A, B, C, D*
k her *(A, B, C)*

should not be told. Disease — a fatal disease, fell like the simoom[1] [5]
upon her frame; and, even while I gazed upon her, the spirit of
change swept over her, pervading her mind, her habits, and her
character, and, in a manner the most subtle and terrible, disturbing
even the[m] identity of her person! Alas! the destroyer came and
went! — and the victim — where is[n] she? I knew her not — or knew
her no longer as Berenicë!

Among the numerous train of maladies superinduced by that
fatal and primary one which effected a revolution of so horrible a
kind in the moral and physical being of my cousin, may be mentioned as the most distressing and obstinate in its nature, a species of
epilepsy not unfrequently terminating in *trance* itself — trance very
nearly resembling positive dissolution, and from which her manner
of recovery was, in most instances, startlingly abrupt. In the mean
time, my own disease — for I have been told that I should call it
by no other appellation — my own disease, then, grew rapidly upon
me, and[o] assumed finally a monomaniac character of a novel and
extraordinary form — hourly and momently[p] gaining vigor — and
at length obtaining over me the most[q] incomprehensible ascendency.
This monomania, if I must so term it, consisted in a morbid irritability of[r] those properties of the mind in metaphysical science
termed the *attentive*. It is more than probable that I am not understood; but I [s]fear, indeed, that it is[s] in no manner possible to convey to the mind of the merely general reader, an adequate idea of
that nervous *intensity of interest* with which, in my case, the powers
of meditation (not to speak technically) busied and[t] buried themselves, in the contemplation of even the most ordinary[u] objects of
the universe.

To muse for long unwearied hours, with my attention riveted to
some frivolous device on[v] the margin or in the typography of a book;
to become absorbed, for the better part of a summer's day, in a
quaint shadow falling aslant upon the tapestry or upon the floor;

---

1 simoom *(A, B, D)*
m the very *(A, B)*
n was *(A, B, C, D)*
o and, aggravated in its symptoms by
the immoderate use of opium, *(A, B, C)*
p momentarily *(A, B)*
q most singular and *(A, B, C)*

r of the nerves immediately affecting
(A, B, C)
s . . . s fear that it is indeed *(A, B, C)*
t and, as it were, *(A, B, C)*
u common *(A, B, C)*
v upon *(A, B, C)*

to lose myself, for an entire night, in watching the steady flame of a lamp, or the embers of a fire; to dream away whole days over the perfume of a flower; to repeat, monotonously, some common word, until the sound, by dint of frequent repetition, ceased to convey any idea whatever to the mind; to lose all sense of motion or physical existence, by means[w] of absolute bodily quiescence long and obstinately persevered in: such were a few of the most common and least pernicious vagaries induced by a condition of the mental faculties, not, indeed, altogether unparalleled, but certainly bidding defiance to anything like analysis or explanation.[6]

Yet let me not be misapprehended. The undue, earnest,[x] and morbid attention thus excited by objects in their own nature frivolous, must not be confounded in character with that ruminating propensity common to all mankind, and more especially indulged in by persons of ardent imagination.[y] It was not even, as might be at first supposed, an extreme condition, or exaggeration of such propensity, but primarily and essentially distinct and different. In the one instance, the dreamer, or enthusiast, being interested by an object usually *not* frivolous, imperceptibly loses sight of this object in a wilderness of deductions and suggestions issuing therefrom, until, at the conclusion of a day-dream *often replete with luxury,* he finds the *incitamentum,* or first cause of his musings, entirely[z] vanished and forgotten. In my case, the primary object was *invariably frivolous,* although assuming, through the medium of my distempered vision, a refracted and unreal importance. Few deductions, if any, were made; and those few pertinaciously returning in[a] upon the original object as a centre.[7] The meditations were *never* pleasurable; and, at the termination of the revery, the first cause, so far from being out of sight, had attained that supernaturally exaggerated interest which was the prevailing feature of the disease. In a word, the powers of mind more particularly exercised were, with me, as I have said before, the *attentive,* and are, with the day-dreamer, the *speculative.*

My books, at this epoch, if they did not actually serve to irritate

---

w   by means/in a state *(A, B, C)*   *changed in B*
x   intense, *(A) canceled in B;* earnest   z   utterly *(A, B)*
first in C   a   in, so to speak, *(A, B, C)*
y   imagination. By no means. *(A)*

BERENICE

the disorder, partook, it will be perceived, largely, in their imaginative and inconsequential nature, of the characteristic qualities of the disorder itself. I well remember, among others, the treatise of the noble Italian, Cælius[b] Secundus Curio, *"De Amplitudine Beati Regni Dei;"* St. Austin's[c] great work, *"The City of God;"* and Tertullian's[d] *"De Carne Christi,"* in which the paradoxical[e] sentence, *"Mortuus est Dei filius; credibile est quia ineptum est; et sepultus resurrexit; certum est quia impossibile est,"* occupied my undivided time, for many weeks of laborious and fruitless investigation.[8]

Thus it will appear that, shaken from its balance only by trivial things, my reason bore resemblance to that ocean-crag spoken of by Ptolemy Hephestion, which,[f] steadily resisting the attacks of human violence, and the fiercer fury of the waters and the winds, trembled only to the touch of the flower called Asphodel.[9] And although, to a careless thinker, it might appear a matter beyond doubt, that the[g] alteration produced by her unhappy malady, in the *moral* condition of Berenicë, would afford me many objects for the exercise of that intense and abnormal[h] meditation whose nature I have been at some trouble in explaining, yet such was not [i]in any degree[i] the case. In the lucid intervals of my infirmity, her calamity, indeed, gave me pain, and, taking deeply to heart that total wreck of her fair and gentle life, I did not fail to ponder, frequently and bitterly, upon the wonder-working means by which so strange a revolution had been so suddenly brought to pass. But these reflections partook not of the idiosyncrasy of my disease, and were[j] such as would have occurred, under similar circumstances, to the ordinary mass of mankind. True to its own character, my disorder revelled in the less important but more startling changes wrought in the *physical* frame of [k]Berenicë — in[k] the singular and most appalling distortion of her personal identity.

During the brightest days of her unparalleled beauty, most

---

b   Cœlius *(A, B, C, D, E) emended editorially*
c   Austin' *(D) misprint*
d   Tertullian *(A, B, C, D) misprint*
e   unintelligible *(A, B, C)*
f   which *(A, D, E) comma added*
from B, C
g   the fearful *(A, B, C)*
h   morbid *(A, B, C)*
i...i   by any means *(A, B, C)*
j   where *(D) misprint*
k...k   Berenice, and in *(A, B, C)*

surely I had never loved her. In the strange anomaly of my existence, feelings,[1] with me, *had never been* of the heart, and my passions *always were* of the mind. Through the gray of the early morning — among the trellised shadows of the forest at noonday — and in the silence of my library at night — she had flitted by my eyes, and I had seen her — not as the living and breathing Berenicë, but as the Berenicë of a dream; not as a being of the [m]earth, earthly,[m] but as the abstraction of such a being; not as a thing to admire, but to analyze; not as an object of love, but as the theme of the most abstruse although desultory speculation. And *now* — now I shuddered in her presence, and grew pale at her approach; yet, bitterly lamenting her fallen and desolate condition, I [n]called to mind[n] that she had loved me long, and, in an evil moment, I spoke to her of marriage.

And at length the period of our nuptials was approaching, when, upon an afternoon in the winter of the year — one of those unseasonably warm, calm, and misty days which are the nurse of the beautiful Halcyon,* — I sat, (and sat, as I thought, alone,) in the inner apartment of the library. But, uplifting my eyes, I saw that[o] Berenicë stood before me.

Was it my own excited imagination — or the misty influence of the atmosphere — or the uncertain twilight of the chamber — or the gray draperies which fell around her figure — that caused [p]in it so vacillating and indistinct an outline?[p] I could not tell.[q] She spoke[r] no word; and I — not for worlds could I have uttered a syllable. An icy chill ran through my frame; a sense of insufferable anxiety oppressed me; a consuming curiosity pervaded my soul; and, sinking back upon the chair, I remained for some time breathless and motionless,[s] with my eyes riveted upon her person. Alas!

* For as Jove, during the winter season, gives twice seven days of warmth, men have called this clement and temperate time the nurse of the beautiful Halcyon. — *Simonides.*[10]

---

1   feelings *(D, E) comma added from A, B, C*
m . . . m   earth — earthly — *(A, B, C)*
n . . . n   knew *(A, B, C)*
o   I saw that *omitted (A, B, C)*
p . . . p   it to loom up in so unnatural a degree? *(A, B, C)*
q   tell. Perhaps she had grown taller since her malady. *(A) changed in B*
r   spoke, however, *(A) changed in B*
s   motionless, and *(A, B, C)*

its emaciation was excessive, and not one vestige of the former being lurked in any single line of the contour. My burning glances at length fell upon the[t] face.

The forehead was high, and very pale, and singularly placid; and the once jetty[u] hair fell partially over it, and overshadowed the hollow temples with [v]innumerable ringlets, now of a vivid yellow,[v] and jarring discordantly, in their fantastic character, with the reigning melancholy of the countenance.[11] The eyes were lifeless, and lustreless, [w]and seemingly pupilless,[w] and I shrank[x] involuntarily from their glassy stare to the contemplation of the thin and shrunken lips. They parted; and in a smile of peculiar meaning, *the teeth* of the changed Berenicë disclosed themselves slowly to my view. Would to God that I had never beheld them, or that, having done so, I had died!

*   *   *   *   *

The shutting of a door disturbed me, and, looking up, I found that[y] my cousin had departed from the chamber. But from the disordered chamber of my brain, had not, alas! departed, and would not be driven away, the white and ghastly *spectrum* of the teeth. Not a speck on[z] their surface — not a shade on their enamel[a]—not an indenture in their edges—but what that brief period of her smile had sufficed to brand in upon my memory. I saw them *now* even more unequivocally than I beheld them *then*. The teeth! — the teeth! — they were here, and there, and everywhere, and visibly and palpably before me; long, narrow, and excessively white, with the pale lips writhing about them,[12] as in the very moment of their first terrible development. Then came the full fury of my *monomania,* and I struggled in vain against its strange and irresistible influence. In the multiplied objects of the external world I had no thoughts but for the teeth. [b]For these I longed with a frenzied desire.[b] All other matters and all different interests became absorbed in their single contemplation. They — they alone

---

t   her *(A, B)*
u   golden *(A, B, C)*
v . . . v   ringlets now black as the raven's ring, *(A);* ringlets now black as the raven's wing, *(B, C)*
w . . . w   *Omitted (A, B, C)*

x   shrunk *(A, B, C)*
y   *Omitted (A, B, C)*
z   upon *(A, B, C)*
a   enamel — not a line in their configuration *(A, B, C)*
b . . . b   *Omitted (A, B, C)*

were present to the mental eye, and they, in their sole individuality, became the essence of my mental life. I held them in every light. I turned them in every attitude. I surveyed their characteristics. I dwelt upon their peculiarities. I pondered upon their conformation. I mused upon the alteration in their ᶜnature. Iᶜ shuddered as I assigned to them, in imagination, a sensitive and sentient power, and, even when unassisted by the lips, a capability of moral expression. Of ᵈMademoiselle Salléᵈ it has been wellᵉ said, *"Que tous ses pas etaient*ᶠ *des sentiments,"*[13] and of Berenicë I more seriously believed *que tous ses dents étaient des idées.*ᵍ ʰ*Des idées!* — ah, here was the idiotic thought that destroyed me! *Des idées!* — ah, *therefore* it was that I coveted them so madly! I felt that their possession could alone ever restore me to peace, in giving me back to reason.ʰ

And the evening closed in upon me thus — and then the darkness came, and tarried, and went — and the day again dawned — and the mists of a second night were now gathering around — and still I sat motionless in that solitary room — and still I sat buried in meditation — and still the *phantasma* of the teeth maintained its terrible ascendency, as, with the most vivid and hideous distinctness, it floated about amid the changing lights and shadows of the chamber. At length there brokeⁱ in upon my dreams aʲ cry as of horror and dismay; and thereunto, after a pause, succeeded the sound of troubled voices, intermingled with many low moanings of sorrow or of pain. I arosᵉᵏ from my seat, and,ˡ throwing open one of the doors of the library, ᵐsaw standingᵐ out in the ante-chamber a servant maiden, all in tears, whoⁿ told me that Berenicë was — no more! ᵒShe had been seized with epilepsyᵒ in the early morning, and now, at the closing in of the night, the grave

---

c . . . c nature — and *(A, B, C)*
d . . . d Mad'selle Sallé *(A, B, C, D)*
accent added from A, B, C, D
e *Omitted (A, B, C)*
f *etoient (A, B) accent added to*
étaient *editorially*
g *idees. (E) accent added from*
A, B, C, D
h . . . h *Omitted (A, B, C) accents*
added from D

i broke forcibly *(A, B, C)*
j a wild *(A, B, C)*
k arose hurriedly *(A, B, C)*
l and *(E) comma added from A,*
B, C, D
m . . . m there stood *(A) changed in B*
n and she *(A, B, C)*
o . . . o Seized with an epileptic fit
she had fallen dead *(A, B, C)*

was ready for its tenant, and all the preparations for the burial were completed.[p]

*   *   *   *   *

I found myself[q] sitting in the library, and again sitting there alone. It seemed that I had newly awakened from a confused and exciting dream. I knew that it was now midnight, and I was well aware[r] that since the setting of the sun[s] Berenicë had been interred. But of that dreary period which[t] intervened I had no positive, at least no definite comprehension. Yet[u] its memory was replete[v] with horror — horror more horrible from being vague, and terror more terrible from ambiguity. It was a fearful page in the record of my existence, written all over with dim, and hideous, and unintelli-

---

p   *After this A, B, C have four paragraphs not used in D and E:*

With a heart full of grief, yet reluctantly, and oppressed with awe, I made my way to the bed-chamber of the departed. The room was large, and very dark, and at every step within its gloomy precincts I encountered the paraphernalia of the grave. The coffin, so a menial told me, lay surrounded by the curtains of yonder bed, and in that coffin, he whisperingly assured me, was all that remained of Berenice. Who was it asked me would I not look upon the corpse? I had seen the lips of no one move, yet the question had been demanded, and the echo of the syllables still lingered in the room. It was impossible to refuse; and with a sense of suffocation I dragged myself to the side of the bed. Gently I uplifted the draperies of the curtains.

As I let them fall they descended upon my shoulders, and shutting me thus out from the living, enclosed me in the strictest communion with the deceased.

The very atmosphere was redolent of death. The peculiar smell of the coffin sickened me; and I fancied a deleterious odor was already exhaling from the body. I would have given worlds to escape — to fly from the pernicious influence of mortality — to breathe once again the pure air of the eternal heavens. But I had no longer the power to move — my knees tottered beneath me — and I remained rooted to the spot, and gazing upon the frightful length of the rigid body as it lay outstretched in the dark coffin without a lid.

God of heaven! — is [was *(C)*] it possible? Is [Was *(C)*] it my brain that reels [reeled *(C)*] — or was it indeed the finger of the enshrouded dead that stirred in the white cerement that bound it? Frozen with unutterable awe I slowly raised my eyes to the countenance of the corpse. There had been a band around the jaws, but, I know not how, it was broken asunder. The livid lips were wreathed into a species of smile, and, through the enveloping gloom, once again there glared upon me in too palpable reality, the white and glistening, and ghastly teeth of Berenice. I sprang convulsively from the bed, and, uttering no word, rushed forth a maniac from that apartment of triple horror, and mystery, and death.

q   myself again *(A, B, C)*

r   aware, *(E) comma deleted to follow A, B, C, D*

s   sun, *(E) comma deleted to follow A, B, C, D*

t   which had *(A, B, C)*

u   But *(C)*

v   rife *(A, B, C)*

gible recollections. I strived to decypher them, but in vain; while ever and anon, like the spirit of a departed sound, the shrill and piercing shriek of a female voice seemed to be ringing in my ears. I had done a deed — what was it? [w]I asked myself the question aloud, and the whispering echoes of the chamber answered me, — "*What was it?*"[w]

On the table beside me burned a lamp, and near it lay a little box.[x] It was[y] of no remarkable character, and I had seen it frequently before, for it was[z] the property of the family physician; but how came it *there,* upon my table, and why did I shudder in regarding it? These things were in no manner to be accounted for, and my eyes at length dropped to the open pages of a book, and to a sentence underscored therein. The words were the singular but simple ones[a] of the poet Ebn Zaiat: — "*Dicebant mihi sodales si sepulchrum amicae visitarem, curas meas aliquantulum fore levatas.*"[b] Why, then, as I perused them, did the hairs of my head erect themselves on end, and the blood of my body [c]become congealed[c] within my veins?

There came a light tap at the library door — and, pale as the tenant of a tomb, a menial entered upon tiptoe. His looks were wild with terror, and he spoke to me in a voice tremulous, husky, and very low. What said he? — some broken sentences I heard. He told of a wild cry disturbing[d] the silence of the night — of the gathering together of the household — of a search in the direction of the sound; and then his tones grew thrillingly distinct as he whispered me of a violated grave — of a disfigured body[e] enshrouded, yet still breathing — still palpitating — *still alive!*[f]

He pointed to my garments; they were muddy and clotted with gore. I spoke not, and he took me gently by the hand:[g] it was indented with the impress of human nails. He directed my atten-

---

w . . . w   And the echoes of the chamber answered me "what was it?" (A, B, C)
x   box of ebony. (A, B, C)
y   was a box (A, B, C)
z   for it was/it being (A, B, C)
a   words (A, B, C)
b   *To the Latin is appended a footnote:* My companions told me I might find some little alleviation of my misery, in visiting the grave of my beloved. (A, B)
c . . . c   congeal (A, B, C)
d   heard in (A, B)
e   body discovered upon its margin — a body (A, B, C)
f   still alive! (A, B, C)
g   hand: but (A, B, C)

tion to some object against the wall. I looked at it for some minutes: it was a spade. With a shriek I bounded to the table, and grasped the[h] box that lay upon it. But I could not force it open; and, in my tremor, it slipped from[i] my hands, and fell heavily, and burst into pieces; and from it, with a rattling sound, there rolled out some instruments of dental surgery, intermingled with [j]thirty-two small,[j] white, and ivory-looking[k] substances that were scattered to and fro about the floor.

NOTES

Title: In Poe's day Berenice was pronounced as four syllables, and rhyming with "very spicy." Hence, a diaeresis has been added to our text.

1.   The words of the motto are quoted again in the text of the story; for the first version of the tale *(A)*, Poe translated them in a footnote he later canceled: "My companions told me I might find some little alleviation of my misery, in visiting the grave of my beloved." The sentence is quoted in French from the *Kitab al-Aghani* (Book of Songs), a tenth-century collection, in D'Herbelot's *Bibliothèque Orientale* (1697), p. 921, s.v. Zaïat. Abou Giafar Mohammed ben Abdalmalek ben Abban, known as Ben Zaïat ("descendant of an oil-merchant"), was a grammarian and poet of Baghdad, who wrote an elegy on the loss of a beloved slave girl. He died about A.D. 218. The source of Poe's Latin version is not known.

2.   See Genesis 9:13 on the rainbow as the symbol of God's covenant with Noah.

3.   Poe's interest in reincarnation is evident also in "Metzengerstein," "Morella," "Ligeia," and several later stories.

4.   The fearless and vigorously beautiful heroine of Scott's *Anne of Geierstein* (1829; new edition, with Introduction by the author, dated 1831) was Baroness of Arnheim; her family and castle had a reputation for magic; seemingly mysterious glimpses of her in the forest by night are described in chapter X of Scott's novel. See notes on Poe's late tale, "The Domain of Arnheim."

5.   The simoon (also spelled simoom), or sirocco, is a destructive wind, hot from crossing the deserts of Africa, which reaches Italy moist and still hot. It is mentioned also in "Al Aaraaf," II, 165; in the 1831 version of "Tamerlane," line 186; in "MS. Found in a Bottle"; and in an early version of "Silence — a Fable."

6.   By "device" Poe means a printer's ornament — not a motto, as Baudelaire mistakenly translated it. There is a parallel passage in "Tamerlane," version of 1829, line 81f.:

---

h the ebony *(A, B, C)*	j . . . j many *(A, B, C)*
i from out *(A, B)*; from out of *(C)*	k glistening *(A, B, C)*

TALES OF THE FOLIO CLUB

> Thus I remember having dwelt
> Some page of early lore upon,
> With loitering eye, till I have felt
> The letters — with their meaning — melt
> To fantasies — with none.

This kind of self-hypnotism may have been an experience of the author. There is another treatment of it in "The Pit and the Pendulum" — "he who ponders over the perfume of some novel flower."

7. Compare "The Conqueror Worm," lines 21-22, "a circle that ever returneth in/To the self-same spot."

8. Poe uses the same words in citing Curio's book as did Isaac D'Israeli in the article "Hell" in *Curiosities of Literature*. Curio (1503-1569), an Italian Protestant, was a cheerful fellow who argued that Hell had a smaller population than Heaven; the British Museum has an edition of his book printed at Basel in 1554. St. Augustine's *De Civitate Dei*, begun in A.D. 413 and finished in 426, argued that the truly eternal city was not the material Rome, but the spiritual City of God. The paradoxical sentence, "The Son of God has died, it is to be believed because it is incredible; and, buried, He is risen, it is sure because it is impossible," is in the fifth section of Tertullian's work *De Carne Christi (On the Flesh of Christ)*, dating from A.D. 202-208. The passage is also quoted in "Marginalia," number 151 (*Graham's*, March 1846, p. 117).

9. Ptolemy Hephestion (Ptolemaeus Chennos) is one of the Mythographi whose works are synopsized by Photius. See a jocularly incorrect reference to him in "A Remarkable Letter." The allusion here is to a passage in Ptolemy's third book, referred to in Bryant's *Antient Mythology* (3rd ed., 1807), V, 204, where Bryant tells of a rock, probably near Gades (modern Cadiz), called Petra Gigonia, which is swayed by a blade of grass. Poe seems to have reasoned if grass, why not better asphodel, a symbol of death. (Asphodels are said to cover the meadows of Hades.) See other references to asphodels in "The Valley Nis," "The Island of the Fay," and "Eleonora."

10. This is a fragment of Simonides (number 37 in the Loeb *Lyra Graeca*, III, 301) preserved in the *Historia Animalium* of Aristotle. Poe used it also in an early version *(A)* of "Morella." Pliny, *Natural History* (Bohn ed. X, 47), following Aristotle, tells us that the birds (who have given their poetic name to the whole kingfisher family) make their nests a week before the summer solstice, and sit for seven days after it upon five eggs, and that at this time the Sicilian sea is usually calm.

11. It has been suggested that Poe had in mind the lady called the "Nightmare Life-in-Death" in the third part of Coleridge's *Ancient Mariner*. The passage appeared thus in the *Lyrical Ballads*, edition of 1800 (that reprinted at Philadelphia in 1802):

> Is that a Death? and are there two?
> Is Death that woman's mate?
> *Her* lips were red, *her* looks were free,
> *Her* locks were yellow as gold
> Her skin was as white as leprosy,

And she was far liker Death than he,
Her flesh made the still air cold.

See Darrell Abel, "Coleridge's 'Life in Death' and Poe's 'Death in Life'" (London N & Q, May 1955). See also "Ligeia" for a change of the color of the heroine's hair. Although natural change of the color of human hair (other than to gray or white) is certainly uncommon, it has occurred. G. M. Gould and W. L. Pyle, *Anomalies and Curiosities of Medicine* (Philadelphia, 1900), pp. 239–240, refer to several cases resulting from severe fevers. Miss Janet Doe, Librarian of the New York Academy of Medicine, kindly supplied me with this reference and others. Poe may have seen a newspaper account or actually have known of a case.

12. Compare "The Pit and the Pendulum": "I saw ... those lips. I saw them writhe with a deadly locution." See also "The Facts in the Case of M. Valdemar": "The upper lip writhed itself away from the teeth."

13. "Her every step was a sentiment." Mlle. Marie Sallé (1714–1756) was a famous dancer, and a friend of Voltaire. The verse, quoted by Bielfeld (Book II, chapter xiv, section 2), who did not name the author, has been found in Louis Fuzelier's "Prologue" to the ballet, *Les Festes grecques et romaines*, 1723, published in *Reçueil general des Operas* (Paris, 1734), volume XIII. Poe's own French means "that all her teeth were ideas."

MORELLA

"Morella" is one of the great stories in Poe's early Arabesque manner. On December 1, 1835, he wrote to Judge Beverley Tucker, "The last tale I wrote was Morella and it was my best. When I write again I will write something better. ... What articles I have published *since Morella* were all written some time ago."

The story involves the idea of metempsychosis, like several other tales by its author.* It also makes use of a widespread superstition that gods and men must answer when their right names are spoken.† Poe also seems to know of a superstition that it is a most unusual, even supernatural, child who takes its first breath after its mother breathes her last.

The name of the heroine is that of a real lady of great learning,

* "Metzengerstein" (where see my notes), "A Tale of the Ragged Mountains," and "The Black Cat" involve regular reincarnation, like "Morella." "Ligeia" (which has many parallels to "Morella") involves something like it, as perhaps does "Eleonora."

† Observe the Romans keeping secret the true names of both Rome and its patron goddess; and Jewish avoidance of speaking the name of God that is printed as Jehovah in the King James version of the Bible.

of whom Poe probably read in an article in *The Lady's Book* for September 1834, called "Women Celebrated in Spain for their Extraordinary Powers of Mind," from which a pertinent paragraph may be abstracted.

> Juliana Morella was born in Barcelona. Her father, being obliged to leave Spain for a homicide, taught his daughter so well that at the age of twelve she publicly maintained theses in philosophy. In her tenth or seventeenth year she is said to have held a public disputation in the Jesuits' college at Lyons. She was profoundly skilled in philosophy, divinity, music, jurisprudence and philology. She entered the convent of St. Praxedia at Avignon. She knew fourteen languages.

This lady, now known as Venerable Mother Juliana Morell (1595–1653), according to the *Catholic Encyclopedia* (1911), was celebrated as the fourth Grace and the tenth Muse in a poem by Lope de Vega.‡ Her name is appropriate to Poe's story, for "morel" is one of the names of the black nightshade, a poisonous weed related to that from which the drug belladonna is made. Poe's heroine seems to have taken a dangerous interest in black magic, for her invocation of the Blessed Virgin (in earlier versions of the story) is appropriate to a repentant witch.

Poe's plot comes almost entirely from a story called "The Dead Daughter" by Henry Glassford Bell, in *The Edinburgh Literary Journal: or, Weekly Register of Criticism and Belles Lettres* of January 1, 1831, reprinted in his book *My Old Portfolio* (1832).§ It tells of the family of Adolphus Walstein, who dwelt

> in one of the wild valleys formed by the Rhætian Alps, which intersect Bohemia . . . [He and his wife] had one only child — a daughter — a pale but beautiful girl . . . She smiled sometimes, but very faintly . . . a lovely smile, — more lovely than it was melancholy . . . there was in her limbs none of the glowing vigour of health. . .
>
> Much did they love that gentle child: they had nothing else in the wide world to love, save an old domestic, and a huge Hungarian dog . . . Paulina . . . was tall beyond her years . . . fragile as the stalk of the white-crowned lilly . . .
>
> [Hers] *was no common countenance* . . . the general expression was such as, once seen, haunted the memory for ever. Perhaps it was the black eye—blacker than the ebon hair — contrasted with the deadly paleness of her white-rose cheek.

‡ There is a summary of the literature about this Dominican nun by S. Griswold Morley in the *Hispanic Review* (1941), 9:137–150.

§ This was discussed by Walter G. Neale in *American Literature* (May 1937). Poe's debt was pointed out in 1885 by John Nichol in his article on Bell in the *Dictionary of National Biography*.

MORELLA

It was deep sunk, too, under her brow ... there was a mystery in it. She had a long thin arm, and tapering fingers ... [The touch of her hand] was in general thrillingly cold, yet at times it was feverishly hot. ...

Paulina ... died upon an autumn evening [when she was thirteen years old]. She had been growing weaker for many a day, and they saw it, but spoke not of it. Nor did she; it seemed almost a pain for her to speak; and when she did, it was in a low soft tone, unaudible almost to all but the ear of affection. Yet was the mind ... busy with ... feverish reverie. She had strange day-dreams ... she dwelt among the mysteries and immaterial shapes of some shadowy realm. ... It was an autumn evening — sunny, but not beautiful — silent, but not serene ... [She] gave a faint moan ... her dark eye became fixed ... and the mother carried her child's body into its desolate home ...

The Hungarian dog howled over the dead body of its young mistress, and the old domestic ... wept as for her own first-born ...

The priests came, and the coffin, and a few of the simple peasants ... The procession winded down the valley. The tinkling of the holy bell mingled sadly with the funeral chant ...

A year has passed away, and ... Walstein's wife bears him another child ... They christened the infant Paulina ... The babe grew, but not in the rosiness of health ... when it wept, it was with a kind of suppressed grief, that seemed almost unnatural to one so young. It was long ere it could walk; when at last it did, it was without any previous effort ...

Often had Philippa, with maternal fondness, pointed out to her husband the resemblance ... between their surviving child and her whom they had laid in the grave ... The resemblance was ... almost supernatural. She was the same tall pale girl, with black, deep, sunk eyes, and long dark ebon hair ... Her manners, too, her disposition, the sound of her voice, her motions, her habits, and ... her expression of countenance ... were the very same ...

One night ... Walstein entered; his eye rested on his daughter ... His Hungarian dog was with him ... as its own [eye] rested keenly on Paulina, the animal uttered a low growl. It was strange that the dog never seemed to love the child* ... Walstein ... knew ... that the second Paulina, born after her sister's death, was *the same Paulina as she whom he had laid in the grave.*

The [first] Paulina ... had frequently dreams of a mysterious meaning, which she used to repeat to her mother ... [Now] the living child ... had dreamt a dream. She recited it, and Philippa shuddered to hear an exact repetition of one she well remembered listening to long ago ... Even in sleep ... Paulina was living over again.

Time still passed on ... She was thirteen ... It was manifest that she, too, was dying ... She never spoke of her deceased sister; indeed she seldom spoke at all; but when they asked if she were well, she shook her head, and stretched an arm towards the churchyard.

To that churchyard her father went one moonlight night ... resolved to open his daughter's grave ... The sexton ... had already dug deep ... "My digging is of no use," said the sexton, "I am past the place where I laid the coffin; and may

---

* The big dog (who came from a home of black magic) sensed that the second Paulina was a revenant.

the Holy Virgin protect me, for there is not a vestige, either of it or the body left."

Walstein groaned convulsively . . . a cold hand was laid upon his shoulder. He . . . saw that his daughter stood beside him . . . fixing her quiet look upon the grave, she said—"Father I shall soon lie there."

It was the thirteenth anniversary of Paulina's death . . . Philippa sat by the sick-bed of her last child. The sufferer . . . said, with a struggle, — "Mother, is it not a mysterious imagination, — but I feel as if I had lived before, and that my thoughts were happier and better than they are now?" Philippa shuddered . . . "It is a dream, Paulina . . . an hour's sleep will refresh you" . . . Paulina *did* sleep, but there was little to refresh in such slumber . . . and her poor mother knew that the moment of dissolution was at hand: . . . a damp distillation stood upon the brow, — it was the last sign of agony which expiring nature gave.

That night Walstein dreamed a dream. Paulina . . . stood opposite his couch . . . The vision became double . . . Walstein trembled and awoke. A strange light glanced under his chamber door . . . an indescribable impulse urged him to rush towards the room in which the body of his daughter lay . . . the door of the chamber was open; the Hungarian dog lay dead at the threshold; *the corpse was gone.*

Nothing essential has been omitted from the above abridgment. Poe's supreme artistic skill is manifest here, for he transmuted the material and supplied a motive and "machinery" which Bell had practically neglected.

Poe composed "Morella" probably late in 1834 or early in 1835. The first manuscript, in a small printlike hand, was not completed. A. H. Quinn (*Poe,* p. 214) regarded it as completed but the presence of an asterisk for the unwritten footnote on the halcyon is decisive. Poe is said to have given it to Mrs. Sarah P. Simmons, a Baltimore neighbor, "who, on many occasions, rendered him financial and other help" between 1831 and 1835.† Her daughter bequeathed it to her physician. He sold it through Eugene L. Didier in 1909. Later Dr. A. S. W. Rosenbach sold it to Henry E. Huntington.‡

TEXTS

(A) Unfinished manuscript about 1835 in the Henry E. Huntington Library; *(B) Southern Literary Messenger,* April 1835 (1:448–450); *(C) Tales of the Grotesque and Arabesque* (1840), I, 9–18; *(D) Burton's Gentleman's Magazine,*

† See the *Baltimore Sun,* March 15, 1909, and Mary E. Phillips, *Edgar Allan Poe the Man* (1926), I, 478. Miss Phillips gives the name of the first recipient's husband as Samuel F. Simmons and her address as in Baltimore. A statement that the story was among the original eleven of the Folio Club is erroneous.

‡ The text of the manuscript, HM 1726, is printed here by permission of The Huntington Library, San Marino, California.

MORELLA [*A*]

November 1839 (5:264–266); *(E)* PHANTASY-PIECES, with manuscript revisions of Poe's book *(C)*, 1842; *(F) Broadway Journal*, June 21, 1845 (1:388–389); *(G)* Mrs. Whitman's copy of the last with manuscript revisions (1848); *(H) Works* (1850), I, 469–474.

Texts *(A)* and *(G)* are given in full. The manuscript, in a small print-like hand, on both sides of one leaf, folio, does not carry Poe's name. Many verbal changes were made from the *Southern Literary Messenger (B)* for the edition of 1840 *(C)*, although none were indicated in the Duane copy. Of the twenty punctuation changes (dashes to commas or semicolons for the most part) made in PHAN-TASY-PIECES *(E)*, only two were adopted in later texts. One of those not adopted was definitely a correction, and is used in the text of this edition. The version in *Burton's (D)* is headed: [*Extracted, by permission of the publishers, Messrs. Lea and Blanchard, from the forthcoming "Tales of the Grotesque and Arabesque."*]

MORELLA [*A*]

Αυτο καθ' αυτο μεθ' αυτου, μονο ειδες αιει ον
Itself — alone by itself — eternally one and single.

PLATO — *Symp.*

With a feeling of deep yet most singular affection I regarded my friend Morella. Thrown by accident into her society many years ago, my soul, from our first meeting, burned with fires it had never known. But the fires were not of Eros — and bitter and tormenting to my eager spirit was the gradual conviction that I could in no manner define their unusual meaning, or regulate their vague intensity. Yet we met, and Fate bound us together at the altar, and I never spoke of love, or dreamed of passion. She, however, shunned society and attaching herself to me alone rendered me happy. It is a happiness to wonder. It is a happiness to think.

Morella's erudition was profound. As I hope for life her talents also were of no common order — her powers of mind were gigantic. I felt this, and in many matters became her pupil. Rare and rich volumes were opened for my use; but my wife, perhaps influenced by her Presburg education, laid before me, as I took occasion to remark, chiefly those speculative writings which have, from causes to me unknown, been neglected in these latter days, and thrown aside, whether properly or not, among the mass of that German morality which is indeed purely wild, purely vague, and at times purely fantastical. These — these speculative writings were, for what reasons I could not imagine, Morella's favourite and constant study, and that in process of time they became my own should be attributed to the simple but effectual influence of habit and example. In all this, if I think aright, my powers of thought predominated. My convictions, or I forget myself, were in no manner acted upon by my imagination; nor was any tincture of the mysticism which I read to be discovered, unless I greatly err, either in my meditations or my deeds. Feeling deeply persuaded of this I abandoned myself more implicitly to the guidance of my wife, and entered with a bolder spirit into the intricacy of her studies. And then — then when poring over forbidden pages I felt the consuming thirst for the unknown, would Morella place her cold hand upon mine, and rake up from the ashes of a dead philosophy words whose singular import burned themselves in upon my memory: and then hour after hour would I linger by her side, and listen to the music of her thrilling voice, until at length its melody was tinged with terror, and I grew pale, and shuddered inwardly at those too unearthly tones — and thus, suddenly, Joy faded into Horror, and the most beautiful became the most hideous as Hinnon became Ge-Henna.

It is unnecessary to state the exact character of those disquisitions which, growing out of the volumes I have mentioned, formed for so long a time almost the sole conversation of Morella and myself. By the learned in what might be called theological morality they will be readily conceived, and by the unlearned they would at all events be little understood. The wild Pantheism of Fitche, the modified Παλιγγενεσια of the Pythagoreans, and above all the doctrines of *Identity* as urged by Schelling were the points of discussion presenting the most of beauty to the imaginative Morella. That kind of identity which is not improperly called 'personal' Mr. Lock determines, truly I think, to consist in the sameness of a rational being. And since by person we understand an intelligent essence having reason, and since there is a consciousness which always accompanies thinking, it it this consciousness which makes every one to be that which he calls 'himself' — thereby distinguishing him from other beings that think, and giving him his personal identity. But the "principium individuationis", the notion of that identity *which at death is or is not lost forever* was to me at all times a consideration of intense interest, not more from the exciting and mystical nature of its consequences, than from the marked and agitated manner in which Morella mentioned them.

But indeed the time had now arrived when my wife's society oppressed me like a spell. I could no longer bear the touch of her wan fingers, nor the low tones of her musical language, nor the lustre of her eyes. And she knew all this, but did not upbraid: she seemed conscious of my weakness or my folly, and smiling called it — Fate. Yet she was woman, and pined away daily. In time the crimson spot settled steadily upon the cheek, and the blue veins upon the pale forehead became prominent: and one instant my nature melted into pity, but in the next I met the glance of her melancholy eyes, and my soul sickened and became giddy with the giddiness of one who gazes downwards into some dreary and fathomless abyss.

Shall I then say that I longed with an earnest and consuming desire for the moment of Morella's decease? I did: but the fragile spirit clung to its tenement of clay for many days — for many weeks and irksome months — until at length my tortured nerves obtained the mastery over my mind, and I grew furious with delay, and with the heart of a fiend I cursed the hours and the bitter moments which seemed to lengthen and lengthen as her gentle life declined, like shadows in the dying of the day.

But one autumnal evening when the winds lay still in Heaven Morella called me to her side. It was that season when the beautiful Halcyon is nursed* — there was a dim mist over all the Earth, and a warm glow upon the waters, and amid the rich November leaves of the forest a rainbow from the firmament had surely fallen. As I came she was murmuring in a low under-tone which trembled with fervor some words of a catholic hymn.

> Sancta Maria! turn thine eyes
> Upon the sinner's sacrifice
> Of fervent prayer, and humble love,
> From thy holy throne above.
>
> At morn, at noon, at twilight dim
> Maria! thou hast heard my hymn:

[* *The footnote was not written out.* ED.]

In Joy and Woe — in Good and Ill
Mother of God! be with me still.

When my hours flew gently by,
And no storms were in the sky,
My soul — lest it should truant be —
Thy love did guide to thine and thee.

Now — when clouds of Fate oe'rcast
All my Present, and my Past,
Let my Future radiant shine
With sweet hopes of thee and thine.

"It is a day of days" — said Morella — "a day of all days, either to live or die. It is a fair day for the sons of Earth and Life — ah! more fair for the daughters of Heaven and Death!" I turned towards her and she continued.

"I am dying — yet shall I live. Therefore for me, Morella, thy wife, hath the charnel-house no terrors — mark me! — not even the terrors of the worm. The days have never been when thou couldst love me; but her whom in life thou didst abhor in death thou shalt adore. I repeat that I am dying — but within me is a pledge of that affection — ah, how little! — which thou didst feel for me — Morella. And *when my spirit departs* shall the child live — thy child and mine, Morella's. But thy days shall be days of sorrow — sorrow, which is the most lasting of impressions, as the cypress is the most enduring of trees. For the hours of thy happiness are past, and Joy is not gathered twice in a life, as the roses of Paestum twice in a year. Thou shalt not, then, play the Teian with Time, but, being ignorant of the flowers and the vine, thou shalt walk the earth with thy shroud around thee, like Moslemin at Mecca".

"How knowest thou this" — I demanded eagerly — "how knowest thou all this, Morella?" But she turned away her face upon the pillow, and a slight tremor coming over her limbs, she thus died, and I heard her voice no more.

Yet, as she had predicted, the child — to which in dying she had given life, and which breathed not till the mother breathed no more — the child, a daughter, lived. And she grew strangely in size, and in intelligence, and I loved her with a love more fervent and more holy than I thought it possible to feel on earth.

[*No more was written of this version.*]

MORELLA [G]

MORELLA. [G]

Αυτο καθ' αυτο μεθ' αυτου, μονο ειδες αιει ον.

Itself, by itself solely, ONE everlastingly, and single.

PLATO. *Sympos.*

With a feeling of deep yet[a] most singular affection I regarded my friend Morella. Thrown by accident into her society many years ago, my soul, from our first meeting, burned with fires it had never before[b] known; but the fires were not of Eros, and bitter and tormenting to my[c] spirit was the gradual conviction that I could in no manner define their unusual meaning, or regulate their vague intensity. Yet we met; and fate bound us together at the altar; and I never spoke of [d]passion, nor thought of love.[d] She, however, shunned society, and, attaching herself to me alone, rendered me happy. It is a happiness to wonder; — it is a happiness to dream.[e]

Morella's erudition was profound. As I hope to live,[f] her talents[g] were of no common order — her powers of mind were gigantic. I felt this, and, in many matters, became[h] her pupil. [i]I soon, however, found that,[j] perhaps on account of her Presburg education,[1] she placed[k] before me a number of those mystical writings which are usually considered the mere dross of the early German literature. These, for what reason[l] I could not imagine, were her[i] favorite and constant study — and that, in process of time they became my own, should be attributed to the simple but effectual influence of habit and example.

Motto: The Greek line is in Roman letters (B); the English portion reads Itself — alone by itself — eternally *one* [*not italicized in A*] and single *(A, B, C, D, E)*
a   but *(B)*
b   Omitted *(A, B)*
c   my eager *(A, B)*
d . . . d   love, or dreamed of passion. *(A);* love, or thought of passion. *(B)*
e   think. *(A)*
f   to live,/for life *(A)*
g   talents also *(A)*
h   because *(H) misprint*
i . . . i   Rare and rich volumes were opened for my use; but my wife, perhaps

influenced by her Presburg education, laid before me, as I took occasion to remark, chiefly those speculative writings which have, from causes to me unknown, been neglected in these latter days, and thrown aside, whether properly or not, among the mass of that German morality which is indeed purely wild, purely vague, and at times purely fantastical. These — these speculative writings were, for what reasons I could not imagine, Morella's *(A)*
j   that,/that Morella, *(B)*
k   she placed/laid *(B)*
l   reasons *(B, C, D, E)*

In all this, ^mif I err not, my reason had little to do.^m My convictions, or I forget myself, were in no manner acted upon by ⁿthe ideal,ⁿ nor was any tincture of the mysticism which I read, to be discovered, unless ^oI am greatly mistaken, either in my deeds or in my thoughts.^o Persuaded^p of this, I abandoned myself^q implicitly to the guidance of my wife, and entered with ^ran unflinching heart^r into the intricacies^s of her studies. And then — then, when, poring^t over forbidden pages, I felt ^ua forbidden spirit enkindling within me^z — would^u Morella place her cold hand upon my own,^v and rake up from the ashes of a dead philosophy ^wsome low, singular words, whose strange meaning^w burned^x themselves in upon my memory. And then, hour after hour, would I linger by her side, and dwell upon^y the music of her^z voice — until, at length, its melody was tainted^a with ^bterror, — and there fell^c a shadow upon my soul — and^d I^b grew pale, and shuddered inwardly^e at those too unearthly tones. And thus, ^fjoy suddenly^f faded into horror, and the most beautiful became the most hideous, as Hinnom^g became Ge-Henna.³

It is unnecessary to state the exact character of those^h disquisitions which, growing out of the volumes I have mentioned, formed, for so long a time, almost the sole conversation of Morella and myself. By the learned in what might be termedⁱ theological morality they will be readily conceived, and by the unlearned they would, at all events, be little understood. The wild Pantheism of Fichte;^j the modified Παλιγγενεσια of the^k Pythagoreans; and,

---

m ... m if I think aright, my powers of thought predominated. *(A)*
n ... n my imagination; *(A, B)*
o ... o I greatly err, either in my meditations or my deeds. *(A)*
p Feeling deeply persuaded *(A, B, C, D, E)*
q myself more *(A, B)*
r ... r a bolder spirit *(A, B)*
s intricacy *(A, B)*
t pouring *(F, G, H) misprint*
u ... u the consuming thirst for the unknown, would *(A); the spirit kindle within me, would *(B)*
v my own,/mine, *(A)*
w ... w words whose singular

import *(A)*
x burnt *(B)*
y dwell upon/listen to *(A)*
z her thrilling *(A, B)*
a tinged *(A, B)*
b ... b terror, and I *(A)*
c there fell/fell like *(B, C, D, E)*
d and *canceled in E*
e inwardly *canceled in E*
f ... f suddenly, Joy *(A)*
g Hinnon *(A, B, C, D, E, F, H) corrected in G*
h these *(B)*
i called *(A)*
j Fitche, *(A, B)*
k *Omitted (H)*

above all, the doctrines of *Identity* as urged by Schelling, were generally[1] the points of discussion presenting the most of beauty to the imaginative Morella. That[m] identity which is [n]termed personal, Mr. Locke, I think, truly defines[n] to consist in the sameness[o] of a rational being. And since by person we understand an intelligent essence having reason, and since there is a consciousness which always accompanies thinking, it is this[p] which makes us all[q] to be that which [r]we call *ourselves*[r] — thereby distinguishing us[s] from other beings that think, and giving us our[t] personal identity. But the [u]*principium individuationis,*[u] the notion of that identity *which at death is or is not lost forever,* was to me,[v] at all times, a consideration of intense interest;[4] not more from the perplexing[w] and exciting[x] nature of its consequences, than from the marked and agitated manner in which Morella mentioned them.

But, indeed, the time had now arrived when [y]the mystery of my wife's manner[y] oppressed me as[z] a spell.[5] I could no longer bear the touch of her wan fingers, nor the low tone[a] of her musical language, nor the lustre of her melancholy[b] eyes. And she knew all this, but did not upbraid; she seemed conscious of my weakness or my folly, and, smiling, called it Fate. [c]She seemed, also, conscious of a cause, to me unknown, for the gradual alienation of my regard; but she gave me no hint or token of its nature.[c] Yet was she[d] woman, and pined away daily. In time, the crimson spot settled steadily upon the cheek, and the blue veins upon the pale forehead became prominent; and, one instant, my nature melted into pity, but, in the next, I met the glance of her meaning[e] eyes, and then[f] my soul

---

l *Omitted (A)*
m That kind of *(A)*
n . . . n not improperly called 'personal' Mr. Lock determines, truly, I think, *(A);* not improperly called *Personal,* I think Mr. Locke truly defines *(B)*
o saneness *(H) misprint*
p this consciousness *(A)*
q us all/every one *(A)*
r . . . r he calls 'himself' *(A)*
s him *(A)*
t us our/him his *(A)*
u . . . u "principium individuationis", *(A);* Principium Individuationis — *(B);*

principium individuationis — *(C, D, F, G, H) comma adopted from A and Poe's manuscript correction in E*
v me — *(F, G, H) comma adopted from B, C, D, E*
w exciting *(A);* mystical *(B, C, D, E)*
x mystical *(A)*
y . . . y my wife's society *(A)*
z like *(A, B)*
a tones *(A)*
b *Omitted (A)*
c . . . c *Omitted (A)*
d was she/she was *(A)*
e melancholy *(A)*
f *Omitted (A, B)*

sickened and became giddy with the giddiness of one who gazes downward[g] into some dreary and unfathomable[h] abyss.

Shall I then say that I longed with an earnest and consuming desire for the moment of Morella's decease? I did; but the fragile spirit clung to its tenement of clay for many days — for many weeks and irksome months — until[i] my tortured nerves obtained the mastery over my mind, and I grew furious through[j] delay, and, with the heart of a fiend,[k] cursed the days, and[l] the hours, and the bitter moments, which seemed to lengthen and lengthen as her gentle life declined — like shadows in the dying of the day.

But one autumnal evening, when the winds lay still in heaven,[6] Morella called me to her bed-side.[m] There[n] was a dim mist over all the earth, and a warm glow upon the waters, and, amid the rich October[o] leaves of the forest, a rainbow from the firmament had surely fallen.[p]

"It is a day of [q]days," she said, as I approached;[q] "a day of all days either to live or die. It is a fair day for the sons of earth and life — ah, more fair for the daughters[r] of heaven and death!"[7]

[s]I kissed her forehead,[s] and she continued:

[t]"I am dying, yet shall I live."

"Morella!"[t]

"The days have never been when thou couldst love me — but[u] her whom in life thou didst abhor, in death thou shalt adore."

"Morella!"[v]

"I repeat that I am dying. But within me is a pledge of that

---

g   downwards *(A)*
h   fathomless *(A, B)*
i   until at length *(A)*
j   with *(A, B)*
k   fiend I *(A, B)*
l   the days, and *omitted (A)*
m   side. *(A, B, C, D) changed in E*
n   It was that season when the beautiful Halcyon is nursed* — there *(A)* [*The footnote was not written out.*]
o   November *(A)*
p   *After this:* As I came she was murmuring in a low under-tone which trembled with fervor some words of a catholic hymn. *This sentence is followed in A, B, C, and D by the hymn as in A*

except that C and D have a *for the* in *the second line. The poem was canceled in E.*
q...q   days" — said Morella — *(A, B, C, D, E)*
r   daughter's *(C) corrected in E*
s...s   I turned towards her *(A, B, C, D, E)*
t...t   "I am dying, yet shall I live. Therefore for me, Morella, thy wife, hath the charnel-house no terrors — mark me! — not even the terrors of the worm. [*the worm. B, C, D, E*] *(A, B, C, D, E)*
u   *Almost illegible in A.*
v   *Omitted (A)*

affection — ah, how little! — which [w]thou didst feel[w] for me, Morella. And [x]when my spirit departs[x] shall the child live — thy child and mine, Morella's. But thy days shall be days of sorrow — that[y] sorrow which is the most lasting of impressions, as the cypress is the most enduring of trees.[8] For the hours of thy happiness are over;[z] and joy is not gathered twice in a life, as the roses of Pæstum twice in a year.[9] Thou shalt no longer,[a] then, play the Teian[10] with time, but, being ignorant of the myrtle[b] and the vine, thou shalt [c]bear about with thee thy shroud on[d] earth, as do[e] the Moslemin at Mecca."[c] [11]

[f]"Morella!" I cried, "Morella! how knowest thou this?"[f] — but she turned away her face upon the pillow, and, a slight tremor coming over her limbs, she thus died, and I heard her voice no more.

Yet, as she had foretold, her[g] child — to which in dying she had given birth, and[h] which breathed not until[i] the mother breathed no more — her[j] child, a daughter, lived. And she grew strangely in stature[k] and [l]intellect, and was the perfect resemblance of her who had departed, and I loved her with a love more fervent[m] than I had[n] believed it possible to feel [o]for any denizen of[o] earth.[l]

But, ere long, the heaven of this pure affection became darkened,[p] and gloom, and horror, and grief, swept[q] over it in clouds. I said the child grew strangely in stature and intelligence. Strange indeed was her rapid increase in bodily size — but terrible,[r] oh!

---

w . . . w you felt *(B, C, D) changed back to A reading in E*
x . . . x *when my spirit departs (A)*
y *Omitted (A)*
z past, *(A)*
a no longer,/not, *(A, B)*
b flowers *(A)*
c . . . c walk the earth with thy shroud around thee, like Moslemin at Mecca". *(A)*
d on the *(H)*
e as do/like *(B)*
f . . . f "How knowest thou this" — I demanded eagerly — "how knowest thou all this, Morella?" *(A)*
g foretold, her/predicted, the *(A)*; foreseen, her *(B)*
h birth and/life, and *(A)*; birth, *(H)*
i till *(A, B)*
j the *(A)*
k size, *(A, B)*
l . . . l in intelligence, and I loved her with a love more fervent and more holy than I thought it possible to feel on earth. *(A) The manuscript ends here.*
m fervent and more intense *(B, C, D) changed in E*
n *Omitted (B)*
o . . . o on *(B)*
p overcast, *(B, C) changed in E;* disturbed, *(D)*
q came *(B)*
r terriable, *(F, G) misprint*

terrible were the tumultuous thoughts which crowded upon me while watching the development of her mental being. Could it be otherwise, when I daily discovered in the conceptions of the child the adult powers and faculties of the woman? — when the lessons of experience fell from the lips of infancy? and when the wisdom or the passions of maturity I found hourly gleaming[s] from its full and speculative eye?[12] When, I say, all this became evident to my appalled senses — when I could no longer hide it from my soul, nor throw it off from those perceptions which trembled to receive it — is it to be wondered at that suspicions, of a nature fearful and exciting, crept in upon my spirit, or that my thoughts fell back aghast upon the wild tales and thrilling theories of the entombed Morella? I snatched from the scrutiny of the world a being whom destiny compelled me to adore, and in the rigorous[t] seclusion of my home,[u] watched with an agonizing anxiety over all which concerned [v]the beloved.[v]

And, as years rolled away, and [w]I gazed, day after day,[w] upon her [x]holy, and mild, and eloquent[x] face, and pored[y] over her maturing form, [z]day after day[z] did I discover new points of resemblance in the child to her mother, the melancholy and the dead. And, hourly, grew darker these shadows[a] of similitude, and[b] more full, and more definite, and more perplexing, and [c]more hideously[c] terrible in their aspect. For that her smile was like her mother's I could bear; but then I shuddered at its too perfect *identity* — that her eyes were [d]like Morella's[d] I could endure; but then they [e]too often looked down[e] into the depths of my soul with Morella's own[f] intense and bewildering meaning. And in the contour of the high forehead, and in the ringlets of the silken hair, and in the wan fingers which buried themselves therein, and in the sad[g] musical tones of her speech, and above all — oh, above all — in the phrases and expressions of the dead on the lips of the loved and

---

s   gleaning *(D) misprint*
t   rigid *(B);* vigorous *(D) misprint*
u   ancestral home, I *(B);* old ancestral home, *(C, D, E)*
v . . . v   my daughter. *(B)*
w . . . w   daily I gazed *(B)*
x . . . x   eloquent and mild and holy *(B)*
y   poured *(F, G, H) misprint*

z . . . z   *Omitted (B)*
a   shadows, as it were, *(B)*
b   and became *(B)*
c . . . c   to me more *(B)*
d . . . d   Morella's own *(B)*
e . . . e   looked down too often *(B)*
f   *Omitted (B)*
g   *Omitted (B)*

the living, I found food for consuming thought and horror — for a worm that *would*[h] not die.[13]

Thus passed away two lustra[i] [14] of her life, [j]and, as yet,[j] my daughter remained nameless upon the earth. "My child" and "my love" were the designations usually prompted by a father's affection, and the rigid seclusion of her days precluded all other intercourse. Morella's name died with her at her death.[15] Of the mother I had never spoken to the daughter; — it was impossible to speak. Indeed, during the brief period of her existence the latter had received no impressions from the outward world save[k] such as might have been afforded by the narrow limits of her privacy. But at length the ceremony of baptism presented to my mind, in its unnerved and agitated condition, a present deliverance from the terrors[l] of my destiny. And at the baptismal font[m] I hesitated for a name. And many titles of the wise and beautiful, of old[n] and modern times, of my own and foreign lands, came thronging to my lips, with[o] many, many fair titles of the gentle, and the happy, and the good. What prompted me, then, to disturb the memory of the buried dead? What demon urged me to breathe that sound, which, in its very recollection was wont to make ebb[p] the purple blood in torrents[q] from the temples to the heart? What fiend spoke from the recesses of my soul, when, amid those dim aisles, and in the silence of the night, I whispered[r] within the ears of the holy man the syllables — Morella? What more than fiend convulsed the features of my child, and overspread them with[s] hues of death, as,[t] starting at that [u]scarcely audible[u] sound, she turned her glassy eyes from the earth to heaven, and, falling prostrate on[v] the black slabs of our[w] ancestral vault, responded — "I am here!"

Distinct, coldly, calmly [x]distinct, fell those few simple sounds

---

h   would *(B)*
i   lustrums *(B, C, D) changed in E*
j . . . j   yet *(B); but (C, D, E)*
k   but *(B, C, D) changed in E*
l   horrors *(B)*
m   fount *(F, G, H) misprint*
n   antique *(B)*
o   lips, with/lips — and *(B, C, D, E)*
p   ebb and flow *(B)*
q   tides *(B)*
r   shrieked *(B, C, D) changed in E*

s   with the *(B, C, D, E)*
t   as,/as *(F, G, H) comma added from B, C, D, E*
u . . . u   *Omitted (B, C, D);* low *(E)*
v   upon *(B)*
w   her *(B)*
x . . . x   distinct — like a knell of death — horrible, horrible death, sank the eternal sounds within my soul. *(B, C, D, E)*

within my ear, and thence, like molten lead, rolled hissingly into my brain.[x] Years — years may pass[y] away, but the memory of that epoch — never! Nor[z] was I indeed ignorant of the flowers and the vine[16] — but the hemlock and the cypress overshadowed me night and day. And I kept no reckoning of time or place, and the stars of my fate faded from heaven, and [a]therefore the earth grew dark, and its figures[a] passed by me, like flitting shadows, and among them all I beheld only — Morella. The winds of the firmament breathed but one sound within my ears, and the ripples upon the sea murmured evermore — Morella. But she died; and with my own hands I bore her to the tomb; and I laughed with a long and bitter laugh as I found no traces of the first, in the charnel where I laid the second — Morella.

NOTES

Motto: This is from Plato's *Symposium*, 211b. Poe found it in Henry Nelson Coleridge's *Introductions to the Study of the Greek Classic Poets* (Philadelphia reprint, 1831), p. 32. The English of earlier versions is from Coleridge, that in later versions is Poe's own. Palmer Holt in *American Literature* (March 1962) points out that Poe often quoted from this book in "Pinakidia" and "Never Bet the Devil Your Head." He also drew from it in some of his poems.

1.   Presburg (Pressburg), where the kings of Hungary were crowned, was the seat of a university and was thought to be a home of black magic. Poe has another character connected with the place in "Von Kempelen and His Discovery."

2.   Compare "Murders in the Rue Morgue," "The vast extent of his reading . . . I felt my soul enkindled by the wild fervor of his imagination."

3.   The following from Thomas Hobbes, *Leviathan* (1651), Part III, Chapter 38, may clarify Poe's allusions:

There was a place near Jerusalem, called the Valley of the Children of Hinnon; in a part whereof, called Tophet, the Jews had committed most grievous idolatry, sacrificing their children to the idol Moloch . . . and wherein Josias had burnt the priests of Moloch upon their own altars . . . the place served afterwards to receive the filth and garbage . . . out of the city; and there used to be fires made, from time to time, to purify the air and take away the stench of carrion. From this abominable place the Jews used . . . to call the place of the damned . . . Gehenna, or Valley of Hinnon . . . Gehenna is . . . usually now trans-

---

y   roll *(B, C, D, E)*
z   Now *(B, C, D, E)*

a . . . a   my spirit grew dark, and the figures of the earth *(B)* lated Hell; and from the fires . . . there burning, we have the notion of everlasting and unquenchable fire.

In the manuscript *(A)* and in the published texts collated Poe followed the spelling Hinnon, as did Hobbes in all the scholarly editions consulted.

4. Poe here expresses one of his own strong interests. Johann Gottlieb Fichte (1762–1814), a follower of Kant, postulated a Moral Will of the Universe, an absolute Ego from which all derives. Poe often misspells the name as Fitche. Palingenesia is "birth again," or metempsychosis. Friedrich Wilhelm Joseph von Schelling (1775–1854) urged his ideas in many places in his writings; Poe alludes indirectly to his theory of identity in the passage dropped from "Loss of Breath" in 1845. John Locke's definition mentioned is in *An Essay Concerning Human Understanding* (1690), II, xxvii, 9.

5. Compare *Politian,* VI, 55, " . . . it oppresses me like a spell."

6. Compare the corresponding paragraph in the early manuscript version of the story *(A, above)* and "Berenicë" at note 10. Poe apparently discovered his mistake when he looked up the quotation for his footnote – and thereupon transferred the allusion, corrected, to the other tale.

7. Compare Genesis 6:2, " . . . the sons of God saw the daughters of men that they were fair."

8. On the cypress – "consecrated to Dis, and consequently placed at the doors of houses as a sign of mourning" – see Pliny, *Natural History,* XVI, 60. These dark trees are used significantly in "Ulalume."

9. See Vergil's *Georgics,* IV, 119, for *biferique rosaria Paesti,* the "rose gardens of Paestum, blooming twice" a year.

10. The Teian is Anacreon of Teos; compare Byron's *Childe Harold,* II, lxiii, 3–4, "Love conquers age . . . /So sings the Teian, and he sings in sooth." This theme is common in the *Anacreontea,* so popular in Moore's version. (Compare "Shadow" at n. 7.)

11. Reference is to a custom of burying one who had made the pilgrimage to Mecca in the robe worn in that city. A similar reference appears in a canceled passage at n. 8 in "The Fall of the House of Usher."

12. Compare "Romance," line 10, "A child – with a most knowing eye."

13. See Isaiah 66:24, " . . . their worm shall not die," and "Ulalume," line 43, "These cheeks, where the worm never dies."

14. A lustrum is five years. Poe was fond of the term, and used it also in "Metzengerstein," "Eleonora," "The Colloquy of Monos and Una," and "Three Sundays in a Week."

15. Compare "Tamerlane," lines 126–127, "Thine image and – a name – a name!/Two separate – yet most intimate things."

16. Compare Byron, "On this day I complete my Thirty-sixth Year," line 6, "The flowers and fruits of love are gone."

KING PEST

This is certainly one of the least valuable of Poe's stories and has received scant praise from the critics. (It horrified Robert Louis Stevenson. Reviewing for *The Academy,* January 2, 1875, the first two volumes of Poe's *Works,* edited by J. H. Ingram, 1874, he showed he was not aware of the factual basis for the most unpleasant incident and, because of Ingram's ordering of the tales, apparently thought "King Pest" was one of Poe's later works.) Yet Poe labored over the tale, as his meticulous revisions indicate; and if it cannot be called a success, it is of some interest as a forerunner of "The Masque of the Red Death." It resembles "Berenicë" in the use of repulsive subject matter.

The story has three major sources that can now be identified, and one that has not yet been found. The first is the incident of a masked ball in Paris, to which a man came in the character of the Cholera, as N. P. Willis had reported in the *New-York Mirror* of June 21, 1832. This is quoted in my introduction to "The Masque of the Red Death." A second parallel is the party given by the Duke of Johannisberger in the first chapter of the sixth book of Benjamin Disraeli's *Vivian Grey.** There some of the guests have exaggerated features, and an unwelcome visitor is forced to drink bumpers of liquor.

Thirdly there is a grim story, almost surely a principal source of Poe's tale, told in the London *Naval Chronicle,*† April 1811:

INEBRIETY.

ANNO 1779, one Mr. Constable of Woolwich, passing through the church-yard of that place, at 12 o'clock at night, was surprised to hear a loud noise like that of several persons singing; at first he thought it proceeded from the church, but on going to the church doors, found them fast shut, and within silent. The noise continuing, he looked round the church-yard, and observed a light in one of the large family tombs; going up to it, he found some drunken sailors, who had got into a vault, and were regaling themselves with bread, cheese, and tobacco, and strong

* This was pointed out by Woodberry, in the Stedman-Woodberry edition of Poe's *Works,* IV (1894–95), 295; and Life (1909), I, 130. For particulars see Ruth Leigh Hudson, "Poe and Disraeli" (*AL,* January 1937).

† April 1811, page 281 — it was inaccurately quoted in *Southey's Commonplace Book* (1850), IV, 386.

beer. They told him they belonged to the Robuste man of war, and, that having resolved to spend a jolly night on shore, they had kept it up in a neighbouring ale-house, till they were turned out by the landlord, and were obliged to take shelter here, to finish their evening. In their jollity, they had opened some of the coffins, and crammed the mouth of one of the bodies full of bread, cheese, and beer. Mr. Constable, with much difficulty, prevailed on them to return to their ship. In their way thither one of them being much in liquor, fell down, and was suffocated in the mud. On which his comrades took him up on their shoulders, bringing him back to sleep in company with the *honest gemmen* with whom he passed the evening. — This story is positively matter of fact.

A fourth source is suggested by Poe's footnote, added in *Tales of the Grotesque and Arabesque* but not used thereafter, in which he seems to refer to some description of the Black Death in the fourteenth century.‡ His story has little kinship with Daniel Defoe's *Journel of the Plague Year,* which concerns the year 1665–66.

The story has no appropriate narrator in the Folio Club, but is earlier than "Morella" according to a letter of the author, December 1, 1835, to Judge Beverley Tucker. "King Pest" probably was written in Baltimore in 1834.

TEXTS

(A) Southern Literary Messenger, September 1835 (1:757–761); *(B)* Duane copy of the last with manuscript changes (1839); *(C) Tales of the Grotesque and Arabesque* (1840), I, 193–212; *(D)* PHANTASY-PIECES (copy of the last with manuscript changes, 1842); *(E) Broadway Journal,* October 18, 1845 (2:219–223); *(F)* Works (1850), II, 363–375.

Griswold's text *(F)* is used, as it shows slight auctorial revisions. The manuscript changes of PHANTASY-PIECES *(D)* are of two kinds, some neatly written, but a few scrawled with a bad pen — or in a bad light — or both. Not all of the scribbled changes have as yet been completely deciphered. There are fifty-one punctuation changes in PHANTASY-PIECES of which thirty-seven substitute commas and semi-colons for dashes. About half were never used in later texts. Except for the period and capitalization changes the marks are not recorded in the variants. The simple title "King Pest" resulting from the PHANTASY-PIECES cancelation of the subtitle was never used elsewhere. Most of the verbal changes in this tale were made for the *Broadway Journal (E)* where Poe used the signature Littleton Barry. See note 41 in "Loss of Breath."

‡ [This fourth source, divined but not found, by Mr. Mabbott, may have been "The Great Plague in the Fourteenth Century," in *Fraser's Magazine* for May 1832, published during the cholera epidemic of that year. The article is a striking description of the devastation wrought by the disease as it passed through Europe and spread over England. Details of its horrors are quoted from "an excellent old writer," identified in a footnote as "Joshua Barnes, B.D. Cantab.," author of *The History of that Most Victorious Monarch Edward IIId. . . . Cambridge,* 1688.]

KING PEST. [*F*]

A TALE CONTAINING AN ALLEGORY.

The gods do bear and well allow in kings
The things which they abhor in rascal routes.
Buckhurst's Tragedy of Ferrex and Porrex

About twelve o'clock, one[a] night in the month of October,[b] and during the chivalrous reign of the third Edward,[1] two seamen belonging to the crew of the "Free and Easy," a trading schooner plying between Sluys and the [c]Thames, and then[c] at anchor in that river, were much astonished to find themselves seated in the taproom[d] of an ale-house in the parish of St. Andrews, London — which ale-house bore for sign the portraiture of a "Jolly Tar."

The room,[e] although ill-contrived, smoke-blackened, low-pitched, and in every other respect agreeing with the general character of such places at the period — was, nevertheless, in the opinion of the grotesque groups scattered here and there within it, sufficiently well adapted to[f] its purpose.

Of these groups our two seamen formed, I think, the most interesting, if not the most conspicuous.

The one who appeared to be the elder, and whom his companion addressed by the characteristic appellation of "Legs," was[g] at the same time much the taller of the two. He might have measured six feet and a half,[h] and an habitual stoop in the shoulders seemed to have been the necessary consequence of an altitude so enormous. — Superfluities in height were, however, more than accounted for by deficiencies in other respects. He was exceedingly[i] thin; and might, as his associates asserted, have answered, when drunk,[j] for a pennant at the mast-head, or, when sober,[k] have served for a jib-boom. But these jests, and others of a similar nature, had evi-

---

Title: King Pest the First. A Tale
containing an Allegory — By — *(A, B);*
King Pest *(D)*
a one sultry *(A, B, C, D)*
b August, *(A, B, C, D)*
c . . . c Thames. It was *(D)*
d tap-room *illegibly changed in D*
e room, it is needless to say,
(A, B, C, D)

f for *(A, B, C, D)*
g was also much the most ill-favored,
and *(A, B, C, D) except that* most *is
changed to* more *in D*
h and a half,/nine inches, *(A, B, C, D)*
i exceedingly, wofully, awfully
(A, B, C, D)
j sober, *(A, B, C, D)*
k stiff with liquor, *(A, B, C, D)*

dently produced, at no time, any effect upon the cachinnatory[1] muscles of the tar. With high cheek-bones, a large hawk-nose, retreating chin, fallen under-jaw, and huge protruding white eyes, the expression of his countenance, although tinged with a species of dogged indifference to matters and things in general, was not the less utterly solemn and serious beyond all attempts at imitation or description.

The younger seaman was, in all outward appearance, the converse[m] of his companion. His stature could not have exceeded four feet. A pair of stumpy bow-legs supported his squat, unwieldly figure, while his unusually short and thick arms, with no ordinary fists at their extremities, swung off dangling from his sides like the fins of a sea-turtle. Small eyes, of no particular color, twinkled far back in his head. His nose remained buried in the mass of flesh which enveloped his round, full, and purple face; and his thick upper-lip rested upon the still thicker one beneath with an air of complacent self-satisfaction, much heightened by the owner's habit of licking them at intervals. He evidently regarded his tall shipmate with a feeling half-wondrous, half-quizzical; and stared up occasionally in his face as the red setting sun stares up at the crags of Ben Nevis.[2]

Various and eventful, however, had been the peregrinations of the worthy couple in and about the different tap-houses of the neighborhood during the earlier hours of the night. Funds even the most ample, are not always everlasting: and it was with empty pockets our friends had ventured upon the present hostelrie.[n]

At the precise period, then, when this history properly commences, Legs, and his fellow, Hugh Tarpaulin, sat, each with both elbows resting upon the large oaken table in the middle of the floor, and with a hand upon either cheek. They were eyeing, from behind a huge flagon of unpaid-for "humming-stuff," the portentous words, "No Chalk," which to their indignation and astonishment were scored over the doorway by means of that very[o] mineral whose presence they purported to deny.[3] Not that the gift of de-

---

1 leaden *(A, B, C, D)*
m antipodes *(A, B, C); changed first to* converse *and then to* reverse *[?] (D)*

n *This appears as* hostelr <ie> *in D.*
o very identical *(A) changed in B*

cyphering written characters — a gift among the commonalty of that day considered little less cabalistical than the art of inditing — could, in strict justice, have been laid to the charge of either disciple of the sea; but there was, to say the truth, a certain twist in the formation of the letters—an indescribable lee-lurch about the whole — which foreboded, in the opinion of both seamen, a long run of dirty weather; and determined them at once, in the allegorical[p] words of Legs himself, to "pump ship, clew up all sail, and scud before the wind."

Having accordingly [q]disposed of[q] what remained of the ale, and looped up the points of their short doublets, they finally made a bolt for the street. Although Tarpaulin rolled twice into the fireplace, mistaking it for the door, yet their escape was at length happily effected — and half after twelve o'clock found our heroes ripe for mischief, and running for life down a dark alley in the direction of St. Andrew's Stair,[4] hotly pursued by the[r] landlady of the "Jolly Tar."

At the epoch of this eventful tale, and periodically,[s] for many years before and after, all England, but more especially the metropolis, resounded with the fearful cry of "Plague!"[t] The city was in a great[u] measure depopulated — and in those horrible regions, in the vicinity of the Thames, where amid the dark, narrow, and filthy lanes and alleys, the Demon of Disease was supposed to have had his nativity, [v]Awe, Terror, and Superstition[v] were alone to be found stalking abroad.

By authority of the king such districts were placed *under ban,* and all persons forbidden, under pain of death, to intrude upon their dismal solitude. Yet neither the mandate of the monarch, nor the huge barriers erected at the entrances of the streets, nor the prospect of that loathsome death which, with almost absolute certainty, overwhelmed the wretch whom no peril could deter from the adventure, prevented the unfurnished and untenanted dwellings from being stripped, by the hand of nightly rapine, of

---

p   pithy *(A, B, C, D)*
q . . . q   drank up *(A, B, C) changed in D*
r   the landlord and *(A, B, C, D)*
s   periodically, *canceled (D)*

t   "Pest! Pest! Pest!" *(A, B);* "Pest!" *(C) changed in D*
u   *Canceled (B)*
v . . . v   awe, terror, and superstition *(A, B, C) capitalized in D*

every article, such as iron, brass, or lead-work, which could in any manner be turned to a profitable account.

Above all, it was usually found, upon the annual winter opening of the barriers, that locks, bolts, and secret cellars, had proved but slender protection to those rich stores of wines and liquors which, in consideration of the risk and trouble of removal, many of the numerous dealers having shops in the neighborhood had consented to trust, during the period of exile, to so insufficient a security.

But there were very few of the terror-stricken people who attributed these doings to the agency of human hands. Pest-spirits, plague-goblins, and fever-demons, were the popular imps of mischief; and tales so blood-chilling were hourly told, that the whole mass of forbidden buildings was,^{w} at length, enveloped in terror as in a shroud, and the plunderer himself was often scared away by the horrors his own depredations had created; leaving the entire vast circuit of prohibited district to gloom, silence, pestilence, and death.

It was by one of the^x terrific barriers already mentioned, and which indicated the region beyond to be under the Pest-ban, that, in scrambling down an alley, Legs and the worthy Hugh Tarpaulin found their progress suddenly impeded.^{y} To return was out of the question, and no time was to be lost, as their pursuers were close upon their heels. With thorough-bred seamen to clamber up the roughly fashioned plank-work was a trifle; and, maddened with the twofold excitement of exercise and liquor, they leaped ^{z}unhesitatingly down within^z the enclosure, and holding on their drunken course with shouts and yellings, were soon bewildered in its noisome and intricate recesses.

Had they not, indeed,^{a} been intoxicated beyond ^{b}moral sense,^{b} their reeling footsteps must have been palsied by the horrors of their situation. The air was^c cold and misty. The paving-stones, loosened from their beds, lay in wild disorder amid the tall, rank grass, which sprang up^d around the feet and ankles. Fallen^e houses

---

w were, (D)
x these (A, B, C, D)
y stopped. [?] (D)
z . . . z down (D)
a indeed, canceled (D)

b . . . b all sense of human feelings, (A, B, C, D)
c was damp, (A, B, C, D)
d up hideously (A, B, C, D)
e Rubbish of fallen (A, B, C, D)

choked up the streets. The most fetid and poisonous smells every-where prevailed; — and by the[f] aid of that ghastly[g] light which, even at midnight, never fails to emanate from a vapory and[h] pesti-lential atmosphere, might be discerned lying in the by-paths and alleys, or rotting in the windowless habitations, the carcass of many a nocturnal plunderer arrested by the hand of the plague in the very perpetration of his robbery.[5]

But it lay not in the power of images, or sensations, or impedi-ments such as[i] these, to stay the course of men who, naturally brave, and at that time especially, brimful of courage and of "humming-stuff!" would have reeled, as straight as their condi-tion might have permitted, undauntedly into the very jaws of[j] Death. Onward — still onward stalked the grim[k] Legs, making the desolate solemnity echo and re-echo with yells like the terrific[l] war-whoop of the Indian: and onward, still onward rolled the dumpy Tarpaulin, hanging on to the doublet of his more active companion, and far surpassing the latter's most strenuous exer-tions in the way of vocal music, by bull-roarings *in basso*,[m] from the profundity of his stentorian[6] lungs.

They had now evidently reached the strong hold of the pesti-lence. Their way at every step or plunge grew more noisome and more horrible — the paths more narrow and more intricate. Huge stones and beams falling momently[n] from the decaying roofs above them, gave evidence, by their sullen and heavy descent, of the vast height of the surrounding [o]houses; and[o] while actual exertion be-came necessary to force a passage through frequent heaps of [p]rub-bish, it was by no means seldom that the hand fell upon a skeleton or rested upon a more fleshly[q] corpse.[p]

Suddenly, as the seamen stumbled against the entrance of a tall[r] and ghastly-looking building, a yell more than usually shrill from

---

f   the occasional *(A, B, C, D)*
g   ghastly and uncertain *(A, B, C, D)*
h   vapory and *canceled (D)*
i   such as/like *(A, B, C, D)*
j   of the Arch-angel *(A, B, C, D)*
k   gigantic *(A, B, C, D)*
l   *Canceled (D)*
m   *basso,* coming forth [?] *(D)*
n   momentarily *(A, B)*

o . . . o   buildings, *(A, B, C);* houses, *(D)*
p . . . p   putrid human corpses. *(A, B, C, D); a footnote which appears in no other texts:* The description here given, of the condition of the *banned* districts, at the period spoken of, is positively *not* exaggerated. *(C, D)*
q   fleshey *(E);* fleshy *(F) misprints*
r   gigantic *(A, B, C, D)*

the throat of the excited Legs, was replied to from within, in a rapid succession of wild, laughter-like, and fiendish shrieks. Nothing daunted at sounds which, of such a nature, at such a time, and in such a place, might have curdled the very blood in hearts less irrevocably[s] on fire, the drunken couple [t]rushed headlong against the door, burst it open,[t] and staggered into the midst of things[7] with a volley of curses.[u]

The room within which they found themselves proved to be the shop of an undertaker; but an open trap-door, in a corner of the floor near the entrance, looked down upon a long range of wine-cellars, [v]whose depths[v] the occasional sound[w] of bursting bottles proclaimed to be well stored with their appropriate contents. In the middle of the room stood a table — in the centre of which again arose a huge tub of what appeared to be punch. Bottles of various wines and cordials, together with[x] jugs, pitchers, and flagons of every shape and quality, were scattered profusely upon the board. Around it, upon coffin-tressels, was seated a company of six. This[y] company I will endeavor to delineate one by one.

Fronting the entrance, and elevated a little above his companions, sat a personage who appeared to be the president of the table. His stature was gaunt and tall, and Legs was confounded to behold in him a figure more emaciated than himself. His face was [z]as yellow as[z] saffron — but no feature[a] excepting one alone, was sufficiently marked to merit a particular description. This one consisted in a forehead so unusually and hideously lofty, as to have the appearance of a bonnet or crown of flesh superadded[b] upon the natural head. His mouth was puckered and dimpled into an[c] expression of ghastly affability, and his eyes, as indeed the eyes of all at table, were glazed over with the fumes of intoxication.

s   irrecoverably *(A, B, C, D)*
t . . . t   burst open the pannels of the door, *(A, B, C, D)*
u   *After this:* It is not to be supposed, however, that the scene which here presented itself to the eyes of the gallant Legs and worthy Tarpaulin, produced at first sight any other effect upon their illuminated faculties than an overwhelming sensation of stupid astonishment. *(A, B, C, D); the last two*

words are changed to surprise *(D)*
v . . . v   from the depths of which *(D)*
w   sounds *(A, B, C, D)*
x   with grotesque *(A, B, C, D)*
y   six. This/six — this *(A, B, C)* *changed in D*
z . . . z   yellower than the yellowest *(A, B, C) changed in D*
a   feature of his visage, *(A, B, C, D)*
b   superseded *(A, B, C, D)*
c   a singular *(A, B, C, D)*

This gentleman was clothed from head to foot in a richly-embroidered black silk-velvet pall,[8] wrapped negligently around his form after the fashion of a Spanish cloak. His head was stuck full of[d] sable hearse-plumes, which he nodded to and fro with a jaunty and knowing air; and, in his right hand, he held a huge human thigh-bone, with which he appeared to have been just knocking down[9] some member of the company for a song.

Opposite him, and with her back to the door, was a lady of no whit the less extraordinary character. Although quite as tall as the [e]person just[e] described, she had no right to complain of his unnatural emaciation. She was evidently in the last stage of a dropsy;[10] and her figure resembled nearly that of[f] the huge puncheon of October beer which stood, with the head driven in, close by her side, in a corner of the chamber. Her face was exceedingly round, red, and full; and the same peculiarity, or rather want of peculiarity, attached itself to her countenance, which I before mentioned in the case of the president — that is to say, only one feature of her face was sufficiently distinguished to need a separate characterization: indeed the acute Tarpaulin immediately observed that the same remark might have applied to each individual person of the party; every one of whom seemed to possess a monopoly of some particular portion of physiognomy. With the lady in question this portion proved to be the mouth. Commencing at the right ear, it swept with a terrific chasm to the left — the short pendants which she wore in either auricle continually bobbing into the aperture. She made, however, every exertion to keep her mouth[g] closed and look[h] dignified, in a dress consisting of a newly starched and ironed shroud coming up close under her chin, with a crimpled[i] ruffle of cambric muslin.

At her right hand sat a diminutive young lady whom she appeared to patronise. This delicate little creature, in the trembling of her wasted fingers, in the livid hue of her lips, and in the slight hectic spot which tinged her otherwise leaden complexion, gave

---

d   full of/all full of tall *(A, B, C, D)*
e . . . e   person who has just been *(A, B, C, D)*
f   that of/in outline the shapeless
proportions of *(A, B, C);* in outline *(D)*
g   jaws *(A, B, C, D)*
h   looked *(C, D)*
i   crimped *(A, B, C, D)*

evident indications of a galloping consumption. An air of extreme *haut ton,* however, pervaded her whole appearance; she wore in a graceful and *dégagé*[j] manner, a large and beautiful winding-sheet of the finest India lawn; her hair hung in ringlets over her neck; a soft smile played about her mouth; but her nose, extremely long, thin, sinuous, flexible and pimpled, hung down far below her under lip, and in spite of the delicate manner in which she now and then moved it to one side or the other with her tongue, gave [k]to her countenance a somewhat equivocal expression.[k]

Over against her, and upon the left of the dropsical lady, was seated a little puffy, wheezing, and gouty old man, whose cheeks reposed[l] upon the shoulders of their owner, like two huge bladders of Oporto wine.[11] With his arms folded, and with one bandaged leg [m]deposited upon[m] the table, he seemed to think himself entitled to some consideration. He evidently prided himself much upon every inch of his personal appearance, but took more especial delight in calling attention to his gaudy-colored surtout.[n] This, to say the truth, must have cost him[o] no little money, and was made to fit him exceedingly well — being fashioned from one of the curiously embroidered silken covers appertaining to those glorious escutcheons which, in England and elsewhere, are customarily hung up, in some conspicuous place, upon the dwellings of departed aristocracy.

Next to him, and at the right hand of the president, was a gentleman in long white hose and cotton drawers. His frame shook, in a ridiculous[p] manner, with a fit of what Tarpaulin called "the horrors." His jaws, which had been newly shaved, were tightly tied up by a bandage of muslin; and his arms being fastened in a similar way at the wrists, prevented him from helping himself too freely to the liquors upon the table; a precaution rendered necessary, in the opinion of Legs, by the peculiarly sottish and wine-bibbing cast of his visage. A pair of prodigious ears, nevertheless, which it was no doubt found impossible to confine, towered away

---

j   *degagé (A, B, C, D, E, F)*
k   . . . k   an expression rather doubtful to her countenance. *(A, B, C, D)*
l   hung down *(A, B, C, D)*

m . . . m   cocked up against *(A, B, C, D)*
n   surcoat. *(A, B, C, D)*
o   cost him/cost *(A, B, C, D)*
p   ludicrous *(A, B, C, D)*

into the atmosphere of the apartment, and were occasionally pricked qup in a spasm, at the sound of the drawing of a cork.q

Fronting him, sixthly and lastly, was situated a singularly stiff-looking personage, who, being afflicted with paralysis, must, to speak seriously, have felt very ill at ease in his unaccommodating habiliments. He was habited, somewhat uniquely, in a new and handsome mahogany coffin. Itsr top or head-pieces pressed upon the skull of the wearer, and extended over it in the fashion of a hood, giving to the entire face an air of indescribable interest. Armholes had been cut in the sides, for the sake not tmore of elegance than oft convenience; butu the dress, nevertheless, prevented its proprietor from sitting as erect as his associates; and as he lay reclining against his tressel, at an angle of forty-five degrees, a pair of huge goggle eyes rolled up their awfulv whites towards the ceiling in absolute amazement at their own enormity.

Before each of the party lay a portion of a skull, which was used as a drinking cup.[12] Overhead was suspended aw human skeleton, by means of a rope tied round one of the legs and fastened to a ring in the ceiling. The other limb confined by no such fetter, stuck off from the body at right angles, causing the whole loose and rattling frame to dangle and twirl aboutx at the caprice of every occasional puff of wind which found its way into the apartment.y In the cranium of this hideous thing lay a quantity of ignitedz charcoal, which threw a fitful but vivid light over the entire scene;[13] while coffins, and other wares appertaining to the shop of an undertaker, were piled high up around the room, and against the windows, preventing anya ray from escaping into the street.

Atb sight of this extraordinary assembly, and of their still more extraordinary paraphernalia, our two seamen did not conduct

---

q . . . q up, or depressed, as the sounds of bursting bottles increased, or died away, in the cellars underneath. (A, B, C, D)
r The (A, B, C, D)
s head-piece of the coffin (A, B, C) changed in D
t . . . t for elegance but for (D)
u Canceled (D)

v Canceled (D)
w an enormous (A, B, C, D)
x about in a singular manner, (A, B, C, D)
y aparment. (E) misprint
z ignited and glowing (A, B, C, D)
a any straggling (A, B, C, D)
b It has been before hinted that at (A, B, C, D)

themselves with that[c] degree of decorum which might have been expected. Legs, leaning[d] against the wall near which he happened to be standing, dropped his lower jaw still lower than usual, and spread open his eyes to their fullest extent: while Hugh Tarpaulin, stooping down so as to bring his nose upon a level with the table, and spreading out a palm upon either knee, burst into a long, loud, and obstreperous[e] roar of very ill-timed and immoderate laughter.

Without, however, taking offence at behavior so excessively rude, the tall president smiled very graciously upon the intruders — nodded to them in a dignified manner with his head of sable plumes — and, arising, took each by an arm, and led him to a seat which some others of the company had placed in the meantime for his accommodation. Legs to all this offered not the slightest resistance, but sat down as he was directed; while the gallant Hugh, removing his coffin tressel from its station near the head of the table, to the vicinity of the little consumptive lady in the winding sheet, plumped down by her side in high glee, and pouring out a skull of red wine, quaffed it[f] to their better acquaintance. But at this presumption the stiff gentleman in the coffin seemed exceedingly nettled; and serious consequences might have ensued had not the president, rapping upon the table with his truncheon, diverted the attention of all present to the following speech:

"It becomes our duty upon the present happy occasion"————

"Avast there!" interrupted Legs, looking very serious, "avast there a bit, I say, and tell us who the devil ye all are, and what business ye have here, rigged off like the foul fiends, and swilling the snug blue ruin[14] stowed away for the winter by my honest shipmate, Will Wimble[15] the undertaker!"

[g]At this unpardonable piece of ill-breeding, all[g] the original company half started to their feet, and uttered the same rapid succession of wild fiendish shrieks which had before caught the attention of the seamen. The president, however, was the first to recover his composure, and at length, turning to Legs with great dignity, recommenced:

---

c that proper *(A, B, C, D)*
d having leant himself back *(A, B, C, D)*
e obstrepons *(E) misprint*
f quaffed it/drank it off *(A, B, C, D)*
g . . . g All [?] *(D)*

"Most willingly will we gratify any reasonable curiosity on the part of guests so illustrious, unbidden though they be. Know then that in these dominions I am monarch, and here rule with undivided empire under the title of 'King Pest the First.'

"This apartment, which you no doubt profanely suppose to be the shop of Will Wimble the undertaker — a man whom we know not, and whose plebeian appellation has never before this night thwarted our royal ears — this apartment, I say, is the Dais-Chamber of our Palace, devoted to the ʰcouncils of ourʰ kingdom, and to other sacred and loftyʰ' purposes.

"The noble lady who sits opposite is Queen Pest,ⁱ our Serene Consort. The other exalted personages whom you behold are all of our family, and wear the insignia of the blood royal under the respective titles of 'His Grace the Arch Duke Pest-Iferous' — 'His Grace the Duke Pest-Ilential' — 'His Grace the Duke Tem-Pest' — and 'Her Serene Highness the Arch Duchess Ana-Pest.'[16]

"As regards," continued he, "your demand of the business upon which we sit here in council, we might be pardoned for replying that it concerns, and concerns *alone,* our own private and regal interest, and is in no manner important to any other than ourself. But in consideration of those rights to which as guests and strangers you may feel yourselves entitled, we will furthermore explain that we are here this night, prepared by deep research and accurate investigation, to examine, analyze, and thoroughly determine the indefinable spirit — the incomprehensible qualities and natureʲ [17] — of those inestimable treasures of the palate, the wines, ales, and liqueurs of this goodly metropolis: by so doing to advance not more our own designs than the true welfare of that unearthly sovereign whose reign is over us all, whose dominions are unlimited, and whose name is 'Death.' "

"Whose name is Davy Jones!"[18] ejaculated Tarpaulin, helping the lady by his side to a skull of liqueur, and pouring out a second for himself.

"Profane varlet!" said the president, now turning his attention to the worthy Hugh, "profane and execrable wretch! — we have

---

h...h *Canceled (D)*
h' lofy *(F) misprint*

i Pest, and *(A, B, C) changed in D*
j nare *(A, B, C, D, E)*

said, that in consideration of those rights which, even in thy[k] filthy person, we feel no inclination to violate, we have condescended to make reply to thy[l] rude and unseasonable inquiries. We,[m] nevertheless, for your unhallowed intrusion upon our councils, believe it our duty to mulct thee[n] and thy[o] companion in each gallon of Black Strap[19] — having imbibed[p] which to the prosperity of our kingdom — at a single draught — and upon your bended knees — ye[q] shall be forthwith free either to proceed upon your way, or remain and be admitted to the privileges of our table, according to your respective and individual pleasures."

"It would be a matter of utter unpossibility,"[r] replied Legs, whom the assumptions and dignity of King Pest the First had evidently inspired with some feelings of respect,[s] and who arose and steadied[t] himself by the table as he spoke — "it would, please your majesty, be a matter of utter unpossibility[u] to stow away in my hold even one-fourth part[v] of that same liquor which your majesty has just mentioned. To say nothing of the stuffs placed on board in the forenoon by way of ballast, and not to mention the various ales and liqueurs shipped this evening at various[w] seaports, I [x]have, at present, a full cargo[x] of 'humming stuff' taken in and duly paid for at the sign of the 'Jolly Tar.' You will, therefore, please your majesty, be so good as to[y] take the will for the deed — for by no manner of means either can I or will I swallow another drop — least of all a drop of that villanous[y'] bilge-water that answers to the hail of 'Black Strap.' "

"Belay that!" interrupted Tarpaulin, astonished not more at the length of his companion's speech than at the nature of his refusal — "Belay that, you lubber! — and I say, Legs, none of your palaver! *My* hull is still light, although I confess you yourself seem to be a little top-heavy; and as for the matter of your share of the

k   your *(D)*
l   your *(A, B, C, D)*
m   We *(E, F) comma added from A, B, C, D*
n   you *(A, B, C, D)*
o   your *(A, B, C, D)*
p   drank *(A, B)*
q   you *(A, B, C, D)*
r   impossibility" — *(A, B)*
s   respcct, *(E) misprint*
t   studied *(A, B)*
u   impossibility *(A, B)*
v   *Omitted (A, B, C, D)*
w   different *(A, B, C, D, E)*
x . . . x   am, at present, full up to the throat *(A, B, C, D)*
y   *Omitted (A, B, C, D)*
y'   villainous *(A, B)*

cargo, why rather than raise a squall I would find stowage-room for it myself, but" ——

"This proceeding," interposed the president, "is by no means in accordance with the terms of the mulct or sentence, which is in its nature Median,[20] and not to be altered or recalled. The conditions we have imposed must be fulfilled to the letter, and that without a moment's hesitation — in failure of which fulfilment we decree that you do here be tied neck and heels together, and duly drowned as rebels in yon hogshead of October beer!"[21]

"A sentence! — a sentence! — a righteous and just sentence![22]— a glorious decree! — a most worthy and upright, and holy condemnation!" shouted the Pest family altogether. The king elevated his forehead into innumerable wrinkles; the gouty little old man puffed like a pair of bellows; the lady of the winding sheet waved her nose to and fro; the gentleman in the cotton drawers pricked up his ears; she of the shroud gasped like a dying fish; and he of the coffin looked stiff and rolled up his eyes.

"Ugh! ugh! ugh!" chuckled Tarpaulin, without heeding the general excitation, "ugh! ugh! ugh! — ugh! ugh! ugh! ugh! — ugh! ugh! ugh![z] — I was saying," said he, "I was saying when Mr. King Pest poked in his marlin-spike,[a] that as for the matter of two or three gallons more or less of[b] Black Strap, it was a trifle to a tight sea-boat like myself not overstowed — but when it comes to drinking the health of the Devil (whom God assoilzie) and going down upon my marrow bones to his ill-favored majesty there, whom I know, as well as I know myself to be a sinner, to be nobody in the whole world, but Tim Hurlygurly[23] the stage-player![c] — why it's[d] quite another guess sort of a thing, and utterly and altogether past my comprehension."

He was not allowed to finish this speech in tranquillity. At the name of Tim Hurlygurly the whole assembly[e] leaped from their seats.

"Treason!" shouted his Majesty[f] King Pest the First.

---

z *One* ugh! *omitted (A, B)*
a marling-spike, *(A, B, C, D)*
b *Omitted (A, B, C, D)*
c stage-player!/organ-grinder *(A, B)*

d its *(A, B, C, E, F) misprint, corrected in D and followed here*
e Junto *(A, B)*
f Serenity *(A, B)*

"Treason!" said the little man with the gout.

"Treason!" screamed the Arch Duchess Ana-Pest.

"Treason!" muttered the gentleman with his jaws tied up.

"Treason!" growled he of the coffin.

"Treason! treason!" shrieked her majesty of the mouth; and, seizing by the hinder part of his breeches the unfortunate Tarpaulin, who had just commenced pouring out for himself a skull of liqueur, she lifted him high[g] into the air, and [h]let him fall[h] without ceremony into the huge open puncheon of his beloved ale. Bobbing up and down, for a few seconds, like an apple in a bowl of toddy, he, at length,[i] finally disappeared amid the whirlpool of foam which, in the already effervescent liquor, his struggles easily succeeded in creating.

Not tamely, however, did the tall seaman behold the discomfiture of his companion. Jostling King Pest through the open trap, the valiant Legs slammed the door down upon him with an oath, and strode towards the centre of the room. Here tearing down the[j] skeleton which swung over the table, he laid it about him with so much energy and good will, that, as the last glimpses of light died away within the apartment, he succeeded in knocking out the brains of the little gentleman with the gout. Rushing then with all his force against the fatal hogshead full of October ale and Hugh Tarpaulin, he rolled it over and over in an instant. Out burst a deluge of liquor so fierce — so impetuous — so overwhelming — that the room was flooded from wall to wall — the loaded table was overturned — the tressels were thrown upon their backs — the tub of punch into the fire-place — and the ladies into hysterics. [k]Piles of death-furniture floundered about.[k] Jugs, pitchers, and carboys mingled promiscuously in the *mélée*,[l] and[m] wicker flagons encountered desperately with bottles of [n]junk.[24] The[n] man with the horrors was drowned upon the spot — the little stiff gentleman

---

g   high up *(A, B, C, D)*
h . . . h   dropped him *(A, B, C, D)*
i   last, *(D)*
j   the huge *(A, B, C, D)*
k . . . k   *Omitted (A, B, C, D)*
l   *melée,* *(A, B, C, D, E, F)*

m   while *(D)*
n . . . n   junk. Piles of death-furniture floundered about. Sculls floated *en masse* — hearse-plumes nodded to escutcheons — the *(A, B, C, D)*

floated[o] off in his coffin — and the victorious Legs, seizing by the waist the fat lady in the shroud, [p]rushed out with her[p] into the street, [q]and made a bee-line for the "Free and Easy,"[q] followed under easy sail by the redoubtable[r] Hugh Tarpaulin, who, having sneezed three or four times, panted and puffed after him with the Arch Duchess Ana-Pest.

NOTES

Subtitle: The allegory referred to in the subtitle has been usually ignored, but see note 16 below.
Motto: The motto is from *Gorboduc,* lines 606–607. This play by Thomas Norton and Thomas Sackville, Lord Buckhurst, was given before Queen Elizabeth I, on January 13, 1561. Its subtitle is "Ferrex and Porrex" and it has been much discussed as "the earliest English tragedy in blank verse." First printed in 1565, it was often reprinted, for example in Dodsley's *Old Plays,* 1744, 1780, and later.

1. Edward III reigned 1327–1377; the Black Death ravaged England several times during his reign.

2. Ben Nevis, 4406 feet high, in the county of Inverness, is the highest mountain in Great Britain, and is visited by countless tourists.

3. "Humming-stuff" is strong drink; "no chalk" means no credit.

4. St. Andrew's Stair probably refers to the approach to St. Andrew's Church, Holborn, not far from 18 Basinghall Street where John Allan had his English place of business.

5. Compare "The Man of the Crowd": "The paving stones lay at random, displaced from their beds by the rankly growing grass. Horrible filth festered in the dammed-up gutters. The whole atmosphere teemed with desolation."

6. In PHANTASY-PIECES, Poe capitalized Stentorian, to show the connection with Stentor, the loud-voiced Greek herald of the *Iliad,* but the change was not adopted in the later editions.

7. "Into the midst of things" is "in medias res" of Horace, *Ars Poetica,* line 148; a commonplace.

8. Compare "A Paean," line 14, "costly broidered pall."

9. Knocking down is not literal; the bone is used as a gavel.

10. "A dropsy" is an obsolete term for an unquenchable thirst, as well as the name of a disease. Poe is capable of the pun.

11. Oporto wine is usually called port.

---

o sailed *(A, B, C, D)*
p . . . p scudded out *(A, B, C, D)*
q . . . q *Omitted (A, B, C, D)*
r redoubted *(A, B)*

12. The Norsemen drank mead from the skulls of brave enemies. Byron had a cup made from the skull of a monk found on his estate. He mentions it in letters of 1809 collected by Moore, and in "Lines Inscribed upon a Cup Formed from a Skull."

13. The skeleton suspended from the ceiling with its cranium full of ignited charcoal is not the most macabre of Poe's hanging lamps. See "Hop-Frog."

14. Blue ruin is cheap gin. Keats used the term in verses on Charles Armitage Brown enclosed in a letter to George and Georgiana Keats dated April 16 or 17, 1819.

15. Will Wimble, in Addison and Steele's *Spectator,* number 108, is a younger son of a nobleman, and a member of Sir Roger De Coverley's Club; being unable to go into trade, he fritters away his time.

16. In the allegory, as worked out by my student, Lynne Chaleff, the six Pests are types of people who are "pests" in the figurative sense of the word. All are "dead" since they are types of deadly futility. (1) King Pest himself, with his high *forehead* and affable expression, is the man of intellect who does nothing with it, and knows only the vanity of wisdom; his Spanish cloak typifies his pride. (2) Queen Pest, into whose huge *mouth* her earrings keep dropping, is the great talker, who repeats only what she has heard, and pretends not to wish to gossip. (3) Arch Duchess Ana-Pest is the bad poet who pokes her *nose* into everything, but is incapable of living a life of her own. (4) Arch Duke Tem-Pest is *cheeky,* is proud of his bandages and a tabard of noble arms, a man of rank and clothes, himself deserving of nothing. (5) Duke Pest-Iferous is a sot who tries not to indulge, but is betrayed by his *ears* when a cork pops. (6) Duke Pest-Ilential, with large *eyes,* sees all, but is wholly sheltered, and recoils from the world.

17. The word "nare" used in the earlier texts, as Ruth Leigh Hudson points out, appears in Disraeli's *Vivian Grey.* See also the motto for "The Folio Club," and the note on the word in "Diddling."

18. Davy Jones is a seaman's name for "the fiend who presides over all the evil spirits of the deep." (OED quotes this definition from Smollett's *Peregrine Pickle,* 1751.)

19. Black Strap is inferior thick port.

20. For the "law of the Medes and the Persians which altereth not" see Esther 1:19, Daniel 6:8, and other passages in the Bible.

21. There is a tradition that the Duke of Clarence, brother of Richard III, was drowned in a butt of Malmsey wine. See Shakespeare, *Richard III,* I, iv, and V, iii.

22. Shylock cries out "A sentence" in *Merchant of Venice,* IV, i, 304.

23. Hurlygurly (or hurdy-gurdy) is a street organ, or the person who plays one; in the first version of Poe's story, the "king" was an organ-grinder. It is amusing to find a boatswain named Hurliguerly as a character in Jules Verne's *Sphinx des Glaces* (1895), a sequel to *Arthur Gordon Pym.*

24. A junk-bottle is made of thick green or black glass. See OED.

OTHER TALES
1836-1839

AUTOGRAPHY

Poe's two early articles called "Autography," published in the *Southern Literary Messenger* in 1836, have a fictional setting, and although the signatures were reproduced from genuine originals, the letters are all made up. Some have a humorous or satirical turn, and because of this and their fictional nature it seems desirable to collect these two papers among the Tales and Sketches. "A Chapter on Autography" in two installments and "An Appendix of Autographs," Poe's three later articles in *Graham's Magazine* for November 1841 to January 1842, are purely factual and critical, and therefore are left for a later volume of this edition.

Poe's articles, as he specifically indicates, although his ascription is false, were conceived in response to a piece in a British magazine. His original was undoubtedly "The Miller Correspondence," in *Fraser's Magazine* for November 1833. A "Rev. George Miller" is there represented as bringing to the magazine office a collection of autograph letters secured from prominent persons by requesting a "character of an imaginary footman" or other servant. Thirty letters are printed, each preceded by a brief comment, usually on the personality the letter suggests. At the end of the article it is unmistakably acknowledged that the whole thing is fictitious.

Poe changed the format slightly, added facsimile signatures, and commented mainly on the handwriting itself as revelatory. The first installment was set up before September 29, 1835, when T. W. White wrote Poe that he was worried about the item concerning James Fenimore Cooper. On October first White wrote to Lucian Minor: "I also send you sheets of the 7th forme of the Messenger. . . . 'Autography' No. 1, I shall not insert . . . I think it unnecessarily severe on Cooper? Read it — and candidly tell me what you think . . . Since scribbling . . . the foregoing . . . I have just seen Mr. Heath . . . He proposes striking out Cooper's and Irving's names . . .

I should not like to shoot so sarcastic an arrow at poor Cooper — however much he deserves it."*

Poe's article appeared in the *Messenger* for February 1836, with the names of both Irving and Cooper. The squib on the latter is so mild that I believe Poe had revised it in proof.

Poe undoubtedly had access to a good many signatures in the files of the *Messenger* office. He treated only living authors, with two exceptions — Chief Justice Marshall — whose name was followed by "Paid" in the list of subscribers published in No. 1 of the *Messenger* — and William Wirt.† For the second installment of the series Poe had the assistance of James F. Otis, lawyer, journalist, and occasional contributor to the *Messenger,* who sent a number of signatures in a letter to Poe from the capital city, June 11, 1836.‡

The first article was reprinted in the *Georgetown Metropolitan,* September 21, October 7, 10, and 12, 1836 — probably by an arrangement with T. W. White, since the signatures were included. The articles were first collected by Harrison in 1902, among Poe's essays.

TEXTS

(A) Southern Literary Messenger, February and August 1836 (2:205–212 and 601–604); *(B) Complete Works,* ed. Harrison (1902), XV, 139–174.

The *Southern Literary Messenger* version *(A)* is followed as it is the sole authorized version. There are no variants, but in the original the title "Autog-

* See David K. Jackson, *Poe and the Southern Literary Messenger* (1934), pp. 101–102. Cooper had drawn bitter criticism upon himself by *A Letter to His Countrymen* (1834) and his satirical novel *The Monikins* (1835), but the former had received a sympathetic notice in the first issue (August 1834) of the *Messenger.*

† William Wirt had died in 1834, the Chief Justice in July 1835. On April 28, 1846, Poe wrote Evert A. Duyckinck that he owned, among others, letters of Marshall and Wirt. From the *Graham's* series of 1841–42 Poe omitted the deceased Carey, Emmons, and Flint, and apologized for including Mellen, who was alive when the notice of him was set up.

‡ This letter is now in the Boston Public Library with the signature clipped out. It enclosed those of Willis, Mellen, Noah, Stone, Miss Gould, and "Jack Downing" used in the August *Messenger* as well as several that Poe used later in *Graham's,* where (December 1841) he reproduced that of Otis himself. A New Englander, nephew of Harrison Gray Otis, the prominent Federalist leader, J. F. Otis was in Washington as a newspaper correspondent. His principal connections were with Portland, Maine; Newburyport, Massachusetts; and Boston, where he died in 1867. [His letter was published by Dwight Thomas in *Poe Studies,* June 1975.]

raphy" was repeated at the beginning of the second installment (Letters xxv–xxxviii), and to it was appended a footnote: "See Messenger for February last."

Reprint

The Metropolitan (Washington and Georgetown), September 21, October 7, 10, and 12, 1836, from *SLM.*

AUTOGRAPHY.

Our friend and particular acquaintance, Joseph Miller, Esq. (who, by the way, signs his name, we think, Joseph A. Miller, or Joseph B. Miller, or at least Joseph C. Miller) paid us a visit a few days ago. His behavior was excessively odd. Walking into our *sanctum* without saying a word, he seated himself with a dogged air in our own exclusive arm-chair, and surveyed us, for some minutes, in silence, and in a very suspicious manner, over the rim of his spectacles. There was evidently something in the wind. "What *can* the man want?" thought we, without saying so.

"I will tell you," said Joseph Miller, Esq. — that is to say, Joseph D. Miller, Joseph E. Miller, or possibly Joseph F. Miller, Esq. "I will tell you," said he. Now, it is a positive fact that we had not so much as attempted to open any of our mouths.

"I will tell you," said he, reading our thoughts.

"Ah, thank you!" we replied, slightly smiling, and feeling excessively uncomfortable — "thank you! — we should like to know."

"I believe," resumed he — resumed Joseph G. Miller — "I believe you are not altogether unacquainted with our family."

"Why, *not* altogether, certainly — pray, sir, proceed."

"It is one of the oldest families in —— in ——"

"In Great Britain," we interposed, seeing him at a loss.

"In the United States," said Mr. Miller — that is, Joseph H. Miller, Esq.

"In the United States! — why, sir, you are joking surely: we thought the Miller family were particularly British — The Jest-Book you know ——"[1]

"You are in error," interrupted he — interrupted Joseph I. Miller — "we are British, but not particularly British. You should know that the Miller family are indigenous every where, and have little connection with either time or place. This is a riddle which you may be able to read hereafter.[2] At present let it pass, and listen to me. You know I have many peculiar notions and opinions — many particularly bright fancies which, by the way, the rabble have thought proper to call whims, oddities, and eccentricities. But, sir, they are not. You have heard of my passion for autographs?"

"We have."

"Well, sir, to be brief. Have you, or have you not, seen a certain rascally piece of business in the London Athenæum?"[3]

"Very possible," we replied.

"And, pray sir, what do you think of it?"

"Think of what?"

"No, sir, not of *what*," said he — said Joseph K. Miller, Esq. getting very angry, "not of *what* at all; but of that absurd, nefarious, and superfluous piece of autographical rascality therein — that is to say in the London Athenæum — deliberately, falsely, and maliciously fathered upon me, and laid to my charge — to the charge of *me*, I say, Joseph L. Miller." Here, Mr. M. arose, and, unbuttoning his coat in a great rage, took from his breast pocket a bundle of MSS. and laid them emphatically upon the table.

"Ah ha!" said we, getting particularly nervous, "we begin to understand you. We comprehend. Sit down! You, Joseph M. — that is to say, Joseph N. Miller — have had — that is to say, ought to have had, eh? — and the London Athenæum is — that is to say, it is not, &c. — and — and — and — oh, precisely!"

"My *dear* sir," said Mr. Miller, affectionately, "you are a fool — a confounded fool. Hold your tongue! *This* is the state of the case. I, Joseph O. Miller, being smitten, as all the world knows, with a passion for autographs, am supposed, in that detestable article to which I am alluding, and which appeared some time ago in the London Athenæum, — am supposed, I say, to have indited sundry epistles, to several and sundry characters of literary notoriety about London, with the sinister design, hope, and intention, of thereby eliciting autograph replies — the said epistles, presumed to be indited by me, each and individually being neither more nor less than one and the same thing, and consisting ——"

"Yes sir," said we, "and consisting ——"

AUTOGRAPHY

"And consisting," resumed Mr. Joseph P. Miller, "of certain silly inquiries respecting the character of certain ——"

"Of certain cooks, scullions, and chambermaids," said we, having now some faint recollection of the article alluded to.

"Precisely," said our visiter — "of certain cooks, scullions, chambermaids, and boot-blacks."

"And concerning whose character you are supposed to be excessively anxious."

"Yes, sir — *I* — excessively anxious! — only think of that! — I, Joseph Q. Miller, excessively anxious!"

"Horrible!" we ejaculated.

"Damnable!" said Mr. M.

"But what papers are *these?*" demanded we, taking courage, and eyeing the bundle of MSS. which our friend had thrown upon the table.

"Those papers," said Mr. Miller, after a pause, and with considerable dignity of manner, "those papers are, to tell you the truth, the result of some — of some ingenuity on the part of your humble servant. They are autographs — but they are *American* autographs, and as such may be of some little value in your eyes. Pray accept them — they are entirely at your service. I beg leave, however, to assure you that I have resorted to no petty arts for the consummation of a glorious purpose. No man can accuse *me*, sir, *me*, Joseph R. Miller, of meanness or of superficiality. My letters have invariably been — have been — that is to say, have been every thing they should be. Moreover, they have not been what they should not be. I have propounded no inquiries about scullions. I wrote not to the sublimated Mr. ——, [here we do not feel justified in indicating more fully the name mentioned by Mr. M.] touching a chambermaid, nor to Mr. ——, in relation to a character. On the contrary, I have adapted my means to my ends. I have — I have — in short, sir, I have accomplished many great and glorious things, all of which you shall behold in the sequel." We bowed, and our visiter continued.

"The autographs here included are, you will perceive, the autographs of our principal *literati*. They will prove interesting to the public. It would be as well to insert the letters in your Messenger,

·2 6 3 ·

with facsimiles of the signatures. Of my own letters eliciting these replies I have unfortunately preserved no copies." Here Mr. M. handed us the MSS.

"Mr. Joseph S. Miller" — we began, deeply penetrated by his kindness.

"Joseph *T*. Miller, if you please," interrupted he, with an emphasis on the T.

"Well, sir," said we — "so be it: Mr. Joseph V. Miller, then, since you will have it so, we are highly sensible of your noble, of your disinterested generosity. We are ———"

"Say no more," interrupted our friend, with a sigh — "say no more, I beseech you. The MSS. are entirely at your service. You have been very kind to me, and when I forget a kindness my name is no longer Joseph W. Miller."

"Then your name *is* — is positively Joseph W. Miller?" — we inquired with some hesitation.

"It is" — he replied, with a toss of the head, which we thought slightly supercilious — "It is — Joseph X. Miller. But why do you ask? Good day! In a style epistolary and non-epistolary I must bid you adieu — that is to say I must depart (and *not* remain) your obedient servant, Joseph Y. Miller."[4]

"Extremely ambiguous!" we thought, as he whipped out of the room — "Mr. Miller! Mr. Miller!" — and we hallooed after him at the top of our voice. Mr. Miller returned at the call, but most unfortunately we had forgotten what we had been so anxious to say.

"Mr. Miller," said we, at length, "shall we not send you a number of the Magazine containing your correspondence?"

"Certainly!" — he replied — "drop it in the Post Office."

"But, sir," said we, highly embarrassed, — "to what — to what address shall we direct it?"

"Address!" ejaculated he — "you astonish me! Address *me*, sir, if you please — Joseph Z. Miller."

The package handed us by Mr. M. we inspected with a great deal of pleasure. The letters were neatly arranged and endorsed, and numbered from one to twenty-four. We print them *verbatim*, and with facsimiles of the signatures, in compliance with our friend's suggestion. The dates, throughout, were overscored, and we have been forced, accordingly, to leave them blank. The remarks appended to each letter are our own.

LETTER I.

Philadelphia, ——.

Dear Sir, — I regret that you had the trouble of addressing me twice respecting the Review of your publication. The truth is it was only yesterday I enjoyed the opportunity of reading it, and bearing public testimony to its merits. I think the work might have a wider circulation if, in the next edition, it were printed *without* the preface. Of your talents and other merits I have long entertained a high opinion.

Respectfully, your faithful servant,

JOSEPH A. MILLER, ESQ.

There is nothing very peculiar in the *physique* of this letter. The hand-writing is bold, large, sprawling, and irregular. It is rather rotund than angular, and is by no means illegible. One would suppose it written in a violent hurry. The t's are crossed with a sweeping scratch of the pen, giving the whole letter an odd appearance if held upside-down, or in any position other than the proper one. The whole air of the letter is *dictatorial.* The paper is of good but not superior quality. The seal is of brown wax mingled with gold, and bears a Latin motto, of which only the words *trans* and *mortuus* are legible.

LETTER II.

Hartford, ——.

My Dear Sir, — Your letter of the — ult. with the accompanying parcel, reached me in safety, and I thank you for that polite attention, which is the more gratifying, as I have hitherto not had the pleasure of your acquaintance. The perusal of the pamphlet afforded me great delight, and I think it displays so much good sense, mingled with so much fine taste, as would render it an acceptable present to readers even more fastidious than myself. The

purely Christian opinions with which the work abounds, will not
fail of recommending it to all lovers of virtue, and of the truth.
I remain yours, with respect and esteem,

L. H. Sigourney.—

Joseph B. Miller, Esq.

Much pains seem to have been taken in the MS. of this epistle.
Black lines have been used, apparently. Every t is crossed and every
i dotted with precision. The punctuation is faultless. Yet the *tout-
ensemble* of the letter has nothing of formality or undue effemi-
nacy. The characters are free, well-sized, and handsomely formed,
preserving throughout a perfectly uniform and beautiful appearance, although generally unconnected with each other. Were one
to form an estimate of the character of Mrs. Sigourney's compositions from the character of her hand writing, the estimate would
not be very far from the truth. Freedom, dignity, precision, and
grace of thought, without abrupt or startling transitions, might be
attributed to her with propriety. The paper is good, the seal small
— of green and gold wax — and without impression.

LETTER III.

New York, ——.

Dear Sir, — I have delayed replying to your letter of the — ult.
until I could find time to make the necessary inquiries about the
circumstances to which you allude. I am sorry to inform you that
these inquiries have been altogether fruitless, and that I am consequently unable, at present, to give you the desired information. If,
hereafter, any thing shall come to light which may aid you in your
researches, it will give me great pleasure to communicate with you
upon the subject.
I am, Dear Sir, your friend and servant,

Joseph C. Miller, Esq.

There is much in the hand-writing here like that of Mrs.

Sigourney, and yet, as a whole, it is very different. In both MSS. perfect uniformity and regularity exist, and in both, the character of the writing is *formed* — that is to say, *decided*. Both are beautiful, and, at a casual glance, both have a somewhat similar *effect*. But Mrs. Sigourney's MS. is one of the most legible, and Mr. Paulding's one of the most illegible in the world. His small a's, t's and c's are all alike, and the *style* of the characters generally is French. No correct notion of Mr. Paulding's literary peculiarities could be obtained from an inspection of his MS. It has probably been modified by strong adventitious circumstances. The paper is of a very fine glossy texture, and of a blue tint, with gilt edges.

LETTER IV.

Boston, ———.

It is due from me to advise you that the communication of the — ult. addressed by you to myself involves some error. It is evident that you have mistaken me for some other person of the same surname, as I am altogether ignorant of the circumstances to which you refer.

I am, sir, very respectfully, your obedient servant,

JOSEPH D. MILLER, ESQ.

The hand writing here is of an odd appearance. The capitals and *long* letters extend far above or below the line, and the rest have a running and diminutive formation, rendering it difficult to distinguish one from another. The words are unusually far apart, and but little matter is contained in much space. At first sight the MS. appears to be hurried — but a few moments' examination will prove that this is not the case. The capital I's might be mistaken for T's. The whole has a clean and uniform appearance. The paper is common, and the seal (of red wax) is oval in shape — probably a shield — the device illegible.

LETTER V.

St. Mark's Place, New York, ———.

Dear Sir,— Your obliging letter of the —— was received in due course of mail, and I am gratified by your good opinion. At the same time my numerous engagements will render it out of my power to send you any communication for your valuable Magazine, 'The Humdrum,' for some months to come at least. Wishing you all success, and with many thanks for your attention.

I remain, sir, your humble servant,

J. Fenimore Cooper

JOSEPH E. MILLER, ESQ.

Mr. Cooper's MS. is bad — very bad. There is no distinctive character about it, and it appears to be *unformed.* The writing will probably be different in other letters. Upon reference we find this to be the fact. In the letter to Mr. Miller, the MS. is of a *petite* and finicky appearance, and looks as if scratched with a steel pen — the lines are crooked. The paper is fine, and of a bluish tint. A wafer is used.

LETTER VI.

New York, ——. My Dear Sir, — I owe you a very humble apology for not answering sooner your flattering epistle of the — ult. The truth is, being from home when your letter reached my residence, my reply fell into the ever open grave of deferred duties.

As regards the information you desire I regret that it is out of my power to aid you. My studies and pursuits have been directed, of late years, in so very different a channel, that I am by no means *au fait* on the particular subject you mention. Believe me, with earnest wishes for your success,

Very respectfully yours,

C. M. Sedgwick

JOSEPH F. MILLER, ESQ.

The penmanship of Miss Sedgwick is excellent. The characters are well-sized, distinct, elegantly, but not ostentatiously formed; and, with perfect freedom of manner, are still sufficiently feminine. The hair strokes of the pen differ little in thickness from the other parts of the MS. — which has thus a uniform appearance it might not otherwise have. Strong common sense, and a scorn of superfluous ornament, one might suppose, from Miss Sedgwick's hand writing, to be the characteristics of her literary style. The paper is very good, blue in tint, and ruled by machine. The seal of red wax, plain.

LETTER VII.

New York, ———.

Dear Sir, — I have received your favor of the ——. The report to which it alludes was entirely without foundation. I have never had, and have not *now,* any intention of editing a Magazine. The Bookseller's statement on this subject originated in a misunderstanding.

Your Poem on "Things in General," I have not had the pleasure of seeing. I have not, however, the least doubt of its — of its — that is to say, of its extreme delicacy of sentiment, and highly original style of thinking — to say nothing at present of that — of that extraordinary and felicitous manner of expression which so particularly characterizes all that — that I have seen of your writings. I shall endeavor, sir, to procure your Poem, and anticipate much pleasure in its perusal.

Very respectfully, your obedient servant,

Fitz. Greene Halleck

JOSEPH G. MILLER, ESQ.

Mr. Halleck's is a free, mercantile hand, and evinces a love for the graceful rather than for the picturesque. There is some *force,* too, in its expression. The *tout ensemble* is pleasing. Mr. H.'s letter is probably written *currente calamo* — but without hurry. The paper is very good, and bluish — the seal of red wax.

LETTER VIII.

Alexandria, Red River, ———, Louisiana.

Dear Sir, — Your polite letter of the — is before me, and the view which you present of the estimation in which you hold my poor labors is every way gratifying. It would afford me great pleasure to send you a few trifles for the Hum-drum, which I have no doubt will prove a very useful periodical if its design is well carried out — but the truth is my time is entirely occupied.   Yours,

Timothy Flint

JOSEPH H. MILLER, ESQ.

The writing in this letter has a *fidgetty appearance,* and would seem to indicate a mind without settled aims — restless and full of activity. Few of the characters are written twice in the same manner, and their *direction* varies continually. Sometimes the words lie perpendicularly on the page — then slope to the right — then, with a jerk, fly off in an opposite way. The thickness, also, of the MS. is changeable — sometimes the letters are very light and fine — sometimes excessively heavy. Upon a casual glance at Mr. F.'s epistle, one might mistake it for an imitation of a written letter by a child. The paper is bad — and wafered.

LETTER IX.

Philadelphia, ———.

Miss Leslie's compliments to Mr. Miller. She has no knowledge of the person spoken of in Mr. Miller's note, and is quite certain there must be some mistake in the statement alluded to.

JOSEPH I. MILLER, ESQ.

Several persons of our acquaintance, between whose mental character and that of Miss Leslie we have fancied a strong similitude, write a hand almost identical with this lady's — yet we are unable to point out much in the MS. itself according with the literary peculiarities of Miss L. Neatness and finish, without over-effeminacy, are, perhaps, the only features of resemblance. We might, also, by straining a point, imagine (from the MS.) that Miss L. regards rather *the effect of her writings as a whole* than the polishing of their constituent parts. The penmanship is rotund, and the words are always finished with an inward twirl. The paper tolerable — and wafered.

LETTER X.

Boston, ——.

Dear Sir, — I have your favor of the ——. For the present I must decline replying to the queries you have propounded. Be pleased to accept my thanks for the flattering manner in which you speak of my Lecture.

I am, Dear Sir, very faithfully, yours,

Edward Everett.

JOSEPH K. MILLER, ESQ.

Here is a noble MS. It has an air of deliberate precision about it emblematic of the statesman; and a mingled solidity and grace speaking the scholar. Nothing can be more legible. The words are at proper intervals — the lines also are at proper intervals, and perfectly straight. There are no superfluous flourishes. The man who writes thus will never grossly err in judgment or otherwise. We may venture to say, however, that he will not attain the loftiest pinnacles of renown. The paper is excellent — stout yet soft — with gilt edges. The seal of red wax, with an oval device bearing the initials E. E., and surrounded with a scroll, on which are legible only the word *cum* and the letters c. o. r. d. a.

LETTER XI.

New York, ——.

My Dear Sir, — I must be pardoned for refusing your request touching your MS. "Treatise on Pigs." I was obliged, some years ago, to come to the resolution not to express opinions of works sent to me. A candid opinion of those whose merit seemed to me small, gave offence, and I found it the best way to avoid a judgment in any case. I hope this will be satisfactory.

I am, my Dear Sir, very respectfully yours,

Washington Irving

JOSEPH L. MILLER, ESQ.

Mr. Irving's hand writing is common-place. There is nothing indicative of genius about it. Neither could any one suspect, from such penmanship, a *high finish* in the author's compositions. This style of writing is more frequently met with than any other. It is a very usual clerk's hand — scratchy and *tapering* in appearance, showing (strange to say) — an eye deficient in a due sense of the *picturesque*. There may be something, however, in the circumstance that the epistle to Mr. Miller is evidently written in a desperate hurry. Paper very indifferent, and wafered.

LETTER XII.

Boston, ———.

Sir, — In reply to your note of the ——, in which you demand if I am "the author of a certain scurrilous attack upon Joseph M. Miller, in the Daily Polyglot of the — ult." I have to say that I am happy in knowing nothing about the attack, the Polyglot, or yourself.

John Neal

JOSEPH M. MILLER.

Mr. Neal's MS. is exceedingly illegible, and very careless. It is necessary to read one half his epistle and guess at the balance. The capitals and long letters, like those of Mr. Palfrey, extend far above and below the line, while the small letters are generally nothing but dots and scratches. Many of the words are run together — so that what is actually a sentence is frequently mistaken for a single word. One might suppose Mr. Neal's mind (from his penmanship) to be bold, excessively active, energetic, and irregular. Paper very common, and wafered.

AUTOGRAPHY

Baltimore, ———.

Dear Sir, — I have received your note of the — ult. and its contents puzzle me no little. I fear it will be impossible to give a definitive reply to an epistle so enigmatically worded. Please write again.

Yours truly,

John P. Kennedy

JOSEPH N. MILLER, ESQ.

This is our *beau ideal* of penmanship. Its prevailing character is *picturesque*. This appearance is given by terminating every letter abruptly, without *tapering,* and by using no perfect angles, and none at all which are not spherical. Great uniformity is preserved in the whole air of the MS. — with great variety in the constituent parts. Every character has the clearness and blackness of a bold wood-cut, and appears to be *placed upon the paper* with singular precision. The long letters do not rise or fall in an undue degree above the line. From this specimen of his hand writing, we should suppose Mr. Kennedy to have the eye of a painter, more especially in regard to the picturesque — to have refined tastes generally — to be exquisitely alive to the proprieties of life — to possess energy, decision, and great talent — to have a penchant also for the *bizarre.* The paper is very fine, clear and white, with gilt edges — the seal neat and much in keeping with the MS. Just sufficient wax, and no more than sufficient, is used for the impression, which is nearly square, with a lion's head in full *alto relievo,* surrounded by the motto *"il parle par tout."*

LETTER XIV.

Philadelphia, ———.

Dear Sir, — Enclosed is your letter of the — ult. addressed to Dr. Robert M. Bird, Philadelphia. From the contents of the note it is evidently not intended for myself. There is, I believe, a Dr. Robert Bird, who resides somewhere in the Northern Liberties — also several Robert Birds in different parts of the city.

Very respectfully, your obedient, humble servant,

Robt. M. Bird

JOSEPH O. MILLER, ESQ.

Dr. Bird's chirography is by no means bad — still it cannot be called good. It is very legible and has force. There is some degree of nervousness about it. It bears a slight resemblance to the writing of Miss Leslie, especially in the curling of the final letters — but is more open, and occupies more space. The characters have the air of not being able to keep pace with the thought, and an uneasy want of finish seems to have been the consequence. A restless and vivid imagination might be deduced from this MS. It has no little of the *picturesque* also. The paper good — *wafered and sealed.*

LETTER XV.

Oak Hill, ———.

Dear Sir, — I have received your polite letter of the ——, and will have no objection to aid you in your enterprise by such information as I can afford. There are many others, however, who would be much better able to assist you in this matter than myself. When I get a little leisure you shall hear from me again.

I am, Dear Sir, with respect, your obedient,

Marshall

JOSEPH P. MILLER, ESQ.

The hand writing of the Chief Justice is not unlike that of Neal — but much better and more legible. The habit of running two words into one (a habit which we noticed in Neal) is also observable in the Chief Justice. The characters are utterly devoid of ornament or unnecessary flourish, and there is a good deal of abruptness about them. They are heavy and black, with very little hair stroke. The lines are exceedingly crooked, running diagonally across the paper. A wide margin is on the left side of the page, with none at all on the right. The whole air of the MS. in its utter simplicity, is strikingly indicative of the man. The paper is a half sheet of course foolscap, wafered.

AUTOGRAPHY

Baltimore, ——.

Dear Sir, — I have received your letter of the — ult. in which you do me the honor of requesting an autograph. In reply, I have to say, that if this scrawl will answer your purpose it is entirely at your service.

Yours respectfully,

JOSEPH Q. MILLER, ESQ.

Mr. Wirt's hand writing has a strong resemblance to that of his friend John P. Kennedy — it is by no means, however, as good, and has too much *tapering* about it to be thoroughly picturesque. The writing is black, strong, clear, and very neat. It is, upon the whole, little in accordance with the character of Mr. W.'s compositions. The lines are crooked. The paper bluish and English — wafered.

LETTER XVII.

Washington, ——.

Dear Sir — In answer to your kind inquiries concerning my health, I am happy to inform you that I was never better in my life. I cannot conceive in what manner the report to which you allude could have originated.

Believe me with the highest respect, your much obliged friend and servant,

JOSEPH R. MILLER, ESQ.

Judge Story's is a very excellent hand, and has the air of being written with great rapidity and ease. It is rotund, and might be characterized as a *rolling hand*. The direction of the letters occasionally varies from right to left, and from left to right. The same peculiarity was observable in Mr. Flint's. Judge Story's MS. is decidedly picturesque. The lines are at equal distances, but lie diagonally on the page. The paper good, of a bluish tint, and folded to form a marginal line. The seal of red wax, and stamped with a common compting-house stamp.

LETTER XVIII.

New York, ——.

My Dear Sir, — I thank you for the hints you have been so kind as to give me in relation to my next edition of the *"Voyage,"* but as that edition has already gone to press, it will be impossible to avail myself of your attention until the sixth impression.

Very respectfully, your obedient servant,

P. M. Reynolds

JOSEPH S. MILLER, ESQ.

We are not partial to Mr. Reynolds' style of chirography. It is a common mercantile hand, in which the words taper off from their beginning to their end. There is much freedom, but no strength about it. The paper good, and wafered.

LETTER XIX.

Portland, ——.

Dear Sir, — I have no knowledge of your owing me the small sum sent in your letter of the ——, and consequently I re-enclose you the amount. You will no doubt be able to discover and rectify the mistake.

Very truly yours,

James Brooks

JOSEPH T. MILLER, ESQ.

Mr. Brooks writes a very good hand, strong, bold, and abrupt — highly indicative of the author's peculiar features of mind. These are nervous common sense, without tinsel or artificiality, and a straight forward directness of conception. The lines are even — and the words at proper intervals. The paper good — and wafered.

AUTOGRAPHY

Washington, ———.

Sir, — I shall be better enabled to answer your letter about "certain mysterious occurrences," of which you desire an explanation, when you inform me explicitly (and I request you will do this) what *are* the mysterious occurrences to which you allude.

J. Q. Adams.

JOSEPH V. MILLER, ESQ.

The chirography of the Ex-President is legible — but has an odd appearance, on account of the *wavering* of the capitals and long letters. The writing is clear, somewhat heavy, and *picturesque* — without ornament. Black lines seem to have been used. A margin is preserved to the right and left. The proportion of the letters is well maintained throughout. The paper common, and wafered.

Philadelphia, ———.

Dear Sir, — I have just received your letter of the ——, in which you complain of my neglect in not replying to your favors of the —— of the —— and of the —— ult. I do assure you, sir, that the letters have never come to hand. If you will be so good as to repeat their contents, it will give me great pleasure to answer them, each and all. The Post Office is in a very bad condition.

Yours respectfully,

Mathew Carey

JOSEPH W. MILLER, ESQ.

Mr. Carey does not write a legible hand — although in other respects a good one. It resembles that of Neal very nearly. Several of the words in the letter to Mr. Miller are run together. The i's are seldom dotted. The lines are at equal distances, and straight. The paper very good — wafered.

LETTER XXII.

Boston, ———.

Dear Sir, — No such person as Philip Philpot has ever been in my employ as a coachman, or otherwise. The name is an odd one, and not likely to be forgotten. The man must have reference to some other Dr. Channing. It would be as well to question him closely.

Respectfully yours,

JOSEPH X. MILLER, ESQ.

Dr. Channing's MS. is very excellent. The letters are bold, well-sized, and beautifully formed. They are, perhaps, too closely crowded upon one another. One might, with some little acumen, detect the high finish of Dr. C.'s style of composition in the character of his chirography. Boldness and accuracy are united with elegance in both. The paper very good, and wafered.

LETTER XXIII.

Philadelphia, ———.

Dear Sir, — I must be pardoned for declining to loan the books you mention. The fact is, I have lost many volumes in this way — and as you are personally unknown to me you will excuse my complying with your request.

Yours, &c.

JOSEPH Y. MILLER, ESQ.

This is a very good MS. — forcible, neat, legible, and devoid of superfluous ornament. Some of the words are run together. The writing slopes considerably. It is too uniform to be picturesque. The lines are at equal distances, and a broad margin is on the left of the page. The chirography is as good at the conclusion as at the commencement of the letter — a rare quality in MSS. — and evincing *indefatigability* of temperament.

AUTOGRAPHY

Washington, ——.

Sir, — Yours of the —— came duly to hand. I cannot send you what you wish. The fact is, I have been so pestered with applications for my autograph, that I have made a resolution to grant one in no case whatsoever.

Yours, &c.

Wm Emmons

JOSEPH Z. MILLER, ESQ.

The writing of the orator is bold, dashing, and chivalrous — the few words addressed to Mr. Miller occupying a full page. The lines are at unequal distances, and run diagonally across the letter. Each sentence is terminated by a long dash — black and heavy. Such an epistle might write the Grand Mogul. The paper is what the English call silver paper — very beautiful and wafered.

[PART II. AUGUST 1836]

Our friend, Joseph A. B. C. D. &c. Miller, has called upon us again, in a great passion. He says we quizzed him in our last article — which we deny positively. He maintains, moreover, that the greater part of our observations on mental qualities, as deduced from the character of a MS., are not to be sustained. The man is in error. However, to gratify him, we have suffered him, in the present instance, to play the critic himself. He has brought us another batch of autographs, and will let us have them upon no other terms. To say the truth, we are rather glad of his proposal than otherwise. We shall look over his shoulder, however, occasionally. Here follow the letters.

LETTER XXV.

Dear Sir, — Will you oblige me by not writing me any more silly letters? I really have no time to attend to them.

Your most obedient servant,

Jared Sparks

JOSEPH A. MILLER, ESQ.

Mr. Sparks' MS. has an odd appearance. The characters are large, round, black, irregular and perpendicular. The lines are close together, and the whole letter wears at first sight an air of confusion — of chaos. Still it is not very illegible upon close inspection, and would by no means puzzle a regular bred devil. We can form no guess in regard to any mental peculiarities from this MS. From its tout-ensemble, however, we might imagine it written by a man who was very busy among a great pile of books and papers huddled up in confusion around him. Paper blueish and fine — sealed, with the initials J. S.

LETTER XXVI.

My Dear Sir, — It gives me great pleasure to receive a letter from you. Let me see, I think I have seen you once or twice in —— where was it? However, your remarks upon "Melanie and other Poems" prove you to be a man of sound discrimination, and I shall be happy to hear from you as often as possible.

Yours truly,

Willis

JOSEPH B. MILLER, ESQ.

Mr. Willis writes a very good hand. What was said about the MS. of Halleck, in the February number, will apply very nearly to this. It has the same grace, with more of the picturesque, however, and, consequently, more force. These qualities will be found in his writings — which are greatly underrated. Mem. Mr. Messenger should do him justice. [Mem. by Mr. Messenger. I have.] Cream colored paper — green and gold seal — with the initials N. P. W.

LETTER XXVII.

Dear Sir, — I have to inform you that "the pretty little poem" to which you allude in your letter is not, as you suppose, of my composition. The author is unknown to me. The poem *is* very pretty.

Yours, &c.

H. F. Gould.

JOSEPH C. MILLER.

AUTOGRAPHY

The writing of Miss Gould resembles that of Miss Leslie very nearly. It is rather more *petite* — but has the same neatness, picturesqueness and finish without over-effeminacy. The literary style of one who writes thus is sure to be forcibly epigrammatic — either in detached sentences — or in the *tout ensemble* of the composition. Paper very fine — wafered.

LETTER XXVIII.

Dear Sir, — Herewith I have the honor of sending you what you desire. If the Essay shall be found to give you any new information, I shall not regret the trouble of having written it.

Respectfully,

JOSEPH D. MILLER, ESQ.

The MS. of Professor Dew is large, bold, very heavy, abrupt, and illegible. It is possible that he never thinks of mending a pen. There can be no doubt that his chirography has been modified, like that of Paulding, by strong adventitious circumstances — for it appears to retain but few of his literary peculiarities. Among the few retained, are *boldness* and *weight*. The abruptness we do not find in his composition — which is indeed somewhat diffuse. Neither is the illegibility of the MS. to be paralleled by any confusion of thought or expression. He is remarkably lucid. We must look for the two last mentioned qualities of his MS. in the supposition that he has been in the habit of writing a great deal, in a desperate hurry, and with a stump of a pen. Paper good — but only a half sheet of it — wafered.

LETTER XXIX.

Dear Sir, — In reply to your query touching the "authenticity of a singular incident," related in one of my poems, I have to inform you that the incident in question is purely a fiction.

With respect, your obedient servant,

JOSEPH E. F. MILLER, ESQ.

The hand-writing of Mr. Mellen is somewhat peculiar, and partakes largely of the character of the signature annexed. It would require no great stretch of fancy to imagine the writer (from what we see of his MS.) a man of excessive sensibility, amounting nearly to disease — of unbounded ambition, greatly interfered with by frequent moods of doubt and depression, and by unsettled ideas of the beautiful. The formation of the G in his signature alone, might warrant us in supposing his composition to have great force, frequently impaired by an undue straining after effect. Paper excellent — red seal.

Dear Sir — I have not the pleasure of your acquaintance, but thank you for the great interest you seem to take in my welfare. I have no relations by the name of Miller, and think you must be in error about the family connection.

Respectfully,

Joseph G. H. Miller, Esq.

The MS. of Mr. Simms resembles, very nearly, that of Mr. Kennedy. It has more slope, however, and less of the picturesque — although still much. We spoke of Mr. K.'s MS. (in our February number) as indicating "the eye of a painter." In our critique on the *Partisan* we spoke of Mr. Simms also as possessing "the eye of a painter," and we had not then seen his hand-writing. The two MSS. are strikingly similar. The paper here is very fine and wafered.

LETTER XXXI.

Dear Sir, — I have received your favor of the —— inst. and shall be very happy in doing you the little service you mention. In a few days I will write you more fully. Very respectfully,

Your most obedient servant,

Joseph J. K. Miller, Esq.

AUTOGRAPHY

Lieutenant Slidell's MS. is peculiar — very neat, very even, and tolerably legible, but somewhat too diminutive. *Black lines* have been, apparently, used. Few tokens of literary manner or character are to be found in this writing. The *petiteness*, however, is most strikingly indicative of a mental habit, which we have more than once pointedly noticed in the works of this author — we mean that of close observation in detail — a habit which, when well regulated, as in the case of Lieut. Slidell, tends greatly to vigor of style. Paper excellent — wafered.

LETTER XXXII.

Dear Sir, — I find upon reference to some MS. notes now lying by me, that the article to which you have allusion, appeared originally in the *"Journal des Sçavans."*

Very respectfully,

Joseph L. M. Miller, Esq.

The writing of Professor Anthon is remarkably neat and beautiful — in the formation of particular letters as well as in the tout-ensemble. The perfect regularity of the MS. gives it, to a casual glance, the appearance of print. The lines are quite straight and at even distances — yet they are evidently written without any artificial aid. We may at once recognise in this chirography the scrupulous precision and finish — the love of elegance — together with the scorn of superfluous embellishment, which so greatly distinguish the compilations of the writer. The paper is yellow, very fine, and sealed with green wax, bearing the impression of a head of Cæsar.

LETTER XXXIII.

Dear Sir, — I have looked with great care over several different editions of Plato, among which I may mention the Bipont edition, 1781–8, 12 vols. oct.; that of Ast, and that of Bekker, reprinted in London, 11 vols. oct. I cannot, however, discover the passage about which you ask me — "is it not very ridiculous?" You must have mistaken the author. Please write again.   Respectfully yours,

Francis Lieber

JOSEPH N. O. MILLER, ESQ.

The MS. of Professor Lieber has nearly all the characteristics which we noticed in that of Professor Dew — besides the peculiarity of a wide margin left at the top of the paper. The whole air of the writing seems to indicate vivacity and energy of thought — but altogether, the letter puts us at fault — for we have never before known a man of minute erudition (and such is Professor Lieber,) who did not write a very different hand from this. We should have imagined a petite and careful chirography. Paper tolerable and wafered.

LETTER XXXIV.

Dear Sir, — I beg leave to assure you that I have *never* received, for my Magazine, *any* copy of verses with so ludicrous a title as "The nine and twenty Magpies." Moreover, if I had, I should certainly have thrown it into the fire. I wish you would not worry me any farther about this matter. The verses, I dare say, are somewhere among your papers. You had better look them up — they may do for the Mirror.

Sarah J Hale

Mr. JOSEPH P. Q. MILLER.

Mrs. Hale writes a larger and bolder hand than her sex generally. It resembles, in a great degree, that of Professor Lieber — and is not easily decyphered. The whole MS. is indicative of a masculine understanding. Paper very good, and wafered.

LETTER XXXV.

Dear Sir, — I am not to be quizzed. You suppose, eh? that I can't understand your fine letter all about "things in general." You want my autograph, you dog — and you sha'nt have it.

Yours respectfully,

M. M. Noah

JOSEPH R. S. MILLER, ESQ.

AUTOGRAPHY

Mr. Noah writes a very good running hand. The lines, however, are not straight, and the letters have too much tapering to please the eye of an artist. The long letters and capitals extend very little beyond the others — either up or down. The epistle has the appearance of being written very fast. Some of the characters have now and then a little twirl, like the tail of a pig — which gives the MS. an air of the quizzical, and devil-me-care. Paper pretty good — and wafered.

LETTER XXXVI.

Mister — I say — It's not worth while trying to come possum over the Major. Your letter's no go. I'm up to a thing or two — or else my name isn't

Jack Downing

Mr. JOSEPH T. V. MILLER.

The Major writes a very excellent hand indeed. It has so striking a resemblance to that of Mr. Brooks, that we shall say nothing farther about it.

LETTER XXXVII.

Dear Sir, — I am exceedingly and excessively sorry that it is out of my power to comply with your rational and reasonable request. The subject you mention is one with which I am utterly unacquainted — moreover, it is one about which I know very little.

Respectfully,

W. L. Stone

JOSEPH W. X. MILLER, ESQ.

Mr. Stone's MS. has some very good points about it — among which is a certain degree of the picturesque. In general it is heavy and sprawling — the short letters running too much together. From the chirography no precise opinion can be had of Mr. Stone's literary style. [Mr. Messenger says no opinion can be had of it in any way.] Paper very good and wafered.

LETTER XXXVIII.

My Good Fellow, — I am not disposed to find fault with your having addressed me, although personally unknown. Your favor (of the —— ultimo) finds me upon the eve of directing my course towards the renowned shores of Italia. I shall land (primitively) on the territories of the ancient Brutii, of whom you may find an account in Lempriére. You will observe (therefore) that, being engrossed by the consequent, necessary, and important preparations for my departure, I can have no time to attend to your little concerns.

Believe me, my dear sir, very faithfully your

JOSEPH Y. Z. MILLER, ESQ.

Mr. Fay writes a passable hand. There is a good deal of spirit — and some force. His paper has a clean appearance, and he is scrupulously attentive to his margin. The MS. however, has an air of *swagger* about it and there are too many dashes — and the tails of the long letters are too long. [Mr. Messenger thinks I am right — that Mr. F. shouldn't try to cut a dash — and that *all* his tales are too long. The swagger he says is respectable, and indicates a superfluity of thought.]

NOTES

1. *Joe Miller's Jests* (London, 1739) is believed to be the work of John Mottley, who ascribed the jokes to Joseph Miller (1684–1738), a Drury Lane comedian. It was constantly revised and reprinted.

2. Compare *Politian*, I, 74–75, "Why, yes it is/And yet it isn't, Ugo, there's a riddle." [Alexander Hammond in *Poe Newsletter*, October 1969 and Roger O'Connor, *ibid.*, June 1970, suggest solutions to Poe's riddle.]

3. The article was not in the London *Athenaeum* but in *Fraser's Magazine*, November 1833. The autograph collector credited was not Joseph, but a Reverend George Miller. I am indebted to W. T. Bandy for pointing this out to me. See also John W. Robertson, *Commentary on the Bibliography of Edgar A. Poe* (1934), II, 152, and Bandy in *AL*, January 1953, p. 536.

4. The phrases "Your servant" and "Your obedient servant" were often spoken by one taking leave, as well as written to close a letter.

AUTOGRAPHY

LETTER I. Robert Walsh (1784–1859) was an industrious man of letters, and in 1836 editor of the Philadelphia *National Gazette*. In 1829 William Wirt had referred Poe to him — Walsh was then editor of the *American Quarterly Review* — for help in finding a publisher for "Al Aaraaf." He generally noticed works immediately upon receipt, and as kindly as possible, as the letter Poe wrote in his person suggests.

II. Mrs. Lydia Huntley Sigourney (1791–1865), "The Sweet Singer of Hartford," wrote or edited more than sixty books during her lifetime. A "poetical contribution, previously unpublished" from her pen had graced the first issue of the *Messenger*. Poe reviewed her *Zinzendorff* in the issue for January 1836.

III. James Kirke Paulding (1778–1860), a prominent New Yorker, a friend of Irving, and one of the Knickerbocker novelists, several times praised Poe's stories. He was an early subscriber and a frequent contributor to the *Messenger*. He had strong Southern sympathies.

IV. John Gorham Palfrey (1796–1881), professor of sacred literature at Harvard, 1831–1839, was editor and chief proprietor, 1835–1843, of the *North American Review*, to which for many years he contributed articles. He is best remembered for his four-volume *History of New England* (1858–75).

V. James Fenimore Cooper (1789–1851), the novelist, was not a favorite author for Poe, but on June 7, 1836, at White's insistence, he wrote to Cooper soliciting "any spare scrap in your port folio" for the *Messenger*. The letter and comment here are so mild that I suspect they were substituted for more biting earlier versions, referred to in White's correspondence about Poe's *jeu d'esprit*.

The *Hum-Drum* is mentioned also in Letter VIII.

VI. Catharine Maria Sedgwick (1789–1867), novelist of New England, was at the time probably the most popular woman writer in America. Her fifth novel, *The Linwoods,* was reviewed in the *Messenger* for December 1835.

VII. Fitz-Greene Halleck (1790–1867), a gifted poet, wrote relatively little after he became secretary to John Jacob Astor in 1832. In the *Messenger,* April 1836, Poe reviewed his small volume *Alnwick Castle, With Other Poems,* together with *The Culprit Fay and Other Poems* by Joseph Rodman Drake. Nelson Adkins, in *Fitz-Greene Halleck* (1930), p. 245, mentions a premature announcement that Halleck was to edit a magazine in New York in 1831.

Diogenes Laertius, *Lives,* VII, "Zeno," 4, says the founder of the Stoics wrote a treatise *On Things in General.*

VIII. Rev. Timothy Flint (1780–1840), Harvard graduate, spent a decade preaching, teaching, and traveling in the Mississippi Valley. He edited the *Western Monthly Review* (Cincinnati), 1827–1830, and in 1833–1834 was connected with the *Knickerbocker Magazine* (New York). He was an early subscriber to the *Messenger,* and a frequent contributor.

The magazine *The Hum-Drum* was also mentioned in Letter V. The fictional hero of "The Literary Life of Thingum Bob" owned a magazine so named, and the *North American Quarterly Humdrum* is mentioned in "Never Bet the Devil Your Head."

OTHER TALES, 1836–1839

IX. Miss Eliza Leslie (1787–1858), a Philadelphia magazinist, had written on cookery and the deportment of young ladies. In 1835 she edited *The Gift ... for 1836,* including in it Poe's "MS. Found in a Bottle." She later wrote much juvenile fiction.

X. Edward Everett (1794–1865), noted orator, edited the *North American Review,* 1820–1824, was a congressman from Massachusetts, 1825–1835, Governor of Massachusetts, 1836–1839, and later President of Harvard.

XI. Washington Irving (1783–1859) was generally considered the foremost American author in 1836. In that year he published *Astoria,* which was reviewed by Poe in the *Messenger* for January 1837.

XII. John Neal (1793–1876) of Portland, Maine, was a critic and novelist, noted for caustic letters. In the *Yankee and Boston Literary Gazette* for September 1829 he had given Poe his "very first words of encouragement" – kind words about "Fairyland." Neal had lived in Baltimore for some years between 1815 and 1823; his quarrel with the poet Pinkney, whose challenge to a duel he declined, was treated in detail by F. L. Pleadwell and myself in *Life and Works of Edward Coote Pinkney* (1926), p. 26.

XIII. John Pendleton Kennedy (1795–1870) was Poe's Baltimore patron. His novel *Horse-Shoe Robinson* (1835) was reviewed in the *Messenger* for May 1835. The remark about an artist may be a personal jest, as his correspondence with Poe at the time concerns a quarrel with William James Hubard (1807–1862) who painted a portrait of Kennedy with his wife and her sister. In a letter of February 11, 1836 Poe says he misdescribed Kennedy's seal, but I can find no clear impression of it.

XIV. Robert Montgomery Bird (1806–1854) was a Philadelphia playwright and novelist. Poe had reviewed his *Calavar* (1834) in the *Messenger,* February 1835, *The Infidel* in June, and *The Hawks of Hawk-Hollow* in December.

The Northern Liberties of Philadelphia was an unfashionable neighborhood.

XV. Chief Justice John Marshall (1755–1835) had assisted Poe to his appointment as a cadet. He died on July 6, 1835.

XVI. William Wirt (1772–1834) had practiced law in Richmond during Poe's childhood there. After serving as Attorney General of the United States, 1817–1829, he settled in Baltimore. He gave kindly counsel to Poe in connection with the publication of "Al Aaraaf."

XVII. Joseph Story (1779–1845), Associate Justice of the Supreme Court, 1811–1845, and a professor of law at Harvard from 1829, wrote some poetry. Before Marshall's death, he had been regarded as a possible successor.

XVIII. Jeremiah N. Reynolds (1799?–1858) was noted for his belief in the hollow earth theory of Symmes used by Poe in "MS. Found in a Bottle," "Hans Phaall," and *Arthur Gordon Pym.* Reynolds' *Voyage of the U.S. Frigate Potomac* was reviewed by Poe in the *Messenger* for June 1835.

XIX. James Brooks (1810–1873) hailed from Maine, was a friend of John Neal, and wrote some of the many imitations of Seba Smith's original "Downing Letters." See Mary A. Wyman, *Two American Pioneers* (1927), pp. 67, 86. See also Letter XXXVI.

AUTOGRAPHY

xx. John Quincy Adams (1767–1848), our sixth President, then currently a member of Congress from Massachusetts, wrote some pleasant poetry. White quoted a letter from him in the first issue of the *Messenger*: "Your design is so laudable, that I would gladly contribute to its promotion; but the periodical literature of the country seems to be rather superabundant than scanty. The desideratum is of quality rather than quantity."

xxi. Mathew Carey (1760–1839), noted publisher and bookseller of Philadelphia, had recently written an autobiography reviewed by Poe in the *Messenger*, February 1836. He subsequently sent it numerous short articles.

xxii. William Ellery Channing (1780–1842), celebrated Unitarian theologian in Boston, during a short residence in Virginia following his graduation from Harvard had gained some insight into the Southern point of view, and his anti-slavery writings from 1835 on were addressed mainly to the Southern conscience.

xxiii. Joseph Hopkinson (1770–1842), a Philadelphia jurist best remembered as the author of "Hail Columbia," was listed in November 1834 as a subscriber to the *Messenger*. Poe had been referred to him by William Wirt in 1829 for advice concerning "Al Aaraaf."

xxiv. William Emmons (born 1792), who lived many years in Kentucky, issued a biography of Van Buren in 1835. He spent his last years in Boston. He was a poetaster like his better known brother Richard, called "Pop" Emmons, to whom Poe referred in a review of "Flaccus" (Thomas Ward) in *Graham's* for March 1843 and in "The Literary Life of Thingum Bob."

xxv. Jared Sparks (1789–1866), editor of the *North American Review*, 1817–1818 and 1824–1830, at this time was editing the writings of George Washington (12 volumes, 1834–1837). Volumes II–VI had been reviewed in the *Messenger* of June 1835. In the comment, the reference to a devil is to a printer's devil.

xxvi. Nathaniel Parker Willis (1806–1867) published *Melanie and Other Poems* in 1835. "Mr. Messenger" here means the *Southern Literary Messenger*, which, in its number of November 1834, reprinted from the Norfolk *American Beacon*, October 10, 1834, a laudatory article on "N. P. Willis" by Hugh Blair Grigsby. Poe from time to time made a good deal of fun of Willis, who later became his good friend.

xxvii. Hannah Flagg Gould (1789–1865) was a New England poetess, now little remembered. Poe reviewed her *Poems* in the *Messenger*, January 1836; and in *Burton's Gentleman's Magazine*, September 1839, he pointed out the similarity of her work to that of Mary Howitt, in a review of the English author's *Birds and Flowers*.

xxxviii. Thomas Roderick Dew (1802–1846), political economist and historian, was a professor at the College of William and Mary and became its president in 1836. An article by him on differences between the sexes was published in the *Messenger* for June 1835, and other contributions followed.

xxix. Grenville Mellen (1799–1841), who moved from New England to New

York, was a minor poet and writer of short stories. He was noted for amiability. A volume of his poems was reviewed in the *Messenger* for May 1836.

xxx. William Gilmore Simms (1806–1870), best known for his historical novels of South Carolina, was a prolific contributor to magazines. Poe's critique of his novel *The Partisan* is in the *Southern Literary Messenger,* January 1836.

xxxi. Alexander Slidell (1802–1848), a naval officer, wrote several books of travel; his *American in England* was reviewed in the *Messenger,* in February, and his *Spain Revisited* in May 1836. In 1838, by legislative authority, he added "Mackenzie" to his name at the request of a maternal uncle.

xxxii. Charles Anthon (1797–1867) was a famous professor of Classics at Columbia College, whose friendship Poe later enjoyed. He had edited Lemprière's *Classical Dictionary* – sixth American edition – in 1827 and a revised and enlarged edition in 1833. The *Journal des Sçavans,* founded in 1665, is mentioned in "Pinakidia," number 125 *(SLM,* August 1836, p. 580). This information probably came from Isaac D'Israeli's article "Literary Journals" in his *Curiosities of Literature.*

xxxiii. Francis Lieber (1800–1872), born and educated in Germany, was a scholar of great attainments. He edited the *Encyclopaedia Americana* (13 volumes, 1829–1833) and became professor of political economy at South Carolina College in 1835. In the *Messenger,* October 1836, is an article, "Classical Bibliography," by Edward William Johnstone, Librarian of South Carolina College. From this, before publication, Poe probably took his description of editions of Plato. The phrase attributed to the philosopher is one of Poe's better jokes.

xxxiv. Sarah Josepha Hale (1788–1879) was the editor of (Godey's) *Lady's Book,* and usually favorable to Poe.

xxxv. Mordecai Manuel Noah (1785–1851), journalist, playwright – and politician – later became a good friend to Poe. An encouraging letter "from the pen of Major Noah, editor of the New York Evening Star" was quoted on the inside of the back cover of the *Messenger* for January 1835, and he subsequently became a contributor.

xxxvi. Jack Downing was a pseudonym used by several satirists who wrote letters ridiculing President Andrew Jackson. Poe, in 1836, thought James Brooks was the "original" Jack, though modern scholars all award the palm to Seba Smith. Brooks was in Washington when James Otis procured the "Downing signature" from him. See also Letter xix above.

xxxvii. William Leete Stone (1792–1844), a New York editor, pamphleteer, and historian, was disliked by Poe, who scathingly reviewed his social satire, *Ups and Downs in the Life of a Distressed Gentleman* in the *Messenger* for June 1836. Examination of the columns of Stone's *New York Commercial Advertiser* has not confirmed a story that he printed a denial of having written this absurdly tautological letter.

xxxviii. Theodore Sedgwick Fay (1807–1898) was connected with the *New-York Mirror.* In the Berg Collection at the New York Public Library there is a copy of Poe's *Poems* (1831) inscribed to "Mr. Theo:ᵉ S. Fay, with the author's compliments." This suggests that Poe ascribed the slight notice of the book in the *New-York Mirror*, May 7, 1831, to Fay. Poe disliked Fay, however, and reviewed his *Norman Leslie* savagely in the *Messenger* for December 1835.

John Lemprière's *Classical Dictionary* (London, 1788) went through many editions, the most recent — in America — being that edited by Charles Anthon in 1833. Poe ridicules Fay for affected and inaccurate learning. The Bruttii occupied the toe of Italy. It is improbable that an American visitor would land at Reggio.

VON JUNG (MYSTIFICATION)

This story is basically a comic anecdote, ridiculing duels — which Poe had already treated with contempt in "Lionizing" — but it is the first work in which he displays an interest in secret writing. The tale also touches upon the relation between a person and his image, or double, which Poe was to consider more seriously in three later stories.* This is a subject of almost universal interest among mankind.

An old joke on the theme of a man's reflection in a mirror may have suggested the action of Poe's tale. It is quoted in a catalogue issued by the bookseller Guido Bruno from a jest book called *Democritus, or the Laughing Philosopher,* published in London, 1770:

An Irishman, having resolved on suicide, caught sight of himself in a large mirror and discharged his pistol at the image. His landlady cried out, "I am ruined and undone forever!" "And so am I," says Paddy, "for I have just now killed the handsomest man in the world."

Poe may well have met with this story or heard it from a different source.

The third element in the tale is a mysterious book that can be understood only by readers who know the key that unlocks its meaning.

There was much interest in the early nineteenth century in the customs of German universities, among which Göttingen was outstanding. A number of Americans, including George Ticknor and

---

* In "Mystification" Poe treats of a real mirror image; in "William Wilson" of a man and his double; in "The Fall of the House of Usher" of a brother and sister who look alike; and in "The Oval Portrait" of a too-lifelike painting.

Edward Everett, studied there; and a character in Poe's Folio Club, Mr. Horribile Dictu, is described as a graduate.†

TEXTS

(A) New York *American Monthly Magazine,* June 1837 (New Series, 3:562–571); *(B) Tales of the Grotesque and Arabesque* (1840), II, 105–122; *(C) Broadway Journal,* December 27, 1845 (2:382–385); *(D) Works* (1856), IV, 251–259. PHANTASY-PIECES, title only.

The *Broadway Journal* text *(C)* is reprinted. Griswold's *(D)* insertion of an "a" before "single combat" does not carry Poe's intended meaning, I am sure. Griswold was followed here (and in omitting "usual" from "his usual stiff and *ultra recherché* air") in the Virginia edition, although it is stated that the *Broadway Journal* text is followed. The final title is in the manuscript Table of Contents in the first volume of PHANTASY-PIECES, but the revised text (in the second volume) is not preserved. The signature "Littleton Barry" was appended in the *Broadway Journal* (see "Loss of Breath," n. 41).

MYSTIFICATION. [*C*]

Slid, if these be your "passados" and "montantes," I'll have none o'them. —
NED KNOWLES.

ªThe Baron Ritzner[1] Von Jungª was of a noble Hungarian family, every member of which (at least as far back into antiquity

† [Just as "Lionizing" was a quiz on Willis, "Mystification" may be a burlesque of Theodore S. Fay, based on "The German Student's Story" which appeared June 11, 1835, in the *New-York Mirror* with a "puff," as a sample of Fay's forthcoming *Norman Leslie,* a book reviewed by Poe in the *Southern Literary Messenger,* December 1835, as "bepuffed, beplastered, and be-Mirrored." Sidney Moss in *Poe's Literary Battles* (1963) ably set forth the details of the literary quarrel between Poe and Fay. That the quarrel bore literary results for Poe in this tale and others is the thesis of Burton Pollin's "Poe's 'Mystification': Its Source in Fay's *Norman Leslie,*" *Mississippi Quarterly,* Spring 1972, pp. 112–130.]

Title: Von Jung, the Mystific (A); Von Jung (B); Mystification PHANTASY-PIECES	Von Jung." If so, these will not fail to remember him, and well; but they may
Motto: Omitted (A, B); and/aud *(D) misprint;* o'/of *(D)*	be at a loss, nevertheless, to understand why I choose to dub the extraordinary
A has an initial paragraph:	personage in question with the odd
I believe there are some young Americans even now in Gotham who were at the University of G——n during "the domination of the Baron Ritzner	title which forms the heading of this article. Thereby hangeth, however, a tale.
	a . . . a My friend, the Baron, *(A);*

MYSTIFICATION

as any certain records extend) was more or less remarkable for talent of some description, — the majority for that species of *grotesquerie* in conception of which Tieck, a scion of the house, has given some vivid, although by no means the most vivid exemplifications.[2] My acquaintance ᵇwith Ritznerᵇ commenced at the magnificent Chateau Jung, into which a train of droll adventures, not to be made public, threw meᶜ during the summer months of the year 18 — . Here it was I obtained a place in his regard, and here, with somewhat more difficulty, a partial insight into his mental conformation. In later days this insight grew more clear, as the intimacy which had at first permitted it became more close; and when, after three years'ᵈ separation, we met at G —— n, I knew all that it was necessary to know of the character of the Baron Ritzner Von Jung.

I remember the buzz of curiosity whichᵉ his advent excited within the college precincts on the night of the twenty-fifth of June. I remember still more distinctly, that while he was pronounced by all parties at first sight "the most remarkable man in the world," no person made any attempt at accounting for this opinion. That he was *unique* appeared so undeniable, thatᶠ it was deemed impertinentᵍ to inquire wherein the uniquity consisted. But, letting this matter pass for the present, I will merely observe that, from the first moment of his setting foot within the limits of the university, he began to exercise over the habits, manners, persons, ʰpurses, andʰ propensities of the whole community which surrounded him, an influence the most ⁱextensive andⁱ despotic, yet at the same time the most indefinitiveʲ and altogether unaccountable. Thus the brief period of his residence at the university forms an era in its annals, and is characterized by all classes of people appertaining to it or its dependencies as "that very extraordinary

---

My friend, the Baron Ritzner Von Jung, *(B)*
b...b with him — with Ritzner — *(A, B)*
c me par hazard *(A, B)*
d years *(B, C, D) corrected from A*
e *Omitted (A)*
f *Omitted (A, B)*

g not pertinent *(A, B)*
h...h purses, moral feelings, intellectual faculties, and physical *(A)*; purses, moral feelings, and physical *(B)*
i...i extensive, the most absolutely *(A)*; extensive and absolutely *(B)*
j indefinitive, inappreciable, *(A)*

epoch forming the domination of the Baron Ritzner Von Jung."[k] [3]

Upon his[1] advent to G —— n, he sought me out in my apartments. He was then of no particular age; — by which I mean that it was impossible to form a guess respecting his age by any data personally afforded. He might have been fifteen or fifty, and *was* twenty-one years and seven months.[m] He was by no means a handsome man — perhaps[n] the reverse. The contour of his face was somewhat angular and harsh. His forehead was lofty and very fair; his nose a snub; his eyes large, heavy, glassy and meaningless. About the mouth there was more to be observed. The lips were gently protruded, and rested the one upon the other after such fashion that it is impossible to conceive any, even the most complex, combination of human features, conveying so entirely,[o] and so singly, the idea of unmitigated gravity, solemnity and repose.[p]

It will be perceived, no doubt, from what I have already said, that the Baron was[q] one of those human anomalies now and then

---

k *After this A and B have another paragraph:*
 I have seen — and be it here borne in mind that the [*Omitted (B)*] gentlemen still living in Gotham who have been with myself witness of these things will have full recollection of the passages to which I now merely allude — I have seen, then, the most outrageously preposterous of events brought about by the most intangible and apparently inadequate of means. I have seen — what, indeed, have I not seen? I have seen Villanova, the danseuse, lecturing in the chair of National Law, and I have seen D——, P——, T——, and Von C——, all enraptured with her profundity. I have seen the protector, the consul, and the whole faculty aghast at the convolutions of a weathercock. I have seen Sontag received with hisses, and a hurdy-gurdy with sighs. I have seen an ox-cart, with oxen, on the summit of the Rotunda. I have seen all the pigs of G——n in periwigs, and all her cows in canonicals. I have seen fifteen hundred vociferous cats in the steeple of St. P——. I have seen the college chapel bombarded — I have seen the college ramparts most distressingly

placarded — I have seen the whole world by the ears — I have seen old Wertemuller in tears — and, more than all, I have seen such events come to be regarded as the most reasonable, commendable, and inevitable things in creation, through the silent, yet all-pervading and magical influence of the dominator Baron Ritzner Von Jung.
l the Baron's *(A, B)*
m *After this:* In stature he was about my own height, say five feet eight inches. *(A);* In stature he was about five feet eight inches. *(B)*
n perhaps rather *(A, B)*
o utterly, *(A)*
p *After this A and B have two more sentences in this paragraph:* My readers have thus the physical Baron before them. What I shall add respecting those mental peculiarities to which I have as yet only partially adverted, will be told in my own words — for I find that, in speaking of my friend, I have been falling unwittingly into one of the many odd literary mannerisms of the dominator Baron Ritzner Von Jung. *(A, B)*
q was neither more nor less than *(A, B)*

to be found, who make the science of *mystification* the study and the business of their lives. For this science a peculiar turn of mind gave him instinctively the cue, while his physical appearance afforded him unusual facilities for carrying his projects into effect. I firmly believe that no student at G —— n, during that renowned epoch so quaintly termed the domination of the Baron Ritzner Von Jung, ever rightly entered into the mystery which overshadowed his character. I truly think that no person at the university, with the exception of myself, ever suspected him to be capable of a joke, verbal or practical: — the old bull-dog at the garden-gate would sooner have been accused, — the ghost of Heraclitus,[4] — or the wig of the Emeritus Professor of Theology. This, too, when it was evident that the most egregious and unpardonable of all conceivable tricks, whimsicalities, and buffooneries were brought about, if not directly by him, at least plainly through his intermediate agency or connivance. The beauty, if I may so call it, of his *art[r] mystifique*[s5] lay in that consummate ability (resulting from an almost intuitive knowledge of human nature, and a[t] most wonderful self-possession,) by means of which he never failed to make it appear that the drolleries he was occupied in bringing to a point, arose partly in spite, and partly in consequence of the laudable efforts he was making for their prevention, and for the preservation of the good order and dignity of Alma Mater. The deep, the poignant, the overwhelming mortification which, upon each such failure of his praiseworthy endeavors, would[u] suffuse every lineament of his countenance, left not the slightest room for doubt of his sincerity in the bosoms of even his most sceptical companions. The adroitness, too, was no less worthy of observation by which he contrived to shift the sense of the grotesque from the creator to the created — from his own person to the absurdities to which he had given rise.[v] In no instance[w] before that of which I speak, have I

---

r   art *(D)*
s   *mystifique, (C, D) comma deleted to follow A, B*
t   the *(A, B)*
u   wonld *(C) misprint*
v   *After this:* How this difficult point was accomplished I have become fully aware by means of a long course of observation on the oddities of my friend, and by means of frequent dissertations on the subject from himself; but upon this matter I cannot dilate. *(A, B)*
w   instance, however, *(A, B)*

known the habitual mystific escape the natural consequence of his manœuvres— an attachment of the ludicrous to his own character and person. Continually enveloped in an atmosphere of whim, my friend appeared to live only for the severities of society; and not even his own household have for a moment associated other ideas than those of the rigid and august with the memory of the Baron Ritzner Von Jung.[x]

During the epoch of [y]his residence at G —— n[y] it really appeared that the demon of the *dolce far niente* lay like an incubus upon the university. Nothing [z]at least, was done,[z] beyond eating and drinking, and making merry.[6] The apartments of the students were converted into so many pot-houses, and there was no pot-house of them all more famous or more frequented than that of the Baron.[a] Our carousals here were many, and boisterous, and long, and never unfruitful of events.

Upon one occasion we had protracted our sitting until nearly daybreak, and an unusual quantity of wine had been drunk. The company consisted of seven or eight individuals besides the Baron and myself. Most of these were young men of wealth, of high con-

---

x   *After this A and B have another paragraph:*
    To enter fully into the labyrinths of the Baron's finesse, or even to follow him in that droll career of practical mystification which gave him so wonderful an ascendency over the mad spirits of G——n, would lead me to a far greater length than I have prescribed to myself in this article. I may dwell upon these topics hereafter, and then not *in petto*. I am well aware that in tracing minutely and deliberately to their almost magical results the operations of an intellect like that of Ritzner, wherein an hereditary and cultivated taste for the bizarre was allied with an intuitive acumen in regard to the every-day impulses of the heart — (acumen which amounted to positive morbidity,) [*entire parenthesis omitted (B)*] an untrodden field would be found to lie open before me, rich in novelty and vigour, of emotion and incident, and abounding in rare food for both speculation and analysis. But this, I have already said, could not be accomplished in little space. Moreover, the Baron is still living in Belgium, and it is not without the limits of the possible that his eye may rest upon what I am now writing. I shall be careful, therefore, not to disclose, *at least thus and here,* [*Phrase not italicized (B)*] the mental machinery which he has a pleasure, however whimsical, in keeping concealed. An anecdote at random, however, may convey some idea of the *spirit* of his *pratique* [practice (B)]. The *method* varied ad infinitum; and in this well-sustained variety lay chiefly the secret of that unsuspectedness with which his multifarious operations were conducted.

y . . . y   the domination *(A, B)*
z . . . z   was done, at least, *(A, B)*
a   the Baron./your humble servant, and the Baron Ritzner Von Jung — for it must be understood that we were chums. *(A, B)*

nection, of great family pride, and all alive with an exaggerated sense of honor. They abounded in the most ultra German opinions respecting the *duello.* To these Quixotic notions some recent Parisian publications, backed by three or four desperate and fatal rencontres[b] at G —— n, had given new vigor and impulse; and thus the conversation, during the greater part of the night, had run wild upon the all-engrossing topic of the times. The Baron, who had been unusually silent and abstracted in the earlier portion of the evening, at length seemed to be aroused from his apathy, took a leading part in the discourse, and dwelt upon the benefits, and more especially upon the beauties, of the received code of etiquette in passages of arms, with an ardor, an eloquence, an impressiveness, and[c] an affectionateness of manner, which elicited the warmest enthusiasm from his hearers in general, and absolutely staggered even myself, who well knew him to be at heart a ridiculer of those very points for which he contended, and especially to hold the entire *fanfaronnade*[d] of duelling[e] etiquette in the sovereign contempt which it deserves.

Looking around me during a pause in the Baron's discourse, (of which my readers may gather some faint idea when I say that it bore resemblance to the fervid, chanting, monotonous, yet musical, sermonic manner of Coleridge,)[7] I perceived symptoms of even more than the general interest in the countenance of one of the party. This gentleman, whom I shall call Hermann, was an original in every respect — except, perhaps, in the single particular that he was [f]a very great fool.[f] He contrived to bear, however, among a particular set at the university, a reputation for deep metaphysical thinking, and, I believe, for some logical talent.[g] [8] As a duellist he

---

b   recontres *(C) misprint*
c   and if I may so speak, *(A, B)*
d   *fanfaronade (A, B, C, D) spelling corrected editorially*
e   *Omitted (A)*
f . . . f   one of the greatest asses in all Christendom. *(A, B)*
g   *After this A and B have:*
His personal appearance was so peculiar that I feel confident my outline of him will be recognized at once by all who have been in company with the model. He was one of the tallest men

I have ever seen, being full six feet and a half. His proportions were singularly *mal-apropos.* His legs were brief, bowed, and very slender; while above them arose a trunk worthy of the Farnesian Hercules. His shoulders, nevertheless, were round, his neck long although thick, and a general stoop forward gave him a slouching air. His head was of colossal dimensions, and overshadowed by a dense mass of straight raven hair, two huge locks of which, stiffly plastered with pomatum, had acquired great renown, even at G —— n. I forget the precise number of victims who had fallen at his hands; but they were many. He was a man of courage undoubtedly. But it was upon his minute acquaintance with the etiquette of the *duello*,[h] and the *nicety* of his sense of honor, that he most especially prided himself. These things were a hobby which he rode to the death. To Ritzner, ever upon the lookout for the grotesque, his peculiarities[i] had for a long time past afforded food for mystification. Of this, however, I was not aware; although, in the present instance, I saw clearly that something of a whimsical nature was upon the *tapis* with my friend,[j] and that Hermann was its especial object.

As the former proceeded in his discourse, or rather monologue,

extended with a lachrymose air down the temples, and partially over the cheek bones — a fashion which of late days has wormed itself (the wonder is that it has not arrived here before) into the good graces of the denizens of Gotham. [*the United States. (B)*] But the face itself was the chief oddity. The upper region was finely proportioned, and gave indication of the loftiest species of intellect. The forehead was massive and broad, the organs of ideality over the temples, as well as those of causality, comparison, and eventuality, which betray themselves above the os frontis, being so astonishingly developed as to attract the instant notice of every person who saw him. The eyes were full, brilliant, beaming with what might be mistaken for intelligence, and well relieved by the short, straight, picturesque-looking eyebrow, which is perhaps one of the surest indications of general ability. The aquiline nose, too, would have done honour to a Hebrew medallion; [The aquiline nose, too, was superb; (B)] certainly nothing more magnificent was ever beheld, nothing more delicate nor more exquisitely modelled. All these things were well enough, as I have said; it was the inferior portions of the visage which abounded in deformity, and which gave the lie instanter to the tittle-tattle of the superior. The upper lip (a huge lip in length) had the appearance of being swollen as by the sting of a bee, and was rendered still more atrocious by a little spot of very black mustachio immediately beneath the nose. The under lip, apparently disgusted with the gross obesity of its fellow, seemed bent upon resembling it as little as might be, and getting as far removed from it as possible. It was accordingly very curt and thin, hanging back as if utterly ashamed of being seen; while the chin, retreating still an inch or two farther, might have been taken for — any thing in the universe but a chin.

In this abrupt transition, or rather descent, in regard to character, from the upper to the lower regions of the face, an analogy was preserved between the face itself and the body at large, whose peculiar construction I have spoken of before. The result of the entire conformation was, that opinions directly conflicting were daily entertained in respect to the personal appearance of Hermann. Erect, he was absolutely hideous, and seemed to be, what in fact he really was, a fool. At table, with his hand covering the lower part of his visage, (an attitude of deep meditation which he much affected,) truly I never witnessed a more impressive *tableau* than his general appearance presented.
h duello, *(A, B)*
i peculiarities, bodily and mental, *(A, B)*
j chum, *(A, B)*

MYSTIFICATION

I perceived the excitement of the latter[k] momently[l] increasing. At length he spoke; offering some objection to a point insisted upon by R., and giving his reasons in detail. To these the Baron replied at length (still maintaining his exaggerated tone of sentiment) and concluding, in what I thought very bad taste, with a sarcasm and a sneer. The hobby of Hermann now took the bit[m] in his teeth. This I could discern by the studied hair-splitting *farrago*[n] of his rejoinder. His last words I distinctly remember. "Your opinions, allow me to say, Baron Von Jung, although in the main correct, are, in many nice points, discreditable to yourself and to the university of which you are a member. In a few respects they are even unworthy of serious refutation. I would say more than this, sir, were it not for the fear of giving you offence (here the speaker smiled blandly,) I would say, sir, that your opinions are not the opinions to be expected from a gentleman."

As Hermann completed this equivocal sentence, all eyes were turned upon the Baron. He became[o] pale, then excessively red, then, dropping his pocket-handkerchief, stooped to recover it, when I caught a glimpse of his countenance, while it could be seen by no one else at the table. It was radiant with the quizzical expression which was its natural character, but which I had never seen it assume except when we were alone together, and when he unbent himself freely. In an instant afterward[p] he stood erect, confronting Hermann; and so total an alteration of countenance in so short a period I certainly never saw[q] before. For a moment I even fancied that I had misconceived him, and that he was in sober earnest. He appeared to be stifling with passion, and his face was cadaverously white. For a short time he remained silent, apparently striving to master his emotion. Having at length seemingly succeeded, he reached a decanter which stood near him, saying, as he held it firmly clenched — "The language you have thought proper to employ, Mynheer Hermann, in addressing yourself to me, is objectionable in so many particulars, that I have neither temper nor time for specification. That my opinions, however, are not the opinions to

---

k   the latter/Hermann *(A, B)*
l   momentarily *(A)*
m reins *(A)*
n farrago *(A, B)*

o became very *(A, B)*
p afterwards *(A, B)*
q witnessed *(A, B)*

be expected from a gentleman, is an observation so directly offensive as to allow me but one line of conduct. Some courtesy, nevertheless, is due to the presence of this company, and to yourself, at this[r] moment, as my guest. You will pardon me, therefore, if, upon this consideration, I deviate slightly from the general usage among gentlemen[s] in similar cases of personal affront. You will forgive me for the moderate tax I shall make upon your imagination, and endeavor to consider, for an instant, the reflection of your person in yonder mirror as the living Mynheer Hermann himself. This being done, there will be no difficulty whatever. I shall discharge this decanter of wine at your image in yonder mirror, and thus fulfil all the spirit, if not the exact letter, of resentment for your insult, while the necessity of physical violence to your real person will be obviated."

With these words he hurled the [t]decanter, full of wine,[t] against the mirror which hung directly opposite Hermann; striking the reflection of his person with great precision, and of course shattering the glass into fragments. The whole company at once started to their feet, and, with the exception of myself and Ritzner, took[u] their departure. As Hermann went out, the Baron whispered me that I should follow him and make an offer of my services. To this I agreed; not knowing precisely what to make of so ridiculous a piece of business.

The duellist accepted my aid with his usual[v] stiff and *ultra recherché*[w] air, and taking my arm, led me to his apartment. I could hardly forbear laughing in his face while he proceeded to discuss,[x] with the profoundest gravity, what he termed "the refinedly peculiar character" of the insult he had received. After a tiresome[y] harangue in his ordinary style, he took down from his bookshelves [z]a number of musty volumes on the subject of the *duello,* and entertained me for a long time with their contents; reading aloud, and commenting earnestly as he read. I can just remember the

---

r   the present *(A, B)*
s   gentleman *(C) misprint*
t . . . t   decanter full of wine
furiously *(A, B)*
u   took their hats for *(A, B)*

v   *Omitted (D)*
w   ultra-recherché *(A, B)*
x   dicuss, *(C) misprint*
y   long *(A)*
z . . . z   a pretty thick octavo, *(A)*

titles of some of the works.[9] There were[a] the "Ordonnance of Philip le Bel on Single Combat;" the "Theatre of Honor," by Favyn, and a treatise "On the Permission of Duels," by Audiguier.[b] He displayed, also, with much pomposity, Brantôme's[c] "Memoirs of Duels," published at Cologne, in 1666, in the types of Elzevir — a precious and unique vellum-paper volume, with a fine margin, and bound by Derôme. But he requested my attention particularly, and with an air of mysterious sagacity, to a thick octavo,[z] written in barbarous Latin by one Hedelin, a Frenchman, and having the quaint title, "*Duelli Lex scripta, et non,[d] aliterque.*"[10] From this he read me one of the drollest chapters in the world concerning "*Injuriæ per applicationem, per constructionem, et per se,*" about half of which, he averred, was strictly applicable to his own "refinedly peculiar" case, although not one syllable of the whole matter could I understand for the life of me. Having finished the chapter, he closed the book, and demanded what I thought necessary to be done. I replied that I had entire confidence in his superior delicacy of feeling, and would abide by what he proposed. With this answer he seemed flattered, and sat down to write a note to the Baron. It ran thus:

SIR, — My friend, Mr. P ——,[e] will hand you this note. I find it incumbent upon me to request, at your earliest convenience, an explanation of this evening's occurrences at your chambers. In the event of your declining this request, Mr. P. will be happy to arrange, with any friend whom you may appoint, the steps preliminary to a meeting.

With sentiments of perfect respect,
Your most humble servant,
JOHAN HERMANN.

To the Baron Ritzner Von Jung,
August 18th, 18 — .

Not knowing what better to do, I called upon Ritzner with

---

a was *(B)*
b Andiguier. *(B, C, D) corrected editorially*
c Brantome's *(B, C, D)*

d *non,/non; (C, D) emended from A, B*
e Mr. P–/M. P– *(C, D) corrected from A, B*

this epistle. He bowed as I presented it; then,[f] with a grave countenance, motioned me to a seat. [g]Having perused the cartel, he wrote the following reply, which I carried to Hermann.[g]

Sir,

Through our common friend, Mr. P., I have received your note of this evening. Upon due reflection I frankly admit the propriety of the explanation you suggest. This being admitted. I still find great difficulty, (owing to the *refinedly peculiar* nature of our disagreement, and of the personal affront offered on my part,) in so wording what I have to say by way of apology, as to meet all the minute exigencies, and[h] all the variable shadows of the case. I have great reliance, however, on that extreme delicacy of discrimination, in matters appertaining to the rules of etiquette, for which you have been so long and[i] so preëminently distinguished. With perfect certainty, therefore, of being comprehended, I beg leave, in lieu of offering any sentiments of my own, to refer you to the opinions of the Sieur Hedelin, as set forth in the ninth paragraph of the chapter of *"Injuriæ[j] per applicationem, per constructionem, et per se,"* in his *"Duelli Lex scripta, et non,[k] aliterque."* The nicety of your discernment in all the matters here treated,[l] will be sufficient, I am assured, to convince you *that the mere circumstance[m] of my[n] referring you* to this admirable passage, ought to satisfy your request, as a man of honor, for explanation.

With sentiments of profound respect,

Your most obedient servant,

Von Jung.[o]

The Herr Johan Hermann.
August 18th, 18 — .

---

f   and, *(A, B)*

g . . . g   He then said that he was aware of the contents of the note, and that, of course, it would be unnecessary for him to peruse it. With this, to my great astonishment, he repeated the letter nearly verbatim, handing me, at the same time, an already written reply. This, which ran as follows, I carried to Hermann. *(A, B) except that* of course, it would be unnecessary for him *is changed to* he did not wish *in B.*

h   and, as it were, *(A, B)*

i   *Omitted (B)*

j   on *"Injuria (A, B);* of *"Injuria (C, D)*

k   *non,/non; (C, D) emended from A, B*

l   treated,/treated of *(A, B)*

m   *circumstance alone (A)*

n   *my/me (C, D) emended from A, B*

o   Von Juns. *(D) misprint*

Hermann commenced the perusal of this epistle with a scowl, which, however, was converted into a smile of the most ludicrous self-complacency as he came to the rigmarole about *Injuriæ per applicationem, per constructionem, et per se.* Having finished reading, he begged me, with the blandest of all possible smiles,[p] to be seated, while he made reference to the treatise in question. Turning to the passage specified, he read it with great care to himself, then closed the book, and desired me, in my character of confidential acquaintance, to express to the Baron Von Jung his exalted sense of his chivalrous behaviour, and, in that of second, to assure him that the explanation offered was of the fullest, the most honorable, and the most unequivocally satisfactory nature.

Somewhat amazed at all this, I made my retreat to the Baron. He seemed to receive Hermann's amicable letter as a matter of course, and after a few words of general conversation, went to an inner room and brought out the everlasting treatise *"Duelli Lex scripta, et non,[q] aliterque."* He handed me the volume and asked me to look over some portion of it. I did so, but to little purpose, not being able to gather the least particle of[r] meaning. He then took the book himself, and read me a chapter aloud. To my[s] surprise, what he read proved to be a most horribly absurd[t] account of a duel between two baboons. He now explained the mystery; showing that the volume, as it appeared *primâ facie,* was written upon the plan of the nonsense verses of Du Bartas; that is to say, the language was ingeniously framed so as to present to the ear all the outward signs of intelligibility, and even of profundity,[u] while in fact not a shadow of meaning existed.[v11] The key to the whole was found in leaving out every second and third word alternately, when there appeared a series of ludicrous quizzes [w]upon single combat as practised in modern times.[w]

The Baron afterwards informed me that he had purposely thrown the treatise in Hermann's way two or three weeks before

---

p airs, *(A, B)*
q *non,/non; (C, D) emended from A, B*
r of definite *(A, B)*
s my extreme *(A)*
t grotesque *(A)*

u profound analysis, *(A, B)*
v existed, except in insulated sentences. *(A, B)*
w . . . w upon the duello. *(A);* upon a single combat as practised in modern times. *(D)*

the adventure, and that he was satisfied, from the general tenor of his conversation, that he had studied it with the deepest attention, and firmly believed it to be a work of unusual merit.[x] Upon this hint he proceeded. Hermann would have died a thousand deaths rather than acknowledge his inability to understand anything[y] and everything in the universe that had ever been written about the *duello*.[z]   Littleton Barry.

NOTES

Motto: This reference to thrusts of the sword in fencing is from a speech of a character named Edward Knowell in Ben Jonson's *Every Man in His Humor*, IV, vii, 145–146, in the version of the folio of 1616 with modernized spelling. Poe also quoted it in a criticism of Cornelius Mathews' *Wakondah* in *Graham's* for February 1842.

1. No source has been found for the Baron's name, but in German the verb *ritzen* means to scratch or crack; hence Poe may suggest that his protagonist cracked jokes. Jung, of course, means young, an appropriate name for the prankster.

2. The prolific and influential German, Johann Ludwig Tieck (1773–1853) — Romantic poet, playwright, novelist, short-story writer, translator, and critic — was frequently mentioned by Poe, and one of his books was a favorite of Roderick Usher's.

3. (Early version only) The danseuse Villanova has not been traced, but Henrietta Sontag, Contessa Rossi (1806–1854), was a celebrated prima donna, and although not faultless, a popular favorite. The Rotunda is the name of the building housing the library, the focus of the campus at the University of Virginia, and Wertemuller's name, a few lines below, may recall that of Poe's friend, the librarian of the University, William Wertenbaker.

4. Heraclitus of Ephesus, known as the weeping philosopher, flourished about 500 B.C. He is mentioned in Poe's early satiric verses "Oh, Tempora! Oh, Mores!"

5. "Mystifique" is Poe's own word for the Baron's peculiar kind of waggery. It is not to be found in French dictionaries.

6. *Dolce far niente* (sweet doing nothing) is a commonplace, but authorities on quotations trace it to Pliny's *Letters*, VIII, ix, 1, "jucundum tamen nihil agere." For "Eat, drink, and be merry" see I Corinthians 15:32. Poe also used it in "The Journal of Julius Rodman," chapter v.

7. Coleridge was at one time a lay preacher. There is a well-known story that he once asked Charles Lamb, "Did you ever hear me preach?" and Lamb replied, "I never heard you do anything else."

x profundity. *(A, B)*   z duello. *(A, B)*
y any *(A, B)*

8. (Early version only) In the long canceled description of Hermann's appearance, reference to the Farnesian Hercules is to a sculpture at Naples, probably a copy of a work by Lysippus. It shows the subject as prodigiously muscular. Poe also names it in a review of J. F. Cooper's *Wyandotté* in *Graham's* for November 1843. For the Hebrew medallions see "Ligeia," note 6.

9. All the following titles except the last refer to actual works. Philip IV of France, called The Fair, during his reign (1285–1314) supervised the issue of about 350 ordinances, many of them repetitions of earlier laws. The book Poe had in mind was Jean Savaron's *Traicte contre les Duels, Avec l'Edict de Phillippes le Bel, de l'an M.CCC.VI, non encores imprimé*, etc. (Paris, 1610). *The Theater of Honour and Knighthood* (London, 1623) is an English translation of a book published in French in 1620 by André Favyn. The work by the Sieur Vital d'Audiguier is *Le Vray et ancien Usage des duels Confirmé par l'exemple des plus illustres combats et deffys qui se soient faits en la Chrestianté* (Paris, 1617), 8vo. Pierre de Bourdeille, abbé de Brantôme, wrote *Anecdotes de la cour de France, touchant les duels*. His works in nine volumes were printed with Elzevir types, 1665–1666, at Leyden. Nicolas-Denis Derôme, born 1731, was the most famous of a family of great bookbinders in France.

10. The *Duelli Lex scripta, et non, aliterque* ("The Law of Duelling, written and unwritten and otherwise") is imaginary, of course. Poe mentions "Hedelin a Frenchman" in "Pinakidia," number 22 (*SLM*, August 1836, p. 575), but he is François Hédelin, abbé d'Aubignac (1604–1676), whose *Conjectures académiques* (1715) discussed multiple authorship of the Homeric poems.

11. Guillaume de Saluste du Bartas (1544–1590) was a French Protestant poet, extravagantly admired in his own day. He was a master of the conceit, but wrote no deliberately meaningless verses. However, Isaac D'Israeli, in his *Curiosities of Literature*, a favorite work with Poe, has a chapter on "Literary Follies" in which he mentions an attempt by Du Bartas to imitate the song of the lark in verse, and in the *next paragraph* tells about "French . . . Nonsense Verses called *Amphigouries*" and gives a sample, not ascribed to any author. A hasty reader might easily have gotten the impression that this was by Du Bartas. Poe used the same allusion in a review of *The Doctor*, by Robert Southey (*SLM*, June 1836); in a review (*Graham's*, August 1841) of Sumner Lincoln Fairfield's *Poems and Prose;* in a review (*Graham's*, March 1844) of R. H. Horne's *Orion;* and in a review (*SLM*, February 1849) of R. W. Griswold's *Female Poets of America*.

LIGEIA

"Ligeia" is a masterpiece of Poe's elaborate early style, surpassing the longer narratives written earlier, and to be surpassed, if at all, only by "The Fall of the House of Usher." Poe himself recognized its excellence: as late as August 9, 1846, he wrote to Philip Pendleton Cooke, " 'Ligeia' may be called my *best* tale";

and writing to Duyckinck, January 8, 1846, he mentioned it as "undoubtedly the best story I have written."

On the copy of the *Broadway Journal* he gave to Mrs. Whitman in 1848 he wrote that the story was suggested by a dream, like the poem "To Helen Whitman" he had sent her, and added, "Observe the eyes in both tale and poem."* It is possible that he meant a vivid daydream, for he may have catered to the lady's known love of the mystical. Yet the fancy of one person changing into another, as old as the legends of Proteus, may occur "in visions of the dark night."

The story was revised with the greatest care. It must be regarded as a thoroughly conscious and complete work of art.

"Ligeia" has two obvious literary inspirations. Primarily it is the reworking of the love theme of Scott's *Ivanhoe,* the story of Rebecca and Rowena. The protagonist's blond wife even bears the name Rowena. Rebecca was unjustly accused of witchcraft; Ligeia studied alchemy — a forbidden knowledge considered akin to witchcraft. The parallel is psychological too. Who does not suppose that Scott's Ivanhoe, married to Rowena, must often have thought sadly of Rebecca?

The second source is in "A Madman's Manuscript" to be found in the eleventh chapter of *Pickwick Papers,* which Poe admired enough to reprint in his review of Dickens' book in the *Southern Literary Messenger,* November 1836. There we find the splendid home, the incipient madness of the hero, the bride's lack of love, the husband's demoniacal hatred, his scorn of the lady's family for cruelly forcing upon her a mercenary marriage, and finally his inability to recall certain facts, in especial to remember the woman's name. There is an extreme parallelism in the following:

I don't remember forms or faces now, but I know the girl was beautiful. I *know* she was; for in the bright moonlight nights, when I start up from my sleep, and all is quiet about me, I see, standing still and motionless in one corner of this cell, a slight and wasted figure, with long black hair, which, streaming down her back, stirs with no earthly wind, and eyes that fix their gaze on me, and never wink or close.

* Poe's comment is quoted in full in my notes on "To Helen Whitman" in this edition, I, 444.

LIGEIA

After "Ligeia" was published Poe sent it to Philip Pendleton Cooke and asked whether the ending of the story was intelligible.† Cooke's comment did not express complete satisfaction, for he said, "I of course 'took' your 'idea' throughout ... your intent is to tell a tale of the 'mighty will' contending with and finally vanquishing Death." But he "was shocked by a violation of the ghostly proprieties ... and wondered how the Lady Ligeia — a wandering essence — could, in quickening *the body of the Lady Rowena* ... become suddenly the visible, bodily, Ligeia." Cooke wished the narrator had only become *gradually* aware that the "blue Saxon eye ... grew daily darker ... a mind of grander powers ... occupied the quickened body," and added, "You may have some theory ... which I have not caught."

Poe replied on September 21, 1839 that because he had already written "Morella" he felt he must be content with a sudden half consciousness on the part of the narrator that Ligeia stood before him. "I should have intimated that the *will* did not perfect its intention — there should have been a relapse ... and Ligeia ... should be at length entombed as Rowena." He added that he would "suffer 'Ligeia' to remain as it is." He was to change his mind five years later. Then he inserted in the story, as a composition of the heroine, his own powerful poem "The Conqueror Worm" (written in 1842 and first published in *Graham's* for January 1843) — a plain indication that the human will was too feeble to enable Ligeia to win. On August 9, 1846, Poe wrote Cooke that he had improved the story.

We cannot doubt that the author intended a story of real magic, as the pentagonal room would suggest. Of course, he did not expect readers to believe the story after they put it down; he wanted temporary suspension of disbelief during its perusal. Reviewing Bird's *Sheppard Lee* in the *Messenger* for September 1836 he had named three wholly incredible notions acceptable in tales of wonder — an invisible person, the elixir of life, and the Wandering Jew. He used the first two, and perhaps the third, in "Ligeia."

---

† Poe's first letter has not survived. Its contents are surmised from Cooke's reply, September 16, 1839 (Harrison, XVII, 49).

It is not surprising to find articles propounding the idea that the story is solely of remorse and hallucination.‡ Poe probably would have been amused. He had provided, by reference to his narrator's use of opium, a way for the matter-of-fact reader to interpret the tale in precisely that way, if he wished. Nobody need dismiss the presence of the hallucinatory element in "Ligeia," even though the documents indicate it was not the primary concern of the author. The pentagonal shape of the bridal chamber is meaningless unless genuine magic be intended.

It is never clear whether the disembodied spirit of Ligeia influenced her husband's mind and led him to seek out the weak Rowena, or whether Ligeia told anyone her true name. The red liquid is not poison, but the *elixir vitae,* the color of which mystical writers believe to be that of a ruby.§

Fanciful interpretations of Poe's story may be found. The heroine is not an orthodox vampire. Her resemblance to a dybbuk is undeniable, but is probably fortuitous, since it is not easy to say how Poe could have met with legends current in Jewish folklore of Poland and Russia.

TEXTS

(A) Baltimore *American Museum,* September 1838 (1:25–37); *(B) Tales of the Grotesque and Arabesque* (1840), I, 171–192; *(C)* PHANTASY-PIECES with manuscript revisions of the last, 1842; *(D)* New York *New World,* February 15,

‡ Roy P. Basler in *College English,* April 1944, and again in *PMLA,* December 1962, at the second place replying to James Schroeter in *PMLA,* September 1961. Schroeter, defending the romantic view, gives a good many references to the "literature," and cites interpretations of the story as one of magic by Woodberry, Clayton Hamilton, and A. H. Quinn. Schroeter also refers to several psychological interpretations, of which only that of D. H. Lawrence in *Studies in Classic American Literature* (1953) is of much interest.

§ Muriel West pointed this out in *Explicator,* October 1963, and again in *Comparative Literature,* Winter 1964. In her later article she quoted Poe's letter to Cooke of September 21, 1839 concerning "Ligeia": "You read my inmost spirit 'like a book,' and with the single exception of D'Israeli, I have had communication with no other person who does." She also suggested that Poe's tale might owe something to D'Israeli's romance "Mejnoun and Leila," but her principal thesis is that Poe felt that he and Isaac D'Israeli had a common understanding of the exceptional relation between the heroine and the hero. She did not mention Poe's "Eleonora," in which more obvious similarities to D'Israeli's tale might be descried.

LIGEIA

1845 (10:100–101); *(E) Broadway Journal,* September 27, 1845 (2:171–176); *(F)* Mrs. Whitman's copy of the last with manuscript revisions, 1848; *(G) Works* (1850), I, 453–468.

The revised copy of the *Broadway Journal (F)* is chosen as the final text. Griswold's variants *(G)* are not surely auctorial, and do not include the important revisions in the last paragraph. Some of the revisions of 1842 *(C)* were abortive. Note that the poem "The Conqueror Worm" was first incorporated in the *New World* version *(D)* in 1845. So few copies of volume 10 of the *New World* survive that this text was lost sight of for many years. See "An Early Publication of Poe's 'Ligeia,'" London *Notes and Queries,* February 28, 1931.

Although except in a few special cases punctuation variants have not been reported in this edition of Poe's works, for reasons set forth in the Introduction it has seemed desirable to present one tale with a record of all the changes of every kind, as an example of Poe at work. The choice has fallen on "Ligeia" not only because Poe took great care in its revision but also because PHANTASY-PIECES *(C)* with Poe's manuscript changes and the hard-to-come-by *New World (D)* text were not collated in the Virginia edition, nor were Poe's changes in the Whitman text recorded there.

The Baltimore *American Museum* printing *(A)* was inconsistent in spelling and at times confused in punctuation. For the *Tales of the Grotesque and Arabesque (B),* thirty-six verbal changes were made, all retained in later printings. (Among other changes "my brain wandered" became "my reason wandered.") Some repetitions were taken care of, several misprints corrected, three capitals changed to lower case, and the spelling of colour, demeanour, etc., was normalized. Forty or more punctuation changes were made — most of them, but not all, improvements.

Alterations for the abortive PHANTASY-PIECES *(C)* were noted in Poe's hand in a copy of *Tales of the Grotesque and Arabesque (B).* Of the sixteen verbal changes all but three were adopted and retained in the later published texts. They included the transposition of the phrases of one sentence, the addition of two long clauses to another, and the italicization of "person" in "the *person* of Ligeia." Poe made twenty-three punctuation changes in PHANTASY-PIECES, seven of which were not used in later printings. All but three of the indicated changes were concerned with the dash.

The *New World* text *(D)* added the poem, the three adjacent paragraphs, and more than fifty verbal changes beyond those in PHANTASY-PIECES. It was by far the most extensive revision Poe ever made in any of the "Ligeia" texts. He reworked a paragraph to make a new one to follow the poem, deleted two complete sentences, and greatly enriched another. He not only deleted words, as in substituting "Shadow" for "dark shadow," "the shackles" for "the iron shackles," but added words, too, as "she habitually uttered" for "she uttered" and "a pall-like canopy" for "a canopy." There were also more than thirty punctuation changes. A few of these corrected errors, some made little difference, and a few he would have been wise not to make.

In the *Broadway Journal (E)* punctuation changes were emphasized, not all improvements. In the sixteen verbal alterations, Poe was still tightening his style when he substituted "preparations" for "preparations for interment," "slow" for "slow but imperceptible," and on other occasions. A number of misprints appeared in this text. Some of them were corrected in the Whitman copy *(F)* where Poe made two final deletions in his story. In three instances the *Broadway Journal* printer used a dash after a period to fill out a line. These dashes have nothing to do with Poe's punctuation and are eliminated in this text. See the variants, and the discussion of variants in the Introduction to this volume.

Griswold's text *(G)* corrected all but two of the typographical errors of the *Broadway Journal* but introduced three new ones, and, as stated above, did not include Poe's manuscript corrections in the last paragraph. Griswold's text shows changes in punctuation and capitalization, particularly in the poem. In eliminating double punctuation at a number of places where *E* and *F* show a dash together with a comma or a semicolon, and in the retention of two necessary commas, the Griswold text follows *A, B, C, D*.

LIGEIA. [*F*]

And the will therein lieth, which dieth not. Who knoweth the mysteries of the will, with its vigor? For God is but a great will pervading all things by nature of its intentness. Man doth not yield himself to the angels, nor unto death utterly, save only through the weakness of his feeble will.

JOSEPH GLANVILL.

I cannot, for my soul, remember how, when, or even precisely where,[a] I first became acquainted with the lady[b] Ligeia. Long years have since elapsed, and my memory is feeble through much suffering. Or,[c] perhaps, I cannot *now* bring these points to mind, because, in truth, the character of my beloved, her rare learning, her singular yet placid cast[d] of beauty, and the thrilling and enthralling eloquence of her low[e] musical language, made their way into my heart by paces[f] so steadily and stealthily progressive[g] that they have been unnoticed and unknown. Yet I believe[h] that I met her [i]first and most[i] frequently in some large, old, decaying city near the Rhine. Of her family — I have surely heard her [j]speak. That it is[j] of a remotely ancient date cannot be doubted. Ligeia! Ligeia![k] Buried in studies of a nature[l] more than all else[m] adapted to deaden impressions of the outward world, it is by that sweet word alone —

Motto: vigor/vigour *(A)*
a where *(A)*
b Lady *(B, C)*
c suffering. Or,/suffering: or, *(A)*
d caste *(G) misprint*
e low, *(A, B, C)*
f paces, *(A)*
g progressive, *(A, B, C, G)*

h know *(A)*
i...i most *(A, B) changed in C*
j...j speak — that they are *(A, B)*
changed in C
k *Omitted (A, B, C)*
l nature, *(A)*
m else, *(A)*

by Ligeia — [n] that I bring before mine eyes in fancy the image of her who is no more. And now, while I write, a recollection flashes upon me that I have *never known* the paternal name of her who was my friend and my betrothed, and who became the partner of my studies, and finally[o] the wife of my bosom.[1] Was it a playful charge on the part of my Ligeia? or was it a test of my strength of affection,[p] that I should institute no inquiries upon this point? or was it rather a caprice of my own — a wildly romantic offering on the shrine of the most passionate devotion? I but indistinctly recall the fact itself — what wonder that I have utterly forgotten the circumstances which originated or attended it? And,[q] indeed, if ever that spirit which is entitled *Romance* — if ever she, the wan[r] and the misty-winged *Ashtophet* of idolatrous Egypt,[2] presided, as they tell, over marriages ill-omened,[s] then most surely she presided over mine.

There is one dear topic, however, on which my memory fails[t] me not. It is the *person*[u] of Ligeia. In stature she was tall, somewhat slender, and,[v] in her latter days,[w] even emaciated. I would in vain attempt to portray[x] the majesty, the quiet ease,[y] of her demeanor,[z] or the incomprehensible lightness and elasticity of her footfall. She came and departed as[a] a shadow. I was never made aware of her entrance into my closed study[b] save by the dear music of her low sweet voice, as she placed her marble[c] hand upon my shoulder. In beauty of face no maiden ever equalled her. It was the radiance of an opium dream[d] — an airy and spirit-lifting vision more wildly divine than the phantasies which hovered about the slumbering souls of the daughters of Delos.[3] Yet her features were not of that regular mould which we have been falsely taught to worship in the classical labors of the heathen.[e] "There is no exquisite beauty," [f]says Bacon, Lord Verulam,[f] speaking truly of all the forms and *genera* of

---

n   Ligeia, *(A)*
o   eventually *(A, B, C)*
p   affection *(A, B, C)*
q   And *(A)*
r   wan, *(A, B, C)*
s   ill-omened *(D)*
t   faileth *(A, B)* changed in C
u   First italicized in C
v   and *(A, B, C)*
w   days *(A, B, C)*

x   pourtray *(A)*
y   ease *(A)*
z   demeanour, *(A)*
a   like *(A, B, C)*
b   study, *(G)*
c   delicate *(A, B, C)*
d   opium dream/opium-dream *(G)*
e   Heathen. *(A)*
f . . . f   saith Verülam, Lord Bacon, *(A);* the umlaut also appears in B, C

beauty,[4] "without some *strangeness* in the proportion."[g] Yet, although I saw that the features of Ligeia were not of a[h] classic regularity — [i] although I perceived that her loveliness was indeed "exquisite," and felt that there was much of "strangeness" pervading it, yet I have tried in vain to detect the irregularity[j] and to trace home my own perception of "the strange." I examined the contour of the lofty and pale forehead — it was faultless — how cold indeed that word when applied to a majesty so divine! — the[k] skin rivalling[l] the purest ivory, the commanding extent[m] and repose, the gentle prominence[5] of the regions above the temples;[n] and then the raven-black, the glossy, the luxuriant and naturally-curling tresses, setting forth the full force of the Homeric epithet, "hyacinthine!"[o] I looked at the delicate outlines of the nose — and nowhere but in the graceful medallions of the Hebrews had I beheld a similar perfection.[6] There were[p] the same luxurious smoothness of surface, the same scarcely perceptible tendency to the aquiline, the same harmoniously curved nostrils[q] speaking the free spirit. I regarded the sweet mouth. Here was indeed the triumph of all things heavenly — the magnificent turn of the short upper lip — the soft, voluptuous slumber[r] of the under — the dimples which sported, and the color[s] which spoke — the teeth glancing back,[t] with a brilliancy almost startling, every ray of the holy light which fell upon them in her serene[u] and placid, yet most exultingly radiant[v] of all smiles. I scrutinized the formation of the chin — and here, too, I found the gentleness of breadth, the softness and the majesty, the fullness[w] and the spirituality, of the Greek — [x] the contour which the God[y] Apollo revealed but in a dream,[z] to Cleomenes, the son of the Athenian.[7] And then I peered into the large eyes of Ligeia.

For eyes we have no models in the remotely antique. It might

---

g proportions." *(A, B, C, D)*
h *Omitted (A, B, C, D)*
i regularity, *(A, B, C)*
j irregularity, *(A, B, C)*
k divine! — the/divine. The *(A)*
l rivaling *(A)*
m breadth *(A)*
n temples, *(A, B, C)*
o "hyacinthine;" *(A)*
p was *(A, B, C)*

q nostril *(A, B, C, D)*
r repose *(A)*
s colour *(A)*
t back *(D)*
u serene, *(A, B, C)*
v radian, *(D) misprint*
w fulness *(A, B, C, G)*
x Greek, *(A)*; Greek, — *(B, C)*
y god *(B, C, D, G)*
z dream *(A)*

have been, too, that in these eyes of my beloved lay the secret to which Lord Verulam[a] alludes. They were, I must believe, far larger than the ordinary eyes of our own[b] race. They were even[c] fuller than the fullest of the gazelle[d] eyes of the tribe of the valley of Nourjahad.[e] [8] Yet it was only at intervals — in moments of intense excitement — that this peculiarity became more than slightly noticeable in Ligeia. And at such moments was her beauty — in my heated fancy thus it appeared perhaps — the beauty of beings either above or apart from the earth — the beauty of the fabulous Houri of the Turk.[9] The hue[f] of the orbs was the most brilliant of black, and,[g] far over them,[h] hung jetty lashes of great length. The brows, slightly irregular in outline, had the same tint.[i] The "strangeness," however, which I[j] found in the eyes,[k] was of a nature distinct from the formation, or the color,[l] or the brilliancy of the features,[m] and must, after all, be referred to the *expression*. Ah, word of no meaning! behind whose vast latitude of mere sound we intrench our ignorance of so much of the spiritual. The expression of the eyes of Ligeia! How[n] for long hours have I pondered upon it! How have I, through the whole of a midsummer[o] night, struggled to fathom it! What was it — that something more profound than the well of Democritus[10] — which lay far within the pupils of my beloved? What *was* it? I was possessed with a passion to discover. Those eyes! those large, those shining, those divine orbs! they became to me twin stars of Leda,[11] and I to them devoutest of astrologers.[p]

There is no point, among the many incomprehensible anomalies of the science of mind, more thrillingly exciting than the fact — never, I believe,[q] noticed in the schools — that[r], in our endeavors[s] to recall to memory something long forgotten,[t] we often find our-

---

a   Verülam *(A, B, C)*
b   *Omitted (A, B, C, D)*
c   even far *(A, B, C, D)*
d   Gazelle *(A, B) changed in C*
e   Nourjabad. *(A)*
f   colour *(A);* color *(B, C)*
g   and *(A, B, C)*
h   them *(A, B, C)*
i   hue. *(A, B, C)*
j   I have *(A)*
k   eyes of my Ligeia *(A);* eyes *(B, C)*
l   colour, *(A)*

m   feature, *(A)*
n   How, *(A, B, C)*
o   mid-summer *(A)*
p   *After this:* Not for a moment was the unfathomable meaning of their glance, by day or by night, absent from my soul. *(A, B, C)*
q   believe *(A)*
r   that *(A, B, C)*
s   endeavours *(A)*
t   forgotten *(A, B, C)*

selves *upon the very verge* of remembrance,[u] without being able, in the end, to remember. And thus[v] how frequently, in my intense scrutiny of Ligeia's eyes, have I felt approaching the full knowledge of[w] their expression — felt it approaching — yet not quite be mine — and so at length entirely[x] depart![y] And (strange, oh strangest mystery of all!) I found, in the commonest objects of the universe, a circle of analogies to that expression. I mean to say that, subsequently to the period when Ligeia's beauty passed into my spirit, there dwelling as in a shrine, I derived,[z] from many existences in the material world, a sentiment[a] such as I felt always aroused[b] within me[c] by her large and luminous orbs. Yet not the more could I define that sentiment, or analyze, or even steadily view it. I recognized[d] it, let me repeat, sometimes[e] in the survey of a rapidly-growing vine — in the contemplation of a moth, a butterfly, a chrysalis, a stream of running water. I have felt it in the ocean;[f] in the falling of a meteor.[12] I have felt it in the glances of unusually aged people.[13] And there are one or two stars in heaven — (one especially, a star of the sixth magnitude, double and changeable, to be found near the large star in Lyra)[g] in a telescopic scrutiny of which I have been made aware of the feeling.[14] I have been filled with it by certain sounds from stringed instruments, and not unfrequently by passages from books. Among innumerable other instances, I well remember something in a volume of Joseph Glanvill, which[h] (perhaps merely from its quaintness — who shall say?) never failed to inspire me with the sentiment; — [i] "And the will therein lieth, which dieth not. Who knoweth the mysteries of the will, with its vigor? For God is but a great will pervading all things by nature of its intentness. Man doth not yield him to the angels, nor unto death utterly, save[j] only through the weakness of his feeble will."

---

u   remembrance *(A, B, C)*
v   thus, *(A, B, C)*
w   of the secret of *(A, B, C)*
x   utterly *(A)*
y   depart. *(A, B, C, D)*
z   derived *(A)*
a   sentiment, *(A)*
b   around *(E, F) misprint, corrected from A, B, C, D;* around, *(G)*
c   me, *(G)*

d   recognised *(G)*
e   *After this:* in the commonest objects of the universe. It has flashed upon me *(A, B, C, D)*
f   ocean, *(A, B, D);* ocean — *(C)*
g   Lyra,) *(G)*
h   which, *(A; parentheses omitted)*
i   sentiment. — *(A);* sentiment, — *(B, C);* sentiment: *(G)*
j   but *(A, B) changed in C*

LIGEIA

Length of years,[k] and subsequent reflection, have enabled me to trace, indeed, some remote connection[l] between this passage in the[m] English moralist and a portion of the character of Ligeia. An *intensity* in thought, action, or speech,[n] was possibly, in her, a result, or at least an index, of that gigantic volition which, during our long intercourse, failed to give other and more immediate evidence of its existence. Of all the[o] women whom I have ever known,[p] she, the outwardly calm, the ever-placid[q] Ligeia, was the most violently a prey to the tumultuous vultures of stern passion. And of such passion I could form no estimate, save by the miraculous expansion of those eyes which at once so delighted and appalled me — [r] by the almost magical melody, modulation, distinctness[s] and placidity of her very low voice — [t] and by the fierce energy[u] (rendered doubly effective by contrast with her manner of utterance)[v] of the wild[w] words which she habitually[x] uttered.

I have spoken of the learning of Ligeia: it was immense — such as I have never known in woman.[15] In[y] the classical tongues was she deeply proficient, and as far as my own acquaintance extended in regard to the modern dialects of Europe, I have never known her at fault. Indeed upon any theme of the most admired, because simply the most abstruse[z] of the boasted erudition of the academy, have I *ever* found Ligeia at fault? How singularly — [a] how thrillingly, this one point in the nature of my wife has forced itself, at this late period[b] only, upon my attention! I said her knowledge was such as I have[c] never known in woman — but where[d] breathes the man who[e] has traversed, and successfully, *all* the wide areas of moral, physical,[f] and mathematical science? I saw not then what I now clearly perceive, that the acquisitions of Ligeia were gigantic,

---

k   years *(G)*
l   connexion *(A, B, C)*
m   the old *(A, B) changed in C*
n   speech *(A)*
o   *Omitted (A, B, C)*
p   known *(B, C)*
q   ever placid *(A)*
r   me, *(A, B, C)*
s   distinctness, *(G)*
t   voice, *(A, B, C)*
u   energy, *(A)*
v   utterance)/utterance,) *(G)*

w   *Omitted (A, B, C)*
x   *Omitted (A, B, C)*
y   In all *(A)*
z   abstruse, *(A, B, C, D)*
a   singularly, *(A, B) changed in C*
b   period, *(A)*
c   had *(A, B, C)*
d   woman — but where/woman. Where *(A, B, C)*
e   who, like her, *(A, B) changed in C*
f   natural, *(A, B, C)*

were astounding;[g] yet I was sufficiently aware of her infinite supremacy to resign myself, with a child-like confidence, to her guidance through the chaotic world of metaphysical investigation at which I was most busily occupied during the earlier years of our marriage. With how vast a triumph — with how vivid a delight — with how much of all that is ethereal in hope — did I *feel*, as she bent over me[h] in studies but little sought[i] — but less known — [j] that delicious vista by slow[k] degrees expanding before me, down whose long, gorgeous, and all untrodden path,[l] I might at length pass onward[m] to the goal of a wisdom too divinely precious not to be forbidden![16]

How poignant, then, must have been the grief with which, after some years, I beheld my well-grounded expectations take wings to themselves and fly[n] away![17] Without Ligeia I was but as a child groping benighted. Her presence, her readings alone, rendered vividly luminous the many mysteries of the transcendentalism[18] in which we were immersed. [o]Wanting the radiant lustre of her eyes, letters, lambent and golden, grew duller than Saturnian lead.[o] [19] And now those eyes shone less and less frequently upon the pages over which I pored.[p] Ligeia grew ill. The wild eyes[q] blazed with a too — too glorious effulgence; the pale fingers became of the transparent waxen hue of the grave,[r] and the blue veins upon the lofty forehead swelled and sank[s] impetuously with the tides of the most gentle emotion. I saw that she must die — [t] and I struggled desperately in spirit with the grim Azrael.[20] And the struggles of the passionate wife[u] were, to my astonishment, even more energetic than my own. There had been much in her stern nature to impress me with the belief that, to her, death would have come without its

---

g   astounding — *(A, B) changed in C*
h   me, *(A)*
i   sought for *(A, B, C)*
j   known *(A)*
k   slow but very perceptible *(A)*; slow but perceptible *(B, C, D)*
l   path *(A)*
m   onwarc *(E, F) misprint, corrected from A, B, C, D, G*
n   flee *(A, B) changed in C*
o . . . o   Letters, lambent and golden, grew duller than Saturnian lead [, *(B)*] wanting the radiant lustre of her eyes. *(A, B) changed in C*
p   poured. *(A)*
q   eye *(A, B, C)*
r   grave — *(A, B) changed in C;* grave; *(D, G)*
s   sunk *(A, B, C)*
t   die; *(C)*
u   Ligeia *(A)*

LIGEIA

terrors; — [v] but not so. Words are impotent to convey any just idea of the fierceness of resistance with which she[w] wrestled with the Shadow.[x] I groaned in anguish at the pitiable spectacle. I would have soothed — I would have reasoned; but,[y] in the intensity of her wild desire for life,[z] — for life — *but* for life — [a] solace and reason were alike the uttermost of folly. Yet [b]not until the last instance,[b] amid the most convulsive writhings of her fierce spirit, was shaken the external placidity of her demeanor. Her voice grew more gentle — grew more low — yet I would not wish to dwell upon the wild meaning of the quietly uttered[c] words. My brain reeled as I hearkened,[d] entranced, to a melody more than mortal — to assumptions and aspirations which mortality had never before known.[21]

That she[e] loved me[f] I should not have doubted; and I might have been easily aware that, in a bosom such as hers,[g] love would have reigned no ordinary passion. But in death only, was I fully impressed with the strength[h] of her affection. For long hours, detaining my hand, would she pour out before me the overflowing[i] of a heart whose more than passionate devotion amounted to idolatry. How had I deserved to be so blessed by such confessions? — how[j] had I deserved to be so cursed with the removal of my beloved in the hour of her making them? But upon this subject I cannot bear to dilate. Let me say only, that in Ligeia's more than womanly abandonment to a love, alas![k] all unmerited, all unworthily bestowed,[l] I at length recognized[m] the principle of her longing[n] with so wildly earnest a desire[o] for the life which was now fleeing so rapidly away. It is this wild longing — it is this eager vehemence[p]

---

v   terrors — *(A, B);* terrors; *(C, G)*
w   Ligeia *(A)*
x   dark shadow. *(A, B, C)*
y   but *(A, B, C)*
z   life *(A, B, C, G)*
a   life, *(A, B, C)*
b . . . b   for an instant, *(A, B, C);* until the last instant, *(D)*
c   quietly uttered/quietly-uttered *(A, B, C, D)*
d   hearkened *(E, F) comma added from A, B, C, D, G*
e   Ligeia *(A)*

f   me, *(A, B, C)*
g   her's, *(G) misprint*
h   intensity *(A)*
i   overflowings *(A, B, C, D)*
j   confessions? — how/confessions. — How *(A)*
k   alas, *(A)*
l   bestowed; *(A)*
m   recognised *(A, B, C, G)*
n   longing, *(A, G)*
o   desire, *(G)*
p   intensity *(A)*

·3 1 7·

of desire for life — *but* for life — that I have no power to portray[q]
— no utterance capable [r]of expressing.[r]

[s]At high noon of the night in which she departed, beckoning
me, peremptorily, to her side, she bade me repeat certain verses
composed by herself not many days before. I obeyed her. — [t] They
were these:[u]

> Lo! 'tis a gala night
> Within the lonesome latter years!
> An angel throng, bewinged, bedight
> In veils, and drowned[v] in tears,
> Sit in a theatre, to see
> A play of hopes and fears,
> While the orchestra breathes fitfully
> The music of the spheres.
>
> Mimes, in the form of God on high,
> Mutter and mumble low,
> And hither and thither fly — [w]
> Mere puppets they, who come and go
> At bidding of vast formless things
> That shift the scenery to and fro,
> Flapping from out their Condor wings
> Invisible Wo!
>
> That motley drama! — oh, be sure
> It shall not be forgot!
> With its Phantom chased[x] forevermore,[y]
> By a crowd that seize it not,
> Through a circle that ever returneth in
> To the self-same spot,[z]

---

q pourtray *(A)*
r . . . r to express. *(A);* of
expression. *(D)*
s . . . s *This material, including the
first paragraph, the poem, and the two
succeeding paragraphs, was introduced
in D. This extensive addition took the
place of the following passage in
A, B, C:*
 Methinks I again behold the
terrific struggles of her lofty, her nearly
idealized nature, with the might and the
terror, and the majesty [, *(B, C)*] of the
great Shadow. But she perished. The
giant *will* succumbed to a power more
stern. And I thought, as I gazed upon
the corpse, of the wild passage in

Joseph Glanvill. [: *(B, C)*] "The will
therein lieth, which dieth not. Who
knoweth the mysteries of the will, with
its vigor? For God is but a great will
pervading all things by nature of its
intentness. Man doth not yield him to
the angels, *nor unto death utterly,* save
only through the weakness of his
feeble will. [" *(B, C)*]
t her. *(G)*
u these: — *(G)*
v drown'd *(D)*
w fly; *(G)*
x chas'd *(D)*
y forever more, *(D);* for evermore, *(G)*
z spot; *(G)*

And much of Madness[a] and more of Sin,[b]
And Horror[c] the soul of the plot.[d]

But see, amid the mimic rout,[e]
    A crawling shape intrude!
A blood-red thing that writhes from out
    The scenic solitude!
It writhes! — it writhes! — with mortal pangs
    The mimes become its food,
And the seraphs sob at vermin fangs
    In human gore imbued.

Out — out are the lights — out all!
    And[f] over each quivering form,
The curtain, a funeral pall,
    Comes down with the rush of a storm,[g]
And the angels, all pallid and wan,
    Uprising, unveiling, affirm
That the play is the tragedy, "Man,"
    And its hero[h] the Conqueror[i] Worm.

"O God!" half shrieked Ligeia, leaping to her feet and extending her arms aloft with a spasmodic movement, as I made an end of these lines — "O God! O Divine Father! — shall these things be undeviatingly so? — shall this Conqueror[j] be not once conquered?[k] Are we not part and parcel in Thee? Who — who knoweth the mysteries of the will with its vigor? Man doth not yield him to the angels, *nor unto death utterly,* save only through the weakness of his feeble will." [22]

And now, as if exhausted with emotion, she suffered her white arms to fall, and returned solemnly to her bed of Death.[l] And as she breathed her last sighs,[m] there came mingled with them[n] a low murmur from her lips. I bent to them my ear[o] and distinguished, again, the concluding words of the passage in Glanvill — [p] "*Man*

---

a Madness, *(D, G)*
b Sin *(G)*
c horror, *(G)*
d plot! *(G)*
e rout *(G)*
f And, *(D)*
g storm — *(G)*
h hero, *(G)*

i conqueror *(G)*
j conqueror *(G)*
k unconquered? *(D) misprint*
l death. *(D)*
m sighs *(D)*
n them, *(D)*
o ear, *(G)*
p Glanvill: — *(G)*

·3 1 9·

doth not yield him to the angels, nor unto death utterly, save only through the weakness of his feeble will."[s]

She died; — [q] and I, crushed into the very dust with sorrow, could no longer endure the lonely desolation of my dwelling in the dim and decaying city by the Rhine. I had no lack of what the world calls[r] wealth.[s] Ligeia had brought me far more, very far more[t] than [u]ordinarily falls[u] to the lot of mortals. After a few months, therefore, of weary and aimless wandering, I purchased, and put in some repair, an abbey, which I shall not name, in one of the wildest and least frequented portions of fair England. The gloomy and dreary grandeur of the building, the almost savage aspect of the domain, the many melancholy and time-honored memories connected with both,[v] had much in unison with the feelings of utter abandonment which had driven me into that remote and unsocial[w] region of the country. Yet[x] although the external abbey, with its verdant decay hanging about it, suffered but little alteration, I gave way,[y] with a child-like perversity, and perchance with a faint hope of alleviating my sorrows, to a display of more than regal magnificence within.[z] For such follies,[a] even in childhood,[b] I had imbibed a taste,[c] and now they came back to me as if in the dotage of grief. Alas, I[d] feel how much even of incipient madness might have been discovered in the gorgeous and fantastic draperies, in the solemn carvings of Egypt, in the wild cornices and furniture,[e] in the Bedlam[f] patterns of the carpets of tufted gold! I had became a bounden slave in the trammels of opium, and my labors and my orders had taken a coloring[g] from my dreams.[23] But these absurdities I must not pause to detail. Let me speak only of that one chamber, ever accursed, whither[h] in a moment of mental

---

q   died — *(A, B) changed in C;*
died: — *(G)*
r   terms *(A, B, C)*
s   wealth — *(A, B) changed in C*
t   more, *(A, B, C, G)*
u . . . u   falls ordinarily *(A, B, C, D)*
v   both *(G)*
w   musical *(A)*
x   Yet, *(A)*
y   way *(A)*
z   within. — *(E, F) End of line dash deleted editorially.*

a   follies *(A, B, C, D)*
b   childhood *(A, B, C, D)*
c   taste *(E, F) comma added from all other texts. The space beside this word, which is at the end of a line, in the* Broadway Journal, *indicates that a comma may have fallen out.*
d   I now *(A)*
e   furniture of Arabesque, *(A)*
f   bedlam *(A, B, C, D)*
g   colouring *(A)*
h   whither, *(A, B, C)*

alienation, I led from the altar as my bride — as the successor of the unforgotten Ligeia — the fair-haired and blue-eyed Lady[i] Rowena Trevanion, of Tremaine.[24]

There is no[j] individual portion of the architecture and decoration of that bridal chamber which is not now visibly before me. Where were the souls of the haughty family of the bride, when,[k] through thirst of gold, they permitted to pass the threshold of an apartment *so* bedecked, a maiden and a daughter so beloved? I have said[l] that I minutely remember the details of the chamber — [m] yet I am sadly forgetful on topics of deep moment — [n] and here there was no system, no keeping, in the fantastic display, to take hold upon the memory. The room lay in a high turret of the castellated abbey,[o] was pentagonal in shape,[25] and of capacious size. Occupying the whole southern face of the pentagon was the sole window — an immense sheet of unbroken glass from Venice — a single pane, and tinted of a leaden hue, so that the rays of either the sun or moon,[p] passing through it, fell with a ghastly lustre on[q] the objects within. Over the upper portion of this huge window,[r] extended the[s] trellice-work of an aged vine,[t] which clambered up the massy walls of the turret. The ceiling, of gloomy-looking oak, was excessively lofty, vaulted, and elaborately fretted with the wildest and most grotesque specimens of a semi-Gothic, semi-Druidical[u] device. From out the most central recess of this melancholy vaulting, depended, by a single chain of gold[v] with long links, a huge censer of the same metal, Saracenic[w] in pattern, and with many perforations so contrived that there writhed in and out of them, as if endued with a serpent vitality, a continual succession of parti-colored[x] fires.

[y] Some few ottomans and golden candelabra,[z] of Eastern figure,[a]

---

i lady *(A)*
j not any *(A, B, C)*
k when *(D)*
l said, *(G)*
m chamber; *(C)*
n moment; *(G)*
o abbey *(D)*
p moon *(G)*
q upon *(A, B, C, D)*
r window *(A, B, C)*
s the open *(A, B, C)*

t vine *(A, B, C, D)*
u semi-druidical *(A)*; semi-Druidicial *(D) misprint*
v gold, *(A, B, C)*
w Arabesque *(A)*; Sarcenic *(D) misprint*
x parti-coloured *(A)*
y *No paragraph division in A, B, C*
z candelabras *(A)*; candelabra *(B, C)*
a figure *(A, B, C)*

were in various stations about — [b] and there was the couch, too — [c] the bridal couch — [d] of an Indian model, and low, and sculptured of solid ebony, with a pall-like[e] canopy above. In each of the angles of the chamber[f] stood on end a gigantic sarcophagus of black granite, from the tombs of the kings over against Luxor,[26] with their aged lids full of immemorial sculpture. But in the draping of the apartment lay, alas! the chief phantasy of all. The lofty walls,[g] gigantic in height — even unproportionably so — [h] were hung from summit to foot, in vast folds,[i] with a heavy and massive-looking[j] tapestry — tapestry of a material which was found alike as a carpet on the floor, as a covering for the ottomans[k] and the ebony bed, as a canopy for the bed, and as the gorgeous volutes of the curtains which partially shaded the window. The[l] material was the richest cloth of gold. It was spotted all over, at irregular intervals, with arabesque[m] figures, about[n] a foot in diameter, and wrought upon the cloth in patterns of the most jetty black. But these figures partook of the true character of the arabesque[o] only when regarded from a single point of view. By a contrivance now common, and indeed traceable to a very remote period of antiquity, they were made changeable in aspect. To one entering the room,[p] they bore the appearance of simple[q] monstrosities; but[r] upon a farther advance, this appearance gradually[s] departed; and[t] step by step, as the visiter[u] moved his station in the chamber, he saw himself surrounded by an endless succession of the ghastly forms which belong to the superstition of the Norman,[v] or arise in the guilty slumbers of the monk.[27] The phantasmagoric effect was vastly heightened by the artificial introduction of a strong continual current of wind behind the draperies — giving a hideous[w] and uneasy animation[x] to the whole.

---

b   about; *(G)*
c   too, *(A, B, C)*
d   couch, *(A, B, C)*
e   *Omitted (A, B, C)*
f   chamber, *(A, B, C, D)*
g   walls — *(A, B) changed in C*
h   so, *(A, B) changed in C*
i   folds *(A)*
j   massy looking *(A);* massive looking *(B, C, D)*
k   ottomans, *(A)*
l   This *(A, B, C, D)*

m   Arabesque *(A)*
n   of about *(A, B, C)*
o   Arabesque *(A)*
p   room *(A, B, C, D)*
q   ideal *(A)*
r   but, *(A, B, C, D)*
s   suddenly *(A, B, C)*
t   and, *(A, B, C, D, G)*
u   visitor *(D)*
v   Northman, *(A, B, C, D)*
w   hidious *(A) misprint*
x   vitality *(A)*

LIGEIA

In halls such as these — in a bridal chamber such as this — [y] I passed, with the Lady[z] of Tremaine, the unhallowed hours of the first month of our marriage — passed them with but little disquietude. That my wife dreaded the fierce moodiness of my temper — that she shunned me[a] and loved me but little — [b] I could not help perceiving;[c] but it gave me rather pleasure than otherwise. I loathed her with a hatred belonging more to demon than to man. My memory flew back, (oh,[d] with what intensity of regret!) to Ligeia, the beloved, [e]the august,[e] the beautiful, the entombed. I revelled in recollections of her purity, of her wisdom, of her lofty, her ethereal nature, of her passionate, her idolatrous love. Now, then, did my spirit fully and freely burn with more than all the fires of her own. In the excitement of my opium dreams[f] (for I was habitually fettered in the[g] shackles of the drug)[h] I would call aloud upon her name, during the silence of the night, or among the sheltered recesses of the glens by day, as if, through[i] the wild eagerness, the solemn passion, the consuming ardor[j] of my longing for the departed,[k] I could restore her[l] to the pathway[m] she had [n]abandoned — ah, *could* it be forever?[o] — upon the earth.[n]

About the commencement of the second month of the marriage, the Lady[p] Rowena was attacked with sudden illness,[q] from which her recovery was slow. The fever which consumed her[r] rendered her nights uneasy; and[s] in her perturbed[t] state of half-slumber, she spoke of sounds, and of motions, in and about the chamber of the turret,[u] which [v]I concluded[v] had no origin save in the distemper of her fancy, or perhaps[w] in the phantasmagoric[x] in-

---

y   this, *(A)*
z   lady *(A)*
a   me, *(A, B, C, D, G)*
b   little, *(A)*
c   perceiving — *(A, B) changed in C*
d   oh *(A)*
e . . . e   *Omitted (A, B, C)*
f   dreams, *(G)*
g   the iron *(A, B, C)*
h   drug,) *(G); parentheses omitted (A)*
i   by *(A)*
j   intensity *(A)*
k   departed Ligeia, *(A, B) changed in C*
l   the departed Ligeia *(A, B) changed in C*

m   pathways *(A)*
n . . . n   abandoned upon earth. *(A, B, C)*
o   for ever? *(D, G)*
p   lady *(A)*
q   illness *(A, B, C, D)*
r   her, *(A, G)*
s   uneasy; and/uneasy, and, *(A,B,C)*
t   pertubed *(E) misprint, corrected in F*
u   turret *(A, D)*
v . . . v   *Omitted (A, B, C)*
w   or perhaps/or, perhaps, *(A, B, C, D)*
x   phantastic *(B, C)*

fluences of the chamber itself. She became at length convalescent — finally[y] well. Yet but a brief period elapsed, ere a second more violent disorder again threw her upon a bed of suffering;[z] and from this attack her frame, at all times feeble, never altogether recovered. Her illnesses were, after this epoch,[a] of alarming character, and of more alarming recurrence, defying alike the knowledge and the great exertions of her physicians.[b] With the increase of the chronic disease[c] which had thus, apparently, taken too sure hold upon her constitution to be eradicated by human means, I could not fail to observe a similar increase in the nervous irritation[d] of her temperament, and in her excitability by trivial causes of fear.[e] She spoke again, and now more frequently and pertinaciously, of the sounds — [f] of the slight sounds — [g] and of the unusual motions among the tapestries,[28] to which she had formerly alluded.[h]

One night,[i] near the closing in of September, she[j] pressed this distressing subject with more than usual emphasis upon my attention. She had just awakened from an unquiet[k] slumber, and I had been watching, with feelings half of anxiety, half of a[l] vague terror, the workings of her emaciated countenance. I sat by the side of her ebony bed, upon one of the ottomans of India. She partly arose, and spoke, in an earnest low whisper, of sounds which she *then* heard, but which I could not hear — [m] of motions which she *then* saw, but which I could not perceive.[29] The wind was rushing hurriedly behind the tapestries, and I wished to show her (what,[n] let me confess it, I could not *all* believe) that those[o] almost inarticulate[p] breathings, and those[q] very gentle variations of the figures upon the wall, were but the natural effects of that customary rushing of the wind.[r] But a deadly pallor,[s] over-spreading her face, had proved

---

y   finally, *(G)*
z   suffering — *(A, B) changed in C*
a   period, *(A)*
b   medical men. *(A, B, C)*
c   disease, *(G)*
d   irritability *(A)*
e   *After this:* Indeed reason seemed fast tottering from her throne. *(A, B, C)*
f   sounds, *(A, B) changed in C*
g   sounds, *(A, B) changed in C*
h   *No paragraph division (A)*

i   It was one night *(A);* One night *(B, C, D)*
j   when she *(A)*
k   an unquiet/a perturbed *(A)*
l   *Omitted (G)*
m   hear, *(A, B) changed in C*
n   what *(D)*
o   those faint, *(A, B, C)*
p   articulate, *(A)*
q   the *(A, B, C)*

to me that my exertions to reassure[t] her would be fruitless. She appeared to be fainting, and no attendants were within call. I remembered where was deposited a decanter of[u] light wine which had been ordered by her physicians, and hastened across the chamber to procure it. But, as I stepped beneath the light of the censer, two circumstances of a startling nature attracted my attention. I had felt that some palpable [v]although invisible[v] object had passed lightly by my person; and I saw that there lay [w]upon the golden carpet, in the very middle of the rich lustre thrown from the censer, a shadow — a faint, indefinite shadow of angelic aspect — such as might be fancied for the shadow of a shade.[w] [30] But I was wild with the excitement of an immoderate dose of opium, and heeded these things but little, nor spoke of them to Rowena. [x]Having found[x] the wine, I recrossed[y] the chamber, and poured out a goblet-ful,[z] which I held to the lips of the fainting lady. She[a] had now partially recovered, however,[b] and [c]took the vessel herself,[c] while I sank upon an[d] ottoman near me, with my eyes fastened[e] upon her person. It was then that I became distinctly aware of a gentle foot-fall[f] upon the carpet, and near the couch; and[g] in a second thereafter, as Rowena was in the act of raising the wine to her lips, I saw, or may have dreamed that I saw, fall within the goblet, as if from some invisible spring[h] in the atmosphere of the room, three or four large drops of a brilliant and ruby colored[i] fluid.[31] If this I saw — not so Rowena. She swallowed the wine unhesitatingly, and I forbore to speak to her of a circumstance which must, after all, I considered, have been but the suggestion of a vivid imagination, rendered morbidly active by the terror of the lady, by the opium, and by the hour.

---

r wind./wind *(D) Period dropped*
s pallor *(A)*
t re-assure *(A)*
u of some *(A, B, C)*
v . . . v *Omitted (A, B, C)*
w . . . w a faint, indefinite shadow upon the golden carpet, in the very middle of the rich lustre thrown from the censer. *(A, B, C; but B and C omit the first comma and A omits the second)*
x . . . x Finding *(A, B, C, D)*

y re-crossed *(A)*
z gobletful, *(B, C)*
a But she *(A)*
b however, *omitted (A)*
c . . . c took, herself, the vessel, *(A, B, C);* took the vessel herself *(D)*
d the *(A, B, C, D)*
e rivetted *(A, B, C)*
f gentle foot-fall/gentle-footfall *(D)*
g and, *(A, B, C)*
h spring, *(D)*
i ruby colored/ruby-colored *(B, C, D)*

· 3 2 5 ·

Yet[j] I cannot conceal it from my own perception that,[k] [l]immediately subsequent to the fall of the ruby-drops,[l] a rapid change for the worse took place in the disorder of my wife;[m] so that, on the third subsequent night, the hands of her menials prepared her for the tomb, and on the fourth, I sat alone, with her shrouded body, in that fantastic[n] chamber which had received her as my bride.[o] Wild visions, opium-engendered,[p] flitted, shadow-like, before me. I gazed with unquiet eye[32] upon[q] the sarcophagi in the angles of the room, upon the varying figures of the drapery,[r] and upon the writhing of the parti-colored[s] fires in the censer overhead. My eyes then fell, as I called to mind the circumstances of a former night, to the spot beneath the glare of the censer where I had seen[t] the faint traces of the shadow. It was there, however, no longer;[u] and[v] breathing with greater freedom, I turned my glances to the pallid and rigid figure upon the bed. Then rushed upon me a thousand memories of Ligeia — and then came back upon my heart, with the turbulent violence of a flood, the whole of that unutterable wo[w] with which I had regarded *her* thus enshrouded. The night waned; and still, with a bosom full of bitter thoughts of the one only and supremely beloved, I remained gazing[x] upon the body of Rowena.

It might have been midnight, or perhaps earlier, or later, for I had taken no note of time, when a sob, low, gentle, but very distinct, startled me from my revery.[y] I *felt* that it came from the bed of ebony — the bed of death. I listened in an agony of superstitious terror — but there was no repetition of the sound.[z] I strained my vision to detect any motion in the corpse — [a] but there was not the slightest[b] perceptible. Yet I could not have been deceived. I *had*[c] heard the noise, however faint, and my soul[d] was awakened within

---

j   Yet — *(B, C)*
k   my own perception that,/myself, *(A);* myself — *(B, C)*
l...l   after this period, *(A, B, C)*
m   wife, *(A)*
n   fantastical *(A)*
o   bride. — *(E, F, G) End of line dash deleted editorially.*
p   opium engendered, *(A, B, C)*
q   upcn *(E, F) misprint, not corrected in F*
r   draperry, *(E) misprint, corrected in F*
s   particolored *(B, C)*

t   beheld *(A, B, C)*
u   longer, *(A, B, C, D)*
v   and, *(A, B, C)*
w   woe *(A)*
x   with mine eyes rivetted *(A, B, C)*
y   revery. — *(E, F) End of line dash deleted editorially.*
z   sound; *(A, B) changed in C*
a   corpse, *(A, B, C)*
b   slightest, *(D)*
c   had *(A)*
d   whole soul *(A, B, C, D)*

me.[e] I resolutely and perseveringly kept my attention riveted[f] upon the body. Many minutes elapsed before any circumstance occurred tending to throw light upon the mystery. At length it became evident that a slight, a very feeble,[g] and barely noticeable tinge of color[h] had flushed up within the cheeks, and along the sunken small veins of the eyelids. Through a species of unutterable horror and awe, for which the language of mortality has no sufficiently energetic expression, I felt[i] my heart cease to beat, my limbs grow rigid where I sat. Yet a sense of duty finally operated to restore my self-possession. I could no longer doubt that we had been precipitate in our preparations[j] — that Rowena still lived. It was necessary that some immediate exertion be made; yet the turret was altogether apart from the portion of the abbey[k] tenanted by the servants — there were none within call — [l] I had no means of summoning them to my aid without leaving the room for many minutes — and this I could not venture to do. I therefore struggled alone in my endeavors to call back the spirit still hovering. In a short period it was certain,[m] however, that a relapse had taken place; the color[n] disappeared from both eyelid and cheek, leaving a wanness even more than that of marble; the lips became doubly shrivelled and pinched up in the ghastly expression of death; a [o]repulsive clamminess and coldness[o] overspread rapidly the surface of the body;[p] and all the usual rigorous stiffness immediately supervened. I fell back with a shudder upon the couch[q] from which I had been so startlingly aroused, and again gave myself up to passionate waking visions of Ligeia.

An hour thus elapsed[r] when[s] (could it be possible?) I was a second time aware of some vague sound issuing from the region of the bed. I listened — in extremity of horror. The sound came again — it was a sigh. Rushing to the corpse, I saw — distinctly saw — a

---

e   me, as *(A, B, C)*
f   rivetted *(A, B, C)*
g   faint, *(A, B, C)*
h   colour *(A)*
i   felt my brain reel, *(A, B) changed in C*
j   preparations for interment *(A, B, C, D)*
k   Abbey *(A, B, C)*

l   call, and *(A);* call, — *(B, C)*
m   was certain,/became evident *(A)*
n   color utterly *(A, B, C)*
o . . . o   coldness surpassing that of ice, *(A)*
p   body, *(A)*
q   ottoman *(A)*
r   elapsed, *(G)*
s   when, *(A, B, C)*

tremor upon the lips. In a minute afterward[t] they[u] relaxed, disclosing a bright line of the pearly teeth. Amazement now struggled in my bosom with the profound awe which had hitherto reigned there[v] alone. I felt that my vision grew dim, that my reason[w] wandered;[x] and it was only by a violent[y] effort that I at length succeeded in nerving myself to the task which duty [z]thus once more[z] had pointed out. There was now a partial glow upon the forehead and[a] upon the cheek and throat;[b] a perceptible warmth pervaded the whole frame;[c] there was even a slight pulsation at the heart. The lady *lived;*[d] and with redoubled ardor[e] I betook myself to the task of restoration. I chafed[f] and bathed the temples[g] and the hands, and used every exertion which experience, and no little medical reading, could suggest. But in vain. Suddenly, the color[h] fled, the pulsation ceased, the lips resumed the expression of the dead, and, in an instant afterward,[i] the whole body took upon itself the icy chilliness,[j] the livid hue, the intense rigidity, the sunken[k] outline, and all[l] the loathsome peculiarities of that which has been, for many days, a tenant of the tomb.

And again I sunk into visions of Ligeia — and again,[m] (what marvel that I shudder while I write?) *again* there reached my ears a low sob from the region of the ebony bed. But why shall I minutely detail the unspeakable horrors of that night? Why shall I pause to relate how, time after time, until near the period of the gray[n] dawn, this hideous drama of revivification[o] was repeated;[p] how each terrific relapse was only into a sterner and apparently more irredeemable death;[q] [r]how each agony wore

---

t after *(A);* after, *(B, C);* afterward, *(D)*
u they slightly *(A, B, C)*
v therein *(A, B, C)*
w brain *(A)*
x wandered, *(A, B, C, D)*
y convulsive *(A, B, C)*
z . . . z thus, once more, *(A, B, C, D)*
a forehead and/forehead, *(A)*
b throat — *(A, B, C)*
c frame — *(A, B, C)*
d lived; *(A, B, C)*
e ardour *(A)*
f chafed, *(A)*
g temples, *(A)*

h colour *(A)*
i afterwards, *(A, B, C)*
j chillness, *(A, B, C);* chileness, *(D) misprint*
k snnken *(D) misprint*
l each and all of *(A, B, C);* ell *(D) misprint*
m again *(A)*
n grey *(A)*
o revivication *(D, E, G) corrected in F*
p repeated, and *(A, B) changed in C*
q death? *(A, B)*
r . . . r *Added in C where the insertion was italicized and with some invisible foe was omitted*

the aspect of a struggle with some invisible foe; and how each struggle was succeeded by I know not what of wild change in the personal appearance of the corpse?[r] Let me hurry to a conclusion.

The greater part of the fearful[s] night had worn away, and [t]she who had been dead,[t] once[u] again stirred — and now more vigorously than hitherto, although arousing from a dissolution more appalling in its utter hopelessness than any. I had long ceased to struggle or to move, and remained sitting rigidly upon the ottoman, a helpless prey to a whirl of violent emotions, of which extreme awe was perhaps the least terrible, the least consuming. The corpse, I repeat, stirred, and[v] now more vigorously than before. The hues of life flushed up with unwonted energy into the countenance — [w] the limbs relaxed — [x] and, save[y] that the eyelids were yet pressed heavily together, and that the bandages and draperies of the grave still imparted their charnel[z] character to the figure, I might have dreamed that Rowena had indeed shaken off, utterly, the fetters of Death. But if this idea was not, even then, altogether adopted, I could at least[a] doubt no longer, when, arising from the bed, tottering, with feeble steps, with closed eyes, and with the manner[b] of one bewildered in a dream, [c]the thing that was enshrouded advanced bodily[d] and palpably into the middle of the apartment.[c]

I trembled[e] not — I stirred not — for a crowd of unutterable fancies connected with the air,[f] the stature,[g] the demeanor[h] of the figure, rushing hurriedly[i] through my brain, [j]had paralyzed — [k] had chilled me into stone.[j] I stirred not — but gazed upon [l]the ap-

s   fearfnl *(E, F) misprint, corrected from A, B, C, D, G*
t . . . t   the corpse of Rowena *(A, B, C)*
u   one *(G) misprint*
v   *Canceled (C)*
w   countenance, *(C)*
x   relaxed, *(C)*
y   and, save/save *(C)*
z   charnal *(A) misprint*
a   could at least/could, at least, *(A, B, C)*
b   air *(A)*
c . . . c   the lady of Tremaine stood bodily and palpably before me. *(A);*

the Lady of Tremaine advanced bodily and palpably into the middle of the apartment. *(B, C)*
d   boldly *(E, G) misprint, corrected in F*
e   spoke *(C)*
f   air — *(C)*
g   *A, B,* and *C* omit the stature,
h   demeanour *(A)*
i   hurridly *(E) misprint, corrected in F*
j . . . j   had sent the purple blood ebbing in torrents from the temples to the heart. *(A)*
k   paralyzed, *(B) changed in C*

parition.[1] There was a mad disorder in my thoughts — a tumult unappeasable. Could it, indeed, be the *living* Rowena who confronted me? [m]Could it indeed be Rowena *at all* — the fair-haired, the blue-eyed Lady Rowena Trevanion of Tremaine?[m] Why, *why* should I doubt it? The bandage lay heavily about the mouth — but then [n]might it not be[n] the mouth of the breathing Lady[o] of Tremaine?[p] And the cheeks — there were the roses as in her noon of life[q] — yes, these [r]might indeed be[r] the fair cheeks of the living Lady[s] of Tremaine. And the chin, with its dimples, as in health, [t]might it not be hers?[t] — but[u] *had she then grown taller since her malady?* What inexpressible madness seized me with that thought? One bound, and I had reached her feet! Shrinking from my touch, she let fall from her head[v] the ghastly cerements which had confined it, and there streamed forth, into the rushing atmosphere of the chamber, huge masses of long and dishevelled[v'] hair; *it*[w] *was blacker than the*[x] *wings of the*[y] *midnight!*[33] And now [z]slowly opened *the eyes*[z] of the figure which stood before me. "Here then,[a] at least," I shrieked aloud, "can I never — can I never be mistaken — these are the full, and the black, and the wild eyes — [b] [c]of my lost love — [c] of the lady[d] — of the LADY[e] LIGEIA!"[f]

NOTES

Title: The name is the feminine (λιγεία) of the Homeric Greek adjective *ligys* (λιγυς), meaning canorous, high-sounding, clear-toned, or shrill. It was used as the name of a spirit in "Al Aaraaf," II, 112, whom Henry B. Hirst, writing under Poe's supervision in the *Saturday Museum*, March 4, 1843, ex-

l . . . l her who was before me. *(A)*	v' disshevelled *(E, F) misprint*
m . . . m *Omitted (A, B, C)*	w hair; *it*/hair. *It (A, B, C)*
n . . . n it was *(A, B);* was it not *(C)*	x *the raven (A, B, C, D, E, G) changed in F*
o lady *(A)*	
p Tremaine. *(A, B, D) changed in C but not followed in D*	y *Omitted (G)*
q health *(A)*	z . . . z the eyes opened *(A, B, C)*
r . . . r were indeed *(A, B, C)*	a then *(A)*
s lady *(A)*	b eyes, *(A, B)*
t . . . t was it not hers? *(A, B, C)*	c . . . c *Omitted (A, B, C)*
u but — but *(A)*	d Lady *(G)*
v head, unloosened, *(A, B, C, D, E, G) changed in F*	e lady *(A, C);* Lady *(B, D)*
	f Ligeia!" *(A, B, C);* LIGEIA." *(G)*

LIGEIA

plained as a "personification of music." The name Ligea was borne by a dryad in Vergil's *Georgics,* IV, 336, and this is probably the significant connection in Poe's poem. It was also the name of a siren, mentioned by Milton, *Comus,* line 880, and in the story this may be in Poe's mind.

Motto: This has never been found. Although the Glanvill quotation in "A Descent into the Maelström" is genuine, that in "Ligeia" is essential to the plot, and hence Poe may have made it up.

1. Ligeia in the story is a magician or alchemist, and in view of the destruction of Morella, when her name was known, we may discern here a hint that perhaps Ligeia, cautiously, never revealed her real name. Her lack of a remembered family name, despite her noble ancestry, suggests that she may have been of Jewish origin and hence had none. Maxwell Morton, in *A Builder of the Beautiful* (1928), p. 58, has pointed out that Ligeia is described as resembling the poet's mother, Elizabeth Arnold Poe, who had a Hebraic nose and large dark eyes. This is hardly accidental, for her son, despite his lack of a conscious memory of her, owned her miniature portrait, and revered her memory.

For "wife of my bosom," a phrase also used in "The Black Cat," compare Deuteronomy 13:6 and 28:54.

2. Ashtophet was, according to *Rees's Cyclopaedia,* a goddess of the Sidonians. In mythology she has been identified with, or assimilated to, Ashtoreth (see 2 Kings 23:13), Astarte, Aphrodite, and eventually Venus. See "The Duc de L'Omelette" above, at note 16, and compare Poe's poems "Eulalie" and "Ulalume" and my notes on them in volume I of this edition.

3. Poe obviously had in mind the following from "A Manuscript Found in a Madhouse" in Bulwer's *Conversations with an Ambitious Student . . .* p. 200 ". . . her face was an angel's. Oh! lovelier far than the visions of the Carian, or the shapes that floated before the eyes of the daughters of Delos." Poe had a similar phrase in a canceled passage in "Silence — A Fable," and must have supposed that the reference was to dreams by night, although Bulwer perhaps had in mind visions inspiring the sculptors of the statues of Aphrodite at Cnidus in Caria, and of Apollo and Artemis at Delos.

4. Bacon (*Essays,* number 43, "Of Beauty") said: "There is no excellent beauty that hath not some strangeness in the proportion." Poe was fond of these words. When he quoted them in the "Anastatic Printing" *(BJ,* April 12, 1845), he said, as he does here, that "the remark is equally applicable to all the forms of beauty." He used the remark with a humorous turn in a canceled passage in "The Man That Was Used Up" *(Burton's,* August 1839); in referring to poetry in a review of William Ellery Channing *(Graham's,* August 1843) and a passage on Shelley in the review of Elizabeth Barrett Barrett's *The Drama of Exile (BJ,* Jan. 4, 11, 1845); and in a discussion of rhyme in "Marginalia," number 147 *(Graham's,* March 1846). Where Bacon has "excellent," Poe wrote "exquisite." See also "The Landscape Garden" at note 13.

5. The "gentle prominence" phrenologists thought to signify love of life; see Edward Hungerford, "Poe and Phrenology" *(AL,* November 1930).

6. For hyacinthine locks compare "The Visionary" at note 6, and see my

notes on Poe's poem "To Helen." Poe referred to the medallions of the Hebrews in canceled passages in early versions of "The Visionary" ("The Assignation") and of "Mystification" at note 8. In his day numismatists called Jewish silver shekels "medallions," and these have graceful outlines, but not of human figures — something one suspects Poe did not know. Walter Blair suggested the sculptured medallions portraying Jewish captives on the Arch of Titus in Rome.

7. Cleomenes, son of Apollodorus the Athenian, is named in its epigraph as the sculptor of the Venus de Medici. The inscription is generally regarded as a Renaissance forgery, although Pliny refers to a sculptor named Cleomenes in the *Natural History*, XXVI, 4. Poe apparently knew some story that the statue was modeled on a vision, and refers to it also in a canceled passage in "The Visionary"; in a review of Sophocles' *Antigone (BJ*, April 12, 1845); and in "Marginalia," number 186 (*Graham's*, December 1846, p. 312).

8. The allusion is to *The History of Nourjahad* by "Sidney Biddulph" (Mrs. Frances Sheridan). Professor G. H. Gerould referred me to a Dublin edition of 1767, pp. 34 and 44; "All parts of the earth shall be explored for women of the most exquisite beauty," and Nourjahad's "seraglio was soon adorned with a number of the most beautiful female slaves, . . . whom he purchased at vast expense." A melodrama, *Illusion, or the Trance of Nourjahad*, was produced at Drury Lane, May 25, 1813.

9. The Houris of the Mahometan Paradise, made of pure musk instead of clay, like mortals, have white skin and black eyes; the name is derived from the eyes. Poe mentions them also in "Israfel" and "The Oval Portrait."

10. Compare Poe's quotation from Glanvill introduced in 1845 as the motto for "A Descent into the Maelström." The idea that Truth lies at the bottom of a well Poe may have found in the article on Democritus in Rees's *Cyclopaedia* (39 v., London, 1819). It has been ascribed to Democritus on the basis of a fragment — "Of truth we know nothing, for truth is in the depths" — quoted by Diogenes Laertius *(Pyrrho*, Book IX, section 72) and others. Poe alluded to the idea, though not to Democritus, in "Letter to Mr. — —," introductory to *Poems* (1831), and in other places . See "The Murders in the Rue Morgue" at note 29.

11. The twins of Leda, mentioned also in "A Valentine" addressed to Frances Sargent Osgood, are the Dioscuri, Castor and Pollux. Poe presumably knew a reference to "the Ledean stars, so famed for love" quoted from Cowley by Isaac D'Israeli in the chapter on "Literary Friendships" in *Curiosities of Literature*.

12. All the natural phenomena named are types of mortality and change. There is another list in the early poem called "Stanzas."

13. Compare the expression of the captain — "the intense, the wonderful, the thrilling evidence of old age" — in "MS. Found in a Bottle," at note 19.

14. The bright star in Lyra — Alpha Lyrae — is Vega. The changeable star Poe means is Epsilon Lyrae, a double double star changing in brightness several times an hour. Lyra (the Harp) is a northern constellation between Hercules and Cygnus.

15. The vast learning of Ligeia may be compared with that of Morella (and, by some, with that of Pierre Bon-Bon). It must trouble those who would find the model for Poe's heroines in his wife.

16. Compare "To Marie Louise," line 23, "Gazing, entranced adown the gorgeous vista." For forbidden knowledge see Genesis, chapters 2 and 3. Here, however, alchemy is meant.

17. See Proverbs 23:5: ". . . riches certainly make themselves wings; they fly away, as an eagle toward heaven."

18. Transcendentalism here means belief in intuitive knowledge.

19. Saturnia is a poetic name for Italy — see Vergil's *Georgics,* II, 173. Italian lead is graphite, than which few things are duller. "Saturn" is the name for lead in alchemy, but Poe's allusion is more pointed.

20. Azrael, the Mahometan angel of death, is also mentioned in "Metzengerstein"; *Politian,* IX, 4; and "Mesmeric Revelation." There is, here and in the third sentence below, an allusion to Hercules who wrestled with Thanatos (Death) to rescue Alcestis.

21. Compare Edward C. Pinkney, "A Health," line 6: "And something more than melody dwells ever in her words." Compare also "The Raven," line 26, for "dreams no mortal ever dared to dream before."

22. The insertion of the poem with its accompanying paragraphs is the indication that Ligeia's struggle cannot succeed. When the poem made its first appearance in the story, the *New World* carried on another page the following comment:

> LIGEIA. — We call attention to the powerful tale in this number of our paper by Edgar A. Poe, entitled LIGEIA. The force and boldness of the conception and the high artistic skill, with which the writer's purpose is wrought out, are equally admirable. Mark the exquisite art, which keeps constantly before the reader the ruined and spectre-haunted mind of the narrator, and so suggests a *possible explanation* of the marvels of the story, without in the least weakening its vigor as an exposition of the mystical *thesis* which the tale is designed to illustrate and enforce.
>
> The story will be, we presume, entirely new to most of our readers. It appeared we believe originally in England, in a volume of which only a small edition was printed. The volume is now out of print. We suggest that some of our enterprising publishers would do well in giving it to the public without delay. In our copy of LIGEIA, the author has put the last hand to his work, and improved it by several important changes and additions. In its present form it has not seen the light before. We shall have the pleasure of laying before our readers hereafter other similar contributions from the same source.

No authoritative record of the English printing mentioned has been found. The poem itself is discussed in detail in the collection of Poems in this edition, I, 323–328.

23. The use of opium is, as usual with Poe, prefatory to a preternatural story.

24. Rowena is the name of the blonde heroine of Scott's *Ivanhoe.* Trevanion probably is from Trevena, a name for Tintagel in Cornwall, associated

with Arthurian romance and magic. [It has also been pointed out (B. Pollin, London *N & Q,* September 1970) that Trevanion was the name of Byron's grandmother.] *Tremaine* is the name of a novel by R. P. Ward, mentioned in "Marginalia," number 221 *(SLM,* May 1849, p. 295), and discusssed in Benjamin Disraeli's *Vivian Grey,* II, x.

25. The pentagon (preferably drawn without lifting the pen) is a powerful figure in magic, and the shape of the chamber is significant.

26. Luxor, on the Nile in Upper Egypt near ancient Thebes, site of the great temple built by Amenhotep III and Ramses II, is mentioned again in "Some Words with a Mummy."

27. In referring to the superstition of the Norman, Poe has in mind Bulwer's "Manuscript Found in a Madhouse" (cited in n. 3 above), p. 201: "I told her that I was more hideous than the demons which the imagination of a Northern savage had ever bodied forth."

28. Compare, for the eerie effect of wind rustling tapestries, "The Fall of the House of Usher."

29. Compare lines in Thomas Tickell's once widely known ballad ghost story, "Colin and Lucy," for "I hear a voice you cannot hear, that says I may not stay; /I see a hand you cannot see, which beckons me away."

30. See "The Raven," lines 79–80, "The air grew denser, perfumed with an unseen censer/Swung by Seraphim." "Shadow of a shade" recalls *Hamlet,* II, ii, 266, "A dream itself is but a shadow."

31. So good a critic as Vincent Buranelli, *Edgar Allan Poe,* p. 73, supposed the drops to be poison, but they are rather a primary corporeal form attained by Ligeia's spirit; and in themselves the elixir of life.

32. Compare "MS. Found in a Bottle," for "he pored, with a fiery unquiet eye."

33. Compare the change of the heroine's hair (from natural causes) in "Berenicë."

THE PSYCHE ZENOBIA
(HOW TO WRITE A
BLACKWOOD ARTICLE)

As originally published in the *American Museum* of Baltimore for November 1838 and as reprinted in the *Broadway Journal* for July 12, 1845 under Poe's editorship, this satirical account of how to write for sensational magazines was designed as one story including another. In this form it is presented here. When Lea and Blanchard published *Tales of the Grotesque and Arabesque*

(1840), however, the narratives were treated as separate units — Poe in his preface said there were twenty-five tales, counting these as two. Griswold's and most subsequent collections have followed that pattern.

The ridiculous story is of special interest because Poe consciously describes some of his own methods. He once said seriously (in his review of Hawthorne's *Twice-Told Tales* in *Graham's*, May 1842) that one invented or selected incidents and other material to fit a preconceived mood or tone. Obviously he realized that the skill of the writer determined how effective the combinations might be. His Mr. Blackwood gave his silly pupil good instruction — Poe used some of his scraps of learning elsewhere in serious as well as comic contexts. But Psyche Zenobia is a fool, and her story is absurd — although the repulsive elements are characteristic of some British magazinists.*

In naming his protagonist, Poe obviously had in mind William Ware's serial begun in March 1836 in the *Knickerbocker Magazine,* published in book form in 1837 as *Letters of Lucius M. Piso from Palmyra, to His Friend Marcus Curtius at Rome,* and later issued with the title *Zenobia.* This popular work had put the great Queen of Palmyra much in the public eye.† Poe's Signora has

* John Esten Cooke about 1852, in his lecture *Poe as a Literary Critic* (edited by N. Bryllion Fagin, 1946), said (p. 11): "This advice, satirically attributed to Mr. Blackwood, Mr. Poe gravely followed... He seems to have carefully gleaned from almost every book which he read, whatever might prove useful to him — in which there was certainly nothing to find fault with — and these facts, quotations, and 'little scraps' he afterwards introduced into his writings with the 'downright improviso air' which he recommends." Poe himself noted in "Marginalia," number 78 (*Democratic Review,* December 1844, p. 585) that "misapplication of quotations is clever, and has a capital effect when well done." [See also Burton R. Pollin, "Poe's Tale of Psyche Zenobia: A Reading for Humor and Ingenious Construction," in *Papers on Poe, Essays in Honor of John Ward Ostrom* (1972), pp. 92–103.]

† Nathaniel Hawthorne gave her name to a character in *The Blithedale Romance* (1852) — who represents Margaret Fuller, an assertor of women's rights — but no connection of Poe's and Hawthorne's use, save as from the same historical prototype, is at all probable. Thomas H. McNeal in the *Modern Language Quarterly* (June 1950) tried to show that Poe's Zenobia was a satire on Margaret Fuller. Poe's tale, however, was printed in 1838, while Miss Fuller was still an obscure writer. She did not become well known until she began to edit *The Dial* in 1840, and the reference to that periodical in Poe's tale was not inserted until 1845. Critical examination of the dates refutes McNeal's notion, but it is mentioned without disapproval in *The Reader's Encyclopedia of American Literature* (1950).

obtained her classic learning from the columns of Lewis Gaylord Clark's magazine; and takes the name of an ancient heroine better known for beauty than courage.

TEXTS

(A) Baltimore *American Museum,* November 1838 (1:301–317); *(B) Tales of the Grotesque and Arabesque* (1840), I, 213–243; *(C)* PHANTASY-PIECES with manuscript revision of last, 1842; *(D) Broadway Journal,* July 12, 1845 (2:1–7); *(E) Works* (1856), IV, 230–250.

The *Broadway Journal* version *(D),* set up as one story including another, is followed. In PHANTASY-PIECES *(C)* Poe changed the titles of both portions of the story, revised a paragraph, a few phrases, and some punctuation. Rearrangement of two paragraphs and more verbal changes were made for the *Broadway Journal* version. Griswold's few changes were not significant. All texts have any body, every body, no body, would'nt, did'nt; the usage is emended editorially. All texts also omit the quotation marks before PIQUANT EXPRESSIONS, which have been inserted editorially.

HOW TO WRITE A BLACKWOOD ARTICLE. [*D*]

"In the name of the Prophet — figs!!"
Cry of the Turkish fig-pedler.

I presume everybody has heard of me. My name is the Signora Psyche Zenobia. This I know to be a fact. Nobody but my enemies ever calls me Suky Snobbs.[1] I have been assured that Suky is but a vulgar corruption of Psyche, which is good Greek, and means "the soul" (that's me, I'm *all* soul) and sometimes "a butterfly," which latter meaning undoubtedly[a] alludes to my appearance in my new crimson satin dress, with the sky-blue Arabian *mantelet,* and the trimmings of green *agraffas,* and the seven flounces of orange-colored *auriculas.*[2] As for Snobbs — any person who should look at me would be instantly aware that my name wasn't Snobbs. Miss Tabitha Turnip propagated that report through sheer envy. Tabitha Turnip indeed! Oh the little wretch! But what can we expect from a turnip? Wonder if she remembers the old adage

---

Title: The Psyche Zenobia *with running title* The Signora Psyche Zenobia *(A);* The Signora Zenobia *(B); changed to present title with running*

title A Blackwood Article *(C)*
Motto: First added in C; Cry of the/Cry of *(E)*
a   *Omitted (A, B, C)*

about 'blood out of a turnip, &c." [Mem: put her in mind of it the first opportunity.] [Mem again — pull her nose.] Where was I? Ah! I have been assured that Snobbs is a mere corruption of Zenobia, and that Zenobia was a queen[3] — (So am I. Dr. Moneypenny, always calls me the Queen of Hearts) — and that Zenobia, as well as Psyche, is good Greek, and that my father was "a Greek,"[4] and that consequently I have a right to our[b] patronymic, which is Zenobia, and not by any means Snobbs. Nobody but Tabitha Turnip calls me Suky Snobbs. I am the Signora Psyche Zenobia.

As I said before, everybody has heard of me. I am that very Signora Psyche Zenobia, so justly celebrated as corresponding secretary to the "*Philadelphia, Regular, Exchange, Tea, Total, Young, Belles, Lettres, Universal, Experimental, Bibliographical, Association, To, Civilize, Humanity.*" Dr. Moneypenny made the title for us, and says he chose it because it sounded big like an empty rum-puncheon. (A vulgar man that sometimes — but he's deep.) We all sign the initials of the society after our names, in the fashion of the R.S.A., Royal Society of Arts — the S.D.U.K., Society for the Diffusion of Useful Knowledge, &c. &c. Dr. Moneypenny says that S stands for *stale,* and that D.U.K. spells duck, (but it don't,) and that S.D.U.K. stands for Stale Duck, and not for Lord Brougham's society[5] — but then Dr. Moneypenny is such a queer man that I am never sure when he is telling me the truth. At any rate we always add to our names the initials P.R.E.T.T.Y.B.L.U.E.-B.A.T.C.H. — that is to say, Philadelphia, Regular, Exchange, Tea, Total, Young, Belles, Lettres, Universal, Experimental, Bibliographical, Association, To, Civilize, Humanity — one letter for each word, which is a decided improvement upon Lord Brougham. Dr. Moneypenny will have it that our initials give our true character — but for my life I can't see what he means.

Notwithstanding the good offices of [c]the Doctor,[c] and the strenuous exertions of the association to get itself into notice, it met with no very great success until I joined it. The truth is, members indulged in too flippant a tone of discussion. The papers read every Saturday evening were characterized less by depth than buffoonery.

---

b   our original *(A, B, C)*   *changed in C*
c . . . c   Dr. Moneypenny, *(A, B)*

They were all whipped syllabub. There was no investigation of first causes, first principles. There was no investigation of anything at all. There was no attention paid to that great point the "fitness of things."[6] In short there was no fine writing like this. It was all low — very! No profundity, no reading, no metaphysics — nothing which the learned call spirituality, and which the unlearned choose to stigmatise as cant. [Dr. M. says I ought to spell "cant" with a capital K — but I know better.][7]

When I joined the society it was my endeavour to introduce a better style of thinking and writing, and all the world knows how well I have succeeded. We get up as good papers now in the P.R.E.T.T.Y.B.L.U.E.B.A.T.C.H. as any to be found even in Blackwood. I say, Blackwood, because I have been assured that the finest writing, upon every subject, is to be discovered in the pages of that justly celebrated Magazine. We now take it for our model upon all themes, and are getting into rapid notice accordingly. And, after all, it's not so very difficult a matter to compose an article of the genuine Blackwood stamp, if one only goes properly about it. Of course I don't speak of the political articles. Everybody knows how *they* are managed, since Dr. Moneypenny explained it. Mr. Blackwood has a pair of tailor's-shears, and three apprentices who stand by him for orders. One hands him the "Times," another the "Examiner,"[8] and a[d] third a "Gulley's New Compendium of Slang-Whang."[9] Mr. B. merely cuts out and intersperses. It is soon done — nothing but Examiner, Slang-Whang, and Times — then Times, Slang-Whang, and Examiner — and then Times, Examiner, and Slang-Whang.

But the chief merit of the Magazine lies in its miscellaneous articles; and the best of these come under the head of what Dr. Moneypenny calls the *bizarreries* (whatever that may mean) and what everybody else calls the *intensities*. This is a species of writing which I have long known how to appreciate, although it is only since my late visit to Mr. Blackwood (deputed by the society) that I have been made aware of the exact method of composition. This method is very simple, but not so much so as the politics. Upon my

---

d the *(A)*

calling at Mr. B.'s, and making known to him the wishes of the society, he received me with great civility, took me into his study, and gave me a clear explanation of the whole process.

"My dear madam," said he, evidently struck with my majestic appearance, for I had on the crimson satin, with the green *agraffas*, and orange-coloured *auriculas*, "My *dear* madam," said he, "sit down. The matter stands thus. In the first place, your writer of intensities must have very black ink, and a very big pen, with a very blunt nib. And, mark me, Miss Psyche Zenobia!" he continued, after a pause, with the most impressive energy and solemnity of manner, "mark me! — *that pen — must — never be mended!* Herein, madam, lies the secret, the soul, of intensity. I assume it[e] upon myself to say, that no individual, of however great genius, ever wrote with a good pen, — understand me, — a good article. You may take it for granted,[f] that when[g] manuscript can be read it is never worth reading. This is a leading principle in our faith, to which if you cannot readily[h] assent, our conference is at an end."

He paused. But, of course, as I had no wish to put an end to the conference, I assented to a proposition so very obvious, and one, too, of whose truth I had all along been sufficiently aware. He seemed pleased, and went on with his instructions.

"It may appear invidious in[i] me, Miss Psyche Zenobia, to refer you to any[j] article, or set of articles, in the way of model or study; yet perhaps I may as well call your attention to a few cases. Let me see.[10] There was '*The Dead Alive,*' a capital thing! — the record of a gentleman's [k]sensations, when entombed before the breath was out of his body — full[k] of[l] taste, terror, sentiment, metaphysics, and erudition. You would have sworn that the writer had been born and brought up in a coffin.[11] Then we had the '*Confessions of an Opium-eater*' — fine, very fine! — glorious imagination — deep philosophy — acute speculation — plenty of fire and fury, and a good spicing of the decidedly unintelligible. That was a nice bit of flummery, and went down the throats of the people delightfully.

---

e *Omitted (E)*
f granted, madam, *(A, B, C)*
g when a *(A, B, C)*
h *Canceled (C)*
i to *(A)*

j an *(E)*
k...k sensa- when entombed before the breath was out of his body — full tions, *(D) dropped line*
l of tact, *(A, B, C)*

They would have it that Coleridge wrote the paper — but not so. It was composed by my pet baboon, Juniper, over a rummer of Hollands and water, 'hot, without sugar.' " [This I could scarcely have believed had it been anybody but Mr. Blackwood, who assured me of it.][12] "Then there was '*The Involuntary Experimentalist*,' all about a gentleman who got baked in an oven, and came out alive and well, although certainly done to a turn.[13] And then there was '*The Diary of a Late Physician*,' where the merit lay in good rant, and indifferent Greek — both of them taking things, with the public.[14] And then there was '*The Man in the Bell*,' a paper by-the-bye, Miss Zenobia, which I cannot sufficiently recommend to your attention.[15] It is the history of a young person who goes to sleep under the clapper of a church bell, and is awakened by its tolling for a funeral. The sound drives him mad, and, accordingly, pulling out his tablets, he gives a record of his sensations. Sensations are the great things after all. Should you ever be drowned or hung, be sure and make a note of your sensations — they will be worth to you ten guineas a sheet. If you wish to write forcibly, Miss Zenobia, pay minute attention to the sensations."

"That I certainly will, Mr. Blackwood," said I.

"Good!" he replied. "I see you are a pupil after my own heart. But I must put you *au fait* to the details necessary in composing what may be denominated a genuine Blackwood article of the sensation stamp — the kind which you will understand me to say I consider the best for all purposes.

"The first thing requisite is to get yourself into such a scrape as no one ever got into before. The oven, for instance, — that was a good hit. But if you have no oven, or big bell, at hand, and if you cannot conveniently tumble out of a balloon, or be swallowed up in an earthquake, or get stuck fast in a chimney, you will have to be contented with simply imagining some similar misadventure. I should prefer, however, that you have the actual fact to bear you out. Nothing so well assists the fancy, as an experimental knowledge of the matter in hand. 'Truth is strange,' you know, 'stranger than fiction' — besides being more to the purpose."[16]

Here I assured him I had an excellent pair of garters, and would go and hang myself forthwith.

A BLACKWOOD ARTICLE

"Good!" he replied, "do so; — although hanging is somewhat hacknied. Perhaps you might do better. Take a dose of Brandreth's[m] pills, and then give us your sensations.[17] However, my instructions will apply equally well to any variety of misadventure, and in your way home you may easily get knocked in the head, or run over by an omnibus, or bitten by a mad dog, or drowned in a gutter. But, to proceed.

"Having determined upon your subject, you must next consider the tone, or manner, of your narration. There is the tone didactic, the tone enthusiastic, the[n] tone natural — all commonplace enough. But then there is the tone laconic, or curt, which has lately come much into use. It consists in short sentences. Somehow thus. Can't be too brief. Can't be too snappish. Always a full stop. And never a paragraph.

"Then there is the tone elevated, diffusive, and interjectional. Some of our best novelists patronize this tone. The words must be all in a whirl, like a humming-top, and make a noise very similar, which answers remarkably well instead of meaning. This is the best of all possible styles where the writer is in too great a hurry to think.

"The tone metaphysical[o] is also a good one.[p] [q]If you know any big words this is your chance for them. Talk of the Ionic and Eleatic schools — of Archytas, Gorgias and Alcmæon.[18] Say something about objectivity and subjectivity. Be sure and abuse a man called[r] Locke.[19] Turn up your nose at things in general, and when you let slip anything a little *too* absurd, you need not be at the trouble of scratching it out, but just add a foot-note, and say that you are indebted for the above profound observation to the '*Kritik*

---

m   Morrison's *(A, B) changed in C*
n   the tone sentimental, and the *(A, B, C)*
o   mystic *(A, B, C)*
p   one./one — but requires some skill in the handling. The beauty of this lies in a knowledge of innuendo. Hint all, and assert nothing. If you desire to say 'bread and butter,' do not by any means say it outright. You may say any thing and every thing *approaching* to 'bread and butter.' You may hint at

'buck-wheat cake,' or you may even go as far as to insinuate 'oat-meal porridge,' but, if 'bread and butter' is your real meaning, be cautious, my *dear* Miss Psyche, not on any account to say 'bread and butter.' "
    I assured him that I would never say it again as long as I lived. He continued. *(A, B, C)*
q . . . q   *Omitted (A, B, C)*
r   named *(E)*

· 3 4 1 ·

der reinen[s] Vernunft,' or to the *'Metaphysische Anfangsgründe[t] der Naturwissenschaft.'*[20] This will look erudite and — and — and frank.[q]

"There are various other tones of equal celebrity, but I shall [u]mention only[u] two more — the tone transcendental[v] and the tone heterogeneous. In the former the merit consists in seeing into the nature of affairs a very great deal farther than anybody else. This second sight is very efficient when properly managed. A little reading of the 'Dial'[w] [21] will carry you a great way.[x] [y]Eschew, in this case, big words; get them as small as possible, and write them upside down. Look over Channing's poems and quote what he says about a 'fat little man with a delusive show of Can.'[22] Put in something about the Supernal Oneness. Don't say a syllable about the Infernal Twoness.[23] Above all, study innuendo.[z] Hint every thing — assert nothing. If you feel inclined to say 'bread and butter' do not by any means say it outright. You may say anything and every thing *approaching* to 'bread and butter.' You may hint at buckwheat cake, or you may even go so far as to insinuate oat-meal porridge, but if bread and butter be your real meaning, be cautious, my *dear* Miss Psyche, not on any account to say 'bread and butter!' "[24]

I assured him that I should never say it again as long as I lived. He kissed me and continued:[y]

"As for the tone heterogeneous, it is merely a judicious mixture, in equal proportions, of all the other tones in the world, and

---

s *reinem (D, E)*
t Anfangsgrunde *(D, E)*
u . . . u only mention *(A, B, C)*
v metaphysical *(A, B, C)*
w the 'Dial'/*'The Sorrows of Werther,' (A);* Coleridge's Table-Talk *(B, C)*
x *After this, in A and B:* If you know any big words this is your chance for them. Talk of the academy and the lyceum, and say something about the Ionic and Italic schools, or about Bossarion, and Kant, and Schelling, and Fitche, and be sure you abuse a man called Locke, and bring in the words *a priori* and *a posteriori.*
   In C: If you know any big words this is your chance for them. Talk of the

Ionic and Eleatic Schools — of Archytas, Gorgias, and Alcmaeon. Say something about objects and subjects. Be sure and abuse a man called Locke. Turn up your nose at things in general; and when you let slip anything very unconscionably absurd, you need not be at the trouble of scratching it out, but just put in a foot-note and say you are indebted for the above profound observation to the 'Kritik der reinen Vernunft' or to the 'Metaphysische Anfangsgrunde der Naturwissenschaft.' This will look erudite and at the same time *frank.*
y . . . y *Omitted (A, B, C)*
z inuendo. *(D, E) misprint*

is consequently made up of everything deep, great, odd, piquant,[a] pertinent, and pretty.

"Let us suppose now you have determined upon your incidents and tone. The most important portion, — in fact the soul of the whole business, is yet to be attended to — I allude to *the filling up.* It is not to be supposed that a lady or gentleman either has been leading the life of a bookworm. And yet above all things it is[b] necessary that your article have an air of erudition, or at least afford evidence of extensive general reading. Now I'll put you in the way of accomplishing this point. See here!" (pulling down some three or four ordinary looking volumes, and opening them at random.) "By casting your eye down almost any page of any book in the world, you will be able to perceive at once a host of little scraps of either learning or *bel-esprit-ism,* which are the very thing for the spicing of a Blackwood article. You might as well note down a few while I read them to you. I shall make two divisions: first, *Piquant Facts for the Manufacture of Similes;* and second, *Piquant Expressions to be introduced as occasion may require.* Write now! — " and I wrote as he dictated.

"PIQUANT FACTS FOR SIMILES. 'There were originally but three Muses — Melete, Mneme, and[c] Aœde — meditation, memory, and singing.'[25] You may make a great deal of that little fact if properly worked. You see it is not generally known, and looks *recherché.* You must be careful and give the thing with a downright improviso air.

"Again. 'The river Alpheus[26] passed beneath the sea, and emerged without injury to the purity of its waters.' Rather stale that, to be sure, but, if properly dressed and dished up, will look quite as fresh as ever.

"Here is something better. 'The Persian Iris appears to some persons to possess a sweet and very powerful perfume, while to others it is perfectly scentless.'[27] Fine that, and very delicate! Turn it about a little, and it will do wonders. We'll have something else in the botanical line. There's nothing goes down so well, especially with the help of a little Latin. Write!

---

a piquant and *(A)*
b it is/is it *(A, B, C)*

c *Omitted (E)*

" '*The Epidendrum Flos Aeris*,[28] of Java, bears a very beautiful flower, and will live when pulled up by the roots. The natives suspend it by a cord from the ceiling, and enjoy its fragrance for years.' That's capital! That will do for the similes. Now for the Piquant Expressions.

"PIQUANT EXPRESSIONS. '*The venerable Chinese novel Ju-Kiao-Li.*'[29] Good! By introducing these few words with dexterity you will evince your intimate[d] acquaintance with the language and literature of the Chinese. With the aid of this you may possibly get along without either Arabic, or Sanscrit, or Chickasaw. There is no passing muster, however, without[e] Spanish, Italian, German, Latin, and Greek. I must look you out a little specimen of each. Any scrap will answer, because you must depend upon your own ingenuity to make it fit into your article. Now write!

" '*Aussi tendre que Zaïre*'[f] — as tender as Zaire — French. Alludes to the frequent repetition of the phrase, *la tendre Zaïre*,[g] in the French tragedy of that name.[30] Properly introduced, will show not only your knowledge of the language, but your[h] general reading and wit. You can say, for instance, that the chicken you were eating (write an article about being choked to death by a chicken-bone) was not altogether *aussi tendre que Zaïre*.[i] Write!

> '*Ven,*[j] *muerte tan escondida,*
> *Que no te sienta venir,*
> *Porque el plazer del morir*
> *No me torne a dar la vida.*'

That's Spanish — from Miguel de Cervantes.[31] 'Come quickly O death! but be sure and don't let me see you coming, lest the pleasure I shall feel at your appearance should unfortunately bring me back again to life.' This you may slip in quite *à propos* when you are struggling in the last agonies with the chicken-bone. Write!

> '*Il pover 'huomo che non se'n era accorto,*
> *Andava combattendo, e era morto.*'

That's Italian, you perceive, — from Ariosto.[32] It means that a

---

d imtitate *(A) misprint*	h you *(E) misprint*
e without French, *(A, B, C)*	i *Zaire.* *(A, B, C, D, E)*
f *Zaire'* *(A, B, C, D, E)*	j *Van (A, B, C, D, E) misprint,*
g *Zaire,* *(A, B, C, D, E)*	*corrected from original*

great hero, in the heat of combat, not perceiving[k] that he had been fairly killed, continued to fight valiantly, dead as he was. The application of this to your own case is obvious — for I trust, Miss Psyche, that you will not neglect to kick for at least an hour and a half after you have been choked to death by that chicken-bone. Please to write!

> 'Und sterb'ich doch, so[l] sterb'ich denn
> Durch sie — durch sie!'

That's German — from Schiller.[33] 'And if I die, at least I die — for thee — for thee!' Here it is clear that you are apostrophising the *cause* of your disaster, the chicken. Indeed what gentleman (or lady either) of sense, *wouldn't* die, I should like to know, for a well fattened capon of the right Molucca breed, stuffed with capers and mushrooms, and served up in a salad-bowl, with orange-jellies *en mosaïques*.[m] Write! (You can get them that way at Tortoni's,)[34] — Write, if you please!

"Here is a nice little Latin phrase, and rare too, (one can't be too *recherché* or brief in one's Latin, it's getting so common,) — *ignoratio elenchi*.[35] He has committed an *ignoratio elenchi* — that is to say, he has understood the words of your proposition, but not the ideas.[n] The man was *a fool*, you see. Some poor fellow[o] whom you addressed[p] while choking with that chicken-bone, and[q] who therefore didn't precisely understand what you were talking about. Throw the *ignoratio elenchi* in his teeth, and, at once, you have him annihilated. If he dare[r] to reply, you can tell him from Lucan (here it is) that[s] speeches are mere *anemonae*[t] *verborum*, anemone words.[36] The anemone, with great brilliancy, has no smell. Or, if he begin[u] to bluster, you may be down upon him with *insomnia Jovis*, reveries of Jupiter — a phrase which [v]Silius Italicus[v] (see here!) applies to thoughts pompous and inflated.[37] This will be sure and cut him to the heart. He can do nothing but roll over and die. Will you be kind enough to write?

---

k   perceivin *(D) misprint*
l   *no (A, B, C, D, E) corrected from*
original quotation
m   *mosaiques. (A, B); mosäiques. (C, D, E)*
n   idea. *(E)*
o   fellow, you perceive, *(A)*

p   address *(E)*
q   *Omitted (A)*
r   dares *(A, B, C)*
s   that his *(A, B, C)*
t   *anemonoe (B); changed in C*
u   begins *(A, B, C)*
v . . . v   Longinus *(A)*

"In Greek we must have something pretty — from Demosthenes, for example. Ανηρ[w] ο φευγων[x] και παλιν μαχησεται.[y] [Aner o pheugon[z] kai palin makesetai.] There is a tolerably good translation of it in Hudibras — [38]

> For he that flies may fight again,
> Which he can never do that's slain.

In a Blackwood article nothing makes so fine a show as your Greek. The very letters have an air of profundity about them. Only observe, madam, the astute[a] look of that Epsilon! That Phi ought certainly to be a bishop![39] Was ever there a smarter fellow than that Omicron? Just twig that Tau! In short, there is[b] nothing like Greek for a genuine sensation-paper. In the present case your application is the most obvious thing in the world. Rap out the sentence, with a huge oath, and by way of *ultimatum,* at the good-for-nothing dunder-headed villain who couldn't understand your plain English in relation to the chicken-bone. He'll take the hint and be off, you may depend upon it."

These were all the instructions Mr. B. could afford me upon the topic in question, but I felt they would be entirely sufficient. I was, at length, able to write a genuine Blackwood article, and determined to do it forthwith. In taking leave of me, Mr. B. made a proposition for the purchase of the paper when written; but as he could [c]offer me only[c] fifty guineas a sheet, I thought it better to let our society have it, than sacrifice it for so paltry[d] a sum. Notwithstanding this niggardly spirit, however, the gentleman showed his consideration for me in all other respects, and indeed treated me with the greatest civility. His parting words made a deep impression upon my heart, and I hope I shall always remember them with gratitude.

"My dear Miss Zenobia," he said, while the[e] tears stood in his eyes, "is there *anything* else I can do to promote the success of your laudable undertaking? Let me reflect! It is just possible that you

w Ανερ *(A, B, D, E) corrected in C
but not followed in later texts*
x φεογων *(A, B, C, D) corrected from E*
y μαχεσεται. *(B, D, E) corrected in C
but not followed in D*
z pheogon *(A, B, C, D) changed to*

follow E
a acute *(A, B, C)*
b there is/there's *(A, B, C)*
c . . . c only offer me *(A, B, C)*
d trivial *(A, B) changed in C*
e *Omitted (A, B, C)*

may not be able, so[f] soon as convenient, to — to — get yourself drowned, or — choked with a chicken-bone, or — or hung, — or — bitten by a — but stay! Now I think me of it, there are a couple of very excellent bull dogs in the yard — fine fellows, I assure you — savage, and all that — indeed just the thing for your money — they'll have you eaten up, *auriculas* and all, in less than five minutes (here's my watch!) — and then only think of the sensations! Here! I say — Tom! — Peter! — Dick, you villain! — let out those" — but as I was really in a great hurry, and had not another moment to spare, I was reluctantly forced to expedite my departure, and accordingly took[g] leave *at once* — somewhat more abruptly, I admit, than strict courtesy would have, otherwise, allowed.

It was my primary object, upon quitting Mr. Blackwood, to get into some immediate difficulty, pursuant to his advice, and with this view I spent the[h] greater part of the day in wandering about Edinburgh, seeking for desperate adventures — adventures adequate to the intensity of my feelings, and adapted to the vast character of the article I intended to write. In this excursion I was attended by my[i] negro-servant Pompey,[40] and my little lap-dog Diana, whom I had brought with me from Philadelphia. It was not, however, until late in the afternoon that I fully succeeded in my arduous undertaking. An important event then happened, of which the following Blackwood article, in the tone heterogeneous, is the substance and result.

A PREDICAMENT.

What chance, good lady, hath bereft you thus? — COMUS.

It was a quiet and still afternoon when I strolled forth in the goodly city of Edina.[41] The confusion and bustle in the streets were terrible. Men were talking. Women were screaming. Children were choking. Pigs were whistling.[42] Carts they rattled. Bulls they bellowed. Cows they lowed. Horses they neighed. Cats they caterwauled. Dogs they danced. *Danced!* Could it then be possible? *Danced!* Alas, thought I, *my* dancing days are over! Thus it is ever.

---

f   as *(A, B, C)*
g   took my *(A, B) changed in C*
h   a *(A, B, C)*
i   one *(E)*

Title: The Scythe of Time *(A, B)*
changed to present title in C
Motto: *First added in C*

What a host of gloomy recollections will ever and anon be awakened in the mind of genius and imaginative contemplation, especially of a genius doomed to the everlasting, and eternal, and continual, and, as one might say, the — *continued* — yes, the *continued and continuous,* bitter, harassing, disturbing, and, if I may be allowed the expression, the *very* disturbing influence of the serene, and godlike, and heavenly, and exalting, and elevated, and purifying effect of what may be rightly termed the[i'] most enviable, the most *truly* enviable — nay! the most benignly beautiful, the most deliciously ethereal, and, as it were, the most *pretty* (if I may use so bold an expression) *thing* (pardon me, gentle reader!) in the world[j] — but I am[k] led away by my feelings. In *such* a mind, I repeat, what a host of recollections are stirred up by a trifle! The dogs danced! *I — I could* not! They frisked — I wept. They capered — I sobbed aloud. Touching circumstances! which cannot fail to bring to the recollection of the classical reader that exquisite passage in relation to the fitness of things, which is to be found in the commencement of the third volume of that admirable and venerable Chinese novel, the *Jo-Go-Slow.*

In my solitary walk through the city I had two humble but faithful companions. Diana, my poodle! sweetest of creatures! She had a quantity of hair over her one eye, and a blue ribband tied fashionably around her neck. Diana was not more than five inches in height, but her head was somewhat bigger than her body, and her tail, being cut off exceedingly close, gave an air of injured innocence to the interesting animal which rendered her a favorite with all.

And Pompey, my negro![l] — sweet Pompey! how shall I ever forget thee? I had taken Pompey's arm. He was three feet in height (I like to be particular) and about seventy, or perhaps eighty, years of age. He had bow-legs and was corpulent. His mouth should not be called small, nor his ears short. His teeth, however, were like pearl, and his large full eyes were deliciously white. Nature had endowed him with no neck, and had placed his ankles (as usual

---

i' he *(D) misprint*   k   am always *(E)*
j   word *(D, E) misprint, corrected*   l   nigger! *(A)*
from *A, B, C*

with that race) in the middle of the upper portion of the feet. He was clad with a striking simplicity. His sole garments were a stock of nine inches in height, and a nearly-new drab overcoat which had formerly been in the service of the tall, stately, and illustrious Dr. Moneypenny. It was a good overcoat. It was well cut. It was well made. The coat was nearly new. Pompey held it up out of the dirt with both hands.

There were three persons in our party, and two of them have already been the subject of remark. There was a third — that third person was myself. I am the Signora[m] Psyche Zenobia. I am *not* Suky Snobbs. My appearance is commanding. On the memorable occasion of which I speak I was habited in a crimson satin dress with a sky-blue Arabian mantelet. And the dress had trimmings of green agraffas, and seven graceful flounces of the orange colored auricula. I thus formed the third of the party. There was the poodle. There was Pompey. There was myself. We were *three*. Thus it is said there were originally but three Furies — Melty, Nimmy and Hetty — Meditation, Memory, and Fiddling.[n]

Leaning upon the arm of the gallant Pompey, and attended at a respectful distance by Diana, I proceeded down one of the populous and very pleasant streets of the now deserted Edina. On a sudden, there presented itself to view a church — a Gothic cathedral — vast, venerable, and with a tall steeple, which towered into the sky. What madness now possessed me? Why did I rush upon my fate? I was seized with an uncontrollable desire to ascend the giddy pinnacle, and thence survey the immense extent of the city.[43] The door of the cathedral stood invitingly open. My destiny prevailed. I entered the ominous archway. Where then was my guardian angel? — if indeed such angels there be. *If!* Distressing monosyllable! what a world of mystery, and meaning, and doubt, and uncertainty is there involved in thy two letters! I entered the ominous archway! I entered; and, without injury to my orange-colored auriculas, I passed beneath the portal, and emerged within the vestibule! Thus it is said the immense river Alfred[o] passed, unscathed, and unwetted, beneath the sea.

---

m   Seignora *(E) misprint*   o   Alceus *(A, B, C)*
n   Singing. *(A, B, C)*

I thought the staircases would never have an end. *Round!* Yes, they went round and up, and round and up and round and up, until I could not help surmising, with the sagacious Pompey, upon whose supporting arm I leaned in all the confidence of early affection — I *could* not help surmising that the upper end of the continuous spiral ladder had been accidentally, or perhaps designedly, removed. I paused for breath; and, in the meantime, an incident occurred of too momentous a nature in a moral, and also in a metaphysical point of view, to be passed over without notice. It appeared to me — indeed I was quite confident of the fact — I could not be mistaken — no! I had, for some moments, carefully and anxiously observed the motions of my Diana — I say that *I could not be* mistaken — Diana *smelt a rat!* At once I[p] called Pompey's attention to the subject, and he — he agreed with me. There was then no longer any reasonable room for doubt. The rat had been smelled — and by Diana. Heavens! shall I ever forget the intense excitement of that moment? Alas! what is the boasted intellect of man? The rat! — it was there — that is to say, it was somewhere. Diana smelled the rat. *I* — I *could* not! Thus it is said the Prussian Isis has, for some persons, a sweet and very powerful perfume, while to others it is perfectly scentless.

The staircase had been surmounted, and there were now only three or four more upward steps intervening between us and the summit. We still ascended, and now only one step remained. One step! One little, little step! Upon one such little step in the great staircase of human life how vast a sum of human happiness or misery often depends! I thought of myself, then[q] of Pompey, and then of the mysterious and inexplicable destiny which surrounded us. I thought of Pompey! — alas, I thought of love! I thought of the many false *steps* which have been taken, and may be taken again. I resolved to be more cautious, more reserved. I abandoned the arm of Pompey, and, without his assistance, surmounted the one remaining step, and gained the chamber of the belfry. I was followed immediately afterwards by my poodle. Pompey alone remained behind. I stood at the head of the staircase, and

---

p   At once I/I *(A, B, C)*   q   and then *(A, B, C)*

encouraged him to ascend. He stretched forth to me his hand, and unfortunately in so doing was forced to abandon his firm hold upon the overcoat. Will the gods never cease their persecution? The overcoat it dropped, and, with one of his feet, Pompey stepped upon the long and trailing skirt of the overcoat. He stumbled and fell — this consequence was inevitable. He fell forwards, and, with his accursed head, striking me full in the —— in the breast, precipitated me headlong, together with himself, upon the hard, filthy and[r] detestable floor of the belfry. But my revenge was sure, sudden and complete. Seizing him furiously by the wool with both hands, I tore out a vast quantity of the black, and crisp, and curling material, and tossed it from me with every manifestation of disdain. It fell among the ropes of the belfry and remained. Pompey arose, and said no word. But he regarded me piteously with his large eyes and — sighed. Ye gods — that sigh! It sunk into my heart. And the hair — the wool! Could I have reached that wool I would have bathed it with my tears, in testimony of regret. But alas! it was now far beyond my grasp. As it dangled among the cordage of the bell, I fancied it still alive. I fancied that it stood on end with indignation. Thus the *happy dandy Flos Aeris* of Java, bears, it is said, a beautiful flower, which will live when pulled up by the roots. The natives suspend it by a cord from the ceiling and enjoy its fragrance for years.

Our quarrel was now made up, and we looked about the room for an aperture through which to survey the city of Edina. Windows there were none. The sole light admitted into the gloomy[r'] chamber proceeded from a square opening, about a foot in diameter, at a height of about seven feet from the floor. Yet what will the energy of true genius not effect? I resolved to clamber up to this hole. A vast quantity of wheels, pinions, and other cabalistic-looking machinery stood opposite the hole, close to it; and through the hole there passed an iron rod from the machinery. Between the wheels and the wall where the hole lay, there was barely room for my body — yet I was desperate, and determined to persevere. I called Pompey to my side.

---

r   filthy and/the filthy, the *(A, B, C)*   r'   gloom *(D) misprint*

"You perceive that aperture, Pompey. I wish to look through it. You will stand here just beneath the hole — so. Now, hold out one of your hands, Pompey, and let me step upon it — thus. Now, the other hand, Pompey, and with its aid I will get upon your shoulders."

He did everything I wished, and I found, upon getting up, that I could easily pass my head and neck through the aperture. The prospect was sublime. Nothing could be more magnificent. I merely paused a moment to bid Diana behave herself, and assure Pompey that I would be considerate and bear as lightly as possible upon his shoulders. I told him I would be tender of his feelings — *ossi tender que beefsteak.*[s] Having done this justice to my faithful friend, I gave myself up with great zest and enthusiasm to the enjoyment of the scene which so obligingly spread itself out before my eyes.

Upon this subject, however, I shall forbear to dilate. I will not describe the city of Edinburgh. Every one has been to Edinburgh — the classic Edina. I will confine myself to the momentous details of my own lamentable adventure. Having, in some measure, satisfied my curiosity in regard to the extent, situation, and general appearance of the city, I had leisure to survey the church in which I was, and the delicate architecture of the steeple. I observed that the aperture through which I had thrust my head was an opening in the dial-plate of a gigantic clock, and must have appeared, from the street, as a large keyhole, such as we see in the face of French watches.[44] No doubt the true object was to admit the arm of an attendant, to adjust, when necessary, the hands of the clock from within. I observed also, with surprise, the immense size of these hands, the longest of which could not have been less than ten feet in length, and, where broadest, eight or nine inches in breadth. They were of solid steel apparently, and their edges appeared to be sharp. Having noticed these particulars, and some others, I again turned my eyes upon the glorious prospect below, and soon became absorbed in contemplation.

---

s   *Zaire. (A, B) changed in C which*
has Beefsteak. *without italics*

A BLACKWOOD ARTICLE

From this, after some minutes, I was aroused by the voice of Pompey, who declared he could stand it no longer, and requested that I would be so kind as to come down. This was unreasonable, and I told him so in a speech of some length. He replied, but with an evident misunderstanding of my ideas upon the subject. I accordingly grew angry, and told him in plain words that he was a fool, that he had committed an *ignoramus e-clench-eye,* that his notions were mere *insommary Bovis,* and his words little better than *an enemy-werrybor'em.* With this he appeared satisfied, and I resumed my contemplations.

It might have been half an hour after this[t] altercation[u] when, as I was deeply absorbed in the heavenly scenery beneath me, I was startled by something very cold which pressed with a gentle pressure upon the back of my neck. It is needless to say that I felt inexpressibly alarmed. I knew that Pompey was beneath my feet, and that Diana was sitting, according to my explicit[v] directions, upon her hind legs in the farthest corner of the room. What could it be? Alas! I but too soon discovered. Turning my head gently to one side, I perceived, to my extreme horror, that the huge, glittering, scimetar-like minute-hand of the clock, had, in the course of its hourly revolution, *descended upon my neck.* There was, I knew, not a second to be lost. I pulled back at once — but it was too late. There was no chance of forcing my head through the mouth of that terrible trap in which it was so fairly caught, and which grew narrower and narrower with a rapidity too horrible to be conceived. The agony of that moment is not to be imagined. I threw up my hands and endeavoured, with all my strength, to force upwards[w] the ponderous iron bar. I might as well have tried to lift the cathedral itself. Down, down, down it came, closer, and yet closer. I screamed to Pompey for aid: but he said that I had hurt his feelings by calling him "an ignorant old squint eye." I yelled to Diana; but she only said "bow-wow-wow," and that "I had told her on no account to stir from the corner." Thus I had no relief to expect from my associates.

Meantime the ponderous and terrific *Scythe of Time* (for I

---

t   my *(A)*   v   express *(A)*
u   altercation with Pompey, *(A)*   w   upward *(E)*

now discovered the literal import of that classical phrase) had not stopped, nor was it[x] likely to stop, in its career. Down and still down, it came. It had already buried its sharp edge a full inch in my flesh, and my sensations grew indistinct and confused. At one time I fancied myself in Philadelphia with the stately Dr. Money-penny, at another in the back parlor of Mr. Blackwood receiving his invaluable instructions. And then again the sweet recollection of better and earlier times came over me, and I thought of that happy period when the world was not all a desert, and Pompey not altogether cruel.

The ticking of the machinery amused me. *Amused me,* I say, for my sensations now bordered upon perfect happiness, and the most trifling circumstances afforded me pleasure. The eternal *click-clack, click-clack, click-clack* of the clock was the most melodious of music in my ears, and occasionally even put me in mind of the grateful sermonic harangues of Dr. Ollapod.[y] [45] Then there were the great figures upon the dial-plate — how intelligent, how intellectual, they all looked! And presently they took to dancing the Mazurka,[z] and I think it was the figure V who performed the most to my satisfaction. She was evidently a lady of breeding. None of your swaggerers, and nothing at all indelicate in her motions. She did the pirouette to admiration — whirling round upon her apex. I made an endeavor to hand her a chair, for I saw that she appeared fatigued with her exertions — and it was not until then that I fully perceived my lamentable situation. Lamentable indeed! The bar had buried itself two inches in my neck. I was aroused to a sense of exquisite pain. I prayed for death, and, in the agony of the moment, could not help repeating those exquisite verses of the poet Miguel De Cervantes:

> Vanny Buren, tan escondida
> Query no te senty venny
> Pork and pleasure, delly morry
> Nommy, torny, darry, widdy ![46]

But now a new horror presented itself, and one indeed sufficient to startle the strongest nerves. My eyes, from the cruel pressure

---

x *Omitted (A, B, C)*
y Morphine. *(B, C)*

z Mauzurka, *(D) misprint, corrected from A, B, C, E*

of the machine, were absolutely starting from their sockets. While I was thinking how I should possibly manage without them, one actually tumbled out of my head, and, rolling down the steep side of the steeple, lodged in the rain gutter which ran along the eaves of the main building. The loss of the eye was not so much as the insolent air of independence and contempt with which it regarded me after it was out. There it lay in the gutter just under my nose, and the airs it gave itself would have been ridiculous had they not been disgusting. Such a winking and blinking were never before seen. This behaviour on the part of my eye in the gutter was not only irritating on account of its manifest insolence and shameful ingratitude, but was also exceedingly inconvenient on account of the sympathy which always exists between two eyes of the same head, however far apart. I was forced, in a manner, to wink and to[a] blink, whether I would or not, in exact concert with the scoundrelly thing that lay just under my nose. I was presently relieved, however, by the dropping out of the other eye. In falling it took the same direction (possibly a concerted plot) as its fellow. Both rolled out of the gutter together, and in truth I was very glad to get rid of them.

The bar was now four[b] inches and a half deep in my neck, and there was only a little bit of skin to cut through. My sensations were those of entire happiness, for I felt that in a few minutes, at farthest, I should be relieved from my disagreeable situation. And in this expectation I was not at all deceived. At twenty-five minutes past five in the afternoon precisely, the huge minute-hand had proceeded sufficiently far on its terrible revolution to sever the small remainder of my neck. I was not sorry to see the head which had occasioned me so much embarrassment at length make a final separation from my body. It first rolled down the side of the steeple, then lodged, for a few seconds, in the gutter, and then made its way, with a plunge, into the middle of the street.[47]

I will candidly confess that my feelings were now of the most singular — nay of the most mysterious, the most perplexing and incomprehensible character. My senses were here and there at one and the same moment. With my head I imagined, at one time, that

a   *Omitted (A, B, C)*   b   three *(A, B, C)*

I the head, was the real Signora Psyche Zenobia — at another I felt convinced that myself, the body, was the proper identity. To clear my ideas upon this topic I felt in my pocket for my snuff-box, but, upon getting it, and endeavoring to apply a pinch of its grateful contents in the ordinary manner, I became immediately aware of my peculiar deficiency, and threw the box at once down to my head. It took a pinch with great satisfaction, and smiled me an acknowledgement in return. Shortly afterwards it made me a speech, which I could hear but indistinctly without^c ears. I gathered enough, however, to know that it was astonished at my wishing to remain alive under such circumstances. In the concluding sentences it ^{d}quoted the noble words of Ariosto — ^{d}

Il pover hommy che non sera corty
And have a combat tenty erry morty;^{e}

^{f}thus comparing me to the hero who, in the heat of the combat, not perceiving that he was dead, continued to contest the battle with inextinguishable valor.^{f} There was nothing now to prevent my getting down from my elevation, and I did so. What it was that Pompey saw so *very* peculiar in my appearance I have never yet been able to find out. The fellow opened his mouth from ear to ear, and shut his two eyes as if he were^g endeavoring to crack nuts between the lids. Finally, throwing off his overcoat, he made one spring for the staircase ^{h}and disappeared.^{h} I hurled after the scoundrel those vehement words of Demosthenes —

Andrew O'Phlegethon, you really make haste to fly,

and then turned to the darling of my heart, to the^i one-eyed! the shaggy-haired Diana. Alas! what^j horrible vision affronted my eyes? *Was* that a rat I saw skulking into his hole? *Are* these the picked bones of the little angel who has been cruelly devoured by the

---

c   without my *(A, B, C)*
d . . . d   compared me to the hero in Ariosto, who, in the heat of combat, not perceiving that he was dead, continued to fight valiantly dead as he was. I remember that it used the precise words of the poet: *(A, B, C)*
e   *morty. (A, B, C. D) The punctuation*
of *E is adopted.*
f . . . f   *Omitted (A, B, C)*
g   was *(A, B, C)*
h . . . h   and — I never saw him again. *(A, B, C)*
i   the *cur*-tailed, the *(A, B, C)*
j   what a *(E)*

monster? Ye Gods! and what *do* I ^kbehold — *is*^k that the departed spirit, the shade, the ghost of my beloved puppy, which I perceive sitting with a grace¹ so melancholy,[48] in the corner? Harken! for she speaks, and, heavens! it is the German of Schiller — [49]

> "Unt stubby duk, so stubby dun
> Duk she! duk she!"

Alas! — and are not her words too true?

> And if I died at least I died
> For thee — for thee.

Sweet creature! she *too* has sacrificed herself in my behalf. Dogless! niggerless, headless, what *now* remains for the unhappy Signora Psyche Zenobia? Alas — *nothing!* I have done.

NOTES

Title: Poe as a boy was undoubtedly familiar with *Blackwood's Edinburgh Magazine* (founded 1817), since his foster father dealt in imported books and periodicals as well as other merchandise. Credited with being the first periodical in English to publish stories and poems, *Blackwood's* provided a source for ideas made use of, one way or another, in many of Poe's stories.

Motto: From a speech ascribed to Dr. Johnson's ghost in *Rejected Addresses: or The New Theatrum Poetarum,* an enormously popular book published, at first anonymously, in 1812 by James and Horace Smith: "A swelling opening is too often succeeded by an insignificant conclusion . . . The pious hawkers of Constantinople . . . solemnly perambulate her streets exclaiming, 'In the name of the Prophet — figs!' " Horace Smith, who was the author of the 10th address entitled "Johnson's Ghost" (see Andrew Boyle's edition, London, 1929, for this and other details), wrote other works that influenced Poe. See the introduction and notes to "A Tale of Jerusalem."

1. One suspects Poe had in mind a passage from Sarah Green's *Romance Readers and Romance Writers* (1810), which begins with an account of one Margaret Marsham, who exclaims: "What then? To add to my earthly miseries am I to be called Peggy? My name is Margaritta! I am sure that if I am called Peggy again, I shall go into a fit." The book is not common now, but is the kind of thing Poe might look into. See G. E. Saintsbury, *The English Novel* (1913), p. 179.

2. The use of these terms probably reflects Poe's acquaintance with Godey's *Lady's Book,* which from its first issue had published colored fashion plates and in the issue for January 1834 had published his story "The Visionary."

---

k . . . k   behold? Is — *is (A, B, C)*   l   grace and face *(A, B, C)*

3. Zenobia was a woman of great beauty and intellectual attainments, who could ride, hunt, lead troops and discuss philosophy as well as any man. Upon the death in A.D. 269 or 268 of her husband Odenathus, ruler of Palmyra, who had regained most of Syria from the Persians and restored it to the Roman empire, she became regent. She shortly proclaimed her son (or stepson) Vaballathus emperor, and herself claimed the title of Septimia Zenobia Augusta, which appears on her coinage. She entered into a tenuous alliance with the martial emperor Aurelian but soon attempted to gain independence. Palmyra was besieged and captured, and Zenobia was taken alive. Her courage failed her, and she laid all blame for her revolt on her ministers — one of them Longinus who wrote *On the Sublime* — and they were executed. Her life was spared, and she was taken to Rome and led as a principal captive in Aurelian's triumph — like a slave girl exposed in the market — fettered and manacled in shackles of gold, so heavy that she could hardly carry them. She was then allowed to retire to a villa at Tivoli. There are rumors of her interest in Judaism (rather than Christianity) but St. Zenobius, Bishop of Florence in the time of St. Ambrose, was reputedly her descendant. See Gibbon's *Decline and Fall of the Roman Empire,* Chapter XI. The principal sources are her biography ascribed to Trebellius Pollio and that of Aurelian ascribed to Vopiscus in the *Scriptores Historiae Augustae.* Poe quotes from the latter in "Epimanes" ("Four Beasts in One").

4. In old slang "a Greek" may mean a hard drinker, a gambler, or an Irishman; since the lady's name is not Irish, the reader may choose between the first two meanings.

5. Henry Peter Brougham (1778–1868), prolific publicist, contributor to the *Edinburgh Review* from its first issue, founder of the Society for the Diffusion of Useful Knowledge in 1825, was an outspoken advocate of social causes, and was Lord Chancellor of England from 1830 to 1834. His *Discourses of Natural Theology* (1835), as well as his vigorous polemics on social and political questions, occasioned much controversy in the press.

6. Compare Fielding's *Tom Jones,* IV, iv, for "the eternal fitness of things," a phrase traced to the ethical theory of Samuel Clarke (1675–1729).

7. Poe often puns on the philosopher Kant and cant. He may well have seen a detailed discussion, "Kant in His Miscellaneous Essays," in *Blackwood's* for August 1830.

8. The *Times* and *Examiner* referred to are the London papers.

9. M. M. Mathews, *A Dictionary of Americanisms* (2 v., Chicago, 1951), defines "slang-whang" as abusive or ranting utterance. *The American Dictionary of Slang* (1967) says it came into use in 1834. John Gully (1783–1863) was a prizefighter who later became a Member of Parliament.

10. The articles mentioned by Mr. Blackwood are genuine, though not all of them appeared in his magazine; most were identified by Lucille King, "Notes on Poe's Sources" (1930).

11. "The Dead Alive" was found by A. H. Quinn *(Poe,* p. 272) in *Fraser's Magazine,* April 1834, but the story outlined comes from "The Buried Alive," published in *Blackwood's,* October 1821, and is used in Poe's "Premature Burial."

12. *Confessions of an English Opium Eater* appeared in the *London Magazine,* beginning in October 1821, and as a book in 1822. The author was Thomas DeQuincey. Poe referred to it in a letter to Thomas W. White, April 30, 1835, and obviously considered it a work of fiction. (Mr. Blackwood's baboon is well named, for Hollands is gin, which is flavored with juniper berries.)

13. "The Involuntary Experimentalist," about a man repairing a boiler which began to be heated, was in *Blackwood's,* October 1837.

14. *Passages from the Diary of a Late Physician* by Samuel Warren began as a serial in *Blackwood's* for August 1830 and later became very popular in book form. The success of the two volumes issued in 1832 led to further chapters, published irregularly in *Blackwood's* and gathered in a third volume with the fifth edition in 1837. Poe discussed the *Diary* when reviewing Warren's *Ten Thousand a Year* in *Graham's* for November 1841.

15. "The Man in the Bell," *Blackwood's,* November 1821, was also mentioned in Poe's letter of April 30, 1835 to White; and probably influenced "The Devil in the Belfry" and the last stanza of "The Bells." The author, "Thomas Mann," was really William Maginn.

16. Poe often quotes "Truth is stranger than fiction" from Byron's *Don Juan,* XIV, ci, 1-2: " 'Tis strange, — but true; for truth is always strange;/ Stranger than fiction."

17. Brandreth's Pills are mentioned also in "Some Words with a Mummy." They were said to remove "acrimonious humors," which the makers regarded as the source of almost all ills of the flesh. "Innocent as bread," they sold for twenty-five cents a box. In the earliest version of the story the reference was to Morrison's Pills, a "Hygeian Vegetable Universal Medicine." This was an English remedy, but also made and sold in this country from 1831. The American proprietor was H. Shepheard Moat. Both nostrums were very widely advertised; this note is based on the columns of a single newspaper, the New York *Sunday Mercury,* April 14, 1844. For other references to these remedies, see "Marginalia," number 212, *SLM,* April 1849, p. 222.

18. The schools are named also in "Bon-Bon." Archytas of Tarentum was a Pythagorean contemporary of Plato, discussed in Book VIII of Diogenes Laertius. Gorgias of Leontini in Sicily long resided at Athens; he was a Sophist and wrote "On Nature, or the Non-Existent." His style was flamboyant in the extreme; he is mentioned again in "The Man of the Crowd." Alcmaeon of Croton was a very minor pupil of Pythagoras, briefly noted by Diogenes Laertius in his Book VIII. Poe mentioned him again in *Eureka.*

19. John Locke is mentioned several times in Poe's tales; here, doubtless, because his *Logic* would repel mystical ideas.

20. The "Critique of Pure Reason" (1781) and "Metaphysical Foundations of Natural Science" (1786) by Immanuel Kant.

21. The *Dial,* 1840–1844, was the chief organ of the Transcendentalists; the editors were successively Margaret Fuller and Emerson. Reference to it first appeared in Poe's story in 1845; the earlier texts refer to Goethe's famous roman-

tic novel or to Coleridge's *Table Talk* (1835) compiled by Henry Nelson Coleridge.

22. *Poems* (1842) by the younger William Ellery Channing was unfavorably reviewed by Poe in *Graham's* for August 1843. The quotation here is somewhat garbled from Channing's "Thoughts": "Thou meetest a common man,/With a delusive show of *can*." Channing, who later dropped his first name, is still well known as the most eccentric of Emerson's friends.

23. Two represents strife and was made the symbol of evil by Pythagoras; compare our expression "the deuce."

24. There is a similar comment on the avoidance of the simplicity of "bread-and-butter" in Poe's review of Richard Henry (later Hengist) Horne's *Orion* in *Graham's* for March 1844.

25. The original three muses' names are traced to Varro, quoted by Servius, in his Commentary on Vergil's *Eclogue* VII, 19–21.

26. On Alpheus see Pomponius Mela, *De Situ Orbis,* II, 7. The story was that the river went underground in the Peloponnesus and rose in Sicily, at the fountain Arethusa.

27. *Iris persica,* a low-growing bulbous iris, notably fragrant, now more frequently found in greenhouses than in gardens.

28. The Epidendron is a kind of orchid. Poe probably took it from Patrick Keith's *System of Physiological Botany* (London, 1816), II, 429, which credits Willdenow. He used it again in "The Thousand-and-Second Tale," where another botanical item is credited to Keith.

29. The Chinese novel *Ju-Kiao-Li or the Two Fair Cousins* (London, 1827) was translated from a French version by M. Abel-Rémusat (Paris, 1826). Poe probably learned of it from Philip Pendleton Cooke's "Leaves from my Scrapbook," part III (*SLM* April 1836, p. 314).

30. Voltaire's tragedy *Zaïre* has no connection with the river Zaire of "Silence — a Fable," which is the Congo.

31. The Spanish verses, which have been ascribed to the Valencian Escrivá, are quoted by Cervantes in *Don Quixote,* II, xxxviii; Professor E. C. Hills told me they have been traced to 1511. See Poe's "Pinakidia," number 112, *SLM,* August 1836. [Edgar C. Knowlton, Jr., in *Poe Studies,* December 1971, has identified Father Dominique Bouhours as Poe's immediate source for a number of items in "Pinakidia," including the stanza quoted here. In the first edition (Paris, 1687) of his work *La Manière de bien penser dans les ouvrages d'esprit,* Bouhours spells the first word of the stanza, *Ven,* correctly while all Poe's authorized texts show the incorrect spelling, *Van* — possibly originally a typographical error; otherwise, however, except for substituting a comma for Bouhours' semicolon in the second line, Poe's text given here follows the spelling and punctuation of Bouhours' first edition. Bouhours was widely influential in the eighteenth century — in *Fraser's Magazine* for September 1834, p. 319, "Father Prout" asks, "Who can pretend to the character of a literary man that has not read ... Bouhours on *La Mannière de bien penser.* . . . ?"]

A BLACKWOOD ARTICLE

32. The Italian lines are *not* by Ariosto, to whom, both here and in "Pina-kidia," number 102 (*SLM*, August 1836, p. 579), Poe ascribes them. [Here again Poe's source is Bouhours; see Knowlton's article, cited above. Again, Bouhours' spelling and punctuation (in his first edition) are followed, except that his amper-sand in the second line is rendered by a simple *e* in all Poe's authorized texts. As Mr. Knowlton points out, John Hoole, in the preface to his eighteenth-century translation of Ariosto's *Orlando Furioso*, traces the couplet to faulty recollection of lines in Berni's version of Bojardo's *Orlando Innamorato*. Hoole quotes, with a translation, the entire stanza (II, xxiv, 60) describing Orlando's "wonderful stroke" which

"sever'd with such art the Pagan foe
(That) the fierce knight, with vigour yet unbroke,
Fought on, though dead, unconscious of the stroke."]

33. The German lines are not from Schiller, but are adapted from Goethe's ballad "Das Veilchen," which was quoted in George Bancroft's "Life and Genius of Goethe" in the *North American Review*, October 1824. Poe quoted them correctly, with a correct ascription, though with a modified translation, as a motto to "The Visionary"; see the notes on that tale, above.

34. Tortoni's was a famous restaurant on the Boulevard des Italiens in Paris; there was also a restaurant of the name in New York. The dish mentioned is also named in "Bon-Bon."

35. *Ignoratio elenchi* is the fallacy of irrelevant conclusion; the arguer seeks to gain his point by diverting attention to something extraneous. See John Stuart Mill, *System of Logic*, V, vii.

36. The phrase *anemonae verborum* is not in Lucan, but, as Miss Emma Katherine Norman (*AL*, March 1934) points out, it is a Latin translation of a phrase in Lucian's *Lexiphanes*, section 23. It is given as Lucian's in a filler in the *Southern Literary Messenger*, April 1836.

37. The phrase ascribed to him is not in Silius Italicus, but is from a Latin version of Longinus, the ninth section (IX.14), of *On the Sublime*. See "Pina-kidia," number 108 (*SLM*, August 1836, p. 579), where, as in the earliest version of his story, Poe gave the right ascription.

38. The Greek line is really one of the *Monosticha* of Menander preserved by Aulus Gellius (*The Attic Nights*, III, 282, in the Loeb edition), but Francis Bacon in *Apophthegms*, number 169, ascribed it to Demosthenes. See *The Works of Francis Bacon*, ed. Spedding, Ellis, Heath (London: Longmans, 1870), vol. VII, p. 118. The "tolerably good translation" is slightly misquoted from Butler's *Hudibras*, III, iii. Poe had used both the Greek and the translation in "Pinakidia," number 94 (*SLM*, August 1836, p. 578).

39. The Greek letter *phi* remotely resembles a chess bishop. Dionysius of Halicarnassus in the fourteenth chapter of *De Compositione Verborum* discussed the beauty of certain letters of the alphabet.

40. A Negro servant in "The Man that was Used Up" is also named Pompey, as is a dog in "The Business Man."

A PREDICAMENT

Title: The title of the early versions is, of course, a commonplace, but Poe may have remembered "The Scythe of Time mows down" from *Paradise Lost,* X, 606.

Motto: Milton, *Comus,* line 277.

41. Edina is Edinburgh.

42. The inn sign of the Pig and Whistle was common.

43. The idea of viewing a city from a steeple is also considered in "Loss of Breath." Hawthorne's "Sights from a Steeple," which appeared in *The Token for 1831,* may be an inspiration for the tale, but Miss Snobbs lived in Philadelphia where it was a custom for sightseers to go into the belfry of Independence Hall.

44. Compare the importance of a key-hole in "The Angel of the Odd."

45. Dr. Ollapod is a character in *The Poor Gentleman,* a farce by George Colman the Younger. The part was sometimes played by William E. Burton, and in the version of Poe's story published when Poe was working for Burton, the name was changed to Dr. Morphine — suggesting the soporific effect of the parson's sermons. Ollapod, an abbreviated form of "olla podrida," primarily means a stew, but is figuratively used for any mixture, such as a literary miscellany. Willis Gaylord Clark began a series in 1835 called "Ollapodiana" for the *Knickerbocker Magazine* edited by his twin brother Lewis. It is barely possible that in the name Ollapod contemporaries might have seen a slighting allusion to the Clarks, as was suggested by Professor William Whipple (*AL,* November 1957).

46. "Pork and pleasure" recalls Dr. Johnson's famous line in his poem on "A Lady coming of Age": "Pride and pleasure, pomp and plenty." Pork in the sense of politician's plunder seems not to have been used so early as the time of Jackson and Van Buren.

47. Compare the fate of Toby Dammit in "Never Bet the Devil Your Head."

48. Note the rhyme in the canceled passage, "grace and face."

49. See text at note 33 and that note, above.

THE DEVIL IN THE BELFRY

This is one of the better grotesques. On the surface it is an extravaganza — Poe called it that in the first publication — a bit of harmless buffoonery, unmarred by repulsive elements, It obviously makes fun of the weighty German scholarship of the time. Yet it has an undercurrent of thought; the effects of discords on the sensitive listener were serious matters for Poe, who was to rework the ending of this story in the final stanza of "The Bells."

The sources from which Poe drew the materials of the farrago have now been rather completely identified. He combined familiar elements of *diablerie* from his minor contemporaries with a curious fancy of Thomas Carlyle, whose *Sartor Resartus* was first published in *Fraser's Magazine* between November 1833 and August 1834.

In Book II, chapter IX, Professor Teufelsdröckh is quoted:

Beautiful it was to sit there, as in my Skyey Tent, musing and meditating; on the high table-land, in front of the Mountains...And then to fancy...the straw-roofed Cottages, wherein stood many a Mother baking bread, with her children round her: — all hidden and protectingly folded up in the valley-folds; yet there and alive, as sure as if I beheld them. Or to see, as well as fancy, the nine Towns and Villages, that lay round my mountain-seat, which, in still weather, were wont to speak to me (by their steeple-bells) with metal tongue; and, in almost all weather, proclaimed their vitality by repeated Smoke-clouds; whereon, as in a culinary horologe, I might read the hour of the day. For it was the smoke of cookery, as kind housewives, at morning, midday, eventide, were boiling their husbands' kettles; and ever a blue pillar rose up into the air, successively or simultaneously, from each of the nine, saying, as plainly as smoke could say: Such and such a meal is getting ready here. Not uninteresting! For you have the whole Borough, with all its love-makings and scandal-mongeries, contentions and contentments, as in miniature, and could cover it all with your hat.*

There are other analogies in a story by Dr. Robert Macnish in *Blackwood's*, October 1826, called "The Barber of Gottingen," where the devil compelled a college barber to shave him, ascended into a high tower, and pulled somebody's nose.† A more serious and remote source may be in "The Man in the Bell" by William Maginn in *Blackwood's*, November 1821, where the hero, shut in a tower and made delirious by the chimes, fancies he sees demons in the belfry. Poe mentioned Maginn's story in a letter to Thomas W. White, April 30, 1835.

As a locale Poe chose a sleepy town of phlegmatic Pennsylvania

* *Fraser's*, August 1834, p. 499. The first edition as a book was published at Boston in 1836, with an unsigned introduction by Ralph Waldo Emerson. Poe mentions reading *Sartor Resartus* in "Marginalia," number 135 (*Godey's*, September 1845, p. 120).
† See Morton, *Builder of the Beautiful*, p. 39.

Dutchmen to be plagued by his mischievous goblin. The local inhabitants are clearly Pennsylvanians of German ancestry, but they are very like the New York Dutchmen (whose ancestors came from Holland) of Washington Irving and the lesser Knicker-bockers.‡

Jean-Paul Weber has pointed out with what detail Poe worked out what may be called the pictorial allegory of his story.§ The whole village is built like a clock, surrounded by the hills as a case. There are sixty houses, like the minutes of an hour. Each home has twenty-four cabbages, like the hours of a day. The seven faces of the great clock are like the days of a week. The un-welcome visitor's large hat and tight garments make him flared at the top, like a minute hand, and at noon he covers up the slowly moving hour hand in the person of the shorter, rotund belfry-man.

The late Professor Carl Schreiber told me he thought the story satirized an excessive emphasis laid on punctuality in Philadelphia. There is reason to think that it was specifically written for its original publication in the Philadelphia *Saturday Chronicle and Mirror of the Times,* May 18, 1839. The number, the first of the fourth volume, has contributions from a good many local men of letters, including Charles West Thomson and John Stevenson Du Solle; and the latter dated his poem "Melancholy" May 14, 1839, which suggests he wrote it by invitation.

TEXTS

(A) Philadelphia *Saturday Chronicle and Mirror of the Times,* May 18, 1839; *(B) Tales of the Grotesque and Arabesque* (1840), I, 157–169; *(C)* the Pedder copy of the last with one manuscript change; *(D)* PHANTASY-PIECES, with manuscript revisions, 1842; *(E) Broadway Journal,* November 8, 1845 (2:271–273); *(F) Works* (1850), II, 383–391.

Griswold's text *(F),* showing one change, is adopted. The unique file of the *Saturday Chronicle (A)* is in the Boston Public Library. The copy of the *Tales of the Grotesque and Arabesque,* inscribed "For Miss Ann and Miss Bessie

‡ "The devil among the Dutchmen" was used as if it was a byword by Poe's friend Lambert A. Wilmer in *Our Press Gang* (1860), p. 387.

§ Weber's essay in *La Nouvelle Revue Française* (August 1958) was translated by Claude Richard and Robert Regan in the latter's *Poe, a Collection of Critical Essays* (1967), p. 80ff.

THE DEVIL IN THE BELFRY

Pedder, from their most sincere friend, The Author," is in the Widener Collection at Harvard.

A footnote was added in the Pedder copy *(C)* and a variation of it in PHANTASY-PIECES *(D)*, but later texts did not adopt either form. Of the four verbal changes made by Poe in *(D)*, three were adopted in later texts, but the eleven punctuation changes were all followed. Among these, five commas were added, two dashes were changed to commas, two colons became dashes, and a comma and a dash were changed to semicolons.

THE DEVIL IN THE BELFRY. [*F*]

What o'clock is it? — *Old Saying.*

Everybody knows, in a general way, that the finest place in the world is — or, alas, *was* — the Dutch borough of Vondervotteimittiss.[a] Yet, as it lies some distance from any of the main roads, being in a somewhat out-of-the-way situation, there are, perhaps, very few of my readers who have ever paid it a visit. For the benefit of those who have *not,* therefore, it will be only proper that I should enter into some account of it. And this is, indeed, the more necessary,[b] as with the hope of enlisting public sympathy in behalf of the inhabitants, I design here to give a history[c] of the calamitous events which have so lately occurred within its[d] limits. No one who knows me will doubt that the duty thus self-imposed will be executed to the best of my ability, with all that rigid impartiality, all that cautious examination into facts, and diligent collation of authorities, which should ever distinguish him who aspires to the title of historian.

By the united aid of medals, manuscripts, and inscriptions, I am enabled to say, positively, that the borough of Vondervotteimittiss has existed, from its origin, in precisely the same condition which it at present preserves.[1] Of the date of this origin, however, I grieve that I can only speak with that species of indefinite definiteness[e] which mathematicians are, at times, forced to put up with in certain algebraic formulæ. The date, I may thus say, in regard

---

Title: The Devil in the Belfry. An Extravaganza. *(A)*
a *Here is added as a footnote:* Qr "Vonder vaat time it is." *(C);* Quaere — Wonder what time it is? *Devil. (D)*

b evident, *(A, B, C, D)*
c history *in petto (A)*
d the *(A, B, C, D)*
e definitiveness *(A, B, C, D)*

to the remoteness of its antiquity, cannot be less than any assignable quantity whatsoever.

Touching the derivation of the name Vondervotteimittiss, I confess myself, with sorrow, equally at fault. Among a multitude of opinions upon this delicate point — some acute, some learned, some sufficiently the reverse — I am able to select nothing which ought to be considered satisfactory.[f] Perhaps the idea of Grogswigg — nearly coincident with that of Kroutaplenttey — is to be cautiously preferred: — It runs: — *"Vondervotteimittiss — Vonder, lege Donder—Votteimittiss, quasi und Bleitziz — Bleitziz obsol: pro Blitzen."* This derivation, to say the truth, is still countenanced by some traces of the electric fluid evident on the summit of the steeple of the House of the Town-Council. I do not choose, however, to commit myself on a theme of such importance, and must refer the reader desirous of[g] information, to the *"Oratiunculæ*[h] *de Rebus Præter-Veteris,"*[i] of Dundergutz. See, also, Blunderbuzzard *"De Derivationibus,"* pp. 27 to 5010, Folio, Gothic edit., Red and Black character, Catch-word and No Cypher; — wherein consult, also, marginal notes in the autograph of Stuffundpuff, with the Sub-Commentaries of Gruntundguzzell.[2]

Notwithstanding the obscurity which thus envelops[j] the date of the foundation of Vondervotteimittiss, and the derivation of its name, there can be no doubt, as I said before, that it has always existed as we find it at this epoch. The oldest man in the borough can remember not the slightest difference in the appearance of any portion of it; and, indeed, the very suggestion of such a possibility is considered an insult. The site of the village is in a perfectly circular valley, about[k] a quarter of a mile in circumference, and entirely surrounded by gentle hills, over whose summit the people have never yet ventured to pass. For this they assign the very good reason that they do not believe there is anything at all on the other side.

Round the skirts of the valley, (which is quite level, and paved throughout with flat tiles,) extends a continuous row of sixty little

---

f   satisfacory. *(A) misprint*
g   of further *(A, B, C, D)*
h   *Oratiunculæ (F) corrected from*
A, B, C, D, E
i   *Præter-Veteris," (F) corrected from*

A, B, C, D, E
j   envelopes *(F) misprint, corrected*
from A, B, C, D, E
k   of about *(A, B, C, D)*

houses. These, having their backs on[1] the hills, must look, of course, to the centre of the plain, which is just sixty yards from the front door of each dwelling. Every house has a small garden before it, with [m]a circular path,[m] a sun-dial, and twenty-four cabbages. The buildings themselves are[n] so precisely alike, that one can in no manner be distinguished from the other. Owing to the[o] vast antiquity, the style of architecture is somewhat odd, but it[p] is not for that reason the less strikingly picturesque. They are fashioned of hard-burned little bricks,[q] red, with black ends, so that the walls look like [r]a chess-board[r] upon a great scale. The gables are turned to the front, and there are cornices, as big as all the rest of the house, over the eaves and over the main doors. The windows are narrow and deep, with very tiny panes and a great deal of sash. On the roof is a vast quantity of tiles with long curly ears. The wood-work, throughout, is of a dark hue,[s] and there is much carving about it, with but a trifling variety of pattern; for, time out of mind, the carvers of Vondervotteimittiss have never been able to carve more than two objects — a time-piece and a cabbage. But these they do exceedingly[t] well, and intersperse them, with singular ingenuity, wherever they find room for the chisel.

The dwellings are as much alike inside as out, and the furniture is all upon one plan. The floors are of square tiles, the [u]chairs and tables[u] of black-looking wood with thin crooked legs and puppy feet. The mantel-pieces are wide and high, and have not only time-pieces and cabbages sculptured over the front, but a real time-piece, which makes a prodigious [v]ticking, on the[v] top in the middle, with a flower-pot containing a cabbage standing on each extremity by way of outrider. Between each cabbage and the time-piece, again, is a little China man having a [w]large stomach[w] with a great round hole in it, through which is seen the dial-plate of a watch.

The fire-places are large and deep, with fierce crooked-looking

---

1   to (A)

m . . . m   circular paths, (A, B, C, D)

n   are all (A, B, C, D)

o   their (A, B, C, D)

p   Omitted (A, B, C, D)

q   brick, (A)

r . . . r   chess-boards (A, B, C, D)

s   a dark hue,/dingy oak, (A)

t   excellently (A, B, C, D)

u . . . u   tables and chairs (A, B, C, D)

v . . . v   tickling, on (A, B, C, D)

w . . . w   big belly (A, B, C, D)

fire-dogs. There is constantly a rousing fire, and a huge pot over it, full of sauer-kraut and pork, to which the good woman of the house is always busy in attending. She is a little fat old lady, with blue eyes and a red face, and wears a huge^x cap like a sugar-loaf, ornamented with purple and yellow ribbons. Her dress is of orange-colored linsey-woolsey, made very full behind and very short in the waist — and indeed very short in other respects, not reaching below the middle^y of her leg. This is somewhat thick, and so are her ankles, but she has a fine pair of green stockings^z to cover them. Her shoes — of pink leather — are fastened each with a bunch of yellow ribbons puckered up in the shape of a cabbage. In her left hand she has a little heavy Dutch watch; in her right she wields a ladle for the sauer-kraut and pork. By her side there stands a fat tabby cat, with a gilt toy repeater³ tied to its tail, which "the boys" have there fastened by way of a quiz.

The boys themselves are, all three of them, in the garden attending the pig. They are each two feet in height. They have three-cornered cocked hats, purple waistcoats reaching down to their thighs, buckskin knee-breeches, red woollen stockings, heavy shoes with big silver buckles, and long surtout^a coats with large buttons of mother-of-pearl. Each, too, has a pipe in his mouth, and a ^blittle dumpy^b watch in his right hand. He takes a puff and a look, and then a look and a puff. The pig — which is corpulent and lazy — is occupied now in picking up the stray leaves that fall from the cabbages, and now in giving a kick behind at the gilt repeater, which the urchins have also tied to *his* tail, in order to make him look as handsome as the cat.

Right at the front door, in a high-backed leather-bottomed armed chair, with crooked legs and puppy feet like the tables, is seated the old man of the house himself. He is an exceedingly puffy little old gentleman, with big circular eyes and a huge double chin. His dress resembles that of the boys — and I need say nothing farther about it. All the difference is, that his pipe is somewhat bigger than theirs, and he can make a greater smoke. Like them,

---

x   high *(A)*
y   middle of the calf *(A, B, C, D)*
z   stocking *(A) misprint*

a   surtouts *(A) misprint*
b . . . b   dumpy little *(A, B, C, D)*

he has a watch, but he carries his[c] watch in his pocket. To say the truth, he has something of more importance than a watch to attend to — and what that is, I shall presently explain. He sits with his right leg upon his left knee, wears a grave countenance, and always keeps one of his eyes, at least, resolutely bent upon a certain remarkable object in[d] the centre of the plain.

This object is situated in the steeple of the House of the Town-Council. The Town-Council are all very little, round, oily,[e] intelligent men, with big saucer eyes and fat double chins, and have their coats much longer and their shoe-buckles much bigger than the ordinary inhabitants of Vondervotteimittiss. Since my sojourn in the borough, they have had several special meetings, and have adopted these[f] three important resolutions: —

"That it is wrong to alter the good old course of things:"

"That there is nothing tolerable out of Vondervotteimittiss:" and —

"That we will stick by our clocks and our cabbages."

Above the session-room of the Council is the steeple, and in the steeple is the belfry, where exists, and has existed time out of mind, the pride and wonder of the village — the great clock of the borough of Vondervotteimittiss. And this is the object to which the eyes of[g] the old gentlemen are turned who sit in the leather-bottomed arm chairs.

The great clock has seven faces — one in each of the seven sides of the steeple[h] — so that it can be readily seen from all quarters. Its faces are large and white, and its hands heavy and black. There is a belfry-man whose sole duty is to attend to[i] it; but this duty is the most perfect of sinecures — for the clock of Vondervotteimittiss was never yet known to have anything the matter with it. Until lately, the bare supposition of such a thing was considered heretical. From the remotest period[j] of antiquity to which the archives[k] have reference, the hours have been regularly struck by the big

c that (A, B, C, D)
d is (A) misprint
e Omitted (A, B, C, D)
f the (A, B, C, D)
g of all (A, B, C, D)

h steeples (E, F) misprint, corrected from A, B, C, D
i Omitted (A, B, C, D)
j periods (A)
k archieves (A) misprint

bell. And, indeed, the case was[1] just the same with all the other clocks and watches in the borough. Never was such a place for keeping the true time. When the large clapper thought proper to say "Twelve o'clock!" all its obedient followers opened their throats simultaneously,[m] and responded like a very echo. In short, the good burghers were fond of their sauer-kraut, but then they were proud of their clocks.

All people who hold sinecure offices are held in more or less respect, and as the belfry-man of Vondervotteimittiss has the most perfect of sinecures, he is the most perfectly respected of any man in the world. He is the chief dignitary of the borough, and the very pigs look up to him with a sentiment of reverence. His coat-tail is *very* far longer — his pipe, his shoe-buckles, his eyes, and his stomach,[n] *very* far bigger — than those of any other[o] old gentleman in the village; and as to his chin, it is not only double, but triple.

I have thus painted the happy estate of Vondervotteimittiss: alas, that so fair a picture should ever experience a reverse!

There has been long a saying among the wisest inhabitants,[p] that "no good can come from over the hills;" and it really seemed that the words had in them something of the spirit of prophecy. It wanted five minutes of noon, on the day before yesterday, when there appeared a very odd-looking object on the summit of the ridge to the eastward. Such an occurrence, of course, attracted universal attention, and every little old gentleman who sat in a leather-bottomed arm-chair, turned one of his eyes with a stare of dismay upon the phenomenon, still keeping the other upon the clock in the steeple.

By the time that it wanted only three minutes to[q] noon, the droll object in question was[r] perceived to be a very diminutive foreign-looking young man. He descended the hills at a great rate, so that everybody had soon a good look at him. He was really the most finnicky little personage that had ever been seen in Vondervotteimittiss. His countenance was of a dark snuff-color, and he

---

l is *(A, B, C, D)*
m simultaneouly, *(A) misprint*
n belly, *(A, B, C, D)*
o *Omitted (A, B, C, D)*

p inhabitans *(A) misprint*
q of *(A, B, C, D)*
r was clearly *(A, B, C, D)*

had a long hooked nose, pea eyes, a wide mouth, and an excellent set of teeth, which latter he seemed anxious of displaying, as he was grinning from ear to ear. What with mustachios[s] and whiskers, there was none of the rest of his face to be seen. His head was uncovered, and his hair neatly done up in *papillotes.* His dress was a tight-fitting swallow-tailed black coat, (from one of whose pockets dangled[t] a vast length of white handkerchief,) black kerseymere knee-breeches, black[u] stockings,[v] and stumpy-looking pumps, with huge bunches of black satin ribbon for bows. Under one arm he carried a huge *chapeau-de-bras,* and under the other a fiddle nearly five times[w] as big as himself. In his left hand was a gold snuff-box, from which, as he capered down the hill, cutting all manner of fantastical steps, he took snuff incessantly with an air of the greatest possible self-satisfaction. God bless me! — here was a sight for [x]the honest[x] burghers of Vondervotteimittiss![4]

To speak plainly, the fellow had, in spite of his grinning, an audacious and sinister kind of face; and as he curvetted right into the village, the odd[y] stumpy appearance of his pumps excited no little suspicion; and many a burgher who beheld him that day, would have given a trifle for a peep beneath the white cambric handkerchief which hung[z] so obtrusively from the pocket of his swallow-tailed coat. But what mainly occasioned a righteous indignation was, that [a]the scoundrelly popinjay,[a] while he cut a fandango here, and a whirligig there, did not seem to have the remotest idea in the world of such a thing as *keeping time* in his steps.

The good people of the borough had scarcely a chance, however, to get their eyes thoroughly open, when, just as it wanted half a minute of noon, the[b] rascal bounced, as I say, right into the midst of them; gave a *chassez*[c] here, and a *balancez* there; and then, after a *pirouette* and a *pas-de-zéphyr,*[d] [5] pigeon-winged himself

---

s moustaches *(B, C);* mustachios [*again*] *(D)*
t dandled *(A)*
u black silk *(A, B, C, D)*
v stocking, *(A) misprint*
w time *(A) misprint*
x . . . x the eyes of the sober *(A, B,*

C, D)*
y old *(A) misprint*
z dandled *(A)*
a . . . a *Canceled (D)*
b the little *(A)*
c *chazzer (A, B, C) changed in D*
d *pas-de-zepher, (A, B, C, D, E, F)*

right up into the belfry of the House of the Town-Council, where the wonder-stricken belfry-man sat smoking in a state of[e] dignity and dismay. But the little chap seized him at once by the nose; gave it a swing and a pull; clapped the big *chapeau-de-bras* upon his head; knocked it down over his eyes and mouth; and then, lifting up the big fiddle, beat him with it so long and so soundly, that what with the belfry-man being so fat, and the fiddle being so hollow, you would have sworn that[f] there was a regiment of double-bass drummers all beating the devil's tattoo up in the belfry of the steeple of Vondervotteimittiss.[6]

There is no knowing to what desperate act of vengeance this unprincipled attack might have aroused the inhabitants, but for the important fact that it now wanted only half a second of noon. The bell was about to strike, and it was a matter of absolute and pre-eminent necessity that every body should look well at [g]his watch.[g] It was evident, however, that just at this moment, the fellow in the steeple was doing something that he had no business to do with the clock. But as it now began to strike, nobody had any time to attend to his manœuvres, for they had all to count the strokes of the bell as it sounded.

"One!" said the clock.

"Von!" echoed every little old gentleman in every leather-bottomed arm-chair in Vondervotteimittiss. "Von!" said his watch also; "von!" said the watch of his vrow, and "von!" said the watches of the boys, and the little gilt repeaters on the tails of the cat and[h] pig.

"Two!" continued the big bell; and

"Doo!" repeated all the repeaters.

"Three! Four! Five! Six! Seven! Eight! Nine! Ten!" said the bell.

"Dree! Vour! Fibe! Sax! Seben! Aight! Noin! Den!" answered the others.

"Eleven!" said the big one.

"Eleben!" assented the little fellows.

"Twelve!" said the bell.

---

e   of stupified *(A, B, C, D)*   g . . . g   their watches. *(A)*
f   *Omitted (A, B, C, D)*   h   and the *(A, B, C, D)*

"Dvelf!"[i] they replied, perfectly satisfied, and dropping their voices.

"Und dvelf[j] it iss!" said all the little old gentlemen, putting up their watches. But the big bell had not done with them yet.

"*Thirteen!*" said he.

"Der Teufel!" gasped the little old gentlemen, turning pale, dropping[k] their pipes, and putting down all their right legs from over their left knees.

"Der Teufel!" groaned they, "Dirteen! Dirteen!! — Mein Gott, [l]it is[l] Dirteen o'clock!!"[7]

[m]Why attempt[m] to describe the terrible scene which ensued? All Vondervotteimittiss flew at once into a lamentable[n] state of uproar.

"Vot is cum'd to mein pelly?" roared all the boys, — "I've been[o] ongry for dis hour!"

"Vot is cum'd to mein kraut?" screamed all the vrows, "It has been done to rags for dis hour!"

"Vot is cum'd to mein pipe?" swore all the little old gentlemen, "Donder and[p] Blitzen! it has been smoked out for dis hour!" — and they filled them up again in a great rage, and, sinking back in their arm-chairs, puffed away so fast and so fiercely that the whole valley was immediately filled with[q] impenetrable smoke.

Meantime the cabbages all turned very red in the face, and it seemed as if[r] old Nick[8] himself had taken possession of everything in the shape of a time-piece. The clocks carved upon the furniture took[s] to dancing as if bewitched, while those upon the mantelpieces could scarcely contain themselves for fury, and kept such a continual striking of thirteen, and such a frisking and wriggling of their pendulums as[t] was really horrible to see. But, worse than all, neither the cats nor the pigs could put up any longer with the[u]

---

i   "Dwelf!" *(A)*
j   Und dvelf/Dwelf *(A)*
k   and dropping *(A)*
l . . . l   it is — it is *(A, B, C, D, E)*
m . . . m   What is the use in attempting *(A);* What is the use of attempting *(B, C, D)*
n   pitiable *(A)*

o   been an *(A, B, C, D)*
p   und *(A, B, C, D)*
q   with an *(A, B, C, D)*
r   if the *(A, B, C, D)*
s   got *(A, B, C, D)*
t   as it *(A, B, C, D)*
u   the outrageous *(A, B, C, D)*

behavior of the little repeaters tied to their tails, and resented it by scampering all over the place, scratching and poking, and squeaking and screeching, and caterwauling and squalling, and flying into the faces, and running under the petticoats of the people, and creating altogether the most abominable din and confusion which it is possible for a reasonable person to conceive. And to make ᵛmatters still more distressing,ᵛ the rascally little scapegrace in the steeple was evidently exerting himself to the utmost. Every now and then one might catch a glimpse of the scoundrel through the smoke. There he sat in the belfry uponʷ the belfryman, who was lying flat upon his back. In his teeth the villainˣ held the bell-rope, which he kept jerking about with his head, raising such a clatter that my ears ring again even to think of it. On his lap lay the big fiddle at which he was scraping out of all time and tune, with bothʸ hands, making a great show, the nincompoop! of playing "Judy O'Flannagan" and "Paddy O'Raferty."ʸ' ⁹

Affairs being thus miserably situated, I left the place in disgust, and now appeal for aid to all lovers of correctᶻ time and fine kraut. Let us proceed in a body to the borough, and restore the ancient order of thingsᵃ in Vondervotteimittiss by ejecting that little fellowᵇ from the steeple.

NOTES

1. The town's stagnation reminds one of the happy state of Nieuw Amsterdam under the rule of the benign and rotund Governor Wouter van Twiller and his council, who smoked their pipes and did nothing as Washington Irving's Diedrich Knickerbocker relates in his *History of New York* (1809).

2. Compare the absurd citations of learned authorities in the chapter "New Amsterdam before the Flood" in the Knickerbocker *History*. But Irving cited actual scholars, Poe's are wholly made up. [There is a character named Grogzwig

---

v . . . v it if he could, more abominable, *(A, B, C, D)*
w upon the belly of *(A, B, C, D)*
x the villain/he *(A, B, C)* changed in D
y both his *(A, B, C, D)*
[*The song titles were first put in quotation marks in E, but as if of a*

single work instead of two — hence I make the needed emendation.]
y' O'Rafferty." *(A, B, C, D)*
z good *(A, B, C, D)*
a thing *(A)* misprint
b chap *(A, B, C, D)*

THE DEVIL IN THE BELFRY

in Dickens' *Nicholas Nickleby,* which Poe reviewed in *Burton's,* December 1839.
– Note contributed by B. Pollin.] The learned nonsense may be rendered *"Vonder,* read Thunder; *Votteimittiss,* as if *and Bleitziz* – obsolete for *Blitzen,* lightning." "Thunder and lightning" is a German oath, mentioned also in "Lionizing."
Dundergutz wrote "Little discussions of the most ancient things"; the bibliographical description is correctly worded in a very old-fashioned way.

3. The repeater is a toy watch.

4. Compare the opening paragraphs of "Hans Pfaall" for the excitement
occasioned in a town in Holland by the arrival of a grotesquely shaped dwarf.
I also find in "The Little Old Man of Coblentz," a story in *The Talisman* for
1829 (New York: Elam Bliss) a description of a being who dances, weighs
nothing, wears an odd costume, has a strange pipe which interests the city
fathers, and carries a gold snuff-box. Note some similarities to the costume of
the devil in "Bon-Bon." *Papillotes* are curl-papers; a *chapeau de bras* is a flat
cocked hat, sometimes carried under the arm. In a review of Charles Lever's
novel *Charles O'Malley* in *Graham's* for March 1842, Poe wrote, "Mr. Dickens
has no more business with the rabble than a seraph with a *chapeau de bras.*"

5. A *pas-de-zephyr* is mentioned in "Loss of Breath."

6. The devil's tattoo is not the title of a musical composition, but a phrase
usually meaning an irritating tapping of the fingers as on a table; "tattoo,"
however, can also mean a beating, thumping, or rapping continuously upon
something *(OED).* The phrase occurs in Disraeli's *Vivian Grey,* Book II, chapter ii: "The Peer sat in a musing mood, playing the Devil's tattoo upon the
library table," and I can cite from the work of a younger New York contemporary of Poe, George W. Pollen, *Writings* (1868), p. 79: "There being no bell,
we were obliged to beat the devil's own tattoo to get up the waiter."

7. "When the clock strikes thirteen" is a locution for never (Archer Taylor,
American N & Q, January 1944). But clocks do strike thirteen on rare occasions,
and the phenomenon is interpreted as a sign of death or very bad luck. See
Elliot O'Donnell, *Ghostly Phenomena* (1910), pp. 33 and 161. Poe's dull
worthies observe only that the thirteenth hour must mean it is one in the
afternoon.

8. In the third of his *Letters on Demonology* of 1830 (New York edition
1842, p. 91), Sir Walter Scott wrote, "The Old Nick, known in England, is ...
[a] genuine descendant of the Northern sea god, Nicksa or Nixas." Another explanation is in Samuel Butler's *Hudibras,* III, i, 1314, that Niccolo Machiavelli
"gave his name to our Old Nick."

9. "Judy O'Flanagan" is the tune to which Thomas Moore's "Sing, sing –
music was given" in *Irish Melodies* was set; see J. W. Lake's edition of Moore's
Poetical Works (Philadelphia, 1835), p. xxiv. The Library of Congress has a
broadside with the original words, beginning, "Good luck, Judy O'Flanagan,/
Dearly she loved nate Looney McTwoulter." The other old Irish tune, "Paddy
O'Rafferty," was set by Beethoven, Opus 224. In "The Bold Dragoon," one of
Irving's *Tales of a Traveller* (1824), the devil is asked to play it.

THE MAN THAT WAS USED UP

This story was so highly regarded by Poe that he gave it a place of honor, second to "The Murders in the Rue Morgue," in both PHANTASY-PIECES and *Prose Romances,* but it has often baffled or repelled commentators. Quinn (*Poe,* p. 283), observing its place of eminence, says "there may be some profound meaning in this satire . . . but it escapes the present writer." There is, however, an important thoughtful element in the tale. The author asks the ancient question, "What is Man?" — and considers the problem of identity. How much of a man still makes a man? The body may be diminished, the spirit is still whole. A relation of the story to the problem of the *principium individuationis* seems unmentioned by my predecessors, but Poe treated other aspects of the problem in "Morella" and "Ligeia." A less fundamental subject of the satire is that greater perfection (in the sense of regularity) is to be found in works of art than in those of Nature, which we know at heart are really better.

The literary source for "The Man that was Used Up" was pointed out by Mr. George Wetzel of Baltimore. This is a striking description of two people whose apparent good looks are not the result of natural gifts, in a once extremely popular book, *Asmodeus, or the Devil upon Two Sticks,* by Alain-René Le Sage.* Of them we learn: "One is a superannuated coquette . . . leaving her hair, eyebrows and teeth on her toilet; the other is an amorous dotard of sixty, . . . he has already laid down his eye . . . and peruke . . . and waits for his man to take off his wooden arm and leg. That beautiful young creature . . . is eldest sister to the gallant . . . her breasts are artificial." Once observed, the parallel of this to "The Man that was Used Up" is unmistakable. There is a plain kinship, too, to the less repulsive but equally false beauty of the heroine of "The Spectacles."

---

* The French original, *Le Diable Boiteux,* first appeared in 1707, and was greatly revised in 1727. The characters are described in the third chapter. I use the English version in a London edition of 1881. Never as popular as his *Gil Blas,* Le Sage's book is now not often read. See London *N & Q,* January 1953.

THE MAN THAT WAS USED UP

The story was timely, for the newspapers were full of references to the troubles with Indians in Florida in 1839, in which the Kickapoo tribe was involved. Readers of historical sources will recall that prisoners were often mutilated by their captors, and some even survived scalping. There are also many allusions to the contemporary scene. The legal troubles of Captain Mann interested journalists in the City of Brotherly Love. So many of the artisans mentioned can now be identified that it seems probable that all were real people, although not all were Philadelphians.

It is not surprising that some readers have thought to find a political satire in "The Man that was Used Up." The basis for this seems to be that the 1840 campaign song beginning "Van, Van's a Used Up Man," in ridicule of Martin Van Buren, is now well remembered by people unaware of how commonly the colloquial phrase "used up," now applied chiefly to supplies, was applied to books, plays, authors, and actors receiving bad notices as well as to politicians in our author's time. The policy of *Burton's Magazine* was to avoid political controversy, and I do not believe Poe violated it on this or any other occasion. His General Smith neither holds nor seeks office.†

TEXTS

(A) Burton's Gentleman's Magazine, August 1839 (5:66–70); *(B) Tales of the Grotesque and Arabesque* (1840), I, 59–74; *(C)* PHANTASY-PIECES with manuscript revisions of last, 1842; *(D) Prose Romances* (1843), pp. 40–48; *(E) Broadway Journal,* August 9, 1845 (2:68–71); *(F) Works* (1856), IV, 315–325.

The version of *Works* (F) is chosen for the text here. In PHANTASY-PIECES Poe added the motto and changed a sentence and a number of words; in *Prose Romances* he deleted three paragraphs and made other verbal changes. More extensive verbal revisions were made for the *Broadway Journal,* and two words were

† In a letter of 1836, Poe said he had had occasion to "use *up*" W. L. Stone's *Ups and Downs* in a review, and in a letter of 1849 he commented: "Lowell is a ranting abolitionist and *deserves* a good using up" (John Ward Ostrom, *The Letters of Edgar Allan Poe,* 1948, pp. 101, 427–428). Phillips *(Poe the Man,* 1926, I, 580) described Poe's story as "on the order of a political farce." William Whipple did more in *University of Texas Studies* 35:91 (1956), for he thought Poe's satire aimed at Richard M. Johnson of Kentucky, an Indian fighter, senator and congressman, and Van Buren's vice-president, 1837–1841. No reference to any commentator seeing any political significance in Poe's tale prior to 1926 has been found.

improved for *Works*. All texts place quotation marks before the conversation pause at the end of sentences, a practice not followed here.

Reprints

The New Mirror, September 9, 1843 (an unauthorized and bowdlerized reprint from *Prose Romances* that has been sought by collectors in lieu of the extremely rare pamphlet); *The Spirit of the Times* (Philadelphia), Sept. 12 and 13, 1845, from *Prose Romances*.

THE MAN THAT WAS USED UP. [*F*]

A TALE OF THE LATE BUGABOO AND KICKAPOO CAMPAIGN.

Pleurez, pleurez, mes yeux, et fondez-vous en eau!
La moitié de ma vie a mis l' autre au tombeau.   CORNEILLE.

I cannot just now remember when or where I first made the acquaintance of that truly fine-looking fellow, Brevet Brigadier General John A. B. C. Smith.[1] Some one *did* introduce me to the gentleman, I am sure — at some public meeting, I know very well — held about something of great importance, no doubt — at[a] some place or other, I[b] feel convinced, — [c]whose name[c] I have unaccountably[d] forgotten. The truth is — that the introduction was attended, upon my part, with a degree of anxious[e] embarrassment which operated to prevent any definite impressions of either time or place. I am constitutionally nervous — this, with me, is a family failing, and I can't help it. In especial, the slightest appearance of mystery — of any point I cannot exactly comprehend — puts me at once into a pitiable state of agitation.

There was something, as it were, remarkable — yes, *remarkable,* although this is but a feeble term to express my full meaning — about the entire individuality of the personage in question.[f] He was, perhaps, six feet in height, and of a presence singularly commanding. There was an *air distingué* pervading the whole man, which spoke of high breeding, and hinted at high birth. [g]Upon

---

Motto: *Omitted (A, B); fondez vous*
(C, D, E, F)
a   and at *(A, B, C, D)*
b   of this I *(A, B, C, D)*
c . . . c   the name of which *(D)*
d   stupidly *(D)*

e   anxious and tremulous *(A, B, C, D)*
f   *After this:* What this something was, however, I found it impossible to say. *(A, B, C, D)*
g . . . g   *Omitted (D)*

this topic — the topic of Smith's personal appearance — I have a kind of melancholy satisfaction in being minute.^g His head of hair would have done honor to a Brutus; — nothing could be more richly flowing, or possess a brighter gloss.[2] It was of a jetty black; — which was also the color, or more properly the no color, of his unimaginable whiskers. You perceive I cannot speak of these latter without enthusiasm; it is not too much to say that they were the handsomest pair of whiskers under the sun. At all events, they encircled, and at times partially overshadowed, a mouth utterly unequalled. Here were the most entirely even, and the most brilliantly white of all conceivable teeth. From between them, upon every proper occasion, issued a voice of surpassing clearness, melody, and strength. In the matter of eyes, ^halso, my acquaintance was^h pre-eminently endowed. Either one of such a pair was worth a couple of the ordinary ocular organs. They were of a deep hazel, exceedingly large and lustrous; and there was perceptible about them, ever and anon, just that amount of interesting obliquity[3] which gives ⁱpregnancy to expression.ⁱ

The bust of the General was unquestionably the finest bust I ever saw. For your life you could not have found a fault with its wonderful proportion. This rare peculiarity set off to great advantage a pair of shoulders which would have called up a blush of conscious inferiority into the countenance of the marble Apollo.[4] I have a passion for fine shoulders, and may say that I never beheld them in perfection before. The^j arms altogether were admirably modelled.^k Nor were the lower limbs less^l superb. These were, indeed, the *ne plus ultra* of good legs. Every connoisseur in such matters admitted the legs to be good. There was neither too much flesh, nor too little, — neither rudeness nor fragility. I could not imagine a more graceful curve than that of the *os femoris,* and there was just that due gentle prominence in the rear of the *fibula* which goes to the conformation of a properly proportioned calf. I

---

h...h my acquaintance was, also, *(A, B, C, D)*
i...i force to the pregnant observation of Francis Bacon — that "there is no exquisite beauty existing in the world without a certain degree of *strangeness* in the expression." *(A)*

j His *(A, B, C, D)*
k modelled, and the fact of his wearing the right in a sling, gave a greater decision of beauty to the left. *(A, B, C)*
l less marvellously *(A, B, C, D)*

wish to God my young and talented friend Chiponchipino, the sculptor, had but seen the legs of Brevet Brigadier General John A. B. C. Smith.

But although men so absolutely fine-looking are neither as plenty as reasons[5] or blackberries, still I could not bring myself to believe that *the remarkable* something to which I alluded just now, — that the odd air of *je ne sais quoi* which hung about my new acquaintance, — lay altogether, or indeed at all, in the supreme excellence of his bodily endowments. Perhaps it might be traced to the *manner;* — yet here again I could not pretend to be positive. There *was* a primness, not to say stiffness, in his carriage — a degree of measured, and, if I may so express it, of rectangular precision, attending his every movement, which, observed in a more diminutive[m] figure, would have had the least little savor in the world, of affectation, pomposity or constraint, but which noticed in a gentleman of his undoubted dimensions,[n] was readily placed to the account of reserve, *hauteur*[o] — of a commendable sense, in short, of what is due to the dignity of colossal proportion.

The kind friend who presented me to General Smith whispered in my ear[p] some few words of comment upon the man. He was a *remarkable* man — a *very* remarkable man — indeed one of the *most* remarkable men of the age. He was an especial favorite, too, with the ladies — chiefly on account of his high reputation for courage.

"In *that* point he is unrivalled — indeed he is a perfect desperado — a downright fire-eater, and no mistake," said my friend, here dropping his voice excessively low, and thrilling me with the mystery of his tone.

"A downright fire-eater, and *no* mistake. Showed *that,* I should say, to some purpose, in the late tremendous swamp-fight away down South, with the Bugaboo and Kickapoo Indians." [Here my friend[q] opened his eyes to some extent.] "Bless my soul! — blood and thunder, and all that! — *prodigies* of valor! — heard of him of course? — you know he's the man —— "

---

m *petite (A, B, C, D)*
n dimension, *(A, B, C, D, E)*
o of hauteur *(A);* hauteur *(B, C)*
p ear, at the instant, *(A, B, C, D)*
q friend placed his forefinger to the side of his nose, and *(A, B, C, D)*

THE MAN THAT WAS USED UP

"Man alive, how *do* you do? why how *are* ye? *very* glad to see ye, indeed!" here interrupted the General himself, seizing my companion by the hand as he drew near, and bowing stiffly but profoundly, as I was presented. I then thought, (and I think so still,) that I never heard a clearer nor a stronger voice nor[r] beheld a finer set of teeth: but I *must* say that I was sorry for the interruption [s]just at that moment,[s] as, owing to the whispers and insinuations aforesaid, my interest had been greatly excited in the hero of the Bugaboo and Kickapoo campaign.

However, the delightfully luminous conversation of Brevet Brigadier General John A. B. C. Smith soon completely dissipated this chagrin. My friend leaving us immediately, we had quite a long *tête-à-tête*,[t] and I was not only pleased but *really* — instructed. I never heard a more fluent talker, or a man of greater general information. With becoming modesty, he forebore, nevertheless, to touch upon the theme I had just then most at heart — I mean the mysterious circumstances attending the Bugaboo war — and, on my own part, what I conceive to be a proper sense of delicacy forbade me to broach the subject; although, in truth, I was exceedingly tempted to do so. I perceived, too, that the gallant soldier preferred topics of philosophical interest, and that he delighted, especially, in commenting upon the rapid march of mechanical invention. Indeed, lead him where I would, this was a point to which he invariably came back.

"There is nothing at all like it," he would say; "we are a wonderful people, and live in a wonderful age. Parachutes and railroads — man-traps and spring-guns![6] Our steam-boats are upon every sea, and the Nassau balloon packet[7] is about to run regular trips (fare either way only twenty pounds sterling) between London and Timbuctoo.[8] And who shall calculate the immense influence upon social life — upon arts — upon commerce — upon literature — which will be the immediate result of the[u] great principles of electro magnetics! Nor, is this all, let me assure you! There is really no end to the march of invention. The most wonderful —

---

r   or *(D)*
s . . . s   *just at that moment, (A,*
B, C, D)

t   *tête-a-tête, (F)* accent added from *A, B, C, D, E*
u   the application of the *(A, B, C, D)*

the most ingenious — and let me add, Mr. — Mr. — Thompson, I believe, is your name — let me add, I say, the most *useful* — the most truly *useful* mechanical contrivances, are daily springing up like mushrooms, if I may so express myself, or, more figuratively, like — ah[v] — grasshoppers — like grasshoppers, Mr. Thompson — about us [w]and ah — ah — ah[w] — around us!"

Thompson, to be sure, is not my name; but it is needless to say that I left General Smith with a heightened interest in the man, with an exalted opinion of his conversational powers, and a deep sense of the valuable privileges we enjoy in living in this age of mechanical invention. My curiosity, however, had not been altogether satisfied, and I resolved to prosecute immediate inquiry among my acquaintances touching the Brevet Brigadier General himself, and particularly respecting the tremendous events[x] *quorum pars magna fuit,*[9] during the Bugaboo and Kickapoo campaign.

The first opportunity which presented itself, and which *(horresco referens)*[10] I did not in the least scruple to seize, occurred at the Church of the Reverend Doctor Drummummupp, where I found myself established, one Sunday, just at sermon time, not only in the pew, but by the side, of that worthy and communicative little friend of mine, Miss Tabitha T. Thus seated, I congratulated myself, and with much reason, upon the very flattering state of affairs. If any person knew anything about Brevet Brigadier General John A. B. C. Smith, that person, it was clear to me, was Miss Tabitha T. We telegraphed a few signals, and then commenced, *sotto voce,* a brisk *tête-à-tête.*[11]

"Smith!" said she, in reply to my very earnest inquiry; "Smith! — why, not General John A. B. C.? Bless me, I thought you *knew* all about *him!* This is a wonderfully inventive age! Horrid affair that! — a bloody set of wretches, those Kickapoos! — fought like a hero — prodigies of valor — immortal renown. Smith! — Brevet Brigadier General John A. B. C.! — why, you know he's the man — "

"Man," here broke in Doctor Drummummupp, at the top of

---

v   like — ah/like *(A, B, C)*
w . . . w   and — ah — ah *(A, C, D);*
and — ah *(B)*

x   events in which he performed so conspicuous a part — *(A, B, C, D)*

his voice, and with a thump that came near knocking[y] the pulpit about our ears;[12] "man that is born of a woman hath but a short time to live; he cometh up and is cut down like a flower!"[13] I started to the extremity of the pew, and perceived by the animated looks of the divine, that the wrath which had [z]nearly proved[z] fatal to the pulpit had been excited by the whispers of the lady and myself. There was no help for it; so I submitted with a good grace, and listened, in all the martyrdom of[a] dignified silence, to the balance of that very capital discourse.

Next evening found me a somewhat late visitor at the Rantipole theatre, where I felt sure of satisfying my curiosity at once, by merely stepping into the box of those exquisite specimens of affability and omniscience, the Misses Arabella[b] and Miranda Cognoscenti. That fine tragedian, Climax,[c] was doing Iago to a very crowded house, and I experienced some little difficulty in making my wishes understood; especially, as our box was next[d] the slips and completely overlooked the stage.

"Smith?" said Miss Arabella, as she at length comprehended the purport of my query; "Smith? — why, not General John A. B. C.?"

"Smith?" inquired Miranda, musingly. "God bless me, did you ever behold a finer figure?"

"Never, madam, but do tell me —— "

"Or so inimitable grace?"

"Never, upon my word! — but pray inform me —— "

"Or so just an appreciation of stage effect?"

"Madam!"

"Or a more delicate sense of the true beauties of Shakespeare? Be so good as to look at that leg!"

"The devil!" and I turned again to her sister.

"Smith?" said she, "why, not General John A. B. C.? Horrid affair that, wasn't it? — great wretches, those Bugaboos — savage and so on — but we live in a wonderfully inventive age! — Smith!

---

y   knocking down (A, B, C, D)
z .'. . z   proved so nearly (A, B, C, D)
a   of a (A, B, C, D)
b   Arabelli (F) misprint, corrected from

A, B, C, D, E
c   Climax, however, (A, B, C, D)
d   next to (A, B, C, D)

— O yes! great man! — perfect desperado — immortal renown — prodigies of valor! *Never heard!*" [This was given in a scream.] "Bless my soul! — why, he's the man —— "

> " _____ mandragora
> Nor all the drowsy syrups of the world
> Shall ever medicine thee to that sweet sleep
> Which thou ow'dst[e] yesterday!"[14]

here roared out Climax just in my ear, and shaking his fist in my face all the time, in a way that I *couldn't* stand, and I *wouldn't.* I left the Misses Cognoscenti immediately, ᶠwent behind the scenes forthwith, and gave the beggarly scoundrel such a thrashing as I trust he will remember to the day of his death.ᶠ

At the *soirée* of the lovely widow, Mrs. Kathleen O'Trump,[15] I wasᵍ confident that I should meet with no similar disappointment. Accordingly, I was no sooner seated at the card-table, with my pretty hostess for a *vis-à-vis,*ʰ than I propounded those questions ⁱthe solution of whichⁱ had become a matter so essential to my peace.

"Smith?" said my partner, "why, not General John A. B. C.? Horrid affair that, wasn't it? — diamonds, did you say? — terrible wretches those Kickapoos! — we are playing *whist,* if you please, Mr. Tattle — however, this is the age of invention, most certainly *the* age, one may say — *the* age *par excellence* — speak French? — oh, quite a hero — perfect desperado! — *no hearts,* Mr. Tattle? I don't believe it! — immortal renown and all that — prodigies of valor! *Never heard!!* — why, bless me, he's the man ——"

"Mann? — *Captain* Mann?"[16] here screamed some little feminine interloper from the farthest corner of the room. "Are you talking about Captain Mann and the duel? — oh, I *must* hear — do tell — go on, Mrs. O'Trump! — do now go on!" And go on Mrs. O'Trump did — all about a certain Captain Mann, who was either shot or hung, or should have been both shot and hung. Yes! Mrs. O'Trump, she went on, and I — I went off. There was no chance

---

e   owd'st *(all texts) corrected from original*
f . . . f   and went behind the scenes for the purpose of giving the scoundrel a sound thrashing. *(A, B, changed in C*

except that C has make no doubt *instead of* trust)
g   was very *(A, B, C, D)*
h   partner, *(A, B, C, D)*
i . . . i   whose solution *(A, B, C)*

of hearing anything farther that evening in regard to Brevet Brigadier General John A. B. C. Smith.

Still I consoled myself with the reflection that the tide of ill luck would not run against me forever, and so determined to make a bold push for information at the rout of that bewitching little angel, the graceful Mrs. Pirouette.

"Smith?" said Mrs. P., as we twirled about together in a *pas de zéphyr*,[j] [17] "Smith? — why not General John A. B. C.? Dreadful business that of the Bugaboos, wasn't it? —terrible creatures, those Indians! — *do* turn out your toes! I really am ashamed of you — man of great courage, poor fellow! — but this is a wonderful age for invention — O dear me, I'm out of breath — quite a desperado — prodigies of valor — *never heard!!* — can't believe it — I shall have to sit down and enlighten[k] you — Smith! why, he's the man ——"

"Man-*Fred*, I tell you!" here bawled out Miss Bas-Bleu,[18] as I led Mrs. Pirouette to a seat. "Did ever anybody hear the like? It's Man-*Fred*, I say, and not at all by any means Man-*Friday*." Here Miss Bas-Bleu beckoned to me in a very peremptory manner; and I was obliged, will I nill I, to leave Mrs. P. for the purpose of deciding a dispute touching the title of a certain poetical drama of Lord Byron's.[19] Although I pronounced, with great promptness, that the true title was Man-*Friday*, and not by any means Man-*Fred*, yet when I returned to seek[l] Mrs. Pirouette she was not to be discovered, and I made my retreat from the house in a very bitter spirit of animosity against the whole race of the Bas-Bleus.

Matters had now assumed a really serious aspect, and I resolved to call at once upon my particular friend, Mr. Theodore Sinivate;[20] for I knew that here at least I should get something like definite information.

"Smith?" said he, in his well-known peculiar way of drawling out his syllables; "Smith? — why, not General John A. B. C.? Savage affair that with the Kickapo-o-o-os,[m] wasn't it? Say! don't you think so? — perfect despera-a-ado — great pity, 'pon my honor!

---

j *zephyr*, *(A, B, C, D, E, F)*   l seek for *(A, B, C, D)*
k tell *(A, B) changed in C*   m Kickapo-o-o-os, *(A, B, C, D)*

— wonderfully inventive age! — pro-o-odigies of valor! By the by, did you ever hear about Captain Ma-a-a-n?"[n]

"Captain Mann be d —— d!" said I, "please to go on with your story."

"Hem! — oh well! — quite° *la même cho-o-ose*, as we say in France. Smith, eh? Brigadier General John A — B — C.? I say" — [here Mr. S. thought proper to put his finger to the side of his nose] — "I say, you don't mean to insinuate now, really and truly, and conscientiously, that you don't know all about that affair of Smith's, as well as I do, eh? Smith? John A — B — C.? Why, bless me, he's the ma-a-an ——"

"*Mr.* Sinivate," said I, imploringly, "*is* he the man in the mask?"[21]

"No-o-o!" said he, looking wise, "nor the man in the mo-o-on."[p]

This reply I considered a pointed and positive insult, and so[q] left the house at once in high dudgeon, with a firm resolve to call my friend, Mr. Sinivate, to a speedy account for his ungentlemanly conduct and ill-breeding.

In the meantime, however, I had no notion of being thwarted touching the information I desired. There was one resource left me yet. I would go to the fountain-head. I would call forthwith upon the General himself, and demand, in explicit terms, a solution of this abominable piece of mystery. Here, at least, there should be no chance for equivocation. I[r] would be plain, positive, peremptory — as short as pie-crust — as concise as Tacitus or Montesquieu.[22]

It was early when I called, and the General was dressing; but I pleaded urgent business, and was shown at once into his bed-room by an old negro valet, who remained in attendance during my visit. As I entered the chamber, I looked about, of course, for the occupant, but did not immediately perceive him. There was a large and exceedingly odd-looking bundle of something which lay close by my feet on the floor, and, as I was not in the best humor in the world, I gave it a kick out of the way.

---

n Mann?" *(A, B, C, D)*
o *toute (A, B, C)*
p mo-o-o-on." *(A, B, C, D, E)*

q I *(A, B, C, D)*
r *Omitted (E) misprint*

THE MAN THAT WAS USED UP

"Hem! ahem! rather civil that, I should say!" said the bundle, in one of the smallest,[s] and altogether the funniest little voices, between a squeak and a whistle, that I ever[t] heard in all the days of my existence.

"Ahem! rather civil that, I should observe."

I fairly shouted with terror, and made off, at a tangent, into the farthest extremity of the room.

"God bless me! my dear fellow," here again whistled the bundle, "what — what — what — why, what *is* the matter? I really believe you don't know me at all." [u]

What *could* I say to all this — what *could* I? I staggered into an arm-chair, and, with staring eyes and open mouth, awaited the solution of the wonder.

"Strange you shouldn't know me though, isn't it?" presently re-squeaked the nondescript,[v] which I now perceived was performing,[w] upon the floor, some inexplicable evolution, very analogous[x] to the drawing on of a stocking. There was only a single leg, however, apparent.

"Strange you shouldn't know me, though, isn't it? Pompey,[23] bring me that leg!" Here Pompey handed the bundle, a very capital cork leg, already[y] dressed, which it screwed on in a trice; and then it stood up[z] before my eyes.[a]

"And a bloody action it *was*," continued the thing, as if in a soliloquy; "but then one musn't fight with the Bugaboos and Kickapoos, and think of coming off with a mere scratch. Pompey, I'll

---

s   smallest, the weakest, *(A, B, C)*
t   I ever/ever I *(A, B, C)*
u   *After this there are three paragraphs:* "No — no — no!" said I, getting as close to the wall as possible, and holding up both hands in the way of expostulation; "don't know you — know you — know you — *don't* know you at all! *Where's* your master?" here I gave an impatient squint towards the negro, still keeping a tight eye upon the bundle.
"He! he! he! he-aw! he-aw! he-aw!" cachinnated that delectable specimen of the human family, with his mouth fairly extended from ear to ear, and with his forefinger held up close to his

face, and levelled at the object of my apprehension, as if he was taking aim at it with a pistol.
"He! he! he! he-aw! he-aw! he-aw! — What, you want Mass Smif? Why, dar's him!" *(A, B, C)* [*in B, C one* he-aw! *is omitted in second paragraph*]
v   bundle, *(A, B, C, D)*
w   per-performing, *(F) misprint*
x   analogous *(E, F) misprint, corrected from A, B, C, D*
y   all ready *(A, B, C, D, E)*
z   upright *(A, B, C, D, E)*
a   eyes. Devil the word could I say. *(A, B, C, D)*

thank you now for that arm. Thomas" [turning to me] "is decidedly the best hand at a cork leg;[b] but if you should ever want an arm, my dear fellow, you must really let me recommend you to Bishop."[24] Here Pompey screwed on an arm.

"We had rather hot work of it, that you may say. Now, you dog, slip on my shoulders and bosom! Pettitt makes the best shoulders, but for a bosom you will have to go to Ducrow."[25]

"Bosom!" said I.

"Pompey, will you *never* be ready with that wig? Scalping is a rough process after all; but then you can procure such a capital scratch at De L'Orme's."[26]

"Scratch!"

"Now, you nigger, my teeth! For a *good* set of these you had better go to Parmly's at once;[27] high prices, but excellent work. I swallowed some very capital articles, though, when the big Buga-boo rammed me down with the butt end of his rifle."

"Butt end! ram down!! my eye!!"

"O yes, by-the-by, my eye — here, Pompey, you scamp, screw it in! Those Kickapoos are not so very slow at a gouge; but he's a belied man, that Dr. Williams,[28] after all; you can't imagine how well I see with the eyes of his make."

I now began very clearly to perceive that the object before me was nothing more nor[c] less than my new acquaintance, Brevet Brigadier General John A. B. C. Smith. The manipulations of Pompey had made, I must confess, a very striking difference in the appearance of the personal man. The voice, however, still puzzled me no little; but even this apparent mystery was speedily cleared up.

"Pompey, you black rascal," squeaked the General, "I really do believe you would let me go out without my palate."

Hereupon the negro, grumbling out an apology, went up to his master, opened his mouth with the knowing air of a horse-jockey, and adjusted therein a somewhat singular-looking machine, in a very dexterous manner, that I could not altogether comprehend.

---

b   leg; he lives in Race street, No. 79 —   c   or *(A, B, C, D)*
stop, I'll give you his card; *(A, B, C, D)*

The alteration, however, in the entire[d] expression of the [e]General's countenance[e] was instantaneous and surprising. When he again spoke, his voice had resumed all[f] that rich melody and strength which I had noticed upon our original introduction.

"D —— n the vagabonds!" said he, in so clear a tone that I positively started at the change, "D —— n the vagabonds! they not only knocked in the roof of my mouth, but took the trouble to cut off at least seven-eighths of my tongue. There isn't Bonfanti's equal, however, in America, for really good articles of this description.[29] I can recommend you to him with confidence," [here the General bowed,] and assure you that I have the greatest pleasure in so doing."

I acknowledged his[g] kindness in my best manner, and[h] took leave of him[i] at once, with a perfect understanding of the true[j] state of affairs — with a full comprehension of the mystery which had troubled me so long. It was evident. It was a clear case. Brevet Brigadier General John A. B. C. Smith was the man —— was *the man that was used up.*

NOTES

Subtitle: The Kickapoo Indians were engaged in the Florida Indian Wars at the time; Poe gave them as allies the Bugaboos here and in an article in *Alexander's Messenger*, March 18, 1840, called "The Railroad War."

Motto: This is from Corneille's tragedy *Le Cid*, III, iii, 7–8, and appears also in "Pinakidia," number 20 (*SLM*, August 1836, p. 575) with the translation: "Weep, weep, my eyes! It is no time to laugh/For half myself has buried the other half."

1. The General's name is an amalgam of commonplace elements, as Betsy Gavin pointed out to me. Compare the names of Joe Miller in "Autography."

2. Although the Roman celebrated for beautiful hair was Cincinnatus (as is mentioned by Suetonius, "Gaius [Caligula]," chapter xxxv), there may have been some tradition of playing Shakespeare's Brutus with long hair.

3. Descartes revealed that, because the first little girl that charmed him squinted, he connected obliquity of vision with beauty. See P. P. Cooke's "Leaves

d whole *(A, B, C)*	g this *(A, B, C)*
e . . . e countenance of the General *(A, B, C, D)*	h and now *(A, B, C, D)*
	i my friend *(A, B, C)*
f the whole of *(A, B, C, D)*	j *Omitted (A, B, C, D)*

from my Scrapbook" (*SLM,* April 1836 and Descartes' *Œuvres,* X, 53. For other uses of the quotation from Bacon in the canceled passage, see "Ligeia," n. 4.

4. The Apollo *par excellence* is the Belvidere Apollo.

5. Reasons, pronounced raisins, is punned upon in Shakespeare's first part of *Henry IV,* II, iv, 265. The phrase is also used in "Revivals," in *Alexander's Messenger,* March 4, 1840.

6. Man traps and spring guns were devices to discourage intruders on private property, especially in England.

7. See the pamphlet by Monck Mason, *Account of the late Aeronautical Expedition from London to Weilburg, Accompanied by Robert Hollond Esq., Monck Mason, Esq. and Charles Green, Aeronaut* (London, 1836; New York, 1837). Poe drew on this account for "The Balloon Hoax," which first appeared in *The Extra Sun,* April 13, 1844. In that tale he refers to "Mr. Monck Mason (whose voyage from Dover to Weilburg in the balloon, 'Nassau,' occasioned so much excitement in 1837)."

8. Timbuctoo, a city of Central Africa (now Tombouctou, Mali), was in Poe's time a type of the most utterly remote place that might be visited by a civilized man.

9. The Latin quotation from the *Æneid,* II, 6, means "Of which things he was a great part."

10. The quotation means, "I shudder recalling it," from the *Æneid,* II, 204, and is used again in "The Conversation of Eiros and Charmion."

11. Tabitha is a feline name and the young lady is catty. Before Morse's successful demonstration in 1844, "telegraph" usually meant a device for visible signaling.

12. Compare Samuel Butler's *Hudibras,* I, i, 11–12, "And pulpit, drum ecclesiastic,/Was beat with fist, instead of a stick."

13. Job 14:1-2.

14. *Othello,* III, iii, 330-333.

15. Mrs. O'Trump is a card-player.

16. Captain Daniel Mann was involved in the five-week trial of Dr. Thomas W. Dyott, who was convicted of fraud. See the Philadelphia *Public Ledger,* May 15 – June 3, 1839 passim; and Cornelia Varner, "Notes on Poe's Use of Contemporary Materials," *Journal of English and Germanic Philology,* January 1933.

17. A *pas de zéphyr* – a ballet step – is mentioned also in "Loss of Breath," "The Devil in the Belfry," and "The Angel of the Odd."

18. Bas-bleu, bluestocking, is also the name of a lady in "Lionizing."

19. *Man-Fred* is a burlesque by Gilbert A'Beckett on Byron's play. It concerns a heroic sweep, in blackface, seeking the heights by climbing chimneys. It was first produced about 1834.

20. What Poe has in mind seems to be a Cockney pronunciation – compare

that of Sam Weller in Dickens' *Pickwick Papers* — of "insinuate." In William E. Burton's article, "Some Account of George Cruikshank," in *Burton's Magazine*, January 1840, the author imagines a bold-faced villain in a London jail remarking, "Vot the 'ell does this 'ere old covey mean by his sinnervations?" Hope for definite direct information from Mr. Sinivate was slight.

21. The Man in the (Iron) Mask is mentioned also in "Lionizing," where see the notes.

22. Poe probably got this comparison from Hugh Blair's *Lectures on Rhetoric* (1783), lecture xviii: "The two most remarkable examples that I know, of conciseness carried as far as propriety will allow ... are Tacitus the [Roman] historian, and the President Montesquieu in *L'Esprit des Loix*." Allusions to one or both of the same examples of conciseness occur in Poe's preface to "Marginalia," in his review of the *Memoirs of Lucien Bonaparte (SLM,* October 1836), and in a canceled passage of "Three Sundays in a Week."

23. Pompey is the name of a Negro servant in "How to Write a Blackwood Article."

24. Most of the tradesmen mentioned here and below apparently were real people. John F. Thomas, a maker of artificial limbs, 79 Race Street, advertised in the Philadelphia *Public Ledger* from April 17, 1839. He stated he had worn an artificial leg for thirty-five years. In the early versions of his tale Poe gave the address. Possible Bishops are Joaquiam Bishop, 213 Cherry St., a maker of chemical instruments; U. C. Bishop, 119 West High St., a furniture dealer; and Gotlieb Bishop, 11 Sassafras Alley, a tailor. Mr. R. N. Williams, Director of the Historical Society of Pennsylvania, found these people in the Directory. I join him in the wish that Gotlieb, whose address is so appealing, was the right man to make an arm.

25. Nicholas Pettitt, 119 North Second Street, was a tailor named in the Philadelphia directory of 1837. Ducrow is not surely identified, but Andrew Ducrow, the great London equestrian performer, was a man of the most noble form, and certainly had a fine bosom.

26. *De l'Orme* is the title of a novel (1830) by G. P. R. James, mentioned in the heading of Poe's review of James's *Memoirs of Celebrated Women (Burton's,* July 1839). Poe used a variation of the name in "Bridal Ballad" in 1841 (Mabbott, I, 309). No wigmaker named De l'Orme has been identified in Philadelphia, New York, or Baltimore.

27. Many American dentists, some in Philadelphia, bore the name Parmly. In 1923 Lawrence Parmly published a book about them, *The Greatest Dental Family.*

28. Note the use of "gouge" here; see "The Gold-Bug" at note 20. The General says Dr. John Williams is "belied," because he had a bad reputation as a quack. He is referred to also in Poe's "Enigmatical and Conundrum-ical" in *Alexander's Messenger,* December 18, 1839. He is described in the Philadelphia *Saturday Courier,* December 21, 1839, as a humbug, who called himself "Oculist to his Majesty" (William IV of England) when he came to America

about 1837. One of his patients sued him because he went to him seeing out of one eye, but under his care became totally blind. Says the Philadelphia *Public Ledger* of December 14, 1839:

> Dr. Williams the Oculist, has been cast in a suit brought by one of his patients to recover $75, the amount paid for an anticipated cure of his eyes. The jury, notwithstanding all of the doctor's patients, blind and nearly blind, testified to his miraculous cures, brought in a verdict against him for $75 and costs.

29. Joseph Bonfanti sold talking *dolls* in New York. He published rhyming advertisements, which were widely copied by newspapers throughout the country, as "Selected Poetry." The following is from a reprint in the *Saturday Herald* of Baltimore, January 1, 1825, or "O'Teague's Description of Jos. Bonfanti's Fancy Store, 279 Broadway," Tune — "Sprig of Shilaleh":

> For jewels and trinkets Bonfanti's the man,
> He sells all that's pretty, he sells all that he can,
>   At his elegant new fancy store in Broadway . . .
> St. Patrick defend us from wizzards and snakes,
> *The deuce of a doll has he got but what spakes.*

THE FALL OF THE HOUSE OF USHER

"The Fall of the House of Usher" is probably the most popular of Poe's earlier tales of wonder. Woodberry says it is unsurpassed for "unity of design" and continues:

> In artistic construction it does not come short of absolute perfection. The adaptation of the related parts and their union in the total effect are a triumph of literary craft; the intricate details, . . . like premonitions and echoes of the theme in music, . . . secure their end with the certainty of harmonic law itself. The sombre landscape . . . the subtle yet not overwrought sympathy between the mansion and the race that had reared it; the looks, traits and pursuits of Usher, . . . and the at first scarce-felt presence of Madeline . . . his sister — all is like a narrowing and ever-intensifying force drawing in to some unknown point; and when this is reached, in the . . . vault . . . the mind, after that midnight scene, expands and breathes freer air, a hundred intimations, each slight in itself, startle and enchain it, until, slowly as obscurity takes shape in a glimmer of light, Usher's dread discloses itself in its concrete and fearful fulfillment, and at once by the . . . stroke of death, house, race and all sink into the black tarn where its glassy image had so long built a shadowy reality.
>
> Never has the impression of total destruction . . . been more strongly given . . . Doom rests upon all things within the shadow of those walls; it is felt to be impending: and therefore, Poe, identifying himself with his reader, places the sure seal of truth on the illusion as he exclaims "From that chamber and that mansion I fled aghast." The mind is already upon the recoil as it turns to view the accomplished fatality . . . [Poe's] work in this kind was done.

THE FALL OF THE HOUSE OF USHER

Woodberry rightly saw what Vincent Buranelli said quite plainly: "Poe is *not* Roderick Usher. He is the creator of Roderick Usher."*

The theme of the tale is succinctly explained by Howard Phillips Lovecraft who wrote:

> *Usher*...hints shudderingly of obscure life in inorganic things,...an abnormally linked trinity of entities at the end of a long and isolated family history – a brother, his twin sister, and their...ancient house all sharing a single soul and meeting one common dissolution at the same moment.

In a later study Richard Wilbur observed: "The House of Usher *is,* in allegorical fact, the physical body of Roderick Usher, and its dim interior *is,* in fact, Roderick Usher's visionary Mind."†

The tale is autobiographical only insofar as it concerns a real brother and sister, James Campbell Usher and Agnes Pye Usher, children of Luke Noble Usher and Harriet Ann L'Estrange Usher, who were actors and the closest friends of Poe's mother. The children were orphaned in 1814, and grew up as neurotics.‡

To what extent Poe modeled his characters on the real Ushers cannot be known. The malady of Roderick Usher, a fear of making any decision, is known clinically, and now sometimes can be cured. Medical theory of Poe's day held that fogs and damp places were conducive to melancholia.§

Poe certainly gives his twins characteristics usually associated

---

* Woodberry, *Poe* (1885), pp. 120–121; *Life* (1909), I, 229–231; Buranelli, p. 138.

† Lovecraft's statement is from the seventh chapter of his long essay, "Supernatural Horror in Literature," originally published in an amateur magazine in 1927, reprinted in *The Outsider and Others* (1939, see p. 530). Wilbur's observation is made in his discussion of allegory in the works of Poe, "The House of Poe," *Anniversary Lectures,* Library of Congress (1959), p. 28. (Wilbur's essay is more easily accessible in Eric Carlson's *The Recognition of Poe,* 1966, pp. 255–277.)

‡ Information reaches me from two independent sources: the Reverend Anson Titus of Somerville, Massachusetts (see Phillips, II, 1611ff), and John P. Poe who about 1890 told my correspondent, Frederick H. Howard, of the poet's use of the younger Ushers in his narrative. He alone reported Mrs. Usher's second given name.

§ My pupil, Lula Nelson Snyder Warden, showed this elaborately in an unpublished master's essay (Columbia University, 1925). [For a more recent study of the atmospheric source of Usher's madness, see Ian Walker in *Modern Language Review,* October 1966.]

with identical twins, but they do not share one sex, and Poe was interested in people who look alike.*

Miss Alterton thought she had found a partial source in the story "Thunder Struck" in the *Passages from the Diary of a Late Physician* (1835) by Dr. Samuel Warren. She pointed out that a number of the details are alike: A beautiful young lady falls into a cataleptic trance; the action takes place in a storm. There is a coffin, an apprehensive waiting for a sound, and the lady coming to life covered with blood. Miss Alterton mentions another idea, that of a gloomy house as a symbol of a family being destroyed by the death of its members, found in "Das Majorat" by E. T. A. Hoffmann. Poe undoubtedly knew Warren's book — he mentions it in "How to Write a Blackwood Article" — and Hoffmann's story had been discussed by Sir Walter Scott in the *Foreign Quarterly Review*, July 1827.†

A suggestion that Poe owed something to William Godwin's *Imogen, a Pastoral Romance* (1784) has been made by Burton R. Pollin.‡ That analogies exist is undeniable, but they all seem to me to be common themes of Gothick romance.

Readers generally have understood the purport of Poe's story, but some details have proved puzzling. Therefore, a scenario is offered. The House of Usher has only one soul which has its abode in the mansion and in the members of the family. Roderick Usher is aware of this, although his sister may not be, and he has concluded that since they are twins, and childless, this soul is interdependent with them and the building. Hence, if one dies, all must perish together. Roderick also fears that he is going mad, and

---

* Compare "Morella," "William Wilson," and "Mystification." The last concerns a mirror-image, something found again in the doubling of the Ushers' house in the waters of the tarn. Familial soul-sharing is not necessarily that of twins. Pliny the Elder in his *Natural History*, VII, 53, tells of two brothers named Corfidius. The elder seemed to die but revived, knowing where his brother had hidden a treasure — and then received word that his brother was really dead.

† See Margaret Alterton, *Origins of Poe's Critical Theory* (1925), pp. 25–26, citing Palmer Cobb's *Influence of E. T. A. Hoffmann on . . . Poe* (1908). See also Woodberry's *Life* (1909), I, 380.

‡ See his reprint of the romance issued in New York in 1964, pp. 88, 104, and 133. This reprint is of the second edition, and first in America, although a copy of the original edition was in a circulating library in New York before 1810. I greatly doubt that Godwin's very rare book was ever seen by Poe.

so summons his friend, the only person he trusts who has no part in the fate of his ancient house. Both brother and sister are dying; the latter seems to die first, but the former is sure that she is still alive because he is. He avoids her actual burial by a temporary entombment. He reads books which deal with unusual ideas about the relation of matter to spirit, of doubles, and of demoniac possession. Roderick also reads a burial service for himself (and his sister), and plays a dirge based on a musical air supposed to have been written on the last day of its composer's life. The reading of the weird romance, *The Mad Trist* — the only purely imaginary book named among the books listed as in Usher's library — probably has a subtle influence too, and climactically "the dragon is slain," for Madeline escapes, but so injured that she reaches her brother only to die with him as the house totters and falls — slowly enough to allow the narrator (who does not share its curse) to escape. As Darrell Abel says, "Throughout the tale, alternative explanations, natural and supernatural, of the phenomena are set forth; and we are induced by the consistently maintained device of a common-sense witness, gradually convinced in spite of his determined scepticism, to accept imaginatively the supernatural explanation."§

Thomas Dunn English, reviewing Poe's *Tales* in the *Aristidean* for October 1845, observed: "The thesis of this tale is the revulsion of feeling consequent upon discovering that for a long period of time we have been mistaking sounds of agony, for those of mirth or indifference." Dr. English had undoubtedly discussed the story with Poe, but probably included ideas of his own.

Several interpretations that I think must be rejected in the light of present knowledge must be mentioned. In *Studies in Classic American Literature* (1923), D. H. Lawrence sought references to incest; but conscious use of such a theme is contrary to Poe's general practice. Some readers have thought vampirism involved, but J. O. Bailey, who inclined to the view,* wrote me that

§ See his fine study "A Key to the House of Usher," *The University of Toronto Quarterly*, January 1949. [See also *Poe Studies* for June 1972 which is devoted to articles on "The Fall of the House of Usher."]

* See his paper "What Happens in the House of Usher" (*AL*, January 1964).

he regarded his idea only as a hypothesis. The ways of vampires are well known in British and American fiction, and Madeline is certainly not an orthodox vampire.†

The merit of the story was recognized immediately. The New York *Evening Star,* September 7, 1839, said, "Mr. Poe's tale of 'The Fall of the House of Usher,' would have been considered a *chef d'œuvre* if it had appeared in the pages of Blackwood." It was copied abroad in *Bentley's Miscellany,* August 1840, and thence into the *Boston Notion* of September 5.‡ Griswold put it in *The Prose Writers of America* (1847), and his example has been followed by countless anthologists to this day.

TEXTS

(A) Burton's Gentleman's Magazine, September 1839 (5:145–152); *(B) Tales of the Grotesque and Arabesque* (1840), I, 75–103; *(C)* PHANTASY-PIECES, copy of last with manuscript changes, 1842; *(D) Tales* (1845), pp. 64–82; *(E)* Griswold's *Prose Writers of America* (1847), pp. 524–530; *(F) Works* (1850), I, 291–309.

The best text, that of *Tales* (D), is followed. It does not differ verbally from *Works* (F), and no changes were made in the J. Lorimer Graham copy of Poe's volume. The version in Griswold's anthology *(E)* was printed with Poe's consent, but the few verbal variants seem not to be the author's changes.

As the variants show, some verbal changes were made in PHANTASY-PIECES *(C)* — twenty punctuation changes were indicated — most of them eliminating dashes; eight of these were used in later editions; but it was for the *Tales* text *(D)* that Poe made his most careful and extensive revisions.

† Lyle H. Kendall in *College English,* March 1963, held that Madeline was a *succubus,* and that Roderick read the black mass from the *Vigiliae.* I find it difficult to take this seriously.

‡The *Broadway Journal,* August 30, 1845, had a humorous comment on this:

We have written paper after paper which attracted no notice at all until it appeared as original in "Bentley's Miscellany" or the "Paris Charivari." The "Boston Notion" once abused us very lustily for having written "The House of Usher." Not long afterwards Bentley published it anonymously, as original with itself, — whereupon "The Notion," having forgotten that we wrote it, not only lauded it *ad nauseam,* but copied it *in toto.*

[In "Poe and the *Boston Notion,*" *English Language Notes,* September 1970, B. Pollin discusses Poe's relation to this paper, but he should have indicated the reprinting of "The Fall of the House of Usher" was noted by Heartman and Canny, p. 160.]

THE FALL OF THE HOUSE OF USHER

Reprints

Bentley's Miscellany (English and American editions), August 1840, from *Tales of the Grotesque and Arabesque*, without acknowledgment; *Boston Notion*, September 5, 1840, from *Bentley's Miscellany; The Oquawka Spectator* (Oquawka, Illinois), August 23 and 30, 1848, from *Burton's Magazine* [described in M. D. McElroy's "Poe's Last Partner," *Papers on Language and Literature*, Summer 1971, which, however, is wrong in saying there was no acknowledgment of authorship; both installments carry Poe's name].

THE FALL OF THE HOUSE OF USHER. [*D*]

> Son cœur est un luth suspendu;
> Sitôt qu'on le touche il résonne.
>
> *De Béranger.*

During the whole of a dull, dark, and soundless day in the autumn of the year, when the clouds hung oppressively low in the heavens, I had been passing alone, on horseback, through a singularly dreary tract of country; and at length found myself, as the shades of the evening drew on, within view of the melancholy House of Usher. I know not how it was — but, with the first glimpse of the building, a sense of insufferable gloom pervaded my spirit.[1] I say insufferable; for the feeling was unrelieved by any of that half-pleasurable, because poetic, sentiment, with which the mind usually receives even the sternest natural images of the desolate or terrible. I looked upon the scene before me — upon the mere house, and the simple landscape features of the domain — upon the bleak walls — upon the vacant eye-like windows — upon a few rank sedges — and upon a few white trunks of decayed trees — with an utter depression of soul which I can compare to no earthly sensation more properly than to the after-dream of the reveller upon opium —[2] the bitter lapse into every-day[a] life — the hideous dropping off of the veil. There was an iciness, a sinking, a sickening of the heart — an unredeemed dreariness of thought which no goading of the imagination could torture into aught of the sublime. What was it — I paused to think —what was it that so unnerved me in the contemplation of the House of Usher? It was a mystery all insoluble; nor could I grapple with the shadowy fancies that

---

Motto: *First added in D; résonne*   a   common *(A, B, C)*
(D, E, F)

crowded upon me as I pondered. I was forced to fall back upon the unsatisfactory conclusion, that while, beyond[b] doubt, there *are* combinations of very simple natural objects which have the power of thus affecting us, still[c] the analysis of this power lies[d] among considerations beyond our depth. It was possible, I reflected, that a mere different arrangement of the particulars of the scene, of the details of the picture, would be sufficient to modify, or perhaps to annihilate its capacity for sorrowful impression; and, acting upon this idea, I reined my horse to the precipitous brink of a black and lurid tarn that lay in unruffled lustre by the dwelling, and gazed down — but with a shudder even more thrilling than before — upon the remodelled and inverted images of the gray sedge, and the ghastly tree-stems, and the vacant and eye-like windows.

Nevertheless, in this mansion of gloom I now proposed to myself a sojourn of some weeks. Its proprietor, Roderick Usher, had been one of my boon companions in boyhood; but many years had elapsed since our last meeting. A letter, however, had lately reached me in a distant part of the country — a letter from him — which, in its wildly importunate nature, had admitted of no other than a personal reply. The MS. gave evidence of nervous agitation. The writer spoke of acute bodily illness — of a [e]mental disorder[e] which oppressed him — and of an earnest desire to see me, as his best, and indeed his only personal friend, with a view of attempting, by the cheerfulness of my society, some alleviation of his malady. It was the manner in which all this, and much more, was said — it was the apparent *heart* that went with his request — which allowed me no room for hesitation; and I accordingly obeyed forthwith[f] what I still considered a very singular summons.[g]

Although, as boys, we had been even intimate associates, yet I really knew little of my friend. His reserve had been always excessive and habitual. I was aware, however, that his very ancient family had been noted, time out of mind, for a peculiar sensibility of temperament, displaying itself, through long ages, in many

---

b beyond a *(E)*
c still the reason, and *(A, B) changed in C*
d lie *(A, B) changed in C*

e . . . e pitiable mental idiosyncrasy *(A, B, C)*
f *Omitted (A, B, C)*
g summons, forthwith. *(A, B, C)*

works of exalted art, and manifested, of late, in repeated deeds of munificent yet unobtrusive charity, as well as in a passionate devotion to the intricacies, perhaps even more than to the orthodox and easily recognisable beauties, of musical science. I had learned, too, the very remarkable fact, that the stem of the Usher race, all time-honored as it was, had put forth, at no period, any enduring branch; in other words, that the entire family lay in the direct line of descent, and had always, with very trifling and very temporary variation, so lain. It was this deficiency, I considered, while running over in thought the perfect keeping of the character of the premises with the accredited character of the people, and while speculating upon the possible influence which the one, in the long lapse of centuries, might have exercised upon the other — it was this deficiency, perhaps, of collateral issue, and the consequent undeviating transmission, from sire to son, of the patrimony with the name, which had, at length, so identified the two as to merge the original title of the estate in the quaint and equivocal appellation of the "House of Usher" — an appellation which seemed to include, in the minds of the peasantry who used it, both the family and the family mansion.[3]

I have said that the sole effect of my somewhat childish experiment — that[h] of looking down within the tarn — had been to deepen the first singular impression. There can be no doubt that the consciousness of the rapid increase of my superstition — for why should I not so term it? — served mainly to accelerate the increase itself. Such, I have long known, is the paradoxical law of all sentiments having terror as a basis. And it might have been for this reason only, that, when I again uplifted my eyes to the house itself, from its image in the pool, there grew in my mind a strange fancy — a fancy so ridiculous, indeed, that I but mention it to show the vivid force of the sensations which oppressed me. I had so worked upon my imagination as really to believe that[i] about the whole mansion and domain there hung an atmosphere peculiar to themselves and their immediate vicinity — an atmosphere which had no affinity with the air of heaven, but which had reeked up from the

---

h *Omitted (A, B, C)*   i that around *(A, B, C)*

decayed trees, and the gray wall[j] and[k] the silent [l]tarn — a pestilent and mystic vapor,[l] dull, sluggish, faintly discernible, and leaden-hued.

Shaking off from my spirit what *must* have been a dream, I scanned more narrowly the real aspect of the building. Its principal feature seemed to be that of an excessive antiquity. The discoloration of ages had been great. Minute fungi overspread the whole exterior, hanging in a fine tangled web-work from the eaves. Yet all this was apart from any extraordinary dilapidation. No portion of the masonry had fallen; and there appeared to be a wild inconsistency between its still perfect adaptation of parts, and the crumbling[m] condition of the individual stones. In this there was much that reminded me of the specious[n] totality of old wood-work which has rotted for long years in some neglected vault, with no disturbance from the breath of the external air. Beyond this indication of extensive decay, however, the fabric gave little token of instability. Perhaps the eye of a scrutinizing observer might have discovered a barely perceptible fissure, which, extending from the roof of the building in front, made its way down the wall in a zigzag direction, until it became lost in the sullen waters of the tarn.

Noticing these things, I rode over a short causeway to the house. A servant in waiting took my horse, and I entered the Gothic archway of the hall. A valet, of stealthy step, thence conducted me, in silence, through many dark and intricate passages in my progress to the *studio*[o] of his master. Much that I encountered on the way contributed, I know not how, to heighten the vague sentiments of which I have already spoken. While the objects around me — while the carvings of the ceilings, the sombre tapestries of the walls, the ebon blackness of the floors, and the phantasmagoric armorial trophies which rattled as I strode, were but matters to which, or to such as which, I had been accustomed from my infancy — while I hesitated not to acknowledge how familiar was all this — I still wondered to find how unfamiliar were the

---

j   walls, *(A)*
k   and in *(E)*
l...l   tarn, in the form of an inelastic vapor or gas — *(A, B, C)*

m   utterly porous, and evidently decayed *(A, B) changed in C*
n   spacious *(E) misprint*
o   studio *(A, B, C)*

fancies which ordinary images were stirring up. On one of the staircases, I met the physician of the family. His countenance, I thought, wore a mingled expression of low cunning and perplexity. He accosted me with trepidation and passed on. The valet now threw open a door and ushered me into the presence of his master.

The room in which I found myself was very large and[p] lofty. The windows were long, narrow, and pointed, and at so vast a distance from the black oaken floor as to be altogether inaccessible from within. Feeble gleams of encrimsoned light made their way through the trellised[q] panes, and served to render sufficiently distinct the more prominent objects around; the eye, however, struggled in vain to reach the remoter angles of the chamber, or the recesses of the vaulted and fretted ceiling. Dark draperies hung upon the walls. The general furniture was profuse, comfortless, antique, and tattered. Many books and musical instruments lay scattered about, but failed to give any vitality to the scene. I felt that I breathed an atmosphere of sorrow. An air of stern, deep, and irredeemable gloom hung over and pervaded all.

Upon my entrance, Usher arose from a sofa on[r] which he had been lying at full length, and greeted me with a vivacious warmth which had much in it, I at first thought, of an overdone cordiality — of the constrained effort of the *ennuyé*[s] man of the world. A glance, however, at his countenance, convinced me of his perfect sincerity. We sat down; and for some moments, while he spoke not, I gazed upon him with a feeling half of pity, half of awe. Surely, man had never before so terribly altered, in so brief a period, as had Roderick Usher! It was with difficulty that I could bring myself to admit the identity of the wan being before me with the companion of my early boyhood. Yet the character of his face had been at all times remarkable. A cadaverousness of complexion; an eye large, liquid, and luminous beyond comparison; lips somewhat thin and very pallid, but of a surpassingly beautiful curve; a nose of a delicate Hebrew model, but with a breadth of nostril unusual in similar formations; a finely moulded chin, speaking, in its want

---

p   and excessively *(A, B, C)*
q   trelliced *(A, B, C);* trellissed *(D)*
corrected from E

r   upon *(A, B, C)*
s   ennuyé *(A)*

of prominence, of a want of moral energy; hair of a more than web-like softness and tenuity; these features, with an inordinate expansion above the regions of the temple, made up altogether a countenance not easily to be forgotten.[4] And now in the mere exaggeration of the prevailing character of these features, and of the expression they were wont to convey, lay so much of change that I doubted to whom I spoke. The now ghastly pallor of the skin, and the now miraculous lustre of the eye, above all things startled and even awed me. The silken hair, too, had been suffered to grow all unheeded, and as, in its wild gossamer texture, it floated rather than fell about the face, I could not, even with effort, connect its Arabesque expression with any idea of simple[t] humanity.

In the manner of my friend I was at once struck with an incoherence — an inconsistency; and I soon found this to arise from a series of feeble and futile struggles to overcome an habitual trepidancy — an excessive nervous agitation. For something of this nature I had indeed been prepared, no less by his letter, than by reminiscences of certain boyish traits, and by conclusions deduced from his peculiar physical conformation and temperament. His action was alternately vivacious and sullen. His voice varied rapidly from a tremulous indecision (when the animal spirits seemed utterly in abeyance) to that species of energetic concision — that abrupt, weighty, unhurried, and hollow-sounding enunciation — that leaden, self-balanced and perfectly modulated guttural utterance, which may be observed in the [u]lost drunkard, or the irreclaimable eater of opium, during the periods of his most intense excitement.[u]

It was thus that he spoke of the object of my visit, of his earnest desire to see me, and of the solace he expected me to afford him. He entered, at some length, into what he conceived to be the nature of his malady. It was, he said, a constitutional and a family evil, and one for which he despaired to find a remedy — a mere nervous affection, he [v]immediately added,[v] which would undoubtedly soon pass. It displayed itself in a host of unnatural sensa-

---

t   simply *(B, C)* *misprint*
u . . . u   moments of the intensest excitement of the lost drunkard, or the

irreclaimable eater of opium. *(A, B, C)*
v . . . v   added in a breath, *(C)*

tions. Some of these, as he detailed them, interested and bewildered me; although, perhaps, the terms, and the general manner of the narration had their weight. He suffered much from a morbid acuteness of the senses;[5] the most insipid food was alone endurable; he could wear only garments of certain texture; the odors of all flowers were oppressive; his eyes were tortured by even a faint light; and there were but peculiar sounds, and these from stringed instruments, which did not inspire him with horror.

To an anomalous species of terror I found him a bounden slave.[6] "I shall perish," said he, "I *must* perish in this deplorable folly. Thus, thus, and not otherwise, shall I be lost. I dread the events of the future, not in themselves, but in their results. I shudder at the thought of any, even the most trivial, incident, which may operate upon this intolerable agitation of soul. I have, indeed, no abhorrence of danger, except in its absolute effect — in terror. In this unnerved — in this pitiable condition — I feel that ᵂthe period will sooner or later arrive when I mustᵂ abandon life and reason together, in ˣsome struggle with the grim phantasm, FEAR."ˣ

I learned, moreover, at intervals, and through broken and equivocal hints, another singular feature of his mental condition. He was enchained by certain superstitious impressions in regard to the dwelling which he tenanted, and whence,ʸ for many years, he had never ventured forth — in regard to an influence whose supposititious force was conveyed in terms too shadowy here to be re-stated — an influence which some peculiarities in the mere form and substance of his family mansion, had, by dint of long sufferance, he said, obtained over his spirit — an effect which the *physique* of the gray walls and turrets, and of the dim tarn into which they all looked down, had, at length, brought about upon the *morale* of his existence.

He admitted, however, although with hesitation, that much of the peculiar gloom which thus afflicted him could be traced to a more natural and far more palpable origin — to the severe and long-continued illness — indeed to the evidently approaching dis-

---

w . . . w   I must inevitably *(A, B, C)*   demon of fear." *(A, B, C)*
x . . . x   my struggles with some fatal   y   from which, *(A, B, C)*

solution — of a tenderly beloved sister — his sole companion for long years — his last and only relative on earth. "Her decease," he said, with a bitterness which I can never forget, "would leave him (him the hopeless and the frail) the last of the ancient race of the Ushers." While[z] he spoke, the lady Madeline (for so was she called) passed slowly through a remote portion of the apartment, and, without having noticed my presence, disappeared. I regarded her with an utter astonishment not unmingled with [a]dread — and yet I found it impossible to account for such feelings.[a] A sensation[b] of stupor oppressed me, as my eyes followed her retreating steps. When[c] a door, at length, closed upon her,[d] my glance sought instinctively and eagerly the countenance of the brother — but he had buried his face in his hands, and I could only perceive that a far more than ordinary wanness had overspread the emaciated fingers through which trickled many passionate tears.

The disease of the lady Madeline had long baffled the skill of her physicians. A settled apathy, a gradual wasting away of the person, and frequent although transient affections of a partially cataleptical character, were the unusual diagnosis. Hitherto she had steadily borne up against the pressure of her malady, and had not betaken herself finally to bed; but, on the closing in of the evening of my arrival at the house, she succumbed (as her brother told me at night with inexpressible agitation) to the prostrating power of the destroyer; and I learned that the glimpse I had obtained of her person would thus probably be the last I should obtain — that the lady, at least while living, would be seen by me no more.

For several days ensuing, her name was unmentioned by either Usher or myself: and during this period I was busied in earnest endeavors to alleviate the melancholy of my friend. We painted and read together; or I listened, as if in a dream, to the wild improvisations of his speaking guitar. And thus, as a closer and still

---

z   As *(A, B, C)*
a . . . a   dread. Her figure, her air, her features — all, in their very minutest development were those — were identically (I can use no other sufficient term) were identically those of the Roderick Usher who sat beside me. *(A, B, C)*
b   feeling *(A, B, C)*
c   As *(A, B, C)*
d   her exit, *(A, B, C)*

closer intimacy admitted me more unreservedly into the recesses of his spirit, the more bitterly did I perceive the futility of all attempt at cheering a mind from which darkness, as if an inherent positive quality,[7] poured forth upon all objects of the moral and physical universe, in one unceasing radiation of gloom.

I shall ever bear about me[e] [8] a memory of the many solemn hours I thus spent alone with the master of the House of Usher. Yet I should fail in any attempt to convey an idea of the exact character of the studies, or of the occupations, in which he involved me, or led me the way. An excited and highly distempered ideality threw a sulphureous[f] lustre over all. His long improvised dirges will ring forever in my ears. Among other things, I hold[g] painfully in mind a certain singular perversion and amplification of the wild air of the last waltz of Von Weber.[9] From the paintings over which his elaborate fancy brooded, and which grew, touch by touch, into vaguenesses at which I shuddered the more thrillingly, because I shuddered knowing not why; — from these paintings (vivid as their images now are before me) I would in vain endeavor to educe more than a small portion which should lie within the compass of merely written words. By the utter simplicity, by the nakedness of his designs, he arrested and overawed attention. If ever mortal painted an idea, that mortal was Roderick Usher. For me at least — in the circumstances then surrounding me — there arose out of the pure abstractions which the hypochondriac contrived to throw upon his canvass,[h] an intensity of intolerable awe, no shadow of which felt I ever yet in the contemplation of the certainly glowing yet too concrete reveries of Fuseli.[10]

One of the phantasmagoric conceptions of my friend, partaking not so rigidly of the spirit of abstraction, may be shadowed forth, although feebly, in words. A small picture presented the interior of an immensely long and rectangular vault or tunnel, with low walls, smooth, white, and without interruption or device.[11] Certain accessory points of the design served well to convey the idea that this excavation lay at an exceeding depth below the sur-

---

e   me, as Moslemin their shrouds at
Mecca, *(A)*
f   sulphurous *(A, B, C)*

g   bear *(A, B, C)*
h   canvas *(A, B, C, E)*

face of the earth. No outlet was observed in any portion of its vast extent, and no torch, or other artificial source of light was discernible; yet a flood of intense rays rolled throughout, and bathed the whole in a ghastly and inappropriate splendor.

I have just spoken of that morbid condition of the auditory nerve which rendered all music intolerable to the sufferer with the exception of certain effects of stringed instruments. It was, perhaps, the narrow limits to which he thus confined himself upon the guitar, which gave birth, in great measure, to the fantastic character of his performances. But the fervid *facility* of his *impromptus*[i] could not be so accounted for. They must have been, and were, in the notes, as well as in the words of his wild fantasias (for he not unfrequently accompanied himself with rhymed verbal improvisations), the result of that intense mental collectedness and concentration to which I have previously alluded as observable only in particular moments of the highest artificial excitement. The words of one of these rhapsodies I have easily remembered.[j] I was, perhaps, the more forcibly impressed with it, as he gave it, because, in the under or mystic current of its meaning, I fancied that I perceived, and for the first time, a full consciousness on the part of Usher, of the tottering of his lofty reason upon her throne. The verses, which were entitled "The Haunted Palace,"[12] ran very nearly, if not accurately, thus:

I.

In the greenest of our valleys,
　　By good angels tenanted,
Once a fair and stately palace —
　　Radiant[k] palace — reared its head.
In the monarch Thought's dominion —
　　It stood there!
Never seraph spread a pinion
　　Over fabric half so fair.

II.

Banners yellow, glorious, golden,
　　On its roof did float and flow;
(This — all this — was in the olden

---

i　impromptus *(A, B, C)*　　　　　　k　Snow-white *(A, B, C)*
j　borne away in memory. *(A, B, C)*

Time long ago)
And every gentle air that dallied,
   In that sweet day,
Along the ramparts plumed and pallid,
   A winged[1] odor went away.

III.

Wanderers in that happy valley
   Through two luminous windows saw
Spirits moving musically
   To a lute's well-tunéd law,
Round about a throne, where sitting
   (Porphyrogene!)
In state his glory well befitting,
   The ruler[m] of the realm was seen.

IV.

And all with pearl and ruby glowing
   Was the fair palace door,
Through which came flowing, flowing, flowing,
   And sparkling evermore,
A troop of Echoes whose sweet[n] duty
   Was but to sing,
In voices of surpassing beauty,
   The wit and wisdom of their king.

V.

But evil things, in robes of sorrow,
   Assailed the monarch's high estate;
(Ah, let us mourn, for never morrow
   Shall dawn upon him, desolate!)
And, round about his home, the glory
   That blushed and bloomed
Is but a dim-remembered story
   Of the old time entombed.

VI.

And travellers now within that valley,
   Through the red-litten windows, see
Vast forms that move fantastically
   To a discordant melody;
While, like a rapid ghastly river,
   Through the pale door,
A hideous throng rush out forever,
   And laugh — but smile no more.

---

1 wingéd *(C)*   m   sovereign *(A, B) changed in C*   n   sole *(A)*

I well remember that suggestions arising from this ballad[n'] led us into a train of thought wherein there became manifest an opinion of Usher's which I mention not so much on account of its novelty, (for other men[o] * have thought thus,)[13] as on account of the pertinacity with which he maintained it. This opinion, in its general form, was that of the sentience of all vegetable things. But, in his disordered fancy, the idea had assumed a more daring character, and trespassed, under certain conditions, upon the kingdom of inorganization.[14] I lack words to express the full extent, or the earnest *abandon* of his persuasion. The belief, however, was connected (as I have previously hinted) with the gray stones of the home of his forefathers. The conditions[p] of the sentience had been here, he imagined, fulfilled in the method of collocation of these stones — in the order of their arrangement, as well as in that of the many *fungi*[q] which overspread them, and of the decayed trees which stood around — above all, in the long undisturbed endurance of this arrangement, and in its reduplication in the still waters of the tarn. Its evidence — the evidence of the sentience — was to be seen, he said, (and I here started as he spoke,) in [r]the gradual yet certain condensation of an atmosphere of their own about the waters and the walls.[r] The result was discoverable, he added, in that silent, yet importunate and terrible influence which for centuries had moulded the destinies of his family, and which made *him* what I now saw him — what he was. Such opinions need no comment, and I will make none.

Our books — the books which, for years, had formed no small portion of the mental existence of the invalid — were, as might be supposed, in strict keeping with this character of phantasm.[15] We pored together over such works as the Ververt et Chartreuse of Gresset;[16] the Belphegor of Machiavelli;[s] [17] the Heaven and Hell

---

*Watson, Dr. Percival, Spallanzani, and especially the Bishop of Landaff. — See "Chemical Essays," vol. v.

---

n' ballad, (D, E, F) comma deleted to follow A, B, C
o No note in A, B, C, E
p condition (A)
q fungi (A, B, C)
r...r Italicized in A, B, C
s After this: the Selenography of Brewster; (A, B, C)

of Swedenborg;[18] the Subterranean Voyage of Nicholas Klimm by[t] Holberg;[19] the Chiromancy of Robert Flud, of Jean D'Indaginé, and of De la Chambre;[20] the Journey into the Blue Distance of Tieck;[21] and the City of the Sun of Campanella.[22] One favorite volume was a small octavo edition of the *Directorium Inquisitorum*,[u] by the Dominican Eymeric de Gironne;[23] and there were passages in Pomponius Mela, about the old African Satyrs and Œgipans, over which Usher would sit dreaming for hours.[24] His chief delight, however, was found in the[v] perusal of an exceedingly rare and curious book in quarto Gothic — the manual of a forgotten church — the *Vigiliae*[w] *Mortuorum secundum Chorum Ecclesiae Maguntinae*.[25]

I could not help thinking of the wild ritual of this work, and of its probable influence upon the hypochondriac, when, one evening, having informed me abruptly that the lady Madeline was no more, he stated his intention of preserving her corpse for a fortnight, (previously to its final interment,) in one of the numerous vaults within the main walls of the building. The worldly[x] reason, however, assigned for this singular proceeding, was one which I did not feel at liberty to dispute. The brother had been led to his resolution (so he told me) by consideration[y] of the unusual character of the malady of the deceased, of certain obtrusive and eager inquiries on the part of her medical men, and of the remote and exposed situation of the burial-ground of the family. I will not deny that when I called to mind the sinister countenance of the person whom I met upon the staircase, on the day of my arrival at the house, I had no desire to oppose what I regarded as at best but a harmless, and by no[z] means an unnatural, precaution.

At the request of Usher, I personally aided him in the arrangements for the temporary entombment. The body having been encoffined, we two alone bore it to its rest. The vault in which we placed it (and which had been so long unopened that our torches, half smothered in its oppressive atmosphere, gave us little oppor-

---

t   de *(A, B) changed in C*
u   *Inquisitorium (A, B, C, D, E, F)*
corrected from the original title
v   the earnest and repeated *(A, B, C)*

w   *Vigilae (A, B) changed in C*
x   wordly *(A, B, C) misprint*
y   considerations *(A, B) changed in C*
z   by no/not by any *(A, B, C)*

tunity for investigation) was small, damp, and entirely[a] without means of admission for light; lying, at great depth, immediately beneath that portion of the building in which was my own sleeping apartment. It had been used, apparently, in remote feudal times, for the worst purposes of a donjon-keep, and, in later days, as a place of deposit for powder, or some[b] other highly combustible substance, as a portion of its floor, and the whole interior of a long archway through which we reached it, were carefully sheathed with copper. The door, of massive iron, had been, also, similarly protected. Its immense weight caused an unusually sharp grating sound, as it moved upon its hinges.

Having deposited our mournful burden upon tressels within this region of horror, we partially turned aside the yet unscrewed lid of the coffin, and looked upon the face of the tenant. A striking[c] similitude between the brother and sister [d]now first arrested my attention; and[d] Usher, divining, perhaps, my thoughts, murmured out some few words from which I learned that the deceased and himself had been twins, and that sympathies of a scarcely intelligible nature had always existed between them. Our glances, however, rested not long upon the dead — for we could not regard her unawed. The disease which had thus entombed the lady in the maturity of youth, had left, as usual in all maladies of a strictly cataleptical character, the mockery of a faint blush upon the bosom and the face, and that suspiciously lingering smile upon the lip which is so terrible in death.[26] We replaced and screwed down the lid, and, having secured the door of iron, made our way, with toil, into the scarcely less gloomy apartments of the upper portion of the house.

And now, some days of bitter grief having elapsed, an observable change came over the features of the mental disorder of my friend. His ordinary manner had vanished. His ordinary occupations were neglected or forgotten. He roamed from chamber to chamber with hurried, unequal, and objectless step. The pallor of his countenance had assumed, if possible, a more ghastly hue —

---

a   utterly *(A)*
b   *Omitted (A, B, C)*
c   A striking/The exact *(A, B, C)*

d...d   even here again startled and confounded me. *(A, B, C)*

but the luminousness of his eye had utterly gone out. The once occasional huskiness of his tone was heard no more; and a tremulous quaver, as if of extreme terror, habitually characterized his utterance. There were times, indeed, when I thought his ᵉunceasingly agitated mindᵉ was laboring with someᶠ oppressive secret, to divulge which he struggled for the necessary courage. At times, again, I was obliged to resolve all into the mere inexplicable vagaries of madness, forᵍ I beheld him gazing upon vacancy for long hours, in an attitude of the profoundest attention, as if listening to some imaginary sound. It was no wonder that his condition terrified — that it infected me. I felt creeping upon me, by slow yet certain degrees, the wild influences of his own fantastic yet impressive superstitions.

It was, especially,ʰ upon retiring to bed late in the night of the seventh or eighth day after the ⁱplacing of the lady Madeline within the donjon,ⁱ that I experienced the full power of such feelings. Sleep came not near my couch — while the hours waned and waned away.²⁷ I struggled to reason off the nervousness which had dominion over me. I endeavored to believe that much, if not all of what I felt, was due to the bewilderingʲ influence of the gloomy furniture of the room — of the dark and tattered draperies, which, tortured into motion by the breath of a rising tempest, swayed fitfully to and fro upon the walls, and rustled uneasily about the decorations of the bed.²⁸ But my efforts were fruitless. An irrepressible tremor gradually pervaded my frame; and, at length, there sat upon my very heart an incubus of utterly causeless alarm.²⁹ Shaking this off with a gasp and a struggle, I uplifted myself upon the pillows, and, peering earnestly within the intense darkness of the chamber, harkened — I know not why, except that an instinctive spirit prompted me — to certain low and indefinite sounds which came, through the pauses of the storm, at long intervals, I knew not whence. Overpowered by an intense sentiment of horror, unaccountable yet unendurable, I threw on my clothes with haste (for

---

e...e mind (C)
f   an (A, B, C)
g   as (A, B, C)
h   most especially, (A, B) changed in C

i...i   entombment of the lady
Madeline, (A)
j   phantasmagoric (A, B, C)

I felt that I should sleep no more during the night), and endeavored to arouse myself from the pitiable condition into which I had fallen, by pacing rapidly to and fro through the apartment.

I had taken but few turns in this manner, when a light step on an adjoining staircase arrested my attention. I presently recognised it as that of Usher. In an instant afterward[k] he rapped, with a gentle touch, at my door, and entered, bearing a lamp. His countenance was, as usual, cadaverously wan — but, moreover,[l] there was a species of mad hilarity in his eyes — an evidently restrained *hysteria*[m] in his whole demeanor. His air appalled me — but anything was preferable to the solitude which I had so long endured, and I even welcomed his presence as a relief.

"And you have not seen it?" he said abruptly, after having stared about him for some moments in silence — "you have not then seen it? — but, stay! you shall." Thus speaking, and having carefully shaded his lamp, he hurried to one of the[n] casements, and threw it freely open to the storm.

The impetuous fury of the entering gust nearly lifted us from our feet. It was, indeed, a tempestuous yet sternly beautiful night, and one wildly singular in its terror and its beauty. A whirlwind had apparently collected its force in our vicinity; for there were frequent and violent alterations in the direction of the wind; and the exceeding density of the clouds (which hung so low as to press upon the turrets of the house) did not prevent our perceiving the life-like velocity with which they flew careering from all points against each other, without passing away into the distance. I say that even their exceeding density did not prevent our perceiving this — yet we had no glimpse of the moon or stars — nor was there any flashing forth of the lightning. But the under surfaces of the huge masses of agitated vapor, as well as all terrestrial objects immediately around us, were glowing in the unnatural[o] light of a faintly luminous and[p] distinctly visible gaseous exhalation which hung about and enshrouded the mansion.

"You must not — you shall not behold this!" said I, shudder-

---

k   afterwards *(A, B, C)*
l   but, moreover,/but *(A, B, C)*
m   hysteria *(A, B, C)*
n   the gigantic *(A, B, C)*
o   *Canceled (C)*
p   yet *(C)*

ingly, to Usher, as I led him, with a gentle violence, from the window to a seat. "These appearances, which bewilder you, are merely electrical phenomena not uncommon — or it may be that they have their ghastly origin in the rank miasma of the tarn. Let us close this casement; — the air is chilling and dangerous to your frame. Here is one of your favorite romances. I will read, and you shall listen; — and so we will pass away this terrible night together."

The antique volume which I had taken up was the "Mad Trist" of Sir Launcelot Canning;[30] but I had called it a[q] favorite of Usher's more in sad jest than in earnest; for, in truth, there is little in its uncouth [r]and unimaginative[r] prolixity which could have had interest for the lofty and spiritual ideality of my friend. It was, however, the only book immediately at hand; and I indulged a vague hope that the excitement which now agitated the hypochondriac, might find relief (for the history of mental disorder is full of similar anomalies) even in the extremeness[s] of the folly which I should read. Could I have judged, indeed, by the wild overstrained air of vivacity with which he harkened, or apparently harkened, to the words of the tale, I might well have[t] congratulated myself upon the success of my design.

I had arrived at that well-known portion of the story where Ethelred, the hero of the Trist, having sought in vain for peaceable admission into the dwelling of the hermit, proceeds to make good an entrance by force. Here, it will be remembered, the words of the narrative run thus:

"And Ethelred, who was by nature of a doughty heart,[31] and who was now mighty withal, on account of the powerfulness of the wine which he had drunken, waited no longer to hold parley with the hermit, who, in sooth, was of an obstinate and maliceful turn, but, feeling the rain upon his shoulders, and fearing the rising of the tempest, uplifted his mace outright, and, with blows, made quickly room in the plankings of the door for his gauntleted hand; and now pulling therewith sturdily, he so cracked, and ripped, and tore all asunder, that the noise of the dry and hollow-sounding wood alarummed and reverberated throughout the forest."

---

q   *Omitted (E)*
r . . . r   *Canceled (C)*

s   utterness *(A)*
t   well have/have well *(A, B, C)*

At the termination of this sentence I started, and for a moment, paused; for it appeared to me (although I at once concluded that my excited fancy had deceived me) — it appeared to me that, from some very remote portion of the mansion,[u] there came, indistinctly, to my ears, what might have been, in its exact similarity of character, the echo (but a stifled and dull one certainly) of the very cracking and ripping sound which Sir Launcelot had so particularly described. It was, beyond doubt, the coincidence alone which had arrested my attention; for, amid the rattling of the sashes of the casements, and the ordinary commingled noises of the still increasing storm, the sound, in itself, had nothing, surely, which should have interested or disturbed me. I continued the story:

"But the good champion Ethelred, now entering within the door, was sore enraged and amazed to perceive no signal of the maliceful hermit; but, in the stead thereof, a dragon of a scaly and prodigious demeanor, and of a fiery tongue, which sate in guard before a palace of gold, with a floor of silver; and upon the wall there hung a shield of shining brass with this legend enwritten —

Who entereth herein, a conqueror hath bin;
Who slayeth the dragon, the shield he shall win;

And Ethelred uplifted his mace, and struck upon the head of[v] the dragon, which fell before him, and gave up his pesty breath, with a shriek so horrid and harsh, and withal so piercing, that Ethelred had fain to close his ears with his hands against the dreadful noise of it, the like whereof was never before heard."

Here again I paused abruptly, and now with a feeling of wild[w] amazement — for there could be no doubt whatever that, in this instance, I did actually hear (although from what direction it proceeded I found it impossible to say) a low and apparently distant, but harsh, protracted, and most unusual screaming or grating sound — the exact counterpart of what my fancy had already conjured up for[x] the dragon's unnatural shriek as described by the romancer.

Oppressed, as I certainly was, upon the occurrence of this second and most extraordinary coincidence, by a thousand conflicting

---

u mansion or of its vicinity, *(A, B, C)*   w utter *(A)*
v sf *(A) misprint*   x as the sound of *(A, B, C)*

sensations, in which wonder and extreme terror were predominant, I still retained sufficient presence of mind to avoid exciting, by any observation, the sensitive nervousness of my companion. I was by no means certain that he had noticed the sounds in question; although, assuredly, a strange alteration had, during the last few minutes, taken place in his demeanor. From a position fronting my own, he had gradually brought round his chair, so as to sit with his face to the door of the chamber; and thus I could but partially perceive his features, although I saw that his lips trembled as if he were murmuring inaudibly. His head had dropped upon his breast — yet I knew that he was not asleep, from the wide and rigid opening of the eye as I caught a glance of it in profile. The motion of his body, too, was at variance with this idea — for he rocked from side to side with a gentle yet constant and uniform sway. Having rapidly taken notice of all this, I resumed the narrative of Sir Launcelot, which thus proceeded:

"And now, the champion, having escaped from the terrible fury of the dragon, bethinking himself of the brazen shield, and of the breaking up of the enchantment which was upon it, removed the carcass from out of the way before him, and approached valorously over the silver pavement of the castle to where the shield was upon the wall; which in sooth tarried not for his full coming, but fell down at his feet upon the silver floor, with a mighty great and terrible ringing sound."

No sooner had these syllables passed my lips, than — as if a shield of brass had indeed, at the moment, fallen heavily upon a floor of silver — I became aware of a distinct, hollow, metallic, and clangorous, yet apparently muffled reverberation. Completely[y] unnerved, I leaped[z] to my feet; but the measured rocking movement of Usher was undisturbed. I rushed to the chair in which he sat. His eyes were bent fixedly before him, and throughout his whole countenance there reigned a[a] stony rigidity. But, as I placed[b] my hand upon his shoulder, there came a strong shudder over his whole person;[c] a sickly smile quivered about his lips; and I saw

---

y   Utterly *(A)*
z   started convulsively *(A, B)*; leapt *(C)*
a   a more than *(A, B) changed in C*

b   laid *(A, B, C)*
c   whole person;/frame; *(A, B, C)*

that he spoke in a low, hurried, and gibbering murmur, as if unconscious of my presence. Bending closely over him,[d] I at length drank in the hideous import of his words.

"Not hear it? — yes, I hear it, and *have* heard it. Long — long — long — many minutes, many hours, many days, have I heard it — yet I dared not — oh, pity me, miserable wretch that I am! — I dared not — I *dared* not speak! *We have put her living in the tomb!* Said I not that my senses were acute? I *now* tell you that I heard her first feeble movements in the hollow coffin. I heard them — many, many days ago — yet I dared not — *I dared not speak!* And now — to-night — Ethelred — ha! ha! — the breaking of the hermit's door, and the death-cry of the dragon, and the clangor of the shield! — say, rather, the rending of her[e] coffin, and the grating of the iron [f]hinges of her prison,[f] and her struggles within the coppered archway of the vault! Oh whither shall I fly?[32] Will she not be here anon? Is she not hurrying to upbraid me for my haste? Have I not heard her footstep[g] on the stair? Do I not distinguish that heavy and horrible beating of her heart?[33] Madman!" — here he [h]sprang furiously[h] to his feet, and shrieked out his syllables, as if in the effort he were giving up his soul — *"Madman![i] I tell you that she now stands without the door!"*

As if in the superhuman energy of his utterance there had been found the potency of a spell — the huge[j] antique pannels[k] to which the speaker pointed, threw slowly back, upon the instant, their ponderous and ebony jaws. It was the work of the rushing gust — but then without those doors there *did* stand the lofty and enshrouded figure of the lady Madeline of Usher. There was blood upon her white robes, and the evidence of some bitter struggle upon every portion of her emaciated frame. For a moment she remained trembling and reeling to and fro upon the threshold — then, with a low moaning cry, fell heavily inward upon the person of her brother, and in her violent[l] and now final death-agonies,

---

d his person, *(A, B, C)*	i "Madman! *(A, B, C)*
e the *(A, B, C)*	j *Canceled (C)*
f . . . f hinges, *(A, B, C)*	k pannels *(all texts)*
g footsteps *(A, B, C)*	l horrible *(A, B, C)*
h . . . h sprung violently *(A, B, C)*	

bore him to the floor a corpse, and a victim to the terrors he had anticipated.[m]

From that chamber, and from that mansion, I fled aghast. The storm was still abroad in all its wrath as I found myself crossing the old causeway. Suddenly there shot along the path a wild light, and I turned to see whence a gleam so unusual could have issued; for the vast house and its shadows were alone behind me. The radiance was that of the full, setting, and blood-red moon, which now shone vividly through that once barely-discernible fissure, of which I have before spoken as extending from the roof of the building, in a zigzag direction, to the base. While I gazed, this fissure rapidly widened — there came a fierce breath of the whirlwind — the entire orb of the satellite burst at once upon my sight — my brain reeled as I saw the mighty walls rushing asunder — there was a long tumultuous shouting sound like the voice of a thousand waters[34] — and the deep and dank tarn at my feet closed sullenly and silently over the fragments of the *"House of Usher."*[n]

NOTES

Motto: This is adapted *(Son* being substituted for *Mon)* from a poem called "Le Refus," lines 41–42, addressed by the popular French lyricist, Pierre-Jean de Béranger (1780–1857) to General Galignani, wherein the poet refused a pension for his "services" in the Revolution of 1830. Poe changes the wording slightly, as he often did, for his own purposes. Killis Campbell thought it an inspiration of Poe's "Israfel." But the motto was not used until 1845; and it is hard to say how Poe could have seen the poem before he met with his quotation in R. M. Walsh's *Sketches of Conspicuous Living Characters of France* (translated from Louis L. de Loménie, 1841), a book he reviewed carefully in *Graham's* for April 1841, and often used. The quotation may be translated, "His heart is a hanging lute; as soon as it is touched, it responds." (See the notes on the poem "Israfel" — Mabbott, I, 177.) A lute is really shaped like a human heart.

1. The solitary horseman was a favorite in the opening scenes of the once popular works of the English novelist, George Payne Rainsford James (1799–1860). However, my correspondent, George Wetzel, points out that there are verbal echoes of the opening of Irving's "Westminster Abbey" in *The Sketch Book:* "One of those sober and rather melancholy days in the latter part of autumn, when the shadows of morning and evening almost mingle together,

m dreaded. *(A, B, C)*
n *At the end is a note in A:* The ballad of "The Haunted Palace,"

introduced in this tale, was published separately, some months ago, in the Baltimore "Museum."

and throw a gloom over the decline of the year, I passed several hours in rambling about Westminster Abbey."

2. The eyelike windows suggest the personality of the house. And the reference to opium is, as always in Poe, a suggestion that unimaginative readers may consider the whole story hallucination.

3. Compare *Politian*, II, 74: "Di Broglio's haughty and time-honored line"; "Berenicë": "Yet there are no towers in the land more time-honored than my gloomy, gray, hereditary halls"; and "Ligeia": "The gloomy and dreary grandeur of the buildings." The author here hints that the family has had the single soul for generations.

4. Compare the heroine's nose in "Ligeia," and the hair of Bedloe in "A Tale of the Ragged Mountains." Phrenologists consider great expansion above the regions of the temple a sign of ideality, or poetic gift. Poe used the word "ideality" in the phrenological sense in his criticism, and may have liked the notion, for he had a high forehead himself.

5. Compare "The Tell-Tale Heart": "What you mistake for madness is but over acuteness of the senses." See also "Colloquy of Monos and Una" at note 19.

6. Compare "I had become a bounden slave," in "Ligeia."

7. Compare *Paradise Lost*, I, 63: "No light, but rather darkness visible."

8. Compare the canceled phrase "as Moslemin their shrouds at Mecca" with "Morella" at note 11.

9. Roderick Usher is playing a dirge for himself, as will be understood when one knows of the early editions of the waltz. In the Library of Congress is a copy called:

Weber's Last Waltz/Composed by him a few hours before his death/for the Piano Forte./Philad.ᵃ Published and sold by Geo. Willig 171 Chesnut (*sic*) St. Folio, one leaf, [circa 1830.]

The waltz was actually composed by Karl Gottlieb Reissiger (1798–1859) and copied out by his friend Karl Maria, Baron von Weber (1786–1826), to play in his concerts in London. Weber died suddenly; the music in his handwriting was believed to be his own composition and was published as such. Poe did not know of the real composer's relation to it. [For added details, see Pollin, *Discoveries in Poe*, pp. 85–86.]

10. Henry Fuseli (1741–1825) was an English painter of Swiss extraction, admired by William Blake, and a master of strange subjects.

11. The painting Poe seems to have imagined, but his inspiration may have been a view through the West Lawn Arcade at the University of Virginia. (This idea has occurred independently to both Richard Wilbur and myself.)

12. "The Haunted Palace," first published, separately, in the Baltimore *American Museum of Science, Literature, and the Arts* for April 1839, is discussed in detail in the volume of Poems (Mabbott, I, 312–318). It may be repeated here, however, that it is not autobiographical, but an allegory of a

deranged mind. Poe's poem was probably inspired by a serious "Ballade" of John Wolcot (Peter Pindar), beginning, "Couldst thou looke into myne harte."

13. Poe's footnote is confusing. His sole authority is Richard Watson (1737–1816), Professor of Chemistry at Cambridge and later Bishop of Llandaff in Wales, author of *An Essay on the Subjects of Chemistry*, which was originally printed in 1771 and collected as the third in the fifth volume of his *Chemical Essays* (1787), V, 127–128. Watson there adds references to the Abbé Lazzaro Spallanzani's *Dissertations Relative to the Natural History of Animals and Vegetables* (translated from the Italian, London, 1784), and to the article by Dr. Thomas Percival on "the perceptive power of vegetables" (1785) included in the *Memoirs of the Literary and Philosophical Society of Manchester* [5 vols, London, 1785–1802], II, 114), as well as to works in Greek or Latin by Joannes Stobaeus, Hieronymus Cardanus, and John Ray. See Harry R. Warfel in *MLN*, February 1939.

14. The kingdom of inorganization is the Mineral Kingdom. See Herbert Smith, "Usher's Madness and Poe's Organicism: A Source" (*AL*, November 1967). He believes that the debt to Watson goes further and that in Watson's scientific essay Poe might have found the idea that "vegetable sentience is simply a major piece of evidence in the organic relatedness of *all matter.*"

15. The books mentioned as in the library of Roderick Usher are all — save *The Mad Trist,* which is integral to the action – actual books. Poe supposed they dealt with ideas about spirit pervading matter, "bipart soul," and the relations of microcosm to macrocosm. Some of them he could not have seen, but he knew of their nature from encyclopedias and perhaps from the conversation of the learned bookseller, William Gowans, with whom he boarded in New York in 1837. Some, I believe, Poe actually had read.

16. A translation by "Father Prout" (Francis Mahony) of Jean-Baptiste-Louis Gresset's poem "Vert-vert, the Parrot," was published in *Fraser's Magazine* for September 1834; and Poe must have seen in *L'Erudition Universelle,* Book II, chapter vi, section 17, Bielfeld's mention of Gresset's *Ververt* and *La Chartreuse.* Bielfeld said these were a special kind of composition, between heroic and burlesque poetry, and having something of the moral, satirical, serious, mocking, and nobly comic. Ververt is a convent parrot who talks ignorantly but sometimes meaningfully of holy things. He visits the waterfront, learns to swear, and is exiled, but, being heartbroken, is taken home again, forgiven, and dies in the arms of the abbess. His poem made the Jesuits expel Gresset, but many readers find it a pious allegory of frail mankind with mystical implications. *La Chartreuse* lacks mystical qualities and Poe had probably not seen it, nor, I suspect, had Bielfeld.

17. "The little novel of Belphegor is pleasantly conceived and pleasantly told," wrote T. B. Macaulay, reviewing a French edition of the works of Machiavelli in the *Edinburgh Review* for March 1827. Written about 1515, the novella was translated into English as early as 1660. The protagonist, a fallen archangel, comes to earth to investigate the complaints of many souls that their wives are to blame for their damnation. In Florence, well supplied with money, he marries the beautiful Onesta Donati, who fleeces him so that he must run away from his

creditors. He "possesses" three ladies in succession, and finally, hearing that his wife is coming after him, he returns to Hell. The demoniac possession is what fascinates Roderick Usher.

Poe canceled "the Selonography of Brewster" mentioned in the early versions but in his manuscript notes for "Hans Phaall" he mentioned it as if it was something to look up. Sir David Brewster (1781–1868), Scottish physicist, distinguished for his work in optics and polarized light, editor, educator, prolific writer on scientific subjects, principal of Edinburgh University, was one of the best known scientists of his day.

18. Emanuel Swedenborg's great work *Heaven and Hell* (1758) deals with visions and mystical experiences.

19. The *Iter Subterraneum* (the "Voyage Underground") by Ludvig Holberg (1684–1754), founder of modern Danish literature, tells of a country inside the earth where the people are trees who walk and talk. Poe presumably found a reference in Bielfeld, Book II, chapter vi, section 45, for in the earliest version of his story he refers to "Nicholas Klimm de Holberg" as if it were a personal name.

20. The works on chiromancy (palmistry) are mentioned by Bielfeld, Book II, chapter xvii, section 10, in a single sentence. They are: *Tractatus de Geomantia,* by Robert Fludd, M.D., 1687; *Discours sur les Principes de la Chiromancie,* by Marin Cureau de la Chambre, 1653 (English translation, 1658); *Introductiones Apotelesmatici . . . in Chiromantiam,* by Joannes ab Indagine of Steinheim, 1522, English translation, 1598. As the title indicates, the first is primarily concerned with geomancy, a method of divination by means of marking the earth with a pointed stick. It is most unlikely that Poe ever saw any of these books, but he obviously knew that these methods of fortune-telling are based on a belief in a mysterious relation between the stars, the configuration of the palms, and so forth; that is, between microcosm and macrocosm.

21. Poe refers to "A Journey into the Blue Distance" in "Marginalia," number 78 (*Democratic Review,* December 1844, p. 585). It is a satirical story within a story – "Das alte Buch und die Reise ins Blaue hinein," a novella by Johann Ludwig Tieck. First published in 1834 in the annual *Urania* (Leipzig) for 1835, it was briefly noticed in "A Glance at the German Annuals" in *Blackwood's Magazine* for February 1835, p. 388:

> The tale by Tieck, which opens the Urania of this year, (Das alte Buch,) the Old Book, is one of those phantasmata in which an attempt is made to blend, somewhat in Tieck's earlier style . . . the dreams of fairy land with the satirical exposure of the vices of modern taste . . . the first half of the tale is written in Tieck's serious vein, full of all his usual vague melancholy and romance . . . while the latter is a mere diatribe against the corruptions of modern times, and particularly of the French school in matters literary.

Further mention of the tale appeared – with the title translated – in a review of Tieck's *Life of a Poet* in *Blackwood's* for September 1837.

The story recounts the adventures of a medieval noble who marries Gloriana, the Faerie Queene. She reigns in a paradise inside a mountain, where dwell the souls of great poets — Dante, Chaucer, Shakespeare. Ugly gnomes have taken over authors like E. T. A. Hoffmann and Victor Hugo, but an emissary of Gloriana has embraced the young Goethe. (This note is by courtesy of my pupil Heidrun Smolka.)

22. The *Civitas Solis* (1623) by the Italian poet and philosopher, Tommaso Campanella, is mentioned by Bielfeld, Book II, chapter vi, section 45. It recounts a visit to the people who inhabit a Utopia in the Sun. Campanella held that the world and all its parts have a spiritual nature.

23. Nicholas Eymeric of Gironne, who became Inquisitor of Aragon in 1356, wrote instructions to priests examining heretics and gave a list of forbidden books such as Usher wished to consult. The first edition of the *Directorium* was printed in 1503.

24. Pomponius Mela, the Latin geographer of the first century A.D., is cited by Poe in a note on "The Island of the Fay." The passages that fascinated Roderick Usher are in *De Situ Orbis,* I, 8, and III, 95:

The Satyrs have nothing human save the form. The form of the Ægipans (goat-pans) as they are named.

The fields, as far as can be seen, are those of the Pans and Satyrs. This opinion is held because, although there is no trace of cultivation therein, no houses of inhabitants, no pathways, a solitude vast by day, and a vaster silence, at night frequent fires gleam, and as if camps widely spread are indicated, cymbals and drums resound, and flutes are heard, sounding more than human.

25. Copies of two quarto editions, printed in Gothic type, of the *Vigiliae mortuorum secundum chorum ecclesiae Maguntinae* ("Vigils for the dead according to the use of the church of Mainz"), are known. There is a copy of one edition in the University Library, Cambridge, England, which has been examined for me. No specimen of either edition is located in America, and I have not found even printed descriptions accessible in Poe's day; but his friend William Gowans was interested in incunabula, and may have spoken of the very rare book. Poe (who knew little of the Roman Catholic Church) may have supposed the work unorthodox, but incorrectly. Prior to the Council of Trent, the texts of Breviaries (with which the *Vigiliae* would commonly be bound) varied somewhat from place to place; but the rites of Mainz in 1500 differed little, and in nothing very important, from those in use in Baltimore in 1839.

26. See "Marginalia," number 77 (*Democratic Review,* December 1844, p. 585), for a rebuke to Bulwer's reference to the "sweet smile . . . of the dying" in *Ernest Maltravers* (1837), IX, vii. See also "Shadow — a Parable."

27. Compare "Al Aaraaf," II, 262: "The night that waned and waned and brought no day."

28. Compare "The Sleeper," lines 22–24: "The bodiless airs, a wizard rout,/ Flit through thy chamber in and out,/And wave the curtain canopy"; and "Ligeia": "a strong continual current of wind behind the draperies — giving a hideous and uneasy animation to the whole."

29. Compare "The Conversation of Eiros and Charmion" at note 5 for "an incubus upon our hearts, and a shadow upon our brains."

30. *The Mad Trist* is a product of Poe's imagination, and part of the plot of his tale. Its fictional author, Sir Launcelot Canning, gets his name from the greatest knight of Arthurian story and from a central figure in the "Rowley" poems of Thomas Chatterton. William Canynges, Mayor of Bristol in the fifteenth century (*DNB*), was a real person about whom Chatterton made up an elaborate legend. "Sir Launcelot Canning" is named as the author of the original rhymed motto for Poe's *Stylus* magazine, discussed at length in the volume of Poems. (See Mabbott, I, 328–329.)

31. Ethelred may get his name from a character in Scott's *Ivanhoe,* who is doughty indeed.

32. Compare Psalm 139:7: "... whither shall I flee from thy presence?"

33. Compare the conclusion of "The Tell-Tale Heart": " 'Villains,' I shrieked ... 'I admit the deed! ... it is the beating of his hideous heart!' "

34. Compare Ezekiel 43:2: "His voice like a noise of many waters," and Revelation 1:15: "as the sound of many waters." See also "The Conversation of Eiros and Charmion" at note 1.

WILLIAM WILSON

The story of "William Wilson" is generally recognized as one of Poe's greatest achievements in prose, and it has always been deservedly popular. Although a work of poetic imagination, clearly containing an allegory, it is told so straightforwardly that he who runs may read it with pleasure as a pure account of extra-ordinary adventures. Some of the adventures are too marvelous for belief in the cold light of reason, but the element of the absolutely incredible is reduced to a minimum. The story may be said to mark the beginning of a trend to realism in the author's fiction.

The main theme, a man's struggle with his conscience, is nothing unusual. But Poe's setting is not commonplace, since the action involves relations between people who look alike and notions about what speculative philosophers term a bipartite soul.

Poe's principal source is now definitely known from his own statement. In a letter to Washington Irving he wrote on October 12, 1839:

I take the liberty of sending you the Octo: No: of the Gents' Magazine, containing the Tale "William Wilson." This is the tale of which I spoke in my former letter, and which is based upon a brief article of your own in the first "Gift" — that for 1836. Your article is called "An Unwritten Drama of Lord

WILLIAM WILSON

Byron." I have hoped that, having thus a right of ownership in my "William Wilson," you will be induced to read it — and I also hope that . . . you will find in it something to appro[v]e.*

The essential parts, for Poe's purposes, of Irving's article follow:

The hero, . . . Alfonso, is a Spanish nobleman. . . . His passions, from early and unrestrained indulgence, have become impetuous and ungovernable, and he follows their impulses with a . . . disregard of consequences.

Soon after his entrance into the world, he finds himself followed, occasionally, in public places, by a person masked and muffled up so as to conceal both countenance and figure. He at first pays but little attention to the circumstance . . . By degrees, however, the frequent intrusion of this silent and observant follower becomes extremely irksome. The mystery, too, which envelopes him, heightens the annoyance. Alfonso is unable to identify him . . . — his name, his country, his place of abode; all are unknown, — and it is impossible even to conjecture his motives for this singular espionage. It is carried, by degrees, to such lengths, that he becomes, as it were, Alfonso's shadow — his second self. Not only the most private actions of the latter pass under the scrutiny of this officious monitor, but his most secret thoughts seem known to him. Speak of him, he stands by his side; think of him, he feels his presence, though invisible, oppress and weigh upon his spirits, like a troubled atmosphere. Waking or sleeping, Alfonso has him in thought or in view. He crosses his path at every turn; like the demon in Faust, he intrudes in his solitude. He follows him in the crowded street, or the brilliant saloon; thwarting his schemes, and marring all his intrigues of love or of ambition. In the giddy mazes of the dance, in which Alfonso is addressing his fair partner with the honeyed words of seduction, he sees the stranger pass like a shadow before him; a voice, like the voice of his own soul, whispers in his ear; the words of seduction die from his lips; he no longer hears the music of the dance.

The hero of the drama becomes abstracted and gloomy. Youth, health, wealth, power — all that promised to give a zest to life, have lost their charm. The sweetest cup of pleasure becomes poison to him. Existence is a burthen. To add to his despair, he doubts the fidelity of the fair but frail object of his affection; and suspects the unknown to have supplanted him in her thoughts.

Alfonso now thirsts only for vengeance, but the mysterious stranger eludes his pursuit, and his emissaries in vain endeavour to discover his retreat. At length he succeeds in tracing him to the house of his mistress, and attacks him with the fury of frantic jealousy, taxes him with his wrongs, and demands *satisfaction*. They fight; his rival scarcely defends himself; at the first thrust he receives the sword of Alfonso in his bosom; and in falling, exclaims, "Are you satisfied!"

The mask and mantle of the unknown drop off, and Alfonso discovers his own image — the spectre of himself — he dies with horror!

The spectre is an allegorical being, the personification of conscience, or of the passions . . .

* Professor Ostrom gave a text of this letter in *American Literature,* November 1952. The "former letter" has not been found.

·4 2 3·

The foregoing sketch of the plot may hereafter suggest a rich theme to a poet or dramatist of the Byron school.†

Poe characteristically took up the challenge, and followed his source rather closely, even to the vagueness about some of his

---

† Irving's article describes the plan of a drama projected by Byron, based on an idea supplied to him by Percy Bysshe Shelley from an old Spanish play. Byron did not carry out his plan, but talked about it with Captain Thomas Medwin, friend of both Byron and Shelley, who wrote down notes on it which he gave to Irving in 1825. In March of that year, Irving enthusiastically outlined the plot in a letter to his brother Peter. Neither Medwin nor Irving knew the right name of the play; Medwin thought it might have been by Pedro Calderon de la Barca and entitled *El Capotado* or *El Embozado*, but Irving was unable to find it under any such title and was still looking for it in 1850, when he asked George Ticknor if he could identify it (see P. M. Irving, *Life and Letters of Washington Irving,* 1826ff., II, 232 and IV, 71–72). Irving never collected his article, which was first printed in the *Knickerbocker* for August 1835 with an acknowledgment to Carey and Hart, who were soon to publish it in *The Gift for 1836.*

Meanwhile Medwin in his *Memoir of Percy Bysshe Shelley* (1833), pp. 84–86, in recounting an anecdote said to have come from Byron, added, "Shelley had been reading a strange drama which was supposed to have been written by Calderon, entitled *El Embozado o el encapatado.* It is so scarce that Washington Irving told me he had sought for it without success in several of the public libraries of Spain." Medwin also gave a brief account of the plot. In his *Life of Percy Bysshe Shelley* (2 vols., 1847), II, 300, he repeated the anecdote in expanded form, including the reference to Irving and a summary of the plot, but this time he gave the supposed title of the play as "the El Encapotado."

Resemblances between Poe's tale and the Spanish play as described were noted in 1880, both by R. H. Stoddard (citing P. M. Irving) and by J. H. Ingram (citing Medwin's *Life of Shelley*) in their respective biographies of Poe, but Stoddard dismissed the resemblance as "probably one of those curious coincidences with which all literature abounds," while Ingram said, "Poe's own tale is most closely paralleled in plot by a rare drama attributed to Calderon, called 'El Encaporado' which Washington Irving had called attention to."

Woodberry (*Poe,* 1885, p. 123n., and *Life,* 1909, I 232n.), mentioning both Stoddard and Ingram as speaking of parallels between "William Wilson" and the Calderon play, identified the play as *El Purgatorio de San Patricio,* in which an important character is "Un Hombre Embozado" — a play that Shelley cites as his source for one passage in *The Cenci.* (In the *Life,* Woodberry also mentions Palmer Cobb's attempt to connect Poe's tale with E. T. A. Hoffmann's "Elixiere des Teufels," of which there is an account in *Blackwood's,* July 1824. This last may be dismissed as peripheral.)

Woodberry like, apparently, most other Poe scholars, was still unaware of Irving's article. Because it had appeared in the same issue of *The Gift* as Poe's "MS. Found in a Bottle," I assumed that it was Poe's immediate source for his plot, and published it in the *Americana Collector* for November 1925, and thence as a separate volume (*An Unwritten Drama of Lord Byron by Washington Irving*) late in that year in an edition of 51 copies. I was not aware that my discovery had been anticipated in *The Curio,* January–February 1888, by John Preston Beecher.

WILLIAM WILSON

hero's evil deeds. But he did use also one or two minor sources, pointed out in the notes below.

Telling the story in the first person, Poe gave his protagonist his own birthday, and had him attend a school of the same name as one he attended. But he describes a different building from the real school, and has his hero commit one crime — cheating at cards — of which nobody who knows of Poe's gambling debts can imagine the author was ever guilty.

Poe's originality in "William Wilson" lies in one idea. Each man has only half a complete soul, and the pair has but one conscience, which abides wholly in the half that belongs to the whisperer.‡

The precise date of the composition of "William Wilson" is uncertain, but it was first published in *The Gift for 1840,* of which the prefatory "Advertisement" is dated "May 1st, 1839." On September 21, 1839 Poe wrote Philip Pendleton Cooke, "This tale ... is perhaps the best, although not the last, I have done." Hence it has been given its present position in this edition.

An adaptation, "James Dixon, ou la funeste resemblance," by Gustave Brunet, was published in the Parisian newspaper *La Quotidienne,* December 3 and 4, 1844 — the earliest known appearance of Poe's influence in France.§

Finally, for the general interpretation of this tale it hardly seems necessary to point out that, as in the case of Roderick Usher, Poe is not William Wilson, but the creator of William Wilson.*

TEXTS

(A) The Gift: a Christmas and New Year's Present for 1840 (1839), pp. 229–253; *(B) Burton's Gentleman's Magazine,* October 1839 (5:205–212); *(C) Tales of the Grotesque and Arabesque* (1840), I, 27–57; *(D)* PHANTASY-PIECES (copy of

‡ "Bi-part soul" is mentioned in "Lionizing" and in "The Murders in the Rue Morgue," and the same notion is used in "The Fall of the House of Usher." Persons who look alike appear in "The Fall of the House of Usher" and in "Morella."

§ It was found in the 1950's by W. T. Bandy; see, *inter alia,* Bandy's "Baudelaire et Edgar Poe: Vue rétrospective," *Revue de Littérature comparée* (Paris), avril-juin 1967, p. 184.

* For an illuminating discussion of Poe's use of narrators in his tales, see James W. Gargano, "The Question of Poe's Narrators," *College English,* December 1963, reprinted in Carlson's *Recognition of Edgar Allan Poe.*

the last with manuscript changes, 1842); *(E) Broadway Journal*, August 30, 1845 (2 : 113–119); *(F) Works* (1850), I, 417–436; *(G) Graham's Magazine*, May 1842 (20 : 298–300), brief extracts in a review of Hawthorne's *Twice-Told Tales*; *(H) Works* (1850), III, 201, from the last.

Griswold's version *(F)* is followed. Besides verbal changes, PHANTASY-PIECES has thirty-three punctuation changes, two abortive. Twelve dashes were removed and ten were added. The most careful and extensive revision occurs in the *Broadway Journal (E)*. The brief extracts in the review of Hawthorne's *Twice-Told Tales (G, H)* follow essentially text *C*, adopting certain changes indicated in PHANTASY-PIECES *(D)* and adapting certain other wording to emphasize Poe's implied claim of plagiary.

Reprint
Spirit of the Times (Philadelphia), September 5, 6 and 8, 1845, probably from the *Broadway Journal*.

WILLIAM WILSON. [*F*]

What say of it? what say of CONSCIENCE grim,
That spectre in my path?

Chamberlayne's Pharonnida.

Let me call myself, for the present, William Wilson. The fair page now lying before me need not be sullied with my real appellation. This has been already too much an object for the scorn — for the horror — for the detestation of my race. To the uttermost regions of the globe have not the indignant winds bruited its unparalleled infamy? Oh, outcast of all outcasts most abandoned! — to the earth art thou not forever[a] dead? to its honors, to its flowers, to its golden aspirations? — and a cloud, dense, dismal, and limitless, does it not hang eternally between thy hopes and heaven?

I would not, if I could, here or to-day, embody a record of my later years of unspeakable misery, and unpardonable crime. This epoch — these later years — took unto themselves a sudden elevation in turpitude, whose origin alone it is my present purpose to assign. Men usually grow base by degrees. From me, in an instant, all virtue dropped bodily as a mantle.[b] From comparatively trivial

Title: William Wilson. A Tale. *(A)*;
William Wilson A Tale. *(From the Gift for* 1840*) (B)*
Motto: *Second* of omitted *(E, F)*, *restored from A, B, C, D; conscience (A);* Conscience *(B);* CHAMBERLAINE'S PHARRONIDA *(A);*

Chamberlaine's Pharronida (B, C, D); *Chamberlain's Pharronida (E, F)* spelling corrected editorially
a for ever *(A, B, F) changed to follow C, D, E*
b *After this:* I shrouded my nakedness in triple guilt. *(A, B, C, D)*

wickedness I passed, with the stride of a giant, into more than the enormities of an Elah-Gabalus.[1] What chance — what one event brought this evil thing to pass, bear with me while I relate. Death approaches; and the shadow which foreruns him has thrown a softening influence over my spirit. I long, in passing through the dim valley, for the sympathy — I had nearly said for the pity — of my fellow men. I would fain have them believe that I have been, in some measure, the slave of circumstances beyond human control. I would wish them to seek out for me, in the details I am about to give, some little oasis of *fatality* amid a wilderness of error. I would have them allow — what they cannot refrain from allowing — that, although temptation may have ere-while existed as great, man was never *thus,* at least, tempted before — certainly, never *thus* fell. ᶜAnd is it therefore that he has never thus suffered?ᶜ Have I not indeed been living in a dream? And am I not now dying a victim to the horror and the mystery of the wildest of all sublunary visions?

I am ᵈthe descendantᵈ of a race whose imaginative and easily excitable temperament has at all times rendered them remarkable; and, in my earliest infancy, I gave evidence of having fully inherited the family character. As I advanced in years it was more strongly developed; becoming, for many reasons, a cause of serious disquietude to my friends, and of positive injury to myself. I grew self-willed, addicted to the wildest caprices, and a prey to the most ungovernable passions. Weak-minded, and beset with constitutional infirmities akin to my own, my parents could do but little to check the evil propensities which distinguished me. Some feeble and ill-directed efforts resulted in complete failure on their part, and, of course, in total triumph on mine. Thenceforward my voice was a household law; and at an age when few children have abandoned their leading-strings, I was left to the guidance of my own will, and became, in all but name, the master of my own actions.

My earliest recollections of a school-lifeᵉ are connected with a large, rambling, ᶠElizabethan house,ᶠ in a misty-looking village of

---

c . . . c   And therefore has he never thus suffered. *(A, B, C) changed in D*
d . . . d   come *(A, B, C) changed in D*
e   school-life/school-life, *(E, F) comma*

deleted to follow A, B, C, D
f . . . f   cottage-built, and somewhat decayed building *(A, B, C, D)*

England, where were a vast number of gigantic and gnarled trees, and where all the houses were excessively ancient.[g] In truth, it was a dream-like and spirit-soothing place, that venerable old town. At this moment, in fancy, I feel the refreshing chilliness of its deeply-shadowed avenues, inhale the fragrance of its thousand shrubberies, and thrill anew with undefinable delight, at the deep hollow note of the church-bell, breaking, each hour, with sullen and sudden roar, upon the stillness of the dusky atmosphere in which the[h] fretted Gothic steeple lay imbedded and asleep.[2]

It gives me, perhaps, as much of pleasure as I can now in any manner experience, to dwell upon minute recollections of the school and its concerns. Steeped in misery as I am — misery, alas! only too real — I shall be pardoned for seeking relief, however slight and temporary, in the weakness of a few rambling details. These, moreover, utterly trivial, and even ridiculous in themselves, assume, to my fancy, adventitious importance, as connected with a period and a locality when and where I recognise the first ambiguous monitions of the destiny which afterwards so fully overshadowed me. Let me then remember.

The house, I have said, was [i]old and irregular.[i] The grounds were extensive, and a[j] high and solid brick wall, topped with a bed of mortar and broken glass, encompassed the whole. This prison-like rampart formed the limit of our domain; beyond it we saw but thrice a week — once every Saturday afternoon, when, attended by two ushers, we were permitted to take brief walks in a body through some of the neighboring fields — and twice during Sunday, when we were paraded in the same formal manner to the morning and evening service in the one church of the village. Of this church the principal of our school was pastor. With how deep a spirit of wonder and perplexity was I wont to regard him from our remote pew in the gallery, as, with step solemn and slow, he ascended the pulpit![3] This reverend man, with countenance so demurely benign, with robes so glossy and so clerically flowing, with wig so minutely powdered, so rigid and so vast, — could this be he

---

g   ancient and inordinately tall. (A, B, C) changed in D
h   the old, (A, B, C, D)

i . . . i   old, irregular, and cottage-built. (A, B, C, D)
j   an enormously (A, B, C, D)

who, of late, with sour visage, and in snuffy habiliments, administered, ferule in hand, the Draconian Laws of the academy?[4] Oh, gigantic paradox, too utterly monstrous for solution!

At an angle of the ponderous wall frowned a more ponderous gate. It was riveted and studded with iron bolts, and surmounted with jagged iron spikes. What impressions of deep awe ᵏdid it inspire!ᵏ It was never opened save for the three periodical egressions and ingressions already mentioned; then, in every creak of its mighty hinges, we found a plenitude of mystery — a world of matter for solemn remark, or forˡ more solemn meditation.

The extensive enclosure was irregular in form, having many capacious recesses. Of these, three or four of the largest constituted the play-ground. It was level, and covered with fine hard gravel. I well remember it had no trees, nor benches, nor anything similar within it. Of course it was in the rear of the house. In front lay a small parterre, planted with box and other shrubs; but through this sacred division we passed only upon rare occasions indeed — such as a first advent ᵐto school or final departure thence,ᵐ or perhaps, when a parent or friend having called for us, we joyfully took our way home for the Christmas or Midsummer holydays.

But the house! — how quaint an old building was this! — to me how veritably a palace of enchantment! There was really no end to its windings — to its incomprehensible subdivisions. It was difficult,ⁿ at any given time, to say with certainty upon which of its two stories one happened to be. From each room to every other there were sure to be found three or four steps either in ascent or descent. Then the lateral branches were innumerable — inconceivable — and so returning in upon themselves, that our most exact ideas in regard to the whole mansion were not very far different from those with which we pondered upon infinity. During the five years of my residence here, I was never able to ascertain with precision, in what remote locality lay the little sleeping apartment assigned to myself and some eighteen or twenty other scholars.

The school-room was the largest in the house — I could not

---

k . . . k   it inspired! (A, B, C) changed
in D
l   for far (A, B)

m . . . m   or final departure from
school, (A)
n   impossible, (A, B, C, D)

who, of late, with sour visage, and in snuffy habiliments, administered, ferule in hand, the Draconian Laws of the academy?[4] Oh, gigantic paradox, too utterly monstrous for solution!

At an angle of the ponderous wall frowned a more ponderous gate. It was riveted and studded with iron bolts, and surmounted with jagged iron spikes. What impressions of deep awe [k]did it inspire![k] It was never opened save for the three periodical egressions and ingressions already mentioned; then, in every creak of its mighty hinges, we found a plenitude of mystery — a world of matter for solemn remark, or for[l] more solemn meditation.

The extensive enclosure was irregular in form, having many capacious recesses. Of these, three or four of the largest constituted the play-ground. It was level, and covered with fine hard gravel. I well remember it had no trees, nor benches, nor anything similar within it. Of course it was in the rear of the house. In front lay a small parterre, planted with box and other shrubs; but through this sacred division we passed only upon rare occasions indeed — such as a first advent [m]to school or final departure thence,[m] or perhaps, when a parent or friend having called for us, we joyfully took our way home for the Christmas or Midsummer holydays.

But the house! — how quaint an old building was this! — to me how veritably a palace of enchantment! There was really no end to its windings — to its incomprehensible subdivisions. It was difficult,[n] at any given time, to say with certainty upon which of its two stories one happened to be. From each room to every other there were sure to be found three or four steps either in ascent or descent. Then the lateral branches were innumerable — inconceivable — and so returning in upon themselves, that our most exact ideas in regard to the whole mansion were not very far different from those with which we pondered upon infinity. During the five years of my residence here, I was never able to ascertain with precision, in what remote locality lay the little sleeping apartment assigned to myself and some eighteen or twenty other scholars.

The school-room was the largest in the house — I could not

---

k . . . k   it inspired! *(A, B, C) changed in D*
l   for far *(A, B)*

m . . . m   or final departure from school, *(A)*
n   impossible, *(A, B, C, D)*

help thinking, in the world. It was very long, narrow, and dismally low, with pointed Gothic windows and a ceiling of oak. In a remote and terror-inspiring angle was a square enclosure of eight or ten feet, comprising the *sanctum,*[o] "during hours," of our principal, the Reverend Dr. Bransby. It was a solid structure, with massy door, sooner than open which in the absence of the "Dominie," we would all have willingly perished by the *peine forte et dure.*[5] In other angles were two other similar boxes, far less reverenced, indeed, but still greatly matters of awe. One of these was the pulpit of the "classical" usher, one of the "English and mathematical." Interspersed about the room, crossing and recrossing in endless irregularity, were innumerable benches and desks, black, ancient, and time-worn, piled desperately with much-bethumbed books, and so beseamed with initial letters, names at full length,[p] grotesque figures, and other multiplied efforts of the knife, as to have entirely[q] lost what little of original form might have been their portion in days long departed. A huge bucket with water stood at one extremity of the room, and a clock of stupendous dimensions at the other.

Encompassed by the massy walls of this venerable academy, I passed, yet not in tedium or disgust, the years of the third lustrum of my life. The teeming brain of childhood requires no external world of incident to occupy or amuse it; and the apparently dismal monotony of a school was replete with more intense excitement than my riper youth has derived from luxury, or my full manhood from crime. Yet I must believe that my first mental development had in it much of the uncommon — even much of the *outré.*[r] Upon mankind at large the events of very early existence rarely leave in mature age any definite impression. All is gray shadow — a weak and irregular remembrance — an indistinct regathering of feeble pleasures and phantasmagoric pains. With me this is not so. In childhood I must have felt with the energy of a man what I now find stamped upon memory in lines as vivid, as deep, and as durable as the *exergues*[s] of the Carthaginian medals.[6]

---

o sanctum, *(A, B, C, D)*

p length, meaningless gashes, *(A, B, C, D)*

q utterly *(A)*

r *outre. (F)*

s exergues *(A, B, C, D)*

Yet in fact — in the fact of the world's view — how little was there to remember! The morning's awakening, the nightly summons to bed; the connings, the recitations; the periodical half-holidays, and perambulations; the play-ground, with its broils, its pastimes, its intrigues; — these, by a mental sorcery long forgotten, were made to involve a wilderness of sensation, a world of rich incident, an universe of varied emotion, of excitement the most passionate and spirit-stirring. *"Oh, le bon temps, que ce siecle de fer!"*[7]

In truth, the ardor,[t] the enthusiasm, and the imperiousness of my disposition, soon rendered me a marked character among my schoolmates, and by slow, but natural gradations, gave me an ascendancy over all not greatly older than myself; — over all with a[u] single exception. This exception was found in the person of a scholar, who, although no relation, bore the same Christian[v] and surname as myself; — a circumstance, in fact,[w] little remarkable; for, notwithstanding a noble descent, mine was one of those every-day appellations which seem, by prescriptive right, to have been, time out of mind, the common property of the mob.[8] In this narrative I have therefore designated myself as William Wilson, — a fictitious title not very dissimilar to the real. My namesake alone, of those who in school-phraseology[x] constituted "our set," presumed to compete with me in the studies of the class — in the sports and broils of the play-ground — to refuse implicit belief in my assertions, and submission to my will — indeed, to interfere with my arbitrary dictation in any respect whatsoever. If there is[y] on earth a supreme and unqualified despotism, it is the despotism of a master-mind[z] in boyhood over the less energetic spirits of its[a] companions.

Wilson's rebellion was to me a source of the greatest embarrassment; the more so as, in spite of the bravado with which in public I made a point of treating him and his pretensions, I secretly felt

---

t ardency, *(A, B, C, D)*
u one *(A, B, C, D)*
v christian *(F) capitalized to follow A, B, C, D, E*
w truth, *(A)*

x school phraseology *(A, B, C, D, E)*
y be *(A, B, C) changed in D*
z master mind *(A, B, C, D, E)*
a his *(A)*

that I feared him, and could not help thinking the equality which he maintained so easily with myself, a proof of his true superiority; since not to be overcome cost me a perpetual struggle. Yet this superiority — even this equality — was in truth acknowledged by no one but myself; our associates,[b] by some unaccountable blindness, seemed not even to suspect it. Indeed, his competition, his resistance, and especially his impertinent and dogged interference with my purposes, were not more pointed than private. He apeared to be[c] destitute alike of the ambition which urged, and of the passionate energy of mind which enabled me to excel. In his rivalry he might have been supposed actuated solely by a whimsical desire to thwart, astonish, or mortify myself; although there were times when I could not help observing, with a feeling made up of wonder, abasement, and pique, that he mingled with his injuries, his insults, or his contradictions, a certain most inappropriate, and assuredly most unwelcome *affectionateness* of manner. I could only conceive this singular behavior to arise from a consummate self-conceit assuming the vulgar airs of patronage and protection.

Perhaps it was this latter trait in Wilson's conduct, conjoined with our identity of name, and the mere accident of our having entered the school upon the same day, which set afloat the notion that we were brothers, among the senior classes in the academy. These do not usually inquire with much strictness into the affairs of their juniors. I have before said, or should have said, that Wilson was not, in the most remote degree, connected with my family. But assuredly if we *had* been brothers we must have been twins; for, after[d] leaving Dr. Bransby's, I casually learned that my namesake[e] was born on the nineteenth of January, 1813[f] — [g]and this is a somewhat remarkable coincidence; for the day is precisely that[g] of my own nativity.[9]

It may seen strange that in spite of the continual anxiety occasioned me by the rivalry of Wilson, and his intolerable spirit of

---

b   companions, *(A)*
c   be utterly *(A, B, C) changed in D*
d   since *(A)*
e   namesake — a somewhat remarkable coincidence — *(A, B, C); all after* namesake *deleted in D*

f   1811 *(A, B);* 1809 *(C) changed back to* 1811 *in D*
g . . . g and this is precisely the day *(A, B, C);* a somewhat remarkable cöincidence; for the day is precisely that *(D)*

contradiction, I could not bring myself to hate him altogether. We had, to be sure, nearly every day a quarrel in which, yielding me publicly the palm of victory, he, in some manner, contrived to make me feel that it was he who had deserved it; yet a sense of pride on[h] my part, and a veritable dignity on[i] his own, kept us always upon what are called "speaking terms," while there were many points of strong congeniality in our tempers, operating to awake in me a sentiment which our position alone, perhaps, prevented from ripening into friendship. It is difficult, indeed, to define, or even to describe, my real feelings towards him. They [j]formed a motley and[j] heterogeneous [k]admixture; — some[k] petulant animosity, which was not yet hatred, some esteem, more respect, much fear, with a world of uneasy curiosity. [l]To the moralist it will be unnecessary[l] to say, in addition, that Wilson and myself were the most inseparable of companions.

It was no doubt the anomalous state of affairs existing between us, which turned all my attacks upon him, (and they were many, either open or covert) into the channel of banter or practical joke (giving pain while assuming the aspect of mere fun) rather than into[m] a more serious and determined hostility. But my endeavors on this head were by no means uniformly successful, even when my plans were the most wittily concocted; for my namesake had much about him, in character, of that unassuming and quiet austerity which, while enjoying the poignancy of its own jokes, has no heel of Achilles in itself,[10] and absolutely refuses to be laughed at. I could find, indeed, but one vulnerable point, and that, lying in a personal peculiarity, arising, perhaps, from constitutional disease, would have been spared by any antagonist less at his wit's end than myself; — my rival had a weakness in the faucial or guttural organs, which precluded him from raising his voice at any time *above a very low whisper*. Of this defect I did not fail to take what poor advantage lay in my power.

Wilson's retaliations in kind were many; and there was one

---

h   upon *(A, B, C, D)*
i   upon *(A, B, C, D)*
j . . . j   were formed of a *(A, B, C);* formed a *(D)*
k . . . k   mixture — some *(A, B, C, D)*

l . . . l   To the moralist fully acquainted with the minute springs of human action, it will be unnecessary *(A, B, C);* It will scarcely be necessary *(D)*
m   into that of *(A, B, C, D)*

form of his practical wit that disturbed me beyond measure. How his sagacity first discovered at all that so petty a thing would vex me, is a question I never could solve; but,[n] having discovered, he habitually practised the annoyance. I had always felt aversion to my uncourtly patronymic, and its very common, if not plebeian prænomen.[o] The words were venom in my ears; and when, upon the day of my arrival, a second William Wilson came also to the academy, I felt angry with him for bearing the name, and doubly disgusted with the name because a stranger bore it, who would be the cause of its twofold repetition, who would be constantly in my presence, and whose concerns, in the ordinary routine of the school business, must inevitably, on account of the detestable coincidence, be often confounded with my own.

The feeling of vexation thus engendered grew stronger with every circumstance tending to show resemblance, moral or physical, between my rival and myself. I had not then discovered the remarkable fact that we were of the same age; but I saw that we were of the same height, and I perceived that we were [p]even singularly alike[p] in general contour of person and outline of feature. I was galled, too, by the rumor touching a relationship, which had grown current in the upper forms. In a word, nothing could more seriously disturb me, (although I scrupulously concealed such disturbance,) than any allusion to a similarity of mind, person, or condition existing between us. But, in truth, I had no reason to believe that (with the exception of the matter of relationship, and in the case of Wilson himself,) this similarity had ever been made a subject of comment, or even observed at all by our schoolfellows. That *he* observed it in all its bearings, and as fixedly as I, was apparent; but that he could discover in such circumstances so fruitful a field of annoyance,[q] can only be attributed, as I said before, to his more than ordinary penetration.

His cue, which was to perfect an imitation of myself, lay both in words and in actions; and most admirably did he play his part. My dress it was an easy matter to copy; my gait and general man-

---

n but *(F) comma added from A, B,*
C, D, E
o praenomen. *(A, B, C) changed in D*

p . . . p not altogether unlike
(A, B, C, D)
q annoyance for myself *(A, B, C, D)*

ner were, without difficulty, appropriated; in spite of his constitutional defect, even my voice did not escape him. My louder tones were, of course, unattempted, but then the key, it was identical; *and his singular whisper, it grew the very echo of my own.*

How greatly this most exquisite portraiture harassed me, (for it could not justly be termed a caricature,) I will not now venture to describe. I had but one consolation — in the fact that the imitation, apparently, was noticed by myself alone, and that I had to endure only the knowing and strangely sarcastic smiles of my namesake himself. Satisfied with having produced in my bosom the intended effect, he seemed to chuckle in secret over the sting he had inflicted, and was characteristically disregardful of the public applause which the success of his witty endeavors might have so easily elicited. That the school, indeed, did not feel his design, perceive its accomplishment, and participate in his sneer, was, for many anxious[r] months, a riddle I could not resolve. Perhaps the *gradation* of his copy rendered it not so readily perceptible; or, more possibly, I owed my security to the masterly air of the copyist, who, disdaining the letter, (which in a painting is all the obtuse can see,) gave but the full spirit of his original for my individual contemplation and chagrin.

I have already more than once spoken of the disgusting air of patronage which he assumed toward[s] me, and of his frequent officious interference with my will. This interference often took the ungracious character of advice; advice not openly given, but hinted or insinuated. I received it with a repugnance which gained strength as I grew in years. Yet, at this distant day, let me do him the simple justice to acknowledge that I can recall no occasion when the suggestions of my rival were on the side of those errors or follies so usual to his immature age and seeming inexperience; that his moral sense, at least, if not his general talents and worldly wisdom, was far keener than my own; and that I might, to-day, have been a better, and thus a happier man, had I [t]less frequently[t] rejected the counsels embodied in those meaning whispers which I then but too cordially hated and too bitterly despised.[u]

---

r   *Canceled (D)*
s   towards *(A, B, C, D)*
t . . . t   more seldom *(A, B, C)*

changed in D
u   derided. *(A, B, C) changed in D*

As it was, I at length grew restive in the extreme under his distasteful supervision, and daily resented more and more openly what I considered his intolerable[v] arrogance. I have said that, in the first years of our connexion as schoolmates, my feelings in regard to him might have been easily ripened into friendship: but, in the latter months of my residence at the academy, although the intrusion of his ordinary manner had, beyond doubt, in some measure, abated, my sentiments, in nearly similar proportion, partook very much of positive hatred. Upon one occasion he saw this, I think, and afterwards avoided, or made a show of avoiding me.

It was about the same period, if I remember aright, that, in an altercation of violence with him, in which he was more than usually thrown off his guard, and spoke and acted with an openness of demeanor rather foreign to his nature, I discovered, or fancied I discovered, in his accent, his air, and general appearance, a something which first startled, and then deeply interested me, by bringing to mind dim visions of my earliest infancy — wild, confused and thronging memories of a time when memory herself was yet unborn. I cannot better describe the sensation which oppressed me, than by saying that[w] I could with difficulty shake off the belief [x]of my having been acquainted with the being who stood before me,[x] at some epoch very long ago — some point of the past even infinitely remote. The delusion, however, faded rapidly as it came; and I mention it at all but to define the day of the last conversation I there held with my singular namesake.

The huge old house, with its countless subdivisions, had several[y] large chambers communicating with each other, where slept the greater number of the students. There were, however, (as must necessarily happen in a building so awkwardly planned,) many little nooks or recesses, the odds and ends of the structure; and these the economic ingenuity of Dr. Bransby had also fitted up as dormitories; although, being the merest closets, they were capable of accommodating but[z] a single individual. One of these small apartments was occupied by Wilson.

---

v   *Canceled (D)*
w   *Canceled (D)*
x . . . x   that myself and the being who stood before me had been acquainted

y   several enormously *(A, B, C, D)*
z   only *(A, B, C, D)*

(A, B, C, D)

WILLIAM WILSON

^aOne night,^a about the close of my fifth year at the school, and immediately after the altercation just mentioned,^b finding every one wrapped in sleep, I arose from bed, and, lamp in hand, stole through a wilderness of narrow passages from my own bedroom to that of my rival. I had long been^c plotting one of those ill-natured pieces of practical wit at his expense in which I had hitherto been so uniformly unsuccessful. It was my intention, now, to put my scheme in operation, and I resolved to make him feel the whole extent of the malice with which I was imbued. Having reached his closet, I noiselessly entered, leaving the lamp, with a shade over it, on the outside. I advanced a step, and listened to the sound of his tranquil breathing. Assured of his being asleep, I returned, took the light, and with it again approached the bed. Close curtains were around it, which, in the prosecution of my plan, I slowly and quietly withdrew, when the bright rays fell vividly upon the sleeper, and my eyes, at the same moment, upon his countenance. I looked; — and a numbness, an iciness of feeling instantly pervaded my frame. My breast heaved, my knees tottered, my whole spirit became possessed with an objectless yet intolerable horror. Gasping for breath, I lowered the lamp in still nearer proximity to the face. Were these, — *these* the lineaments of William Wilson? I saw, indeed, that they were his, but I shook as if^d with a fit of the ague, in fancying they were not. What *was* there about them to confound me in this manner? I gazed; — while my brain reeled with a multitude of incoherent thoughts. Not thus he appeared — assuredly not *thus* — in the vivacity of his waking hours. The same name! the same contour of person! the same day of arrival at the academy! And then his dogged and meaningless imitation of my gait, my voice, my habits, and my manner! Was it, in truth, within the bounds of human possibility, that *what I now saw*^e was the result, merely,^f of the habitual practice of this sarcastic imitation? Awe-stricken, and with a creeping shudder, I extinguished the lamp, passed silently from the chamber, and left, at once, the halls of that old academy, never to enter them again.

---

a . . . a   It was upon a gloomy and tempestuous night of an early autumn, *(A, B, C, D)*
b   mentioned, that, *(A, B, C, D)*
c   long been/been long *(A, B, C, D)*
d   *Omitted (A, B, C, D)*
e   *witnessed (A, B, C)* changed in D
f   result, merely,/result *(A, B, C, D)*

After a lapse of some months, spent at home in mere idleness, I found myself a student at Eton. The brief interval had been sufficient to enfeeble my remembrance of the events at Dr. Bransby's, or at least to effect a material change in the nature of the feelings with which I remembered them. The truth — the tragedy — of the drama was no more. I could now find room to doubt the evidence of my senses; and seldom called up the subject at all but with wonder at the extent of human credulity, and a smile at the vivid force of the imagination which I hereditarily possessed. Neither was this species of skepticism likely to be diminished by the character of the life I led at Eton. The vortex of thoughtless folly into which I there so immediately and so recklessly plunged, washed away all but the froth of my past hours, ingulfed[g] at once every solid or serious impression, and left to memory only the veriest levities of a former existence.

I do not wish, however, to trace the course of my miserable profligacy here — a profligacy which set at defiance the laws, while it eluded the vigilance of the institution. Three years of folly, passed without profit, had but given me rooted habits of vice, and added, in a somewhat unusual degree, to my bodily stature, when, after a week of soulless dissipation, I invited a small party of the most dissolute students to a secret carousal in my chambers.[h] We met at a late hour of the night; for our debaucheries were to be faithfully protracted until morning. The wine flowed freely, and there were not wanting other and[i] perhaps more dangerous seductions; so that the gray dawn had already faintly appeared in the east, while our delirious extravagance was at its height. Madly flushed with cards and intoxication, I was in the act of insisting upon a toast of more than wonted[j] profanity, when my attention was suddenly diverted by the violent, although partial unclosing of the door of the apartment, and by the eager voice [k]of a servant from without.[k] He said that some person, apparently in great haste, demanded to speak with me in the hall.

---

g   engulfed *(A, B, C, D, E)*
h   chamber. *(A, B, C) changed in D*
i   other and/other, *(A, B, C) changed in D*

j   intolerable *(A, B, C) changed in D*
k . . . k   from without of a servant. *(A, B, C, D)*

Wildly excited with wine,[1] the unexpected interruption rather delighted than surprised me. I staggered forward at once, and a few steps brought me to the vestibule of the building. In this low and small room there hung no lamp; and now no light at all was admitted, save that of the exceedingly feeble dawn which made its way through the[m] semi-circular window. As I put my foot over the threshold, I became aware of the figure of a youth about my own height, and[n] habited in a white kerseymere[o] morning frock,[11] cut in the novel fashion of the one I myself wore at the moment. This the faint light enabled me to perceive; but the features of his face I could not distinguish. Upon[p] my entering, he strode hurriedly up to me, and, seizing me by the arm with a gesture of petulant impatience, whispered the words "William Wilson!" in my ear.

I grew perfectly sober in an instant.

There was that in the manner of the stranger, and in the tremulous shake of his uplifted finger, as he held it between my eyes and the light, which filled me with unqualified amazement; but it was not this which had so violently moved me. It was the pregnancy of solemn admonition in the singular, low, hissing utterance; and, above all, it was the character, the tone, *the key,* of those few, simple, and familiar, yet *whispered*[q] syllables, which came with a thousand thronging memories of by-gone days, and struck upon my soul with the shock of a galvanic battery. Ere I could recover the use of my senses he was gone.

Although this event failed not of a vivid effect upon my disordered imagination, yet was it evanescent as vivid. For some weeks, indeed, I busied myself in earnest inquiry, or was wrapped in a cloud of morbid speculation. I did not pretend to disguise from my perception the identity of the singular individual who thus perseveringly interfered with my affairs, and harassed me with his insinuated counsel. But who and what was this Wilson? — and whence came he? — and what were his purposes? Upon neither of these points could I be satisfied — merely ascertaining, in regard to

l   the potent *Vin de Barac,* (A, B, C, D)

m   a *(A, B, C, D)*

n   and (what then peculiarly struck my mad fancy) *(A, B, C, D)*

o   cassimere *(A, B, C, D)*

p   Immediately upon *(A, B, C, D)*

q   whispered *(A, B, C, D)*

him, that a sudden accident in his family had caused his removal from Dr. Bransby's academy on the afternoon of the day in which I myself had eloped. But in a brief period I ceased to think upon the subject, my attention being all absorbed in a contemplated departure for Oxford. Thither I soon went, the uncalculating vanity of my parents furnishing[r] me with an outfit and annual establishment, which would enable me to indulge at will in the luxury already so dear to my heart — to vie in profuseness of expenditure with the haughtiest heirs of the wealthiest earldoms in Great Britain.

Excited by such appliances to vice, my constitutional temperament broke forth with redoubled ardor, and I spurned even the common restraints of decency in the mad infatuation of my revels. But it were absurd to pause in the detail of my extravagance. Let it suffice, that among spendthrifts I out-Heroded[s] Herod,[12] and that, giving name to a multitude of novel follies, I added no brief appendix to the long catalogue of vices then usual in the most dissolute university of Europe.

It could hardly be credited, however, that I had, even here, so utterly fallen from the gentlemanly estate, as to seek acquaintance with the vilest arts of the gambler by profession, and, having become an adept in his despicable science, to practise it habitually as a means of increasing my already enormous income at the expense of the weak-minded among my fellow-collegians. Such, nevertheless, was the fact. And the very enormity of this offence against all manly and honorable sentiment proved, beyond doubt, the main if not the sole reason of the impunity with which it was committed. Who, indeed, among my most abandoned associates, would not rather have disputed the clearest evidence of his senses, than have suspected of such courses, the gay, the frank, the generous William Wilson — the noblest and most liberal commoner at Oxford — him whose follies (said his parasites) were but the follies of youth and unbridled fancy — whose errors but inimitable whim — whose darkest vice but a careless and dashing extravagance?

I had been now two years successfully busied in this way, when there came to the university a young *parvenu* nobleman, Glendin-

---

r   furnished *(A)*   s   out-heroded *(A, B, C) capitalized in D* ning[13] — rich, said report, as Herodes Atticus — his riches, too, as easily acquired.[14] I soon found him of weak intellect, and, of course, marked him as a fitting subject for my skill. I frequently engaged him in play, and contrived, with the[t] gambler's usual art, to let him win considerable sums, the more effectually to entangle him in my snares. At length, my schemes being ripe, I met him (with the full intention that this meeting should be final and decisive) at the chambers of a fellow-commoner, (Mr. Preston,)[15] equally intimate with both, but who, to do him justice, entertained not even a remote suspicion of my design. To give to this a better coloring, I had contrived to have assembled a party of some eight or ten, and was solicitously careful that the introduction of cards should appear accidental, and originate in the proposal of my contemplated dupe himself. To be brief upon a vile topic, none of the low finesse was omitted, so customary upon similar occasions[t'] that it is a just matter for wonder how any are still found so besotted as to fall its victim.

We had protracted our sitting far into the night, and I had at length effected the manœuvre of getting Glendinning as my sole antagonist. The game, too, was my favorite *écarté*.[u] The rest of the company, interested in the extent of our play, had abandoned their own cards, and were standing around us as spectators. The *parvenu*, who had been induced by my artifices in the early part of the evening, to drink deeply, now shuffled, dealt, or played, with a wild nervousness of manner for which his intoxication, I thought, might partially, but could not altogether account. In a very short period he had became my debtor to a large amount,[v] when, having taken a long draught of port, he did precisely what I had been coolly anticipating — he[w] proposed to double our already extravagant stakes. With a well-feigned show of reluctance, and not until after my repeated refusal had seduced him into some angry words which gave a color of *pique* to my compliance, did I finally comply. The result, of course, did but prove how entirely

---

t a *(A, B, C, D)*
t' occasions, *(F) comma deleted to follow A, B, C, D, E*
u *ecarte. (F)*

v amount of money, *(A, B, C) changed in D*
w *Omitted (A)*

the prey was in my toils: in less than an^x hour he had quadrupled his debt. For some time his countenance had been losing the florid tinge lent it by the wine; but now, to my astonishment, I perceived that it had grown to a pallor^y truly fearful. I say, to my astonishment. Glendinning had been represented to my eager inquiries as immeasurably wealthy; and the sums which he had as yet lost, although in themselves vast, could not, I supposed, very seriously annoy, much less so violently affect him. That he was overcome by the wine just swallowed, was the idea which most readily presented itself; and, rather with a view to the preservation of my own character in the eyes of my associates, than from any less interested motive, I was about to insist, peremptorily, upon a discontinuance of the play, when some expressions at my elbow from among the company, and an ejaculation evincing utter despair on the part of Glendinning, gave me to understand that I had effected his total ruin under circumstances which, rendering him an object for the pity of all, should have protected him from the ill offices even of a fiend.

What now might have been my conduct it is difficult to say. The pitiable condition of my dupe had thrown an air of embarrassed gloom over all; and, for some moments, a profound^z silence was maintained, during which I could not help feeling my cheeks tingle with the many burning glances of scorn or reproach cast upon me by the less abandoned of the party. I will even own that an intolerable weight of anxiety was for a brief instant lifted from my bosom by the sudden and extraordinary interruption which ensued. The wide, heavy folding doors of the apartment were all at once thrown open, to their full extent, with a vigorous and rushing impetuosity that extinguished, as if by magic, every candle in the room. Their light, in dying, enabled us just to perceive that a stranger had entered, about^a my own height, and closely muffled in a cloak. The darkness, however, was now total; and we could only *feel*^{b} that he was standing in our midst. Before any one of us could recover from the extreme astonishment into

---

x   a single *(A, B, C, D)*
y   palor *(C) corrected in D*
z   profound and unbroken *(A, B, C, D)*

a   of about *(A, B, C, D)*
b   feel *(A, B, C, D)*

which this rudeness had thrown all, we heard the voice of the intruder.

"Gentlemen," he said, in a low, distinct, and never-to-be-forgotten *whisper* which thrilled to the very marrow of my bones, "Gentlemen, I make no apology for this behavior, because in thus behaving, I am but fulfilling a duty. You are, beyond doubt, uninformed of the true character of the person who has to-night won at *écarté*[c] a large sum of money from Lord Glendinning. I will therefore put you upon an expeditious and decisive plan of obtaining this very necessary information. Please to examine, at your leisure, the inner linings of the cuff of his left sleeve, and the several little packages which may be found in the somewhat capacious pockets of his embroidered morning wrapper."[16]

While he spoke, so profound was the stillness that one might have heard a pin drop[d] upon the floor. In ceasing, he [e]departed at once,[e] and as abruptly as he had entered. Can I — shall I describe my sensations? Must[f] I say that I felt all the horrors of the damned? Most assuredly I had[g] little time[h] for reflection. Many hands roughly seized me upon the spot, and lights were immediately re-procured. A search ensued. In the lining of my sleeve were found all[i] the court cards essential in *écarté*,[j] and, in the pockets of my wrapper, a number of packs, fac-similes of those used at our sittings, with the single exception that mine were of the species called, technically, *arrondées*;[k] the honors being slightly convex at the ends, the lower cards slightly convex at the sides. In this disposition, the dupe who cuts, as customary, at the length[l] of the pack, will invariably find that he cuts his antagonist an honor; while the gambler, cutting at the breadth,[m] will, as certainly, cut nothing for his victim which may count in the records of the game.[17]

Any[n] burst of indignation upon this[o] discovery would have

---

c   *ecarte (F)*
d   dropping *(A, B, C) changed in D*
e . . . e   at once departed *(A, B, C, D)*
f   Must/ — must *(A, B, C, E) changed in D*
g   had but *(A, B)*
h   time given *(A, B, C, D, E)*

i   all of *(A, B, C, D)*
j   *ecarte (F)*
k   *arrondé; (A); arrondees; (F)*
l   breadth *(A, B, C, D)*
m   length, *(A, B, C, D)*
n   Any outrageous *(A, B, C, D)*
o   this shameful *(A, B, C, D)*

affected me less than the silent contempt, or the sarcastic composure, with which it was received.

"Mr. Wilson," said our host, stooping to remove from beneath his feet an exceedingly luxurious cloak of rare furs, "Mr. Wilson, this is your property." (The weather was cold; and, upon quitting my own room, I had thrown a cloak over my dressing wrapper, putting it off upon reaching the scene of play.) "I presume it is supererogatory to seek here (eyeing the folds of the garment with a bitter smile) for any farther evidence of your skill. Indeed, we have had enough. You will see the necessity, I hope, of quitting Oxford — at all events, of quitting instantly my chambers."

Abased, humbled to the dust as I then was, it is probable that I should have resented this galling language by immediate personal violence, had not my whole attention been ᵖat the momentᵖ arrested by a fact of the most startling character. The cloak which I had worn was of a rare description of fur; how rare, how extravagantly costly, I shall not venture to say. Its fashion, too, was of my own fantastic invention; for I was fastidious to ᑫan absurd degree ofᑫ coxcombry, in matters of this frivolous nature. When, therefore, Mr. Preston reached me that which he had picked up upon the floor, and near the folding-doors of the apartment, it was with an astonishment nearly bordering upon terror, that I perceived my own already hanging on my arm, (where I had no doubt unwittingly placed it,) and that the one presented me was but its exact counterpart in every, ʳin even the minutest possibleʳ particular. The singular being who had so disastrously exposed me, had been muffled, I remember, in a cloak; and none had been worn at all by any of the members of our party, with the exception of myself. Retaining some presence of mind, I took the one offered me by Preston; placed it, unnoticed, over my own; left the apartment with a resolute scowl of defiance; and, next morning ere dawn of day, commenced a hurried journey from Oxford to the continent, in a perfect agony of horror and of shame.

I fled in vain. My evil destiny pursued me as if in exultation, and proved, indeed, that the exercise of its mysterious dominion

---

p . . . p immediately *(A)*   r . . . r *Canceled (D)*
q . . . q a degree of absurd *(A, B, C, D)*

had as yet only begun. Scarcely had I set foot in Paris, ere I had fresh evidence of the detestable interest taken by this Wilson in my concerns. Years flew, while I experienced no relief. Villain! — at Rome, with how untimely, yet with how spectral an officiousness, stepped he in between me and my ambition! At Vienna, too — at Berlin — and at Moscow! Where, in truth, had I *not* bitter cause to curse him within my heart? From his inscrutable tyranny did I at length flee, panic-stricken, as from a pestilence; and to the very ends of the earth *I fled in vain.*

And again, and again, in secret communion with my own spirit, would I demand the questions "Who is he? — whence came he? — and what are his objects?" But no answer was there found. And now I scrutinized, with a minute scrutiny, the forms, and the methods, and the leading traits of his impertinent supervision. But even here there was very little upon which to base a conjecture. It was noticeable, indeed, that, in no one of the multiplied instances in which he had of late crossed my path, had he so crossed it except to frustrate those schemes, or to disturb those actions, which, if[s] fully carried out, might have resulted in bitter mischief. Poor justification this, in truth, for an authority so imperiously assumed! Poor indemnity for natural rights of self-agency so pertinaciously, so insultingly denied!

I had also been forced to notice that my tormentor, for a very long period of time, (while scrupulously and with miraculous dexterity maintaining his whim of an identity of apparel with myself,) had so contrived it, in the execution of his varied interference with my will, that I saw not, at any moment, the features of his face. Be Wilson what he might, *this*, at least, was but the veriest of affectation, or of folly. Could he, for an instant, have supposed that, in my admonisher at Eton — in the destroyer of my honor at Oxford, — in him who thwarted my ambition at Rome, my revenge at[t] Paris, my passionate love at Naples, or what he falsely termed my avarice in Egypt, — that in this, my arch-enemy and evil genius, I could fail to recognise the William Wilson of my school-boy[u] days, — the namesake, the companion, the rival, — the hated[v] and

---

s *Omitted (A, B, C, D)* u schoolboy *(A, B, C, D, E)*
t in *(A, B, C, D)* v hatred *(C, D) misprint*

dreaded rival at Dr. Bransby's? Impossible! — But let me hasten to the last eventful scene of the drama.

Thus far I had succumbed supinely[w] to this imperious domination. The sentiment[x] of deep awe with which I habitually regarded the elevated character, the majestic wisdom, the apparent omnipresence and omnipotence of Wilson, added to a feeling of even terror, with which certain other traits in his nature and assumptions inspired me, had operated, hitherto, to impress me with an idea of my own utter [y]weakness and[y] helplessness, and to suggest an implicit, although bitterly reluctant submission to his arbitrary[z] will. But, of late days, I had given myself up entirely to wine; and its maddening influence upon my hereditary temper rendered me more and more impatient of control. I began to murmur, — to hesitate, — to resist. And was it only fancy which induced me to believe that, with the increase of my own firmness, that of my tormentor underwent a proportional diminution? Be this as it may, I now began to feel the inspiration[a] of a burning hope, and at length nurtured in my secret thoughts a stern and desperate resolution that I would submit no longer to be enslaved.

It was at Rome, during the Carnival of 18 — , that I attended a masquerade in the palazzo of the Neapolitan Duke Di Broglio.[18] I had indulged more freely than usual in the excesses of the wine-table; and now the suffocating atmosphere of the crowded rooms irritated me beyond endurance. The difficulty, too, of forcing my way through the mazes of the company contributed not a little to the ruffling of my temper; for I was anxiously seeking (let me not say with what unworthy motive) the young, the gay, the beautiful wife of the aged and doting Di Broglio. With a too unscrupulous confidence she had previously communicated to me the secret of the costume in which she would be habited, and now, having caught a glimpse of her person, I was hurrying to make my way into her presence. At this moment I felt a light hand placed[b] upon my shoulder, and that ever-remembered, low, damnable *whisper*[c] within my ear.

---

w *Canceled (D)*
x sentiments *(A, B, C, D)*
y...y *Canceled (D)*
z *Canceled (D)*

a inspirations *(A)*
b laid *(A)*
c whisper *(A, B, C, D)*

In ^dan absolute frenzy^d of wrath, I turned at once upon him who had thus interrupted me, and seized him violently by the collar. He was attired, as I had^e expected, ^fin a costume altogether similar to my own;^f wearing a ^gSpanish cloak of blue velvet, begirt about the waist with a crimson belt sustaining a rapier. A mask of black silk entirely covered his face.^g

"Scoundrel!" I said, in a voice husky with rage, while every syllable I uttered seemed as new fuel to my fury; "scoundrel! impostor! accursed villain! you shall not — you *shall*^h not dog me unto death! Follow me, or I stab you where you^i stand!" — and I broke my way from the ball-room^j into a small ante-chamber adjoining, dragging him unresistingly with me as I went.

Upon entering, I thrust him furiously from me. He staggered against the wall, while I closed the door with an oath, and commanded him to draw. He hesitated but for an instant; then, with a slight sigh, drew in silence, and put himself upon his defence.

The contest was brief indeed. I was frantic with every species of wild excitement, and felt within my single arm the energy and^k power of a multitude. In a few seconds I forced him by sheer strength against the wainscoting, and thus, getting him at mercy, plunged my sword, with brute ferocity, repeatedly through and through his bosom.

At that^l instant some person tried the latch of the door. I hastened to prevent an intrusion, and then immediately returned to my dying antagonist. But what human language can adequately portray *that* astonishment, *that* horror which possessed me at the spectacle then presented to view?^m ^nThe brief moment in which I averted my eyes had been sufficient to produce, apparently, a material change in the arrangements^o at the upper or farther end of the room. A large ^pmirror, — so at first it seemed to me in my con-

---

d . . . d   a perfect whirlwind *(A, B, C, D)*
e   *Omitted (A)*
f . . . f   like myself; *(A, B, C, D)*
g . . . g   large Spanish cloak, and a mask of black silk which entirely covered his features. *(A, B, C, D)*
h   shall *(C, D)*
i   I *(A)*
j   room *(A, B, C, D)*

k   and the *(A, B, C, D)*
l   this *(A, B, C, D)*
m   view?/view. *(A, B, C) changed in D*
n   The brief/[*Here begin G and H*]
o   arrangement *(G, H)*
p . . . p   mirror, it appeared to me, now *(A, B, C, G, H);* mirror (so at first it appeared to me in my confusion) now *(D)*

fusion — now[p] stood where none had been perceptible before; and, as I stepped up to it in extremity of terror, mine own image, but with features all pale and dabbled in blood, [q]advanced[r] to meet me with a feeble and tottering gait.[q]

Thus it appeared, I say, but was not. [s]It was my antagonist — it[s] was Wilson, who then stood before me in the agonies of his[t] dissolution. [u]His mask and cloak lay, where he had thrown them, upon the floor. Not a thread in all his raiment — not a line in all the marked and singular lineaments of his face which was not, even in the most absolute identity, *mine own!*[u] [19]

It was Wilson; but he spoke no longer in a whisper, and I could have fancied that I myself was speaking while he said:

"You have conquered, and I yield. Yet, henceforward art thou also dead — dead to the [v]World, to Heaven and to Hope![v] In me didst thou exist — and, in my death, see by this image, which is thine own,[w] how utterly thou hast murdered thyself."[20]

NOTES

Title: Poe actually knew of two men named William Wilson with whom John Allan did business; one was a Quaker living at Kendal, the other an agent for Washington College (now Washington and Lee) at Lexington, Virginia. See Killis Campbell's *Mind of Poe*, p. 146.

Motto: Compare the quotation from Poe's *Politian* in note 3, below. The two lines of the motto here are not from William Chamberlayne's *Pharonnida* (1659) — all Poe's texts, as well as Harrison, and Mabbott, I, 319-320, misspell the title of the poem — but are perhaps a confused echo of a passage from a play by the same author, *Love's Victory* (1658), V, 2746f.: "Conscience waits on me like the frighting shades/Of ghosts when gastly [sic] messengers of death," etc. S. W. Singer had brought out an edition of Chamberlayne's two works in three volumes in 1820. See Kenneth S. Rothwell in *Modern Language Notes*, April 1959.

---

q . . . q   advanced, with a feeble and tottering gait, to meet me. *(A, B, C, D, G, H)*

r   *advanced, (G, H)*

s . . . s   It *(G, H)*

t   *Omitted (G, H)*

u . . . u   Not a line in all the marked and singular lineaments of that face which was not, even identically, mine own! His mask and cloak lay, where he had thrown them, upon the floor. *(A, B, C, D, G, H); after* Not *is added* a thread in all the raiment — not; *and* mine own! *is italicized (D); the last sentence is italicized (G, H)* [*This is the end of the passage in the review.*]

v . . . v   *world and its hopes.* *(A, B, C, D)*

w   *thine own,/thine, (A)*

WILLIAM WILSON

1. Elah-Gabalus, more properly Elagabalus, was the the sobriquet of a Roman Emperor (218–222), described by Lemprière (see under "Heliogabalus") as a monster of cruelty and depravity. Poe alludes to him also in "Epimanes" and in "Mellonta Tauta."

2. In his sketch of Poe in the *Saturday Museum* of March 4, 1843, Henry B. Hirst, almost certainly with Poe's approval, pointed out that Poe really attended the Manor House School of the Reverend John Bransby at Stoke Newington and that these passages are based on the author's experience there, and Griswold in his "Memoir," p. xxiv, picked this up. But Poe romanticized it all (especially in revisions) and confused the actual building with neighboring Fleetwood House, a large mansion. Poe also gave St. Mary's Church a steeple instead of a cupola. And the schoolmaster is a composite of Bransby and the Reverend George Gaskin, rector of the church, a secretary of the Society for Promoting Christian Knowledge. (See Phillips, *Poe the Man*, I, 150–160, for illustrations and discussion.) The British author, Edward Shanks, *Edgar Allan Poe* (1937), p. 27, remarks on the cupola.

3. With the description of the minister entering the pulpit compare *Politian*, VII, 55–56, "A spectral figure, solemn, and slow, and noiseless – /Like the grim shadow Conscience."

4. Draconian laws, propounded by the Athenian Draco about 624 B.C., were notoriously severe, punishing a great many offenses by death. The word here probably means unvarying, since English schoolboys were chastised bareskin with a rod for every kind of misbehavior.

5. The *peine forte et dure* was pressing to death, the penalty for refusing to plead guilty or not guilty to a capital charge, something endured by courageous persons to save their estates from confiscation. Poe's friend Henry B. Hirst later wrote a poem called *The Penance of Roland* (1849) on this grim subject.

6. In referring to "the exergues of the Carthaginian medals" Poe had in mind two statements made in Baron Bielfeld's chapter "Les Médailles et Monnoies," in *L'Érudition Universelle*, Book III, Chapter XI, sections 11 and 12. He defines the exergue as the portion of the design found beneath the ground on which are placed the figures portrayed. Bielfeld describes "Les Puniques ou Carthaginoises" as including coins having on one side a standing spearman and the inscription Kart-hago, and on the other a horse's head in profile and in exergue "XLII." *Médaille* (like medal) formerly meant an old coin not current. Poe apparently supposed the exergue less liable to be worn by circulation than the rest of the coin, for in a review of Henry Lord Brougham's *Critical and Miscellaneous Writings* in *Graham's Magazine* for March 1842, he says, "Fifty years hence it will be difficult . . . to make out the deepest indentations of the *exergue*." The coin described is now assigned to the Vandal King of Carthage, Gelimir (A.D. 530–534); XLII is the denomination. The exergue is very large, filling almost half of the design.

7. The quotation is from Voltaire's satires, "Le Mondain," line 21, and means, "Oh, what a good time it was, that age of iron." Poe probably saw it in Bielfeld, Book III, Chapter v, section 14.

8. There is some evidence that Poe's own name annoyed him; some Southerners so pronounce "poor." "Poh!" is an expression of disgust, and there is an inelegant pun on French and Scottish *pot*. See Phillips, I, 137, 820; Quinn, *Poe,* p. 38; and Sidney P. Moss, *Poe's Literary Battles,* p. 195.

9. Poe was really born January 19, 1809, but gave the years 1811 and 1813 on occasion. Notice that the variants at this place show all three dates for the characters named "William Wilson."

10. Thetis dipped her son Achilles in the Styx to make him invulnerable, holding him by one ankle – that spot was not protected. Paris killed him by shooting him with an arrow in "the tendon of Achilles."

11. Kerseymere (cassimere) is a kind of woolen cloth. The word is derived from Kashmir.

12. The quotation about Herod, from *Hamlet,* III, ii, 16, is a great favorite with Poe. See "Metzengerstein."

13. Colonel Melvin Helfers told me that Glendinning was the name of Poe's successor as Sergeant Major in the First Artillery.

14. Tiberius Claudius Atticus Herodes was the greatest rhetorician of the second century of our era. His wealth was easily acquired, for his father discovered a vast treasure, which the Emperor Trajan advised him "to use." The rhetorician became a friend of the Emperor Hadrian, and built public works in Greek cities, especially in his native Athens, where the Odeon, or Music Hall, still stands.

15. One of Poe's Richmond schoolmates, and his lifelong friend, was John T. L. Preston.

16. Poe here used an incident from "The Gamesters," a chapter contributed anonymously by David Watson to William Wirt's "Old Bachelor" series of 1810–1813, published in book form in 1814. Watson's paper tells the troubles of a gentleman whose identical twin is a scoundrel. Coming to a group of old friends, the good brother is indignantly driven away because they suppose him to be his twin whom they have caught cheating at cards. See Richard Beale Davis in *American Literature,* November 1944.

17. In early versions of his tale, Poe misdescribed the marked cards. His source of information has not been discovered.

18. In "The Mysterious Stranger," one of Irving's *Tales of a Traveller* (1824), mention is made of the Broglio, the piazzetta in front of the Doge's Palace in Venice; the unnamed hero of that story is a young nobleman from Naples. Poe has a character named the Duke di Broglio in his play, *Politian.* The Ducs de Broglie, long settled in France, descended from an Italian family originally named Broglio. In the preface to his translation of Poe's play, *Politien* (Paris, 1924), p. 13, H. R. Woestyn notices an analogue of "William Wilson" to *La Nuit de Décembre* (1835) by Louis-Charles-Alfred de Musset, where the

climax is at the end of "un bal masqué ... dans le palais di Broglio." This may well be fortuitous, since Poe is not known to have mentioned Alfred de Musset.

19.   This and the preceding paragraph Poe quotes as "parallel passages" in a review of Hawthorne's *Twice-Told Tales* (*Graham's,* May 1842), intimating that they were plagiarized in "Howe's Masquerade." Since that story was printed in the *Democratic Review* for May 1838, the charge is manifestly absurd. See Horace E. Thorner, "Hawthorne, Poe, and a Literary Ghost," *New England Quarterly,* March 1934, for an entertaining demonstration that the similar episodes may have, ultimately, a common source far back of Calderon. [See also Robert Regan's persuasive essay, "Hawthorne's 'Plagiary'; Poe's Duplicity," *Nineteenth Century Fiction,* December 1970.]

20.   Woodberry, in the Stedman and Woodberry edition of Poe's *Works,* IV, 358, 359, points out as a possible inspiration of Poe the last paragraph of *The Man of Two Lives* by "Edward Sydenham," a pen name of James Boaden (1762–1839), whose book first appeared in London in 1828 and was reprinted in Boston the next year. The paragraph reads:

"Here I shall close this narrative. I have reached that point of my existence when the connection of the two lives was *dropt* entirely. I describe the scenes only in which it influenced my present being. The world at large will not perhaps regret that this amazing privilege has been peculiar to myself. I do not think that they ought. Yet in fact most men are permitted *two lives* even here; *one* of *action* with its usual attendant *error,* – the *other of Reflection* and, as it ought to prove, of *Atonement.* To carry on the parallel, neither are *they* without a mysterious friend and guide, to whom the *Magnetic Mesmer* was but a shade, who comes upon them unannounced and knows them through all disguises. He is plain too and generally alarming in his addresses and urges them to take the only course that conducts to their real interest, their peace, their honor and their final happiness. The reader *feels* that I can only here mean the power of *Conscience.*"

Woodberry says nothing else in Boaden's book is like Poe's, and it is not sure that Poe was acquainted with it.

THE CONVERSATION
OF EIROS AND CHARMION

This is the first of what may be called Poe's Platonic Dialogues between spirits in Heaven; the others are "The Colloquy of Monos and Una" and "The Power of Words." They have been much admired by some critics. Duyckinck included all three among the dozen stories he chose for Poe's *Tales* of 1845. And C. Alphonso Smith (*Poe: How to Know Him,* 1921, p. 295) called them "soaring meditations that compass . . . life and death . . . the natural and the supernatural, . . . the . . . arches that span the spaces between."*

"The Conversation of Eiros and Charmion" was popular enough to be translated into French in Poe's lifetime (by Isabelle Meunier as "Le Colloque d'Eiros et Charmion" in *La Démocratie pacifique*, Paris, July 3, 1847). The subject, the destruction of the world by fire as prophesied in the Bible, has often occupied both serious divines and fanatics. In the 1830's it was of especial interest to Americans: William Miller of Low Hampton, Washington County, New York, announced in 1831 that the world's end would occur in 1843, and impressed increasing numbers of followers throughout the decade. In 1833 there were showers of meteors, and later a succession of comets. Many people in all ages have regarded comets with fear, and perhaps as forerunners of the world's end. Poe speculated about how the comet might be its cause. (He apparently took his own ideas fairly seriously when he wrote this tale, for in his little sketch called "A Prediction" in 1848, he remarks on changing his earlier hypothesis.)

In Poe's day comets aroused far greater popular interest than in the last half century, when no really important comet has appeared. In the early nineteenth century several were seen. There was a very brilliant comet in 1811. The famous Halley's Comet returned in 1835. And there was much discussion of Encke's comet because, although it has no tail and is so small that it can be seen with the naked eye only under the most favorable conditions, its periodicity had been calculated, and it had returned in 1833 and 1838, and was expected again in 1842.†

The excitement of 1838 called forth a story that almost certainly set Poe to thinking. This is "The Comet" by S. Austin Jr. in

---

* Lucian of Samosata wrote *Dialogues of the Dead,* and in Poe's day Walter Savage Landor's *Imaginary Conversations* were much talked about. But Poe's have no satirical or historical purpose and are, I feel, more in Plato's manner. Two of Walt Whitman's early stories seem to be modeled on Poe's, namely "The Angel of Tears" and "A Spirit Record."

† It may be remarked here that Quinn's suggestion (*Poe,* p. 187) that Poe's story was to some extent inspired by the famous Leonid meteors of 1833 which aroused great excitement in Baltimore seems to me unacceptable. Poe and his first readers were better acquainted with comets than we are today.

EIROS AND CHARMION

The Token and Atlantic Souvenir for 1839.‡ In it Austin describes the discovery of a comet; the disputes of astronomers; the excitement of press and people; and philosophical discussions when it becomes known that the visitant must strike the earth. At last the comet is seen as of huge size, and stirs up tremendous tides that overwhelm humanity.

Poe decided that Austin's "machinery" would not work. In view of the known tenuosity of comets, it is doubtful if one ever stirred a tide commensurable by man. Furthermore, the Biblical prophecies promise that there will be no second flood, but call for the destruction of the world by fire. (Poe in 1829 called comets "carriers of the fire" in "Al Aaraaf," I, 94.) He must have read in proof a review in the *Southern Literary Messenger,* April 1836, called "Slavery in the United States" in which Judge Beverley Tucker wrote of a comet that it might "prove the messenger of that dispensation which, in the end of all things, is to wrap our earth in flames."§

Poe also seems to have consulted Thomas Dick's *Christian Philosopher* (1823), from which the following extracts are pertinent:

> The atmosphere is now ascertained to be a compound substance, formed of two very different ingredients, termed *oxygen gas* and *nitrogen gas*. Of 100 measures of atmospheric air, 21 are oxygen, and 79 nitrogen. The one, namely, oxygen is the principle of combustion and the vehicle of heat, and is absolutely necessary for the support of animal life, and is the most powerful and energetic agent in nature; the other is altogether incapable of supporting either flame or animal life. Were we to breathe oxygen air, without any mixture or alloy, our animal spirits would be raised, and the fluids in our bodies would circulate with greater rapidity; but we would soon infallibly perish by the rapid ... accumulation of heat in the animal frame. If the nitrogen were extracted from the air, and the whole atmosphere contained nothing but oxygen or vital air, combustion would not proceed in that gradual manner which it now does, but with the most dreadful and irresistible rapidity ...
>
> Should the Creator issue forth his Almighty Fiat — "Let the nitrogen of the atmosphere be completely separated from the oxygen, and let the oxygen exert its native energies without control, wherever it extends;" — from what we know

---

‡ Ingram, *Life and Letters,* p. 131, pointed out this source.
§ See Harrison's *Complete Works* of Poe, VIII, 267; in 1902 the article was thought to be Poe's work.

·453·

of its nature, we are warranted to conclude, that instantly a universal conflagration would commence throughout all the kingdoms of nature.*

Poe's imagination supplied a comet with an affinity for nitrogen. Like Dick, he calls the atmosphere a compound, where the word mixture is proper.†

Poe's story was presumably written about October or November 1839. A few years after its first printing, it became timely for republication. The Great Comet of 1843 was first observed on February 28, and was kept under observation until April 19. It was extremely bright in March, and passed less than one solar radius above the Sun's surface. Its tail was the longest on record, two hundred million miles — about twice the distance between the Earth and the Sun.‡

Poe inserted his story, with a new title, in the *Philadelphia Saturday Museum* of April 1, 1843 — the date may be significant. On another page of that paper was a short article about the story:

DESTRUCTION OF THE WORLD.

We invite attention to the singular article, on another page, entitled "The Destruction of the World." It details an imaginary conversation supposed to occur between two departed spirits, at a period subsequent to the Great Catastrophe which few doubt will, at some future epoch, take place.

The views embodied in this conversation are in strict accordance with philosophical speculation. The danger to be apprehended from collision with a comet is, to be sure, very little, and, from the gaseous nature of these erratic bodies, it has been contended that even actual contact would not have a fatal result; but the purport of the article in question seems to be the suggestion of a mode in which, through the cometary influence, the destruction of the earth might be brought about, and brought about in accordance with Prophecy.

From the celestial visitant now present, we have, of course, nothing to fear. It is now receding from the earth with a rapidity absolutely inconceivable, and, in a very short period, will be lost, and perhaps forever, to human eyes. But it came unheralded, and to-morrow its counterpart, or some wonder even more startling, *may* make its appearance. A firm reliance upon the wisdom and goodness of the Deity is by no means inconsistent with a due sense of the manifold and multiform perils by which we are so fearfully environed.

* This source was pointed out by Margaret Alterton, *Origins of Poe's Critical Theory* (1925), p. 141. Like her, I use the stereotyped edition of Dick's *Complete Works* (Cincinnati, 1855), II, 32 and 135.

† See Harrison's edition, IV, 276, for Professor W. LeConte Stevens' discussion of what is unscientific in "The Conversation of Eiros and Charmion."

‡ This I was told by Professor Stanley P. Wyatt Jr.

EIROS AND CHARMION

This piece I consider Poe's own. It is reproduced here from the unique exemplar of the original paper in the library of the University of North Carolina, where I discovered it in 1940.

TEXTS

(A) Burton's Gentleman's Magazine, December 1839 (5:321–323); (B) Tales of the Grotesque and Arabesque (1840), II, 213–222; (C) Philadelphia Saturday Museum, April 1, 1843; (D) Tales (1845), pp. 110–115; (E) Works (1850), II, 286–291; PHANTASY-PIECES, title only.

The text of Tales (D) is followed. Griswold's version (E) was taken from it, without verbal change. The motto introduced in the Philadelphia Saturday Museum version (C) was adopted in later texts but the change of title was not. A number of verbal changes in (C) were not followed when Poe prepared his text for Tales (D).

THE CONVERSATION
OF EIROS AND CHARMION. [D]

Πυρ σοι προσοισω
I will bring fire to thee.

Euripides — Androm:

EIROS.

Why do you call me Eiros?

CHARMION.

So henceforward will you[a] always be called. You must forget, too, *my* earthly name, and speak to me as Charmion.

EIROS.

This is indeed no dream!

CHARMION.

Dreams are with us no more; — but of these mysteries anon. I rejoice to see you looking life-like and rational. The film of the shadow has already passed from off your eyes. Be of heart, and fear nothing. Your allotted days of stupor have expired; and, to-morrow, I will myself induct you into the full joys and wonders of your novel existence.

Title: The Destruction of the World. (A Conversation between two Departed Spirits.) *(C)*

Motto: *This first appeared in C.*
a will you/you will *(C)*

EIROS.

True — I feel no stupor — none at all. The wild sickness and the terrible darkness have left me, and I hear no longer that mad, rushing, horrible sound, like the "voice of many waters." [1] Yet my senses are bewildered, Charmion, with the keenness of their perception of *the new*.

CHARMION.

A few days will remove all this; — but I fully understand you, and feel for you. It is now ten earthly years since I underwent what you undergo — yet the remembrance of it hangs by me still. You have now suffered all of pain, however, which you will suffer in Aidenn.[2]

EIROS.

In Aidenn?

CHARMION.

In Aidenn.

EIROS.

ᵇOh God! — pity me,ᵇ Charmion! — I am overburthened with the majesty of all things — of the unknown now known — of the speculative Future merged in the august and certain Present.

CHARMION.

Grapple not now with such thoughts. To-morrow we will speak of this. Your mind wavers, and its agitation will find relief in the exercise of simple memories. Look not around, nor forward — but back. I am burning with anxiety to hear the details of that stupendous event which threw you among us. Tell me of it. Let us converse of familiar things, in the old familiar[3] language of the world which has so fearfully perished.

EIROS.

Most fearfully, fearfully! — this is indeed no dream.

CHARMION.

Dreams are no more. Was I much mourned, my Eiros?

---

b . . . b   Pity me, my *(C)*

EIROS AND CHARMION

EIROS.

Mourned, Charmion? — oh deeply. To that last hour of all, there hung a cloud of intense gloom and devout sorrow over your household.

CHARMION.

And that last hour — speak of it. Remember that, beyond the naked fact of the catastrophe itself, I know nothing. When, coming out from among mankind, I passed into Night through the Grave — at that period, if I remember aright, the calamity which overwhelmed you was utterly unanticipated. But, indeed, I knew little of the speculative philosophy of the day.

EIROS.

The individual calamity was, as you say, entirely unanticipated; but analogous misfortunes had been long a subject of discussion with astronomers. I need scarce tell you, my friend, that, even when you left us, men had agreed to understand those passages in the most holy writings which speak of the final destruction of all things by fire, as having reference to the orb of the earth alone.[4] But in regard to the immediate agency of the ruin, speculation had been at fault from that epoch in astronomical knowledge in which the comets were divested of the terrors of flame. The very moderate density of these bodies had been well established. They had been observed to pass among the satellites of Jupiter, without bringing about any sensible alteration either in the masses or in the orbits of these secondary planets. We had long regarded the wanderers as vapory creations of inconceivable tenuity, and as altogether incapable of doing injury to our substantial globe, even in the event of contact. But contact was not in any degree dreaded; for the elements of all the comets were accurately known. That among *them* we should look for the agency of the threatened fiery destruction had been for many years considered an inadmissible idea. But wonders and wild fancies had been, of late days, strangely rife among mankind; and, although it was only with a few of the ignorant that actual apprehension prevailed, upon the announcement by astronomers of a *new* comet, yet this announcement was generally received with I know not what of agitation and mistrust.

The elements of the strange orb were immediately calculated, and it was at once conceded by all observers, that its path, at perihelion, would bring it into very close proximity with the earth. There were two or three astronomers, of[c] secondary note, who resolutely maintained that a contact was inevitable. I cannot very well express to you the effect of this intelligence upon the people. For a few short days they would not believe an assertion which their intellect, so long employed among worldly considerations, could not in any manner grasp. But the truth of a vitally important fact soon makes its[d] way into the understanding of even the most stolid. Finally, all men saw that astronomical knowledge lied not, and they awaited the comet. Its approach was not, at first, seemingly rapid; nor was its appearance of very unusual character. It was of a dull red, and had little perceptible train. For seven or eight days we saw no material increase in its apparent diameter, and but a partial alteration in its color. Meantime, the ordinary affairs of men were discarded, and all interests absorbed in a growing discussion, instituted by the philosophic, in respect to the cometary nature. Even the grossly ignorant aroused their sluggish capacities to such considerations. The learned *now* gave their intellect — their soul — to no such points as the allaying of fear, or to the sustenance of loved theory. They sought — they panted for right views. They groaned for perfected[e] knowledge. *Truth* arose in the purity of her strength and exceeding majesty, and the wise bowed down and adored.

That material injury to our globe or to its inhabitants would result from the apprehended contact, was an opinion which hourly lost ground among the wise; and the wise were now freely permitted to rule the reason and the fancy of the crowd. It was demonstrated, that the density of the comet's *nucleus*[f] was far less than that of our rarest gas; and the[g] harmless passage [h]of a similar visitor[h] among the satellites of Jupiter was a point strongly insisted upon, and[i] which served greatly to allay terror. Theologists, with an earnestness fear-enkindled, dwelt upon the biblical prophecies, and

---

c   and these of *(A, B, C)*
d   it *(B) misprint*
e   perfect *(C)*
f   nucleus *(A, B, C)*

g   its *(A, B)*
h...h   Omitted *(A, B, C)*
i   and one *(A)*

expounded them to the people with a directness and simplicity of which no previous instance had been known. That the final destruction of the earth must be brought about by the agency of fire, was urged with a spirit that enforced every where conviction; and that the comets were of no fiery nature (as all men now knew) was a truth which relieved all, in a great measure, from the apprehension of the great calamity foretold. It is noticeable that the popular prejudices and vulgar errors in regard to pestilences and wars — errors which were wont to prevail upon every appearance of a comet — were now altogether unknown. As if by some sudden convulsive exertion, reason had at once hurled superstition from her throne. The feeblest intellect[j] had derived vigor from excessive interest.

What minor evils might arise from the contact were points of elaborate question. The learned spoke of slight geological disturbances, of probable alterations in climate, and consequently in vegetation; of possible magnetic and electric influences. Many held that no visible or perceptible effect would in any manner be produced. While such discussions were going on, their subject gradually approached, growing larger[k] in apparent diameter, and of a more brilliant lustre. Mankind grew paler as it came. All human operations were suspended.

There was an epoch in the course of the general sentiment when the comet had attained, at length, a size surpassing that of any previously recorded visitation. The people now, dismissing any lingering hope that the astronomers were wrong, experienced all the certainty of evil. The chimerical aspect of their terror was gone. The hearts of the stoutest of our race beat violently within their bosoms. A very few days sufficed, however, to merge even such feelings in sentiments more unendurable. We could no longer apply to the strange orb any *accustomed* thoughts. Its *historical* attributes had disappeared. It oppressed us with a hideous *novelty* of emotion. We saw it not as an astronomical phenomenon in the heavens, but as an incubus[5] upon our hearts,[1] and a shadow upon our brains.[m] It had taken, with inconceivable rapidity, the charac-

---

j   understanding *(A)*
k   larger and larger *(C)*

l   heart, *(A, C)*
m   brain. *(A, B, C)*

ter of a gigantic mantle of rare flame, extending from horizon to horizon.

Yet a day, and men breathed with greater freedom. It was clear that we were already within the influence of the comet; yet we lived. We even felt an unusual elasticity of frame and vivacity of mind. The exceeding tenuity of the object of our dread was apparent; for[n] all heavenly objects were plainly visible through it. Meantime, our vegetation had perceptibly altered; and we gained faith, from this predicted circumstance, in the foresight of the wise. A wild luxuriance of foliage, utterly unknown before, burst out upon every vegetable thing.

Yet another day — and the evil was not altogether upon us. It was now evident that its nucleus would first reach us. A wild change had come over all men; and the first sense of *pain* was the wild signal for general lamentation and horror. This first sense of pain lay in a rigorous constriction of the breast and lungs, and an insufferable dryness of the skin. It could not be denied that our atmosphere was radically affected; the conformation of this atmosphere and the possible modifications to which it might be subjected, were now the topics of discussion. The result of investigation sent an electric thrill of the intensest terror through the universal heart of man.

It had been long known that the air which encircled us was a compound of oxygen and nitrogen gases, in the proportion of twenty-one measures of oxygen, and seventy-nine of nitrogen, in every one hundred of the atmosphere.[6] Oxygen, which was the principle of combustion, and the vehicle of heat, was absolutely necessary to the support of animal life, and was the most powerful and energetic agent in nature. Nitrogen, on the contrary, was incapable of supporting either animal life or flame. An unnatural excess of oxygen would result, it had been ascertained, in just such an elevation of the animal spirits as we had latterly experienced. It was the pursuit, the extension of the idea, which had engendered awe. What would be the result of *a total extraction of the nitrogen?* A combustion irresistible, all-devouring, omni-prevalent, immedi-

n   *Omitted (A, B, C)*

ate; — the entire° fulfillment, in all their^p minute and terrible^q details, of the fiery and horror-inspiring denunciations of the prophecies of the Holy Book.

Why need I paint, Charmion, the now disenchained frenzy of mankind? That tenuity in the comet which had previously inspired us with hope, was now^r the source of the bitterness of despair. In its impalpable gaseous character we clearly perceived the consummation of Fate. Meantime a day again passed — bearing away with it the last shadow of Hope. We gasped in the rapid modification of the air. The red blood bounded tumultuously through its strict channels. A furious delirium possessed all men; and, with arms rigidly^s outstretched towards the threatening heavens, they trembled and shrieked aloud. But the nucleus of the destroyer was now upon us; — even here in Aidenn, I shudder while I speak.[7] Let me be brief — brief as the ruin that overwhelmed. For a^t moment there was a wild lurid light alone, visiting and penetrating all things. Then — let us bow down, Charmion, before the excessive majesty of the great^u God! — then, there came a shouting and^v pervading sound, as if from the mouth itself^w of HIM; while the whole incumbent^x mass of ether in which we existed, burst at once into a species of intense flame, for whose surpassing brilliancy and all-fervid heat even the angels in the high^y Heaven of pure knowledge have no name. Thus ended all.

NOTES

Title: The two speakers are named for Cleopatra's faithful handmaidens, of whom Lalage reads in *Politian*, IV, 20–27. They are mentioned in Plutarch's "Antony," chapter 85, in Shakespeare's *Antony and Cleopatra,* and in Dryden's *All for Love.* Shakespeare used the spelling "Charmian," Dryden has Charmion, but all call the other girl Iras.

Motto: This is from the *Andromache* of Euripides, line 257.

1. The quotation is from Revelation 14:2. Compare "The Fall of the House of Usher" at n. 34.

o *Omitted (C)*	u the great *omitted (C)*
p its *(A, B)*	v shouting and/great *(A, B, C)*
q and terrible *omitted (C)*	w mouth itself/very mouth *(C)*
r at length *(C)*	x circumambient *(C)*
s immoveably *(A, B); omitted (C)*	y great *(A, B)*
t a short *(A, B)*	

2. Here is Poe's earliest use of the name Aidenn (from the Arabic *Adn*, Eden) for Heaven, used later in "The Raven" and in "The Power of Words."

3. Compare Charles Lamb's poem "The Old Familiar Faces."

4. See II Peter 3:10, "The earth also, and the works that are therein, shall be burned up." For the idea that the prophecy refers only to the surface of the earth — "to the crust of this orb alone" — compare Poe's review (referring the reader to "the excellent observations of Dr. Dick") of Henry Duncan's *Sacred Philosophy of the Seasons* in *Burton's*, March 1840. Compare also "Marginalia," number 21 (*Democratic Review*, November 1844, p. 487).

5. Compare "The Fall of the House of Usher" at n. 29 for "there sat upon my very heart an incubus of utterly causeless alarm."

6. Compare the excerpt from Dick's work, above.

7. Compare "The Man that was Used Up" at n. 10, where Poe uses Vergil's phrase, *horresco referens.*

WHY THE LITTLE FRENCHMAN
WEARS HIS HAND IN A SLING

This little piece is a mere comic anecdote, and almost the slightest story that Poe ever wrote. The chief inspiration of the tale was obviously a character in a once famous story by General George Pope Morris called "The Little Frenchman and his Water Lots." That first appeared in the *New-York Mirror* of December 31, 1836, and gave its name to a collection of Morris's stories published in 1838. It was decidedly popular, but Poe's friend Lambert A. Wilmer did not care for it, and wrote: "General M[orris] can do nothing without 'a little Frenchman' . . . If there had been no little Frenchman, I doubt if the General's wit had found any opportunity for development."*

Morris's story (from which Poe took nothing but the stock character and his dialect) recounts the sad adventures of one Monsieur PooPoo, a Parisian who comes to New York, has a toy shop,

---

* *The Quacks of Helicon* (1841), p. 43. Morris included in his volume several other tales of little Frenchmen.

and saves $5000. He is led by a craze for land speculation to buy at auction with his savings sixty lots on Long Island, "with valuable water privileges." Visiting them, he learns that at high tide they are *under water*. He then returns to Paris as poor as he had come from it.

Poe's Irish hero appropriately comes from Connaught, for men from that most westerly province of Ireland are proverbially the most pugnacious and wildest of "Wild Irishmen."

No source for the chief incident has been suggested, and it is the kind of thing that might have occurred in real life.

Poe's story can hardly be earlier than the appearance of its inspiration, but no more exact dating than 1837–1839 is as yet possible. For it, alone among Poe's Tales, no first publication in a periodical has been discovered. That there was an earlier printing than that in *Tales of the Grotesque and Arabesque* is almost indubitable.† The story is wholly uncontroversial, and precisely the kind of thing editors of the time appreciated. Indeed, it was one of the first of Poe's stories to be pirated in London. It appeared in *Bentley's Miscellany,* July 1840, with the title "The Irish Gentleman and the Little Frenchman."

In 1837 or 1838 Poe was in touch with friends in Baltimore, where some of them presumably were editing the *Saturday Visiter,* a paper of which not a single issue of 1837 through 1839 is located. May this have been where the tale first appeared?

TEXTS

(A) [Unlocated periodical, 1837–1839]; *(B) Tales of the Grotesque and Arabesque* (1840), II, 183–191; *(C) Broadway Journal,* September 6, 1845 (2:129–131); *(D) Works* (1850), II, 473–478. PHANTASY-PIECES, title only.
Griswold's version *(D)* shows auctorial changes and is followed. In the *Broadway Journal (C)* the tale was signed Littleton Barry (see "Loss of Breath," n. 41). In "Why the Little Frenchman Wears His Hand in a Sling" variants in spelling are recorded because Poe's changes show him working out a dialect for his story. As all texts insert apostrophes erratically in it's, didn't, couldn't, and wouldn't, the text is corrected by the editor and such misprints are not recorded.

† In preparing a Table of Contents for the revised and expanded version of *Tales of the Grotesque and Arabesque,* to be called PHANTASY-PIECES in 1842, Poe canceled the titles of two stories which had not yet appeared in magazines.

Reprint

Bentley's Miscellany (English and American editions), July 1840, from *Tales of the Grotesque and Arabesque* as "The Irish Gentleman and the Little Frenchman," without acknowledgment.

WHY THE LITTLE FRENCHMAN
WEARS HIS HAND IN A SLING. [D]

It's on my wisiting cards sure enough (and it's them that's all o' pink satin paper) that inny gintleman that plases may behould the intheristhin[a] words, "Sir Pathrick O'Grandison, Barronitt,[b] 39 Southampton Row, Russell[c] Square, Parrish o' Bloomsbury." [1] And shud ye be wantin[d] to diskiver who is the pink of purliteness quite, and the laider of the hot tun[2] in the houl city o' Lonon[e] — why it's jist mesilf.[f] And fait[g] that same is no wonder at all at all, (so be plased to stop curlin[h] your nose,) for every inch o' the six wakes that I've been a gintleman, and left aff wid the bog-throthing to take up wid the Barronissy, it's Pathrick that's been living like a houly imperor, and gitting the iddication and the graces. Och! and wouldn't it be a blessed thing for your sperrits if ye cud lay your two peepers jist, upon Sir Pathrick O'Grandison, Barronitt, when he is all riddy drissed for the hopperer, or stipping into the Brisky[3] for the drive into the Hyde Park. But it's the iligant big figgur that I ave,[i] for the rason[j] o' which all the ladies fall in love wid me. Isn't it my own swate silf[k] now that'll missure the six fut, and the three inches more nor that, in me stockings, and that am excadingly will proportioned all over to match? And is it ralelly[l] more than the three fut and a bit that there is, inny how, of the little ould furrener Frinchman that lives jist over the way, and that's a oggling and a goggling the houl day, (and bad luck to him,) at the purty widdy Misthress Tracle[4] that's my own nixt door neighbor, (God bliss her) and a most particuller frind and ac-

---

a	intheristhing *(B)*	g	faith *(B)*
b	Barronit, *(B)*	h	curling *(B)*
c	Russel *(B)*	i	have, *(B)*
d	wanting *(B)*	j	reason *(B)*
e	London *(B)*	k	self *(B)*
f	meself. *(B)*	l	really *(B)*

quaintance?ᵐ You percave the little spalpeen is summat down in the mouth, and wears his lift hand in a sling; and it's for that same thing, by yur lave, that I'm going to give you the good rason.

The truthⁿ of the houl matter is jist simple enough; for the very first day that I com'd from Connaught, and showd my swate little silf in the strait to the widdy, who was looking through the windy, it was a gone case althegither wid the heart o' the purty Misthress Tracle. I percaved it, ye see, all at once, and no mistake, and that's God's thruth. First of all it was up wid the windy in a jiffy, and thin she threw open her two peepers to the itmost, and thin it was a little gould spy-glass that she clapped tight to one o' them, and divil may burn me if it didn't spake to me as plain as a peeper cud spake, and says it, through the spy-glass, "Och! the tip o' the mornin to ye, Sir Pathrick O'Grandison, Barronitt, mavourneen; and it's a nate gintleman that ye are, sure enough, and it's mesilfᵒ and me fortenᵖ jist that'll be at yur sarvice, dear, inny time o' day at all at all for the asking." And it's not mesilfᵖ ye wud have to be bate in the purliteness; so I made her a bow that wud haʳ broken yur heart althegither to behould, and thin I pulled aff me hat with a flourish, and thin I winked at her hard wid both eyes, as much as to say, "Thrue for you, yer a swate little crature, Mrs. Tracle, me darlint, and I wish I may be drownthed dead in a bog, if it's not mesilf,ˢ Sir Pathrick O'Grandison, Barronitt, that'll make a houl bushel o' love to yur leddy-ship, in the twinkling o' the eye of a Londonderry purraty."

And it was the nixt mornin, sure,ᵗ jist as I was making up me mind whither it wouldn't be the purlite thing to sind a bit o' writinᵘ to the widdy by way of a love-litter, when up cum'd the delivery sarvant wid an illigant card, and he tould me that the name on it (for I niver cud rade the copper-plate printinᵛ on account of being lift handed) was all about Mounseer, the Count, A Goose, Look-aisy, Maiter-di-dauns,⁵ and that the houl ofʷ the

---

m	acquaintance? (C)	s	meself, (B)
n	thruth (B)	t	sure enough, (B)
o	meself (B)	u	writing (B)
p	fortin (B, C)	v	printing (B)
q	meself (B)	w	o' (B)
r	have (B)		

divilish lingo was the spalpeeny long name of the little ould furrener Frinchman as lived over the way.

And jist wid that in cum'd the little willian[x] himself,[y] and thin he made me a broth of a bow, and thin he said he had ounly taken the liberty of doing me the honor of the giving me a call, and thin he went on to palaver at a great rate, and divil the bit did I comprehind what he wud be afther the tilling me at all at all, excipting and saving that he said "pully wou, woolly wou," and tould me, among a bushel o' lies, bad luck to him, that he was mad for the love o' my widdy Misthress Tracle, and that my widdy Mrs. Tracle had a puncheon for *him.*[6]

At the hearin of this, ye may swear, though, I was as mad as a grasshopper, but I remimbered that I was Sir Pathrick O'Grandison, Barronitt, and that it wasn't althegither gentaal to lit the anger git the upper hand o' the purliteness, so I made light o' the matter and kipt dark, and got quite sociable wid the little chap, and afther a while what did he do but ask me to go wid him to the widdy's saying he wud give me the feshionable inthroduction[z] to her leddyship.

"Is it there ye are?" said I thin to mesilf,[a] "and it's thrue for you, Pathrick, that ye're the fortunnittest mortal in life. We'll soon see now whither it's your swate silf,[b] or whither it's little Mounseer Maiter-di-dauns, that Misthress Tracle is head and ears in the love wid."

Wid that we wint aff to the widdy's, next door, and ye may well say it was an illigant place; so it was. There was a carpet all over the floor, and in one corner there was a forty-pinny and a jews-harp[7] and the divil knows what ilse, and in another corner was a sofy, the beautifullest thing in all natur, and sitting[c] on the sofy, sure enough, there was the swate little angel, Misthress Tracle.

"The tip o' the morning to ye," says I, "Mrs. Tracle," and thin[d] I made sich an iligant obaysance that it wud ha quite althegither bewildered the brain o' ye.

---

x	willain *(B)*	b	silf, dear, *(B)*
y	himsilf, *(C)*	c	sittin *(B)*
z	introduction *(B)*	d	then *(B)*
a	meself — *(B)*		

"Wully woo, pully woo, plump in the mud," [8] says the little furrenner Frinchman, "and sure[e] Mrs. Tracle," says he, that he did, "isn't this gintleman here jist his reverence[f] Sir Pathrick O'Grandison, Barronitt,[9] and isn't he althegither and entirely the most purticular frind and acquintance[g] that I have in the houl world?"

And wid that the widdy, she gits up from the sofy, and makes the swatest curtchy nor iver was seen; and thin down she sits[h] like an angel; and thin, by the powers, it was that little spalpeen Mounseer Maiter-di-dauns that plumped his silf[i] right down by the right side of her. Och hon! I ixpicted the two eyes o' me wud ha cum'd out of my head on the spot, I was so dispirate mad! Howiver, "Bait who!" says I, after a while. "Is it there ye are, Mounseer Maiter-di-dauns?" and so down I plumped on the lift side of her leddyship, to be aven wid the willain. Botheration! it wud ha done your heart good to percave the illigant double wink that I gived her jist thin right in the face wid both eyes.

But the little ould Frinchman he niver beginned to suspect me at all at all, and disperate hard it was he made the love to her leddyship. "Woully wou," says he, "Pully wou," says he, "Plump in the [j]mud," says he.[j]

"That's all to no use, Mounseer Frog, mavourneen," thinks I; and I talked as hard and as fast as I could all the while, and throth[k] it was mesilf[l] jist that divarted her leddyship complately and intirely, by rason of the illigant conversation that I kipt up wid her all about the dear[m] bogs of Connaught. And by and by she gived[n] me such[o] a swate smile, from one ind of her mouth to the ither,[p] that it made me as bould as a pig, and I jist took hould of the ind of her little finger in the most dillikittest manner in natur, looking at her all the while out o' the whites of my eyes.

And then[q] ounly[r] percave the cuteness of the swate angel, for no

---

e	sure enough *(B)*	l	meself *(B)*
f	riverence *(B, C)*	m	swate *(B)*
g	acquaintance *(B)*	n	giv'd *(B)*
h	gits agin *(B)*	o	sich *(B)*
i	self *(B)*	p	other, *(B)*
j . . . j	mud." *(B)*	q	thin *(B)*
k	troth *(B)*	r	ounly to *(B, C)*

sooner did she obsarve that I was afther the squazing of her flipper, than she up wid it in a jiffy, and put it away behind her back, jist as much as to say, "Now thin, Sir Pathrick O'Grandison, there's a bitther chance for ye, mavourneen, for it's not altogether[s] the gentaal thing to be afther the squazing of my flipper right full in the sight of that little furrenner Frinchman, Mounseer Maiter-di-dauns."

Wid that I giv'd her a big wink jist to say "lit Sir Pathrick alone for the likes o' them thricks," and thin I wint aisy to work, and you'd have died wid the divarsion to behould how cliverly I slipped my right arm betwane the back o' the sofy, and the back of her leddyship, and there, sure enough, I found a swate little flipper all a waiting to say, "the tip o' the mornin to ye, Sir Pathrick O'Grandison, Barronitt."[t] And wasn't it mesilf,[u] sure, that jist giv'd it[v] the laste little bit of a squaze in the world, all in the way of a commincement, and not to be too rough wid her leddyship? and och, botheration, wasn't it the gentaalest and dilikittest[w] of all the little squazes that I got in return? "Blood and thunder, Sir Pathrick, mavoureen," [x] thinks I to myself,[y] "fait[z] it's jist the mother's son of you, and nobody else at all at all, that's the handsomest[a] and the fortunittest young bogthrotter that ever cum'd out of Connaught!" And wid that I giv'd the flipper a big squaze, and a big squaze it was, by the powers, that her leddyship giv'd to me back. But it would[b] ha split the seven sides of you wid the laffin to behould, jist then[c] all at once, the consated[d] behavior[e] of Mounseer Maiter-di-dauns. The likes o' sich a jabbering, and a smirking, and a parly-wouing as he begin'd wid her leddyship, niver was known before upon arth; and divil may burn me if it wasn't me[f] own very two peepers that cotch'd him tipping her the wink out of one eye. Och hon? if it wasn't mesilf[g] thin that was[h] mad as a Kilkenny cat[10] I shud like to be tould who it was!

---

s	althegither *(B)*	a	handsommest *(B)*
t	Barronit." *(B)*	b	wud *(B)*
u	meself, *(B)*	c	thin *(B, C)*
v	*Omitted (B)*	d	concated *(B, C)*
w	delikittest *(B)*	e	behaviour *(B, C)*
x	mavourneen," *(B, C)*	f	my *(B)*
y	meself, *(B);* mesilf *(C)*	g	meself *(B)*
z	faith *(B)*	h	was as *(B)*

"Let me infarm you, Mounseer Maiter-di-dauns," said I, as purlite[i] as iver ye seed, "that it's not the gintaal thing at all at all,
and not for the likes o' you inny how, to be affter[j] the oggling
and a goggling at her leddyship in that fashion," and jist wid that
such another squaze as it was I giv'd her flipper, all as much as to
say, "isn't it Sir Pathrick now, my jewel, that'll be able to the
protecting[k] o' you, my darlint?" and then[l] there cum'd another
squaze back, all by way of the answer. "Thrue for you, Sir Pathrick," it said as plain as iver a squaze said in the world, "Thrue
for you, Sir Pathrick, mavourneen, and it's a proper nate gintleman ye are — that God's truth,"[m] and wid that she opened her two
beautiful peepers till I belaved they wud ha com'd out of her hid[n]
althegither and intirely, and she looked first as mad as a cat at
Mounseer Frog, and thin as smiling as all out o' doors at mesilf.[o]

"Thin," says he, the willian, "Och hon! and a wolly-wou,[p]
pully-wou," and then[q] wid that he shoved up his two shoulders till
the divil the bit of his hid[r] was to be diskivered, and then[s] he let
down the two corners of his purraty-trap,[11] and thin not a haporth[t]
more of the satisfaction could I git out o' the spalpeen.

Belave me, my jewel, it was Sir Pathrick that was unrasonable
mad thin,[u] and the more by token that [v]the Frinchman[v] kept an[w]
wid his winking[x] at the widdy; and the widdy she kipt an[y] wid the
squazing of my flipper, as much as to say, "At him again Sir
Pathrick O'Grandison, mavourneen;" so I just[z] ripped out wid a
big oath, and says I,[a]

"Ye little spalpeeny frog of a bog-throtting son of a bloody
noun!" — and jist thin what d'ye think it was that her leddyship
did? Troth she jumped up from the sofy as if she was bit, and
made off[b] through the door, while I turned my head round affter

---

i   purlit (B)
j   after (B)
k   proticting (B, C)
l   thin (B)
m   thruth" — (B)
n   head (B)
o   meself. (B)
p   woolly-wou, (B, C)
q   thin (B, C)
r   head (B)

s   thin (B, C)
t   a haporth/the bit (B)
u   thin, sure enough, (B)
v . . . v   he (B); the Finchman (C)
w   kept an/kept on (B); kipt an (C)
x   winking and blinking (B)
y   kipt an/kept on (B); kip tan (C)
z   jist (B, C)
a   I, sure enough — (B)
b   aff (B, C)

her, in a complete[c] bewilderment and botheration, and followed her wid me two peepers. You percave I had a reason[d] of my own for[e] knowing that she couldn't git down the stares[f] althegither and entirely;[g] for I knew very well that I had hould of her hand, for divil the bit had I iver lit it go. And says I,

"Isn't it the laste little bit of a mistake in the world that ye've been afther the making, yer leddyship? Come back now, that's a darlint, and I'll give ye yur flipper." But aff she wint down the stairs like a shot, and then I turned round to the little Frinch[h] furrenner. Och hon! if it wasn't his spalpeeny little paw[i] that I had hould of in my own — why thin — thin it wasn't — that's all.

And maybe[j] it wasn't mesilf[k] that jist died then outright wid the laffin, to behould the little chap when he found out that it wasn't the widdy at all at all[l] that he had[m] hould of all the time,[n] but only Sir Pathrick O'Grandison. The ould divil himself[o] niver behild sich[p] a long face as he pet an![q] As for Sir Pathrick O'Grandison, Barronitt, it wasn't for the likes of his riverence to be afther the minding of[r] a thrifle of a mistake. Ye may jist say, though (for it's God's thruth) that afore I lift hould of the flipper of the spalpeen, (which was not till afther her leddyship's futmen had kicked us both down the stairs,) I gived it such a nate little broth of a squaze, as made it all up into raspberry jam.

"Wouly-wou," says he, "pully-wou," says he — "Cot tam!"

And that's jist the thruth of the rason why he wears his left[s] hand in a sling.[t]

NOTES

1. The narrator is a namesake of the hero of Samuel Richardson's novel *Sir Charles Grandison* (1753). His London address is that of a house in which John Allan and his family resided for a time, according to a letter of September

---

c   complate *(B, C)*
d   rason *(B, C)*
e   for the *(B, C)*
f   stairs *(B, C)*
g   intirely — *(B)*
h   French *(B)*
i   flipper *(B)*
j   And maybe/Maybe *(B)*
k   meself *(B)*

l   at all *omitted (B)*
m   had had *(C)*
n   of all the time,/of, *(B)*
o   himsilf *(C)*
p   such *(B)*
q   on! *(B)*
r   *Omitted (B, C)*
s   lift *(B, C)*
t   *signed* LITTLETON BARRY *(C)*

12, 1817, quoted by Quinn (*Poe*, p. 77). The landlord was a Frenchman, Henry Dubourg, whose sisters' school Edgar Poe attended as a boy.

2. *Haut ton.*

3. The vehicle driven in Hyde Park by the baronet is a britska (the word is spelled in several ways), a light four-wheel carriage with a calash top, originally designed in Poland.

4. Mrs. Tr[e]acle is appropriately named for her sweetness.

5. The dancing master Luchesi is pretty surely named for a Baltimore character of whom John H. Hewitt in *Shadows on the Wall* (1877), p. 68, wrote:

> Frederick Lucchesi ... held a prominent position as teacher of music ... I remember him when he played the piccolo in the band at West Point ... He was a small boy then ... and excited the admiration of all by his skill in handling his tiny instrument.

Mr. John D. Kilbourne, Librarian of the Maryland Historical Society, wrote that the Baltimore *Sun* of September 4, 1869, records his death on the previous day in his fifty-eighth year. He was a native of Lucca in Italy, but a resident of Baltimore for thirty-five years. In 1837 and 1840, the Directory calls him a musician; in 1842, a music teacher; in 1845 and later, a Professor of Music. Playing the piccolo, however well, is regarded as comic by literary convention, and Frenchmen often bore Italian names. Luchesi is also the name of a minor character in "The Cask of Amontillado."

6. Luchesi probably said, *"Pouvez-vous, voulez-vous,"* and thought the widow had a *"penchant"* for him.

7. The pianoforte (or forty-penny!) and the jew's harp show that the widow had a catholic taste in music.

8. "Plump in the mud" may be *"Tout à la mode."*

9. In *Politian*, II, 91, San Ozzo is called "his reverence," although he is without ecclesiastical connections.

10. Two Kilkenny cats in Irish legend fought with each other until only their tails were left.

11. The purraty-trap is the trap for "praties" (potatoes), hence the mouth.

PREFACE
for *Tales of the Grotesque and Arabesque*

In 1839 Poe finally found publishers for his collected short stories, and composed a brief preface which is placed here in the present edition, since it was obviously written after the stories that precede it. The two volumes, called *Tales of the Grotesque and*

Arabesque, were dedicated thus: "Dedication. These Volumes are Inscribed to Colonel William Drayton, of Philadelphia, with every Sentiment of Respect, Gratitude, and Esteem, By his obliged Friend and Servant, THE AUTHOR." Drayton had been Poe's commanding officer at Fort Moultrie, and the poet as sergeant-major had constantly dealt with him directly. Their friendship was renewed when both lived in Philadelphia, but the precise reason for the dedication must be a matter of conjecture. Drayton's descendants knew and were proud of the poet's connection, but preserved no reminiscences beyond the fact that Poe sometimes called on his old commander (Quinn, *Poe,* p. 129). Possibly Drayton had helped Poe financially.

The Preface is not candid, for the stories had not been composed in two or three, but in at least eight years. Poe also seems to have been unduly worried about critics who protested against his work as Germanic. I have found one pertinent criticism, in the *Richmond Compiler,* February, 1836, which (anent "The Duc de L'Omelette") said:

> Mr. Poe is too fond of the wild — unnatural and horrible! Why will he not permit his fine genius to soar into purer, brighter, and happier regions? Why will he not disenthral himself from the spells of German enchantment and supernatural imagery? There is room enough for the exercise of the highest powers, upon the multiform relations of human life, without descending into the dark mysterious and unutterable creations of licentious fancy.

The criticism is reprinted in the *Southern Literary Messenger,* April 1836, p. 345. No file of the *Compiler* for February 1836 is now available.

See also Poe's letter of November 11, 1839 to Dr. Snodgrass, where he says he hopes to refute those who accuse him of Germanism by praise from Washington Irving who "heads the school of the *quietists.*"

TEXT

The text is from the only authorized version, *Tales of the Grotesque and Arabesque* (1840), I, [5]–6.

PREFACE

PREFACE.

The epithets "Grotesque" and "Arabesque" will be found to indicate with sufficient precision the prevalent tenor of the tales here published.[1] But from the fact that, during a period of some two or three years, I have written five-and-twenty short stories[2] whose general character may be so briefly defined, it cannot be fairly inferred — at all events it is not truly inferred — that I have, for this species of writing, any inordinate, or indeed any peculiar taste or prepossession. I may have written with an eye to this re-publication in volume form, and may, therefore, have desired to preserve, as far as a certain point, a certain unity of design. This is, indeed, the fact; and it may even happen that, in this manner, I shall never compose anything again. I speak of these things here, because I am led to think it is this prevalence of the "Arabesque" in my serious tales, which has induced one or two critics to tax me, in all friendliness, with what they have been pleased to term "Germanism" and gloom. The charge is in bad taste, and the grounds of the accusation have not been sufficiently considered. Let us admit, for the moment, that the "phantasy-pieces"[3] now given *are* Germanic, or what not. Then Germanism is "the vein" for the time being. To morrow I may be anything but German, as yesterday I was everything else. These many pieces are yet one book. My friends would be quite as wise in taxing an astronomer with too much astronomy, or an ethical author with treating too largely of morals. But the truth is that, with a single exception,[4] there is no one of these stories in which the scholar should recognise the distinctive features of that species of pseudo-horror which we are taught to call Germanic, for no better reason than that some of the secondary names of German literature have become identified with its folly.[5] If in many of my productions terror has been the thesis, I maintain that terror is not of Germany, but of the soul, — that I have deduced this terror only from its legitimate sources, and urged it only to its legitimate results.

There are one or two of the articles here, (conceived and executed in the purest spirit of extravaganza,) to which I expect no serious attention, and of which I shall speak no farther. But for the rest I cannot conscientiously claim indulgence on the score of hasty effort. I think it best becomes me to say, therefore, that if I have sinned, I have deliberately sinned. These brief compositions are, in chief part, the results of matured purpose and very careful elaboration.[6]

NOTES

1. Grotesque decoration (so called as found in ancient grottoes, as the Italians termed excavations) combines plant, animal, and human motifs. Arabesque uses only flowers and calligraphy. Poe was not the first person to apply these two words to literary works. Quinn (*Poe,* p. 289) pointed out that Poe took them from Sir Walter Scott's essay "On the Supernatural in Fictitious Composition" (*Foreign Quarterly Review,* July 1827).

2. There are twenty-five tales, if "How to Write a Blackwood Article" and "A Predicament" are counted as two.

3. Poe adopted this phrase as the title for the collection of his stories he planned in 1842.

4. "Metzengerstein."

5. The German authors of secondary rank include G. A. Bürger and E. T. A. Hoffmann.

6. The slightest story is "Why the Little Frenchman Wears His Hand in a Sling." The author worked very hard on "Loss of Breath" and "King Pest," which tend to please his readers the least.

THE

PROSE ROMANCES OF EDGAR A. POE,

AUTHOR OF "THE GOLD-BUG," "ARTHUR GORDON PYM," "TALES
OF THE GROTESQUE AND ARABESQUE,"
ETC. ETC. ETC.

UNIFORM SERIAL EDITION.

EACH NUMBER COMPLETE IN ITSELF.

No. I.

CONTAINING THE

MURDERS IN THE RUE MORGUE,

AND THE

MAN THAT WAS USED UP.

PHILADELPHIA:
PUBLISHED BY WILLIAM H. GRAHAM,
NO. 98 CHESTNUT STREET.
1843.

Price 12½ cents.

THE FOLIO CLUB

There is a Machiavelian plot
Though every nare olfact it not

Butler

THE Folio Club is, I am sorry to say, a mere Junto of Dunderheadism. I
think too the members are quite as ill-looking as they are stupid. I also believe it
their settled intention to abolish Literature, subvert the Press, and overturn the
Government of Nouns and Pronouns. These are my private opinions which I now take
the liberty of making public.

Yet when, about a week ago, I first became one of this diabolical association, no
person could have entertained for it more profound sentiments of admiration and
respect. Why my feelings in this matter have undergone a change will appear, very
obviously, in the sequel. In the meantime I shall vindicate my own character, and the
dignity of Letters.

I find, upon reference to the records, that the Folio Club was organized as such on the ―― day of ―― in the year ――. I like to begin with the beginning, and have a partiality for dates. A clause in the Constitution then adopted forbade the members to be otherwise than erudite and witty: and the avowed objects of the Confederation were 'the instruction of society, and the amusement of themselves'. For the latter purpose a meeting is held monthly at the house of some one of the association, when each individu-al is expected to come prepared with a 'Short Prose Tale' of his own composition. Each ar-ticle that produced is read by its ~~respective~~ author to the company assembled over a glass of wine at ~~every late~~ dinner. Much rivalry will of course ensue ―― more particularly as the writer of the 'Best Thing' is appointed President of the Club pro tem., an office endowed with many dignities and little expense, and which endures until its occupant is dispos-sessed by a superior morceau. The Father of the Tale held, on the contrary, to be the least meritorious, is bound to furnish the dinner and wine at the next similar meeting of the Society. This is found an excellent method of occasionally supplying the body with a new members, in the place of some unfortunate who, forfeiting two or three entertainments

FIRST PAGE OF THE INTRODUCTION TO POE'S EARLIEST PROJECTED COLLECTION (1833)

The Houghton Library

PHANTASY-PIECES

by

Edgar Allan Poe.

[Including all the author's late tales with a new edition of the "Grotesque and Arabesque"]

Seltsamen tochter Jovis,
Seinem schosskinde,
Der Phantasie.　　Göthe

Two
~~Three~~ Volumes.

Contents

To Printer — In printing the Tales preserve the order of the Table of Contents.

POE'S SECOND PROJECTED COLLECTION (1842)
H. Bradley Martin

" Sundry citizens of this good land, meaning well, and hoping well, prompted by a certain something in their nature, have trained themselves to do service in various Essays, Poems, Histories, and books of Art, Fancy, and Truth."

ADDRESS OF THE AMERICAN COPY-RIGHT CLUB.

WILEY AND PUTNAM'S

LIBRARY OF AMERICAN BOOKS.

NO. II.

TALES.

BY

EDGAR A. POE.

NEW YORK AND LONDON.

WILEY AND PUTNAM, 161 BROADWAY: 6 WATERLOO PLACE.

Price, Fifty Cents.

INTERLUDE: 1840

INSTINCT VERSUS REASON

There is no doubt of Poe's authorship of this sketch, first published in *Alexander's Weekly Messenger,* Philadelphia, January 29, 1840. It was discovered by Clarence Saunders Brigham, who reprinted it in the *Proceedings of the American Antiquarian Society* for April 1942. It is included in *Edgar Allan Poe's Contributions to Alexander's Weekly Messenger,* by Clarence S. Brigham, published by the Society in 1943. Poe did not publish the piece again, but used the material in a different and far more dramatic story, "The Black Cat" — where the emphasis is laid on the superstition that black cats are witches.

In the present story the heroine — for we may call so clever an animal by that name — is not Poe's beloved Caterina, who lived with his family from at least 1844 until 1849, but her predecessor. Caterina is said to have been very large and a tortoise shell (Mary Gove Nichols, in the London *Sixpenny Magazine,* February 1863, quoted by Woodberry, *Life,* 1909, II, 218). Compare Poe's references to the self-satisfied nature of feline pets in "Bon-Bon"; and the unsigned "Desultory Notes on Cats" (Philadelphia *Public Ledger,* July 19, 1844), assigned (by implication) by Eli Bowen to Poe's pen.

TEXT

The only authorized text, that of *Alexander's Weekly Messenger,* January 29, 1840, is followed.

INSTINCT VS REASON — A BLACK CAT.

The line which demarcates the instinct of the brute creation from the boasted reason of man, is, beyond doubt, of the most shadowy and unsatisfactory character — a boundary line far more difficult to settle than even the North-Eastern or the Oregon.[1] The question whether the lower animals do or do not reason, will possibly never be decided — certainly never in our present condition of knowledge. While the self-love and arrogance of man will persist in denying the reflective power to beasts, because the granting it seems to derogate from his own vaunted supremacy, he yet perpetually finds himself involved in the paradox of decrying instinct as an inferior faculty, while he is forced to admit its infinite superiority, in a thousand cases, over the very reason which he claims exclusively as his own. Instinct, so far from being an inferior reason, is perhaps the most exacted[2] intellect of all. It will appear to the true philosopher as the divine mind itself acting *immediately* upon its creatures.

The habits of the lion-ant, of many kinds of spiders, and of the beaver, have in them a wonderful analogy, or rather similarity, to the usual operations of the reason of man — but the instinct of some other creatures has no such analogy — and is referable only to the spirit of the Deity itself, acting *directly,* and through no corporal organ, upon the volition of the animal. Of this lofty species of instinct the coral-worm affords a remarkable instance. This little creature, the architect of continents, is not only capable of building ramparts against the sea, with a precision of purpose, and scientific adaptation and arrangement, from which the most skillful engineer might imbibe his best knowledge — but is gifted with what humanity does not possess — with the absolute spirit of prophecy. It will foresee, for months in advance, the pure accidents which are to happen to its dwelling, and aided by myriads of its brethren, all acting as if with one mind (and *indeed* acting with only one — with the mind of the Creator) will work diligently to counteract influences which exist alone in the future. There is also an immensely wonderful consideration connected with the cell of the bee. Let a mathematician be required to solve the problem of the shape best calculated in such a cell as the bee wants, for the two requisites of strength and space — and he will find himself involved in the very highest and most abstruse questions of analytical research. Let him be required to tell the number of sides which will give to the cell the greatest space, with the greatest solidity, and to define the exact angle at which, with the same object in view, the roof must incline — and to answer the query, he must be a Newton or a Laplace. Yet since bees were, they have been continually solving the problem.[3] The leading distinction between instinct and reason seems to be, that, while the one is infinitely the more exact, the more certain, and the more far-seeing in its sphere of action — the sphere of action in the other is of the far wider extent. But we are preaching a homily, when we merely intended to tell a short story about a cat.

The writer of this article is the owner of one of the most remarkable black cats in the world — and this is saying much; for it will be remembered that black cats are all of them witches. The one in question has not a white hair about her, and is of a demure and sanctified demeanor. That portion of the kitchen which she most frequents is accessible only by a door, which closes with what is termed a thumb-latch; these latches are rude in construction, and some force and dexterity are always requisite to force them down. But puss is in the daily habit of opening the door, which she accomplishes in the following way. She first springs from the ground to the guard of the latch (which resembles the guard over a gun-trigger,) and through this she thrusts her left arm to hold on with. She now, with her right hand, presses the thumb-latch until it yields, and here several attempts are frequently requisite. Having forced it down, however, she seems to be aware that her task is but half accomplished, since, if the door is not pushed open before she lets go, the latch will again fall into its socket. She, therefore, screws her body round so as to bring her hind feet immediately beneath the latch, while she leaps with all her strength from the door — the impetus of the spring forcing it open, and her hind feet sustaining the latch until this impetus is fairly given.

We have witnessed this singular feat a hundred times at least, and never without being impressed with the truth of the remark with which we commenced this article — that the boundary between instinct and reason is of a very shadowy nature. The black cat, in doing what she did, must have made use of all the perceptive and reflective faculties which we are in the habit of supposing the prescriptive qualities of reason alone.

NOTES

1. The Maine-New Brunswick boundary dispute was settled by the Webster-Ashburton Treaty of 1842; the Oregon boundary was established at the 49th parallel in 1846.

2. This word is probably a misprint for "exalted."

3. Speculations about the allegedly unreasoned actions of members of the animal kingdom are found in Poe's poem, "Romance" of 1829, and culminate in "The Raven" fifteen years later. Poe again referred to the coralites, the ant-lion, and the bees in the third chapter of "The Journal of Julius Rodman" and in "The Thousand-and-Second Tale of Scheherazade." The great scientists Isaac Newton and the Marquis de Laplace hardly need comment.

PETER PENDULUM
(THE BUSINESS MAN)

This little story must have been generally understood, when first published, as a deliberate parody on the *Charcoal Sketches* of Joseph C. Neal (1807–1847), a Philadelphia editor. These pictures of characters in low life, often with alliterative names, first came out in his own *Pennsylvanian* and other papers, and were very popular. Collected in book form in 1838, they were even pirated in England. Since Neal is almost completely forgotten, and copies of his books are not common, I quote the following from E. A. Duyckinck:

> The forte of Mr. Neal was a certain genial humor, devoted to the exhibition of a peculiar class of citizens falling under the social history description of the genus "loafer." ... laggards in the rear of civilization, who lack energy or ability to make an honorable position in the world, and who fall quietly into decay, complaining of their hard fate in the world ... small spendthrifts, inferior pretenders to fashion, bores, half-developed inebriates ... enjoying the minor miseries and social difficulties of life ... Mr. Neal ... interpreted their ailments, repeated their slang ... A quaint vein of speculation wrapped up this humorous dialogue ... The alliterative and extravagant titles of the sketches take off something from the reality ... it would be painful to ... laugh at real misery while we may be amused with comic exaggeration.*

Duyckinck reprints "P. Pilgarlick Pigwiggen, Esq." — a tale of a poetaster, arrested for debt, who consents to accompany an

* E. A. and G. L. Duyckinck, *Cyclopædia of American Literature* (1855), II, 456.

officer to jail "on condition he were taken there by the alley-way."
Neal had a certain wry compassion for his characters, who are never
wholly impossible people. Poe's parody — which is hardly better
than its models — is pure burlesque, and, although some of the
incidents are founded on fact, others obviously could not happen.
Poe's kindred tale called "Diddling" includes only incidents that
probably had really occurred, and is not in Neal's manner.

The first version of the story was presumably composed shortly
before its publication early in 1840. The title and the name of the
protagonist were changed and the tale was expanded by the addition of six paragraphs at the end when it appeared in the *Broadway Journal* five years later. The new material includes something
founded on a real event of November 1842. It seems somewhat
unlikely that Poe would have written so much new material for his
own weekly in the summer of 1845, and it is possible that the tale
was revised for one of the papers of which only imperfect files are
preserved — the *Philadelphia Saturday Museum* of 1843 or the
New York *Sunday Times* of 1844.

TEXTS

(A) Burton's Gentleman's Magazine, February 1840 (6:87–89); *(B) Broadway
Journal,* August 2, 1845 (2:49–52); *(C) Works* (1856), IV, 326–335. PHANTASY-
PIECES, title only.

The Griswold version *(C)* is followed as it shows presumably auctorial changes.

The early form was considerably revised for the *Broadway Journal.* The
name Peter Pendulum, already omitted from the title as listed for PHANTASY-
PIECES, was omitted from the body of the tale, and in several places Peter Proffit
was substituted. Six paragraphs were added at the end.

THE BUSINESS MAN. [C]

Method is the soul of business. — OLD SAYING.

Iᵃ am a business man. I am a methodical man. Method is *the*
thing, after all. But there are no people I more heartily despise,

---

Title: PETER PENDULUM,	*Motto:* Not in A
THE BUSINESS MAN. *(A); In C the*	a My name is Pendulum — Peter
running title on some pages is Method	Pendulum. I *(A)*
is the Soul of Business.	

than your eccentric fools who prate about method without understanding it; attending strictly to its letter, and violating its spirit.[1] These fellows are always doing the most out-of-the-way things in what they call an orderly manner. Now here — I conceive[b] is a positive paradox.[2] True method appertains to the ordinary and the obvious alone, and cannot be applied to the *outré*. What definite idea can a body attach to such expressions as "methodical[c] Jack o' Dandy," or "a systematical Will o' the Wisp?"

My notions upon this head might not have been so clear as they are,[d] but for a fortunate accident which happened to me when I was a very little boy. A good-hearted old Irish nurse (whom I shall not forget in my will) took me up one day by the heels, when I was making more noise than was necessary, and, swinging me round two or three times, d —— d my eyes for "a shreeking little spalpeen," and then knocked my head into a cocked hat against the bed-post. This, I say, decided my fate, and made my fortune. A [e]bump arose[e] at once on my sinciput, and turned out to be as pretty an organ of *order* as one shall see on a summer's day. Hence that positive appetite for system and regularity which has made me the distinguished man of business that I am.

If there is any thing on earth I hate, it is a genius. Your geniuses are all arrant asses — the greater the genius the greater the ass — and to this rule there is no exception whatever. Especially, you cannot make a man of business out of a genius, any more than money out of a Jew, or the best nutmegs out of pineknots.[3] The creatures are always going off at a tangent into some fantastic employment, or ridiculous speculation, entirely at variance with the "fitness of things,"[4] and having no business whatever to be considered as a business at all. Thus you may tell these characters immediately by the nature of their occupations. If you ever[f] perceive a man setting up as a merchant or a manufacturer; or going into the cotton or tobacco trade, or any of those eccentric pursuits; or getting to be a dry-goods dealer, or soap-boiler, or something of that kind; or pretending to be a lawyer, or a blacksmith, or a physician — anything

---

b   conceive it *(A)*
c   "a methodical *(A, B)*
d   are, nor should I have been so

well to do in the world as I am, *(A)*
e . . . e tremendous bump got up *(A)*
f   you ever/ever you *(A)*

out of the usual way — [g] you may set him down at once as a genius, and then, according to the rule-of-three, he's an ass.[5]

Now[h] I am not in any respect a genius, but a regular business man. My Day-book and Ledger will[i] evince this in a minute. They are well kept, though I say it myself; and, in my general habits of accuracy and punctuality, I am not to be beat by a clock. More-over, my occupations have been always made to chime in with the ordinary habitudes of my fellow-men. Not that I feel[j] the least indebted, upon this score, to my exceedingly weak-minded parents, who, beyond doubt, would have made an arrant genius of me at last, if my guardian angel had not come, in good time, to the rescue. In biography the truth is everything, and in auto-biography it is especially so — yet I scarcely hope to be believed when I state, how-ever solemnly, that my poor father put me, when I was about fif-teen years of age, into the counting-house of what he[k] termed "a respectable hardware and commission merchant doing a capital bit of business!" A capital bit of fiddlestick! However, the consequence of this folly was, that in two or three days, I had to be sent home to my button-headed family in a high state of fever, and with a most violent and dangerous pain in the sinciput, all round about my[l] organ of order. It was nearly a gone case with me then — just touch-and-go for six weeks — the physicians giving me up and all that sort of thing. But, although I suffered much, I was a thankful boy in the main. I was saved from being a "respectable hardware and commission merchant, doing a capital bit of business," and I felt grateful to the protuberance which had been the means of my salvation, as well as to the kind-hearted female[m] who had originally put these means within my reach.[n]

The most of boys run away from home at ten or twelve years of age, but I waited till I was sixteen. I don't know that I should have [o]gone, even[o] then, if I had not happened to hear [p]my old

---

g way — if ever, in short, you see a conceited fellow running heels-over-head into the patent-blacking, or linen-draping, or dog-meat line, *(A)*
h Now my name is Peter Pendulum, and *(A)*
i would *(A)*

j feel in *(A)*
k he ridiculously *(A)*
l my big *(A)*
m Irish female *(A)*
n *After this:* I shall remember that fine old nurse in my will. *(A)*
o . . . o even gone just *(A)*

mother talk[p] about setting me up on my own hook in the grocery way. The *grocery* way! — only think of that! I resolved to be off forthwith, and try and establish myself in some *decent* occupation, without dancing attendance any longer upon the caprices of these eccentric old people, and running the risk of being made a genius of in the end. In this project I succeeded perfectly well at the first effort, and by the time I was fairly eighteen, found myself doing an extensive and profitable business in the Tailor's[q] Walking-Advertisement line.

I was enabled to discharge the onerous duties of this profession, only by that rigid adherence to system which formed the leading feature of my mind. A scrupulous *method* characterized my actions as well as my accounts. In my case, it was method — not money — which made the man: at least all of him that was not made by the tailor whom I served. At nine, every morning, I called upon that individual for the clothes of the day. Ten o'clock found me in some fashionable promenade or other place of public amusement. The precise regularity with which I turned my handsome person about, so as to bring successively into view every portion of the suit upon my back, was the admiration of all the knowing men in the trade. Noon never passed without my bringing home a customer to the house of my employers, Messrs. Cut and Comeagain.[6] I say this proudly, but with tears in my eyes — for the firm proved themselves the basest of ingrates. The little account about which we quarrelled and finally parted, cannot, in any item, be thought overcharged, by gentlemen[r] really conversant with the nature of the business. Upon this point, however, I feel a degree of proud satisfaction in permitting the reader to judge for himself. My bill ran thus:[7]

Messrs. Cut and Comeagain, Merchant Tailors.

	To Peter Proffit,[s] *Walking Advertiser,*[t]	Drs.
July[u] 10.	To promenade, as usual, and customer brought home,	$oo 25
July 11.	To do do do	25
July 12.	To one lie, second class; damaged black cloth sold for invisible green,	25

p . . . p   old Mrs. Pendulum talking *(A)*   s   *Pendulum, (A)*
q   Tailors' *(A)*   t   *Advertisement, (A)*
r   gentleman *(C) misprint, corrected*   u   July *given only once (A)*
from A, B

July	13.	To one lie, first class, extra quality and size; recommending milled sattinet as broadcloth,		75
July	20.	To purchasing bran new paper shirt collar or dickey, to set off gray Petersham,[8]		2
Aug.[v]	15.	To wearing double-padded bobtail frock, (thermometer 706[w] in the shade.)		25
Aug.	16.	Standing[x] on one leg three hours, to show off new-style[y] strapped pants[9] at 12½ cents per leg per hour,		37½
Aug.	17.	To promenade, as usual, and large customer brought home[z] (fat man,)		50
Aug.	18.	To do do (medium size,)		25
Aug.	19.	To do do (small man and bad pay,)		6[a]
				$2 96½ [b]

The item chiefly disputed in this bill was the very moderate charge of two pennies for the dickey. Upon my word of honor, this *was not* an unreasonable price for that dickey. It was one of the cleanest and prettiest little dickeys I ever saw; and I have good reason to believe that it effected the sale of three Petershams. The elder partner of the firm, however, would allow me[c] only one penny of the charge, and took it upon himself to show in what manner four of the same sized conveniences could be got out of a sheet of foolscap. But it is needless to say that I stood upon the *principle*[d] of the thing. Business is business, and should be done in a business way. There was no *system* whatever in swindling me out of a penny — a clear fraud of fifty per cent. — no *method* in any respect.[e] I left at once the employment of Messrs. Cut and Comeagain, and set up in the Eye-Sore line by myself — one of the most lucrative, respectable and independent of the ordinary occupations.

My strict integrity, economy, and rigorous business habits, here again came into play. I found myself driving a flourishing trade, and soon became a marked man upon 'Change.' The truth is, I never dabbled in flashy matters, but jogged on in the good old sober routine of the calling — a calling in which I should, no doubt,

---

v   Aug. *given only once (A)*
w   206 *(A)*
x   To standing *(A)*
y   new-touch *(A)*
z   home, *omitted (C) restored from A, B*
a   6¼ *(A)*
b $2 96 ¾ *(A)*

c   *Omitted (A)*
d   principle *(A)*
e   *After this:* My organ of order revolted. So, thanks to that kind old Irish lady, (whom I shall be sure to remember in my will,) *(A)*

have remained to the present hour, but for a little accident which happened to me in the prosecution of one of the usual business operations of the profession. Whenever a rich old hunks, or prodigal heir, or bankrupt corporation, gets into the notion of putting up a palace, there is no such thing in the world as stopping either of them, and this every intelligent person knows. The fact in question is indeed the basis of the Eye-Sore trade. As soon, therefore, as a building project is fairly afoot by one of these parties, we merchants secure a nice corner of the lot in contemplation, or a prime little situation just adjoining or right in front. This done, we wait until the palace is half-way up, and then we pay some tasty architect to run us up an ornamental mud hovel, right against it; or a Down-East or Dutch Pagoda, ᶠor a pig-sty, or anᶠ ingenious little bit of fancy work, either Esquimau, Kickapoo, or Hottentot.[10] Of course, we can't afford to take these structures down under a bonus of five hundred per cent. upon the prime cost of our lot and plaster. *Can we?* I ask the question. I ask it of business men. It would be irrational to suppose that we can. And yet there was a rascally corporation which asked me to do this very thing — this *very thing!* I did not reply to their absurd proposition, of course; but I felt it a duty to go that same night, and lamp-black the whole of their palace. For this, the unreasonable villains clapped me intoᵍ jail; and the gentlemen of the Eye-Sore trade could not well avoid cutting my connection when I came out.

The Assault and Battery business, into which I was now forced to adventure for a livelihood, wasʰ somewhat ill-adaptedⁱ to the delicate nature of my constitution; but I went to work in it with a good heart, and found my account, here as heretofore, in those stern habits of methodical accuracy which had been thumped into me by that delightful old nurse — I would indeed be the basest of men not to remember her well in my will. By observing, as I say, the strictest system in all my dealings, and keeping a well-regulated set of books, I was enabled to get over many serious difficulties, and, in the end, to establish myself very decently in the profession. The truth is, that few individuals, in anyʲ line, did a snugger little

f ... f   or any *(A)*
g   in *(A)*
h   was one *(A)*

i   illy adapted *(A)*
j   my *(A)*

business than I. I will just copy ᵏa page or so outᵏ of my Day-Book; and this will save me the necessity of blowing my own trumpet — a contemptible practice, of which no high-minded man will be guilty. Now, the Day-Book is a thing that don't lie.

"Jan. 1. — New Year's day. Met Snap[11] in the street, groggy. Mem — he'll do. Met Gruff shortly afterwards, blind drunk. Mem — he'll answer too. Entered both gentlemen in my Ledger, and opened a running account with each.

"Jan. 2. — Saw Snap at the Exchange, and went up and trod on his toe. Doubled his fist and knocked me down. Good! — got up again. Some trifling difficulty with Bag, my attorney. I want the damages at a thousand, but he says that, for so simple a knock-down, we can't lay them at more than five hundred. Mem — must get rid of Bag — no *system* at all.

"Jan. 3. — Went to theˡ theatre, to look for Gruff. Saw him sitting in a side box, in the second tier, between a fat lady and a lean one. Quizzed the whole partyᵐ through an opera-glass, till I saw the fat lady blush and whisper to G.[12] Went round, then, into the box, and put my nose within reach of his hand. Wouldn't pull it — no go. Blewⁿ it, and tried again — no go. Sat down then, and winked at the lean lady, when I had the high satisfaction of finding him lift me up by the nape of the neck, and fling me over into the pit. Neck dislocated, and right leg capitally splintered. Went home in high glee, drank a bottle of champagne, and booked the young man for five thousand. Bag says it'll do.

"Feb. 15. — Compromised the case of Mr. Snap. Amount entered in Journal — fifty cents — which see.

"Feb. 16. — Cast by that villain, Gruff, who made me a present of five dollars. Cost of suit, four dollars and twenty-five cents. Nett profit — see Journal — seventy-five cents."

Now, here is a clear gain, in a very brief period, of no less than one dollar and twenty five cents — this isᵒ in the mere cases of Snap and Gruff; and I solemnly assure the reader that these extracts are taken at random from my Day-Book.

---

k . . . k   out a page or so *(A)*   n   Wiped *(A)*
l   to the/tot he *(B) misprint*   o   *Omitted (A)*
m   set *(A)*

It's an old saying, and a true one, however, that money is nothing in comparison with health. I found the exactions of the profession somewhat too much for my delicate state of body; and, discovering, at last, that I was knocked [p]all out of[p] shape, so that I didn't[q] know very well what to make of the matter, and so that[r] my friends, when they met me in the street, couldn't tell that I was Peter Proffit[s] at all, it occurred to me that the best expedient I could adopt, was to alter my line of business. [t]I turned my attention, therefore, to Mud-Dabbling, and continued it for some years.[t]

The worst of this occupation is[t′] that too many people take a fancy to it, and the competition is in consequence excessive. Every ignoramus of a fellow who finds that he hasn't brains in sufficient quantity to make his way as a walking advertiser, or an eye-sore-prig, or a salt and batter man, thinks, of course, that he'll answer very well as a dabbler of mud. But there never was entertained a more erroneous idea than that it requires no brains to mud-dabble. Especially, there is nothing to be made in this way without *method.* I did[u] only a retail business myself, but my old habits of *system* carried[v] me swimmingly along. I selected my street-crossing, in the first place, with great deliberation, and I never put down a broom in any part of the town *but that.* I took[w] care, too, to have a nice little puddle at hand, which I could[x] get at in a minute. By these means I[y] got to be well known as a man to be trusted; and this is one-half the battle, let me tell you, in trade. Nobody ever failed[z] to pitch *me* a copper, and got[a] over *my* crossing with a clean pair of pantaloons. And, as my business habits, in this respect, were[b] sufficiently understood, I never met[c] with any attempt at imposition. I wouldn't have[d] put up with it, if I had.[e] Never imposing upon

---

p . . . p out of all *(A)*
q did't *(C) misprint, corrected from A, B*
r so that omitted *(A)*
s Pendulum *(A)*; Profit *(C) misprint, corrected from B and from C above*
t . . . t I am now, therefore, in the Mud-Dabbling way, and have been so for some years. *(A)*
t′ occupation, is, *(B, C) corrected from A*
u do *(A)*
v carry *(A)*
w take *(A)*
x can *(A)*
y I have now *(A)*
z fails *(A)*
a gets *(A)*
b are *(A)*
c meet *(A)*
d *Omitted (A)*
e did. *(A)*

any one myself, I suffered[f] no one to play the possum with me. The frauds[g] of the banks [h]of course I couldn't[h] help.[13] Their[i] suspension put[j] me to ruinous inconvenience. These, however, are not individuals, but corporations; and corporations, it is very well known, have neither bodies[k] to be kicked, nor souls[14] to be damned.[l]

I was making money at this business, when, in an evil moment, I was induced to merge[m] in the Cur-Spattering — a somewhat analogous, but, by no means, so respectable a profession. My location, to be sure, was an excellent one, being central, and I had capital blacking and brushes. My little dog, too, was quite fat and up to all varieties of snuff. He had been in the trade a long time, and, I may say, understood it. Our general routine was this; — Pompey, having rolled himself well in the mud, sat upon end at the shop door, until he observed a dandy approaching in bright boots. He then proceeded to meet him, and gave the Wellingtons a rub or two with his wool. Then the dandy swore very much, and looked about for a boot-black. There I was, full in his view, with blacking and brushes. It was only a minute's work, and then came a sixpence. This did moderately well for a time; — in fact, I was not avaricious, but my dog was. I allowed him a third of the profit, but he was advised to insist upon half. This I couldn't stand — so we quarrelled and parted.

I next tried my hand at the Organ-grinding for a while, and may say that I made out pretty well. It is a plain, straight-forward business, and requires no particular abilities. You can get a music-mill for a mere song, and, to put it in order, you have but to open the works, and give them three or four smart raps with a hammer. It improves the tone of the thing, for business purposes, more than you can imagine. This done, you have only to stroll along, with the mill on your back, until you see tan-bark in the street, and a knocker wrapped up in buckskin. Then you stop and grind; looking as if you meant to stop and grind till doomsday. Presently a window opens, and somebody pitches you a sixpence, with a re-

---

f   suffer *(A)*
g   rauds *(B) misprint*
h . . . h   I can't, of course, *(A)*
i   Their infamous *(A)*
j   has put *(A)*

k   posteriors *(A)*
l   *Here A ends, paragraphs 18–23 are first known from B*
m   merge it *(B)*

quest to "Hush up and go on," &c. I am aware that some grinders have actually afforded to "go on" for this sum; but for my part, I found the necessary outlay of capital too great, to permit of my "going on" under a shilling.

At this occupation I did a good deal; but, somehow, I was not quite satisfied, and so finally abandoned it. The truth is, I labored under the disadvantage of having no monkey — and American streets are *so* muddy, and a Democratic rabble is *so* obtrusive, and so full of demnition mischievous little boys.

I was now out of employment for some months, but at length succeeded, by dint of great interest, in procuring a situation in the Sham-Post.[15] The duties, here, are simple, and not altogether unprofitable. For example: — very early in the morning I had to make up my packet of sham letters. Upon the inside of each of these I had to scrawl a few lines — on any subject which occurred to me as sufficiently mysterious — signing all the epistles Tom Dobson, or Bobby Tompkins, or anything in that way. Having folded and sealed all, and stamped them with sham postmarks — New Orleans, Bengal, Botany Bay, or any other place a great way off — I set out, forthwith, upon my daily route, as if in a very great hurry. I always called at the big houses to deliver the letters, and receive the postage. Nobody hesitates at paying for a letter — especially for a double one — people are *such* fools — and it was no trouble to get round a corner before there was time to open the epistles. The worst of this profession was, that I had to walk so much and so fast; and so frequently to vary my route. Besides, I had serious scruples of conscience. I can't bear to hear innocent individuals abused — and the way the whole town took to cursing Tom Dobson and Bobby Tompkins, was really awful to hear. I washed my hands of the matter in disgust.[15]

My eighth and last speculation has been in the Cat-Growing way. I have found this a most pleasant and lucrative business and, really, no trouble at all. The country, it is well known, has become infested with cats — so much so of late, that a petition for relief, most numerously and respectably signed, was brought before the legislature at its late[n] memorable session. The assembly,

---

n   last *(B)*

at this epoch, was unusually well-informed, and, having passed many other wise and wholesome enactments, it crowned all with the Cat-Act. In its original form, this law offered a premium for cat-*heads,* (fourpence a-piece) but the Senate succeeded in amending the main clause, so as to substitute the word *"tails"* for "heads." This amendment was so obviously proper, that the house concurred in it *nem. con.*[16]

As soon as the Governor had signed the bill, I invested my whole estate in the purchase of Toms and Tabbies. At first, I could only afford to feed them upon mice (which are° cheap), but they fulfilled the Scriptural injunction at so marvellous a rate,[17] that I at length considered it my best policy to be liberal, and so indulged them in oysters and turtle. Their tails, at aᵖ legislative price, now bring me in a good income: for I have discovered a way, in which, by means of Macassar oil, I can force three crops in a year.[18] It delights me to find, too, that the animals soon get accustomed to the thing, and would rather have the appendages cut off than otherwise. I considerᵖ' myself, therefore, a made man, and am bargaining for a country seat on the Hudson.[19]

NOTES

Title: Peter Pendulum, in the title of the first version, took his name from a character in sketches published by Joseph Dennie in the *Farmer's Museum* of Walpole, New Hampshire, about 1795–1799. See the Duyckinck *Cyclopædia,* I, 562.

Motto: Lord Chesterfield, in a letter of February 5, 1750, wrote, "Despatch is the soul of business."

1. See II Corinthians 3:6, and Romans 7:6, on spirit and letter. There is similar phrasing in Poe's "Mystification."

2. A character in "Lionizing" is called Sir Positive Paradox.

3. Compare Poe's model hexameters (Mabbott, I, 393–394) for Jews (money-lenders) and pine-knots.

4. Compare "How to Write a Blackwood Article" at n. 6.

5. Some have thought there is a personal allusion to John Allan's wish to put Poe in his countinghouse. See Agnes Bondurant, *Poe's Richmond* (1942), p. 49.

o   which are/whichare *(B) misprint*   p'   consider, *(C) corrected from B*
p   the *(B)*

6. Dr. Kutankumagen is a Russian medico in Dickens' *Mudfog Papers* (1838), much given to bleeding patients.

7. In the first text this bill was made out by Peter Pendulum. [The new name for the narrator may have come from Poe's associations in Washington. He was there in March 1843 (see Mabbott I, 553). Professor Pollin has found in the *Congressional Globe* of March 10, 1843, an account of Mr. Proffit of Indiana (George H. Proffitt) speaking on a Naval Appropriations Bill.]

8. A kind of greatcoat about 1812, named for Viscount Petersham, later fourth Earl of Harrington, who is said to have designed it.

9. The word "pants" here is earlier than any recorded by lexicographers. See *American N & Q*, April 1967.

10. Compare references to bad architecture in "Philosophy of Furniture," and in *Doings of Gotham*, Letter V.

11. Snap is also the name of a character in Poe's Folio Club.

12. Compare "The Spectacles": "... the stern decrees of Fashion had, of late, imperatively prohibited the use of the opera-glass to stare at a lady."

13. The reference is to the frequent suspension of banks during the Jackson and Van Buren administrations. In a letter to Thomas Wyatt, April 1, 1841 (formerly in the Koester Collection, now at the University of Texas), Poe mentioned deferring his own plans for the "Penn Magazine" and accepting the position offered him at *Graham's* because of the bank suspensions. [Professor Joseph J. Moldenhauer published this letter in *American Literature*, January 1971.]

14. That corporations have no souls can be traced to a dictum of Sir Edward Coke (1552–1634) in the Case of Sutton's Hospital, 10 Report 32.

15. The Sham-Post incident is not in the first version, and seems to have been suggested by a story in the *Saturday Evening Post*, November 12, 1842:

> PENNY ROGUES. The New York Sun says: "A subscriber has shown us several letters received by himself and friends from pretended letter carriers, who thus extorted 18 3/4 cents on each letter from them, as postage. The letters of course proved a hoax, and even the postmark was not imitated."

The odd sum of money is one and a half New York "shillings" or Spanish-American silver reals. In Poe's day, Mexican silver circulated in the United States in greater quantity perhaps than our own coins, and was legal tender. New York shillings were still money of account in the Fulton Fish Market in the 1960's.

16. *Nem[ine] con[tradicente]* is "without opposition"; Poe's dislike of meddling politicians is well known.

17. The Scriptural injunction, "Be fruitful and multiply," is in Genesis 1:22.

18. Macassar oil was a popular hair tonic; the word antimacassar was coined to describe a cloth put on the back of a chair to protect it from the oil. The following is from an article on "Puffing" in the *New-York Mirror*, June 27, 1835: "What more delicate and insinuating than the manner in which the marvellous effects of the incomparable oil of Macassar are introduced to the reader? And

what, in fact, more poetical than that sublime image of the table upon which the oil was spilled by accident, and which was the next day covered with mahogany colored hair?"

19. Mansions on the Hudson were marks of affluence. Washington Irving's Sunnyside may still be visited, and General George Pope Morris's Undercliff was described, with an engraved illustration, in *Burton's,* March 1840.

CABS

This jeu d'esprit was first printed in *Alexander's Weekly Messenger,* April 1, 1840; and reprinted by its discoverer, Clarence S. Brigham, in *Proceedings of the American Antiquarian Society* for April 1942. Like "Instinct vs Reason" it is included in Brigham's *Edgar Allan Poe's Contributions to Alexander's Weekly Messenger.* Because of its fanciful nature it is here collected among the Tales and Sketches. Brigham observed that it is most unlikely that anyone associated with Alexander's paper except Poe would have brought the two great French naturalists, Buffon and Cuvier, into a discussion of cabdrivers. The little piece is perhaps a first sketch for the second of the articles headed "A Moving Chapter" in the Philadelphia *Public Ledger,* July 18, 1844, assigned to Poe's pen with great plausibility by his friend Eli Bowen.

TEXT

The sole authorized text, that of *Alexander's Weekly Messenger,* April 1, 1840, is reproduced.

CABS.

These anomalous vehicles, of which we Americans know so little by personal inspection, and so much through the accounts of the travelled, and the pages of the novelist, are about to be introduced among us "as a regular thing." In New-York they are already gaining ground, and *going over* it. The cab proper, as used in London, is an affair *sui generis,* and has very little affinity with any thing else in nature. It resembles, in some respect, the old-fashioned sedan chair, and carries two inside passengers, who sit vis a vis, with the coachman at top. The bottom nearly touches the pavement, and the entire vehicle has an outré appearance. Those in New York at present, are of a bright chocolate color, and look very stylish. Their charge is twenty five cents for any distance under two miles. The cab-introduction will bring about among us a peculiar race of people — the cabman. These creatures are not mentioned in Buffon, and Cuvier has entirely forgotten them. They bear a droll kind of resemblance to the human species — but their faces are all fashioned of brass, and they carry both their brains and their souls in their pockets.

NOTES

None is needed for this *jeu d'esprit.* T.O.M.

PHILOSOPHY OF FURNITURE

This sketch includes a slight narrative element, and is closely akin to "Landor's Cottage." That story is an idealized description of Poe's cottage at Fordham, but to what extent the "Philosophy of Furniture" portrays a room in one of Poe's Philadelphia homes cannot be known. However, Lambert A. Wilmer records that Poe "kept a piano to gratify" Virginia Poe's "taste for music, at a time when his income could scarcely afford such an indulgence."[*]

Even if Poe could never afford such a modestly luxurious home as that in "Philosophy of Furniture," he had one opportunity to act as a "decorist." When Marie Louise Shew moved to 51 (now 17 West) Tenth Street soon after May 1, 1847, she tells us: "I gave him *carte blanche* to furnish the music-room and library as he pleased. I had hung the pictures myself, . . . placing over the piano a large painting by Albano. Mr. Poe admired it for hours, and . . . was much pleased at my request, and my uncle said he had never seen him so cheerful."[†]

[*] "Recollections of Edgar A. Poe" in the Baltimore *Daily Commercial,* May 23, 1866; see p. 32 in my edition of Wilmer's *Merlin* (1941), where the article is reprinted.
[†] See Ingram, *Life and Letters,* p. 361; and Phillips, *Poe the Man,* II, 1268. The latter names the uncle, Hiram Barney, a lawyer. The authenticity of the picture by Francesco Albani can be doubted.

PHILOSOPHY OF FURNITURE

Poe's "Philosophy of Furniture" was probably written in March or April 1840.

TEXTS

(A) Burton's Gentleman's Magazine, May 1840 (6:243–245); *(B) Broadway Journal,* May 3, 1845 (1:273–275; *(C) Works* (1850), II, 299–305.

Griswold's version *(C)* which restores the first title is followed. Poe's care in revising this piece is evident. The appreciable number of changes he made in the *Burton's Gentleman's Magazine* text *(A)* for the *Broadway Journal (B)* included the elimination of the opening paragraph and the rephrasing of sentences, as well as changes in words and italicization.

Both the *Broadway Journal (B)* and the Griswold *(C)* texts have an error in "Americans of modern means," where modest or moderate is obviously intended. As there is no evidence to substantiate a change from Poe's early use of moderate, it is adopted for this text.

Reprints
Spirit of the Times (Philadelphia), May 16, 1840, from *Burton's Gentleman's Magazine; New-York Mirror* (Weekly), May 17, 1845, prefaced by: "The following Essay on a subject that, in New York at least, has more of May-day in it than dog-wood blossoms, birds or willow buds, is well worth copying entire from our excellent contemporary, the *Broadway Journal.*"

PHILOSOPHY OF FURNITURE. [C]

In the internal decoration, if not in the external architecture of their residences, the English are supreme. The Italians have but little sentiment beyond marbles and colors. In France, *meliora probant, deteriora sequuntur*[1] — the people are too much a race of gad-abouts to[a] maintain those household proprieties of which, indeed, they have a delicate appreciation, or at least the elements of a proper sense. The Chinese and most of the eastern races have a

---

Title: The Philosophy of Furniture *(A)*; House Furniture *(B)*

The earliest text (A) begins with a paragraph eliminated in later texts: "Philosophy," says Hegel, "is utterly useless and fruitless, and, *for this very reason,* is the sublimest of all pursuits, the most deserving of our attention, and the most worthy of our zeal" — a somewhat Coleridegy assertion, with a rivulet of deep meaning in a meadow of words. It would be wasting time to disentangle the paradox — and the more so as no one will deny that Philosophy has its merits, and is applicable to an infinity of purposes. There is reason, it is said, in the roasting of eggs, and there is philosophy even in furniture — a philosophy nevertheless which seems to be more imperfectly understood by Americans than by any civilized nation upon the face of the earth.

a   to study and *(A)*

·495·

warm but inappropriate fancy. The Scotch are *poor* decorists.[2] The Dutch [b]have, perhaps, an indeterminate[b] idea that a curtain is not a cabbage. In Spain they are *all* curtains — a nation of hangmen.[c] The Russians do[d] not furnish. The Hottentots and Kickapoos are very well in their way. The Yankees alone are preposterous.[3]

How this happens, it is not difficult to see. We have no aristocracy of blood, and having therefore as a natural, and indeed as an inevitable thing, fashioned for ourselves an aristocracy of dollars, the *display of wealth* has here to take the place and perform the office of the heraldic display in monarchical countries. By a transition readily understood, and which might have been as readily[e] foreseen, we have been brought to merge in simple *show* our notions of taste itself.

To speak less abstractly.[f] In England, for example, no mere parade of costly appurtenances would be so likely as with us, to create an impression of the beautiful in respect to the appurtenances themselves — or of taste as regards[g] the proprietor: — this for the reason, first, that wealth is not, in England, the loftiest object of ambition as constituting a nobility; and secondly, that there, the true nobility of [h]blood, confining itself within the strict limits of legitimate taste,[h] rather avoids than affects that mere[i] costliness in which a *parvenu*[j] rivalry may at any time[k] be successfully attempted.[l] The people *will*[m] imitate the nobles, and the result is a thorough diffusion of the proper[n] feeling. But in America, [o]the coins current being the sole arms of the[o] aristocracy, their display may be said, in general,[p] to be the sole means of aristocratic distinction; and the populace, looking always upward[q] for models, are insensibly led to confound the two entirely separate ideas of magnificence and beauty. In short, the cost of an article of furniture has at length come to be, with us, nearly the sole test of its

b . . . b have merely a vague *(A)*
c *hang*men. *(A)*
d no *(A) misprint*
e as readily/easily *(A)*
f abstractedly. *(A)*
g respects *(A)*
h . . . h blood *(A)*
i that mere *omitted (A)*
j parvenu *(A)*
k at any time *omitted (A)*
l attempted, confining itself within the rigorous limits, and to the analytical investigation, of legitimate taste. *(A)*
m naturally *(A)*
n the proper/a right *(A)*
o . . . o dollars being the supreme insignia of *(A)*
p general terms, *(A)*
q always upward/up *(A)*

merit in a decorative point of view — and this test, once established, has led the way to many analogous errors, readily traceable to the one primitive folly.

There could be nothing[r] more directly offensive to the eye of an artist than the interior of what is termed in the United [s]States — that is to say, in Appallachia — [t] a[s] well-furnished apartment. Its most usual defect is a[t] want of keeping. We speak of the keeping of a room as we would of the keeping of a picture — for both the picture and the room are amenable to those undeviating principles which regulate all varieties of art; and very nearly the same laws by which we decide on[u] the higher merits of a painting, suffice for [v]decision on[v] the adjustment of a chamber.

A want of keeping is observable sometimes in the character of the several pieces of furniture, but generally in their colors or modes of adaptation to use. *Very*[w] often the eye is offended by their inartistical arrangement. Straight lines are too prevalent — too uninterruptedly continued — or clumsily interrupted at right angles. If curved lines occur, they are repeated into unpleasant uniformity. [x]By undue precision, the appearance of many a fine apartment is utterly spoiled.[x]

Curtains are rarely well disposed, or well chosen in respect to[y] other decorations. With formal furniture, curtains are out of place; and an extensive[z] volume of drapery of any kind is, under any circumstances, irreconcilable with good taste — the proper quantum, as well as the proper adjustment, depending[a] upon the character of the general effect.

Carpets are better understood of late than of ancient days, but we still very frequently err in their patterns and colors. [b]The soul of the apartment is the carpet.[b] From it are deduced not only the hues but the forms of all objects incumbent. A judge at common law may be[c] an ordinary man; a good judge of a carpet *must*

---

r   scarcely any thing *(A)*
s . . . s States, a *(A)*
t   a preposterous *(A)*
u   upon *(A)*
v . . . v   a decision upon *(A)*
w   Very *(A)*
x . . . x   Undue precision spoils the

appearance of many a room. *(A)*
y   to the *(A)*
z   excessive *(A)*
a   depends *(A)*
b . . . b   A carpet is the soul of an
apartment. *(A)*
c   *may be (A)*

be a genius. Yet we[d] have heard discoursing[e] of carpets, with the air[f] *"d'un mouton qui rêve,"*[g] [5] fellows who[h] should not and who could not be entrusted with the management of their own *moustaches.*[i] Every one knows that a large floor *may*[j] have a covering of large figures, and that[k] a small one [l]*must* have a covering[l] of small — yet this is not all the knowledge in the world. As regards texture, the Saxony is alone admissible. Brussels is the preterpluperfect tense of fashion, and Turkey is taste in its dying agonies.[6] Touching pattern — a carpet should *not* be bedizzened out like a Riccaree Indian[7] — all red chalk, yellow ochre, and cock's feathers. In brief — distinct grounds, and vivid circular or cycloid[m] figures, *of no meaning,* are here Median laws.[8] The abomination of flowers, or representations of well-known objects of any kind, should not[n] be endured within the limits of Christendom. Indeed, whether on carpets, or curtains, or tapestry,[o] or ottoman coverings, all upholstery of this nature should be rigidly Arabesque. As for those[p] antique floor-cloths still[q] [r]occasionally seen[r] in the dwellings of the rabble — cloths of huge, sprawling, and radiating devices,[s] stripe-interspersed, and glorious with all hues, among which no ground is intelligible — these[t] are but the wicked invention of a race of time-servers and money-lovers — children of Baal and worshippers of Mammon — Benthams,[u] who, to [v]spare thought and economize[v] fancy, first cruelly invented the Kaleidoscope,[9] and then established [w]joint-stock companies[w] to twirl it by steam.

Glare is a leading error in the philosophy of American household decoration — an error easily recognised as deduced from the perversion of taste just specified. We are violently enamored of gas and of glass. The former is totally inadmissible within doors.

---

d I *(A)*
e fellows discourse *(A)*
f visage of a sheep in a reverie — *(A)*
g *réve," (C) accent corrected*
from A, B
h fellows who/ — who *(A)*
i mustachios. *(A)*
j should *(A)*
k *Omitted (A)*
l...l *Omitted (A)*
m or cycloid *omitted (A)*
n never *(A)*

o paper-hangings, *(A)*
p As for those/Those *(A)*
q which are still *(A)*
r...r seen occasionally *(A)*
s devises, *(C) misprint, corrected*
from A, B
t *Omitted (A)*
u men *(A)*
v...v save trouble of thought and
exercise of *(A)*
w...w a patent company *(A)*

PHILOSOPHY OF FURNITURE

Its harsh and unsteady light offends.[x] No one[y] having both brains and eyes will use it. A mild, or what artists term a cool light, with its consequent warm shadows, will do wonders for even an ill-furnished apartment. Never was a more lovely thought than that of the astral lamp. We[z] mean, of couse, the astral lamp proper[a] — the lamp of Argand, with its original plain ground-glass shade, and its tempered and uniform moonlight rays.[10] The cut-glass shade is a weak invention of the enemy. The eagerness with which we have adopted it, partly on account of its *flashiness,* but principally on account of its *greater cost,* is a good commentary on[b] the proposition with which we[c] began. It is not too much to say, that the deliberate employer of a cut-glass shade, is[d] either radically deficient in taste, or blindly subservient to the caprices of fashion. The light proceeding from one of these gaudy abominations is unequal, broken, and painful. It alone is sufficient to mar a world of good effect in the furniture subjected to its influence. Female loveliness, in especial, is more than one-half disenchanted beneath its evil eye.

In the matter of glass, generally, we proceed upon false principles. Its leading feature is *glitter* — and in that one word how much of all that is detestable do we express! Flickering, unquiet lights, are *sometimes* pleasing — to children and idiots always so — but in the embellishment of a room they should be scrupulously avoided. In truth, even strong *steady* lights are inadmissible. The huge and unmeaning glass chandeliers, prism-cut, gas-lighted,[e] and without shade, which dangle[f] in our most fashionable drawing-rooms, may be cited as the quintessence of [g]all that is false in taste or preposterous in[g] folly.

The rage for *glitter* — because its idea has become, as we[h] before observed, confounded with that of magnificence in the abstract — has led us,[i] also, to the exaggerated employment of mirrors. We line our dwellings with great British plates, and then imagine

x   is positively offensive. (A)
y   man (A)
z   I (A)
a   proper, and do not wish to be misunderstood (A)
b   upon (A)
c   I (A)

d   is a person (A)
e   gas-litten, (A)
f   dangle by night (A)
g . . . g   false taste, as so many concentrations of preposterous (A)
h   I (A)
i   Omitted (A)

we have done a fine thing. Now the slightest thought will be sufficient to convince any one who has an eye at all, of the ill effect of numerous looking-glasses, and especially of large ones. Regarded apart from its reflection, the mirror presents a continuous, flat, colorless, unrelieved surface, — a thing always [j]and obviously unpleasant.[j] Considered as a reflector, it is potent in producing a monstrous and odious uniformity: and the evil is here aggravated, not in merely[k] direct proportion with the augmentation of its sources, but in a ratio constantly increasing. In fact, a room with four or five mirrors arranged at random, is, for all purposes of artistic[l] show, a room of no shape at all. If we add to this evil,[m] the attendant glitter upon glitter, we have a perfect farrago of discordant and displeasing effects. The veriest [n]bumpkin, on[n] entering an apartment so bedizzened, would be instantly aware of something wrong, although he might be altogether unable to assign a cause for his dissatisfaction. But let the same person[o] be led into a room tastefully furnished, and he would be startled into an exclamation of [p]pleasure and surprise.[p]

It is an evil growing out of our republican institutions, that here a man of large purse has usually a very little soul which he keeps in it. The corruption of taste is a portion or[q] a pendant of the dollar-manufacture. As we grow rich, our ideas grow rusty. It is, therefore, not among *our* aristocracy that we must [r]look (if at all, in Appallachia,)[r] for the spirituality of a British *boudoir*. But we[s] have seen apartments in the tenure of Americans [t]of moderate means,[t] [11] which, in negative merit at least, might vie with any of the *or-molu'd* cabinets of our friends across the water. Even *now*,[u] there is present to our[v] mind's eye a small and not ostentatious chamber with whose decorations no fault can be found. The proprietor lies asleep on[w] a sofa — the weather is cool — the time is

j . . . j unpleasant, and obviously so. *(A)*
k not in merely/in no *(A)*
l artistical *(A)*
m evil, *omitted (A)*
n . . . n bumpkin, not addle-headed, upon *(A)*
o individual *(A)*
p . . . p surprise and of pleasure. *(A)*
q and *(A)*
r . . . r look if at all, in the United States, *(A)*
s I *(A)*
t . . . t — men of exceedingly moderate means yet *rarae aves* of good taste — *(A)*; of modern means, *(B, C) misprint, emended by the editor*
u *now*,/now *(A)*
v my *(A)*
w upon *(A)*

near midnight: we[x] will make a sketch of the room [y]during his slumber.[y]

It is oblong — some thirty feet in length and twenty-five in breadth — a shape affording the best (ordinary)[z] opportunities for the adjustment of furniture. It has but one [a]door — by no means a wide one — which[a] is at one end of the parallelogram, and but two windows, which are at the other. These latter are large, reaching down[b] to the floor — have[c] deep recesses — and open on[d] an Italian *veranda*. Their panes are of a crimson-tinted glass, set in rose-wood framings, [e]more massive[e] than usual. They are curtained within the recess, by a thick silver tissue adapted to the shape of the window, and hanging [f]loosely in small[f] volumes. Without the recess are curtains of an exceedingly rich crimson silk, fringed with a deep network of gold, and lined with the silver tissue, which [g]is the material of[g] the exterior blind. There are no cornices; but the folds of the whole fabric (which are sharp rather than massive, and have an airy appearance,) issue from beneath a broad entablature of rich giltwork, which encircles the room at the junction of the ceiling and walls. The drapery is thrown open also, or closed, by means of a thick rope of gold loosely enveloping it, and resolving itself readily into a knot; no pins or other such devices are apparent. The colors of the curtains and their[h] fringe — the tints of crimson and gold — [i]appear everywhere in profusion, and determine[i] the *character* of the room.[j] The carpet — of Saxony material — is quite half an inch thick, and is of the same crimson ground, relieved simply by the appearance[k] of a gold cord (like that festooning the curtains) [l]slightly relieved above the surface of the *ground,* and[l] thrown upon it in such a manner as to form a[m] succession of short irregular [n]curves — one occasionally[n] overlaying the other.[o]

---

x I *(A)*

y . . . y ere he awakes. *(A)*

z *Omitted (A)*

a . . . a door, which *(A)*

b downwards *(A)*

c are situated in *(A)*

d upon *(A)*

e . . . e of a kind somewhat broader *(A)*

f . . . f loosely, but having no *(A)*

g . . . g forms *(A)*

h its *(A)*

i . . . i form *(A)*

j room, and appear every where in profusion. *(A)*

k *appearance (A)*

l . . . l *Omitted (A)*

m a close *(A)*

n . . . n curves, no one *(A)*

o *After this:* This carpet has no border. *(A)*

ᵖThe walls are prepared with a glossy paper of a silver gray tint, spottedᵖ with small Arabesque devices of a fainter hueᑫ of the prevalent crimson. Many paintings relieve the expanse of the paper. These are chiefly landscapes of an imaginative cast — such as the fairy grottoes of Stanfield,[12] or the lake of the Dismal Swamp ofʳ Chapman.[13] ˢThere are, nevertheless, three or four female heads, of an ethereal beauty — portraits in the manner of Sully.ˢ [14] The tone of each pictureᵗ is warm, but dark. There are no "brilliant effects." ᵘ*Repose* speaks in all.ᵘ Not oneᵛ is of small size. Diminutive paintings give that *spotty* look to a room, which is the blemish of so many a fine work of Art overtouched. The frames are broad but not deep,ʷ and richly carved, without being ˣ*dulled* orˣ filagreed. ʸThey haveʸ the whole lustre of burnishedᶻ gold. They lie flat onᵃ the walls, and do not hang off with cords. The designs themselves ᵇare often seen to better advantageᵇ in this latter position, but the general appearance of the chamber is injured. ᶜBut one mirror — and this not a very large one — is visible. In shape it is nearly circular — and it is hung so that a reflection of the person can be obtained from it in none of the ordinary sitting-places of the room.ᶜ Two large lowᵈ sofas of rose-wood and crimson silk, gold-flowered,ᵉ form the only ᶠseats, with the exception of two light conversation chairs, also of rose-wood.ᶠ There is a ᵍpianoforte, (rose-wood, also,)ᵍ without ʰcover, and thrown open.ʰ An octagonal table, formed altogetherⁱ of the richest gold-threaded marble, is placed near one of the ʲsofas. Thisʲ is also without cover — the drapery of the curtains has been thought sufficient. Four

---

p . . . p The paper on the walls is of a glossy, silvery hue, intermingled *(A)*
q   tint *(A)*
r   of our own *(A)*
s . . . s *Omitted (A)*
t   *Omitted (A)*
u . . . u *Omitted (A)*
v   one of the pictures *(A)*
w   *but not deep, (A)*
x . . . x *Omitted (A)*
y . . . y Their profuse gilding gives them *(A)*
z   *Omitted (A)*
a   upon *(A)*

b . . . b may, sometimes, be best seen *(A)*
c . . . c *No* mirror is visible — nor chairs. *(A)*
d   *Omitted (A)*
e   *Omitted (A)*
f . . . f seats. *(A)*
g . . . g piano-forte — also of rose-wood, and *(A)*
h . . . h cover. Mahogany has been avoided. *(A)*
i   entirely *(A)*
j . . . j sofas — this table *(A)*

large and gorgeous Sèvres[k] vases, in which bloom[l] a profusion[m] of sweet and vivid flowers,[n] occupy the [o]slightly rounded[o] angles of the room. A tall[p] candelabrum, bearing a small antique lamp with highly[q] perfumed oil, is standing near the head of my sleeping friend. Some light and graceful hanging shelves, with golden edges and crimson silk cords and gold tassels, sustain two or three hundred magnificently bound books.[15] Beyond these things, there is no furniture, if we except an Argand lamp, with a plain crimson-tinted ground-glass[r] shade, which depends from the lofty vaulted[s] ceiling by a single slender[t] gold chain, and throws a tranquil[u] but magical radiance over all.[16]

NOTES

In the canceled paragraph, the remark ascribed to Hegel may represent the general view of that sage rather than his exact words. Poe has the same allusion in "Marginalia," number 245 (*SLM,* June 1849, p. 337). For reason in roasting an egg, compare Pope's "Second Epistle of the Second Book of Horace," line 85: "The vulgar boil, the learned roast an egg."

1. The Latin commonplace from Ovid's *Metamorphoses,* VII, 20–21, means "approve the better, follow the worse," and was used by Poe again in a review of *A Grammar of the English Language* by Hugh A. Pue in *Graham's* for July 1841.

2. "Decorist" does not appear in any of the major dictionaries of Poe's time, or of ours — with the exception of the OED, which lists it, giving as the single example Poe's use in "The Assignation." He used the word again in a review of Bulwer's *Night and Morning* in *Graham's,* April 1841.

3. Compare mention in "The Business Man" of "an ornamental mud-hovel ... Dutch pagoda ... or an ingenious little bit of fancy work, either Esquimau, Kickapoo or Hottentot." There is also a humorous account of pretentious architecture in Brooklyn in the fifth letter of *Doings of Gotham.*

4. Appalachia (variously spelled) and Allegania were proposed as new national names for this country, and were much discussed in 1845 when Poe revised this article. See also "Marginalia," number 184 (*Graham's,* December 1846, p. 312).

5. Compare "Never Bet the Devil Your Head," at note 24.

k	Sevres *(A)*		q	strongly *(A)*
l	grow *(A)*		r	glass *(A)*
m	number *(A)*		s	Omitted *(A)*
n	flowers in full bloom, *(A)*		t	Omitted *(A)*
o ... o	Omitted *(A)*		u	subdued *(A)*
p	tall and magnificent *(A)*			

6. Compare "Taste kicking *in articulo mortis*" in Poe's "Fifty Suggestions," Number 26 (*Graham's,* June 1849).

7. Ricaree is the name used by George Catlin and others for the Arikara tribe of Plains Indians; they are also mentioned in "The Journal of Julius Rodman," chapter IV.

8. For the unchanging laws of the Medes and Persians see Daniel 6:8.

9. Poe's unsympathetic references to Jeremy Bentham (1748–1832), the utilitarian philosopher, are frequent (see "Diddling," "Mellonta Tauta," and the preface to "Marginalia"). The Kaleidoscope was invented by Sir David Brewster, a Scottish physicist, in 1816; there were two articles on it in *Blackwood's,* in May and June 1818, occasioned by disputes over the patent and over schemes of mechanizing the device.

10. Aimé Argand, a Swiss, invented the lamp named for him in 1784; it has the hollow wick and glass chimney typical of oil lamps generally used in America in the nineteenth and early twentieth centuries.

11. In the canceled passage, the Latin phrase meaning "rare birds" has been traced to *"rara avis in terris,"* Juvenal's figurative use in his *Satires,* VI, 165. Poe uses the whole Latin phrase in "Hop-Frog."

12. William Clarkson Stanfield, R.A. (1793–1867), painted romantic scenes; his illustration of *Comus* in the Summer House at Buckingham Palace was famous. He is also mentioned in "The Landscape Garden."

13. John Gadsby Chapman (1808–1889), a native of Alexandria, Virginia, had held an exhibition of his paintings there in 1831. His "Lake of the Dismal Swamp" was exhibited in New York, 1836, at the National Academy of Design, as number 177, the year he became an Academician. An engraving of it by James Smillie was published soon after by Bancroft and Holley. (See Georgia Stamm Chamberlain, *Studies on John Gadsby Chapman,* 1963, p. 40.) The painting may well have recalled a memory of Poe's boyhood; see his early poem "The Lake," Mabbott I, 82ff.

14. One of Poe's Richmond schoolmates was a nephew of Thomas Sully (1783–1872), whom Poe knew as a friend in Philadelphia. Poe admired Sully, and called his portrait of Fanny Kemble "one of the finest things in the world" in his review of *The Gift* for 1836 in the *Southern Literary Messenger,* September 1836. Poe's friend Robert Sully studied under his uncle for a time and also became an artist. One of his paintings is thought to have inspired "The Oval Portrait."

15. Poe himself had a hanging bookshelf in the cottage at Fordham, according to the reminiscences of Mrs. Mary Gove Nichols, published originally in the London *Sixpenny Magazine,* February 1863 – quoted in Woodberry's *Life* (1909), II, 214.

16. At this point in the sequence of Poe's tales the reader feels that no room described in such fond detail by the author would be complete without its hanging lamp. Unlike some of the others this one has nothing sinister or perhaps even significant about it. It is simply as if he had written Edgar A. Poe after one of his manuscripts.

THE MAN OF THE CROWD

Here is a powerful treatment of the mystery hidden in every human soul, which no other soul ever knows completely. Some part of what is hidden is evil, at least in tendency. It may be observed that the protagonist, who is never named, and is unknowable apart from the crowd, himself is neither rich nor poor; rather, he wears a costume suggesting both wealth and poverty. Is he not Everyman?*

Poe's story is in the manner of the early *Sketches by Boz* of Charles Dickens† — that is, of the more serious stories; and indeed is in particular a kind of answer to a passage in "The Drunkard's Death." This reads:

> Strange tales have been told in the wanderings of dying men; tales so full of guilt and crime, that those who stood by the sick person's couch have fled in horror and affright, lest they should be scared to madness by what they heard and saw; and many a wretch has died alone, raving of deeds the very name of which has driven the boldest man away.

But Dickens saw and described real places and people in London, and moralized about the evils of social inequality and injustice. Poe adopted the setting and envisioned the people, and considers the lonely spirit of evil. Dickens relates just what his drunkard did before drowning himself. Poe's wicked man's deeds are unknown; he does not die, but lives on in the midst of the crowd, of which he is a type, but not truly part. Poe contends that "much of sorrow and more of sin" will never be told.

Poe's story is dated in the first publication "November 1840." This is probably reliable. The circumstances of the first printing need explanation. Poe's connection with *Burton's Gentleman's Magazine* ended with the issue for June 1840. In November of that

---

* I am indebted to my student Anna Milani for this idea. In "Marginalia," number 194 (*Graham's*, January 1848, p. 24), Poe suggests that someone might "revolutionize . . . human thought . . . opinion, and . . . sentiment" by publishing "a very little book . . . 'My Heart Laid Bare'." But, he adds, "this little book must be *true to its title* . . . No man ever will dare write it . . . The paper would shrivel and blaze at every touch of the fiery pen."

† He reviewed *Watkins Tottle, and Other Sketches . . . By Boz* in the *Southern Literary Messenger* for June 1836.

year, George R. Graham, proprietor of *The Casket,* bought the *Gentleman's* from Burton, and under Graham's editorship Poe's story appeared in both *The Casket* and the *Gentleman's* for December. Both issues carried the new heading "Graham's Magazine" on the first page of text, but each retained its individual title page and serial number, and the *Gentleman's* had eight additional pages concluding a continued story begun some months before. Otherwise, the two issues were identical. Each, however, served to complete a volume. With the issue for January 1841, Graham began publishing *Graham's Lady's and Gentleman's Magazine (The Casket and Gentleman's United),* numbered in sequence with the old *Casket,* and within a few months he added Poe to his staff.

TEXTS

(A) The Casket for December 1840 (17:267–270) and [Burton's] *Gentleman's Magazine* for December 1840 (7:267–270), both captioned on first page of text "Graham's Magazine"; *(B) Tales* (1845), pp. 219–228; *(C)* J. Lorimer Graham copy of the last with one manuscript correction; *(D) Works* (1850), II, 398–407; PHANTASY-PIECES, title only.

Text *(C)* is followed. The Lorimer Graham correction is merely insertion of a period at the end of the final footnote — something done independently by Griswold or his printer in *Works (D)*. The spelling *decrepid* was a recognized variant. There were five printer's end-of-line dashes in the first printing (*A*); two were eliminated for *Tales,* but three were allowed to remain. In *B* and *C* and in our text they fall within the line.

THE MAN OF THE CROWD. [C]

Ce grand malheur, de ne pouvoir être seul.

La Bruyère.

It was well said of a certain German book that *"er lasst sich nicht lesen"* — it does not permit itself to be read.[1] There are some secrets which do not permit themselves to be told. Men die nightly in their beds, wringing the hands of ghostly confessors, and looking them piteously in the eyes — die with despair of heart and convulsion of throat, on account of the hideousness of mysteries which

---

Title: *In the Table of Contents this is*   (*B, C*)
listed as The Man in the Crowd.   Motto: *French unaccented (A)*

will not *suffer themselves* to be revealed. Now and then, alas, the conscience of man takes up a burthen so heavy in horror that it can be thrown down only into the grave. And thus the essence of all crime is undivulged.

Not long ago, about the closing in of an evening in autumn, I sat at the large bow window of the D —— Coffee-House in London.[2] For some months I had been ill in health, but was now convalescent, and, with returning strength, found myself in one of those happy moods which are so precisely the converse of *ennui* — moods of the keenest appetency, when the film from the mental vision departs — the αχλυς ος πριν επηεν —[3] and the intellect, electrified, surpasses as greatly its every-day condition, as does the vivid yet candid reason of Leibnitz,[a] the mad and flimsy rhetoric of Gorgias.[4] Merely to breathe was enjoyment; and I derived positive pleasure even from many of the legitimate sources of pain. I felt a calm but inquisitive interest in every thing. With a cigar in my mouth and a newspaper in my lap, I had been amusing myself for the greater part of the afternoon, now in poring over advertisements, now in observing the promiscuous company in the room, and now in peering through the smoky panes into the street.

This latter is one of the principal thoroughfares of the city, and had been very much crowded during the whole day. But, as the darkness came on, the throng momently increased; and, by the time the lamps were well lighted,[b] two dense and continuous tides of population were rushing past the door. At this particular period of the evening I had never before been in a similar situation, and the tumultuous sea of human heads filled me, therefore, with a delicious novelty of emotion. I gave up, at length, all care of things within the hotel, and became asborbed in contemplation of the scene without.

At first my observations took an abstract and generalizing turn. I looked at the passengers in masses, and thought of them in their aggregate relations. Soon, however, I descended to details, and regarded with minute interest the innumerable varieties of figure, dress, air, gait, visage, and expression of countenance.

---

a   Combe, *(A)*   b   litten *(A)*

INTERLUDE: 1840

By far the greater number of those who went by had a satisfied business-like demeanor, and seemed to be thinking only of making their way through the press. Their brows were knit, and their eyes rolled quickly; when pushed against by fellow-wayfarers they evinced no symptom of impatience, but adjusted their clothes and hurried on. Others, still a numerous class, were restless in their movements, had flushed faces, and talked and gesticulated to themselves, as if feeling in solitude on account of the very denseness of the company around. When impeded in their progress, these people suddenly ceased muttering, but redoubled their gesticulations, and awaited, with an absent and overdone smile upon the lips, the course of the persons impeding them. If jostled, they bowed profusely to the jostlers, and appeared overwhelmed with confusion. — There was nothing very distinctive about these two large classes beyond what I have noted. Their habiliments belonged to that order which is pointedly termed the decent. They were undoubtedly noblemen, merchants, attorneys, tradesmen, stock-jobbers — the Eupatrids[5] and the common-places of society — men of leisure and men actively engaged in affairs of their own — conducting business upon their own responsibility. They did not greatly excite my attention.

The tribe of clerks was an obvious one and here I discerned two remarkable divisions. There were the junior clerks of flash houses — young gentlemen with tight coats, bright boots, well-oiled hair, and supercilious lips. Setting aside a certain dapperness of carriage, which may be termed *deskism*[c] for want of a better word, the manner of these persons seemed to me an exact fac-simile of what had been the perfection of *bon ton* about twelve or eighteen months before. They wore the cast-off graces of the gentry; — and this, I believe, involves the best definition of the class.

The division of the upper clerks of staunch firms, or of the "steady old fellows," it was not possible to mistake. These were known by their coats and pantaloons of black or brown, made to sit comfortably, with white cravats and waistcoats, broad solid-looking shoes, and thick hose or gaiters. — They had all slightly bald heads, from which the right ears, long used to pen-holding, had an

---

c   deskism *(A)*

odd habit of standing off on end. I observed that they always removed or settled their hats with both hands, and wore watches, with short gold chains of a substantial and ancient pattern. Theirs was the affectation of respectability; — if indeed there be an affectation so honorable.

There were many individuals of dashing appearance, whom I easily understood[d] as belonging to the race of swell pick-pockets, with which all great cities are infested. I watched these gentry with much inquisitiveness, and found it difficult to imagine how they should ever be mistaken for gentlemen by gentlemen themselves. Their voluminousness of wristband, with an air of excessive frankness, should betray them at once.

The gamblers, of whom I descried not a few, were still more easily recognisable. They wore every variety of dress, from that of the desperate thimble-rig bully,[6] with velvet waistcoat, fancy neckerchief, gilt chains, and filagreed buttons, to that of the scrupulously inornate clergyman, than which nothing could be less liable to suspicion. Still all were distinguished by a certain sodden swarthiness of complexion, a filmy dimness of eye, and pallor and compression of lip. There were two other traits, moreover, by which I could always detect them; — a guarded lowness of tone in conversation, and a more than ordinary extension of the thumb in a direction at right angles with the fingers. — Very often, in company with these sharpers, I observed an order of men somewhat different in habits, but still birds of a kindred feather. They may be defined as the gentlemen who live by their wits. They seem to prey upon the public in two battalions — that of the dandies and that of the military men. Of the first grade the leading features are long locks and smiles; of the second frogged coats and frowns.

Descending in the scale of what is termed gentility, I found darker and deeper themes for speculation. I saw Jew pedlars, with hawk eyes flashing from countenances whose every other feature wore only an expression of abject humility; sturdy professional street beggars scowling upon mendicants of a better stamp, whom despair alone had driven forth into the night for charity; feeble and ghastly invalids, upon whom death had placed a sure hand, and

---

d   set down (A)

who sidled and tottered through the mob, looking every one beseechingly in the face, as if in search of some chance consolation, some lost hope; modest young girls returning from long and late labor to a cheerless home, and shrinking more tearfully than indignantly from the glances of ruffians, whose direct contact, even, could not be avoided; women of the town of all kinds and of all ages — the unequivocal beauty in the prime of her womanhood, putting one in mind of the statue in^e Lucian,[7] with the surface of Parian marble, and the interior filled with filth — the loathsome and utterly lost leper in rags — the wrinkled, bejewelled and paint-begrimed beldame, making a last effort at youth — the mere child of immature form, yet, from long association, an adept in the dreadful coquetries of her trade, and burning with a rabid ambition to be ranked the equal of her elders in vice;[8] drunkards innumerable and indescribable — some in shreds and patches, reeling, inarticulate, with bruised visage and lack-lustre eyes — some in whole although filthy garments, with a slightly unsteady swagger, thick sensual lips, and hearty-looking rubicund faces — others clothed in materials which had once been good, and which even now were scrupulously well brushed — men who walked with a more than naturally firm and springy step, but whose countenances were fearfully pale, whose eyes hideously wild and red, and who clutched with quivering fingers, as they strode through the crowd, at every object which came within their reach; beside these, pie-men, porters, coal-heavers, sweeps; organ-grinders, monkey-exhibiters and ballad mongers, those who vended with those who sang; ragged artizans and exhausted laborers of every description, and^f all full of a noisy and inordinate vivacity which jarred discordantly upon the ear, and gave an aching sensation to the eye.

As the night deepened, so deepened to me the interest of the scene; for not only did the general character of the crowd materially alter (its gentler features retiring in the gradual withdrawal of the more orderly portion of the people, and its harsher ones coming out into bolder relief, as the late hour brought forth every species of infamy from its den,) but the rays of the gas-lamps, feeble at first in their struggle with the dying day, had now at

e of (A)   f and still (A)

length gained ascendancy, and threw over every thing a fitful and garish lustre. All was dark yet splendid — as that ebony to which has been likened the style of Tertullian.[9]

The wild effects of the light enchained me to an examination of individual faces; and although the rapidity with which the world of light[g] flitted before the window, prevented me from casting more than a glance upon each visage, still it seemed that, in my then peculiar mental state, I could frequently read, even in that brief interval of a glance, the history of long years.

With my brow to the glass, I was thus occupied in scrutinizing the mob, when suddenly there came into view a countenance (that of a decrepid old man, some sixty-five or seventy years of age,) — a countenance which at once arrested and absorbed my whole attention, on account of the absolute idiosyncracy of its expression. Any thing even remotely resembling that expression I had never seen before. I well remember that my first thought, upon beholding it, was that Retzsch,[h] had he viewed it, would have greatly preferred it to his own pictural incarnations of the fiend.[10] As I endeavored, during the brief minute of my original survey, to form some analysis of the meaning conveyed, there arose confusedly and paradoxically within my mind, the ideas of vast mental power, of caution, of penuriousness, of avarice, of coolness, of malice, of blood-thirstiness, of triumph, of merriment, of excessive terror, of intense — of supreme despair. I felt singularly aroused, startled, fascinated. "How wild a history," I said to myself, "is written within that bosom!"[11] Then came a craving desire to keep the man in view — to know more of him. Hurriedly putting on an overcoat, and seizing my hat and cane, I made my way into the street, and pushed through the crowd in the direction which I had seen him take; for he had already disappeared. With some little difficulty I at length came within sight of him, approached, and followed him closely, yet cautiously, so as not to attract his attention.

I had now a good opportunity of examining his person. He was short in stature, very thin, and apparently very feeble. His clothes, generally, were filthy and ragged; but as he came, now

---

g   life *(A)*   *corrected editorially*
h   Retzch, *(A, B, C, D) misprint,*

and then, within the strong glare of a lamp, I perceived that his linen, although dirty, was of beautiful texture; and my vision deceived me, or, through a rent in a closely-buttoned and evidently second-handed *roquelaire*[i] which enveloped him,[12] I caught a glimpse [j]both of a diamond and of a dagger.[j] These observations heightened my curiosity, and I resolved to follow the stranger whithersoever he should go.[13]

It was now fully night-fall, and a thick humid fog hung over the city, [k]soon ending[k] in a settled and heavy rain. This change of weather had an odd effect upon the crowd, the whole of which was at once put into new commotion, and overshadowed by a world of umbrellas. The waver, the jostle, and the hum increased in a tenfold degree. For my own part I did not much regard the rain — the lurking of an old fever in my system rendering the moisture somewhat too dangerously pleasant. Tying a handkerchief about my mouth, I kept on. For half an hour the old man held his way with difficulty along the great thoroughfare; and I here walked close at his elbow through fear of losing sight of him. Never once turning his head to look back, he did not observe me. By and bye he passed into a cross street, which, although densely filled with people, was not quite so much thronged as the main one he had quitted. Here a change in his demeanor became evident. He walked more slowly and with less object than before — more hesitatingly. He crossed and re-crossed the way[l] repeatedly without apparent aim; and the press was still so thick that, at every such movement, I was obliged to follow him closely. The street was a narrow and long one, and his course lay within it for nearly an hour, during 'which the passengers had gradually diminished to about that number which is ordinarily seen at noon in Broadway near the Park — [14] so vast a difference is there between a London populace and that of the most frequented American city. A second turn brought us into a square, brilliantly lighted,[m] and overflowing with life. The old manner of the stranger re-appeared. His chin fell upon his breast, while his eyes rolled wildly from under his knit brows, in every direction, upon those who hemmed him in.

---

i   roquelaire *(A)*
j . . . j   either of a diamond, or of a dagger. *(A)*

k . . . k   threatening to end *(A)*
l   street way *(A)*
m   litten, *(A)*

He urged his way steadily and perseveringly. I was surprised, however, to find, upon his having made the circuit of the square, that he turned and retraced his steps. Still more was I astonished to see him repeat the same walk several times — once nearly detecting me as he came round with a sudden movement.[15]

In this exercise he spent another[n] hour, at the end of which we met with far less interruption from passengers than at first. The rain fell fast; the air grew cool; and the people were retiring to their homes. With a gesture of[o] impatience, the wanderer passed into a bye-street comparatively deserted. Down this, some quarter of a mile long, he rushed with an activity I could not have dreamed of seeing in one so aged, and which put me to much trouble in pursuit. A few minutes brought us to a large and busy bazaar, with the localities of which the stranger appeared well acquainted, and where his original demeanor again became apparent, as he forced his way to and fro, without aim, among the host of buyers and sellers.

During the hour and a half, or thereabouts, which we passed in this place, it required much caution on my part to keep him within reach without attracting his observation. Luckily I wore a pair of caoutchouc[p] over-shoes, and could move about in perfect silence. At no moment did he see that I watched him. He entered shop after shop, priced nothing, spoke no word, and looked at all objects with a wild and vacant stare. I was now utterly amazed at his behaviour, and firmly resolved that we should not part until I had satisfied myself in some measure respecting him.

A loud-toned clock struck eleven, and the company were fast deserting the bazaar. A shop-keeper, in putting up a shutter, jostled the old man, and at the instant I saw a strong shudder come over his frame. He hurried into the street, looked anxiously around him for an instant, and then ran with incredible swiftness through many crooked and people-less lanes, until we emerged once more upon the great thoroughfare whence we had started — the street of the D —— Hotel. It no longer wore, however, the same aspect. It was still brilliant with gas; but the rain fell fiercely,

---

n   about an *(A)*   p   gum *(A)*
o   of what seemed to be petulant *(A)*

and there were few persons to be seen. The stranger grew pale.[q] He walked moodily some paces up the once populous avenue, then, with a heavy sigh, turned in the direction of the river, and, plunging through a great variety of devious ways, came out, at length, in view of one of the principal theatres. It was about being closed, and the audience were thronging from the doors. I saw the old man gasp as if for breath while he threw himself amid the crowd; but I thought that the intense agony of his countenance had, in some measure, abated. His head again fell upon his breast; he appeared as I had seen him at first. I observed that he now took the course in which had gone the greater number of the audience — but, upon the whole, I was at a loss to comprehend the waywardness of his actions.

As he proceeded, the company grew more scattered, and his old uneasiness and vacillation were resumed. For some time he followed closely a party of some ten or twelve roisterers; but from this number one by one dropped off, until three only remained together, in a narrow and gloomy lane little frequented. The stranger paused, and, for a moment, seemed lost in thought; then, with every mark of agitation, pursued rapidly a route which brought us to the verge of the city, amid regions very different from those we had hitherto traversed. It was the most noisome quarter of London, where every thing wore the worst impress of the most deplorable poverty, and of the most desperate crime. By the dim light of an accidental lamp, tall, antique, worm-eaten, wooden tenements were seen tottering to their fall,[16] in directions so many and capricious that scarce the semblance of a passage was discernible between them. The paving-stones lay at random, displaced from their beds by the rankly-growing grass. Horrible filth festered in the dammed-up gutters. The whole atmosphere teemed with desolation. Yet, as we proceeded, the sounds of human life revived by sure degrees, and at length large bands of the most abandoned of a London populace were seen reeling to and fro. The spirits of the old man again flickered up, as a lamp which is near its death-hour. Once more he strode onward with elastic tread. Suddenly a corner was turned, a blaze of light burst upon our sight, and we

---

q   deadly pale. (A)

stood before one of the huge suburban temples of Intemperance — one of the palaces of the fiend, Gin.[17]

It was now nearly day-break; but a number of wretched inebriates still pressed in and out of the flaunting entrance. With a half shriek of joy the old man forced a passage within, resumed at once his original bearing, and stalked backward and forward, without apparent object, among the throng. He had not been thus long occupied, however, before a rush to the doors gave token that the host was closing them for the night. It was something even more intense than despair that I then observed upon the countenance of the singular being whom I had watched so pertinaciously. Yet he did not hesitate in his career, but, with a mad energy, retraced his steps at once, to the heart of the mighty London. Long and swiftly he fled, while I followed him in the wildest amazement, resolute not to abandon a scrutiny in which I now felt an interest all-absorbing. The sun arose while we proceeded, and, when we had once again reached that most thronged mart of the populous town, the street of the D ——— Hotel, it presented an appearance of human bustle and activity scarcely inferior to what I had seen on the evening before. And here, long, amid the momently increasing confusion, did I persist in my pursuit of the stranger. But, as usual, he walked to and fro, and during the day did not pass from out the turmoil of that street. And, as the shades of the second evening came on, I grew wearied unto death, and, stopping fully in front of the wanderer, gazed at him steadfastly in the face.[18] He noticed me not, but resumed his solemn walk, while I, ceasing to follow, remained absorbed in contemplation. "This old man," I said at length, "is the type and the genius of deep crime. He refuses to be alone. *He is the man of the crowd.* It will be in vain to follow; for I shall learn no more of him, nor of his deeds. The worst heart of the world is a grosser book than the 'Hortulus Animæ,'* [r] and perhaps it is but one of the great mercies of God that *'er lasst sich nicht lesen.'* " [19]

* The *"Hortulus Animæ cum Oratiunculis Aliquibus Superadditis"* of Grünninger.

[r] *Footnote added first in B. The Lorimer Graham (C) correction is merely the addition of a period at the* *end of the footnote. A is dated at the end* November, 1840.

INTERLUDE: 1840

NOTES

Motto: "That great evil, to be unable to be alone," is from La Bruyère's *Les Caractères,* section 99, "De l'homme." It is also quoted in "Metzengerstein."

1. This quotation recurs at the end of the tale, and is discussed in note 19.

2. Poe's descriptions frequently echo Dickens' language. The most striking parallels are quoted in the notes below; others, less important, might be found. Hervey Allen in *Israfel* (1926), II, 515, thought Poe's story "reveals impressions of the visit to London with the Allans," but while a schoolboy of twelve, of a refined American family, might observe large crowds in London streets by day, he would know nothing of gin-shops at first hand.

3. The Greek phrase means "the mist that previously was upon [them]." It is adapted from the *Iliad,* V, 127, where Athene removes the haze from the eyes of Diomedes, to permit him to distinguish the gods in battle. Poe used the same words in his "American Novel-Writing" (not collected by Harrison) in the *Pittsburgh Literary Examiner and Western Monthly Review* for August 1839.

4. In a review of Mrs. Sigourney's *Letters to Young Ladies* (*Southern Literary Messenger,* July 1836), Poe accuses Leibnitz of "a multiplicity of errors" on the subject of the faculty of Memory, but in another review quotes him approvingly. However, the philosopher named at this point in the earlier versions of this tale is George Combe (1788–1858), now chiefly remembered as a phrenologist. He was also a moral philosopher, advocating the study of the natural world as a guide to human conduct. He visited America in 1838. Poe referred to him favorably in a review of Amos Dean's *Philosophy of Human Life* in *Burton's,* February 1840, and as "George Combe – than whom a more candid reasoner never, perhaps, wrote or spoke," in a review of Macaulay's *Critical and Miscellaneous Essays* in *Graham's,* June 1841. Gorgias of Leontini, on the other hand, was a statesman and sophist of the time of Plato, who gave his name to a Socratic dialogue on rhetoric. His style was elaborate, to the point of absurdity. He is named also in "How to Write a Blackwood Article."

5. Eupatrids are persons belonging to the noblest families.

6. Thimble rig is the shell game.

7. The passage referred to in Lucian of Samosata is in the twenty-fourth section of his *Somnium* ("The Dream," also called "The Cock") and is used by Poe in a review of Lord Brougham's *Historical Sketches of Statesmen Who Flourished in the Time of George III* in *Burton's,* September 1839, and in "Fifty Suggestions," number 21.

8. One source of the description of the prostitutes is in "The Pawnbroker's Shop" in *Sketches by Boz:*

> In the next box is a young female, whose attire, miserably poor, but extremely gaudy, wretchedly cold, but scrupulously fine, but too plainly bespeaks her station in life. The rich satin gown with its faded trimmings – the worn-out thin shoes, and pink silk stockings – the summer bonnet in winter, and the sunken face where a daub of rouge only serves as an index to the ravages of squandered health ... and where the practised smile is a wretched mockery of the misery of the heart – cannot be mistaken.

9. Jean-Louis Guez de Balzac (1594–1655) said this of the style of Tertullian (A.D. 160–230), according to *Menagiana* (second edition, Paris, 1694), p. 86. Poe probably used it at second hand.

10. Friedrich August Moritz Retzsch (1779–1857) was a German painter and engraver, noted especially for his illustrations of Goethe's *Faust*. In his long review of Henry F. Chorley's *Memorials of Mrs. Hemans* (*SLM*, October 1836), Poe notes that "Retzsch and Flaxman were Mrs. H's favorites among modern artists. "

11. Compare "To Helen Whitman," line 42: "What wild heart-histories seem to lie enwritten."

12. A roquelaire (usually spelled *roquelaure*) is a knee-length cloak, mentioned also in "The Cask of Amontillado."

13. This is an echo of St. Luke 9:57, "I will follow thee whithersoever thou goest."

14. City Hall Park in Poe's day was the center of life in New York City.

15. The source of much of the description of the old man and his behavior is in Dickens' "Thoughts about People," which describes at St. James's Park a man who "walked up and down before the little patch of grass on which the chairs are placed for hire, not as if he were doing it for pleasure or recreation, but as if it were a matter of compulsion."

16. Compare Gray's "Impromptu," line 14: "Turrets and arches nodding to their fall." There is a similar description of dilapidated streets and houses in Poe's "King Pest."

17. This paragraph and the next owe much to Dickens' sketch of "Gin-Shops" which Poe admired enough to reprint in full in his review of *Watkins Tottle* (*SLM*, June 1836). Pertinent parts are:
The filthy and miserable appearance of this part of London can hardly be imagined by those ... who have not witnessed it. Wretched houses, with broken windows patched with rags and paper, every room let out to a different family, and in many instances to two, or even three ... filth every where — a gutter before the houses and a drain behind them — clothes drying at the windows, slops emptying from the ditto; girls of fourteen or fifteen, with matted hair, walking about bare-footed, and in old white great coats, almost their only covering; boys of all ages, in coats of all sizes, and no coats at all; men and women, in every variety of scanty and dirty apparel, lounging about, scolding, drinking, smoking, squabbling, fighting, and swearing.
You turn the corner. What a change! All is light and brilliancy. The hum of many voices issues from that splendid gin-shop. . . .
It is growing late, and the throng of men, women, and children who have been constantly going in and out, dwindles down to two or three occasional stragglers — cold wretched-looking creatures, in the last stage of emaciation and disease. The knot of Irish laborers ... become furious in their disputes; . . . Some of the party are borne off to the station-house, and the remainder slink home to beat their wives for complaining, and kick the children for daring to be hungry.

18. Compare "Silence — a Fable": "And the lynx ... lay down at the feet of the Demon, and looked at him steadily in the face."

19. The German quotation appears also (applied to a book by "Mr. Mathews") in the forty-sixth of Poe's "Fifty Suggestions." The Latin work here mentioned is certainly the *Ortulus anime cum oratiunculis* printed at Strassburg by Johann Reinhard Grüninger, January 31, 1500 (no. 8937 in Hain's *Repertorium Bibliographicum,* Stuttgart, 1826–38), of which there is a copy in the British Museum. Poe's spelling of the title and the printer's name are retained here as given in all his texts. They are those of his probable source, Isaac D'Israeli's "Religious Nouvellettes" in *Curiosities of Literature.* D'Israeli there describes the book as having indecorous illustrations. Poe presumably had some other source for his German sentence, which has not yet been found. I have not emended *er* because, although *Buch* is neuter (calling for *es*), the word *hortulus* is masculine. At the beginning of his story Poe translated the German literally, "It does not permit itself to be read." Here he took this to mean that the book was too shocking for a reader to peruse it completely; but the meaning of his source may have been that the book referred to was execrably printed, or that no copy was available. It will be recalled that in 1837 Poe boarded with the learned bookseller William Gowans, who took an interest in incunabula, of which Grüninger's "small octavo in Gothic type" is an example.

TALES: 1841-1842

THE MURDERS IN THE RUE MORGUE

This story is a great literary monument. It may not be the first detective story, but it is the first story deliberately written as such to attain worldwide popularity. It is the ancestor of a vast number of works which have given much harmless pleasure to all sorts and conditions of men.* The piece has a fault, shared by too many later detective stories, of one too gory passage, something avoided in the far finer tale, "The Purloined Letter," which Poe himself valued more highly.

In a letter to his friend Philip Pendleton Cooke, August 9, 1846, Poe humorously commented on being given undue credit for unraveling mysteries he invented for the purpose, and so not mysterious to him at all:

> You are right about the hair-splitting of my French friend [Dupin] : — that is all done for effect. These tales of ratiocination owe most of their popularity to being something in a new key. I do not mean to say they are not ingenious — but people think they are more ingenious than they are — on account of their method and *air* of method . . . Where is the ingenuity of unravelling a web which you yourself (the author) have woven for the express purpose of unravelling? The reader is made to confound the ingenuity of the supposititious Dupin with that of the writer of the story.

On this subject it would be hard to say anything better, but the ingenuity Poe so modestly mentions deserves a good deal of admiration. Poe's source for his detective is the philosophic protagonist of Voltaire's *Zadig* — a story in which the hero describes a dog he has never seen and later explains:

---

* G. K. Chesterton has remarked that normal people have "a healthy interest in murder," but Poe himself, writing to P. P. Cooke, ascribed the popularity of his detective stories to the novelty of his method. E. D. Forgues mentioned it in his review of Poe's *Tales* (New York and London, 1845) in the *Revue des Deux Mondes,* October 1846, and the Goncourt brothers, under date of July 16, 1856, "after having read Poe," recorded in their famous journal their impression that here was "a new literary world, signs of the literature of the twentieth century — love giving place to deductions . . . the interest of the story moved from the heart to the head . . . from the drama to the solution." Brander Matthews cites this passage in "Poe and the Detective Story," *Scribner's,* September 1907.

I saw an animal's tracks on the sand, and I judged ... they were ... of a small dog. The long shallow furrows printed on the little ridges of sand between the tracks of the paws informed me that the animal was a bitch with pendent dugs, who hence had puppies recently. Other tracks ... which seemed ... to have scraped the surface of the sand beside the forepaws, gave me the idea that the bitch had very long ears: and [since] ... the sand was always less hollowed by one paw than by the three others, I concluded that our ... bitch was somewhat lame.

A similar incident follows about a horse.†

A possible factual source for Poe's story was pointed out in the London *Notes and Queries,* May 12, 1894, by W. F. Waller, who found in the *Annual Register for 1834* a short article, "New Mode of Thieving," telling of a robber monkey. This was synopsized from the Ipswich *Shrewsbury Chronicle,* August 22, 1834. Poe probably did not see the English provincial newspaper, but perhaps read some fuller account than that in the *Register.* The original article was copied out for me several years ago from the office file by the then editor, and reads:

An extraordinary burglary — attended by very singular circumstances, and perpetrated by a curious felon — occurred in this town on Monday night. Mr. Smith, with his lady, resides in the apartments of Mrs. Weaver in Mardol. After Mrs. S. retired to her bed-room, and before her husband had desisted from his supper enjoyments, some of the family was alarmed by a scream from her bed-room, and one of the inmates (a female) proceeding thither, was attacked on entering the door, by a Monkey (or a Ribbed-face Baboon) which threw her down, and placing his feet upon her breast, held her pinned firmly to the ground. The screams of Mrs. Smith brought up her husband, who, seeing the condition of the prostrate female, assailed the monkey, and compelled him to quit his hold on the female, and thereby drew all his vengeance upon himself. The brute took up his position on the wash-basin stand; and every attempt to dislodge him brought to the ground some fragile articles of furniture — glasses, basins, and jugs — till, on Mr. Smith attempting to go into another room for his pistols, the monkey leaped on his back with the speed of lightning, made various efforts to reach his throat, broke his watch guard assunder in rage, and, dropping to the

† See *Zadig* (1748), chapter 3; this source — the tale was first published anonymously in 1747 under another title — was pointed out by Forgues in his review cited above; Brander Matthews retells both stories in his article in *Scribner's.* Poe mentioned *Zadig* in "Hop-Frog." Voltaire's source — it was asserted by his confirmed enemy, Elie Fréron, in *L'Année littéraire,* 1767 (1:145), an attribution often repeated — was in the adventures of the Three Princes of Serendip, as translated into French from the Persian by the Chevalier de Mailly in 1719. The princes describe an unseen camel from circumstantial clues.

ground, bit his leg, and again fled to the basin-stand. Mr. Smith pursued him and flung him off many times in his leaping attacks. After skirmishing a considerable time, the worried animal dashed through the window, carrying the frame and glass along with him. Mr. Smith grasped at its hind legs, when the brute bit him through the thumb. A gold watch was taken off the table; but whether by the animal, or by some of the persons who were called into the room by the strange contest, has not yet been proved. One man has been committed for cross examination. When the watchman arrived, the room where this skirmishing took place was strewed with fractured chairs, tables, glasses etc. But where did this Baboon come from? The animal had been danced through this town two or three days by itinerant showmen; and had either escaped from them or been let loose for the sake of his plundering. Some persons suspect this animal was trained ... to pursue such adventures. It appears he had dropped from the eaves of the house to the window-sill of Mrs. Smith's chamber, and got into the room through the window, which was left partly open. The owner recovered the animal from the housetops next morning, and escaped to Ludlow.

There is also a story, still sometimes told by stage comedians, about a barber's pet monkey who, in the absence of his master from the shop, essayed to shave a customer with disastrous results. The victim later reproaches the barber, saying, "I'll never let your father [or grandfather] shave me again." In an old printed version before me the monkey after the fiasco ran up the chimney for safety, coming down only when his victim left the shop.‡

There is also a well-known story of a pet monkey, who, imitating his master shaving himself, cut his own throat. Professor Charles Duffy of the University of Akron, Ohio, called my attention to a poem on this, "The Monkey" by David Humphreys (1752–1818), one of the Hartford Wits, to be seen in Duyckinck's *Cyclopaedia of American Literature*, I, 378.

Still another among numerous possible sources is one pointed out by John Robert Moore in *American Literature,* March 1936, an incident in Sir Walter Scott's *Count Robert of Paris* (1831), chapter xxv, where the villainous philosopher Agelastes is strangled by Sylvan, an orangutan (who makes strange hoarse unintelligible sounds), whom he had once hit with a staff. This "crime" remained

‡ The version referred to is a quarto broadside called *A Wonderful Monkey of Liverpool, Who turn'd Barber To Shave the Irish Gentleman* ... "Printed at Pitts, Toy Warehouse, 6, Great st Andrew street, seven Dials" [London], which I bought from Dobell's Catalogue 216:344. Since the long "s" is used, it is hardly later than 1830. I have heard the story told variously on the stage in recent years in New York and Atlantic City.

unsolved, for Sylvan escaped and returned to his owners.

In *Notes and Queries* (London) for September 1966 Patrick Diskin demonstrates that Poe might have received suggestions from two stories by J. S. LeFanu in the *Dublin University Magazine* for March and November 1838 and a story by J. C. Mangan in the same journal for October and December 1838.

Finally, mention must be made of a "factual" source in a "real" Parisian murder, which I regard as an absurd hoax and, like Killis Campbell, relegate to a footnote.§

Orangs were popular in America, having been occasionally exhibited as early as 1831. I have seen reference to one named Mlle. Fanny — were French names often given to performing apes? Poe alludes to orangs in other stories — "Hop-Frog" and "The System of Doctor Tarr and Professor Fether."

The source of the name of Poe's detective has occasioned considerable discussion. The form of the given names, "C. Auguste" (for César Auguste), is decidedly unusual, and was obviously taken from that of Monsieur C. Auguste Dubouchet, a friend who was seeking a position as a teacher of French. A letter to Poe, September 30, 1840, from Dr. Socrates Maupin, a prominent physician of Richmond, gives the applicant's name.* Dupin, however, is a com-

§ Killis Campbell, in a footnote in his *Mind of Poe*, p. 165, mentions an anonymous article in the *Washington Post*, October 3, 1912. This article, "Facts Behind Poe's Story," credited as "From a Foreign Exchange," relates how a courtesan, Rose Delacourt, was found in her Montmartre apartment, stabbed through the heart with a sword, which pierced the mattress of her bed three or four inches. Suicide was out of the question. Yet the door was locked and bolted inside; the single window likewise was locked, inside, and there was a sheer drop of sixty feet from it to the pavement. One theory was that a monkey had climbed down the chimney, but the flue was too small "to have admitted an ape big enough to have done the deed" and "there were no soot marks in the room." Other theories of removal and replacement of a windowpane, door panel, or a plank in the floor, or use of magnets on the lock were found untenable. No date of the demise of Mlle. Delacourt is given, and I think the nameless "foreign" author of these absurd "facts" found *his* source in Poe's story.

* This was pointed out by W. T. Bandy in *PMLA*, September 1964. He prints Maupin's letter; and refers to discussions by Campbell (*Mind of Poe*, p. 173), who remarked that Dupin was the family name of George Sand, and by Quinn (*Poe*, p. 310), who found that Marie Dupin was the heroine of "Marie Laurente," a story in *Burton's*, September 1838, concerning the French detective Vidocq (see note 28 below). Poe mentions the historian Du Pin (Louis-Ellies Dupin) in a footnote to "Al Aaraaf," I, 105. Bandy himself suggests a combination of *Du*bouchet and Mau*pin*, an ingenious but unconvincing fancy.

mon name in France, although not of Frenchmen in America. The person Poe had in mind was almost surely André-Marie-Jean-Jacques Dupin (1783–1865), a French politician described as a person of antithetical qualities, a living encyclopedia, and a lover of legal methods, in *Sketches of Living Characters of France,* translated by R. M. Walsh (1841), a book reviewed by Poe in the issue of *Graham's* in which his story appeared.†

Poe wrote his story hastily. The manuscript shows more changes than do most of his surviving manuscripts, which appear to be copies carefully made for the printer rather than working drafts.‡ The name of the street, Rue Morgue, was a brilliant afterthought. The first references in the text give it as the sole reading, but it appears as a change from Rue Trianon in later portions. This bears out the statement of Dr. Thomas Dunn English that "The incidents . . . are purely imaginary. Like all the rest [of the tales], it is written backwards."§

The first printing was done by Barrett and Thrasher, 33 Carter's Alley, and the revised proof read in the office of the *Saturday Evening Post,* Chestnut Street above Third, Philadelphia. An apprentice, J. M. Johnston, who heard it, was so delighted that he "picked it [the manuscript] from the waste-basket, asked and obtained leave to keep it."* Poe's story was received enthusiastically when published on March 15, 1841.

A few years later the story served to awaken French interest in Poe. It was not the first of his tales to be noticed in France — that was "William Wilson" — but "The Murders" fell into the hands of two Parisian journalists who printed different adapations, each

---

† Howard Haycraft, in *Murder for Pleasure* (1941), p. 23, picked the same Dupin, without reference to Poe's review. For another probable use of Walsh's translation see the note on the motto of "The Fall of the House of Usher," p. 417 above.

‡ "The Purloined Letter" is another story that seems to have been completed too near the publisher's deadline to permit copying. See the introduction to that story in this edition.

§ From his review of "Poe's Tales" in the *Aristidean* for October 1845, written after discussion with the author.

* Johnston's account, written July 26, 1881, is printed by Harrison in *Complete Works* (1902), IV, 295f. This manuscript was acquired by George W. Childs, who gave it to the Drexel Institute. It is now in the Richard Gimbel Collection of the Free Library of Philadelphia.

as if original with himself. The first was "Un Meurtre sans exemple dans les fastes de la justice," signed G. B. (Gustave Brunet) in *La Quotidienne*, June 11, 12, 13, 1846. The second was "Une sanglante énigme" signed O. N. (for Old Nick, pen name of E. D. Forgues) in *Le Commerce*, October 12, 1846. In *La Presse* of October 14, 1846, there appeared an article pointing out the parallels as if they were plagiarisms. Forgues (whose review of Poe's *Tales* appeared at almost the same time) revealed *his* source as the American Poe in the next day's issues of *Le Commerce* and *Le National*. A lawsuit brought by Forgues against M. de Girardin, editor of *La Presse,* was dismissed by a court on December 9, and this gave further publicity to Edgar Poe.†

An abridged translation by Isabelle Meunier, acknowledging the American author of the tale, appeared in *La Démocratie pacifique,* January 31, 1847, as "L'Assassinat de la rue Morgue."

Poe himself, in "Marginalia," number 176 (*Graham's,* November 1846, p. 246), called attention to what he thought his story inspired: an incident in Eugène Sue's *Mysteries of Paris* (*Les Mystères de Paris,* 1842–43).

TEXTS

(A) Manuscript, March 1841; *(B) Graham's Magazine* for April 1841 (18:166–179); *(C) Prose Romances* (1843), pp. 9–40; *(D) Tales* (1845), pp. 116–150; *(E)* J. Lorimer Graham copy of the *Tales* with manuscript changes; *(F) Works* (1850), I, 178–212. PHANTASY-PIECES, title only.

The best text is that of the J. Lorimer Graham copy of the *Tales* (E), in which, however, Poe changed only two words. Griswold did not have it in time for use, and the 1850 text of the *Works (F)* was set up from a copy of the 1845 volume *(D)* with no changes. Later issues of *Works* (see under Sources) show three new errors in this tale, which are recorded in our variants. Also recorded in the variants and corrected in the text are six comma errors introduced in *Prose Romances (C),* and carried unfortunately into all later authorized texts.

The manuscript *(A),* now in the Free Library of Philadelphia, consists of seventeen numbered small folio leaves, with writing on only one side. Those

† An amusing account of the newspaper battle in *L'Entre'Acte,* October 20, 1846, was quoted by Griswold in his "Memoir," p. xxxv. I follow Louis Seylaz, *Poe et les premiers symbolistes français* (Lausanne, 1923), pp. 39–42. Seylaz consulted the original periodicals. Some earlier discussions are decidedly inaccurate. J. H. Wigmore's entertaining account in the *Cornell Law Quarterly,* February 1928, is acknowledged by the author to be inconclusive.

THE MURDERS IN THE RUE MORGUE

numbered 5 and 9 are each made up of pieces of paper fastened together. [Through the courtesy of Mr. Howell J. Heaney, Rare Book Librarian, the manuscript has been recently consulted. Scholars should be made aware of the fact that *The Murders in the Rue Morgue facsimile of the MS in the Drexel Institute,* copyright 1895, is reduced in size and has some distortions. This "facsimile" is useful for reference but should not be relied upon.]

In our list of recorded variant readings cancelations in the MS are enclosed in angle brackets, < >; additions are enclosed in arrows, ↑ ↓; and square brackets, [ ], enclose matter lost by mutilation and restored from other texts. The manuscript *(A)* was certainly used in setting up the *Graham's* text *(B)*. See Ernest Boll, "The Manuscript of 'The Murders in the Rue Morgue' and Poe's Revisions," *Modern Philology,* May 1943, for a history of the manuscript and a careful study of Poe's changes.

Translations

La Quotidienne, June 11, 12, 13, 1846, as "Un Meurtre sans exemple dans les fastes de la justice," signed G.B.; *Le Commerce,* October 12, 1846, as "Une sanglante énigme," signed O.N.; *La Démocratie pacifique,* January 31, 1847, as "L'Assassinat de la rue Morgue," by Isabelle Meunier.

THE MURDERS IN THE RUE MORGUE. [*E*]

What song the Syrens sang, or what name Achilles assumed when he hid himself among women, although puzzling questions, are not beyond *all* conjecture.

Sir Thomas Browne.

The[a] mental features discoursed of as the analytical[a'] are, in themselves, but little susceptible of analysis. We appreciate them

---

Title: The Murders in the Rue <Trianon-Bas> Morgue. *(A)*
Beneath the title, in the same script, is By Edgar A. Poe.
Motto: Omitted (A, B)
In early versions there is an opening paragraph:

It is not improbable that a few farther steps in phrenological science will lead to a belief in the existence, if not to the actual discovery and location of an organ of *analysis.* If this power (which may be described, although not defined, as the capacity for resolving thought into its elements) be not, in fact, an essential portion of what late philosophers term ideality, then there are indeed many good reasons for supposing it a primitive faculty. That it may be a constituent of ideality is here suggested in opposition to the vulgar dictum (founded ↑ however ↓ upon the assumptions of grave authority), <however)> that the calculating and discriminating powers (causality and comparison) are at variance with the imaginative — that the three, in short, can hardly coexist. But, although thus opposed to received opinion, the idea will not appear ill-founded when we observe that the processes of invention or creation are strictly akin with the processes of resolution — the former being nearly, if not absolutely, the latter conversed. *(A, B, C) In the third sentence* however *was transposed in the manuscript (A); in the second sentence* be not *became* is not *in Prose Romances (C).*
a It cannot be doubted that the *(A, B, C)*
a' analytical, *(C, D, E, F) corrected from A, B*

only in their effects. We know of them, among other things, that they are always to their possessor, when inordinately possessed, a source of the liveliest enjoyment. As the strong man exults in his physical ability, delighting in such exercises as call his muscles into action,[1] so glories the analyst in that moral activity which *disentangles*. He derives pleasure from even the most trivial occupations bringing his talent into play. He is fond of enigmas, of conundrums, of hieroglyphics; exhibiting in his solutions of each[b] a degree of *acumen*[c] which appears to the ordinary apprehension præternatural.[2] His results, brought about by the very soul and essence of method, have, in truth, the whole air of intuition.

The faculty of re-solution[d] is possibly much invigorated by mathematical study, and especially by that highest branch of it which, unjustly, and merely on account of its retrograde operations, has been called, as if *par excellence,* analysis. Yet to calculate is not in itself to analyse. A chess-player, for example, does the one without effort at the other. It follows that the game of chess, in its effects upon mental character, is greatly misunderstood. I am not now writing a treatise, but simply prefacing a somewhat peculiar narrative by observations very much at random; I will, therefore, take occasion to assert that the higher powers of the reflective intellect are more decidedly and more usefully tasked[e] by the unostentatious game of draughts than by all the elaborate frivolity of chess. In this latter, where the pieces have different and *bizarre*[f] motions, with various and variable values, what[g] is only complex is mistaken (a not unusual error) for what[h] is profound. The *attention* is here called powerfully into play. If it flag for an instant, an oversight is committed, resulting in injury or defeat. The possible moves being not only manifold but involute, the chances of such oversights are multiplied; and in nine cases out of ten it is the more concentrative rather than the more acute player who conquers. In draughts, on the contrary, where the moves are *unique*[i] and have but little variation, the probabilities of inadvertence are dimin-

---

b   each and all *(A, B)*
c   acumen *(A, B)*
d   of re-solution/in question *(A, B, C)*
e   taxed *(A, B)*

f   bizarre *(A, B)*
g   that which *(A, B, C)*
h   that which *(A, B, C)*
i   unique *(A, B)*

ished, and the mere attention being left comparatively unemployed, what advantages are obtained by either party are obtained by superior *acumen*.[j] To be less abstract — Let us suppose a game of draughts where the pieces are reduced to four kings, and where, of course, no oversight is to be expected. It is obvious that here the victory can be decided (the players being at all equal) only by some *recherché*[k] movement, the result of some strong exertion of the intellect. Deprived of ordinary resources, the analyst throws himself into the spirit of his opponent, identifies himself therewith, and not unfrequently sees thus, at a glance, the sole methods (sometimes indeed absurdly simple ones) by which he may seduce into [l]error or hurry into miscalculation.[l]

Whist has long been noted for its influence upon what is[m] termed the calculating power;[n] and men of the highest order of intellect have been known to take an apparently unaccountable delight in it, while eschewing chess as frivolous. Beyond doubt there is nothing of a similar nature so greatly tasking the faculty of analysis. The best chess-player in Christendom *may* be little more than the best player of chess; but proficiency in whist implies capacity for success in all those more important undertakings where mind struggles with mind. When I say proficiency, I mean that perfection in the game which includes a comprehension of *all*[o] the sources whence[p] legitimate advantage may be derived. These are not only manifold but multiform, and lie frequently among recesses of thought altogether inaccessible to the ordinary understanding. To observe attentively is to remember distinctly; and, so far, the concentrative chess-player will do very well at whist; while the rules of Hoyle (themselves based upon the mere mechanism of the game) are sufficiently and generally comprehensible.[3] Thus to have a retentive memory, and to proceed by "the book," are points commonly regarded as the sum total of good playing. But it is in matters beyond the limits of mere rule that[q]

---

j   acumen. *(A, B)*
k   recherché *(A, B)*
l...l   miscalculation or hurry into error. *(A, B, C)*
m   are *(A, B)*
n   powers; *(A, B)*

o   all *(A, B, C)*
p   (whatever be their character) from which *(A, B);* (whatever be their character) whence *(C)*
q   where *(A, B)*

the skill of the analyst is evinced. He makes, in silence, a host of observations and inferences. So, perhaps, do his companions; and the difference in the extent of the information obtained$^{q'}$ lies not so much in the validity^r of the inference as in the quality of the observation. The necessary knowledge is that of *what* to observe. Our player confines himself not at all; nor, because the game is the object, does he reject deductions^s from things external to the game. He examines the countenance of his partner, comparing it carefully with that of each of his opponents. He considers the mode of assorting the cards in each hand; often counting trump by trump, and honor by honor, through the glances bestowed by their holders upon each. He notes every variation of face as the play progresses, gathering a fund of thought from the differences in the expression of certainty, of surprise, of triumph, or of^t chagrin. From the manner of gathering up a trick he judges whether the person taking it^u can make another in the suit.^{v} He recognises what is^w played through feint, by the air with which it is thrown upon the table. A casual or inadvertent word; the accidental dropping or turning of a card,^{x} with the accompanying anxiety or carelessness in regard to its concealment; the counting of the tricks, with the order of their arrangement; embarrassment, hesitation, eagerness or trepidation — all afford, to his apparently intuitive perception, indications of the true state of affairs. The first two or three rounds having been played, he is in full possession of the contents of each hand, and thenceforward puts down his cards with as absolute a precision of purpose as if the rest of the party had turned outward^y the faces of their own.^{4}

The analytical power should not be confounded with simple ingenuity; for while the analyst is necessarily ingenious, the ingenious man is often remarkably^z incapable of analysis.^{a} The con-

---

q' obtained, *(C, D, E, F)*
corrected from A, B
r falsity *(A, B, C)*
s deductions <arising> *(A)*
t *Omitted in later issues of F*
u ↑ it ↓ *(A)*
v *After this:* <Embarrasment, hesitation, eagerness, or

trepidation.> *(A)*
w <a card> ↑ what is ↓ *(A)*
x <anything important,> ↑ a card, ↓ *(A)*
y outwards *(A)*
z utterly *(A, B)*
a *After this:* I have spoken of this latter faculty as that of resolving thought

structive or combining power, by which ingenuity is usually manifested, and to which the phrenologists (I believe erroneously) have assigned a separate organ, supposing it a primitive faculty, has been so frequently seen in those whose intellect bordered otherwise upon idiocy, as to have attracted general observation among writers on morals. Between ingenuity and the analytic ability there exists a difference far greater, indeed, than that between the fancy and the imagination, but of a character very strictly analogous. It will be found, in fact, that the ingenious are always fanciful, and the *truly*[b] imaginative never otherwise than[c] analytic.

The narrative which follows will appear to the[d] reader somewhat in the light of a commentary upon the propositions just advanced.

Residing in Paris during the spring[e] and part of the summer[f] of 18 — , I there [g]became acquainted[g] with a Monsieur C. Auguste Dupin. This young gentleman was of an excellent — indeed of an illustrious family, but, by a variety of untoward events, had been reduced to such poverty that the[h] energy of his character succumbed beneath[i] it, and he ceased to bestir himself in the world, or to care for the retrieval of his fortunes. By courtesy of his creditors, there still remained in his possession a small remnant of his patrimony; and, upon the income arising from this, he managed, by means of a rigorous[j] economy, to procure the necessaries[k] of life, without troubling himself about its superfluities. Books, indeed, were his sole luxuries, and in Paris these are easily obtained.

[l]Our first meeting was at an obscure library in the Rue Montmartre, where the accident of our both being in search of the same

---

into its elements, and it is only necessary to glance upon this idea to perceive the necessity of the distinction just mentioned. *(A, B, C)*

b   <highly> ↑ *truly* ↓ *(A)*
c   than profoundly *(A, B, C)*
d   the <reflective> *(A)*
e   <autumn> ↑ spring ↓ *(A)*
f   <winter> ↑ summer ↓ *(A)*

g . . . g   contracted an intimacy *(A, B, C)*
h   the quondam *(A, B);* the *quondam (C)*
i   <before> ↑ beneath ↓ *(A)*
j   vigorous *(B) misprint*
k   necessaries <, without> *(A)*
l   ¶ *inserted before this sentence (A)*

very rare and very remarkable volume[l'] brought us into closer communion. We saw each other again and again. I was deeply interested in the little family history which he detailed to me with all that[m] candor[n] which a Frenchman [o]indulges whenever mere[o] self is his[p] theme. I was astonished, too, at the vast extent of his reading; and, above all, I felt[q] my soul enkindled within me by the wild fervor, and[r] the vivid freshness of his imagination. Seeking in Paris the objects I then sought, I felt that the society of such a man would be to me a treasure beyond price; and this feeling I frankly confided to him. It was at length arranged that we should live together during my stay in the city; and as my worldly circumstances were somewhat less embarrassed than his own, I was permitted to be at the expense of renting, and furnishing in a style which suited the rather fantastic gloom of our common temper, a time-eaten and grotesque mansion, long deserted through superstitions into which we did not inquire, and tottering to its fall[5] in a retired and desolate portion of the Faubourg St. Germain.

Had the routine of our life at this place been known to the world, we should have been regarded as madmen — although, perhaps, as madmen of a harmless nature. Our seclusion was perfect. We admitted no visitors.[s] Indeed the locality of our retirement had been carefully kept a secret from my own former associates; and it had been many years since Dupin had ceased to know or be known in Paris. We existed within ourselves alone.

It was a freak of fancy in my friend (for what else shall I call it?) to be enamored of the Night for her own sake; and into this *bizarrerie,* as into all his others, I quietly fell; giving myself up to his wild whims with a perfect[t] *abandon.* The sable divinity would not herself dwell with us always; but we could counterfeit her presence.[6] At the first dawn of the morning we closed all the massy shutters of our old building,[t'] lighting[u] a couple of tapers which,

---

l' volume, *(C, D, E, F)*
corrected from A, B
m the *changed to* that *(A);* the *(B, C)*
n candor <of a Frenchman in> *(A)*
o . . . o <only> indulges ↑ only ↓ when *(A);* indulges only when *(B, C)*
p the *in later issues of F*

q felt <all> *(A)*
r and what I could only term *(A, B, C)*
s visitors whomsoever. *(A, B, C)*
t a perfect/an utter *(A, B)*
t' building; *(C, D, E, F)*
comma adopted from A, B
u lighted *(F)*

strongly perfumed, threw out only the ghastliest and feeblest of rays. By the aid of these we then busied our souls in dreams[7] — reading, writing, or conversing, until warned by the clock of the advent of the true Darkness. Then we sallied forth into the streets, arm in arm, continuing the topics of the day, or roaming far and wide until a late hour, seeking, amid the wild lights and shadows of the populous city, that infinity of mental excitement which quiet observation can[v] afford.

At such times I could not help remarking and admiring (although from his rich ideality I had been prepared to expect it[w]) a peculiar analytic ability in Dupin. He seemed, too, to take an eager delight in its exercise — if not exactly in its display — and did not hesitate[x] to confess the pleasure thus derived. He boasted to me, with a low chuckling laugh, that most men, in respect to himself, wore windows in their bosoms,[8] and was wont to follow up such assertions by direct and very startling proofs of his intimate knowledge of my own. His manner at these moments was frigid and abstract; his eyes were vacant in expression; while his voice, usually a rich tenor, rose into a treble which would have sounded petulantly but for the deliberateness and entire distinctness of the enunciation. Observing him in these moods, I often dwelt meditatively upon the old philosophy of the Bi-Part Soul,[9] and amused myself with the fancy of a double Dupin — the creative and the resolvent.

Let it not be supposed, from what I have just said, that I am detailing any mystery, or penning any romance. What I have described in the Frenchman[x'] was merely[y] the result of an excited, or perhaps of a diseased intelligence. But of the character of his remarks at the periods in question an example will best convey the idea.

We were strolling one night down a long dirty street, in the vicinity of the Palais Royal.[10] Being both, apparently, occupied with thought, neither of us had spoken a syllable for fifteen minutes at least. All at once Dupin broke forth with these words:

---

v   could *(A);* would *(B)*
w   it *omitted (A, B, C)*
x   hesitute *misprint in later issues of F*

x'   Frenchman, *(C, D, E, F)*
     corrected from A, B
y   but *(A, B, C)*

"He is a very little fellow, that's true, and would do better for the *Théâtre²* *des Variétés.*" [11]

"There can be no doubt of that," I replied unwittingly, and not at first observing (so much had I been absorbed in reflection) the extraordinary manner in which the speaker had chimed in with my meditations. In an instant afterward[a] I recollected myself, and my astonishment was profound.

"Dupin," said I, gravely, "this is beyond my comprehension. I do not hesitate to say that I am amazed, and can scarcely credit my senses. How was it possible you should know I was thinking of —— ?" Here I paused, to ascertain beyond a doubt whether he really knew of whom I thought.

—— "of Chantilly," said he, "why do you pause? You were remarking to yourself that his diminutive figure unfitted him for tragedy." [12]

This was precisely what had formed the subject of my reflections. Chantilly was a *quondam*[b] cobbler of the Rue St. Denis, [13] who, becoming stage-mad, had attempted the *rôle*[c] of Xerxes, in Crébillon's[d] tragedy so called, [14] and been notoriously Pasquinaded for his pains.

"Tell me, for Heaven's[e] sake," I exclaimed, "the method — if method there is[f] — by which you have been enabled to fathom my soul in this matter." In fact I was even more startled than I would have been willing to express.

"It was the fruiterer," replied my friend, "who brought you to the conclusion that the mender of soles was not of sufficient height for Xerxes *et id genus omne.*" [15]

"The fruiterer! — you astonish me — I know no fruiterer whomsoever."[g]

"The man who ran up against you as we entered the street — it may have been fifteen minutes ago."

I now remembered that, in fact, a fruiterer, carrying upon his head a large basket of apples, had nearly thrown me down, by

---

z	*Théâtre (A)*	d	Crebillon's *(A, B)*
a	afterwards *(A)*	e	God's *(A, B, C)*
b	quondam *(A, B)*	f	be *(A, B, C)*
c	rôle *(A, B)*	g	whatever." *(A)*

accident, as we passed from the Rue C —— into the thoroughfare where we[h] stood; but what this had to do with Chantilly I could not possibly understand.

There was not a particle of *charlatanerie*[i] about Dupin. "I will explain," he said, "and that you may comprehend all clearly, we will first retrace the course of your meditations, from the moment in which I spoke to you until that of the *rencontre*[j] with the fruiterer in question. The larger links of the chain run thus — Chantilly, Orion, Dr. Nichol,[k] [16] Epicurus, Stereotomy, the street stones, the fruiterer."

There are few persons who have not, at some period of their lives, amused themselves in retracing the steps by which particular conclusions of their own minds have been attained. The occupation is often full of interest; and he who attempts it for the first time is[l] astonished by the apparently illimitable distance and incoherence between the starting-point and the goal.[17] What, then, must have been my amazement when I heard the Frenchman speak what he had just spoken, and when I could not help acknowledging that he had spoken the truth. He continued:

"We had been talking of horses, if I remember aright, just before leaving the Rue C ——. This was the last subject we discussed. As we crossed into this street, a fruiterer, with a large basket upon his head, brushing quickly past us, thrust you upon a pile of paving-stones collected at a spot where the causeway is undergoing repair. You stepped upon one of the loose fragments, slipped, slightly strained your ankle, appeared vexed or sulky, muttered a few words, turned to look[m] at the pile, and then proceeded in silence. I was not particularly attentive to what you did; but observation has become with me, of late, a species of necessity.

"You kept your eyes upon the ground — glancing, with a petulant expression, at the holes and ruts in the pavement, (so that I saw you were still thinking of the stones,) until we reached the little alley called Lamartine,[18] which has been paved, by way of

---

h we now *(A, B)*
i *charlatânerie (B, C, D, E, F),* *corrected from A*
j rencontre *(A, B)*

k Nichols, *(C, D, E, F) corrected* *from A, B*
l is <invariably> *(A)*
m look back *(A)*

experiment, with the overlapping and riveted blocks.[19] Here your countenance brightened up, and, perceiving your lips move, I could not doubt that you murmured[n] the [o]word 'stereotomy,' a term very affectedly applied to this species of pavement.[o] I knew that you could not [p]say to yourself 'stereotomy' without[p] being brought to think of atomies, and thus of the theories of Epicurus;[20] and since,[q] when we discussed this subject not very long ago, I mentioned to you how singularly, yet with how little notice, the vague guesses of that noble Greek had met with confirmation in the late nebular cosmogony, I felt that you could not avoid casting your eyes upward[r] to the great *nebula*[s] in Orion,[21] and I certainly expected that you would do so. You did look up; and I was now[t] assured that I had correctly followed your steps. But in that bitter *tirade* upon Chantilly, which appeared in yesterday's '*Musée*,' the satirist, making some disgraceful allusions to the cobbler's change of name upon assuming the buskin, quoted a[u] Latin line[v] about which[w] we have often conversed. I mean the line

[x]Perdidit antiquum litera prima sonum[x]

I had told you that this was in reference to Orion, formerly written Urion; and, from certain pungencies connected with this explanation, I was aware that you could not have forgotten it.[22] It was clear, therefore, that you would not fail to combine the two ideas of Orion and Chantilly. That you did combine them I saw by the character of the smile which passed over your lips. You thought of the poor cobbler's immolation. So far, you had been stooping in your gait; but now I saw you draw yourself up to your full height. I was then sure that you reflected upon the diminutive figure of Chantilly. At this point I interrupted your meditations to remark

---

n murmured to yourself *(A, B, C)*
o . . . o word stereotomic. You continued the same inaudible murmur, with a knit brow, as is the <habit> ↑ custom ↓ of a man tasking his memory, until I considered that you sought the Greek derivation of the word stereotomy. *(A, B, C)*
p . . . p find this without *(A, B, C)*
q as, *(A, B)*

r upwards *(A)*
s nebula *(A, B)*
t was now/now was *(A, B, C)*
u a very peculiar *(A, B, C)*
v Latin line/<line> ↑ Latin verse ↓ *(A)*
w about which/upon whose meaning *(A, B)*; upon the meaning of which *(C)*
x . . . x *Latin italicized (A, B, C)*

that as, in fact, he *was* a very little fellow — that Chantilly — he would do better at the *Théâtre des Variétés.*" [y]

Not long after this, we were looking over an evening edition of [z]the "Gazette des Tribunaux,"[z] when the following paragraphs arrested our attention.

"EXTRAORDINARY MURDERS. — This morning, about three o'-clock, the inhabitants of the Quartier St. Roch were aroused from sleep by a succession of terrific shrieks, issuing, apparently, from the fourth story of a house in the Rue Morgue, known to be in the sole occupancy of one Madame L'Espanaye, and her daughter, Mademoiselle Camille L'Espanaye. After some delay, occasioned by a fruitless attempt to procure admission in the usual manner, the gateway was broken in with a crowbar,[a] and eight or ten of the neighbors entered, accompanied by two *gendarmes.*[b] By this time the cries had ceased; but, as the party rushed up the first flight of stairs, two or more rough voices, in angry contention, were dis-tinguished, and[c] seemed to proceed from the upper part of the house. As the second landing was reached, these sounds, also, had ceased, and everything remained perfectly quiet. The party spread themselves, and hurried from room to room. Upon arriving at a large back chamber in the fourth story, (the door of which, being found locked, with the key inside, was forced open,) a spectacle presented itself which struck every one present not less with horror than with astonishment.

"The apartment was in the wildest disorder — the furniture broken and thrown about in all directions. There was only one bedstead; and from this the bed had been removed, and thrown into the middle of the floor. On a chair lay a razor, besmeared with blood. On the hearth were two or three long and thick tresses of grey human hair, also dabbled in blood, and seeming to have been pulled out[d] by the roots. On[e] the floor were found four Napoleons, an ear-ring of topaz, three large silver spoons, three[f] smaller of *métal*[g] *d'Alger,*[23] and two bags, containing nearly four thousand

---

y   Théâtre des Variétés." *(A)*
z . . . z   "Le Tribunal" *(A, B, C)*
a   crow-bar. *(A, B, C)*
b   <gens d'armes.> ↑ *gendarmes.* ↓ *(A)*
c   <proceeding> and *(A)*

d   <up> ↑ out ↓ *(A)*
e   Upon *(A, B, C, D, F)*
f   <and> three *(A)*
g   *metal (A, B)*

francs in gold. The drawers of a *bureau,* which stood in one corner, were open, and had been, apparently, rifled, although many articles still remained in them. A small iron safe was discovered under the *bed* (not under the bedstead). It was open, with the key still in the door. It had no contents beyond a few old letters, and other papers of little consequence.

"Of Madame L'Espanaye no traces were here seen; but an unusual quantity of soot being observed in the fire-place, a search was made in the chimney, and (horrible to relate!)[24] the corpse of the daughter, head downward,[h] was dragged therefrom; it having been thus forced up the narrow aperture for a considerable distance.[25] The body was quite warm. Upon examining it, many excoriations were perceived, no doubt occasioned by the violence with which it had been thrust up and disengaged. Upon the face were many severe scratches, and, upon the throat, dark bruises, and deep indentations of finger nails, as if the deceased had been throttled to death.

"After a thorough investigation of every portion of the house, without farther discovery, the party made its way into a small paved yard in the rear of the building, where lay the corpse of the old lady, with her throat so entirely cut that, upon an attempt to raise her, the head fell off.[i] The body, as well as the head, was[j] fearfully mutilated — the former so much so as scarcely to retain any semblance of humanity.

"To this horrible mystery there is not as yet, we believe, the slightest clew."[k]

The next day's paper had these additional particulars.

"*The Tragedy in the Rue Morgue.* Many individuals have been examined in relation to this most extraordinary and frightful affair." [The word '*affaire*' has not yet, in France, that levity of import which it conveys with us,] "but nothing whatever has transpired to throw light upon it. We give below all the material testimony elicited.[26]

"*Pauline Dubourg,* laundress, deposes that she has known both the deceased for three years, having washed for them during that

---

h downwards, *(A)*
i off and rolled to some distance. *(A, B)*

j <were> ↑ was ↓ *(A)*
k *At first appearance in the MS this word is spelled* clew

period. The old lady and her daughter seemed on good terms — very affectionate towards[1] each other. They were excellent pay. Could not speak in regard to their mode or means of living. Believed that Madame L. told fortunes for a living. Was reputed to have money put by. Never met any persons in the house when she called for the clothes or took them home. Was sure that they had no servant in employ. There appeared to be no furniture in any part of the building except in the fourth story.

"*Pierre Moreau*, tobacconist, deposes that he has been in the habit of selling small quantities of tobacco and snuff to Madame L'Espanaye for nearly four years. Was born in the neighborhood, and has always resided there. The deceased and her daughter had occupied the house in which the corpses were found, for more than six years. It was formerly occupied by a jeweller, who under-let the upper rooms to various persons. The house was the property of Madame L. She became dissatisfied with the abuse of the premises by her tenant, and moved into them herself, refusing to let any portion. The old lady was childish. Witness had seen the daughter some five or six times during the six years. The two lived an exceedingly retired life — were reputed to have money. Had heard it said among the neighbors that Madame L. told fortunes — did not believe it. Had never seen any person enter the door except the old lady and her daughter, a porter once or twice, and a physician some eight or ten times.

"Many other persons, neighbors, gave evidence to the same effect. No one was spoken of as frequenting the house. It was not known whether there were any living connexions of Madame L. and her daughter. The shutters of the front windows were seldom opened. Those in the rear were always closed, with the exception of the large back room, fourth story. The house was a good house — not very old.

"*Isidore* [m]*Musèt, gendarme,*[m] deposes that he was called to the house about three o'clock in the morning, and found some twenty or thirty persons at the gateway,[n] endeavoring to gain admittance. Forced it open, at length, with a bayonet — not with a crowbar.[o]

---

1   toward *(B)*
m ... m   *Musèt,* gendarme, *(A, B)*

n   <front door> ↑ gateway, ↓ *(A)*
o   crow-bar. *(A, B, C)*

Had but little difficulty in getting it open, on account of its being a double or folding gate,[p] and bolted neither at bottom nor top. The shrieks were continued until the gate[q] was forced — and then suddenly ceased. They seemed to be[r] screams of some person (or persons) in great agony — were loud and drawn out, not short and quick. Witness led the way up stairs. Upon reaching the first landing, heard two voices in loud and angry contention — the one a gruff voice, the other much shriller — a very strange voice. Could distinguish some words of the former, which was that of a Frenchman. Was positive that it was not a woman's voice. Could distinguish the words 'sacré'[s] and 'diable.' The shrill voice was that of a foreigner. Could not be sure whether it was the voice of a man or of a woman. Could not make out what was said, but believed the language to be Spanish.[t] The state of the room and of the bodies was described by this witness as we described them yesterday.

"*Henri Duval*, a neighbor, and by trade a silver-smith,[u] deposes that he was one of the party who first entered the house. Corroborates the testimony of Musèt[v] in general. As soon as they forced an entrance, they reclosed the door, to keep out the crowd, which collected very fast, notwithstanding the lateness of the hour. The shrill voice, this witness thinks, was that of an Italian. Was certain it was not French. Could not be sure that it was a man's voice. It might have been a woman's. Was not[w] acquainted with the Italian language. Could[x] not distinguish the words, but[y] was convinced by the intonation that the speaker was an Italian. Knew Madame L. and her daughter. Had conversed with both frequently. Was sure that the shrill voice was not that of either of the deceased.

" —— *Odenheimer, restaurateur.*[z] This witness volunteered his testimony. [a]Not speaking French, was examined through an inter-

---

p <door,> ↑ gate, ↓ *(A)*
q <door> ↑ gate ↓ *(A)*
r be the *(A)*
s 'sacre' *(A)*
t *After this:* Might have distinguished some words if he had been acquainted with the Spanish. *(A)*

u silversmith, *(A)*
v Musêt *(A)*
w ↑ not ↓ *(A)*
x <, and, although he> Could *(A)*
y ↑ but ↓ *(A)*
z restaurateur. *(A, B)*
a . . . a *Inserted (A)*

preter.[a] Is a native of Amsterdam. Was passing the house at the time of the shrieks. They lasted for several minutes — probably ten. They were long and loud — very awful and distressing. Was one of those who entered the building. Corroborated the previous evidence in every respect but one. Was sure that the shrill voice was that of a man — of a Frenchman. Could not distinguish the words uttered. They were loud and quick — [b]unequal — spoken[b] apparently in fear as well as in anger. The voice was harsh — not so much shrill as harsh. Could not call it a shrill voice. The gruff voice said repeatedly *'sacré,'*[c] *'diable,'* and once *'mon Dieu.'*

"*Jules Mignaud,* banker, of the firm of Mignaud et Fils, Rue Deloraine. Is the elder Mignaud. Madame L'Espanaye had some property. Had opened an account with his banking house in the spring of the year —— (eight years previously). Made frequent deposits[d] in small sums. Had checked for nothing until the third day before her death, when she took out in person the sum of 4000 francs. This sum was paid in gold, and a clerk sent home with the money.

"*Adolphe Le Bon,* clerk to[e] Mignaud et Fils, deposes that on the day in question, about noon, he accompanied Madame L'Espanaye to her residence with the 4000 francs, put up in two bags. Upon the door being opened, Mademoiselle L. appeared and took from his hands one of the bags, while the old lady relieved him of the other. He then bowed and departed. Did not see any person in the street at the time. It is a bye-street[f] — very lonely.

"*William Bird,* tailor, deposes that he was one of the party who entered the house. Is an Englishman. Has lived in Paris two years. Was one of the first to ascend the stairs. Heard the voices in contention. The gruff voice was that of a Frenchman. Could make out several words, but cannot now remember all. Heard distinctly *'sacré'*[g] and *'mon Dieu.'* There was a sound at the moment as if of several persons struggling — a scraping and scuffling sound. The shrill voice was very loud — louder than the gruff one. Is sure that

---

b ... b unequal — sometimes quick, sometimes deliberate — spoken *(A, B)*
c *'sacre'* *(A)*
d deposites *(A, B)*

e to Messieurs *(A)*
f bye street *(A, B, C)*
g *'sacre'* *(A)*

it was not the voice of an Englishman. Appeared to be that of a German. Might have been a woman's voice. [h]Does not understand German.[h]

"Four of the above-named witnesses, being recalled, deposed that the door of the chamber in which was found the body of Mademoiselle L. was locked on the inside when the party reached it. Every thing was perfectly silent — no groans or noises of any kind. Upon forcing the door no person was seen. The windows, both of the back and front room, were down and firmly fastened from within. A door between the two rooms was closed, but not locked. The door leading from the front room into the passage was [i]locked, with the key on the inside.[i] A small room in the front of the house, on the fourth story, at the head of the passage, was[j] open, the door being ajar. This room was crowded with old beds, boxes, and so forth. These were carefully removed and searched. There was not an inch of any portion of the house which was not carefully searched. Sweeps were sent up and down the chimneys. The house was a four story one, with garrets (*mansardes*.)[k] A trap-door[l] on the roof was nailed down very securely — did not appear to have been opened for years. The time elapsing between the hearing of the voices in contention and the breaking open of[m] the room door, was variously stated by the witnesses. Some made it as short as three minutes — some as long as five. The door was opened with difficulty.

"*Alfonzo Garcio,* undertaker, deposes[n] that he resides in the Rue Morgue.[o] Is a native of Spain. Was one of the party who entered the house. Did not proceed up stairs. Is nervous, and was apprehensive of the consequences of agitation. Heard the voices in contention. The gruff voice was that of a Frenchman. Could not distinguish what was said. The shrill voice was that of an Englishman — is sure of this. Does not understand the English language, but judges by the intonation.

---

h ... h *Inserted (A)*
i ... i <open — not wide open, but ajar.> ↑ locked with the key on the inside. ↓ *(A)*
j   was <also> *(A)*
k   ↑ *(mansardes).* ↓ *(A)*

l   trap door *(A, B)*
m   *Omitted (A)*
n   deposed *(A)*
o   < — (the street of the murder.)> <↑Trianon. ↓ > ↑ Morgue. ↓ *(A)*

[p]"*Alberto Montani,* confectioner, deposes that he was among the first to ascend the stairs. Heard the voices in question. The gruff voice was that of a Frenchman. Distinguished several words. The speaker appeared to be expostulating. Could not make out the words of the shrill voice.[q] Spoke quick and unevenly. Thinks it the voice of a Russian. Corroborates the general testimony. Is an Italian. Never conversed with a native of Russia.[p]

"Several witnesses, recalled, here testified that the chimneys of all the rooms on the fourth story were too narrow to admit the passage of a human being. By 'sweeps' were meant cylindrical[r] sweeping-brushes, such as are employed by those who clean chimneys. These brushes were passed up and down every flue in the house. There is no back passage by which any one could have descended while the party proceeded up stairs. The body of Mademoiselle L'Espanaye was so firmly wedged in the chimney that it could not be got down until four or five of[s] the party united their strength.

"*Paul Dumas,* physician, deposes that he was called to view the bodies about day-break. They were both then[t] lying on the sacking of the bedstead in the chamber where Mademoiselle L. was found. The corpse of the young lady was much bruised and excoriated. The fact that it had been thrust up the chimney would sufficiently account for these appearances. The throat was greatly chafed. There were several deep scratches just below the chin, together with a series of livid spots which were evidently the impression of fingers. The face was fearfully discolored, and the eye-balls protruded. The tongue had been partially bitten through. A large bruise was discovered upon the pit of the stomach, produced, apparently, by the pressure of a knee. In the opinion of M. Dumas, Mademoiselle L'Espanaye had been throttled to death by some person or persons unknown. The corpse of the mother was horribly mutilated. All the bones of the right leg and arm were more or less shattered. The left *tibia*[u] much splintered, as well as all the ribs of the left side. Whole body dreadfully bruised and discolored.

p . . . p *Inserted in the margin (A)*
q ↑ voice. ↓ *(A)*
r ↑ cylindrical ↓ *(A)*
s or *(B) misprint*
t both then/then both *(A)*
u tibia *(A, B)*

It was not possible to say how the injuries had been inflicted. A heavy club of wood, or a broad bar of iron — a chair — any large, heavy, and obtuse weapon would^v have produced such results, if wielded by the hands of a very powerful man. No woman could have inflicted the blows with any weapon. The head of the deceased, when seen by witness, was entirely separated from the body, and was also greatly shattered. The throat had evidently been cut with some very sharp instrument — probably with a razor.

"*Alexandre Etienne,* surgeon, was called with M. Dumas to view the bodies. Corroborated the testimony, and the opinions of M. Dumas.

"Nothing farther of importance was elicited, although several other persons were examined. A murder so mysterious, and so perplexing in all its particulars, was never before committed in Paris — if indeed a murder has been committed at all. The police are entirely at fault — an unusual occurrence in affairs of this nature. There is not, however, the shadow of a clew^w apparent."

The evening edition of the paper stated that the greatest excitement still continued in the Quartier St. Roch^x — that the premises in question had been carefully re-searched, and fresh examinations of witnesses instituted, but all to no purpose. A postscript, however, mentioned that Adolphe Le Bon had been arrested and imprisoned — although nothing appeared to criminate him, beyond the facts already detailed.

Dupin seemed singularly interested in the progress of this affair — at least so I judged from his manner, for he made no comments.^{y} It was only after the announcement that Le Bon had been imprisoned, that he asked me my opinion respecting the murders.^{z}

I could merely agree with all Paris in considering them^a an insoluble mystery.^{b} I saw no means by which it would be possible to trace^c the murderer.

"We must not judge of the means," said Dupin, "by this shell^d

---

v could *(A)*
w clue *(A)*
x <Rue Trianon> ↑ Quartier St. Roch ↓ *(A)*
y comments whatever. *(A, B)*
z the murders./it. *(A, B, C)*

a it *(A, B, C)*
b *After this:* <In regard to the perpetrator of the butchery> *(A)*
c trace <him> *(A)*
d <*bizarrerie*> ↑ shell ↓ *(A)*

of an examination. The Parisian police, so much extolled for *acumen,*[e] are cunning, but no more. There is no method in their proceedings, beyond the method of the moment. [f]They make a vast parade of measures; but, not unfrequently, these are so ill[g] adapted to the objects[h] proposed, as to put us in mind of Monsieur Jourdain's calling for his *robe-de-chambre*[i] — *pour mieux entendre la musique.*[f] [27] The results attained by them are not unfrequently surprising, but, for the most part, are brought about by simple diligence and activity. When these qualities are unavailing, their schemes fail. Vidocq, for example,[j] was a good guesser, and a persevering man.[28] But, without[k] educated thought, he erred continually by the very intensity of his investigations. He impaired his vision by holding the object too close. He might see, perhaps, one or two points with unusual clearness, but in so doing he, necessarily, lost sight of the matter as a whole. Thus there is such a thing as being too profound. Truth is[l] not always[m] in a well. In fact, as regards the more[n] important knowledge, I do believe that she is invariably superficial. The depth lies[o] in the valleys where we seek her, and not[p] upon the mountain-tops[q] where she is found.[29] The modes and sources of this kind of error are well typified in the contemplation of[r] the heavenly bodies. To look at a star by glances — to view it in a side-long[s] way, by turning toward[t] it the exterior portions of the *retina*[u] (more susceptible of feeble impressions of light than the interior), is to behold the star distinctly — is to have the best appreciation of its lustre — a lustre which grows dim just in proportion as we turn our vision *fully* upon it. A greater number of rays actually fall upon the eye in the latter case, but, in the former, there is the more refined capacity for comprehension. By undue profundity we perplex and enfeeble thought; and it is possi-

---

e   acumen, *(A, B)*
f . . . f   *Inserted in right-hand margin (A)*
g   illy *(A, B)*
h   <results> ↑ objects ↓ *(A)*
i   *robe de chambre (A)*
j   ↑ for example ↓ *(A)*
k   without <an> *(A)*
l   <does> ↑ is ↓ *(A)*
m   always <lie> *(A)*

n   <most> ↑ more ↓ *(A)*
o   lies <oftener> *(A)*
p   <than> ↑ and not ↓ *(A)*
q   mountain tops *(A, B)*
r   of <a star> *(A)*
s   side long *(A)*
t   towards *(A)*
u   retina <is to see it distinctly — is> *(A)*; retina *(B)*

ble to make even Venus herself vanish from the firmament by a scrutiny too sustained, too concentrated, or[v] too direct.[30]

"As for these murders, let us enter into some examinations for ourselves, before we make up an opinion respecting them. An inquiry will afford us amusement," [I thought this an odd term, so applied, but said nothing] "and, besides, Le Bon once rendered me a service for which I am not ungrateful. We will go and see the premises with our own eyes. I know G —— ,[31] the [w]Prefect of Police,[w] and shall have no difficulty in obtaining the necessary permission."

The[x] permission was obtained, and we proceeded at once to the Rue Morgue. This is one of those miserable thoroughfares which intervene between the Rue Richelieu and the Rue St. Roch. It was late in the afternoon when we reached it; as[y] this quarter[z] is at a great distance from that in which we resided. The house was[a] readily found; for there were still many persons gazing up at the closed shutters, with an objectless curiosity, from the opposite side of the way. It was an ordinary[b] Parisian house, with a gateway, on one side of which was a glazed watch-box, with a sliding panel in the window, indicating a *loge de concierge*. Before going in we walked up the street, turned down an alley, and then, again turning, passed in the rear of the building — Dupin, meanwhile, examining the whole neighborhood, as well as the house, with a minuteness of attention for which I could see no possible object.

Retracing our steps, we came again to the front of the dwelling, rang, and, having shown our credentials, were admitted by the agents in charge. We went up stairs — into the chamber where the body of Mademoiselle L'Espanaye had been found, and where both the deceased still lay. The disorders of the room had, as usual, been suffered to exist. I saw nothing beyond what had been stated in the [c]"Gazette des Tribunaux."[c] Dupin scrutinized every thing — not excepting the bodies of the victims. We then went into the other rooms, and into the yard; a *gendarme*[d] accompanying us

---

v   and *(A, B)*
w ... w   *Préfet de Police, (A, B)*
x   This *(A, B)*
y   it; as/it for *(A, B)*
z   Quartier *(A)*

a   we *(A, B)*
b   ordinary <French hou> *(A)*
c ... c   "Tribunal." *(A, B, C)*
d   gendarme *(A, B)*

throughout. The[e] examination occupied us until dark, when we took our departure. [f]On our way home my companion stepped in for a moment at the office of one of the daily papers.[f]

I have said that the whims of my friend were manifold, and that *Je les ménageais:*[g] — for this phrase there is no English equivalent.[32] It was his humor, now, to decline all conversation on the subject of the murder, until[h] about [i]noon the next day.[i] He then asked me, suddenly, if I had observed any thing *peculiar* at the scene of the atrocity.

There was something in his manner of emphasizing the word "peculiar," which caused me to shudder, without knowing why.

"No, nothing *peculiar,*" I said; "nothing more, at least, than we both saw stated in the paper."

[j] "The 'Gazette,' "[j] he replied, "has not entered, I fear, into the unusual horror of the thing. But dismiss[k] the idle opinions of this print. It appears to me that this mystery is considered insoluble, for the very reason[l] which should cause it to be regarded as easy of solution — I mean for the *outré* character of its features. The police are confounded by the seeming absence of motive — not for the murder itself — but for the atrocity of the murder. They are [m]puzzled, too, by[m] the seeming impossibility of reconciling the voices heard in contention, with the facts that no one was discovered up stairs but the assassinated Mademoiselle L'Espanaye, and that there were no means of egress without the notice of the party ascending. The wild disorder of the room; the corpse thrust, with the head downward,[n] up the chimney; the frightful mutilation of the body of the old lady; these considerations, with those just mentioned, and others which I need not mention, have sufficed to paralyze the powers, by putting completely at fault the boasted *acumen,*[o] of the government agents. They have fallen into the gross but common[p] error of confounding the unusual with the

e   Our *(A, B, C)*
f ... f   *Inserted in right-hand margin (A)*
g   *menagais: (A,B); ménagais (C,D,E,F)*
h   until after we had taken a bottle of wine together *(A, B, C)*
i ... i   <midnight.> ↑ noon the next

day. ↓ *(A)*
j ... j   "Le Tribunal," *(A, B, C)*
k   we will not revert to *(A, B)*
l   reasons *(A)*
m ... m   puzzled by *(A, B, C)*
n   downwards *(A)*
o   acumen, *(A, B)*
p   ↑ but common ↓ *(A)*

abstruse. But it is by these deviations from the^q plane of the ordinary, that^r reason feels its way, if at all, in its search for^s the true.[33] In investigations such as we are now pursuing, it should not be so much^t asked 'what has occurred,' as^u 'what has occurred that^v has never occurred before.' ^{w} In fact, the facility with which I shall arrive, or have arrived, at the solution of this mystery, is in ^{x}the direct ratio of^x its apparent insolubility in the eyes of the police."

I stared at the speaker in mute astonishment.^{y}

"I am now awaiting," continued he, looking toward^z the door of our apartment — "I am now awaiting a person who, although perhaps not the perpetrator of these butcheries, must have been^a in some measure implicated in their perpetration. Of the worst portion of the crimes committed, it is probable that he is innocent. I hope that I am right in this supposition; for upon it I build my expectation of reading the entire riddle. I look for the man here — in this room — every moment. It is true that he may not arrive; but the probability is that he will. Should he come, it will be necessary to detain him. Here are pistols; and we both know how to use them when^b occasion demands their use."

I took the pistols, scarcely knowing what I did, or believing what I heard, while Dupin went on, very much as if in a soliloquy. I have already spoken of his abstract manner at such times. His discourse was addressed to myself; but his voice, although by no means loud, had that intonation which is commonly employed in speaking to some one at a great distance. His eyes, vacant in expression, regarded only the wall.

"That the voices heard in contention," he said, "by the party upon the stairs, were not the voices of the women themselves, was fully proved by the evidence. This relieves us of all doubt upon

---

q   the common-place — by these prominences from the *(A)*
r   that <true> *(A)*
s   after *(A, B)*
t   ↑ so much ↓ *(A)*
u   <but> ↑ as ↓ *(A)*
v   which *(A, B, C)*
w   *After this:* <Just in proportion as this matter has appeared insoluble to the police, has been that facility with which I have arrived at its solution.> *(A)*
x ... x   an exact ratio with *(A)*; exact ratio with *(B, C)*
y   *After this:* He continued. *(A, B, C)*
z   towards *(A)*
a   ↑ been ↓ *(A)*
b   when <the> *(A) deletion is made in pencil*

the question whether the old lady[c] could have first destroyed the daughter, and afterward[d] have committed suicide. I speak of this point chiefly for the sake of method; for the strength of Madame L'Espanaye would have been utterly unequal to the task of thrusting her daughter's corpse up the chimney as it was found; and the nature of the wounds upon her own person entirely preclude the idea of self-destruction. Murder, then, has been committed by some third party; and the voices of this third party were those heard in contention. Let me now advert — not to the whole testimony respecting these voices — but to what was *peculiar*[e] in that testimony. Did you observe any thing peculiar about it?"

I remarked that, while all the witnesses agreed in supposing the gruff voice to be that of a Frenchman, there was much disagreement in regard to the shrill, or, as one individual termed it, the harsh voice.

"That was the evidence itself," said Dupin, "but it was not the peculiarity of the evidence. You have observed nothing distinctive.[f] Yet there *was* something to be observed.[g] The witnesses, as you remark, agreed about the gruff voice; they were here unanimous. But in regard to the shrill voice, the peculiarity is — not that they disagreed — but that, while an Italian, an Englishman, a Spaniard, a Hollander, and a Frenchman attempted to describe it, each one spoke of it as that *of a foreigner.* Each is sure that it was not the voice of one of his own countrymen. Each likens it — not to the voice of an individual of any nation with whose language he is conversant — but the converse. The Frenchman supposes it the voice of a Spaniard, and 'might have distinguished some words *had he been acquainted with the Spanish.*' The Dutchman maintains it[h] to have been that of a Frenchman; but we find it stated that '*not understanding French this witness was examined through an interpreter.*' The Englishman thinks it the voice of a German, and '*does not understand German.*' The Spaniard 'is sure' that it was[i] that of

---

c ↑ lady ↓ *(A)*
d afterwards *(A)*
e peculiar *(A, B)*
f *After this:* Re-employing my own words I may say that you have pointed out no prominence above the plane of

the ordinary, by which reason may feel her way. *(A, B, C) Except* its way *for* her way *(C)*
g pointed out. *(A, B, C)*
h <the voice> ↑ it ↓ *(A)*
i is *(A, B, C)*

an Englishman, but 'judges by the intonation' altogether, *'as he has no knowledge of the English.'* The Italian believes it the voice of a Russian, but *'has never conversed with a native of Russia.'* A second Frenchman differs, moreover, with the first, and is positive that the voice was[j] that of an Italian; but, *not being cognizant of that tongue,* is, like the Spaniard, 'convinced by the intonation.' Now, how strangely unusual must that voice have really been, about which such testimony as this *could* have been elicited[k]! — in whose *tones,* even, denizens of the five great divisions of Europe could recognise nothing familiar! You will say that it might have been the voice of an Asiatic — of an African. Neither Asiatics nor Africans abound in Paris; but, without[l] denying the inference, I will[m] now merely call your attention to three points.[n] The voice is termed by one witness 'harsh rather than shrill.' It is represented by two others to have been 'quick and *unequal.'* No words — no sounds[o] resembling words — were[p] by any witness mentioned as distinguishable.

"I know not," continued Dupin, "what impression I may have made, so far, upon your own understanding; but I do not hesitate to say that legitimate deductions even from this portion of the testimony — the portion respecting the gruff and shrill voices — are in themselves sufficient to engender a suspicion which should[q] give direction to all farther[r] progress in the investigation of the mystery. I said 'legitimate deductions;' but my meaning is not thus fully expressed. I designed to imply that the deductions are[s] the *sole* proper ones, and that the suspicion arises[t] *inevitably* from them as the single result. What the suspicion is, however, I will not say just yet. I merely wish you to bear in mind that, with myself, it was sufficiently forcible to give a definite form — a certain tendency — to my inquiries in the chamber.

"Let us now transport ourselves, in fancy, to this[u] chamber.

---

j   is (*A, B, C*)
k   <given> ↑ elicited ↓ (*A*)
l   not [*erasure*] ↑ without ↓ (*A*)
m   will just (*A, B, C*)
n   points which have relation to this topic. (*A, B, C*)
o   no sounds/<nothing> ↑ no

sounds ↓ (*A*)
p   <was> ↑ were ↓ (*A*)
q   should bias, or (*A, B, C*)
r   further (*A*)
s   were (*A, B, C*)
t   arose (*A, B, C*)
u   that (*A, B*)

What shall we first seek here? The means of egress employed by the murderers. It is not too much to say that[v] neither of us believe in præternatural events. Madame and Mademoiselle L'Espanaye were not destroyed by spirits. The doers of the[w] deed were material, and escaped materially. Then how? Fortunately, there is but one mode of reasoning upon the[x] point, and that mode *must* lead us to a definite decision. — Let us examine, each by each, the possible means of egress. It is clear that the assassins were in the room where [y]Mademoiselle L'Espanaye was found,[y] or at least in the room adjoining, when the party ascended the stairs. It is then only from these two apartments that we have to seek[z] issues. The police have laid bare the floors, the ceilings, and the masonry of the walls, in every direction. No *secret* issues could have escaped their vigilance. But, not trusting to *their*[a] eyes, I examined with my own. There were, then, *no* secret issues. Both doors leading from the rooms into the passage were securely locked, with the keys inside. Let us turn to the chimneys. These, although of ordinary width for some eight or ten feet above the hearths, will not admit, throughout their extent, the body of a large cat. The impossibility of egress, by[b] means already stated,[c] being thus absolute, we are reduced to the windows. Through those of the front room no one could have escaped without notice from the crowd in the street. The murderers *must* have passed, then, through those of the back room. Now, brought to this conclusion in so unequivocal a manner as we are, it is not our part, as reasoners, to reject it on account of apparent impossibilities. It is only left for us to prove that these apparent[d] 'impossibilities' [e]are, in reality,[e] not such.

"There are two windows in the chamber. One of them is unobstructed by furniture, and is wholly visible. The lower portion of the other is hidden from view by the head of the unwieldy bedstead which is thrust close up against it. The former was found securely fastened from within. It resisted the utmost force of those

---

v   that we *(A, B)*
w   the dark *(A, B, C)*
x   this *(A)*
y . . . y   <the crime was committed,>
↑ Mademoiselle l'Espanaye was found, ↓ *(A)*

z   seek for *(A, B, C)*
a   their *(A, B)*
b   by the *(A)*
c   ↑ stated ↓ *(A)*
d   *Omitted (A, B)*
e . . . e   are *(A, B)*

who endeavored to raise it. A large gimlet-hole had been pierced in its frame to the left, and a very stout nail was found fitted therein, nearly to the head. Upon examining the other window, a similar nail was seen similarly fitted in it; and a vigorous attempt to raise this sash[e'] failed also. The police were now entirely satisfied that egress had not been[f] in these directions. And, *therefore,* it was thought a matter of supererogation to withdraw the nails and open the windows.

"My own examination was somewhat more particular, and was so for the reason I have just given — because here it was, I knew, that all apparent impossibilities *must* be proved to be not such in reality.

"I proceeded to think thus — *à[g] posteriori.* The murderers *did* escape from one of these windows. This being so, they could not have re-fastened the sashes from the inside, as they were found fastened; — the consideration which put a stop, through its obviousness, to the scrutiny of the police in this quarter. Yet the sashes *were* fastened. They *must,* then, have the power of fastening themselves. There was no escape from this conclusion. I stepped to the unobstructed casement, withdrew the nail with some difficulty, and attempted to raise the sash. It resisted all my efforts, as I had[h] anticipated. A concealed spring must, I now knew, exist; and this corroboration of my idea convinced me that my premises, at least, were correct, however mysterious still appeared the circumstances attending the nails. A careful search soon brought to light the hidden spring. I pressed it, and, satisfied with the discovery, forbore to upraise the sash.

"I now replaced the nail and regarded it attentively. A person passing out through this window might have reclosed it, and the spring would have caught — but the nail could not have been replaced. The conclusion was plain, and again narrowed in the field of my investigations. The assassins *must* have escaped through the other window. Supposing, then, the springs upon each sash to be the same, as was probable, there *must* be found a difference be-

e' sash, *(C, D, E, F)*
corrected from A, B
f been <made> *(A)*

g *a (A, B)*
h ↑ had ↓ *(A)*

tween the nails, or at least between the modes of their fixture. Getting upon the sacking of the bedstead, I looked over the head-board minutely at the second casement. Passing my hand[i] down behind the board, I readily discovered and pressed the spring, which was, as I had supposed, identical in character with its neighbor. I now looked at the nail. It was as stout as the other, and apparently fitted in in[j] the same manner — driven in nearly up to the head.

"You will say that I was puzzled; but, if you think so, you must have misunderstood the nature of the inductions. To use a sporting phrase, I had not [k]been once[k] 'at fault.' The scent had never for an instant been lost. There was no flaw in any link of the chain. I had traced[l] the secret to its ultimate result, — and that result was *the nail.* It had, I say, in every respect, the appearance of its fellow in the other window; but this fact was an absolute nullity (conclusive as it might seem to be) when compared with the consideration that here, at this point, terminated the clew.[m] 'There *must* be something wrong,' I said, 'about the[n] nail.' I touched it; and the head, with about a quarter[o] of an inch of the shank, came off in my fingers. The rest of the shank was in the gimlet-hole, where it had been broken off. [p]The fracture was an old one (for its edges were incrusted with rust), and[p] had apparently been accomplished by the blow of a hammer, which had partially imbedded, in the top of the bottom sash, the head portion of the nail. I now carefully replaced this head portion in the indentation whence I had taken it, and the resemblance to a perfect nail was [q]complete — the fissure was invisible.[q] [r]Pressing the spring, I[r] gently raised the sash for a few inches; the head went up with it, remaining firm in its bed. I closed the window, and the semblance of the whole nail was again perfect.

"The riddle, so far, was now unriddled. The assassin[s] had escaped through the window which looked upon the bed. Dropping[s']

---

i   arm *(A)*
j   *Omitted (B, C, D, E, F) restored from manuscript (A)*
k . . . k ↑ been ↓ once <been> *(A)*
l   tracked *(A)*
m   clue. *(A)*
n   this *(A)*

o   a quarter/the eighth *(A, B)*
p . . . p *Written over an erasure in A*
q . . . q complete. *(A, B, C)*
r . . . r I *(A, B)*
s   assassins *(A, B, C)*
s' Droping *(D, E, F) misprint*

· 5 5 3 ·

of its own accord upon his[t] exit (or perhaps purposely closed),[u] it had become fastened by the spring; and it was the retention of this spring which had been mistaken by the police for that of the nail, — farther inquiry being thus considered unnecessary.

"The next question is that of the mode of descent. Upon this point I had been[v] satisfied in my walk with you around the building. About [w]five feet and a half[w] from the casement in question there runs[x] a lightning-rod. From this rod it would have been impossible for any one to reach the window itself, to say nothing of entering it. I observed, however, that the shutters of the fourth story were of the peculiar kind called by Parisian carpenters *ferrades* — a kind rarely employed at the present day, but frequently seen upon very old mansions[y] at Lyons and Bourdeaux. They are in the form of an ordinary door, (a single, not a folding door) except that the upper[z] half is latticed or worked in open trellis — thus affording an excellent hold for the hands. In the present instance these shutters are fully three feet and a half broad. When we saw them from the rear of the house, they were both about half open — that is to say, they stood off at right angles from the wall. It is probable that the police, as well as myself, examined the back of the tenement; but, if so, in looking at these *ferrades* in the line of their breadth (as they must have done), they did not perceive this great breadth itself, or, at all events, failed to take it into due consideration. In fact, having once satisfied themselves that no egress could have been made in this quarter, they would naturally bestow here a very cursory examination. It was clear to me, however, that the shutter belonging to the window at the head of the bed, would, if swung fully [a]back to the wall,[a] reach to within two feet[b] of the lightning-rod. It was also evident that, by exertion of a very unusual degree of activity and courage, an entrance into the window,[c] from the rod, might have been thus effected. — By reaching to the distance of two[d] feet and a half (we now suppose the shutter

---

t   their *(A, B, C)*
u   closed by them) *(A, B, C)*
v   been <sufficiently> *(A)*
w . . . w <six feet> < ↑ eight ↓ >
↑ five feet and a half ↓ *(A)*
x   ran *(A, B)*

y   <houses> ↑ mansions ↓ *(A)*
z   lower *(A, B, C, D, F)*
a . . . a   open, *(A)*
b   two feet/four feet and a half *(A)*
c   window, <might have> *(A)*
d   <four> two *(A)*

open to its whole extent) a robber might have taken a firm grasp upon the trellis-work. Letting go, then, his hold upon the rod, placing his feet securely[e] against the wall, and springing boldly from it, he might have swung the shutter so as to close it, and, if we imagine the window open at the time, might even have swung himself into the room.

"I wish you to bear especially in mind that I have spoken of a *very* unusual degree of activity as requisite to success in so hazardous and so difficult a feat. It is my design to show you, first, that the thing might possibly have been accomplished: — but, secondly and *chiefly*, I wish to impress upon your understanding the *very extraordinary* — the almost præternatural character of that agility which could have accomplished it.

"You will say, no doubt, using the language of the law, that 'to make out my case,' I should rather undervalue, than insist upon a full estimation of the activity required in this matter. This may be the practice in law, but it is not the usage of reason. My ultimate object is only the truth. My immediate purpose is to lead you to place in juxta-position, that *very unusual* activity of which I have just spoken, with[f] that *very peculiar* shrill (or harsh) and *unequal* voice, about whose nationality[g] no two persons could be found to agree, and in whose utterance no syllabification[h] could be detected."

At these words a vague and half-formed conception of the meaning of Dupin flitted over my mind. I seemed to be upon the verge of comprehension, without power to comprehend — as men, at times, find themselves upon the brink of remembrance, without being able, in the end, to remember. My friend went on with his discourse.[i]

"You will see," he said, "that I have shifted the question from the mode of egress to that of ingress.[j] It was my design to suggest[k] the idea that both were effected in the same manner, at the same point. Let us now revert[l] to the interior of the room. Let us survey

---

e   firmly *(A, B)*
f   <and> ↑ with ↓ *(A)*
g   <language> ↑ nationality ↓ *(A)*
h   syllabi ↑ fi ↓ cation *(A)*
i   discourse. <for it had now assumed

all the character of such.> *(A)*
j   <ingress> *not clear* ingress. *(A)*
k   convey *(A, B, C, D, F)*
l   revert in fancy *(A, B, C)*

the appearances here. The drawers of the bureau, it is said, had been rifled, although many articles of apparel still remained within them. The conclusion here is absurd. It is a mere guess — a very silly one — and no more. How are we to know that the articles found in the drawers were not all these drawers had originally contained? Madame L'Espanaye and her daughter lived an exceedingly retired life — saw no company — seldom went out — had little use for numerous changes of habiliment. Those found were at least of as good quality as any likely to be possessed by these ladies. If a thief had taken any, why did he not take the best — why did he not take all? In a word, why did he abandon four thousand francs in gold to encumber himself with a bundle of linen? The gold *was* abandoned. Nearly the whole sum mentioned by Monsieur Mignaud, the banker, was discovered, in bags, upon the floor. I wish you, therefore, to discard from your thoughts the blundering idea of *motive,*[m] engendered in the brains of the police by that portion of the evidence which speaks of money delivered at the door of the house. Coincidences ten times as remarkable as this (the delivery of the money, and murder committed within three days upon the party receiving it), happen to[n] all of us every hour[o] of our lives, without attracting even[p] momentary notice. Coincidences, in general, are great stumbling-blocks in the way of that class of thinkers who have been educated to know nothing[q] of the theory of probabilities — that theory to which the most glorious objects of human research are indebted for the most glorious of illustration. In the present instance, had the gold been gone, the fact of its delivery three days before would have formed something more than a coincidence. It would have been corroborative of this idea of motive. But, under the real circumstances of the case, if we are to suppose gold the motive of this outrage, we must also imagine the perpetrator so vacillating an idiot as to have abandoned his gold and his motive together.

"Keeping now steadily in mind the points to which I have drawn your attention — that peculiar voice, that unusual agility,

---

m   *motive* <which has been> *(A)*
n   to each and *(A, B)*
o   <day> ↑ hour ↓ *(A)*

p   even a *(A, B, C)*
q   nothing and care less *(A, B, C)*

and that startling absence of motive in a murder[r] so singularly atrocious as this — let us glance at the butchery itself. Here is a woman strangled to death by manual strength, and thrust up a chimney, head downward.[s] Ordinary assassins employ no such modes of murder as this. Least of all, do they thus dispose of the murdered. In the manner of thrusting the corpse up the chimney, you will admit that there was something *excessively outré* — something altogether irreconcilable with our common notions of human action, even when we suppose the actors the most depraved of men. Think, too, how great[t] must have been[u] that strength which could have thrust the body *up* such an aperture so forcibly that the united vigor of several persons was found barely sufficient to drag it *down!*

[v]"Turn, now, to other indications of the employment of a vigor most marvellous. On the hearth[w] were thick tresses — very thick tresses — of grey human hair. These had been [x]torn out by the roots.[x] You are aware of the great force necessary in tearing thus from the head even twenty or thirty hairs together. You saw the locks in question as well as myself. Their roots (a hideous sight!) were clotted with fragments of the flesh of the scalp — sure token of the prodigious power[y] which had been exerted in uprooting perhaps half[z] a million of hairs at a time.[34] The throat of the old lady was not merely cut, but the head absolutely severed from the body: the instrument was a mere razor.[a] I wish you also to look[b] at the *brutal*[c] ferocity of these deeds. Of the bruises upon the body of Madame L'Espanaye I do not speak. Monsieur Dumas, and his worthy coadjutor Monsieur Etienne, have pronounced that they were inflicted by some obtuse instrument; and so far these gentlemen are very correct. The obtuse instrument was clearly the stone pavement in the yard, upon which the victim had fallen from the window which looked in upon the bed. This idea, however simple

---

r butchery *(A)*
s downwards. *(A)*
t how great/what *(A, B, C)*
u been the degree of *(A, B, C)*
v *Not a new paragraph in A*
w <sacking of the bedstead>
↑ hearth ↓ *(A)*
x . . . x *torn out by the roots. (A, B, C)*

y ↑ power ↓ *(A)*
z *Omitted (A, B, C)*
a *After this:* Here again we have evidence of that vastness of strength upon which I would fix your attention. *(A, B, C)*
b look, and to look steadily *(A, B, C)*
c brutal *(A)*

it may now seem, escaped the police for the same reason that the breadth of the shutters escaped them — because, by the affair of the nails, their perceptions had been hermetically sealed against the possibility of the windows having ever been opened at all.

"If now, in addition to all these things, you have properly reflected upon the odd disorder of the chamber, we have gone so far as to combine the ideas of ᵈan agility astounding, a strength superhuman,ᵈ a ferocity brutal, a butchery without motive, a *grotesquerie*ᵉ in horror absolutely alien from humanity, and a voice foreign in tone to the ears of menᶠ of many nations, and devoid of all distinct or intelligible syllabification. What result, then, has ensued? What impression have I made upon your fancy?"

I ᵍfelt a creeping of the fleshᵍ as Dupin asked me the question. "A madman," I said, "has done this deed — some raving maniac, escaped from a neighboring *Maison de Santé*."

"In some respects," he replied, "your idea is not irrelevant. But the voices of madmen, even in their wildest paroxysms, are never found to tally with that peculiar voice heard upon the stairs. Madmen are of some nation, and their language, however incoherent in its words, has always the coherence of syllabification. Besides, the hair of a madman is not suchʰ as I now hold in my hand. I disentangled this little tuft from the ⁱrigidly clutched fingersⁱ of Madame L'Espanaye. Tell me what you can make of it."

"Dupin!"ʲ I said, completely unnerved; "this hair is most unusual — this is no *human* hair."

"I have not asserted that it is,"ᵏ said he; "but, before we decideˡ this point, I wish you to glance atᵐ the little sketchⁿ I have here traced upon this paper. It is a *fac-simile*ᵒ drawing of what has been described in one portion of the testimony as 'dark bruises, and deep indentations of finger nails,'ᵖ upon the throat of Mademoiselle

---

d . . . d a strength superhuman, an agility astounding, *(A, B, C)*
e   grotesquerie *(A)*
f   man *(A) uncertain*
g . . . g   shuddered *(A, B, C)*
h   such hair *(A, B, C)*
i . . . i   among the tresses remaining upon the head *(A, B, C)*

j   "Dupin!"/"Good God," *(A, B, C)*
k   was," *(A, B, C)*
l   decide upon *(A, B)*
m   <your eyes> upon *(A)*
n   sketch which *(B, C)*
o   fac-simile *(A, B, C)*
p   finger-nails' *(A)*

L'Espanaye, and in another, (by Messrs.[q] Dumas and Etienne,) as a 'series of livid spots, evidently the impression of fingers.'

"You will perceive," continued my friend, spreading out the paper upon the table before us, "that[r] this drawing gives the idea of a firm and fixed hold. There is no *slipping* apparent. Each finger has retained — possibly until the death of the victim — the fearful grasp by which it originally imbedded itself. Attempt, now, to place all your fingers, at[s] the same time, in the respective[t] impressions as you see them."

I made the attempt in vain.

"We are possibly not giving this matter a fair trial," he said. "The paper is spread out upon a plane surface; but the human throat is cylindrical. Here is a billet of wood, the circumference of which is about that of the throat. Wrap the drawing around it, and try the experiment again."

I did so; but the difficulty was even more obvious than before. "This," I said, "is the mark of no human hand."

[u]"Read now," replied Dupin, "this[u] passage from Cuvier."[35]

It was a minute anatomical and generally descriptive account of the large fulvous[v] Ourang-Outang of the East Indian Islands. The gigantic stature, the prodigious strength and activity,[w] the wild ferocity, and the imitative propensities of these mammalia are sufficiently well known to all. I understood the full horrors[x] of the murder at once.

"The description of the digits," said I, as I made an end of reading, "is in exact accordance with this drawing. I see that no animal but an Ourang-Outang, of the species[y] here mentioned, could have impressed the indentations as you have traced them. This tuft of tawny[z] hair, too,[a] is identical in character with that of the beast of Cuvier. But I cannot possibly comprehend the particulars of this frightful mystery. Besides, there were *two*[b] voices

---

q	Messieurs *(A)*	w	↑ and activity, ↓ *(A)*
r	"you will perceive that *(A, B, C)*	x	horror *(A)*
s	at one and *(A, B, C)*	y	class *(A)*
t	*Omitted (A, B, C)*	z	yellow *(A, B, C)*
u . . . u	"Assuredly it is not," replied	a	hair, too,/hair *(A, B)*
	Dupin — "read now this *(A, B, C)*	b	two *(A, B)*
v	↑ fulvous ↓ <tawny> *(A)*		

heard in contention, and one of them was unquestionably the voice of a Frenchman."

"True; and you will remember an expression attributed almost unanimously, by the evidence, to this voice, — the expression, 'mon Dieu!' This, under the circumstances, has been justly characterized by one of the witnesses ᶜ(Montani, the confectioner,)ᶜ as an expression of remonstrance or expostulation. Upon these two words, therefore, I have mainly built my hopes of a full solution of the riddle. A Frenchman was cognizant of the murder. It is possible — ᵈindeed it isᵈ far more than probable — that he was innocent of all participation in the bloody transactions which took place. The Ourang-Outang may have escaped from him. He may have traced it to theᵉ chamber; ᶠbut, under the agitating circumstances which ensued, he could never have re-captured it. It is still at large.ᶠ I will not pursue these guesses — for I have no right to call them moreᵍ — since the shades of reflection upon which they are based are scarcely of sufficient depth to be appreciable by my ownʰ intellect, and since I could not pretend to make them intelligible to the understanding of another.ⁱ We will call them guesses then,ʲ and speak of them as such. If the Frenchman in question isᵏ indeed, as I suppose, innocent of this atrocity, this advertisement, which I left last night, upon our return home, at the office of 'Le Monde,' ˡ(a paper devoted to the shipping interest, and much soughtᵐ by sailors,)ˡ will bring him to our residence."

He handed me a paper, and I read thus:

CAUGHTⁿ — *In the Bois de Boulogne, early in the morning of the —— inst., (the morning of the murder,) a very large, tawnyᵒ Ourang-Outang of the Bornese species. The owner, (who is ascertained to be a sailor, belonging to a Maltese vessel,) may have the animal again, upon identifying it satisfactorily, and paying a few*

---

c . . . c *Omitted (A)*
d . . . d   it is indeed *(A)*
e   this *(A, B)*
f . . . f *Inserted in left-hand margin (A)*
g   more than <such> ↑ guesses ↓ *(A);* more than guesses *(B, C)*
h   my own/own *(C) misprint*
i   another than myself. *(A, B, C)*

j   ↑ then, ↓ *(A)*
k   be *(A, B)*
l . . . l *Inserted in right-hand margin (A)*
m   sought for *(B, C)*
n   <Found> ↑ CAUGHT ↓ *(A)*
o   *tawny-colored (A, B, C)*

charges arising from its capture and keeping. Call at No. —— , Rue
——,' Faubourg St. Germain — au troisième.[p] [36]

"How was it possible," I asked, "that you should know the man to be a sailor, and belonging to a Maltese vessel?"

"I do *not* know it," said Dupin. "I am not *sure* of it. Here, however, is a small piece of ribbon, which[q] from its form, and from its greasy appearance, [r]has evidently been[r] used in tying the hair in one of[s] those long *queues* of which sailors are so fond. Moreover, this knot is one which few besides sailors can tie, and is peculiar to the Maltese. I picked the ribbon up at the foot of the lightning-rod. It could not have belonged to either of the deceased. Now if, after all, I am wrong in my induction from this ribbon, that the Frenchman was a sailor belonging to a Maltese vessel, still I can have done no harm in saying[t] what I did in the advertisement. If I am in error, he will merely suppose that I have been misled by some circumstance into which he will not take the trouble to inquire. But if I am right, a great point is gained. Cognizant [u]although innocent of the murder,[u] the Frenchman will naturally hesitate about replying to the advertisement — about demanding the Ourang-Outang. He will reason thus: — 'I am innocent; I am poor; my Ourang-Outang is of great value — to one in my circumstances a fortune of itself — why should I lose it[v] through idle apprehensions of danger? Here it is, within my grasp. It was found in the Bois de Boulogne — at a vast distance from the scene of that butchery. How can it ever be suspected that a brute beast should have done the deed? The police are at fault — they have failed to procure the slightest clew.[w] Should they even trace the animal, it would be impossible to prove me cognizant of the murder, or to implicate me in guilt on account of that cognizance. Above all, *I am known.* The advertiser designates me as the possessor of the beast. I am not sure to what limit[x] his knowledge may extend. Should I avoid claiming a property of so great[y] value, which it is

---

p   *troisieme. (A, B); troisième. (C, D, E,*
F)
q   which has evidently, *(A, B, C)*
r . . . r   been *(A, B, C)*
s   ↑ one of ↓ *(A)*
t   stating *(A, B, C)*

u . . . u   of the murder, although not
guilty, *(A, B, C)*
v   <him> ↑ it ↓ *(A)*
w   clue. *(A)*
x   extent *(A)*
y   great a *(A, B, C)*

known that I possess, I will render ᶻthe animal at least,ᶻ liable to suspicion. It is not my policy to attract attention ᵃeither to myself orᵃ to the beast. I will answer the advertisement, get the Ourang-Outang, and keep itᵇ close until this matter has blown over.' "

At this moment we heard a step upon the stairs.

"Be ready," said Dupin, "with your pistols, but neither ᶜuse them nor showᶜ them until at a signal from myself."

The front door of the house had been left open, and the visiter had entered, without ringing,ᵈ and advanced several steps upon the staircase. Now, however, he seemed to hesitate. Presently we heard him descending. Dupin was moving quickly to the door, when we again heard him coming up. He did not turn back a second time, but stepped up with decision,ᵉ and rapped at the door of our chamber.

"Come in," said Dupin, in a cheerful and hearty tone.

A manᶠ entered. He was a sailor, evidently, — a tall, stout, and muscular-looking person,ᵍ with a certain dare-devil expression of countenance, not altogether unprepossessing. His face, greatly sunburnt, was more than half hidden byʰ whisker and *mustachio.*ⁱ He had with himʲ a huge oaken cudgel, but appeared to be otherwise unarmed. He bowed awkwardly, and bade us "good evening," in French accents, which, although somewhat Neufchatel-ish,³⁷ were still sufficiently indicative of a Parisian origin.

"Sit down, my friend,"ᵏ said Dupin. "I suppose you have called about the Ourang-Outang. Upon my word, I almost envy you the possession of him; a remarkably fine, and no doubt a very valuable animal. How old do you suppose him to be?"

The sailor drew a long breath, with the air of a man relieved of some intolerable burden, and then replied, in an assured tone:

"I have no way of telling — but he can't be more than four or five years old. Have you got him here?"

---

z . . . z <the animal> at least ↑ the animal ↓ *(A)*
a . . . a ↑ either to myself or ↓ *(A)*
b <him> ↑ it ↓ *(A)*
c . . . c show them nor use *(B)*
d ringing or rapping, *(A, B, C)*
e with decision,/quickly *(A, B)*

f A man/The visiter *(A, B, C)*
g person,/man *(A, B);* man, *(C)*
h by a world of *(A, B, C)*
i *mustache. (A)*
j *Omitted (A) a slip of the pen*
k freind," *(D, E, F) misprint*

"Oh no; we had no conveniences for keeping him here. He is at a livery stable in the Rue Dubourg, just by.[38] You can get him in the morning. Of course you are prepared to identify the property?"[l]

"To be sure I am, sir."

"I shall be sorry to part with him," said Dupin.

"I don't mean that you should be at all this trouble for nothing, sir," said the man. "Couldn't expect it. Am very willing to pay a reward for the finding of the animal — that is to say, any thing[m] in reason."

"Well," replied my friend, "that is all very fair, to be sure. Let me think! — what should I[n] have?[o] Oh! I will tell you. My reward shall be this. You shall give me all the information in your power about these murders[p] in the Rue Morgue."[q]

Dupin said the[r] last words in a very low tone, and very quietly. Just as quietly, too, he walked toward[s] the door, locked it, and put the key in his pocket. He then drew a pistol from [t]his bosom[t] and placed it, without the least flurry, upon the table.

The sailor's face flushed up [u]as if he were struggling with suffocation.[u] He started to his feet and grasped his cudgel; but the next moment he fell back into his seat, trembling violently,[v] and with the[w] countenance of[x] death itself. He spoke not a[y] word. I pitied him from the bottom of my heart.

"My friend," said Dupin, in a kind tone, "you are alarming yourself unnecessarily — you are indeed. We mean you no harm whatever. I pledge you the honor of a gentleman, and of a Frenchman, that we intend you no injury. I perfectly well know that you are innocent of the atrocities in the Rue Morgue.[z] It will not do, however, to deny that you are in some measure implicated in them.

---

l   property." *(A)*
m   thing/reward *(A, B)*
n   should I/reward ought I to *(A, B);* ought I to *(C)*
o   have. *(A)*
p   these murders/that affair *(A);* that affair of the murder *(B, C)*
q   <Trianon.">↑ Morgue." ↓ *(A)*
r   these *(A, B, C)*
s   towards *(A, B, C)*

t . . . t   <his coat pocket> ↑ his bosom ↓ *(A)*
u . . . u   with an ungovernable tide of crimson. *(A, B, C)*
v   convulsively, *(A, B)*
w   a *(A)*
x   as colorless as that of *(A)*
y   a single *(A, B)*
z   <Trianon.> ↑ Morgue. ↓ *(A)*

From what I have already said, you must know that I have had means of information about this matter — means of which you could never have dreamed. Now the thing stands thus. You have done nothing which you could have avoided — nothing, certainly, which renders you culpable. You were not even guilty of robbery, when you might have robbed with impunity. You have nothing to conceal. You have no reason for concealment. On the other hand, you are bound by every principle of honor to confess all[a] you know. An innocent man is now imprisoned, charged with that crime of which you can point out the perpetrator."

The sailor had recovered his presence of mind, in a great measure, while Dupin uttered[b] these words; but his original boldness of bearing was all gone.

"So help me God," said he, after a brief pause, "I *will* tell you all[c] I know about[d] this affair; — but I do not expect you to believe one half[e] I say — I would be a[f] fool indeed if I did. Still, I *am* innocent, and I will make a clean breast[g] if I die for it."

[h]What he stated was, in substance, this. He had lately made a voyage to the Indian Archipelago. A [i]party, of which he formed one,[i] landed at Borneo, and passed into the interior on[j] an excursion of pleasure. Himself and a companion had captured the Ourang-Outang. This companion dying, the animal fell into his own exclusive possession. After great trouble, occasioned by the intractable ferocity of his captive during the home voyage, he at length succeeded in lodging it[k] safely at his own residence in Paris, where, not to attract toward[l] himself the unpleasant curiosity of his neighbors, he kept it carefully secluded, until such time as it should recover from a wound in the foot, received from a splinter on board ship. His ultimate design was to sell it.

Returning home from some sailors'[m] frolic on the night, or

---

a all that *(A, B, C)*
b [utter]ed *(A) manuscript torn here and later*
c all that *(A, B, C)*
d [abo]ut *(A)*
e half that *(A, B, C)*
f would [be a] *(A)*
g [brea]st *(A)*
h *Before this:* I do not propose to follow the man in the circumstantial narrative which he now detailed. *(A, B, C)*
i...i party ↑ of which he formed one ↓ *(A)*
j upon *(A)*
k <him> ↑ it ↓ *(A)*
l towards *(A, B, C)*
m sailor's *(A)*

rather in the morning of the murder, he found the beast[n] occupying his own bed-room, into which it[o] had broken from a closet adjoining, where it[p] had been, as[q] was thought, securely confined. Razor[r] in hand, and fully lathered, it[s] was sitting before a looking-glass, attempting the operation of shaving, in which it[t] had no doubt previously watched its[u] master through the key-hole[v] of the closet. Terrified at the sight of so dangerous a weapon in the[w] possession of an animal so ferocious, and so well able to use it, the man, for some moments, was at a loss what to do. He had been accustomed, however, to quiet the creature, even in its fiercest moods, by the use of a[x] whip, and to this he now resorted. Upon sight of it, the Ourang-Outang sprang at once through the door of the chamber, down the stairs, and thence, through a window, unfortunately open, into the street.

The Frenchman followed in despair; the ape, razor still in hand, occasionally stopping to look back and gesticulate at its[y] pursuer, until the latter had nearly come up with it.[z] It[a] then again made off. In this manner the chase continued for a long time. The streets were profoundly quiet, as it was nearly three o'clock in the morning. In passing down an alley in the rear of the Rue Morgue,[b] the fugitive's attention was arrested by a light[c] gleaming from the open window of Madame L'Espanaye's chamber, in the fourth story of her house. Rushing to the building, it[d] perceived the lightning-rod, clambered up with inconceivable agility, grasped the shutter, which was thrown fully back against the wall, and, by its means, swung itself[e] directly upon the headboard[f] of the bed. The whole feat did not occupy a minute. The shutter was kicked open again by the Ourang-Outang[g] as it[h] entered the room.

---

n	the beast/his prisoner *(A, B, C)*	y	his *(A, B, C)*
o	he *(A, B, C)*	z	him. *(A, B, C)*
p	he *(A, B, C)*	a	He *(A, B, C)*
q	as it *(A, B, C)*	b	Trianon *(A)* *[Not changed]*
r	The beast, razor *(A, B, C)*	c	light (the only one apparent except
s	*Omitted (A, B, C)*		those of the town-lamps) *(A, B)*
t	he *(A, B, C)*	d	he *(A, B, C)*
u	his *(A, B, C)*	e	himself *(A, B, C)*
v	key hole *(A)*	f	head-board *(A, B, C)*
w	*Omitted (A)*	g	ape *(A)*
x	a strong wagoner's *(A, B)*	h	he *(A, B, C)*

The sailor, in the meantime, was both rejoiced and perplexed. He had strong hopes of now recapturing[i] the brute,[j] as it could scarcely escape from the trap into which it had ventured, except by the rod, where it[k] might be intercepted as it[l] came down. On the other hand, there was much cause for anxiety as to what it[m] might do in the house. This latter reflection urged the man [n]still to follow the fugitive.[n] A lightning-rod is ascended without difficulty, especially by a sailor; but, when he had arrived as high as the window, which lay far to his left, his career was stopped; the most that he could accomplish was to reach over so as to obtain a glimpse of the interior of the room. At this glimpse he nearly fell from his hold[o] through excess of horror. Now it was that those hideous shrieks arose upon the night, which had startled from slumber the inmates of the Rue Morgue.[p] Madame L'Espanaye and her daughter, habited in their night clothes,[q] had apparently been occupied in arranging some papers in the iron chest[r] already mentioned, which had been wheeled into the middle of the room. It was open, and its contents lay beside it on the floor. [s]The victims must have been sitting with their backs toward[s] the window; and, from[t] the time elapsing between the [u]ingress of the beast[v] and the screams,[u] it seems probable that it[w] was not immediately perceived. The flapping-to of the shutter[x] would naturally have been[y] attributed to the wind.

As the sailor looked in, the gigantic animal[z] had seized Madame L'Espanaye by the hair, (which was[a] loose, as she had been combing it,) and was flourishing the razor about her face, in imitation of the motions of a barber. The daughter lay prostrate and motionless; she had swooned. The screams and struggles of the old

---

i   re-capturing *(A)*
j   ape *(A, B, C)*
k   <his master could intercept him>
↑ it ↓ *(A)*
l   <he> ↑ it ↓ *(A)*
m   the brute *(A, B, C)*
n . . . n   <to ascend.> ↑ still to follow the fugitive. ↓ *(A)*
o   hold <in horror> *(A)*
p   Trianon. *(A)* [*Not changed*]
q   night-clothes, *(A)*
r   iron-chest *(A)*

s . . . s   Their backs must have been towards *(A, B, C)*
t   by *(A, B)*
u . . . u   screams and the ingress of the ape, *(A, B)*
v   ape *(C)*
w   he *(A, B, C)*
x   shutter they *(A, B)*
y   *Omitted (A, B)*
z   beast *(A, B, C)*
a   <had> was *(A)*

lady (during which the hair was torn from her head) had the effect of changing the probably pacific purposes of the Ourang-Outang into those of[b] wrath. With one determined sweep of its[c] muscular arm it[d] nearly severed her head from her body. The sight of blood inflamed[e] its[f] anger into phrenzy. Gnashing its[g] teeth, and flashing fire from its[h] eyes, it[i] flew upon the body of the girl, and imbedded its[j] fearful talons in her throat, retaining its[k] grasp until she expired. Its[l] wandering and wild glances fell[m] at this moment upon[n] the head of the bed, over which the face[o] of its[p] master, rigid with[q] horror, was[r] just discernible. The fury of the beast, who no doubt bore still in mind the dreaded whip, was instantly converted into fear.[s] Conscious of having deserved punishment, it[t] seemed desirous [u]of concealing[u] its[v] bloody deeds, and skipped about the chamber in an[w] agony of nervous agitation; throwing down and breaking the furniture as it[x] moved, and dragging the bed from the bedstead. In conclusion, it[y] seized first the corpse of the daughter, and thrust it up the chimney, as it was found; then that of the old lady, [z]which it immediately hurled through the window headlong.[z]

As the ape approached the casement[a] with its mutilated burden, the sailor shrank[b] aghast to the rod, and, rather gliding than clambering down it, hurried at once home — dreading the consequences of the butchery, and gladly abandoning, in his terror, all solicitude about the fate of the Ourang-Outang. The words heard by the party upon the staircase were the Frenchman's exclamations of

---

b of ungovernable *(A, B)*
c his *(A, B, C)*
d he *(A, B, C)*
e enflamed *(A)*
f his *(A, B, C)*
g his *(A, B, C)*
h his *(A, B, C)*
i he *(A, B, C)*
j his *(A, B, C)*
k his *(A, B, C)*
l His *(A, B, C)*
m <adverted> ↑ fell ↓ *(A)*
n <to> ↑ upon ↓ *(A)*
o the face/those *(A, B)*
p his *(A, B, C)*

q rigid with/glazed in *(A, B)*
r were *(A, B)*
s dread. *(A, B)*; terror. *(C)*
t he *(A, B, C)*
u . . . u to conceal *(B)*
v his *(A, B, C)*
w an apparent *(A, B, C)*
x he *(A, B, C)*
y he *(A, B, C)*
z . . . z with which he rushed to the window precipitating it immediately therefrom. *(A, B, C)*
a the casement/him *(A, B, C)*
b shrunk *(B, C)*

horror and affright, commingled with the fiendish jabberings of the brute.

I have scarcely anything to add. The Ourang-Outang must have escaped from the chamber, by the rod, just before the breaking of the door. It^c must have closed the window as it^d passed through it. It^e was subsequently caught by the owner himself, who obtained for it^f a very large sum at the *Jardin des Plantes*.[39] Le Bon was instantly released, upon our narration of the circumstances (with some comments from Dupin) at the *bureau* of the Prefect of^g Police. This functionary, however well disposed to my friend, could not altogether conceal his chagrin at the turn which affairs had taken, and was fain to indulge in a sarcasm or two, about^h the propriety of every person minding his own business.

"Let him talk," said Dupin, who had not thought it necessary to reply. "Let him discourse; it will ease his conscience. I am satisfied with having defeated him in his own castle. ^{i}Nevertheless, that he failed in the solution of this mystery, is by no means that matter for wonder which he supposes it; for,^{j} in truth, our friend the Prefect is somewhat too cunning to be profound.^{i} ^{k}In his wisdom is no *stamen*.^{k} It is all head and no body, like the pictures of the Goddess Laverna, — or, at best,^{l} all head and shoulders, like a codfish.[40] But he is a good creature^m after all. I like him especially for one master stroke^n of cant, by which he has attained his^o reputation for ingenuity.^{p} I mean the way^q he has '*de nier ce qui est, et d'expliquer ce qui n'est pas.*'" * [41]

*Rousseau — Nouvelle Heloise.

---

c   He *(A, B, C)*
d   he *(A, B, C)*
e   He *(A, B, C)*
f   him *(A, B, C)*
g   Prefect of/*chêf de (A); Prefet de (B)*
h   in regard to *(A, B, C)*
i...i   In truth, he is too cunning to be acute. *(A, B)*
j   it; for,/it. *Nil sapientiæ odiosius acumine nimio*, is, perhaps, the only line in the puerile and feeble Seneca not absolutely unmeaning; and *(C)*
k...k   There is no *stamen* in his

wisdom. *(A, B)*
l   least *(A, B)*
m   fellow, *(A, B)*
n   master-stroke *(A)*
o   that *(A, B, C)*
p   ingenuity./ingenuity which he possesses. *(A, B, C)*
q   way <which> *(A)*
Footnote first appears in C.
Dated at end: Philadelphia, March, 1841. *(B)*

THE MURDERS IN THE RUE MORGUE

Title: There is no Rue Morgue in Paris; the grim name is a stroke of genius, and came as an afterthought when the manuscript was almost finished. The earlier names, Trianon and Trianon-Bas, are also made up, but need no comment. Many of Poe's inaccuracies — a few of them flagrant errors — in details of his French setting have been criticized. Forgues, in his review cited above, noted some that would startle Parisian readers but conceded that Poe, in giving his details for verisimilitude, was writing primarily for Americans and that tales of the very unusual have frequently been laid in distant lands. Charles Baudelaire, sympathetic to Poe, did not let the "errors" bother him, but remarked in a footnote to his translation, "Do I need to point out that Edgar Poe never came to Paris?"

Motto: This is from *Urn-Burial*, chapter V, paragraph 3, and refers to the difficult questions which Suetonius, in his life of Tiberius (chapter LXX), says that the Emperor enjoyed putting to literary scholars. Poe had used the Browne quotation in "American Novel-Writing" in the Pittsburgh *Literary Examiner* for August 1839, and he used it again in a review of Wilmer's *Quacks of Helicon* in *Graham's* for August 1841, and in an article on "American Poetry" in the *Aristidean* for November 1845.

The first paragraph of the three early versions of the story, containing a reference to phrenology, was removed in 1845 — as was a reference in "The Black Cat." By that time Poe seems to have come to a disbelief in the "science of bumps." See my discussion at note 2 in "The Imp of the Perverse."

1. Compare Psalm 19:5, "...rejoiceth as a strong man to run a race."

2. Poe first italicized *acumen* in *Prose Romances* (1843) here and elsewhere throughout the tale, as if it had come to have some special significance for him.

3. Edmond Hoyle (1672–1769) wrote fundamental books on card playing which have been reprinted, revised, collected, adapted, and imitated extensively in the two centuries since his death. The Berg Collection at the New York Public Library has a small volume called *The Card Games of Hoyle, complete,* London, 1828 *(The Pocket Hoyle),* in which "Edgar A. Poe" is written, but it is not Poe's signature and the volume is classified as a forgery.

4. After his disastrous experience at the University, Poe seems never to have gambled. He played whist with his French Jesuit friends at Fordham; and with the children of neighbors there played Dr. Busby (a game resembling Old Maid) according to an interview of Mrs. Minnie Phelps, reprinted in the New York *Commercial Advertiser,* June 18, 1897.

5. Compare *Politian,* XI, 33, "these tottering arcades"; and "The Man of the Crowd, " at n. 16.

6. The turning of day into night is said to have been a custom of the French historian François-Eudes de Mézeray (1610–1683) — see *The Percy Anecdotes* (New York, 1832), p. 382. It was also reported of Edward Young, author of *Night Thoughts,* as a student at Oxford, according to a reminiscence of Dr. Ridley, cited in Mitford's "Life" in the Aldine edition of *The Poetical Works of*

Edward Young (1844), I, xii. The notion that Poe himself did something of the kind has been printed by irresponsible persons.

7. Compare *Politian*, VI, 21, "Give not thy soul to dreams"; and "The Colloquy of Monos and Una": "And now it was . . . that we wrapped our spirits, daily, in dreams."

8. In *Stanley* (1838), II, 237–242, by "William Landor" (Horace Binney Wallace), Poe probably found the story that Momus, god of laughter, reproached Vulcan for not making his human automata with windows in their bosoms. (J. J. Cohane contributed this note.) The classical source is Lucian, *Hermotimus,* section 20.

9. "Bi-Part Soul" was earlier mentioned in "Lionizing," and the idea appears in "The Fall of the House of Usher" and "William Wilson."

10. The Palais Royal, built for Richelieu in 1629–1634 and subsequently a residence of the Orléans princes, is a hollow rectangle with long, plain outside walls, but it encloses a park with gardens and galleries. By 1832, when N. P. Willis was in Paris, it had become "a public haunt . . . of pleasure and merchandise." See Willis, *Pencillings by the Way,* letter IX.

11. The Théâtre des Variétés is factual, a place of light entertainment.

12. Chantilly bears the name of a city famous for lace, hence appropriate to one of delicate or diminutive stature.

13. Rue St. Denis, like rue Montmartre, rue Richelieu, and rue St. Roch, is an actual street name, borrowed with little regard for geography.

14. In 1833 Poe quoted Crébillon's *Xerxes* (1714) in his motto for "Epimanes." For other references to Crébillon see the last note to "The Purloined Letter."

15. "Mender of bad soles" is a pun from the cobbler in Shakespeare's *Julius Caesar*, I, i, 15. *Et id genus omne* means "and all that sort of thing."

16. Dr. John Pringle Nichol (1804–1859), Regius Professor of astronomy at Glasgow University, published in 1837 *Views of the Architecture of the Heavens in a Series of Letters to a Lady,* an attractively written popular presentation of the findings and theories of current astronomy as stimulated by and growing out of the discoveries of Sir William Herschel, his son John, and their contemporaries. Nichol quotes frequently from both Herschels, discusses Sir William's work on the Orion nebula, and describes the nebular hypothesis. Nichol's book went through a number of editions, one of them issued in New York in 1840. Apparently Poe was greatly impressed by it. He cites it frequently in *Eureka*. Nichol lectured in the United States in 1848–49.

17. Thomas Hobbes, *Leviathan* (1651), I, 3, says: "This train of thoughts, or mental discourse, is of two sorts. The first is unguided, without design, and inconstant . . . And yet in the wide ranging of the mind, a man may oft times perceive the way of it, and the dependence of one thought upon another. For in a discourse of our present civil war, what could seem more impertinent than to ask, (as one did,) what was the value of a Roman penny? Yet the coherence to me was manifest enough. For the thought of the war introduced the thought of

the delivering up the King to his enemies. The thought of that brought in the thought of the delivering up of Christ, and that again the thought of the thirty pence, which was the price of that treason."

18. Poe thought the voluminous poet Lamartine a bore, and slyly gave his name to a little alley.

19. For Poe's interest in street paving, see his essay on that subject, published in the *Broadway Journal*, April 19, 1845.

20. Epicurus held that "everything, whether material or spiritual, is made out of atoms" (George Sarton, *History of Science*, I, 1952, p. 590.) In *Eureka*, discussing the cosmogony of Laplace, Poe said: "His original idea seems to have been a compound of the true Epicurean atoms with the false nebulae of his contemporaries, and thus his theory presents us with the singular anomaly of absolute truth deduced, as a mathematical result, from a hybrid datum of ancient imagination intertangled with modern inacumen."

21. The Orion nebula, discovered in 1610, became the starting point in 1774 for the remarkable survey of the heavens by William Herschel and his son John, so frequently quoted by Dr. Nichol (see note 16 above).

22. The quotation means "the first letter has lost its original sound" and is from a story in Ovid's *Fasti*, Book V, lines 493–536, concerning the birth of the "Bœotian Orion" which accounts for the early spelling "Urion."

23. "Métal d'Alger" is an inexpensive alloy of lead, tin, and antimony, used in place of silver. A Napoleon is a twenty-franc gold piece.

24. The Latin form of the interjection, *horribile dictu,* is a commonplace, found in Florus, *Epitome* I, chapter XI (section 16). For Mr. Horribile Dictu see "The Folio Club," above.

25. The body of Mademoiselle L'Espanaye was found with the head downwards because Poe wanted to make it obvious that she did not herself attempt to escape by climbing into the chimney.

26. The names of the witnesses are assigned supposedly as typical of their nationalities, but some may have had a special meaning for Poe. As a little boy he went to the school of the Misses Dubourg at 146 Sloane Street, Chelsea, in London – and he names a laundress for them. Pierre Moreau's family name is that of the president of the Electors of Paris who received the keys of the Bastille at the hands of the mob, governed Paris for three days, and "persuaded the Electors to place Lafayette in command of the National Guard." He was a publisher and bookseller in Philadelphia, 1794–1798, but then returned to France to avoid deportation under the Alien Act *(DAB)*. The silversmith has the surname of the notorious highwayman Claude Duval (1643–1670), which is also that of Peter S. Duval, Philadelphia lithographer, who made the plates for *The Conchologist's First Book* (see Mabbott I, 499, 548, 549). My student, Joan Bahrs, has pointed out that Le Bon, the innocent man accused, is "the good." The tailor's name echoes that of William Byrd, founder of an aristocratic family, whose tobacco warehouse on the James became the nucleus of Richmond, Virginia; Robert Montgomery Bird was a well-known Philadelphia writer in Poe's

day. Paul Dumas is presumably named for Alexandre Dumas, novelist. Nothing appropriate about Musèt (whose name bears an unorthodox accent), Odenheimer, Mignaud, Garcio (Garcia is the common Spanish name), Montani, or Etienne, has been propounded. Mignaud's address, rue Deloraine, is fictional.

27. In Molière's *Bourgeois Gentilhomme,* Act I, Scene ii, the protagonist calls for his *robe de chambre,* the better to enjoy chamber music.

28. François-Eugène Vidocq (1775–1857), head of the detective service under Napoleon I and later, utilized ex-convicts like himself in suppressing crime. Whether he wrote any of the books ascribed to him is doubtful. [A series of stories, "Unpublished Passages in the Life of Vidocq," ascribed to "J. M. B.," appeared in *Burton's* in 1838 and 1839. One of these was "Marie Laurent," mentioned in the introduction above; another one, "Doctor Arsac," October 1838, is proposed as another source for Poe's tale by I. V. K. Ousby in *Poe Studies,* December 1972.]

29. Compare "Letter to Mr. ——— " introductory to *Poems* (1831): "As regards the greater truths, men oftener err by seeking them at the bottom than at the top; the depth lies in the huge abysses where wisdom is sought -- not in the palpable palaces where she is found. The ancients were not always right in hiding the goddess in a well." The reference is to the well of Democritus, referred to also in the motto for "A Descent into the Maelström" and in "Ligeia" at note 10.

30. On seeing something better by not looking at it too directly, compare "Al Aaraaf," II, 72–74, "ponder/With half closing eyes/On the stars" and "The Island of the Fay" (1841), "mused with half-shut eyes."

One paragraph removed from the passage quoted above in "Letter to Mr. ——— " (1831), Poe says (of Coleridge): "He goes wrong by reason of his very profundity, and of his error we have a natural type in the contemplation of a star. He who regards it directly and intensely sees, it is true, the star, but it is the star without a ray — while he who surveys it less inquisitively is conscious of all for which the star is useful to us below — its brilliancy and its beauty." In Chapter III of *The Narrative of Arthur Gordon Pym,* Poe speaks of making a white slip of paper in some measure perceptible "by surveying it slightly askance." In "Hans Pfaall" (*SLM,* February 1835, and *Tales,* 1840) in a passage later canceled, Poe first juxtaposes the well, or abyss, and star references: "I believed, and still do believe, that truth, is frequently, of its own essence, superficial, and that, in many cases, the depth lies more in the abysses where we seek her, than in the actual situations wherein she may be found. Nature herself seems to afford me corroboration of these ideas. In the contemplation of the heavenly bodies it struck me very forcibly that I could not distinguish a star with nearly as much precision, when I gazed upon it with, earnest, direct and undeviating attention, as when I suffered my eye only to glance in its vicinity alone." In a review of Alexander Slidell's *The American in England* (*SLM,* February 1836), he says, "The old adage about 'Truth in a well...' should be swallowed *cum grano salis* at times," and goes on in the same paragraph to add, "a star may be seen more distinctly in a sidelong survey."

Poe's assertion of the effectiveness of indirect vision in certain cases was supported by the observations of scientists. In a paper by John F. W. Herschel and James South, read before the Royal Society of London on January 15, 1824, is the following: "A rather singular method of obtaining a view, and even a rough measure of the angles of stars of the last degree of faintness, has often been resorted to, viz. to direct the eye to another part of the field. In this way, a faint star in the neighbourhood of a large one, will often become very conspicuous, so as to bear a certain illumination, which will yet *totally disappear*, as if suddenly blotted out, when the eye is turned full upon it, and so on, appearing and disappearing alternately, as often as we please. The small companion of 23 (h) Ursæ Majoris, is a remarkable instance ... The lateral portions of the retina, less fatigued by strong lights, and less exhausted by perpetual attention, are probably more sensible to faint impressions than the central ones, which may serve to account for this phænomenon." (See *Philosophical Transactions* for 1824, part III, pp. 15–16, published in 1825.) Sir David Brewster quoted this passage in his *Treatise on Optics* (see first American edition, Philadelphia, 1833, p. 249), but he had alluded to the phenomenon earlier, as "observed by several astronomers, both with regard to faint stars and to the satellites of Saturn" in his *Optics* (Edinburgh, 1828), p. 43, and he mentioned it again in his *Letters on Natural Magic* (1832), pp. 24–25. Upon the last book Poe leaned heavily for his "Maelzel's Chess-Player." See W. K. Wimsatt, Jr., "Poe and the Chess Automaton" *(AL,* May 1939).

31. It is perhaps significant that the Prefect in Poe's stories of Dupin is called G – – , for Henri-Joseph Gisquet was prefect of police in Paris, 1831–1836. This fact was confirmed for me by Professor Beatrice F. Hyslop who consulted the Archives of the Prefecture of the Police in Paris. Baudelaire in 1865 identified G –– as Gisquet in a footnote to "The Mystery of Marie Roget." E. L. Didier (who misspelled the name "Grisquet") noticed his death in February 1866 as that of Poe's original; see *The Poe Cult* (1909), p. 37. Poe may well have heard of Gisquet from his friend James Pedder, an Englishman who had resided for some time in France. Since he and Poe are known to have been much together for several years in Philadelphia, we must not assume that Poe learned all he knew of the French from printed sources.

32. The meaning here of the French phrase is "I humored him cautiously."

33. In comparing *outré* and *ordinary* crimes in "The Mystery of Marie Rogêt" (at note 41) Dupin repeats this idea in almost the same language. Compare Poe's elaboration of this sentence in *Eureka*, where in a footnote he cited "The Murders in the Rue Morgue": "Now, I have elsewhere observed that it is by just such difficulties as the one now in question – such roughnesses – such peculiarities – such protuberances above the plane of the ordinary – that Reason feels her way, if at all, in the search for the True."

34. Vernon Rendall told me a human head has only about 60,000 hairs.

35. Georges Cuvier (1769–1832), the great French natural historian, in his famous *Règne Animal* (1817), I, 102, placed the Orang immediately after Man. Dupin, in character, naturally named the French work. But Poe himself read the following from Thomas Wyatt's compilation, *A Synopsis of Natural History* ...

Arranged as a Text Book for Schools (Philadelphia, 1839), page 31, under Mammalia, Order II, Quadrumans, Family I, Simia; Tribe I:

 Genus I. Pithecus, Geoff. *Ourangs.* No tail, nor callosities, nor cheek-pouches. Of all animals the ourang is considered as approaching most nearly to man in the form of his head, height of forehead and volume of brain . . . The body of the Ourang-Outang is covered with coarse red hair, the face bluish, and the hinder thumbs very short compared with the toes. (Cochin-China, Malacca, Borneo.)

Poe "edited" Wyatt's book, as he revealed in a review in *Burton's,* July 1839, and made use of it in "The Gold-Bug," "The Tell-Tale Heart," "The Thousand-and-Second Tale," and "The Sphinx." Poe has something on orangs ("men of the forest") again in "The System of Doctor Tarr and Professor Fether," and in "Hop-Frog."

36. "Au troisième" means literally "on the third" but was used for what we call the fourth floor. In "The Purloined Letter" Poe gives the full address, no. 33, rue Dunôt.

37. "Neufchatel-ish" means uncouth, countrified. The people of Neufchâtel are Protestants, somewhat cut off from Catholic France, and speak French as an acquired language, which remains still enmeshed in the local dialect. This note is by courtesy of Professor Jean-Albert Bédé.

38. No such street as the rue Dubourg existed in Paris in 1841. See *Galignani's New Paris Guide* dated that year.

39. The Jardin des Plantes, or Botanical Garden, includes the famous Paris zoological collection.

40. Laverna was the Roman goddess of thefts, represented as a head without a body, mentioned by Horace, *Epistolae,* I, xvi, 60. There is another reference to her in "Fifty Suggestions," Number 31 (*Graham's,* June 1849). The Latin sentence listed in the variants was inserted in *Prose Romances* (1843) but omitted in the later versions. Poe subsequently used it as the motto for "The Purloined Letter"; see my note on it there.

41. "To deny what is, and explain what is not." Poe used the quotation again in "Fifty Suggestions," number 28 (*Graham's,* June 1849). It comes from the second footnote to Letter xi in Part VI of Rousseau's *La Nouvelle Héloïse.* The note concerns Plato's explanation of ghostly apparitions and concludes with the comment, "C'est une manie commune aux philosophes de tous les âges de nier ce qui est et d'expliquer ce qui n'est pas."

A DESCENT INTO THE MAELSTRÖM

This story, first published in *Graham's Magazine* for May 1841, is deservedly one of the most popular of Poe's tales. We all love stories of hairbreadth escapes, and this, says Woodberry (*Life,*

A DESCENT INTO THE MAELSTRÖM

I, 306), "is to be classed with the 'MS. Found in a Bottle,' and is the best of its kind." It is also an example of Poe's creative craftsmanship in taking certain elements from four specific sources that have been clearly identified and fusing them with details of his own imagining into "a unified production of great power," * further improved by the cutting and polishing he gave it in two revisions.

The reviewer of "Poe's Tales" in the *Aristidean* for October 1845, writing after discussions with Poe, said the story was "noted for the boldness of its subject — a subject never dreamed of before"; but only the solution was novel.† Poe's chief inspiration — the plot together with a challenge — came undoubtedly from the story in *Fraser's Magazine* of September 1834 called "The Maelstrom: a Fragment," by Edward Wilson Landor, who subsequently published *Adventures in the North of Europe* (2 vols., London, 1836) and *Lofoden, or, The Exiles of Norway* (London, 1849). The tale in *Fraser's* is long and diffuse, with several characters and much pious conversation, but it tells of a ship that was destroyed in a whirlpool off the coast of Norway. The hero refers to spectators observing the disaster from Mount Helseggen, and his own sensation as he went down in the pool. But he fainted, and when he found himself safe on land — the only survivor — he did not know how he had escaped destruction. It was characteristic of Poe, in response to the magazinist's failure, to devise the machinery for the rescue.

---

* The quoted words are those of W. T. Bandy, in *American Literature,* January 1953, pp. 534–536, where he points out that "Le Maelstrom" in *Le Magasin Universel,* April 1836, discussed as a clue to the source of Poe's plot by Arlin Turner (see below), is actually an adaptation of a story published two years before in *Fraser's Magazine.*

† The discovery of Poe's major sources may be traced through W. T. Bandy's article, cited above; Arlin Turner's important paper in the *Journal of English and Germanic Philology,* July 1947, which synopsizes the earlier literature and demonstrates — mentioning specific titles — that Poe used details from at least four different sources; and the Stedman-Woodberry edition of Poe's *Works* (volume IV, 1894, pp. 290–291), which points out both that Poe relied much more extensively on the article "Maelstrom" in the *Encyclopaedia Britannica* (3rd–6th editions, 1797–1836) than his citation for one brief quotation indicates, and that the *Britannica* article itself was lifted almost verbatim, without acknowledgment, from *The Natural History of Norway* (London, 1755), a translation from the Danish original (1752–53) of Erich Pontoppidan, Bishop of Bergen.

For details, he went to the *Encyclopaedia Britannica,* and possibly to *The Mariner's Chronicle* (New Haven: Durrie and Peck, 1834), a one-volume compilation of "narratives of the most remarkable disasters at sea ... and other extraordinary and interesting occurrences." This volume, which was stereotyped and often reprinted, reproduced (pp. 439–440) the *Britannica* article "Maelstrom" in its entirety, without acknowledgment, and appended as a final paragraph (p. 441) a description by "an American captain" of his first-hand observation of "this celebrated phenomenon." Poe used some of the American captain's material, though whether he took it from *The Mariner's Chronicle,* or from a later newspaper article, or indeed from some earlier publication, has not been determined.‡ His greatest debt is to the *Britannica,* where he found the articles "Maelstrom," "Norway," and "Whirlpool." He quotes only the first directly, but the last probably suggested to him his hero's means of preservation. The method seems to have been Poe's own invention, as were some other vivid bits of description — usually erroneous — that he added to his recognizable borrowings.§

Poe's story was completed very shortly before its publication, probably in March or April 1841.* On July 12 of that year he wrote to J. E. Snodgrass: "You flatter me about the 'Maelström.' It was finished in a hurry, and therefore its conclusion is imperfect."

‡ Killis Campbell (*Mind of Poe,* p. 166) suggested as one of Poe's possible sources "an account of the Drontheim Whirlpool in *Alexander's Weekly Messenger,* October 10, 1838," which, as Arlin Turner observed, Poe might have seen earlier in *The Mariner's Chronicle* (New Haven, 1834). The same material was found by my correspondent George Wetzel in the Baltimore *Sun* of September 13, 1838, where, like the article in Alexander's paper, it was part of a letter "from a gentleman in Florida to Hon. A. B. Woodward, Judge of Middle Florida." Since Judge Woodward — author among other things of *A System of Universal Science* (1816) — had been dead since 1827, the letter must have been a number of years old, and like most of the narratives collected in *The Mariner's Chronicle* may well have been published several times before.

§ In *Natural History,* October 1935, Frank C. Jordan called attention to "strange ways of the moon" and other unorthodox phenomena in Poe's tale. Poe himself, in "A Reviewer Reviewed," pointed out that the manner in which the hero is saved is as imaginary as the hero, and as the reference to Archimedes.

* Some scholars formerly assigned Poe's story to a much earlier date, chiefly on the unreliable testimony of J. H. B. Latrobe, who many years afterward said it had been one of the stories submitted in the *Visiter* contest of 1833 (see his remarks in Sara Sigourney Rice, *Poe, A Memorial Volume,* 1877, p. 59). Jay B. Hubbell, in

A DESCENT INTO THE MAELSTRÖM

TEXTS

(A) Graham's Magazine for May 1841 (18:235–241); *(B) Tales* (1845), pages 83–99; *(C)* J. Lorimer Graham copy of *Tales* with manuscript revisions about 1849; *(D) Works* (1850), I, 161–177. PHANTASY-PIECES, title only.

The J. Lorimer Graham copy of the *Tales (C)* with Poe's manuscript changes is followed. The 1850 edition of *Works (D)* has no changes from *Tales* (1845) *(B)*. The text of the Virginia edition (1902), ostensibly following the Lorimer Graham copy of the 1845 volume, omits Poe's three manuscript changes in the last paragraph, and for some reason adopts nine of the ten changes (obviously misprints) in later issues of Griswold. These are not recorded in Stewart's variants.

Reprints

An annual called *The Irving Offering, a Token of Affection for 1851* has a reprint of the earliest version *(A)* at pages 101–127, pretty surely unauthorized but generally sought by collectors as the first edition in book form of that version of the tale.

Boston Museum, May 26, 1849, from *Graham's Magazine*.

Translations

Revue britannique, September 1846, signed O.N.; *La Démocratie pacifique*, September 24, 25, 1847, by Isabelle Meunier.

A DESCENT INTO THE MAELSTRÖM. [*C*]

The ways of God in Nature, as in Providence, are not as *our* ways; nor are the models that we frame any way commensurate to the vastness, profundity, and unsearchableness of His works, *which·have a depth in them greater than the well of Democritus.*

Joseph Glanville.

We had now reached the summit of the loftiest crag. For some minutes the old man seemed too much exhausted to speak.

"Not long ago," said he at length, "and I could have guided you on this route as well as the youngest of my sons; but, about three years past, there happened to me an event such as never happened before to mortal man — or at least such as no man ever survived to tell of — and the six hours of deadly terror which I then

---

PMLA, September 1954, recorded that Latrobe's reminiscences of Poe in the New York *Old Guard*, June 1866, differed essentially from what he told later, and William H. Graveley, Jr., showed me an unprinted study in which he gave further instances of Latrobe's inaccuracies in matters of detail. It is likely that the septuagenarian Latrobe was confused by his memory of "MS. Found in a Bottle."

Motto: *Omitted (A)*

endured have broken me up body and soul. You suppose me a *very old man* — but I am not. It took less than a single day to change these hairs from a jetty black to white,[1] to weaken my limbs, and to unstring my nerves, so that I tremble at the least exertion, and am frightened at a shadow. Do you know I can scarcely look over this little cliff without getting giddy?"

The "little cliff," upon whose edge he had so carelessly thrown himself down to rest that the weightier portion of his body hung over it, while he was only kept from falling by the tenure of his elbow on its extreme and slippery edge — this "little cliff" arose, a sheer unobstructed precipice of black shining rock, some fifteen or sixteen hundred feet from the world of crags beneath us. Nothing[a] would have tempted me to within half a dozen yards of its brink. In truth so deeply was I excited by the perilous position of my companion, that I fell at full length upon the ground, clung to the shrubs around me, and dared not even glance upward at the sky — while I struggled in vain to divest myself of the idea that the very foundations of the mountain were in danger from the fury of the winds. It was long before I could reason myself into sufficient courage to sit up and look out into the distance.[2]

"You must get over these fancies," said the guide, "for I have brought you here that you might have the best possible view of the scene of that event I mentioned — and to tell you the whole story with the spot just under your eye."

"We are now," he continued, in that particularizing manner which distinguished him — "we are now close upon the Norwegian coast — in the sixty-eighth degree of latitude — in the great province of Nordland — and in the dreary district of Lofoden. The mountain upon whose top we sit is Helseggen, the Cloudy. Now raise yourself up a little higher — hold on to the grass if you feel giddy — so — and look out, beyond the belt of vapor beneath us, into the sea."

I looked dizzily, and beheld a wide expanse of ocean, whose waters wore so inky a hue as to bring at once to my mind the Nubian geographer's account of the *Mare Tenebrarum*.[3] A panorama

---

a   No consideration (*A*)

more deplorably desolate no human imagination can conceive. To the right and left, as far as the eye could reach, there lay out-stretched, like ramparts of the world, lines of horridly black and beetling cliff, whose character of[b] gloom was but the more forcibly illustrated by the surf which reared high up against it its white and ghastly crest, howling and shrieking for ever. Just opposite the promontory upon whose apex we were placed, and at a[c] distance of some five or six miles out at sea, there was visible a small, bleak-looking island; or, more properly, its position was discernible through the wilderness of surge in which it was enveloped. About two miles nearer the land, arose another of smaller size, hideously craggy and barren, and encompassed at various intervals by a cluster of dark rocks.

The appearance of the ocean, in the space between the more distant island and the shore, had something very unusual about it. Although, at the time, so strong a gale was blowing landward that a brig in the remote offing lay to under a double-reefed trysail, and constantly plunged her whole hull out of sight, still there was here nothing like a regular swell, but only a short, quick, angry cross dashing of water in every direction — as well in the teeth of the wind as otherwise. Of foam there was little except in the immediate vicinity of the rocks.

"The island in the distance," resumed the old man, "is called by the Norwegians Vurrgh. The one midway is Moskoe. That a mile to the northward is Ambaaren. Yonder are Iflesen, Hoeyholm, Kieldholm, Suarven, and Buckholm. Farther off — between Moskoe and Vurrgh — are Otterholm, Flimen, Sandflesen, and Skarholm.[d] These are the true names of the places — [4] but why it has been thought necessary to name them at all, is more than either you or I can understand. Do you hear any thing? Do you see any change in the water?"

We had now been about ten minutes upon the top of Helseg-

---

b   of irredeemable *(A)*
c   the *(A)*
d   *Some of the names are variously spelled but four have been emended, since the printed versions show erroneous forms. Three may be misprints from*

Poe's handwriting, namely:
Iflesen/Islesen, Hoeyholm/Hotholm, Kieldholm/Keildhelm. *In the case of* Skarholm/Stockholm *the error was in Poe's source. See notes on this word and* Vurrgh.

gen, to which we had ascended from the interior of Lofoden, so that we had caught no glimpse of the sea until it had burst upon us from the summit. As the old man spoke, I became aware of a loud and gradually increasing sound, like the moaning of a vast herd of buffaloes upon an American prairie;[5] and at the same moment I perceived that what seamen term the *chopping* character of the ocean beneath us[d'] was rapidly changing into a current which set to the eastward. Even while I gazed, this current acquired a monstrous velocity. Each moment added to its speed — to its headlong impetuosity. In five minutes the whole sea, as far as Vurrgh, was lashed into ungovernable fury; but it was between Moskoe and the coast that the main uproar held its sway. Here the vast bed of the waters, seamed and scarred into a thousand conflicting channels, burst suddenly into phrensied convulsion — heaving, boiling, hissing — gyrating in gigantic and innumerable vortices, and all whirling and plunging on to the eastward with a rapidity which water never elsewhere assumes except in precipitous descents.[6]

In a few minutes more, there came over the scene another radical alteration. The general surface grew somewhat more smooth, and the whirlpools, one by one, disappeared, while prodigious streaks of foam became apparent where none had been seen before. These streaks, at length, spreading out to a great distance, and entering into combination, took unto themselves the gyratory motion of the subsided vortices, and seemed to form the germ of another more vast. Suddenly — very suddenly — this assumed a distinct and definite existence, in a circle of more than half a mile[e] in diameter. The edge of the whirl was represented by a broad belt of gleaming spray; but no particle of this slipped into the mouth of the terrific funnel, whose interior, as far as the eye could fathom it, was a smooth, shining, and jet-black wall of water, inclined to the horizon at an angle of some forty-five degrees, speeding dizzily round and round with a swaying and sweltering motion, and sending forth to the winds an appalling voice, half shriek, half roar, such as not even the mighty cataract of Niagara ever lifts up in its agony to Heaven.

The mountain trembled to its very base, and the rock rocked.

---

d' us, (B, C, D) *corrected from A*   e half a mile/a mile (A, B, D)

I threw myself upon my face, and clung to the scant herbage in an excess of nervous agitation.

"This," said I at length, to the old man — "this *can* be nothing else than the great whirlpool of the Maelström."

"So it is sometimes termed," said he. "We Norwegians call it the Moskoe-ström, from the island of Moskoe in the midway."

The ordinary accounts of this vortex had by no means prepared me for what I saw. That of Jonas Ramus, which is perhaps the most circumstantial of any, cannot impart the faintest conception either of the magnificence, or of the horror of the scene — or of the wild bewildering sense of *the novel* which confounds the beholder. I am not sure from what point of view the writer in question surveyed it, nor at what time; but it could neither have been from the summit of Helseggen, nor during a storm. There are some passages of his description, nevertheless, which may be quoted for their details, although their effect is exceedingly feeble in conveying an impression of the spectacle.[7]

"Between Lofoden and Moskoe," he says, "the depth of the water is between thirty-six and forty fathoms; but on the other side, toward Ver (Vurrgh) this depth decreases so as not to afford a convenient passage for a vessel, without the risk of splitting on the rocks, which happens even in the calmest weather. When it is flood, the stream runs up the country between Lofoden and Moskoe with a boisterous rapidity; but the roar of its impetuous ebb to the sea is scarce equalled by the loudest and most dreadful cataracts; the noise being heard several leagues off, and the vortices or pits are of such an extent and depth, that if a ship comes within its attraction, it is inevitably absorbed and carried down to the bottom, and there beat to pieces against the rocks; and when the water relaxes, the fragments thereof are thrown up again. But these intervals of tranquillity are only at the turn of the ebb and flood, and in calm weather, and last but a quarter of an hour, its violence gradually returning. When the stream is most boisterous, and its fury heightened by a storm, it is dangerous to come within a Norway mile of it.[8] Boats, yachts, and ships have been carried away by not guarding against it before they were within its reach. It likewise happens frequently, that whales come too near the stream, and are overpowered by its violence; and then it is impossible to describe their howlings and bellowings in their fruitless struggles to disengage themselves. A bear once, attempting to swim from Lofoden to Moskoe, was caught by the stream and borne down, while he roared terribly, so as to be heard on shore. Large stocks of firs and pine trees, after being absorbed by the current, rise again broken and torn to such a degree as if bristles grew upon them. This plainly shows the bottom to consist of craggy rocks, among which they are whirled to and fro. This stream is regulated by the flux and reflux of the sea — it being constantly high and low water every six hours. In the year 1645, early in the morning of Sexagesima Sunday,[9] it raged with such noise and impetuosity that the very stones of the houses on the coast fell to the ground."

In regard to the depth of the water, I could not see how this could have been ascertained at all in the immediate vicinity of the vortex. The "forty fathoms" must have reference only to portions of the channel close upon the shore either of Moskoe or Lofoden. The depth in the centre of the Moskoe-ström must be immeasurably greater; and no better proof of this fact is necessary than can be obtained from even the sidelong glance into the abyss of the whirl which may be had from the highest crag of Helseggen. Looking down from this pinnacle upon the howling Phlegethon[10] below, I could not help smiling at the simplicity with which the honest Jonas Ramus records, as a matter difficult of belief, the anecdotes of the whales and the bears; for it appeared to me, in fact, a self-evident thing, that the largest ship of the line in existence, coming within the influence of that deadly attraction, could resist it as little as a feather the hurricane, and must disappear bodily and at once.

The attempts to account for the phenomenon — some of which, I remember, seemed to me sufficiently plausible in perusal — now wore a very different and unsatisfactory aspect. The idea generally received is that this, as well as three smaller vortices among the Ferroe islands,[11] "have no other cause than the collision of waves rising and falling, at flux and reflux, against a ridge of rocks and shelves, which confines the water so that it precipitates itself like a cataract; and thus the higher the flood rises, the deeper must the fall be, and the natural result of all is a whirlpool or vortex, the prodigious suction of which is sufficiently known by lesser experiments." — These are the words of the Encyclopædia Britannica.[12] Kircher and others imagine that in the centre of the channel of the Maelström is an abyss penetrating the globe, and issuing in some very remote part — the Gulf of Bothnia being somewhat decidedly named in one instance. This opinion, idle in itself, was the one to which, as I gazed, my imagination most readily assented; and, mentioning it to the guide, I was rather surprised to hear him say that, although it was the view almost universally entertained of the subject by the Norwegians, it nevertheless was not his own. As to the former notion he confessed his inability to comprehend it; and here I agreed with him — for, however conclusive on paper, it becomes altogether unintelligible, and even absurd, amid the thunder of the abyss.

"You have had a good look at the whirl[13] now," said the old man, "and if you will creep round this crag, so as to get in its lee, and deaden the roar of the water, I will tell you a story that will convince you I ought to know something of the Moskoe-ström."

I placed myself as desired, and he proceeded.

"Myself and my two brothers once owned a schooner-rigged smack of about seventy tons burthen, with which we were in the habit of fishing among the islands beyond Moskoe, nearly to Vurrgh. In all violent eddies at sea there is good fishing, at proper opportunities, if one has only the courage to attempt it; but among the whole of the Lofoden coastmen, we three were the only ones who made a regular business of going out to the islands, as I tell you. The usual grounds are a great way lower down to the southward. There fish can be got at all hours, without much risk, and therefore these places are preferred. The choice spots over here among the rocks, however, not only yield the finest variety, but in far greater abundance; so that we often got in a single day, what the more timid of the craft could not scrape together in a week. In fact, we made it a matter of desperate speculation — the risk of life standing instead of labor, and courage answering for capital.

"We kept the smack in a cove about five miles higher up the coast than this; and it was our practice, in fine weather, to take advantage of the fifteen minutes' slack to push across the main channel of the Moskoe-ström, far above the pool, and then drop down upon anchorage somewhere near Otterholm, or Sandflesen, where the eddies are not so violent as elsewhere. Here we used to remain until nearly time for slack-water again, when we weighed and made for home. We never set out upon this expedition without a steady side wind for going and coming — one that we felt sure would not fail us before our return — and we seldom made a mis-calculation upon this point. Twice, during six years, we were forced to stay all night at anchor on account of a dead calm, which is a rare thing indeed just about here; and once we had to remain on the grounds nearly a week, starving to death, owing to a gale which blew up shortly after our arrival, and made the channel too boisterous to be thought of. Upon this occasion we should have been driven out to sea in spite of everything, (for the whirlpools threw us round and round so violently, that, at length, we fouled our anchor and dragged it) if it had not been that we drifted into one of the innumerable cross currents — here to-day and gone to-morrow — which drove us under the lee of Flimen, where, by good luck, we brought up.

"I could not tell you the twentieth part of the difficulties we encountered 'on the grounds' — it is a bad spot to be in, even in good weather — but we made shift always to run the gauntlet of the Moskoe-ström itself without accident; although at times my heart has been in my mouth when we happened to be a minute or so behind or before the slack. The wind sometimes was not as strong as we thought it at starting, and then we made rather less way than we could wish, while the current rendered the smack unmanageable. My eldest brother had a son eighteen years old, and I had two stout boys of my own. These would have been of great assistance at such times, in using the sweeps, as well as afterward in fishing — but, somehow, although we ran the risk ourselves, we had not the heart to let the young ones get into the danger — for, after all is said and done, it *was* a horrible danger, and that is the truth.

"It is now within a few days of three years since what I am going to tell you occurred. It was on the tenth day of July, 18 — , a day which the people of this part of the world will never forget — for it was one in which blew the most terrible hurricane that ever came out of the heavens. And yet all the morning, and indeed until late in the afternoon, there was a gentle and steady breeze from the south-west, while the sun shone brightly, so that the oldest seaman among us could not have foreseen what was to follow.

"The three of us — my two brothers and myself — had crossed over to the islands about two o'clock P. M., and had soon nearly loaded the smack with fine fish, which, we all remarked, were more plenty that day than we had ever known them. It was just seven, *by my watch,* when we weighed and started for home, so as to make the worst of the Ström at slack water, which we knew would be at eight.

"We set out with a fresh wind on our starboard quarter, and for some time spanked along at a great rate, never dreaming of danger, for indeed we saw not the slightest reason to apprehend it. All at once we were taken aback by a breeze from over Helseggen. This was most unusual — something that had never happened to us before — and I began to feel a little uneasy, without exactly knowing why. We put the boat on the wind, but could make no headway at all for the eddies, and I was upon the point of proposing to return to the anchorage, when, looking astern, we saw the whole horizon covered with a singular copper-colored cloud that rose with the most amazing velocity.

"In the meantime the breeze that had headed us off fell away, and we were dead becalmed, drifting about in every direction. This state of things, however, did not last long enough to give us time to think about it. In less than a minute the storm was upon us — in less than two the sky was entirely overcast — and what with this and the driving spray, it became suddenly so dark that we could not see each other in the smack.

"Such a hurricane as then blew it is folly to attempt describing. The oldest seaman[f] in Norway never experienced any thing like it. We had let our sails go by the run before it cleverly took us; but, at the first puff, both our masts went by the board as if they had been sawed off — the mainmast taking with it my youngest brother, who had lashed himself to it for safety.

f   seamen *(A)*

"Our boat was the lightest feather of a thing that ever sat upon water. It had a complete flush deck, with only a small hatch near the bow, and this hatch it had always been our custom to batten down when about to cross the Ström, by way of precaution against the chopping seas. But for this circumstance we should have foundered at once — for we lay entirely buried for some moments. How my elder brother escaped destruction I cannot say, for I never had an opportunity of ascertaining. For my part, as soon as I had let the foresail run, I threw myself flat on deck, with my feet against the narrow gunwale of the bow, and with my hands grasping a ring-bolt near the foot of the foremast. It was mere instinct that prompted me to do this — which was undoubtedly the very best thing I could have done — for I was too much flurried to think.

"For some moments we were completely deluged, as I say, and all this time I held my breath, and clung to the bolt. When I could stand it no longer I raised myself upon my knees, still keeping hold with my hands, and thus got my head clear. Presently our little boat gave herself a shake, just as a dog does in coming out of the water, and thus rid herself, in some measure, of the seas. I was now trying to get the better of the stupor that had come over me, and to collect my senses so as to see what was to be done, when I felt somebody grasp my arm. It was my elder brother, and my heart leaped for joy, for I had made sure that he was overboard — but the next moment all this joy was turned into horror — for he put his mouth close to my ear, and screamed out the word 'Moskoe-ström!'

"No one ever will know what my feelings were at that moment. I shook from head to foot as if I had had the most violent fit of the ague. I knew what he meant by that one word well enough — I knew what he wished to make me understand. With the wind that now drove us on, we were bound for the whirl of the Ström, and nothing could save us!

"You perceive that in crossing the Ström *channel,* we always went a long way up above the whirl, even in the calmest weather, and then had to wait and watch carefully for the slack — but now we were driving right upon the pool itself, and in such a hurricane as this! 'To be sure,' I thought, 'we shall get there just about the slack — there is some little hope in that' — but in the next moment

I cursed myself for being so great a fool as to dream of hope at all. I knew very well that we were doomed, had we been ten times a ninety-gun ship.

"By this time the first fury of the tempest had spent itself, or perhaps we did not feel it so much, as we scudded before it, but at all events the seas, which at first had been kept down by the wind, and lay flat and frothing, now got up into absolute mountains. A singular change, too, had come over the heavens. Around in every direction it was still as black as pitch, but nearly overhead there burst out, all at once, a circular rift of clear sky — as clear as I ever saw — and of a deep bright blue — and through it there blazed forth the full moon with a lustre that I never before knew her to wear.[14] She lit up every thing about us with the greatest distinctness — but, oh God, what a scene it was to light up!

"I now made one or two attempts to speak to my brother — but, in some manner which I could not understand, the din had so increased that I could not make him hear a single word, although I screamed at the top of my voice in his ear. Presently he shook his head, looking as pale as death, and held up one of his fingers, as if to say 'listen!'

"At first I could not make out what he meant — but soon a hideous thought flashed upon me. I dragged my watch from its fob. It was not going. I glanced at its face by the moonlight, and then burst into tears as I flung it far away into the ocean. *It had run down at seven o'clock! We were behind the time of the slack, and the whirl of the Ström was in full fury!*

"When a boat is well built, properly trimmed, and not deep laden, the waves in a strong gale, when she is going large, seem always to slip from beneath her — which appears very strange to a landsman — and this is what is called *riding,* in sea phrase. Well, so far we had ridden the swells very cleverly; but presently a gigantic sea happened to take us right under the counter, and bore us with it as it rose — up — up — as if into the sky. I would not have believed that any wave could rise so high. And then down we came with a sweep, a slide, and a plunge, that made me feel sick and dizzy, as if I was falling from some lofty mountain-top in a dream.[15] But while we were up I had thrown a quick glance around — and that one glance was all sufficient. I saw our exact position in an instant. The Moskoe-ström whirlpool was about a quarter of a mile dead ahead — but no more like the every-day Moskoe-ström, ᵍthan the whirl as you now see it is like a mill-race.ᵍ If I had not known where we were, and what we had to expect, I should not have recognised the place at all. As it was, I involuntarily closed my eyes in horror. The lids clenched themselves together as if in a spasm.

"It could not have been more than two minutes afterward until we suddenly felt the waves subside, and were enveloped inʰ foam. The boat made a sharp half turn to larboard, and then shot off in its new direction like a thunderbolt. At the same moment the roaring noise of the water was completely drowned in a kind of shrill shriek — such a sound as you might imagine given out by the waste-pipes of many thousand steam-vessels, letting off their steam all together. We were now in the belt of surf that always surrounds the whirl; and I thought, of course, that another moment would plunge us into the abyss — down which we could only see indistinctly on account of the amazing velocity with which we were borne along. The boat did not seem to sink into the water at all, but to skim like an air-bubble upon the surface of the surge. Her starboard side was next the whirl, and on the larboard arose the world of ocean we had left. It stood like a huge writhing wall between us and the horizon.

"It may appear strange, but now, when we were in the very jaws of the gulf, I felt more composed than when we were only approaching it. Having made up my mind to hope no more, I got rid of a great deal of that terror which unmanned me at first. I suppose it was despair that strung my nerves.

"It may look like boasting — but what I tell you is truth — I began to reflect how magnificent a thing it was to die in such a manner, and how foolish it was in me to think of so paltry a consideration as my own individual life, in view of so wonderful a manifestation of God's power. I do believe that I blushed with shame when this idea crossed my mind. After a little while I became possessed with the keenest curiosity about the whirl itself. I

---

g . . . g   than a mill-race is like the whirl   h   in a wilderness of (A)
as you now see it. (A)

positively felt a *wish* to explore its depths, even at the sacrifice I was going to make; and my principal grief was that I should never be able to tell my old companions on shore about the mysteries I should see. These, no doubt, were singular fancies to occupy a man's mind in such extremity — [16] and I have often thought since, that the revolutions of the boat around the pool might have rendered me a little light-headed.

"There was another circumstance which tended to restore my self-possession; and this was the cessation of the wind, which could not reach us in our present situation — for, as you saw yourself, the belt of surf is considerably lower than the general bed of the ocean, and this latter now towered above us, a high, black, mountainous ridge. If you have never been at sea in a heavy gale, you can form no idea of the confusion of mind occasioned by the wind and spray together. They blind, deafen, and strangle you, and take away all power of action or reflection. But we were now, in a great measure, rid of these annoyances — just as death-condemned felons in prison are allowed petty indulgences, forbidden them while their doom is yet uncertain.

"How often we made the circuit of the belt it is impossible to say. We careered round and round for perhaps an hour, flying rather than floating, getting gradually more and more into the middle of the surge, and then nearer and nearer to its horrible inner edge. All this time I had never let go of the ring-bolt. My brother was at the stern, holding on to a large[i] empty watercask which had been securely lashed[j] under the coop of the counter, and was the only thing on deck that had not been swept overboard when the gale first took us. As we approached the brink of the pit he let go his hold upon this, and made for the ring, from which, in the agony of his terror, he endeavored to force my hands, as it was not large enough to afford us both a secure grasp. I never felt deeper grief than when I saw him attempt this act — although I knew he was a madman when he did it — a raving maniac through sheer fright. I did not care, however, to contest the point with him. I thought[k] it could make no difference whether either of us held

---

i   small *(A, B, D)*   k   knew *(A, B, D)*
j   lashed aft *(A)*

on at all; so I let him have the bolt, and went[1] astern to the cask.[17] This there was no great difficulty in doing; for the smack flew round steadily enough, and upon an even keel — only swaying to and fro, with the immense sweeps and swelters of the whirl. Scarcely had I secured myself in my new position, when we gave a wild lurch to starboard, and rushed headlong into the abyss. I muttered a hurried prayer to God, and thought all was over.

"As I felt the sickening sweep of the descent, I had instinctively tightened my hold upon the barrel, and closed my eyes. For some seconds I dared not open them — while I expected instant destruction, and wondered that I was not already in my death-struggles with the water. But moment after moment elapsed. I still lived. The sense of falling had ceased; and the motion of the vessel seemed much as it had been before[m] while in the belt of foam, with the exception that she now lay more along. I took courage, and looked once again upon the scene.

"Never shall I forget the sensations of awe, horror, and admiration with which I gazed about me. The boat appeared to be hanging, as if by magic, midway down, upon the interior surface of a funnel vast[n] in circumference, prodigious[o] in depth, and whose perfectly smooth sides might have been mistaken for ebony, but for the bewildering rapidity with which they spun around, and for the gleaming and ghastly radiance they shot forth, as the rays of the full moon, from that circular rift amid the clouds which I have already described, streamed in a flood of golden glory along the black walls, and far away down into the inmost recesses of the abyss.[18]

"At first I was too much confused to observe anything accurately. The general burst of terrific grandeur was all that I beheld. When I recovered myself a little, however, my gaze fell instinctively downward. In this direction I was able to obtain an unobstructed view, from the manner in which the smack hung on the inclined surface of the pool. She was quite upon an even keel — that is to say, her deck lay in a plane parallel with that of the water — but this latter sloped at an angle of more than forty-five degrees, so that we seemed to be lying upon our beam-ends. I could not help observ-

---

l   went, myself, *(A)*
m   before, *(A, B, D)*

n   prodigious *(A)*
o   immeasurable *(A)*

ing, nevertheless, that I had scarcely more difficulty in maintaining my hold and footing in this situation, than if we had been upon a dead level; and this, I suppose, was owing to the speed at which we revolved.

"The rays of the moon seemed to search the very bottom of the profound gulf; but still I could make out nothing distinctly, on account of a thick mist in which everything there was enveloped, and over which there hung a magnificent rainbow, like that narrow and tottering bridge which Mussulmen say is the only pathway between Time and Eternity.[19] This mist, or spray, was no doubt occasioned by the clashing of the great walls of the funnel, as they all met together at the bottom — but the yell that went up to the Heavens from out of that mist, I dare[p] not attempt to describe.

"Our first slide into the abyss itself, from the belt of foam above, had carried us a great distance down the slope; but our farther descent was by no means proportionate. Round and round we swept — not with any uniform movement — but in dizzying swings and jerks, that sent us sometimes only a few hundred feet[q] — sometimes nearly the complete circuit of the whirl. Our progress downward, at each revolution, was [r]slow, but very perceptible.[r]

"Looking about me upon the wide waste of liquid ebony on which we were thus borne, I perceived that our boat was not the only object in the embrace of the whirl. Both above and below us were visible fragments of vessels, large masses of building timber and trunks of trees, with many smaller articles, such as pieces of house furniture, broken boxes, barrels and staves. I have already described the unnatural curiosity which had taken the place of my original terrors. It appeared to grow upon me as I drew nearer and nearer to my dreadful doom. I now began to watch, with a strange interest, the numerous things that floated in our company. I *must* have been delirious — for I even sought *amusement* in speculating upon the relative velocities of their several descents toward the foam below. 'This fir tree,' I found myself at one time saying, 'will certainly be the next thing that takes the awful plunge and disappears,' — and then I was disappointed to find that the wreck of

---

p   will *(A)*
q   yards *(A, B, D)*

r . . . r   very perceptible, but slow. *(A)*

a Dutch merchant ship overtook it and went down before. At length, after making several guesses of this nature, and being deceived in all — this fact — the fact of my invariable miscalculation — set me upon a train of reflection that made my limbs again tremble, and my heart beat heavily once more.[20]

"It was not a new terror that thus affected me, but the dawn of a more exciting *hope*. This hope arose partly from memory, and partly from present observation. I called to mind the great variety of buoyant matter that strewed the coast of Lofoden, having been absorbed and then thrown forth by the Moskoe-ström. By far the greater number of the articles were shattered in the most extraordinary way — so chafed and roughened as to have the appearance of being stuck full of splinters — but then I distinctly recollected that there were *some* of them which were not disfigured at all. Now I could not account for this difference except by supposing that the roughened fragments were the only ones which had been *completely absorbed* — that the others had entered the whirl at so late a period of the tide, or, for some reason, had descended so slowly after entering, that they did not reach the bottom before the turn of the flood came, or of the ebb, as the case might be. I conceived it possible, in either instance, that they might thus be whirled up again to the level of the ocean, without undergoing the fate of those which had been drawn in more early, or absorbed more rapidly. I made, also, three important observations. The first was, that, as a general rule, the larger the bodies were, the more rapid their descent; — [s] the second, that, between two masses of equal extent, the one spherical, and the other *of any other shape,* the superiority in speed of descent[t] was with the sphere; — [u] the third, that, between two masses of equal size, the one cylindrical, and the other of any other shape, the cylinder was absorbed the more slowly. Since my escape, I have had several conversations on this subject with an old school-master of the district; and it was from him that I learned the use of the words 'cylinder' and 'sphere.' He explained to me — although I have forgotten the explanation — how what I observed was, in fact, the natural conse-

---

s   descent; — /descent — (A, B, D)   u   sphere; —/ sphere — (A, B, D)
t   speed of descent/speed (A)

quence of the forms of the floating fragments — and showed me how it happened that a cylinder, swimming in a vortex, offered more resistance to its suction, and was drawn in with greater difficulty than an equally bulky body, of any form whatever.*[v]

"There was one startling circumstance which went a great way in enforcing these observations, and rendering me anxious to turn them to account, and this was that, at every revolution, we passed something like a barrel, or else the broken[w] yard or the mast of a vessel, while many of these things, which had been on our level when I first opened my eyes upon the wonders of the whirlpool, were now high up above us, and seemed to have moved but little from their original station.

"I no longer hesitated what to do. I resolved to lash myself securely to the water cask upon which I now held, to cut it loose from the counter, and to throw myself with it into the water. I attracted my brother's attention by signs, pointed to the floating barrels that came near us, and did everything in my power to make him understand what I was about to do. I thought at length that he comprehended my design — but, whether this was the case or not, he shook his head despairingly, and refused to move from his station by the ring-bolt. It was impossible to force[x] him; the emergency admitted[y] no delay; and so, with a bitter struggle, I resigned him to his fate, fastened myself to the cask by means of the lashings which secured it to the counter, and precipitated myself with it into the sea, without another moment's hesitation.

"The result was precisely what I had hoped it might be. As it is myself who now tells you this tale — as you see that I *did* escape — and as you are already in possession of the mode in which this escape was effected, and must therefore anticipate all that I have farther to say — I will bring my story quickly to conclusion. It might have been an hour, or thereabout, after my quitting the smack, when, having descended to a vast distance beneath me, it made three or four wild gyrations in rapid succession, and, bearing my loved brother with it, plunged headlong, at once and forever,

---

* See Archimedes, "De Incidentibus in Fluido." — lib. 2.[21]

v	*Footnote omitted (A)*
w	the broken/the *(A, B, D)*

x	reach *(A, B, D)*
y	admitted of *(A, B, D)*

into the chaos of foam below. The cask[z] to which I was attached sank[a] very little farther than half the distance between the bottom of the gulf and the spot at which I leaped overboard, before a great change took place in the character of the whirlpool.[b] The slope of the sides of the vast funnel became momently less and less steep. The gyrations of the whirl [c]grew, gradually, less and less violent. By degrees, the froth and the rainbow disappeared, and the bottom of the gulf seemed slowly to uprise.[c] The sky was clear, the winds had gone down, and the full moon was setting radiantly in the west, when I found myself on the surface of the ocean, in full view of the shores of Lofoden, and above the spot where the pool of the Moskoe-ström *had been.* It was the hour of the slack — but the sea still heaved in mountainous waves from the effects of the hurricane. I was borne violently into the channel of the Ström, and in a few minutes was hurried down the coast into the 'grounds' of the fishermen. A boat picked me up — exhausted from fatigue — and (now that the danger was removed) speechless from the memory of its horror. Those who drew me on board were my old mates and daily companions — but they knew me no more than they would have known a traveller from the spirit-land. My hair which[d] had been raven-black the day before, [e]was as white as you see it now.[e] They say too that the whole expression of my countenance had changed. I told them my [f]story. They[f] did not believe it. I now tell it to *you* — and [g]I can scarcely expect you to put[g] more faith in it than did the merry fishermen of Lofoden." [22]

NOTES

Title: Poe's is the only use cited by the *Oxford English Dictionary* of the diaeresis over the "o" in Maelstrom.

Motto: This is from Joseph Glanvill's *Essays on Several Important Sub-*

---

z   barrel *(A, B, D)*
a   sunk *(A, B, D)*
b   *After this:* The froth and the rainbow disappeared. *(A)*
c . . . c   grew feeble and fluctuating — then ceased altogether — then finally reversed themselves with a gradually accelerating motion. And then the bottom of the gulf uprose — and its turgid aspect had in great measure departed. *(A)*
d   *Omitted (A)*
e . . . e   and now it is white as you see. *(A)*
f . . . f   story — they *(A, B, D)*
g . . . g   you will put no *(A)*

jects (London, 1676), p. 15, in an essay "Against Confidence in Philosophy and Matters of Speculation": "The *ways* of God in *Nature* (as in *Providence)* are not as *ours* are: Nor are the models that we frame any way commensurate to the vastness and profundity of his Works; which have a *Depth* in them greater than the *Well of Democritus.*" Compare "Ligeia" at note 10, and for the proverbial well of Democritus see that note. Poe also ascribes to Glanvill the motto he uses for "Ligeia," but that passage has not been located. All texts of "A Descent into the Maelström" add "e" to Glanvill.

1. Byron's note on the opening lines of *The Prisoner of Chillon* (1816) records the story that the hair of Ludovico Sforza grew "white in a single night." It is a commonplace belief not given credence by medical men.

2. Reason is first introduced as in the mind of the narrator, later it shines forth as the chief characteristic of the old Norseman.

3. Poe has in mind here, and in "Eleonora" and "Mellonta Tauta," a reference in his favorite Jacob Bryant's *Antient Mythology* (third edtion, 1807), IV, 79: "By the Nubian geographer the Atlantic is uniformly called ... Mare Tenebrarum." For more on the Nubian geographer see "Eleonora," note 4.

4. The islands mentioned are all actual members of the Lofoten group. Poe's source for the spelling "Vurrgh" has not been found; he may have had it orally from a Scottish or Scandinavian friend; the *Britannica* and its source gave Ver, the *National Geographic Atlas* gives Væroy. All Poe's texts follow the *Britannica* article in the flagrantly erroneous listing of "Stockholm" for Skarholm, which is correctly given on p. 78 of *The Natural History of Norway* (1755), the English translation of the Danish original of Erich Pontoppidan, Bishop of Bergen. The spellings of the other island names, as emended, conform to the spellings in this translation.

5. The references to the West here and elsewhere in this tale add to the evidence Killis Campbell presented that Poe was not "out of space, out of time," but very much in touch with the life and thought of his day ("Poe in Relation to His Times," *Studies in Philology,* July 1923). For a view that gives more significance to these references, see Edwin Fussell, *Frontier: American Literature and the American West* (1965), pp. 162–163.

6. Poe echoes the American captain *(Mariner's Chronicle,* New Haven, 1834, p. 441): "foaming, tumbling, rushing to its vortex, very much concave; ... the noise too, hissing, roaring, dashing, all pressing on the mind at once, presented the most awful, grand, and solemn sight I ever experienced."

7. Jonas Ramus (1649–1718), "pastor ... in the diocese of Aggerhuus" according to Bishop Pontoppidan, who quotes him extensively, "has deserved highly of his country for his Description of Norway, published in quarto at Copenhagen 1715" *(Natural History of Norway,* London, 1755, p. xiii). Poe's quotation, however, is from the *Encyclopaedia Britannica, s.v.* Maelstrom, which is lifted bodily — except for its errors — from the London Pontoppidan.

8. A Norway mile is equal to about four and one half of our miles.

9. Sexagesima Sunday is the second Sunday before the beginning of Lent.

10. Phlegethon is the "fiery" river in Hades. See *Paradise Lost,* II, 580.

11. The Faeroe Islands, between Iceland and the north of Scotland.

12. Poe meagerly acknowledged his source here — the source of most of his color — and of the substance of his next sentence. Athanasius Kircher (1602–1680) and later Jonas Ramus wished to connect the Maelstrom with Charybdis, and it was Kircher, according to Pontoppidan (London, 1755, p. 83) who maintained that the Maelstrom was "a sea-vortex, attracting the flood under the shore of Norway, where, through another abyss, it is discharged into the gulph of Bothnia."

13. Compare Coleridge's *Ancient Mariner,* VII, stanza x, "Upon the whirl, where sank the Ship."

14. Frank Jordan (*Natural History,* October 1935) pointed out that in July the moon "would barely rise above the southern horizon for an observer in Norway," and furthermore that in July in the Land of the Midnight Sun "moonlight would be superfluous."

15. Compare "MS. Found in a Bottle": "At times we gasped for breath at an elevation beyond the albatross — at times became dizzy with the velocity of our descent."

16. Like the narrator of "MS. Found in a Bottle" (at n. 25) the Norwegian fisherman in extreme peril found himself intensely curious about the phenomena he saw. Acute observation led to reasoning, and at length to action. Compare the experience of the narrator in "The Pit and the Pendulum" at n. 17.

17. The idea of using a cask, as Arlin Turner pointed out, probably came from the *Britannica* article "Whirlpool," which describes a "whirlpool among the Orcades" (Orkneys):

> Wherever it appears, it is very furious; and boats, etc. would inevitably be drawn in and perish with it; but the people who navigate them are prepared for it, and always carry an empty vessel, a log of wood, or some such thing, in the boat with them; as soon as they perceive the whirlpool, they toss this within its vortex, keeping themselves out. This substance, whatever it be, is immediately received into the centre, and carried under water; and as soon as this is done, the surface of the place where the whirlpool was becomes smooth, and they row over it with safety.

18. Compare the American captain's description in *The Mariner's Chronicle* (New Haven, 1834), p. 441: "Imagine to yourselves an immense circle running round, of a diameter of one and a half miles, the velocity increasing ... gradually changing its dark blue color to white." — Another factual error pointed out by Frank Jordan: the real Maelstrom does not form a funnel.

19. "Musselmen'" is a common but incorrect form for Mussulmans (Mahometans), also used by Poe in "Never Bet the Devil Your Head." The bridge referred to is called Al Siraat, and is described in the fourth section of Sale's "Preliminary Discourse" to his translation of the Koran.

20. The old Norseman's "train of reflection" moves with great attention to detail and verisimilitude through the following paragraphs.

21. The work of Archimedes of Syracuse (in the Oxford edition of 1792) is called *De iis quae in humido vehuntur.* Poe himself indicated, according to "A Reviewer Reviewed," that it contains nothing resembling his "quotation," which he made up to justify the solution of his plot. Killis Campbell (*MLN,* December 1927, p. 520) was the first to point out the fictional character of Poe's reference ("meaning, I take it . . . *De Insidentibus in Humido*"), but the actual source of Poe's citation was probably Isaac D'Israeli's 1839 revision of *The Literary Character,* which was published both separately and in later editions of his *Curiosities of Literature.* In chapter XI D'Israeli mentions "the two books of Archimedes, *De insidentibus in fluido.*" Poe does not follow D'Israeli's spelling.

22. Observe Poe's device in the last sentence – added in 1845 – to excuse incredulous readers.

THE ISLAND OF THE FAY

This charming fantasy is one of the most beautiful of Poe's stories. It was originally published as a plate article in *Graham's Magazine,* accompanying a steel engraving by John Sartain "after an original by Martin." The Martin named was undoubtedly the contemporary English artist John Martin, whose powerfully imaginative historical paintings and later mezzotint illustrations of the Bible and "Paradise Lost" were enthusiastically admired by some and as vehemently condemned by others. John Sartain had known Martin in London, thought highly of him, and owned a number of his etchings. Certainly Sartain's engraving and Poe's story are closely interrelated; probably each contributed to the development of the other.*

Poe may have obtained something from a well-known story about William Blake, repeated as an introduction to a poem of ten quatrains signed "A" in the *New-York Mirror,* June 21, 1834:

THE FAIRY'S FUNERAL

Reading, the other day, Macnish's very interesting volume on the "Philosophy of Sleep," I was much struck with his brief, but very characteristic account

* See F. DeWolfe Miller, *AL,* May 1942; John Sartain's *Reminiscences of a Very Old Man* (1899), pp. 15–17; and Thomas Balston, *John Martin 1789–1854: His Life and Works* (London, 1947). [Burton R. Pollin has gathered evidence on which to base a persuasive argument that Martin's "original" was a simple etching illustrating one of his pamphlets (1828) on a water supply for London, and that Sartain in his engraving greatly elaborated and adapted Martin's work in response to suggestions from Poe. See his article in *The Mystery and Detection Annual* (Beverly Hills, 1972).]

of the painter Blake. He was remarkable for his "habit of conversing with angels, demons and heroes, and taking their likenesses." . . . One of his visions appeared to me so particularly poetical in its conception, that I was irresistibly impelled to . . . give it a poetic dress.

"Did you ever see a fairy's funeral, madam?" he once said to a lady . . . "Never, sir," was the answer. "I have," said Blake, "but not before last night. I was walking alone in my garden; there was great stillness among the branches and flowers, and more than common sweetness in the air; I heard a low and pleasant sound, and knew not whence it came. At last I saw the broad leaf of a flower move, and underneath I saw a procession of creatures of the size and color of green and gray grasshoppers, bearing a body laid out on a rose-leaf, which they buried with songs, and then disappeared. It was a *fairy funeral.*"†

Suggestions of tone and color, and the annual cycle, may owe something to "A Fairy Tale" in the *Southern Literary Messenger* for January 1836.‡ A lonely fairy, "placed by Titania on this lower earth," was alternately rejoiced and desolated, year after year, by the spring blossoming and autumn death of the special flower to which she had given her heart, until "she wished never again to fix her heart upon the perishing flowers of Earth . . . and she sighed for another home." When "the time of her sojourn was over . . . she slept" and on awakening found herself in Fairy-land: ". . . The longings of her heart were over. She had found a home utterly free from the chilling shadows of mortality."

Poe drew also upon a dream fantasy — perhaps his own — which he described in the early versions (1835, 1840) of "Hans Pfaall" — a passage later canceled:

And out of this melancholy water arose a forest of tall eastern trees like a wilderness of dreams. And I bore in mind that the shadows of the trees which fell upon the lake remained not on the surface where they fell — but sunk slowly

---

† Poe might have seen the anecdote in Robert Macnish's book itself (Glasgow, 1830) — it appeared on pages 227–228 of the New York edition of 1834 — or he might even have seen it in the source cited by Macnish, volume II of Allan Cunningham's *Lives of the Most Eminent British Painters* . . . (London, 1829), pages 137–138 of the edition issued by J. and J. Harper (New York, 1831).

‡ David K. Jackson called this story to my attention. See his *Poe and the Southern Literary Messenger* (1934), p. 106. The author was probably Margaret Mercer, a sister of Charles Fenton Mercer, congressman from Virginia for many years. The story may also have influenced Poe's "Eleonora," which has much in common with "The Island of the Fay." [Professor Pollin thinks both tales are indebted to La Motte-Fouqué's *Undine*, in Grenville Mellen's translation, which was reviewed by Poe in *Burton's* for September 1839. See his article "Undine in the Works of Poe," *Studies in Romanticism,* Winter 1975.]

THE ISLAND OF THE FAY

and steadily down, and commingled with the waves, while from the trunks of the trees other shadows were continually coming out, and taking the places of their brothers thus entombed. "This then," I said thoughtfully, "is the very reason why the waters of this lake grow blacker with age, and more melancholy as the hours run on."

Poe's story was written presumably about April 1841, while the June issue of *Graham's Magazine* was being prepared.

TEXTS

(A) *Graham's Magazine* for June 1841 (18:253–255); *(B)* *Broadway Journal*, October 4, 1845 (2:188–190); *(C)* *Works* (1850), I, 360–365. PHANTASY-PIECES, title only.

Griswold's text *(C)* is followed. It contains a new footnote and one other verbal change.

THE ISLAND OF THE FAY. [C]

Nullus enim locus sine genio est. — *Servius.*

*"La musique,"*ᵃ says Marmontel, ᵇin those "Contes Moraux" * ᶜ which, in all our translations, we have insisted upon calling "Moral Tales," as if in mockery of their spiritᵇ — *"la musique est le seul*

---

* Moraux is here derived from *mœurs,* and its meaning is *"fashionable,"* or, more strictly, "of manners."

Motto: *Poe at first used a version of his "Sonnet — To Science."*
    SCIENCE, true daughter of old Time thou art,
      Who alterest all things with thy peering eyes!
    Why prey'st thou thus upon the poet's heart,
      Vulture, whose wings are dull realities?
    How should he love thee, or how deem thee wise
      Who wouldst not leave him, in his wandering,
    To seek for treasure in the jewelled skies,
      Albeit be [*sic*] soared with an undaunted wing?
    Hast thou not dragged Diana from her car?
      And driven the Hamadryad from the wood?
    Has thou not spoilt a story in each star?
      Hast thou not torn the Naiad from her flood?
    The elfin from the grass? — the dainty *fay,*
    The witch, the sprite, the goblin — where are they?
                Anon. (A)

a *No part of the quotation is italicized (A)*
b . . . b with the same odd confusion of thought and language which leads

him to give his very equivocal narratives the title of *"Contes Moraux" (A)*
c *Note omitted (A)*

des talens qui jouissent de lui-même;[d] *tous les autres veulent des témoins.*"[e][1] He here confounds the pleasure derivable from sweet sounds with the capacity for creating them. No more than any other *talent,* is that for music susceptible of complete enjoyment, where there is no second party to appreciate its exercise. And it is only in common with other talents that it produces *effects* which may be fully enjoyed in solitude. The idea which the *raconteur* has either failed to entertain clearly, or has sacrificed in its expression to his national love of *point,* is, doubtless, the very tenable one that the higher order of music is the most thoroughly estimated when we are[f] exclusively alone. The proposition, in this form, will be admitted at once by those who love the lyre for its own sake, and for its spiritual uses. But there is one pleasure still within the reach of fallen mortality — and perhaps only one — which owes even more than does music to the accessory sentiment of seclusion. I mean the happiness experienced in the contemplation of natural scenery. In truth, the man who would behold aright the glory of God upon earth must in solitude behold that glory. To me, at least, the presence — not of human life only — but of life in any other form than that of the green things which grow upon the soil and are voiceless — is a stain upon the landscape — is at war with the genius of the scene. I love, indeed, to regard the dark valleys, and the grey rocks, and the waters that silently smile,[2] and the forests that sigh in uneasy slumbers, and the proud watchful mountains that look down upon all — I love to regard these as themselves but the colossal members of one vast animate and sentient whole — a whole whose form (that of the sphere) is the most perfect and[g] most inclusive of all; whose path is among associate planets; whose meek handmaiden is the moon; whose mediate sovereign is the sun; whose life is eternity; whose thought[h] is that of a God; whose enjoyment is knowledge; whose destinies are lost in immensity; whose cognizance of ourselves is akin with our own cognizance of the *animalculæ*[i] which infest the brain — a being which we, in

---

d lui même; *(A); lui même; (B, C)*
e temoins." *(A); temoins." (B, C)*
f are the most *(A)*
g and the *(A)*

h intelligence *(A)*
i animalculæ in crystal, or of those
(A); animalculæ (C)

consequence, regard as purely inanimate and material, much in the same manner as these *animalculæ*[j] must thus regard us.

Our telescopes, and our mathematical investigations assure us on every hand — notwithstanding the cant of the more ignorant of the priesthood — that space, and therefore that bulk, is an important consideration in the eyes of the Almighty. The cycles in which the stars move are those best adapted for the evolution, without collision, of the greatest possible number of bodies. The forms of those[k] bodies are accurately such as, within a given surface, to include the greatest possible amount of matter; — while the surfaces themselves are so disposed as to accommodate a denser population than could be accommodated on the same surfaces otherwise arranged. Nor is it any argument against bulk being an object with God, that space itself is infinite; for there may be an infinity of matter to fill it. And since we see clearly that the endowment of matter with vitality is a principle — indeed, as far as our judgments[l] extend, the *leading* principle in the operations of Deity — it is scarcely logical to imagine it[m] confined to the regions of the minute, where we daily trace it, and [n]not extending[n] to those of the august. As we find cycle within cycle without end — yet all revolving around one far-distant centre which is the Godhead, may we not analogically suppose, in the same manner, life within life, the less within the greater, and all within the Spirit Divine?[3] In short, we are madly erring, through self-esteem, in believing man, in either his temporal or future destinies, to be of more moment in the universe than that vast "clod of the valley" [4] which he tills and contemns, and to which he denies a soul for no more profound reason than that he does not behold it in[o] operation.† [p] [5]

These fancies, and such as these, have always given to my meditations among the mountains, and the forests, by the rivers and the ocean, a tinge of what the every-day world would not fail to term the fantastic. My wanderings amid such scenes have been many,

† Speaking of the tides, Pomponius Mela, in his treatise *"De Sitû Orbis,"* says "either the world is a great animal, or" &c.

j	animalculæ *(A);* animalculœ *(C)*	n . . . n	that it does not extend *(A)*
k	these *(A)*	o	it in/its *(A)*
l	jndgments *(B) misprint*	p	*Note omitted (A)*
m	that it is *(A)*		

and far-searching, and often solitary; and^q the interest with which
I have strayed through many a dim deep valley, or gazed into the
reflected Heaven of many a bright lake, has been an interest
greatly deepened by the thought that I have strayed and gazed
alone. What flippant Frenchman‡ ^r was it who said, in allusion to
the well-known work of Zimmerman, that, *"la solitude est une
belle chose; mais il faut quelqu'un pour vous dire que la solitude
est une belle chose?"*[6] The epigram cannot be gainsayed;^s but the
necessity is a thing that does not exist.

It was during one of my lonely journeyings, amid a far-distant
region of mountain locked within mountain, and sad rivers and
melancholy tarns writhing or sleeping within all — that I chanced
upon a certain^t rivulet and island.^u I came upon them suddenly in
the leafy June, and threw myself upon the turf, beneath the
branches of an unknown odorous shrub, that I might doze as I
contemplated the scene. I felt that thus only should I look upon it
— such was the character of phantasm which it wore.

On all sides — save to the west, where the sun was about sinking — arose the verdant walls of the forest. The little river which
turned sharply in its course, and was thus immediately lost to sight,
seemed to have no exit from its prison, but to be absorbed by the
deep green foliage of the trees to the east — while in the opposite
quarter (so it appeared to me as I lay at length and glanced upward) there poured down noiselessly and continuously into the
valley, a rich golden and crimson water-fall from the sunset fountains of the sky.[7]

About midway in the short vista which my dreamy vision took
in, one small circular island, profusely^v verdured, reposed upon
the bosom of the stream.

> So blended bank and shadow there,
> That each seemed pendulous in air —

so mirror-like was the glassy water, that it was scarcely possible to

‡ Balzac — in substance — I do not remember the words.

q aud *(B) misprint*
r *Note omitted (A, B)*
s gainsayed; *(A, B, C)*
t a certain/the *(A)*

u island./the island which are the
subject of our engraving. *(A)*
v fantastically *(A)*

say at what point upon the slope of the emerald turf its crystal dominion began.[8]

My position enabled me to include in a single view both the eastern and western extremities of the islet; and I observed a singularly-marked difference in their aspects.[9] The latter was all one radiant harem of garden beauties. It glowed and blushed beneath the eye of the slant sunlight, and fairly laughed with flowers. The grass was short, springy, sweet-scented, and Asphodel-interspersed.[10] The trees were lithe, mirthful, erect — bright, slender and graceful — of eastern figure and foliage, with bark smooth, glossy, and parti-colored.[11] There seemed a deep sense of life and[w] joy about all; and although no airs blew from out the Heavens,[12] yet every thing had motion through the gentle sweepings to and fro of innumerable butterflies, that might have been mistaken for tulips with wings.§

The other or eastern end of the isle was whelmed in the blackest shade. A sombre, yet beautiful and peaceful gloom here pervaded all things. The trees were dark in color and mournful in form and attitude — wreathing themselves into sad, solemn, and spectral shapes, that conveyed ideas of mortal sorrow and untimely death. The grass wore the deep tint of the cypress, and the heads of its blades hung droopingly, and, hither and thither among it, were many small unsightly hillocks, low, and narrow, and not very long, that had the aspect of graves, but were not; although over and all about them the rue and the rosemary clambered.[13] The shade of the trees fell heavily upon the water, and seemed to bury itself therein, impregnating the depths of the element with darkness. I fancied that each shadow, as the sun descended lower and lower, separated itself sullenly from the trunk that gave it birth, and thus became absorbed by the stream; while other shadows issued momently from the trees, taking the place of their predecessors thus[x] entombed.[14]

This idea, having once seized upon my fancy, greatly excited it, and I lost myself forthwith in revery. "If ever island were en-

§ Florem putares nare per liquidum æthera. — *P. Commire.*

w   and of *(A)*   x   *Omitted (A)*

chanted," said I to myself, "this is it. This is the haunt of the few gentle Fays who remain from the wreck of the race. Are these green tombs theirs? — or do they yield up[y] their sweet lives as mankind yield up their own? In dying, do they not rather waste away mournfully; rendering unto God [z]little by little their existence,[z] as these trees render up shadow after shadow,[15] exhausting their substance[a] unto dissolution? What the wasting tree is to the water that imbibes its shade, growing thus blacker by what it preys upon, may not the life of the Fay be to the death which ingulfs it?"[b]

As I thus mused, with half-shut eyes,[16] while the sun sank rapidly[c] to rest, and eddying currents careered round and round the island, bearing upon their bosom large, dazzling, white flakes[d] of the bark of the sycamore — flakes which, in their multiform positions upon the water, a quick imagination might have converted into any thing it pleased — while I thus mused, it appeared to me that the form of one of those very Fays about whom I had been pondering, made its way slowly into the darkness from out the light at the western end of the island. She stood erect in a singularly fragile canoe, and urged it with the mere phantom of an oar. While within the influence of the lingering sunbeams, her attitude seemed indicative of joy — but sorrow deformed it as she passed within the shade. Slowly she glided along, and at length rounded the islet and re-entered the region of light. "The revolution which has just been made by the Fay," continued I, musingly, "is the cycle of the brief year of her life. She has floated through her winter and through her summer. She is a year nearer unto[e] Death: for I did not fail to see that as she came into the shade, her shadow fell from her, and was swallowed up in the dark water, making its blackness more black."

And again the boat appeared, and the Fay; but about the attitude of the latter there was more of care and uncertainty, and less of elastic joy. She floated again from out the light, and into the

---

y   up at all *(A)*
z . . . z   their existence little by little, *(A)*
a   substances *(A, B)*
b   it — but what fairy-like form is this which glides so solemnly along the

water?" *(A)*
c   sank rapidly/rapidly sank *(A)*
d   flakes, *(C) comma deleted to follow A, B*
e   to *(A)*

gloom (which deepened momently) and again her shadow fell from her into the ebony water, and became absorbed into its blackness. And again and again she made the circuit of the island, (while the sun rushed down to his slumbers) and at each issuing[f] into the light, there was more sorrow about her person, while it grew feebler, and far fainter, and more indistinct; and at each passage into the gloom, there fell from her a darker shade, which became whelmed in a shadow more black. But at length, when the sun had utterly departed, the Fay, now the mere ghost of her former self, went disconsolately with her boat into the region of the ebony flood — and that she issued thence at all I cannot say, — for darkness fell over all things, and I beheld her magical figure no more.

NOTES

Mottoes: For the first version Poe used his own "Sonnet — To Science" marked as anonymous, altering the ending to adapt it to the tale. The motto in later versions, which means "No place is without its genius," is slightly misquoted from Servius' Commentary on Vergil's *Æneid*, V, 95. Poe's form is precisely like that in Victor Hugo's *Notre-Dame de Paris* (1831), Book VII, chapter V, near the end, which obviously is his source. Burton Pollin called my attention to this source. [See his *Discoveries in Poe*, pp. 21–22.]

1. See Jean-François Marmontel (1723–1799), *Contes Moraux*, "La Bergère des Alpes," in *Oeuvres Complètes* (Paris, 1818), III, 272, and in *Contes* (Paris, 1829), II, 78. There is an English translation by C. Dennis and R. Lloyd, about 1790, but Poe probably took his quotation from Bulwer's *Ernest Maltravers* (1837), Book VII, chapter 2; it means, "Music is the only talent which gives pleasure of itself; all the others require witnesses."

2. Compare "Al Aaraaf," II, 132–133: "To lone lake that smiles,/In its dream of deep rest."

3. Compare the last sentence of *Eureka:* "In the meantime bear in mind that all is Life — Life — Life within Life — the less within the greater, and all within the *Spirit Divine*."

4. For "clods of the valley" see Job 21:33.

5. Pomponius Mela, *De situ orbis*, III, i, "Mundus...si...unum animal est: an..." Poe took his quotation from Hugh Murray's *Encyclopædia of Geography*, as Richard Wilbur pointed out to me. On p. 37 of the London (1834) edition we find that Pomponius Mela speculated on the cause of the tides: "... either the world is a great animal whose breathings excite the alternate move-

---

f   issuing forth *(A)*

ments; or it contains deep caves, into which the waters are alternately absorbed and ejected." Murray continues: "He does, however mention the theory that supposes them influenced by the moon . . ."

6. Johann Georg von Zimmermann's first essay on *Solitude (Einsamkeit)* was not published until 1756. The flippant remark that "solitude is a fine thing, but one needs somebody to tell that solitude is a fine thing" was made about something else, for it comes from "Entretien Premier" in *Les Entretiens* of Jean-Louis Guez de Balzac (Leyden, 1659), p. 62, and Balzac thought he had said it before. Poe, as his footnote indicates, quoted from memory. Balzac wrote: "La solitude est certainement une belle chose; mais il y a plaisir d'avoir quelqu'un qui scache respondre, à qui on puisse dire de temps en temps, que c'est une belle chose!"

7. Compare "The Valley Nis" (first version of "The Valley of Unrest"), lines 38–42, "the gorgeous clouds do fly/ . . . Rolling like a waterfall/O'er th' horizon's fiery wall."

8. The couplet is altered from Poe's own "City in the Sea." Compare "Landor's Cottage": " . . . *so* clear was this heaven, so perfectly, at times, did it reflect all objects above it, that where the true bank ended and where the mimic one commenced, it was a point of no little difficulty to determine."

9. For a discussion of Poe's treatment of the west in this story, see Edwin Fussell, *Frontier: American Literature and the American West* (1965), pp. 164–165.

10. Poe mentions "the quiet asphodel" in "The Valley Nis," line 26. It is usually a symbol of death, as it is in "Berenicë," but the flower is used with a difference in "Eleonora" and perhaps here.

11. Compare the last paragraph of "The Domain of Arnheim": " . . . there is a dream-like intermingling to the eye of tall slender Eastern trees — "

12. Compare "The Valley of Unrest," lines 17–18, "Ah, by no wind those clouds are driven/That rustle through the unquiet Heaven." The footnote below is the eleventh line of Père Jean Commire's "Papilio et Apis," which I find in *Johannis Commirii Carmina* (Paris, 1714), I, 308. Poe, however, probably found it with a translation among "Some Ingenious Thoughts" in Isaac D'Israeli's *Curiosities of Literature:* "P. Commire, a pleasing writer of Latin verse, says of the flight of a butterfly, ' . . . IT FLIES, and swims a flower in liquid air!' "

13. Compare "For Annie," lines 63–64, "A rosemary odor,/Commingled with pansies" which also alludes to Ophelia's speech in *Hamlet,* IV, v, 175–186.

14. Compare the canceled passage from "Hans Pfaall" quoted in the introduction above.

15. An echo of St. Matthew 22:21, "Render . . . unto God the things that are God's."

16. Compare "Al Aaraaf," II, 72–73, "Bright beings! that ponder,/With half-closing eyes."

THE COLLOQUY OF
MONOS AND UNA

This is the second of Poe's trilogy of dialogues of blessed spirits in Heaven; the others are "The Conversation of Eiros and Charmion" of 1839 and "The Power of Words" of 1845. In the present story, "we find him recording another of his imaginative excursions beyond the bourne of mortality, and in this sense it belongs with his other stories of burial and resurrection" (see Patrick Quinn, *The French Face of Poe,* page 273). Once again Poe is saying what he has said and will say again not only in his tales but in his poems, and what he later expresses so well in "The Premature Burial" (1844): "The boundaries that divide Life from Death are at the best shadowy and vague. Who shall say where the one ends and the other begins?"

Emphasized here is Poe's proclamation of his rejection of the idea of Progress, expressed also in his "Sonnet — To Science" and "The Island of the Fay." He joined the ancients in the fable of the Golden Age, rejected the idea of egalitarian democracy, and feared the increasing ugliness of urban industrial growth. For some of his later treatments of these matters, compare "Some Words with a Mummy," "Mellonta Tauta," and especially his comment in the *Columbia Spy* for May 18, 1844 (reprinted in *Doings of Gotham*): "The old mansions are doomed ... The spirit of Improvement has withered them with its acrid breath."

"The Colloquy of Monos and Una" was probably written in May or June, 1841.

TEXTS

(A) Graham's Magazine for August 1841 (19:52–55); *(B) Tales* (1845), pp. 100–109; *(C) Works* (1850), II, 276–285. PHANTASY-PIECES, title only.

The version of 1845 *(B)* is followed, with the correction of one misprint. Griswold's text *(C)* does not differ from it verbally. No changes were made in the J. Lorimer Graham copy of *Tales.*

THE COLLOQUY OF MONOS AND UNA. [B]

Μελλοντα ταυτα

Sophocles — Antig:

These things are in the future.

Una. "Born again?"

Monos. Yes, fairest and best beloved Una, "born again."[1] These were the words upon whose mystical meaning I had so long pondered, rejecting the explanations of the priesthood, until Death himself resolved for me the secret.

Una. Death!

Monos. How strangely, sweet Una, you echo my words! I observe, too, a vacillation in your step — a joyous inquietude in your eyes. You are confused and oppressed by the majestic novelty of the Life Eternal.[2] Yes, it was of Death I spoke. And here how singularly sounds that word which of old was wont to bring terror to all hearts — throwing a mildew upon all pleasures!

Una. Ah, Death, the spectre which sate at all feasts![3] How often, Monos, did we lose ourselves in speculations upon its nature! How mysteriously did it act as a check to human bliss — saying unto it "thus far, and no farther!"[4] That earnest mutual love, my own Monos, which burned within our bosoms — how vainly did we flatter ourselves, feeling happy in its first upspringing, that our happiness would strengthen with its strength![5] Alas! as it grew, so grew in our hearts the dread of that evil hour which was hurrying to separate us forever! Thus, in time, it became painful to love. Hate would have been mercy then.

Monos. Speak not here of these griefs, dear Una — mine, mine forever now!

Una. But the memory of past sorrow — is it not present joy?[6] I have much to say yet of the things which have been. Above all, I burn to know the incidents of your own passage through the dark Valley and Shadow.

Monos. And when did the radiant Una ask anything of her Monos in vain? I will be minute in relating all — but at what point shall the weird narrative begin?

Motto: *Omitted (A)*

THE COLLOQUY OF MONOS AND UNA

Una. At what point?

Monos. You have said.

Una. Monos, I comprehend you. In Death we have both learned the propensity of man to define the indefinable. I will not say, then, commence with the moment of life's cessation — but commence with that sad, sad instant when, the fever having abandoned you, you sank into a breathless and motionless torpor, and I pressed down your pallid eyelids with the passionate fingers of love.

Monos. One word first, my Una, in regard to man's general condition at this epoch. You will remember that one or two of the wise among our forefathers — wise in fact, although not in the world's esteem — had ventured to doubt the propriety of the term "improvement," as applied to the progress of our civilization. There were periods in each of the five or six centuries immediately preceding our dissolution, when arose some vigorous intellect, boldly contending for those principles whose truth appears now, to our disenfranchised reason, so utterly obvious — principles which should have taught our race to submit to the guidance of the natural laws, rather than attempt their control. At long intervals some master-minds appeared, looking upon each advance in practical science as a retro-gradation in the true utility. Occasionally the poetic intellect — that intellect which we now feel to have been the most exalted of all — since those truths which to us were of the most enduring importance could only be reached by that *analogy* which speaks in proof-tones to the imagination alone, and to the unaided reason bears no weight — occasionally did this poetic intellect proceed a step farther in the evolving of the vague idea of the philosophic, and find in the mystic parable that tells of the tree of knowledge, and of its forbidden fruit, death-producing, a distinct intimation that knowledge was not meet for man in the infant condition of his soul.[7] And these men — the poets — living and perishing amid the scorn of the "utilitarians" —[8] of rough pedants, who arrogated to themselves a title which could have been properly applied only to the scorned — these men, the poets, pondered piningly, yet not unwisely, upon the ancient days when our wants were not more simple than our enjoyments were keen — days when *mirth* was a word unknown, so solemnly[a] deep-toned was happiness — holy, august and blissful days, when blue rivers ran undammed, between hills unhewn, into far forest solitudes, primæval, odorous, and unexplored.

Yet these noble exceptions from the general misrule served but to strengthen it by opposition. Alas! we had fallen upon the most evil of all our evil days.[9] The great "movement" — that was the cant term — went on: a diseased commotion, moral and physical. Art — the Arts — arose supreme, and, once enthroned, cast chains upon the intellect which had elevated them to power. Man, because he could not but acknowledge the majesty of Nature, fell into childish exultation at his acquired and still-increasing dominion over her elements. Even while he stalked a God in his own fancy, an infantine imbecility came over him. As might be supposed from the origin of his disorder, he grew infected with system, and with abstraction. He enwrapped himself in generalities. Among other odd ideas, that[b] of universal equality gained ground; and in the face of analogy and of God — in despite of the loud warning voice of the laws of *gradation* so visibly pervading all things in Earth and Heaven — wild attempts at an omni-prevalent Democracy were made. Yet this evil sprang necessarily from the leading evil, Knowledge. Man could not both know and succumb.[10] Meantime huge smoking cities arose, innumerable. Green leaves shrank before the hot breath of furnaces. The fair face of Nature was deformed as with the ravages of some loathsome disease. And methinks, sweet Una, even our slumbering sense of the forced and of the far-fetched might have arrested us here. But now it appears that we had worked out our own destruction[11] in the perversion of our *taste,* or rather in the blind neglect of its culture in the schools. For, in truth, it was at this crisis that taste alone — that faculty which, holding a middle position between the pure intellect and the moral sense, could never safely have been disregarded — it was now that taste alone could have led us gently back to Beauty, to Nature, and to Life. But alas for the pure contemplative spirit and majestic intuition of Plato! Alas for the μουσική which he justly regarded as an all-sufficient education for the soul! Alas for

a   solomnly (*B, C*) misprint, corrected   b   those (*A*)
from *A*

him and for it! — since both were most desperately needed when both were most entirely forgotten or despised.* [12]

Pascal, a philosopher whom we both love, has said, how truly! — *"que tout notre raisonnement se réduit*[c] *à céder au sentiment;"*[13] and it is not impossible that the sentiment of the natural, had time permitted it, would have regained its old ascendancy over the harsh mathematical reason of the schools. But this thing was not to be. Prematurely induced by intemperance of knowledge, the old age of the world drew on. This the mass of mankind saw not, or, living lustily although unhappily, affected not to see. But, for myself, the Earth's records had taught me to look for widest ruin as the price of highest civilization. I had imbibed a prescience of our Fate from comparison of China the simple and enduring, with Assyria the architect, with Egypt the astrologer, with Nubia, more crafty than either, the turbulent mother of all Arts.[14] In history† [15] of these regions I met with a ray from the Future. The individual artificialities of the three latter were local diseases of the Earth, and in their individual overthrows we had seen local remedies applied; but for the infected world at large I could anticipate no regeneration save in death. That man, as a race, should not become extinct, I saw that he must be *"born again."*

And now it was, fairest and dearest, that we wrapped[d] our spirits,[e] daily, in dreams.[16] Now it was that, in twilight, we discoursed of the days to come, when the Art-scarred surface of the Earth,

---

* "It will be hard to discover a better [method of education] than that which the experience of so many ages has already discovered; and this may be summed up as consisting in gymnastics for the body, and *music* for the soul." — Repub. lib. 2. "For this reason is a musical education most essential; since it causes Rhythm and Harmony to penetrate most intimately into the soul, taking the strongest hold upon it, filling it with *beauty* and making the man *beautiful-minded*. . . . . He will praise and admire *the beautiful;* will receive it with joy into his soul, will feed upon it, and *assimilate his own condition with it.*" — Ibid. lib. 3. Music (μουσικη) had, however, among the Athenians, a far more comprehensive signification than with us. It included not only the harmonies of time and of tune, but the poetic diction, sentiment and creation, each in its widest sense. The study of *music* was with them, in fact, the general cultivation of the taste — of that which recognizes the beautiful — in contra-distinction from reason, which deals only with the true.

† "History," from ιστορειν, to contemplate.

---

c   *rèduit (A, B, C)*   e   souls, *(A)*
d   busied *(A)*

having undergone that purification‡ which alone could efface its rectangular obscenities, should clothe itself anew in the verdure and the mountain-slopes and the smiling waters of Paradise, and be rendered at length a fit dwelling-place for man:[17] — for man the Death-purged — for man to whose now exalted intellect there should be poison in knowledge no more — for the redeemed, regenerated, blissful, and now immortal, but still for the *material*, man.

Una. Well do I remember these conversations, dear Monos; but the epoch of the fiery overthrow was not so near at hand as we believed, and as the corruption you indicate did surely warrant us in believing. Men lived; and died individually. You yourself sickened, and passed into the grave; and thither your constant Una speedily followed you. And though the century which has since elapsed, and whose conclusion brings us thus together once more, tortured our slumbering senses with no impatience of duration, yet, my Monos, it was a century still.

Monos. Say, rather, a point in the vague infinity. Unquestionably, it was in the Earth's dotage that I died. Wearied at heart with anxieties which had their origin in the general turmoil and decay, I succumbed to the fierce fever. After some few days of pain, and many of dreamy delirium replete with ecstasy,[18] the manifestations of which you mistook for pain, while I longed but was impotent to undeceive you — after some days there came upon me, as you have said, a breathless and motionless torpor; and this was termed *Death* by those who stood around me.

Words are vague things. My condition did not deprive me of sentience. It appeared to me not greatly dissimilar to the extreme quiescence of him, who, having slumbered long and profoundly, lying motionless and fully prostrate in a midsummer noon, begins to steal slowly back into consciousness, through the mere sufficiency of his sleep, and without being awakened by external disturbances.

I breathed no longer. The pulses were still. The heart had ceased to beat. Volition had not departed, but was powerless. The

‡ The word *"purification"* seems here to be used with reference to its root in the Greek πυρ, fire.

senses were unusually active, although eccentrically so — assuming often each other's functions at random.[19] The taste and the smell were inextricably confounded, and became one sentiment, abnormal and intense. The rose-water with which your tenderness had moistened my lips to the last, affected me with sweet fancies of flowers — fantastic flowers, far more lovely than any of the old Earth, but whose prototypes we have here blooming around us. The eyelids, transparent and bloodless, offered no complete impediment to vision. As volition was in abeyance, the balls could not roll in their sockets — but all objects within the range of the visual hemisphere were seen with more or less distinctness; the rays which fell upon the external retina, or into the corner of the eye, producing a more vivid effect than those which struck the front or interior surface. Yet, in the former instance, this effect was so far anomalous that I appreciated it only as *sound* — sound sweet or discordant as the matters presenting themselves at my side were light or dark in shade — curved or angular in outline. The hearing, at the same time, although excited in degree, was not irregular in action — estimating real sounds with an extravagance of precision, not less than of sensibility. Touch had undergone a modification more peculiar. Its impressions were tardily received, but pertinaciously retained, and resulted always in the highest physical pleasure. Thus the pressure of your sweet fingers upon my eyelids, at first only recognised through vision, at length, long after their removal, filled my whole being with a sensual delight immeasurable. I say with a sensual delight. *All* my perceptions were purely sensual. The materials furnished the passive brain by the senses were not in the least degree wrought into shape by the deceased understanding. Of pain there was some little; of pleasure there was much; but of moral pain or pleasure none at all. Thus your wild sobs floated into my ear with all their mournful cadences, and were appreciated in their every variation of sad tone; but they were soft musical sounds and no more; they conveyed to the extinct reason no intimation of the sorrows which gave them birth; while the large and constant tears which fell upon my face, telling the bystanders of a heart which broke, thrilled every fibre of my frame with ecstasy alone. And this was in truth the *Death* of which these bystanders spoke reverently, in low whispers — you, sweet Una, gaspingly, with loud cries.

They attired me for the coffin — three or four dark figures which flitted busily to and fro. As these crossed the direct line of my vision they affected me as *forms;* but upon passing to my side their images impressed me with the idea of shrieks, groans, and other dismal expressions of terror, of horror, or of wo. You alone, habited in a white robe, passed in all directions musically about me.[20]

The day waned; and, as its light faded away, I became possessed by a vague uneasiness — an anxiety such as the sleeper feels when sad real sounds fall continuously within his ear — low distant bell-tones, solemn, at long but equal intervals, and commingling with melancholy dreams. Night arrived; and with its shadows a heavy discomfort. It oppressed my limbs with the oppression of some dull weight, and was palpable. There was also a moaning sound, not unlike the distant reverberation of surf, but more continuous, which, beginning with the first twilight, had grown in strength with the darkness. Suddenly lights were brought into the room, and this reverberation became forthwith interrupted into frequent unequal bursts of the same sound, but less dreary and less distinct. The ponderous oppression was in a great measure relieved; and, issuing from the flame of each lamp, (for there were many,) there flowed unbrokenly into my ears a strain of melodious monotone. And when now, dear Una, approaching the bed upon which I lay outstretched, you sat gently by my side, breathing odor from your sweet lips, and pressing them upon my brow, there arose tremulously within my bosom, and mingling with the merely physical sensations which circumstances had called forth, a something akin to sentiment itself — a feeling that, half appreciating, half responded to your earnest love and sorrow; but this feeling took no root in the pulseless heart, and seemed indeed rather a shadow than a reality, and faded quickly away, first into extreme quiescence, and then into a purely sensual pleasure as before.

And now, from the wreck and the chaos of the usual senses, there appeared to have arisen within me a sixth, all perfect. In its exercise I found a wild delight — yet a delight still physical, inasmuch as the understanding had in it no part. Motion in the animal frame had fully ceased. No muscle quivered; no nerve thrilled; no artery throbbed. But there seemed to have sprung up in the brain, *that* of which no words could convey to the merely human intelligence even an indistinct conception.[f] Let me term it a mental pendulous pulsation.[21] It was the moral embodiment of man's abstract idea of *Time*. By the absolute equalization of this movement — or of such as this — had the cycles of the firmamental orbs themselves, been adjusted. By its aid I measured the irregularities of the clock upon the mantel, and of the watches of the attendants. Their tickings came sonorously to my ears. The slightest deviations from the true proportion — and these deviations were omniprævalent — affected me just as violations of abstract truth were wont, on earth, to affect the moral sense. Although no two of the time-pieces in the chamber struck the individual seconds accurately together, yet I had no difficulty in holding steadily in mind the tones, and the respective momentary errors of each. And this — this keen, perfect, self-existing sentiment of *duration* — this sentiment existing (as man could not possibly have conceived it to exist) independently of any succession of events — this idea — this sixth sense, upspringing from the ashes of the rest, was the first obvious and certain step of the intemporal soul upon the threshold of the temporal Eternity.

It was midnight; and you still sat by my side. All others had departed from the chamber of Death. They had deposited me in the coffin. The lamps burned flickeringly; for this I knew by the tremulousness of the monotonous strains. But, suddenly these strains diminished in distinctness and in volume. Finally they ceased. The perfume in my nostrils died away. Forms affected my vision no longer. The oppression of the Darkness uplifted itself from my bosom. A dull shock like that of electricity[22] pervaded my frame, and was followed by total loss of the idea of contact. All of what man has termed sense was merged in the sole consciousness of entity, and in the one abiding sentiment of duration. The mortal body had been at length stricken with the hand of the deadly *Decay*.

f   definition. *(A)*

Yet had not all of sentience departed; for the consciousness and the sentiment remaining supplied some of its functions by a lethargic intuition. I appreciated the direful change now in operation upon the flesh, and, as the dreamer is sometimes aware of the bodily presence of one who leans over him, so, sweet Una, I still dully felt that you sat by my side. So, too, when the noon of the second day came, I was not unconscious of those movements which displaced you from my side, which confined me within the coffin, which deposited me within the hearse, which bore me to the grave, which lowered me within it, which heaped heavily the mould upon me, and which[g] thus left me, in blackness and corruption, to my sad and solemn[h] slumbers with the worm.[23]

And here, in the prison-house which has few secrets to disclose,[24] there rolled away days and weeks and months;[i] and the soul watched narrowly each second as it flew, and, without effort, took record of its flight — without effort and without object.[j]

A year passed. The consciousness of *being* had grown hourly more indistinct, and that of mere *locality* had, in great measure, usurped its position. The idea of entity was becoming merged in that of *place*. The narrow space immediately surrounding what had been the body, was now growing to be the body itself. At length, as often happens to the sleeper (by sleep and its world alone is *Death* imaged) — at length, as sometimes happened on Earth to the deep slumberer, when some flitting light half startled him into awaking, yet left him half enveloped in dreams — so to me, in the strict embrace of the *Shadow*, came *that* light which alone might have had power to startle — the light of enduring *Love*. Men toiled at the grave in which I lay darkling.[25] They upthrew the damp earth. Upon my mouldering bones there descended the coffin of Una.[26]

And now again all was void. That nebulous light had been extinguished. That feeble thrill had vibrated itself into quiescence. Many *lustra* had supervened. Dust had returned to dust.[27] The worm had food no more. The sense of being had at length

g   *Omitted (A)*
h   sad and solemn/sad *(A)*
i   solemn months, *(A)*
j   *After this:* Meantime the worm,

with its convulsive motion, writhed untorturing and unheeded about me. *(A)*

THE COLLOQUY OF MONOS AND UNA

utterly departed, and there reigned in its stead — instead of all things — dominant and perpetual — the autocrats *Place* and *Time*. For *that* which *was not* — for that which had no form — for that which had no thought — for that which had no sentience — for that which was soulless, yet of which matter formed no portion — for all this nothingness, yet for all this immortality, the grave was still a home, and the corrosive hours,²⁸ co-mates.

NOTES

Title: The names are the usual Greek masculine and Latin feminine adjectives for "one," used as substantives. The title was suggested by Bulwer's "Monos and Daimonos" (One and Demon), upon which Poe's own "Silence — a Fable" is based. Poe mentions Bulwer's story in reviewing his *Rienzi* in the *Southern Literary Messenger*, February 1836.

Motto: This is from the *Antigone* of Sophocles, line 1333; it appeared as a heading to the ninth book of Bulwer's *Ernest Maltravers* (1837). Poe used the phrase *mellonta tauta* as the title for a story in 1848.

1. See the Gospel according to St. John, 3:3: "Except a man be born again, he cannot see the kingdom of God." Phrases from the King James version of the Bible were part of Poe's working vocabulary. This tale probably contains more of them than any of his other stories.

2. Compare St. John 17:3, "This is life eternal."

3. Spectre — more usually skeleton — at the feast has long been a commonplace expression for a cause of disturbing thoughts in the midst of enjoyment. The phrase has been traced to a record by Herodotus (Bk. II, ch. 78) of an ancient Egyptian custom of displaying a skeleton, or corpse, or mummy, or a representation of one, at feasts as a reminder of mortality. See also "The Dinner of the Seven Wise Men" in Plutarch's *Moralia,* vol. II, p. 359 in the Loeb edition; and Petronius' *Satyricon* 35, p. 53 in the Loeb edition for the custom as adopted by the Romans. There is a corpse at the feast in Poe's "Shadow," but there it is an essential part of the plot.

4. Compare Job 38:11, "Hitherto shalt thou come, but no further."

5. An echo of Pope's "Essay on Man," II, 136: "Grows with his growth, and strengthens with his strength," echoed also in "Never Bet the Devil Your Head" and "The Black Cat."

6. Compare Vergil's *Æneid* I, 203, *Haec olim meminisse iuvabit:* "Someday it will be pleasant to remember these things." For the valley of the shadow see Psalm 23:4, and the note on "Eldorado," line 21 (Mabbott I, 464).

7. See Genesis 2:17 and 3:3–5 for the tree of knowledge.

8. Poe rarely lost an opportunity to speak with disfavor of the Utilitarians —

Bentham, Mill, and their followers. See "Philosophy of Furniture," "Diddling," the Preface to "Marginalia," and "Mellonta Tauta."

9. See *Paradise Lost,* VII, 25, for "fallen on evil days."

10. All Poe's authorized texts have this sentence as it appears here. A suggestion has been made, however, that Poe meant to write "Man could not both know and *not* succumb": see Genesis 2 : 17, cited in note 7 above.

11. Compare Philippians 2 : 12 ". . . work out your own salvation."

12. The quotations in the footnote are from Plato's *Republic,* II, 17 (376e) and III, 12 (401d–402a). See also "Marginalia," number 239 (*SLM,* June 1849, p. 336) for discussion of the word translated "music."

13. The phrase is from Blaise Pascal's *Pensées,* VII, 4, and means that "all our reasoning is forced to give way to feeling (or intuition)."

14. Many scholars in Poe's day thought the culture of Nubia and Ethiopia older than that of Egypt. See, for example, in the *Edinburgh Review* for January 1835 an article on "Ancient and Modern Nubians" which mentions "Nubian temples evidently anterior to the maturity of Egyptian art," and in the issue of October 1835 a review of G. A. Haskins' *Travels in Ethiopia . . . Illustrating the Antiquities, Arts, and History of the Ancient Kingdom of Meroë* (London, 1835).

15. Poe commented, in his review of Bulwer's *Rienzi* mentioned above: "History, from ισ[τ]ορειν [the *tau* is omitted – a misprint – in the *SLM*], to contemplate, seems, among the Greeks, to have embraced not only the knowledge of past events, but also Mythology, Esopian and Milesian fables, *Romance,* Tragedy and Comedy." Poe closely follows Bielfeld, Book III, chap. IV, sec. 1.

16. Compare "Give not thy soul to dreams," from *Politian,* VI, 21, and "we then busied our souls in dreams," from "Murders in the Rue Morgue."

17. Poe thought the destruction of the world, prophesied in Revelation 21 : 1, applied only to the surface of the globe. See "The Conversation of Eiros and Charmion," note 4, and "Marginalia," number 21 (*Democratic Review,* November 1844, p. 487).

18. Dr. George W. Rawlings of Richmond, Poe's physician in 1849, related that his patient said when his mind was quite clear that the fantasies of mania were always delightful, he saw nothing but visions of beauty and heard sweetest music. (From the manuscript "Recollections of Poe" by various persons, collected about 1880 by Father John Bannister Tabb and now number 361 in the Ingram Collection at the University of Virginia.)

19. For acuteness of the senses, compare "The Fall of the House of Usher" and "The Tell-Tale Heart." The evidence of synesthesia ("senses assuming each other's functions") here is not the only place it occurs in Poe's works. See Mabbott I, 38, 64, 107, and 161–162: "Tamerlane" [*A*], line 373, with Poe's footnote and my note on line 373; "Al Aaraaf," part II, lines 41 and 47; and "Fairy Land" [II], lines 22–29 with the pertinent notes. [For a later discussion, see Robert D. Jacobs, *Poe: Journalist and Critic* (1969), pp. 409–410.]

20. Compare this paragraph with "The Haunted Palace" (1839), lines 19–20 and 43–44.

21. For other uses of the word "pendulous" see "The Island of the Fay" at note 8 and "Marginalia," number 47 (*Democratic Review,* December 1844, p. 581): "the pendulous character of the long branches" of the weeping willow.

22. By 1841, the science of electricity had progressed considerably beyond "the new Galvanic Battery" mentioned in Poe's early tale "A Decided Loss," notably through the discoveries in the 1830's by Michael Faraday and Joseph Henry concerning induced currents.

23. Compare "Irenë" (1831), line 62, and "The Sleeper" (1841), line 47. See Mabbott I, pp. 185, 188.

24. See *Hamlet,* I, v, 14, "to tell the secrets of my prison house," and compare the title of Poe's sketch, "Some Secrets of the Magazine Prison-House."

25. "Darkling" here means "in the dark," as Keats used it in the "Ode to a Nightingale," stanza vi: "Darkling I listen."

26. Poe may have had in mind a legend ascribed to "an ancient chronicle of Tours" that when, in 1164, Heloise was laid in the tomb of Abelard his arms opened to receive her. The legend is recounted by Isaac D'Israeli in "Abelard and Eloisa" (*Curiosities of Literature,* first series), an article from which Poe drew "the two reprehensible lines in Pope's Eloisa" quoted in "Pinakidia," number 89 (*SLM,* August 1836, p. 578). D'Israeli found the legend in a note by André Duchesne in his 1616 edition of Abelard's works. Duchesne's extensive annotation is reprinted in J. P. Migne's *Patrologiae cursus completus,* vol. 178 (1856); the legend appears in column 176.

27. Compare Genesis 3:19: "... dust thou art, and unto dust shalt thou return."

28. "Corrosive hours" is repeated from "The Coliseum," line 32.

NEVER BET YOUR HEAD
(NEVER BET THE DEVIL YOUR HEAD)

Poe spoke of the "witty exaggerated into the burlesque" as a way to attain celebrity in the Magazines in a letter to Thomas W. White, April 30, 1835.* This comic story conforms very well to the author's peculiar ideas of what constituted humor. Relatively few readers share his belief that *any* impossible combination of events is laughable; and the tale is never, or hardly ever, anthologized. Nevertheless there are amusing hits at those commentators who give a profound meaning to mere extravagancies of imagination. Poe wrote an illuminating comment on his story in

* For a discussion see Walter Fuller Taylor, "Israfel in Motley," *Sewanee Review,* July–September, 1934.

a letter referring to it of September 19, 1841, to Dr. Joseph Evans Snodgrass: "You are mistaken about 'The Dial.' I have no quarrel in the world with that illustrious journal, nor it with me. I am not aware that it ever mentioned me by name, or alluded to me either directly or indirectly. My slaps at it were only in 'a general way.' The tale in question is a mere Extravaganza levelled at no one in particular, but hitting right and left at things in general."

The source for the principal incident is a brief account in the second chapter of *The Posthumous Papers of the Pickwick Club:*

> Now it so happened that Mr. Pickwick and his three companions had resolved to make Rochester their first halting-place; ... they agreed to occupy the seat at the back of the coach ...
>
> "Heads, heads, take care of your heads," cried the loquacious stranger, as they came out under the low archway, which, in those days, formed the entrance to the coach-yard. "Terrible place – dangerous work; other day, five children – mother – tall lady, eating sandwiches – forgot the arch – crash, knock – children look round, mother's head off ... head of a family off; shocking, shocking."†

Covered bridges were common in America, especially in the northeast, and were usually wooden.‡ Poe's substitution of one for a British archway is typical, for it may be supposed his transcendental protagonist was from New England.

The story was presumably written in the early summer of 1841. Poe apparently planned to include it in PHANTASY-PIECES, the collection he projected in 1842, for he listed it in the table of contents between "The Mask of the Red Death" and "Eleonora."

TEXTS

(A) Graham's Magazine for September 1841 (19:124–127); *(B) Broadway Journal,* August 16, 1845 (2:85–88); *(C) Works* (1850), II, 408–417. PHANTASY-PIECES, title only.

The text followed is Griswold's *(C)* which shows one apparently auctorial change from *(B).*

Reprints

New York *Brother Jonathan,* September 4, 1841, from *Graham's Magazine; Jonathan's Miscellany,* September 7, 1841, from *Brother Jonathan.*

† Poe had reviewed Dickens' book appreciatively in the *Southern Literary Messenger,* November 1836. My quotation is from the Philadelphia edition (1836), pp. 26–27.

‡ See Clara E. Wagemann, *Covered Bridges of New England* (1931). Age and motor traffic have now eliminated most of them.

NEVER BET THE DEVIL YOUR HEAD. [C]

A TALE WITH A MORAL.

"Con *tal que las costumbres de un autor,*" says Don Thomas[a] De Las Torres, in the preface to his "Amatory Poems," "*sean puras y castas, importa muy poco que no sean igualmente severas sus obras*"[1] — meaning, in plain English, that, provided the morals of an author are pure, personally, it signifies nothing what are the morals of his books. We presume that Don Thomas[b] is now in Purgatory for the[c] assertion. It would be a clever thing, too, in the way of poetical justice, to keep him there until his "Amatory Poems" get out of print, or are laid definitely[d] upon the shelf through lack of readers. Every fiction *should have* a[e] moral; and, what is more to the purpose, the[f] critics have discovered that every fiction *has*. [g]Philip Melancthon, some time ago, wrote a commentary upon the "Batrachomyomachia" and proved that the poet's object was to excite a distaste for sedition. Pierre La Seine, going a step farther, shows that the intention was to recommend to young men temperance in eating and drinking. Just so, too, Jacobus Hugo has satisfied himself that by Euenis, Homer meant to insinuate John Calvin; by Antinöus, Martin Luther; by the Lotophagi, Protestants in general; and, by the Harpies, the Dutch.[2] Our more modern Scholiasts are equally acute.[g] These[h] fellows demonstrate a hidden meaning in "The Antediluvians,"[3] a parable in "Powhatan,"[4] new views in "Cock Robin," and trancendentalism in "Hop O' My Thumb."[5] [i]In short, it has been shown[i] that no man can sit down to write without a very profound design. Thus to authors in general much trouble is spared. A novelist, for example, need have no care of his moral. It is there — that is to say, it is somewhere — and the moral and the critics can take care of themselves. When the proper time arrives, all that the gentleman intended,

---

Title: Never Bet Your Head. A Moral Tale. *(A);* Never Bet Your Head. (PHANTASY-PIECES)
a   Tomas *(A)*
b   Torres *(A)*
c   so heterodox an *(A)*

d   definitively *(A)*
e   its *(A)*
f   our modern *(A)*
g...g   *Omitted (A)*
h   These ingenious *(A)*
i...i   It has been proved *(A)*

and all that he did not intend, will be brought to light, in the "Dial," or the "Down-Easter," [6] together with all that he ought to have intended, and the rest that he clearly meant to intend: — so that it will all come very straight in the end.

There is no just ground, therefore, for the charge brought against me by certain ignoramuses — that I have never written a moral tale, or, in more precise words, a tale with a moral. They are not the critics predestined to bring me out, and *develop* my morals: — that is the secret. By and by the "North American Quarterly Humdrum" [7] will make them ashamed of their stupidity. In the meantime, by way of staying execution — by way of mitigating the accusations against me — I offer the sad history appended; — a history about whose obvious moral there can be no question whatever, since he who runs may read it in the large capitals which form the title of the tale. I should have credit for this arrangement — a far wiser one than that of La Fontaine and others, who reserve the impression to be conveyed until the last moment, and thus sneak it in at the fag end of their fables.

[j]*Defuncti injuriâ ne afficiantur* was a law of the twelve tables, and[j] *De mortuis nil nisi bonum* is an excellent injunction — even if the dead in question be nothing but dead small beer.[8] It is not my design, therefore, to vituperate my deceased friend, Toby Dammit. He was a sad dog, it is true, and a dog's death it was that he died; but he himself was not to blame for his vices. They grew out of a personal defect in his mother. She did her best in the way of flogging him while an infant — for duties to her well-regulated mind were always pleasures, and babies, like tough steaks, [k]or the modern Greek olive trees,[k] are invariably the better for beating — [9] but, poor woman! she had the misfortune to be left-handed, and a child flogged left-handedly had better be left unflogged. The world revolves from right to left. It will not do to whip a baby from left to right. If each blow in the proper direction drives an evil propensity out, it follows that every thump in an opposite one knocks its quota of wickedness in. I was often present at Toby's chastisements, and, even by the way in which he kicked, I could per-

---

j . . . j *Omitted (A)*   k . . . k *Omitted (A)*

ceive that[1] he was getting worse and worse every day. At last I saw, through the tears in my eyes, that there was no hope of the villain at all, and one day when he had been cuffed until he grew so black in the face that one might have mistaken him for a little African, and no effect had been produced beyond that of making him wriggle himself into a fit, I could stand it no longer, but went down upon my knees forthwith, and, uplifting my voice, made prophecy of his ruin.

The fact is that his precocity in vice was awful. At five months of age he used to get into such passions that he was unable to articulate. At six months,[m] I caught him gnawing[n] a pack of cards.[10] At seven months,[o] he was in the constant habit of catching and kissing the female babies. At eight months[p] he peremptorily refused to put his signature to the Temperance pledge. Thus he went on increasing in iniquity, month after month, until, at the close of the[q] first year, he not only insisted upon wearing *moustaches,*[r] [11] but had contracted a propensity for cursing and swearing, and for backing his assertions by bets.

Through this latter most ungentlemanly practice, the ruin which I had predicted to Toby Dammit overtook him at last. The fashion had "grown with his growth and strengthened with his strength,"[12] so that, when he came to be a man, he could scarcely utter a sentence without interlarding it with a proposition to gamble. Not that he actually *laid* wagers — no. I will do my friend the justice to say that he would as soon have laid eggs. With him the thing was a mere formula — nothing more. His expressions on this head had no meaning attached to them whatever. They were simple if not altogether innocent expletives — imaginative phrases wherewith to round off a sentence. When he said "I'll bet you so and so," nobody ever thought of taking him up; but still I could not help thinking it my duty to put him down. The habit was an immoral one, and so I told him. It was a vulgar one — this I begged him to believe. It was discountenanced by society — here I said nothing but the truth. It was forbidden by act of Congress — here I

1	*Omitted (A)*	p	*Omitted (A)*
m	*Omitted (A)*	q	his *(A)*
n	knawing *(C) emended from A, B*	r	Melnotte frocks, *(A)*
o	*Omitted (A)*		

had not the slightest intention of telling a lie. I remonstrated — but to no purpose. I demonstrated — in[s] vain. I entreated — he smiled. I implored — he laughed. I preached — he sneered. I threatened — he swore. I kicked him — [t] he called for the police. I pulled his [u]nose — he blew it, and offered to bet the Devil his head that I would not venture to try that experiment[u] again.

Poverty was another vice which the peculiar physical deficiency of Dammit's mother had entailed upon her son. He was detestably poor; and this was the reason, no doubt, that his expletive expressions about betting[u'] seldom took a pecuniary turn. I will not be bound to say that I ever heard him make use of such a figure[v] of speech as "I'll bet you a dollar." It was usually "I'll bet you what you please," or "I'll bet you what you dare," or "I'll bet you a trifle," or else, more significantly still, *"I'll bet the Devil[w] my head."*

This latter form seemed to please him[x] best: — perhaps because it involved the least[y] risk; for Dammit had become excessively parsimonious. Had any one taken him up, his head was small, and thus his loss would have been[z] small too. But these are my own reflections, and I am by no means sure that I am right in attributing them to him. At all events the phrase in question grew daily in favor, notwithstanding the gross impropriety of a man[a] betting his brains like bank-notes: — but this was a point which my friend's perversity of disposition would not permit him to comprehend. In the end, he abandoned all other forms of wager, and gave himself up to *"I'll bet the Devil[b] my head,"* with a pertinacity and exclusiveness of devotion that displeased not less than it surprised me. I am always displeased by circumstances for which I cannot account. Mysteries force a man to think, and so injure his health. The truth is, there was something in *the air* with which Mr. Dammit was wont to give utterance to his offensive expression — something in his *manner* of enunciation — which at first interested, and after-

---

s	but in *(A)*	w	*the Devil/you (A)*
t	him — /him and *(A)*	x	him the *(A)*
u...u	nose, and he bet me that I	y	the least/less *(A)*
	dared not do it *(A)*	z	have been/be *(A)*
u'	betting, *(B, C) corrected from A*	a	man's *(A, B)*
v	a figure/figures *(A)*	b	*the Devil/ you (A)*

wards made me very uneasy — something which, for want of a more definite term at present, I must be permitted to call *queer;* but which Mr. Coleridge would have called mystical, Mr. Kant pantheistical, Mr. Carlyle twistical, and Mr. Emerson hyperquizzitistical.c [13] I began not to like it at all. Mr. Dammit's soul was in a perilous state. I resolved to bring all my eloquence into play to save it. I vowed to serve him as St. Patrick, in the Irish chronicle, is said to have served the dtoad, that is to say, "awaken himd to a sense of hise situation." [14] I addressed myself to the task forthwith. Once more I betook myself to remonstrance. Again I collected my energies for a final attempt at expostulation.

When I had made an end of my lecture, Mr. Dammit indulged himself in some very equivocal behavior. For some moments he remained silent, merely looking me inquisitively in the face. But presently he threw his head to one side, and elevated his eyebrows to great extent. Then he spread out the palms of his hands and shrugged up his shoulders. Then he winked with the right eye. Then he repeated the operation with thef left. Then he shut them both up very tight.g Then he opened them both so very wide that I became seriously alarmed for the consequences. Then, applying his thumb to his nose, he thought proper to make an indescribable movement with the rest of his fingers. Finally, setting his arms a-kimbo, he condescended to reply.

I can call to mind only the heads of his discourse. He would be obliged to me if I would hhold my tongue.h He wished none of my advice. He despised all my insinuations. He was old enough to take care of himself. iDid I still think him baby Dammit? Did I mean to say anything against his character? Did I intend to insult him? Was I a fool?i Was my maternal parent aware, in a word, of my absence from the domiciliary residence? He would put this latter question to me as to a man of veracity, and he would bind

---

c   hyper-fizzitistical. *(A)*
d ...d   snakes and toads when he "awakened them *(A)*
e   their *(A)*
f   his *(A)*
g   tight, as if he was trying to crack nuts between the lids. *(A)*
h ... h   keep my opinions within my

own bosom. *(A)*
i ... i   Did I mean to say anything against his character? Did I intend to insult him? Did I take him for an idiot? Did I still think him baby Dammit? Was I a fool? — or was I not? Was I mad? — or was I drunk? *(A)*

himself to abide by my reply. Once more he would demand explicitly if my mother knew that I was out. My confusion, he said, betrayed me, and he would be willing to bet the Devil[j] his head that she did not.

Mr. Dammit did not pause for my rejoinder. Turning upon his heel, he left my presence with undignified precipitation. It was well for him that he did so. My feelings had been wounded. Even my anger had been aroused. For once I would have taken him up upon his insulting wager. I would have won [k]for the Arch-Enemy Mr. Dammit's little head — for the fact is, my mamma *was* very[k] well aware of my merely[l] temporary absence from home.

But[m] *Khoda shefa midêhed* — [15] Heaven gives relief — as the Musselmen say when you tread upon their toes. It was in pursuance of my duty that I had been insulted, and I bore the insult like a man. It now seemed to me, however, that I had done all that could be required of me, in the case of this miserable individual, and I resolved to trouble him no longer with my counsel, but to leave him to his conscience and[n] himself. But although I forebore to intrude with my advice, I could not bring myself to give up his society altogether. I even went so far as to humor some of his less reprehensible propensities; and there were times when I found myself lauding his wicked jokes, as epicures do mustard, with tears in my eyes: — [16] so profoundly did it grieve me to hear his evil talk.

One fine day, having strolled out together, arm in arm, our route led us in the direction of a river. There was a bridge, and we resolved to cross it. It was roofed over, by way of protection from the weather, and the arch-way, having but few windows, was thus very uncomfortably dark. As we entered the passage, the contrast between the external glare, and the interior gloom, struck heavily upon my spirits. Not so upon those of the unhappy Dammit, who offered to bet the Devil[o] his head that I was hipped.[17] He seemed to be in an unusual[p] good humor. He was excessively lively — so much so that I entertained I know not what of uneasy suspicion. It is not impossible that he was affected with the tran-

j the Devil *omitted (A)*	m *Omitted (A)*
k . . . k his little head. My maternal	n and to *(A)*
parent was *very (A)*	o the Devil/me *(A)*
l *Omitted (A)*	p extravagantly *(A)*

scendentals. I am not well enough versed, however, in the diagnosis of this disease to speak with decision upon the point; and unhappily there[q] were none of my friends of the "Dial" present. I suggest the idea, nevertheless, because of a certain [r]species of austere[r] Merry-Andrewism which seemed to beset my poor friend, and caused him to make quite a Tom-Fool of himself.[18] Nothing would serve him but wriggling and skipping about under and over everything that came in his way; now shouting out, and now lisping out, all manner of odd little and big words, yet preserving the gravest face in the world all the time. I really could not make up my mind whether to kick or to pity him. At length, having passed nearly across the bridge, we approached the termination of the foot way, when our progress was impeded by a turnstile of some height. Through this I made my way quietly, pushing it around as[s] usual. But this turn would not serve the turn of Mr. Dammit. He insisted upon leaping the stile, and said he could cut a pigeon-wing over it[t] in the air. Now this, conscientiously speaking, I did not think he could do. The best pigeon-winger over all kinds of style, was my friend Mr. Carlyle, and as I knew *he* could not do it, I would not believe that[u] it could be done by Toby Dammit. I therefore told him, in so many words, that he was a braggadocio, and could not do what he said. For this, I had reason to be sorry afterwards; — for he straightway [v]offered to *bet the Devil*[v] *his head* that he could.

I was about to reply, notwithstanding my previous resolutions, with some remonstrance against his impiety, when I heard, close at my elbow, a slight cough, which sounded very much like the ejaculation *"ahem!"* I started, and looked about me in surprise. My glance at length fell into a nook of the frame-work of the bridge, and upon the figure of a little lame old gentleman of venerable aspect.[19] Nothing could be more reverend than his whole appearance; for, he not only had on a full suit of black, but his shirt was perfectly clean and the collar turned very[w] neatly down over a white cravat, while his hair was parted in front like a girl's.

---

q   th ere *(B) misprint*
r . . . r   austere species of *(A)*
s   as is *(A)*
t   it while *(A)*

u   *Omitted (A)*
v . . . v   *bet me (A)*
w   *Omitted (A)*

His hands were clasped pensively together over his stomach, and his two eyes were[x] carefully rolled up into the top of his head.[20]

Upon observing him more closely, I perceived that he wore a black silk apron over his small-clothes; and this was a thing which I thought very odd. Before I had time to make any remark, however, upon so singular a circumstance, he interrupted me with a second *"ahem!"*

To this observation[y] I was not immediately prepared to reply. The fact is, remarks of this laconic[z] nature are nearly unanswerable. I have known a[a] Quarterly Review *non-plused*[b] by the word *"Fudge!"*[21] I am not ashamed to [c]say, therefore, that[c] I turned to Mr. Dammit for assistance.

"Dammit," said I, "what are you about? don't you hear? — the gentleman says *'ahem!'* " I looked sternly at my friend while I thus addressed him; for to say the truth, I felt particularly puzzled, and when a man is particularly[d] puzzled[e] he must knit his brows and look savage, or else he is pretty sure to look like a fool.

"Dammit," observed I — although this sounded very much like an oath, than which nothing was farther from my thoughts — "Dammit," I suggested — "the gentleman says *'ahem!'* "

I do not attempt to defend my remark on the score of profundity; I did not think it profound myself; but I have noticed that the effect of our speeches is not always proportionate with their importance in our own eyes; and if I had shot Mr. D. through and through with a Paixhan bomb,[22] or knocked him in the head with [f]the "Poets and Poetry of America," [23] he[f] could hardly have been more discomfited than when I addressed him with those simple words — "Dammit, what are you about? — don't you hear? — the gentleman says *'ahem!'* "

"You don't say so?" gasped he at length, after turning more colors than a pirate runs up, one after the other, when chased by a man-of-war. "Are you quite sure[g] he said *that?* Well, at all events I am in for it now, and may as well put a bold face upon the matter. Here goes, then — *ahem!"*

---

x   *Omitted (A)*
y   observation of his *(A)*
z   *Omitted (A)*
a   a profound *(A)*
b   stumped *(A)*
c . . . c   say that *(A)*

d   *Omitted (A)*
e   pnzzled *(B) misprint*
f . . . f   one of Dr. McHenry's epics, he *(A)*
g   sure that *(A)*

At this the little old gentleman seemed pleased — God only knows why. He left his station at[h] the nook of the bridge, limped forward with a gracious air, took Dammit by the hand and shook it cordially, looking all the while straight up in his face with an air[i] of the most unadulterated benignity which it is possible for the mind of man to imagine.

"I am quite sure you will[j] win it, Dammit," said he, with the frankest of all smiles, "but we are obliged to have a trial you know, for the sake of mere form."

"Ahem!" replied my friend, taking off his coat with a deep sigh, tying a pocket-handkerchief[k] around his waist, and producing an unaccountable alteration in his countenance by twisting up his eyes, and bringing down the corners of his mouth — "ahem!" And "ahem," said he again, after a pause; and not another[l] word more than "ahem!" did I ever know him to say after that. "Aha!" thought I, without expressing myself aloud — "this is quite a remarkable silence on the part of[m] Toby Dammit, and is no doubt a consequence of his[n] verbosity upon a previous occasion. One extreme induces another. I wonder if he has forgotten the many unanswerable questions which he propounded to me so fluently on the day when I gave him my last lecture? At all events, he is cured of the transcendentals."

"Ahem!" here replied Toby, just as if he had been reading my thoughts, and looking like a very old sheep in a reverie.[24]

The old gentleman now took him by the arm, and led him more into the shade of the bridge — a few paces back from the turnstile. "My good fellow," said he, "I make it a point of conscience to allow you this much run. Wait here, till I take my place by the stile, so that I may see whether you go over it handsomely, and transcendentally, and don't omit any flourishes of the pigeon-wing. A mere form, you know. I will say 'one, two, three, and away.' Mind you start at the word 'away.'" Here he took his position by the stile, paused a moment as if in profound reflection, then[o] *looked up* and, I thought, smiled very slightly, then tight-

---

h in *(A)*
i an air/a countenance *(A)*
j you will/you'll *(A)*
k pocket-hankerchief *(B) misprint*

l not another/devil the *(A)*
m of my friend, *(A)*
n his great *(A)*
o then looked down, then *(A)*

ened the strings of his apron, then took a long look at Dammit,[p] and finally gave the word as agreed upon —

One — two — three — and away!

Punctually at the word "away," my poor friend set off in a strong gallop. The stile[q] was not very high, like Mr. Lord's[r] — nor yet[s] very low, like that of Mr. Lord's[t] reviewers,[25] but upon the whole I made sure that he would clear it. And then what if he did not? — ah, that was the question — what if he did not? "What right," said I, "had the old gentleman to make any other gentleman jump? The little old dot-and-carry-one! who is *he?* If he *asks me*[u] to jump, I won't do it, that's flat, and I don't care who *the devil he is.*" The bridge, as I say, was arched and covered in, in a very ridiculous manner, and there was a most uncomfortable echo about it at all times — an echo which I never before so particularly observed as when I uttered the four last words of my remark.

But what I said, or what I thought, or what I heard, occupied only an instant.[v] In less than five seconds from his starting, my poor Toby had taken the leap. I saw him run nimbly, and spring grandly from the floor of the bridge, cutting the most awful flourishes with his legs as he went up. I saw him high in the air, pigeon-winging it to admiration just over the top of the stile; and of course I thought it an unusually singular thing that he did not *continue* to go over. But the whole leap was the affair of a moment,[w] and, before I had a chance to make any profound reflections, down came[x] Mr. Dammit on the flat of his back, on the same side of the stile from which he had started. At[y] the same instant I saw the old gentleman limping off at the top of his speed, having caught and wrapped up in his apron something that fell heavily into it from the darkness of the arch just over the turnstile. At all this I was much astonished; but I had no leisure to think, for Mr.

p Dammit, then put his fore-finger to the side of his nose, *(A)*
q style *(A)*
r Pue's *(A)*
s yet to say *(A)*
t Pue's *(A)*
u me *(A)*
v instant of time. *(A)*
w moment, as they always say in the crack historical novels, *(A)*
x downcame *(B) misprint*
y In *(B)*

Dammit lay particularly still, and I concluded that his feelings had been hurt, and that he stood in need of my assistance. I hurried up to him and found that he had received what might be termed a serious injury. The truth is, he had been deprived of his head, which after a close search I could not find anywhere; — so I determined to take him home, and send for the homœopathists.[z] In the meantime[a] a thought struck me, and I threw open an adjacent window of the bridge; when the sad truth flashed upon me at once. About five feet just above the top of the turnstile, and crossing the arch of the foot-path so as to constitute a brace, there extended a flat[b] iron bar, lying with its breadth horizontally, and forming one of a series that served to strengthen the structure throughout its extent. With the edge of this brace it appeared evident that the neck of my unfortunate friend had come precisely in contact.

He did not long survive his terrible loss. The homœopathists[c] did not give him little enough physic,[26] and what little they did give him he hesitated to take. So in the end he grew worse, and at length died, a lesson[d] to all riotous livers. I bedewed his grave with my tears, worked a *bar* sinister[27] on his family escutcheon, and, for the general expenses of his funeral, sent in my very moderate bill to the transcendentalists.[e] The scoundrels refused to pay it, so I had Mr. Dammit dug up at once, and sold him for dog's meat.

NOTES

Title: The title phrase seems to have been a fairly common expression in Poe's day. Only a few years after the publication of this tale the *New World*, March 8, 1845, reported of the Shakespearean lecturer Henry Norman Hudson: "Mr. Hudson was determined to emphasize his assertion – so leaning forward and bringing his hand down vigorously upon the table before him, he added in a loud and earnest tone, *'I'll wager my head on it!'* "

1. The Spanish quotation means "As long as the habits of an author are pure and chaste, it matters very little if his works are less austere" – a doctrine being disputed at the time by English and American critics. Texts *A, B,* and *C*

---

z homœopathics. *(A)*
a mean time *(B)*
b flat and sharp *(A)*
c homœopathics *(A)*

d lession *(C) misprint, corrected* from *A, B*
e transcendendalists. *(B) misprint*

all give the erroneous spelling *importo* for *importa.* The sentence may be found in *Cuentos en verso castellano* by Tomás Hermenegildo de las Torres (Zaragoza, 1828), pp. v–vi. Poe used it again in "Fifty Suggestions," number 19 (*Graham's,* May 1849).

2. Compare "Pinakidia," numbers 131 and 142 (*SLM,* August 1836, p. 580), which (as pointed out by Palmer Holt, *AL,* March 1962) Poe took from H. N. Coleridge's *Introductions to the Study of the Classic Poets.* See the Philadelphia edition (Carey & Lea, 1831), p. 189, where a footnote says:

> Philip Melancthon wrote a commentary on the Battle of the Frogs and Mice, and conceived the scope of the poet to have been to excite a hatred of tumults and seditions in the minds of the readers.

> Pierre la Seine thought the object was to recommend to young men temperance in eating and drinking; — *Why,* I do not find written. Fabric[ius, *Bibliotheca Graeca*]. Lib. ii, c.2. s.3.

Another passage in a note on p. 89 reads:

> Jacobus Hugo was of opinion that Homer under divine influence prophesied the destruction of Jerusalem under that of Troy; the life, miracles and passion of our Saviour, and the history of the Church under the Emperors in the Iliad. He thinks Homer secretly meant the Dutch by the Harpies, John Calvin by *Euenis,* Martin Luther by Antinous and *Lades,* and the Lutherans generally by the Lotophagi. Fabric. lib i. c.6. s.15.

> Jacobus Hugo (Jacques Hugues) published his *Vera historia Romana* at Rome in 1655. Melancthon's commentary appeared in an edition of the Pseudo-Homeric *Batrachomyomachia* (Paris, 1542); and Pierre La Seine (Pietro Lasena, an Italian scholar of French descent) wrote *Homeri Nepenthes, seu, de abolendo luctu* (Lyons, 1624).

3. *The Antediluvians, or The World Destroyed,* a narrative poem in ten books (London, 1839; Philadelphia, 1840), was by Dr. James McHenry (1785–1845), poet, novelist, and contributor of criticism to Robert Walsh's *American Quarterly Review.* Two articles of his in the *American Quarterly* (March 1832 and June 1834) unfavorably criticizing Willis and Bryant and American literature in general had stirred up violent antagonism, and in July 1834 an article by Willis Gaylord Clark in the *Knickerbocker* very nearly demolished him. McHenry's epic, *The Antediluvians,* was reviewed most unfavorably in *Blackwood's* for July 1839, and again unfavorably in *Graham's* for February 1841. (This review was taken for Poe's work and reprinted by Harrison, *Complete Works,* X, 105; but Poe wrote no reviews for *Graham's* before the April number.) In "An Appendix of Autographs," *Graham's,* January 1842, Poe complained of the unfair tactics of Professor Wilson, the editor of *Blackwood's,* and of a cabal of American enemies of Doctor McHenry, and called his poem "the only tolerable American epic." One suspects Poe decided to be on the side of a poet disliked by Lewis Gaylord Clark and his cohorts; and, between the time he composed his tale and "An Appendix of Autographs" for *Graham's,* looked into *The Antediluvians.* He let only one of his two original references stand in revising "Never Bet." McHenry died on July 25, 1845, and was given a brief but kindly obituary in the *Broadway Journal* of August 23, 1845.

4. Seba Smith's *Powhatan: A Metrical Romance* was unfavorably reviewed by Poe in *Graham's* for July 1841.

5. The old nursery rhyme "Who Killed Cock Robin?" and the fairy tale "Hop o' My Thumb" (from Charles Perrault's collection) have been part of children's literature in English since the early eighteenth century.

6. *The Dial,* founded in 1840, was the organ of the Transcendentalists, including Emerson and Margaret Fuller. *Down-Easter* is a fictitious title possibly suggesting John Neal's old *Yankee,* founded in Portland, or suggested by the title of one of his novels, *The Down-Easters* (1833).

7. *The Humdrum* burlesques the serious quarterlies, particularly the *North American Review.* Poe used the same made-up title in "Autography" (*SLM,* February 1836, letters v and viii), and in "The Literary Life of Thingum Bob," the hero purchases the *Hum-Drum.*

8. The first statement, just as it is here, appeared in "Pinakidia," No. 25 (*SLM,* August 1836, p. 575). "Let the dead suffer no injury" is not in the early Roman laws, but is of uncertain origin. "Nothing but good of the dead" is a maxim of the early Greek philosopher Chilo, recorded by Diogenes Laertius, *Lives of the Philosophers* (I, "Chilo," 2), and mentioned by Plutarch as one of the laws of Solon (*Lives,* Solon, sec. 21). For both quotations see "Fifty Suggestions," number 9 (*Graham's,* May 1849).

9. The comparison of babies to steaks is again used in "Fifty Suggestions," number 20. For the olive trees, compare "Sweepings from a Drawer" by "W. Landor" (Horace Binney Wallace) in *Burton's,* November 1839: "Some schoolmasters seem to think of their pupils as the modern Greeks do of their olive trees, that the more they are beaten the more they thrive."

10. "Knawing" for gnawing is listed in the OED as a spelling used occasionally in the fifteenth century and more commonly in the sixteenth and seventeenth centuries. It is now considered obsolete.

11. The "Melnotte frocks" mentioned in the canceled passage were fashionable coats named after Claude Melnotte, the hero of Bulwer's play *The Lady of Lyons* (1838).

12. Adapted from Pope's *Essay on Man,* II, 136; the passage is also used in "The Colloquy of Monos and Una" and "The Black Cat," in serious contexts.

13. Most of Poe's numerous references to Coleridge, Kant, Carlyle, and Emerson make fun of what he considered vagueness, obscurity, or confusion of style.

14. The remark about St. Patrick is used also in "Fifty Suggestions," number 12 (*Graham's,* May 1849).

15. Mr. Francis Paar informed me that the phrase is correct modern Persian; but the proper plural of Mussulman is Mussulmans.

16. The bit about mustard echoes the section "Rake" in James Puckle's little book *The Club; or, A Gray Cap for a Green Head* (1711), and is used also in

"Fifty Suggestions," number 18 (*Graham's*, May 1849). A delightful illustrated edition of *The Club* was issued by the Chiswick Press in 1834.

17. "Affected with hypochondria; morbidly depressed." OED.

18. Buffoonery. William Maginn's comment in *Fraser's*, January 1836, p. 37, is quoted by the OED: "Nothing is more distasteful ... than the undiscriminating Merryandrewism of an ingrained vulgarian." Both Merry Andrews and Tom Fools are buffoons.

19. In *Le Diable boiteux* (1707) of Alain-René Le Sage, the demon Asmodeus is lame. In popular representations of the Devil, identifying marks often include a cloven hoof. It is suggested in "Von Kempelen and His Discovery."

20. In the *Yankee,* December 1829, reviewing Robert Montgomery's poems, John Neal said a certain portrait of the author made him look "like a hero of a French cookery-book — with his hair parted in the middle like a girl's, and tumbled up in huge masses at the temples." A satirical drawing of Montgomery by Daniel Maclise, accompanying Maginn's amusing text in *Fraser's* for January 1832, not only shows Montgomery's hair arrangement but also "hands clasped ... over his stomach" and eyes upturned. The drawing is labeled "The author of Satan." It is probably not accidental that Poe made the Devil look like this religious poetaster. (See also "Loss of Breath," note 15.)

21. [There is probably some connection here with Thomas Moore's books on the adventures of the Fudge Family, which undoubtedly influenced "Lionizing."]

22. General Henri-Joseph Paixhans (1783–1854) designed field guns to fire explosive shells in the Napoleonic wars.

23. Poe here substituted for his earlier reference to McHenry the title of R. W. Griswold's *Poets and Poetry of America,* a royal octavo of over 400 pages, often called "The Big Book." The first three editions appeared in 1842 and contained three of Poe's poems; a tenth edition was issued in 1849. (See Mabbott, I, 584, for a listing of Poe's contributions to the first and later editions.)

24. Compare *"Un mouton qui rêve,"* in "Philosophy of Furniture" at n. 5.

25. Poe "used up" William W. Lord's *Poems* (one of which burlesqued Poe) in the *Broadway Journal,* May 24, 1845 (see Mabbott, I, 314–315, 352). The author ridiculed in the earlier version is Hugh A. Pue, a Philadelphian, whose *Grammar ... Addressed to Every American Youth,* published by the author, Poe denounced in *Graham's* for July 1841.

26. The use of very small doses was a conspicuous characteristic of homeopathy, a system of therapeutics based on the theory that like cures like. It was still new in the United States in the 1830's and like Mesmerism and phrenology was attracting attention.

27. A bar sinister, sometimes called a baton, is a sign of illegitimacy in heraldry. There is a double entendre, since a sinister bar was unluckily fatal to Toby Dammit.

ELEONORA

"Eleonora" is a story of happiness lost and regained, and a favorite of romantic readers. But like the more somber prose poems "Shadow" and "Silence" it is cryptic, and Poe was not quite satisfied with it. Reviewing the annual in which it first appeared, he called it a tale "which is not ended so well as it might be — a good subject spoiled by hurry in the handling."* Since he made no radical changes in revision, he clearly never decided upon a better ending.

Critics have been more lenient. Woodberry wrote, "In this alone of all his tales is there . . . the warmth, the vital sense of human love. The myth . . . is pictorial, like a medieval legend . . . Here love came to the boy and girl, beneath the fantastic trees . . . Symbolism has seldom been more simple and pure . . . more absolute master of the things of sense for the things of the spirit than in this unreal scene."†

Dr. Thomas Holley Chivers, likening the story to the Ossianic poems, spoke of the "flower-gemmed Valley" where Poe "spent, with the Morning Star of his Soul . . . his youth," and added, "This Tale . . . revealing . . . the freshest as well as the loftiest emotions of his soul . . . contains the rudiments of many of his afterthoughts."‡

Poe probably expected readers to suppose his story partly inspired by Dr. Johnson's *Rasselas,* which was subtitled "The Happy Valley," but Poe took little else from the lexicographer. Poe's plot reminds many of Bernardin de St. Pierre's *Paul et Virginie* (1788). There a boy and girl grow up together in idyllic surroundings on the island of Mauritius. They reach the age of discretion, fall in

---

* See the review of *The Gift for 1842* in *Graham's Magazine,* November 1841.

† *Poe* (1885), p. 168. Unaware that annuals were usually on sale well before the beginning of the year for which they were issued, Woodberry connected the illness of Eleonora with that of Virginia Poe, whose first serious hemorrhage occurred in January 1842. He was also reminded of the thirteenth century romance, *Aucassin and Nicolette,* a work not published in America until after Poe's time.

‡ *Life of Poe* (first printed in 1952), p. 79. Poe regarded "Ossian" highly, although aware the poems are modern.

love, and see the world in a new light. They are separated, and the beauty departs. Finally they are reunited, but the girl soon dies.§

In tone and color, like "The Island of the Fay," to which it is akin, "Eleonora" may have taken something from Miss Mercer's "Fairy Tale" (*SLM*, January 1836), quoted in the introduction to the former story, above.

Some autobiographical element in Poe's story is undeniable — the two cousins and the girl's mother parallel the poet's personal life. May Garrettson Evans saw the story's relation to the unfolding of Poe's love when the family lived in Amity Street, Baltimore; and John C. French thought the scene of "Eleonora" partly inspired by the clear stream and wooded hills at the valley of Gwynn's Falls in Baltimore County about a mile and a half west of Poe's home, to which the two young people probably walked.* A. H. Quinn thought the story Poe's way of telling Virginia that she was his mate for eternity.†

Since Poe expressed dissatisfaction with the first form of "Eleonora," we cannot seek for a completely consistent plot in it, but the deletion of two fairly long passages and some of the careful changes in wording may indicate one in the revised version. Yet there are several interpretations of the action even in that. The simplest is that it is a story of reincarnation: the virtuous Eleonora is permitted to return as Ermengarde. The time element is awkward, however, and the hero hears Eleonora after his marriage. A notion of "bipart" soul in Eleonora, the uniting of both parts in

§ See Sinclair Snow in *Romance Notes*, Autumn 1963. Marguerite Mespoulet sent me this suggestion independently. *Paul and Virginia* in English translation was extremely popular in Poe's time. The basic plot, however, is an old one — witness I. D'Israeli's "Mejnoun and Leila" (in his *Romances,* first American edition, Philadelphia, 1803), retelling a traditional Arabian love story from the version by the twelfth-century Persian poet Nizami. Kais and Leila, educated together, are separated by Leila's father. Kais, deprived of his love, loses his mind and wanders in the desert, becoming known as "Mejnoun" ("Madman"). Leila dies of grief, and shortly afterward Mejnoun dies at her grave and is buried beside her. Some of D'Israeli's exotic details may be reflected in "Eleonora."

* See articles in the *Maryland Historical Magazine*, December 1941, and March 1955, respectively.

† *Poe*, p. 329. Professor Wightman F. Melton, in the *South Atlantic Quarterly*, April 1912, pointed out parallels between "Eleonora" and "Annabel Lee"; verbal resemblances, however, are rather to "The Raven."

Ermengarde, may be intended — the hint of that in the first version was canceled later.

A second interpretation is ethical. As a child Eleonora accepted vows that her husband should not have taken. Mature, in Heaven, she is allowed to absolve him of them, for there "the Spirit of Love reigneth," and in this world too.‡

A third view is based on the hint of the hero's madness — Ermengarde is hallucinatory. Poe usually gave his less romantic readers some reason for a matter-of-fact explanation in his stories, but "Eleonora" seems to me primarily a fairy tale.

The allegorical undercurrent in "Eleonora" may be interpreted in several ways. Some feel the allegory is of childhood and maturity — as hinted in the reference to the riddle of the Sphinx. Some would even see the idea of paradise lost and regained. And the interpretation has been offered that the artist's career is shadowed forth, as he emerges from a world of unreality into a real world of manhood and action.§ It can be observed that "Eleonora" is perhaps the last of Poe's tales in his extreme arabesque manner.

Poe wrote to his friend Snodgrass on January 17, 1841, "I have one or two articles *in statu pupillari* that would make you stare, at least, on account of the utter oddity of their conception. To carry out the conception is a difficulty which — may be overcome." Poe presumably had "Eleonora" ready during the first two months of the year, for on February 22, 1841, one of the editors of *The Gift* wrote, " . . . the work is now in the hands of the printer."*

TEXTS

(A) The Gift: A Christmas and New Year's Present for 1842 (1841), pp. 154–162; *(B) Broadway Journal*, May 24, 1845 (1:322–324); *(C) Works* (1850), I, 446–452. PHANTASY-PIECES, title only.

The version of the *Broadway Journal* is followed; Griswold's version *(C)* shows no author's correction, and introduces a misprint.

‡ A student, Mr. Richard Oliver, thought the motto inserted in the second version strengthens this view, which I prefer myself.

§ Thanks are due to my students Greta Boxer, Eileen O'Connor, Adrienne Rosignana, and Patricia Walsh for suggestions on interpretation.

* Edward L. Carey to Charles West Thomson, quoted by Heartman and Canny, *A Bibliography of . . . Poe* (1943), p. 68.

TALES, 1841–1842

Reprints

Boston Notion, September 4, 1841; *Roberts' Semi-Monthly Magazine* as "Eleonora – A Fable," September 15, 1841; *New-York Weekly Tribune,* September 18, 1841; *New-York Daily Tribune,* September 20, 1841; *Literary Souvenir* (Lowell, Mass.), November 13, 1841 and July 9, 1842. All from *The Gift.*

ELEONORA. [B]

Sub conservatione formae specificae salva anima.
Raymond Lully.

I am come of a race noted for vigor of fancy and ardor of passion.[a] Men have called me mad; but the question is not yet settled, whether madness is or is[b] not the loftiest[c] intelligence — whether much that is glorious — whether all that is profound — does[d] not spring from disease of thought — from *moods*[e] of mind exalted at the expense of the general intellect.[1] They who dream by day are cognizant of many things which escape [f]those who dream only[f] by night. In their grey visions they obtain glimpses of eternity, and thrill, in awaking,[g] to find that they have been upon the verge of the great secret. In snatches, they learn something of the wisdom which is of good, and more of the[h] mere knowledge which is of evil.[2] They penetrate, however rudderless or compassless, into the vast ocean of the "light ineffable"[3] and again, like the adventurers[i] of the Nubian geographer,[4] *"agressi sunt mare tenebrarum, quid in eo esset exploraturi."*

We will say, then, that I am mad. I grant, at least, that there are two distinct conditions of my mental existence — the condition of a lucid reason, not to be disputed, and belonging to the memory of events forming the first[j] epoch of my life — and a condition of shadow and doubt, appertaining to the present, and to the recollection of what constitutes the second great era of my being. Therefore, what I shall tell of the earlier period, believe;

Title: Eleonora. A Fable. *(A)*
Motto: *Not in A*
a   *After this:* Pyrros is my name. *(A)*
b   is or is/be or be *(A)*
c   loftier *(A)*
d   do *(A)*

e   moods *(A)*
f ...f   the dreamers *(A)*
g   waking, *(C)*
h   that *(A)*
i   adventures *(C) misprint*
j   first *(B) misprint*

and to what I may relate of the later time, give only such credit as may seem due; or doubt it altogether; or, if doubt it ye cannot,[k] then play unto its riddle the Oedipus.[1] [5]

She whom I loved in youth, and of whom I now pen calmly and distinctly these remembrances, was the sole daughter of the only sister of my mother long departed. Eleonora was the name of my cousin. We had always dwelled together, beneath a tropical sun, in the Valley of the[m] Many-Colored Grass.[6] No unguided footstep ever came upon that vale; for it lay[n] far away up among a range of giant hills that hung beetling around about it, shutting out the sunlight from its sweetest recesses. No path was trodden in its vicinity; and, to reach our happy home, there was need of putting back, with force, the foliage of many thousands of forest trees, and of crushing to death the glories of many millions of fragrant flowers. Thus it was that we lived all alone, knowing nothing of the world without the valley, — I, and my cousin, and her mother.

From the dim regions beyond the mountains at the upper end of our encircled domain, there crept out a narrow and deep river, brighter than all save [o]the eyes of Eleonora;[o] and, winding stealthily about in mazy courses, it passed away, at length, through a shadowy gorge, among hills still dimmer than those whence[p] it had issued. We called it the "River of Silence:" for there seemed to be a hushing influence in its flow. No murmur arose from its bed, and so gently it wandered along[p'] that the pearly pebbles upon which we loved to gaze, far down within its bosom, stirred not at all, but lay in a motionless content, each in its own old station, shining on gloriously forever.[7]

The[q] margin of the river, and of the many dazzling rivulets that glided, through devious ways, into its channel, as well as[r] the spaces that extended from the margins[s] away down into the depths of the streams until they reached the bed of pebbles at the bottom, — these spots, not less than the whole surface of the valley, from the river to the mountains that girdled it in, were carpeted all by a

---

k   dare not, *(A)*
l   Sphynx. *(A)*
m   *Omitted (A);* he *(B) misprint*
n   lay singularly *(A)*
o . . . o   Eleonora's eyes; *(A)*

p   from which *(A)*
p'   along, *(B, C) corrected from A*
q   And the *(A)*
r   as well as/and *(A)*
s   brinks *(A)*

soft green grass, thick, short, perfectly even, and vanilla-perfumed,[8] but so besprinkled throughout with the yellow buttercup, the white daisy, the purple violet, and the ruby-red asphodel, that its exceeding beauty spoke to our hearts, in loud tones, of the love and of the glory of God.

And, here and there, in groves about this grass, like wildernesses of dreams, sprang up fantastic trees, whose tall slender stems stood not upright, but slanted gracefully towards[t] the light that peered at noon-day into the centre of the valley. Their bark was speckled with the vivid alternate splendor[u] of ebony and silver, and was smoother than all save the cheeks of Eleonora;[9] so that but for the brilliant green of the huge leaves that spread from their summits in long tremulous lines, dallying with the Zephyrs,[10] one might have fancied them giant serpents of Syria doing homage to their Sovereign the Sun.[11]

Hand in hand about this valley, for fifteen years, roamed I with Eleonora before Love entered within our hearts. It was one evening at the close of the third lustrum of her life, and of the fourth of my own, that we sat, locked in each other's embrace, beneath the serpent-like trees, and looked down within the waters of the River of Silence at our images therein. We spoke no words during the rest of that sweet day; and our words even[v] upon the morrow were tremulous and few. We had drawn the God Eros from that wave,[12] and now we felt that he had enkindled within us the fiery souls of our forefathers. The passions which had for centuries distinguished our race[v'] came thronging with the fancies for which they had been equally noted, and together breathed a delirious bliss over the Valley of the Many-Colored Grass. A change fell upon all things. Strange brilliant flowers, star-shaped, burst out upon the trees where no flowers had been known before. The tints of the green carpet deepened; and when, one by one, the white daisies shrank away, there sprang up, in place of them, ten by ten of the ruby-red asphodel.[13] And life arose in our paths; for the tall flamingo, hitherto unseen, with all gay glowing birds,

---

t	toward *(A)*	v	*Omitted (A)*
u	splendours *(A)*	v'	race, *(B, C) corrected from A*

ELEONORA

flaunted his scarlet plumage before us. The[w] golden and silver fish haunted the river, out of the bosom of which issued, little by little, a murmur that swelled, at length, into a lulling melody more divine than that of the harp of Æolus[14] — sweeter than all save the voice of Eleonora. And now, too, a[x] voluminous cloud, which we had long watched in the regions of Hesper,[15] floated out thence, all gorgeous in crimson and gold, and settling in peace above us, sank, day by day, lower and lower, until its edges rested upon the tops of the mountains, turning all their dimness into magnificence, and shutting us up, as if forever, within a magic prison-house of grandeur and of glory.[16]

The loveliness of Eleonora was that of the [y]Seraphim; but she[y] was a maiden artless and innocent as the brief life she had led among the flowers.[17] No guile disguised the fervor of love which animated her heart, and she examined with me its inmost recesses as we walked together in the Valley of the Many-Colored Grass, and discoursed of the mighty changes which had lately taken place therein.[z]

At length, having spoken one day, in tears, of the last sad change which must befall Humanity, she thenceforward dwelt only upon this one sorrowful theme, interweaving it into all our converse, as, in the songs of the bard of Schiraz,[a] [18] the same images are found occurring, again and again, in every impressive variation of phrase.

She had seen that the finger of Death was upon her bosom —

---

w us. The/us; and *(A)*
x a vast and *(A)*
y . . . y seraphim — and here, as in all things referring to this epoch, my memory is vividly distinct. In stature she was tall, and slender even to fragility; the exceeding delicacy of her frame, as well as of the hues of her cheek, speaking painfully of the feeble tenure by which she held existence. The lilies of the valley were not more fair. With the nose, lips, and chin of the Greek Venus, she had the majestic forehead, the naturally-waving auburn hair, and the large luminous eyes of her kindred. Her beauty, nevertheless, was of that nature which leads the heart to wonder not less than to love. The grace of her motion was surely ethereal. Her fantastic step left no impress upon the asphodel — and I could not but dream as I gazed, enrapt, upon her alternate moods of melancholy and of mirth, that two separate souls were enshrined within her. So radical were her changes of countenance, that at one instant I fancied her possessed by some spirit of smiles, at another by some demon of tears. *New paragraph.* She *(A)*
z place therein./place. *(A)*
a Shiraz *(A)*

that, like the ephemeron,[b] she had been made perfect in loveliness only to die;[19] but the terrors of the grave, to her, lay solely in a consideration which she revealed to me, one[c] evening at twilight, by the banks of the River of Silence. She grieved to think that, having entombed her in the Valley of the Many-Colored Grass, I would quit forever its happy recesses, transferring the love which now was[d] so passionately her own to some maiden of the outer and every-day world. And, then and there, I threw myself hurriedly at the feet of Eleonora, and offered up a vow, to herself and to Heaven, that I would never bind myself in marriage to any daughter of Earth — that I would in no manner prove recreant to her dear memory, or to the memory of the devout affection with which she had blessed me. And I called the Mighty Ruler of the Universe to witness the pious solemnity of my vow. And the curse which I invoked of *Him*[e] and of her, a saint in Helusion,[f] [20] should I prove traitorous to that promise, involved a penalty the exceeding great horror of which will not permit me to make record of it here. And the bright eyes of Eleonora grew brighter at my words; and she sighed as if a deadly burthen[g] had been taken from her breast; and she trembled and very bitterly wept; but she made acceptance of the vow, (for what was she but a child?) and it made easy to her the bed of her death. And she said to me, not many days afterwards, tranquilly dying, that, because of what I had done for the comfort of her spirit, she would watch over me in that spirit when departed, and, if so it were permitted her, return to me visibly in the watches of the night; but, if this thing were, indeed, beyond the power of the souls in Paradise, that she would, at least, give me frequent indications of her presence; sighing upon me in the evening winds, or filling the air which I breathed with perfume from the censers of the angels.[21] And, with these words upon her lips, she yielded up her innocent life, putting an[h] end to the first epoch of my own.

Thus far I have faithfully said. But as I pass the barrier in Time's path formed by the death of my beloved, and proceed with[i]

b	ephemera, *(A)*	f	Elysium, *(A)*
c	one still *(A)*	g	burden *(A)*
d	now was/was now *(A)*	h	*Omitted (A)*
e	*Him*/him, *(A)*	i	into *(A)*

the second era of my existence, I feel that a[j] shadow gathers over my brain, and I mistrust the perfect sanity of the record. But let me on. — Years dragged themselves along heavily, and still[k] I dwelled within the Valley of the Many-Colored [l]Grass; — but a[l] second change had come upon all things. The star-shaped flowers shrank into the stems of the trees, and appeared no more. The tints of the green carpet faded; and, one by one, the ruby-red asphodels withered away; and there sprang up, in place of them, ten by ten, dark eye-like violets that [m]writhed uneasily[22] and were ever encumbered with dew.[m] And Life departed from our paths; for the tall flamingo flaunted no longer his scarlet plumage before us, but flew sadly from the vale into the hills, with all the gay glowing birds that had arrived in his company. And the golden and silver fish swam down through the gorge at the lower end of our domain and bedecked the sweet river never again. And the lulling melody that had been softer than the wind-harp of Æolus and more divine than all save the voice of Eleonora, it died[23] little by little away, in murmurs growing lower and lower, until the stream returned, at length, utterly, into the solemnity of its original silence. And then, lastly the voluminous cloud uprose, and, and, abandoning the tops of the mountains to the dimness of old, fell back into the regions of Hesper, and took away all its manifold golden and gorgeous glories from the Valley of the Many-Colored Grass.

Yet the promises of Eleonora were not forgotten; for I heard the sounds of the swinging of the censers of the angels; and streams of a holy perfume floated ever and ever about the valley; and at lone hours, when my heart beat heavily, the winds that bathed my brow came unto me laden with soft sighs; and indistinct murmurs filled often the night air; and once — oh, but once only! I was awakened from a slumber like[n] the slumber of death by the pressing of spiritual lips upon my[o] own.

But the void within my heart refused, even thus, to be filled. I longed[p] for the love which had before filled it to overflowing. At length the valley *pained* me through its memories of Eleonora,

---

j a vague *(A)*	m ... m quivered uneasily. *(A)*
k still, with the aged mother of	n like unto *(A)*
Eleonora, *(A)*	o mine *(A)*
l ... l Grass. A *(A)*	p longed — I madly pined *(A)*

and I left it forever for the vanities and the turbulent triumphs of the world.

*　　*　　*　　*　　*

I found myself within a strange[q] city, where all things might have served to blot from recollection the sweet dreams I had dreamed so long in the Valley of the Many-Colored Grass. The pomps and pageantries of a stately court, and the mad clangor of arms, and the radiant loveliness of woman, bewildered and intoxicated my brain. But as yet my soul had proved true to its[r] vows, and the indications of the presence of Eleonora were still given me in the silent hours of the night. Suddenly, these manifestations they[s] ceased; and the world grew dark before mine[t] eyes; and I stood aghast at the burning thoughts which possessed — at the terrible temptations which beset me; for there came from some far, far[u] distant and unknown land, into the gay court of the king I served, a[v] maiden to whose beauty my whole recreant heart yielded at once — at whose footstool I bowed down without a struggle, in the most ardent, in the most abject worship of love. What indeed was [w]my passion[w] for the young girl of the valley in comparison with the [x]fervor, and the delirium, and the spirit-lifting[x] ecstasy of adoration[24] with which I poured out my whole[y] soul in tears at the feet of the ethereal[z] Ermengarde? — Oh bright was the seraph[a] Ermengarde! [b]and in that knowledge I had room for none other. — Oh divine was the angel Ermengarde! and as I looked down into the depths of her memorial eyes[25] I thought only of them — and *of her.*[b]

---

q　strange Eastern *(A)*
r　her *(A)*
s　*Omitted (A)*
t　my *(A)*
u　far, far/far *(A)*
v　a fair-haired and slender *(A)*
w . . . w　the passion I had once felt *(A)*
x . . . x　madness, and the glow, and the fervour, and the spirit-stirring *(A)*
y　*Omitted (A)*
z　lady *(A)*
a　lady *(A)*
b . . . b　I looked down into the blue depths of her meaning eyes, and I thought only of them, and of her. Oh, lovely was the lady Ermengarde! and in that knowledge I had room for none other. Oh, glorious was the wavy flow of her auburn tresses! and I clasped them in a transport of joy to my bosom. And I found rapture in the fantastic grace of her step — and there was a wild delirium in the love I bore her when I started to see upon her countenance the radical transition from tears to smiles that I had wondered at in the long-lost Eleonora. I forgot — I despised the horrors of the curse I had so blindly invoked, and I wedded the lady Ermengarde. *(A)*

ELEONORA

I wedded; — nor dreaded the curse I had invoked; and its bitterness was not visited upon me.[26] ᶜAnd once — but once again inᶜ the silence of the night, there cameᵈ through my lattice the soft sighs which had forsaken me; and they modelled themselves into ᵉfamiliar andᵉ sweet voice, saying:

"Sleep in peace! — for the Spirit of Love reigneth and ruleth, and, in taking to thy passionate heart her who is Ermengarde, thou art absolved, for reasons which shall be made known to thee in Heaven, of thy vows unto Eleonora."

Suggestions," number 23 (*Graham's,* May 1849), on the relation of genius to madness. Poe there quotes inaccurately Dryden's *Absalom and Achitophel,* line 163, "Great wits are sure to madness near allied."

2. For the knowledge of good and evil see Genesis 2:17.

3. "Light ineffable" may be an echo of *Paradise Lost,* V, 734, "Lightning Divine, ineffable."

4. The Nubian geographer is the author of *Geographia Nubiensis* (Paris, 1619), catalogued by the British Museum under "Nubian Geography" and described as "an abridgment in Latin of Al Idrisi's *Nuzhat Al Mushtak*" — a compilation completed in the middle of the twelfth century by the Arab scientist, poet, and traveler for Roger II of Sicily. Poe follows Bryant's *Antient Mythology* (3rd ed. 1807), IV, 79. The quotation means, "They were come into the sea of shades, to find out what is in it." *Mare Tenebrarum* is the name regularly used for the Atlantic Ocean by "the Nubian," who is also mentioned in "A Descent into the Maelström," "Mellonta Tauta," and *Eureka.*

5. The Sphinx, a monster half woman and half beast, asked travelers, "What goes on four legs, two, and three legs?" Those unable to answer, she threw from a cliff near Thebes in Bœotia. Oedipus replied, "A baby crawls, a man walks, and an old man uses a staff," whereupon the monster jumped from the cliff herself. There is another reference to Oedipus solving an enigma in "Thou Art the Man."

6. Compare Shelley's *Adonais,* line 462, "Life, like a dome of many-colored glass," and Miss Mercer's description of the fairy's crystal grotto: "The few rays of light that penetrated through its deep shade, fixed in its vaulted roof an unfading rainbow. Its floor was inlaid with many colored pebbles..."

7. The River of Silence typifies the mystery surrounding life. It resembles Alph with its "mazy motion" in Coleridge's "Kubla Khan." (Sam S. Baskett, *MLN,* May 1958, points out other resemblances to details in "Kubla Khan.") Compare also a canceled line after "Al Aaraaf," II, 40, "Far down within the crystal of the lake."

8. The "Epidendron Flos Aeris," mentioned in "How to Write a Blackwood Article" and "The Thousand-and-Second Tale of Scheherazade," has a perfume like vanilla, but is not a grass. See the notes on those two stories.

9. Compare a passage in "The Island of the Fay," where "the trees are lithe,...bright, slender, and graceful...with bark smooth, glossy and particolored."

10. For dalliance with Zephyrs, gentle western winds, compare Milton's "L'Allegro," line 19, "Zephyr with Aurora playing."

11. The giant serpents may refer to the hundred-headed Typhon, but no quite satisfactory explanation has been found. Compare also a phrase in Sir Thomas Browne's *Religio Medici,* II, xi, "A piece of divinity in us...that... owes no homage to the sun."

12. The Neo-Platonist Iamblichus drew Eros and Anteros (Love and Love

ELEONORA

Returned) in the form of youths from their fountains at Gadara, according to Eunapius, *Vitae Philosophorum,* cited by Byron in his note on *Manfred,* II, ii, 93.

13. Poe often refers to asphodels — classically associated with death or the dead (see "The Valley Nis," line 26, and note, Mabbott I, 192, 194) — but those in "Eleonora" are not pale, as in nature, but red, being transformed by the power of love.

14. The harp of Æolus — god of the winds — refers to the sound of the wind in the trees. It is mentioned also in "The Poetic Principle."

15. Hesperus, the evening star; Hesperia, the region of the west.

16. Compare "The Coliseum," line 9, "grandeur, gloom, and glory: [and, Mr. Pollin suggests, the third text of "To Helen," line 9, in *Graham's,* September 1841, where "the glory that was Greece" appeared, to join for the first time "the grandeur that was Rome"].

17. Poe echoes William Cullen Bryant's extremely popular "Death of the Flowers," lines 28–30, "And we wept that one so lovely should have a life so brief;/ ... So gentle and so beautiful, should perish with the flowers."

18. The bard of Shiraz in Persia was Shams-ud-din Mahomet, known by the sobriquet Hafiz (Rememberer [of the Koran by heart]), whose pen name appears in every one of his poems. He was a Sufi, and his lines in praise of wine and women are believed to be mystical expositions of his philosophy. He died about A.D. 1389.

19. An ephemeron is any insect that lives only one day in the mature state.

20. In "Pinakidia," number 80 (*SLM,* August 1836, p. 578), Poe records that "Bochart derives Elysium from the Phoenician Elysoth, joy, through the Greek 'Ηλυσιον." Samuel Bochart's typically chimerical etymology is in *Geographia Sacra* (1707), XXXIV, col. 600, which Poe knew surely at second hand through H. N. Coleridge's *Introductions,* p. 141. Poe uses "Helusion" in "Shadow — a Parable," and in a review of R. H. Horne's *Orion* in *Graham's* for March 1844.

21. Compare "The Raven," lines 79–80, "perfumed from an unseen censer/ Swung by seraphim."

22. For the violets compare "The Valley Nis" (1831), lines 29–30, "Helen, like thy human eye/There th' uneasy violets lie."

23. Observe the Gallicism of "the lulling melody ... it died" and, below, "These manifestations, they ceased." Poe uses this device from time to time.

24. Compare the similar effective use of the article repeated in the last sentence of "Ligeia."

25. Here "memorial eyes" means those that awaken memory.

26. This sentence is cited in Mabbott I, 484, as one of "three examples of rhyming prose of the most serious kind"; the others are in "Morella" and "The Masque of the Red Death." The last clause of the sentence echoes Exodus 20:5: "visiting the iniquity of the fathers upon the children ... "

A SUCCESSION OF SUNDAYS
(THREE SUNDAYS IN A WEEK)

Poe prided himself on the variety of his subjects. This is his only tale that can possibly be read as a simple happy love story. Probably because of its superficial comedy — reminiscent of "Lionizing" — it has been more popular with ordinary readers than with professed critics.

The natural phenomenon on which the plot is based is something noticed when Spanish and Portuguese navigators reached China by different routes. Rabelais, Book II, chapter 1, mentions a "week of three Thursdays." Poe's attention was probably attracted by an unsigned article, "Three Thursdays in One Week" in the Philadelphia *Public Ledger,* October 29, 1841, and by a reference to "three Sundays within nine days" in an article signed "Naval" in that paper on November 17, 1841.* He added a satirical element that must have been easily understood by his first readers: Dionysius Lardner, LL.D. (1793–1859), appointed in 1827 professor of natural philosophy and astronomy in the newly established University of London, founder and editor of the *Cabinet Cyclopaedia* of more than 130 volumes, left London in 1840 for the United States and began to deliver lectures on scientific subjects that proved immensely popular with American audiences. His lectures were announced in the Philadelphia *Saturday Evening Post* of November 20, 1841, the issue immediately preceding that containing Poe's story. Poe certainly thought him a quack, for in "Marginalia," number 38 (*Democratic Review,* November 1844), he discussed a pretentious "demonstration" of the lecturer. However, many of Poe's notes in "The Thousand-and-Second Tale of Scheherazade" come from a pamphlet by Lardner.†

---

* See Fannye N. Cherry in *American Literature,* November 1930. I am indebted to Archer Taylor, cited in the note to the title, below, for the reference to Rabelais.

† See my article in *American N & Q,* November 1943, and see also the amusing skit and portrait in *Fraser's Magazine,* July 1832. There was some scandal attached to Lardner's name in America, as he was accompanied by a Mrs. Heaviside who had run away with him, and, according to the *Saturday Evening Post* of January 16,

The story has an element of autobiography also, for Poe had married his cousin; and it may not be purely fanciful to see something of John Allan in Uncle Rumgudgeon.

Poe's tale was presumably published almost immediately after he wrote it.‡

TEXTS

(A) Philadelphia *Saturday Evening Post,* November 27, 1841, as "A Succession of Sundays"; *(B) Broadway Journal,* May 10, 1845 (1:293–295); *(C) Works* (1850), II, 376–382. PHANTASY-PIECES, title only.

The text of *Works (C)* is followed with slight corrections from the first form *(A)*. The *Broadway Journal* version *(B)* differs verbally from *C* only in having more typographical errors. An examination of the Philadelphia *Saturday Evening Post* text *(A)* shows that the tale was thoroughly revised for the *Broadway Journal.* Some pointings, such as *would'nt, must'nt* and *is'nt* have been normalized for this text.

Reprints

Spirit of the Times (Philadelphia), May 14, 1845; *Star of Bethlehem* (Lowell, Mass.), June 7, 1845. Both from the *Broadway Journal.*

THREE SUNDAYS IN A WEEK. [*C*]

"You hard-hearted, dunder-headed, obstinate, rusty, crusty, musty, fusty, old savage!"[1] said I, in fancy, one afternoon, to my grand uncle Rumgudgeon — [2] shaking my fist[a] at him in imagination.

Only in imagination. The fact is,[a'] some trivial discrepancy *did* [b]exist, just then,[b] between what I said[c] and what I had not the

---

1841, was then with him in New York. Lardner, after making $200,000, retired in 1845 to France with the lady. See *A Gallery of Illustrious Literary Characters . . .* (reprinted from *Fraser's Magazine;* edited by William Bates, London, 1873), pp. 72–73.

‡ This story seems to have been the first of Poe's tales to be translated into Spanish — as "La Semana de los tres Domingos" in *El Museo Universal,* Madrid, February 15, 1857, where the author was not named. See J. DeLancey Ferguson, *American Literature in Spain* (1916), p. 56.

Title: A Succession of Sundays *(A) and*	a' is,/is that *(A)*
PHANTASY-PIECES.	b . . . b exist *(A)*
a first *(C) misprint*	c said just then *(A)*

courage to say — between what I did and what I had half a mind to do.

The old porpoise, as I opened the drawing-room[d] door, was sitting with his feet upon[e] the mantel-piece, and a bumper of port in his paw, making strenuous efforts to accomplish the ditty,

Remplis ton verre vide![f]
Vide[g] *ton verre plein!*[3]

"My *dear* uncle," said I, closing the door gently, and approaching him wth the blandest of smiles, "you are always so *very* kind and considerate, and have evinced your benevolence in so many — so *very* many ways — that — that I feel I have only to suggest this little point to you once more to make sure of[h] your full acquiescence."

"Hem!" said he, "good boy! go on!"

"I am sure, my dearest uncle, [you confounded old rascal!] that you have no design really, seriously, to oppose my union with Kate. This is merely a joke of yours, I know — ha! ha! ha! — how *very* pleasant you are at times."

"Ha! ha! ha!" said he, "curse you! yes!"

" [i]To be sure — of course! [i] I *knew* you were jesting. Now, uncle, all that Kate and myself wish at present, is that you would oblige us with your advice as[j] — as regards the *time* — *you* know, uncle — in short, when will it be most convenient for yourself, that the wedding shall — shall — come off, you know?"

"Come off, you scoundrel! — what do you mean by that? — Better wait till it goes on."

"Ha! ha! ha! — he! he! he! — hi! hi! hi! — ho! ho! ho! — hu! hu! hu!4 — oh, that's good! — oh, that's capital — *such* a wit! But all we want[k] just[l] *now,* you know, uncle, is that you would indicate the time precisely."

"Ah! — precisely?"[m]

---

d dining-room *(A)*
e up on *(A)*
f vuide, *(A) misprint* [*The quotation is not italicized in A*]
g vuide *(A) misprint*
h make sure of/procure *(A)*
i . . . i Of course, *(A)*

j advice as/advice — you are so *very* competent to advise us, uncle — and — and *(A)*
k wish *(A)*
l *just (A)*
m *precisely." (A)*

"Yes, uncle — that is, if it would be quite agreeable to your-self."

"Wouldn't it answer, Bobby, if I were to leave it at random — some time within a year or so, for example? — *must* I say pre-cisely?"

"*If* you please, uncle — precisely."

"Well, then, Bobby, my boy — you're a fine fellow, aren't you? — since you *will* have the exact time, I'll — why,[n] I'll oblige you for once."

"Dear[o] uncle!"

"Hush, [p]sir!" [drowning my voice] — "I'll[p] oblige you for once. You shall have my consent — and the *plum,*[q] [5] we mustn't forget the plum — let me see![r] when shall it be? To-day's Sunday — isn't it? [s]Well, then, you[s] shall be married precisely — *precisely,* now mind! — *when three Sundays come* [t]*together in a week!*[t] Do you hear me, sir! *What* are you gaping at? I say, you shall have Kate and her[u] plum when three [v]Sundays come together in a week[v] — but not *till* then — you young scapegrace — not *till* then, if I die for it. You know me — *I'm a man of my word* — now be off!" Here he swallowed his bumper[w] of port, while I rushed from the room in despair.

A very "fine old English gentleman," [6] was my grand-uncle Rumgudgeon, but unlike him of the song, he had his weak points. He was a little, pursy, pompous, passionate, semicircular some-body, with a red nose, a thick skull, a long purse, and a strong sense of his own consequence. With the best heart in the world, he [x]con-trived, through a predominant whim of *contradiction,*[x] to earn for himself, among those who only knew him superficially, the character of a curmudgeon.[y] Like many excellent people, he seemed possessed with[z] a spirit of *tantalization,* which might easily, at a casual glance, have been mistaken for malevolence. To every

---

n *Omitted (A)*
o *Dear (A)*
p . . . p sir! — I'll *(A)*
q plum, Bobby, *(A)*
r see now, *(A)*
s . . . s Well then, I have it. You *(A)*
t . . . t *in succession! (A)*

u and her plum/(and the plum) *(A)*
v . . . v *Sundays come in succession (A)*
w tumbler *(A)*
x . . . x contrived *(A)*
y curmudgeon, merely through a predominant whim of *contradiction. (A)*
z by *(A)*

request, a positive "No!" [a] was his immediate answer; but in the end — in the long, long end — there were exceedingly few requests which he refused. Against all attacks upon his purse he made the most sturdy defence; but the amount extorted from him, at last [b]was, generally,[b] in direct[c] ratio with the length of the siege and the stubbornness of the resistance. In charity no one gave more liberally or with a[d] worse grace.

For the fine arts, and especially for the belles lettres,[e] he entertained a profound contempt. With this he had been inspired by Casimir Périer,[f] whose pert little query *"A quoi un poète est-il[g] bon?"* [7] he was in the habit of quoting, with a very droll pronunciation, as the *ne plus ultra* of logical wit. Thus my own inkling[8] for the Muses had[h] excited his entire displeasure. He assured me one day, when I[i] asked him for a new copy of Horace, that the translation[j] of *"Poeta nascitur non fit"*[9] was "a[k] nasty poet for nothing fit" — a remark[l] which I took in high[m] dudgeon. His repugnance to "the humanities" had, also, much[n] increased of late, by an accidental bias in favor of what he supposed to be natural science. Somebody had accosted him in the street, mistaking him for no less a personage than Doctor Dubble L. Dee, the lecturer upon quack physics.[10] This set him off at a tangent; and just at the epoch of this story — for story it is getting[o] to be after all — my grand-uncle Rumgudgeon was accessible and pacific only upon points which happened to chime in with the caprioles of the hobby he was riding. For the rest, he laughed with his arms and legs, and his politics were stubborn and easily understood. He thought, with Horsley, that "the people have[p] nothing to do with the laws but to obey them." [11]

I had lived with the old gentleman all my life. My [q]parents, in

---

a   "No!" *(A)*
b ...b   was always *(A)*
c   exact *(A)*
d   *Omitted (A)*
e   *belles lettres, (A)*
f   Perier, *(A, B, C)*
g   *poete est il (A, B, C)*
h   *Omitted (A)*

i   I had *(A)*
j   meaning *(A)*
k   "a/a *(B) misprint*
l   a remark/an insult *(A)*
m   very serious *(A)*
n   been much *(A)*
o   growing *(A)*
p   had *(A)*

dying,[q] had bequeathed me to him as a rich legacy.[r] [12] I believe[s] the old villain loved me as his own child — nearly if not quite as well as he loved Kate — but it was a dog's existence that he led me, after all. From my first year until my fifth, he obliged me with very regular floggings. From five to fifteen, he threatened me, hourly, with the House of Correction. From fifteen to twenty, not a day passed in which he did not [t]promise to[t] cut me off with a shilling. I was a sad dog, it is true — but then it was a part of my nature — a point of my faith. In [u]Kate, however, I had[u] a firm friend, and I knew it. She was a good girl, and told me very sweetly that I might have her (plum and all) whenever I could badger my grand uncle Rumgudgeon[v] into the necessary consent. Poor girl! — she was barely fifteen, and without this consent, her little amount in the funds was not[w] come-at-able until five immeasurable summers had "dragged their slow length[x] along." [13] What then, to do? At fifteen, or even at twenty-one[y] (for I had now passed[z] my fifth olympiad)[a] five years in prospect are very much the same as five hundred. In vain we besieged the old gentleman with importunities. Here was a *pièce de résistance*[b] (as Messieurs Ude and Careme[c] would say)[14] which suited his perverse fancy to a T. It would have stirred the indignation of Job himself, to see how much like an old mouser he behaved to us two poor wretched little mice. In his heart he wished for nothing more ardently than our[d] union. He had made up his mind to this all along. In fact, he would have given ten thousand pounds from his own pocket (Kate's plum was *her own*) if he could have[e] invented anything like an[f] excuse for complying with our very natural wishes. But then we had been so imprudent as to broach the subject *ourselves*.

---

q . . . q parents *(A)*

r legacy, in dying. *(A)*

s believed *(A)*

t . . . t swear a round oath that he would *(A)*

u . . . u Kate I had, however, *(A)*

v Rumgudgeon, *(B, C) comma deleted to follow A*

w was not/would not be *(A)*

x lengths *(A)*

y twenty *(A)*

z reached *(A)*

a lustrum) *(A)*

b *piece de resistance (A, B, C)*

c Careme *(A, B);* Carene *(C) misprint*

d our own *(A)*

e have discovered or *(A)*

f a decent *(A)*

Not to oppose it under such circumstances, I sincerely believe was not in his power.[g]

I have said already that he had his weak points; but, in speaking of these, I must not be understood as referring to his [h]obstinacy: which[h] was one of his strong points — *"assurément ce n'était*[i] *pas sa foible."*[15] When I [j]mention his weakness I have[j] allusion to a *bizarre* old-womanish superstition which beset him. He was great in dreams, portents, *et id genus omne*[16] of rigmarole. He was excessively punctilious, too, upon small points of [k]honor, and, after his own fashion, was a man of his word, beyond doubt.[17] This[k] was, in fact, one of his hobbies. The *spirit* of his vows he made no scruple of setting at naught, but the *letter*[l] was a bond inviolable. Now it was this latter peculiarity in his disposition, of which Kate's ingenuity enabled us one fine day, not long after our interview in the dining-room, to take a very unexpected advantage; and, having thus, in the fashion of all modern bards and orators, exhausted in *prolegomena,*[m] all the time at my command, and nearly [n]all the room at my disposal,[n] I will sum [o]up in a few words[o] what constitutes the whole[p] pith of the story.[q] [18]

It happened then — so the Fates ordered it — that among the naval acquaintances of my betrothed, were[r] two gentlemen who had just set foot upon[s] the shores of England, after a year's absence, each, in foreign travel. In company with these gentlemen, my cousin and I, preconcertedly, paid uncle[t] Rumgudgeon a visit on the afternoon of Sunday, October the tenth,[u] [19] — just three weeks after the memorable decision which had so cruelly defeated our hopes. For about half an hour the conversation ran upon or-

---

g his power./the power of my dear, good, obstinate, tantalistical, old uncle Rumgudgeon. *(A)*

h . . . h obstinacy. That *(A);* obstinacy: that *(B)*

i *n'tail (A) misprint [The French is not accented in A, B, C]*

j . . . j mentioned his weaknesses I had *(A)*

k . . . k honor — although sufficiently loose in regard to large ones. He was *a man of his word,* beyond doubt, but it was after his own fashion to

Keep the word of promise to the ear,

But break it to the hope, *(A)*

l *letter* of his word *(A)*

m prolegomend, *(A)*

n . . . n every inch of the space assigned me, *(A)*

o . . . o up *(A)*

p *Omitted (A)*

q story./story in as concise a style as that of Tacitus or Montesquieu. *(A)*

r there were *(A)*

s on *(A)*

t old Uncle *(A)*

u 10th, *(A)*

dinary topics; but at last, we contrived, quite naturally, to give it the following turn:[v]

Capt. Pratt. " [w]Well, I have been absent just one year. Just one year to-day, as I live — let me see! yes! — this is October the tenth. You remember, Mr. Rumgudgeon, I called, this day year, to[w] bid you good-bye. And by the way,[x] it *does* seem something like a coincidence, does it not — that our friend, Captain Smitherton, here, has been absent exactly a year also — a year to-day?"

Smitherton.[y] "Yes! just one year to a fraction. You will remember, Mr. Rumgudgeon, that I called with Capt. Pratt[z] on this very day, last year,[20] to pay[a] my parting respects."

Uncle. "Yes, yes, yes — I remember it very[b] well — very queer indeed! Both of you gone just one year. A very strange coincidence, indeed! Just what Doctor [c]Dubble L. Dee would denominate an extraordinary concurrence of events. Doctor Dub — " [c]

Kate. [Interrupting.][d] "To be sure, papa, it *is* something strange; but then Captain Pratt and Captain Smitherton didn't go altogether[e] the same route, and that makes a difference you know."

Uncle. "I don't know any such thing, you huzzy! How should I? I think it only makes the matter more remarkable. Doctor Dubble[f] L. Dee — "

Kate. "Why, papa, Captain Pratt went round Cape Horn, and Captain Smitherton doubled the Cape of Good Hope."

Uncle. "Precisely! — the one went east and the other went west, you jade, and they both have gone quite round the world. By the by, Doctor Dubble[g] L. Dee — "

Myself, [*hurriedly.*] "Captain Pratt, you must come and spend the evening with us to-morrow — you and Smitherton[h] — you can tell us all about your voyage, and we'll have a game of whist, and — "

---

v *After this is another paragraph:*
  Uncle. — And so, Captain Pratt, you have been absent from London a whole year — a whole year to a day, as I live. Let me see — yes — this is October the tenth. *(A)*
w ... w A whole year to-day, sir, — precisely. You remember I called to *(A)*
x way, Mr. Rumgudgeon, *(A)*
y *Capt. Smitherton. (A)*

z Pratol *(B, C) misprint, corrected from A*
a pay you *(A)*
b *Omitted (A)*
c ... c Double L. Dee — *(A)*
d *Omitted (A)*
e alttogether *(B) misprint*
f Double *(A)*
g Double *(A)*
h Captain Smitherton *(A)*

Pratt.[i] "Whist, my dear fellow — you forget.[j] To-morrow will be Sunday. Some other evening — "

Kate. "Oh, no, fie! — Robert's[k] not *quite* so bad as that. *To-day's* Sunday."

Uncle. "To be sure — to be sure!"

Pratt.[l] "I beg both your pardons[m] — but I can't be so much mistaken. I know[n] to-morrow's Sunday, because — "

[o]*Smitherton, (much surprised.)*[o] "What *are* you all thinking about? Wasn't *yesterday* Sunday, I should like to know?"

All. "Yesterday, indeed! you *are* out!"

Uncle. "To-day's[p] Sunday, I say — don't *I* know?"

Pratt.[q] "Oh no! — to-morrow's Sunday."

Smitherton.[r] "You are *all* mad — every one of you. I am as positive that yesterday was Sunday, as I am that I sit upon this chair."

Kate, (jumping up eagerly.) "I see it — I see it all. Papa, this is a judgment upon you, about — about you know what. Let me alone, and I'll explain it all in a minute. It's a very simple thing, indeed. Captain Smitherton says that yesterday was Sunday: so it was; he is right. Cousin Bobby, and uncle and I, say that[s] to-day is Sunday: so it is; we are right. Captain Pratt maintains that to-morrow will be Sunday: so it will; he is right, too. The fact is, we are all right, and thus [t]*three Sundays have come together in a week.*" [t]

[u]*Smitherton, (after a pause.)* "By[u] the by, Pratt, Kate [v]has us completely.[v] What fools we two are! Mr. Rumgudgeon, the matter stands thus: the earth you know is twenty-four thousand miles in [w]circumference. Now[w] this globe of the earth turns upon its own axis — revolves — spins round — these twenty-four thousand miles

i *Captain Pratt. (A)*	s *Omitted (A)*
j forget yourself. *(A)*	t . . . t three Sundays' have come
k Bobby's *(A)*	together. *(A)*
l *Capt. Pratt. (A)*	u . . . u *Smitherton.* Oh yes, by *(A)*
m pardon's *(B)* misprint	v . . . v is quite rational. *(A)*
n *know (A)*	w . . . w circumference —
o . . . o *Capt. Smitherton (in surprise.)*	*Uncle.* — To be sure! — Doctor
(A)	Double —
p *Today's (A)*	*Smitherton.* — Twenty-four thousand
q *Capt. Pratt. (A)*	miles in circumference. Now *(A)*
r *Capt. Smitherton. (A)*	

of extent, going from west to east, in precisely twenty-four hours. Do you understand, Mr. Rumgudgeon?"

Uncle. "To be sure — to be sure — Doctor Dub — " [x]

[y]*Smitherton, (drowning his voice.)*[y] "Well, sir; that is at the rate of one thousand miles per hour. Now, suppose that[z] I sail from this position a thousand miles east. Of course,[a] I anticipate the rising of the sun here at London, by just one hour. [b]I see the sun rise one hour before you do.[b] Proceeding, in the same direction, yet another thousand miles, I anticipate the rising by two hours — another thousand, and I anticipate it by three hours, and so on, until I go entirely round the globe, and back to this spot, when, having gone twenty-four thousand miles east, I anticipate the rising of the London sun by no less than twenty-four hours; that is to say, I am a day *in advance* of your time. [c]Understand, eh?"

Uncle. "But Dubble L. Dee — "

Smitherton, (speaking very loud.)[c] Captain Pratt, on the contrary, when he had sailed a thousand miles west of this position, was an hour, and when he had sailed twenty-four thousand miles west, was twenty-four hours, or one[d] day, *behind* the time at London. Thus, with me, yesterday was Sunday — thus, with you, today is Sunday — and thus, with Pratt, to-morrow will be Sunday. And what is more, Mr. Rumgudgeon, it is positively clear that we are *all right;* for there can be no philosophical[e] reason assigned why the idea of one of us[f] should have preference over that of the other."

Uncle. "My eyes! — well, Kate — well, Bobby! — this *is* a judgment upon me, as you say.[g] [h]But I am a man of my word[h] — *mark that!* you shall have her, boy[i] (plum and all,) when you please. Done up, by Jove! Three Sundays all in a row! I'll go, and take Dubble[j] L. Dee's opinion upon *that.*"

x   Doub — *(A)*
y ... y   *Smitherton. (A)*
z   Now, suppose that/Now *(A)*
a   Of course, *omitted (A)*
b ... b   *Omitted (A)*
c ... c   *Omitted (A)*
d   a *(A)*
e   philosophical or just *(A)*

f   one of us/one *(A)*
g   *After this:* I always *was* a great old scoundrel. *(A)*
h ... h   *But I am a man of my word (A)*
i   my boy, *(A)*
j   Double *(A)*

TALES, 1841–1842

Title: The final title is a proverbial phrase for "never," especially used among the rural Irish. See Archer Taylor in *American Notes & Queries,* January 1944.

1. Compare "Crusty . . . Rusty . . . Musty . . . Fusty Christopher" in Tennyson's verses "To Christopher North" quoted in full in a review of *Poems by Alfred Tennyson* (London, 1833) in the *Quarterly Review* (London), April 1833, p. 95.

2. The gudgeon is a small fish, notable for being easily caught; hence a gudgeon is a person easily taken in.

3. Charles Nizard, *Des Chansons populaires* (1867), I, 104, says the lines were written by one of the "Dîners du Vaudeville," founded in 1796. They mean "Refill your empty glass, Empty your full glass."

4. In a letter to Beverley Tucker, December 1, 1835, Poe indicates that he thinks the *grotesque* is humorous, and refers to this silly way of recording laughter as having been "most effective" in "a *critique* in Blackwood's Mag." His memory served him ill. The review was identified by Kenneth L. Daughrity (*AL,* November 1930) as "The Age – A Poem – In Eight Books" in *Blackwood's* for January 1830, where Professor Wilson ridiculed the author's trade but did not use the odd kind of laughter.

5. A plum – eighteenth and early nineteenth century slang – is one hundred thousand pounds.

6. The "Fine Old English Gentleman," popular in Poe's day, was based on a ballad ascribed to the period of James I and subsequently included in many collections. Pepys heard it on June 16, 1668 (*Diary,* Bell edition, London, 1896, III, 50); Thomas D'Urfey collected a version of it, with music, in *Songs Compleat and Diversive,* III, 271–273 (1719), and the same year in *Wit and Mirth;* Henry Phillips revived it in his own adaptation for nineteenth century concerts; C. H. Purday, a music seller, published a version and sued Phillips for infringement of copyright (Phillips, *Musical and Personal Recollections,* 1864, I, 197–211); *Fraser's* (March 1834, pp. 373–374) commented on the copyright squabble and published comparative excerpts; and Charles Dickens parodied the verses with lines "to be said or sung at all Conservative Dinners" in the *Examiner* (London), August 7, 1841. Poe very probably saw the comment in *Fraser's,* since he drew other material from issues of the same year, and he may possibly have seen Dickens' parody.

7. "What is a poet good for?" Casimir-Pierre Périer (1777–1832) was a French statesman, premier 1831–32 under Louis Philippe. His *Opinions et discours* were published by his family in 1838. Poe quoted the same remark in reviewing Fouqué's *Undine* in *Burton's,* September 1839.

8. Inclination. Now obsolete in this sense.

9. "A poet is born, not made" is not, as often supposed, from Horace but is derived from Florus, *De Qualitate Vitae,* Fragment 8: "Each year new consuls and proconsuls are made, but not every year is a king or a poet born." (Steven-

son's *Home Book of Quotations,* 1967.) See also "Fifty Suggestions," number 10 (*Graham's,* May 1849).

10. Undoubtedly Dionysius Lardner; see general introductory note above.

11. Samuel Horsley (1733–1806), then Bishop of Rochester, made his remark on November 11, 1795, during the debate in the House of Lords on the Treasonable Practices bill. See *The Parliamentary History of England,* XXXII, 258. Poe used it again in "Fifty Suggestions," number 45 (*Graham's,* June 1849).

12. An allusion to Shakespeare's *Julius Caesar,* III, ii, 142, "Bequeathing it as a rich legacy."

13. See Pope, *Essay on Criticism,* II, 157, "A needless Alexandrine ends the song/That, like a wounded snake, drags its slow length along."

14. Louis-Eustache Ude and Marie-Antoine Carême were prominent writers of French cookbooks, current in Poe's time. An article in the London *Quarterly Review* for July 1835 (pp. 117–155) reviewing Brillat-Savarin's *Physiologie du goût* (Paris, 1835) and Ude's book *The French Cook* (12th edition, London, 1833) was noticed in the *Southern Literary Messenger* for December 1835, with the comment, "This article is written in the most exquisite spirit of banter and is irresistibly amusing." It contains, among other pleasant bits, the statement: "*Pièces de résistance,* says Lady Morgan on Carême's authority, came in with the National Convention," and quotes Lady Morgan's description of a dinner by Carême at Baron Rothschild's.

15. "Certainly it was not his weak point." Poe uses here an early form of *faible* current in the time of Molière. Compare "Whatever may be the *foible* of Dr. Lardner's intellect, its *forte* is certainly not originality" in "Marginalia," number 38 (*Democratic Review,* November 1844, p. 491), cited in the introduction above, and "X-ing a Paragrab," paragraph 1.

16. "And all that sort of thing."

17. The passage that follows this in the first version echoes *Macbeth,* V, viii, 21–22: "That keep the word of promise to our ear/And break it to our hope."

18. For the canceled reference to Tacitus and Montesquieu, see "The Man that Was Used Up," note 22.

19. October 10, 1841 fell on a Sunday.

20. Compare "Ulalume," line 86, "on *this* very night of last year."

LIFE IN DEATH
(THE OVAL PORTRAIT)

In its final form "The Oval Portrait" is one of the briefest and best known of the arabesques. It was much shortened when recast from the first version called "Life in Death," published in *Graham's Magazine* for April 1842.

The central idea is the very ancient one that the spirit may take up its residence in a facsimile. This was doctrinal to the Ancient Egyptians, who made statues for the *ka* (what modern Occultists call the astral body), and to modern primitive peoples who are afraid of photography. "The Oval Portrait" is the latest of Poe's stories to deal with relations between a person and his double or his image.*

Poe's inspiration was a painting by his friend Robert M. Sully, as his granddaughter, Miss Julia Sully of Richmond, has revealed. She wrote that the picture was an oval portrait, two-thirds life-size, of a girl holding in her hand a locket that hung on a ribbon about her bare neck.†

Poe also may have known a story of Tintoretto (1518–1594), who is said to have painted a portrait of his beloved daughter, Maria Robusti, herself a gifted painter, on her deathbed.‡

In her *Origins of Poe's Critical Theory*, p. 20, Margaret Alterton pointed out a parallel between the opening of Poe's "Life in Death" (see the variants, below) and that of a story called "Buried Alive" in *Blackwood's* for October 1821: "I had been for some time ill of a low and lingering fever. My strength gradually wasted, but the sense of life seemed to become more and more acute as my corporeal powers became weaker. I could see by the looks of the doctor that he despaired of my recovery."

There also may well be a slight autobiographical element in the tale. It may be recalled that Virginia Poe cared little for her husband's poetry, as the heroine of the story was jealous of her husband's painting. But Virginia ruptured a blood vessel while singing in January 1842, and her serious illness greatly disturbed her husband. "Life in Death," published about March 15, presumably was written only a few weeks before its publication, since

---

* "Morella," "Mystification," "The Fall of the House of Usher," and "William Wilson" preceded it.

† See Phillips, *Poe the Man*, I, 691. Miss Phillips was in touch with Miss Sully and located the picture in an antique shop on Fourth Avenue, New York; but it was sold sometime after 1920, and she did not obtain a photograph.

‡ This suggestion of my friend Jay B. Hubbell was recorded in my *Selected Poetry and Prose of . . . Poe* (1951), p. 421. The story appears in various accounts — see, for example, the *Nouvelle Biographie générale* (1866), but we have not yet found it in print where Poe could easily have seen it.

Poe was editing the magazine in which it appeared and had no cause to delay releasing it — even, indeed, may have been pressed for copy.

Poe's subsequent revision indicates that he may, as with "Eleonora," have considered it "a good subject spoiled by hurry in the handling." Revising consisted largely of pruning, but in this case pruning so drastic that one of the two principal themes of the original version was almost completely eliminated, thus changing the focus of the tale and greatly intensifying its effect. He probably decided that the story does not involve any impossibility for which unimaginative readers might prefer an explanation that it is all hallucinatory.§

§ A succession of interpretations of the meaning of the story may be mentioned. Patrick Quinn, in *The French Face of Edgar Poe* (1957), p. 261, holds that "The interest that lies at the heart of this story is a typical Poe interest, and it has no relevance to moral ideas." On p. 266 he explains that "in the living economy of matter as Poe conceived it, the Whole — 'vast, animate and sentient' — continues always to exist, although its parts die in feeding one another and in so bringing about new living structures. In 'The Oval Portrait,' the life of the woman was drained from her body, but instead of being dissipated this life was transferred to her portrait. The quantity of life remains constant. This principle is as basic to the story as it is to the cosmological treatise *Eureka*." Later he adds, "To see the organic in the inorganic — this is one of the typical modulations in our experience of the world which Poe makes possible in his stories."

David Rein ("Poe and Virginia Clemm," *Bucknell Review*, May 1958) analyzes "Berenicë," "Morella," "Ligeia," "The Fall of the House of Usher," and "Eleonora" in order to show that "Poe was expressing his feelings about his own marriage to Virginia, was confirming what the biographical evidence indicates, that Virginia did not adequately qualify as his wife." He interprets "The Oval Portrait" as "a remorseful story about a young artist who mistreated his wife" and holds that it marks an abrupt change in Poe's feelings toward Virginia after the threat of loss occasioned by her illness.

In *Modern Language Notes*, January 1959, Seymour Gross studies Poe's changes, pointing out that "all of Poe's revisions tighten up the moral framework of the tale," which he calls "a parable of the moral deadliness of artistic monomania." Quoting A. H. Quinn (*Poe*, p. 331) on the similarity of its theme to Hawthorne's story "The Birthmark" (March 1843) which, Quinn said, "is apparent, but Hawthorne's treatment is so different that there can be no question of plagiarism," Gross goes on to remark that Poe quite probably saw in Hawthorne's story "a memorably deft and suggestive handling of a theme which he himself had botched in 'Life in Death' " — and was thereby challenged to do as well in polishing and tightening his own imperfect tale.

[G. R. Thompson in his introduction to *Great Short Works of Edgar Allan Poe*, 1970, p. 39, says that "The Oval Portrait" "has a carefully constructed dramatic and ironic frame around it, so that the tale can also be read as the dream of a man delirious from pain and lack of sleep." See also his paper in *English Language Notes*, December 1968.]

TEXTS

(A) Graham's Magazine for April 1842 (20:200–201); *(B) Broadway Journal,* April 26, 1845 (1:264–265); *(C) Works* (1850), I, 366–369. PHANTASY-PIECES, title only.

The last version, Griswold's *(C)*, is adopted for this edition. The revision of the first version *(A)* for the *Broadway Journal (B)* included the deletion of the long first paragraph (here printed following the notes) and other excisions.

J. H. Ingram, in England, reprinted the earliest version of the tale, although he used Poe's second title.

Reprint

New York *Weekly News,* May 10, 1845, from the *Broadway Journal.* (See G. Thomas Tanselle, *Publications of the Bibliographical Society of America,* Second Quarter 1962, p. 252.)

THE OVAL PORTRAIT. [*C*]

The chateau into which my valet[a] had ventured to make forcible entrance, rather than permit me, in my desperately wounded condition, to pass a night in the open air, was one of those[b] piles of commingled gloom and grandeur[1] which have so long frowned among the Apennines,[c] not less in fact than in the fancy of Mrs. Radcliffe.[2] To all appearance it had been temporarily and very lately abandoned.[d] We[e] established ourselves in one of the smallest and least sumptuously furnished apartments. It lay[f] in a remote turret of the building. Its decorations were rich, yet tattered and antique. Its walls were hung with tapestry and bedecked with manifold and multiform armorial trophies, together with an unusually great number of very spirited modern paintings in frames of rich golden arabesque. In these paintings, which depended from the walls not only in their main surfaces, but in very many

---

Title: Life in Death. *(A;* PHANTASY-PIECES)
Motto: Egli è *vivo* e parlerebbe se non osservasse la rigola del silentio.
    Inscription beneath an Italian picture of St. Bruno (A)
a   my valet/Pedro *(A)*
b   those fantastic *(A)*
c   Appennines, *(A);* Appenines, *(B, C) corrected editorially*
d   *After this:* Day by day we expected

the return of the family who tenanted it, when the misadventure which had befallen me would, no doubt, be received as sufficient apology for the intrusion. *(A)*
e   We/Meantime, that this intrusion might be taken in better part, we had *(A)*
f   lay high *(A)*

nooks which the bizarre architecture of the chateau rendered necessary — in these paintings my incipient delirium, perhaps, had caused me to take deep interest; so that[g] I bade Pedro[3] to close the heavy shutters of the room — since it was already night — to light the tongues of a tall candelabrum which stood by the head of my bed — and to throw open far and wide the fringed curtains of black velvet which enveloped the bed itself. I wished all this done that I might resign myself, if not to sleep, at least alternately to the contemplation of these pictures, and the perusal of a small volume which had been found upon the pillow, and which purported to criticise and describe them.

Long — long I read — and devoutly, devotedly[h] I gazed.[i] Rapidly and gloriously the hours flew by, and the deep midnight came. The position of the candelabrum displeased me, and outreaching my hand with difficulty, rather than disturb my slumbering valet, I [j]placed it so[j] as to throw its rays more fully upon the book.

But the action produced an effect altogether unanticipated. The rays of the numerous candles (for there were many) now fell within a niche of the room which had hitherto been thrown into deep shade by one of the bed-posts. I thus saw in vivid light a picture all unnoticed before. It was the portrait of a young girl just ripening[k] into womanhood. I glanced at the painting hurriedly, and then closed my eyes. Why I did this was not at first apparent even to my own perception. But while my lids remained thus shut, I ran over in mind my reason for so shutting them. It was an impulsive movement to gain time for thought — to make sure that my vision had not deceived me — to calm and subdue my fancy for a more sober and more certain gaze. In a very few moments I again looked fixedly at the painting.

That I now saw aright I could not and would not doubt; for

---

g   that having swallowed the opium, as before told, *(A)*
h   devoutly *(C) misprint, corrected from A, B*
i   *After this:* I felt meantime, the voluptuous narcotic stealing its way to my brain. I felt that in its magical influence lay much of the gorgeous richness and variety of the frames — much of the ethereal hue that gleamed from the canvas — and much of the wild interest of the book which I perused. Yet this consciousness rather strengthened than impaired the delight of the illusion, while it weakened the illusion itself. *(A)*
j . . . j   so placed it *(A)*
k   ripened *(A)*

the first flashing of the candles upon that canvass had seemed to dissipate the dreamy stupor which was stealing over my senses, and to startle [l]me at once into waking life.[l] [4]

The portrait, I have already said, was that of a young girl. It was a mere head and shoulders, done in what is technically termed a *vignette* manner; much in the style of the favorite heads of Sully.[5] The arms, the bosom and even the ends of the radiant hair, melted imperceptibly into the vague yet deep shadow which formed the back ground of the whole. The frame was oval, [m]richly gilded and filagreed in *Moresque*.[m] As a thing[n] of art nothing could be more admirable than the painting itself.[o] [6] But it could have been neither the execution of the work, nor the immortal beauty of the countenance, which had so suddenly and so vehemently moved me. Least of all, could it have been that my fancy, shaken from its half slumber, had mistaken the head for that of a living person. I saw at once that the peculiarities of the design, of the *vignetting,* and of the frame, must have instantly dispelled such idea — must have prevented even its momentary entertainment. Thinking earnestly upon these points, I remained, for an hour[p] perhaps, half sitting, half reclining, with my vision riveted upon the portrait. At length, satisfied with[q] the true secret of its effect, I fell back within the bed. I had found the spell of the picture in an absolute[r] *life-likeliness* of expression, which, at first startling, finally confounded, subdued and appalled me.[s] With[t] deep and reverent awe I replaced the candelabrum in its former position. The cause of my deep agitation being thus shut from view, I sought eagerly the volume which discussed the paintings and their histories. Turning to the number which designated the oval portrait, I there read the vague and quaint words which follow:

"She was a maiden of rarest beauty, and not more lovely than full of glee. And evil was the hour when she saw, and loved, and

l . . . l me into waking life as if with the shock of a galvanic battery. *(A)*

m . . . m richly, yet fantastically gilded and filagreed. *(A)*

n work *(A)*

o *After this:* The loveliness of the face surpassed that of the fabulous Houri. *(A)*

p an hour/some hours *(A)*

q of *(A)*

r an absolute/a perfect *(A)*

s *After this:* I could no longer support the sad meaning smile of the half-parted lips, nor the too real lustre of the wild eye. *(A)*

t With a *(A)*

wedded the painter. He, passionate, studious, austere, and having already a bride in his Art; she a maiden of rarest beauty, and not more lovely than full of glee: all light and smiles, and frolicksome as the young fawn: loving and cherishing all things: hating only the Art which was her rival: dreading only the pallet and brushes and other untoward instruments which deprived her of the countenance of her lover. It was thus a terrible thing for this lady to hear the painter speak of his desire to portray[u] even his young bride. But she was humble and obedient, and sat meekly for many weeks in the dark high turret-chamber where the light dripped upon the pale canvass only from overhead. But he, the painter, took glory in his work, which went on from hour to hour, and from day to day. And he was a passionate, and wild, and moody man, who became lost in reveries; so that he *would* not see that the light which fell so ghastlily[v] in that lone turret withered the health and the spirits of his bride, who pined visibly to all but him. Yet she smiled on and still on, uncomplainingly, because she saw that the painter, (who had high renown,) took a fervid and burning pleasure in his task, and wrought day and night to depict her who so loved him, yet who grew daily more dispirited and weak. And in sooth some who beheld the portrait spoke of its resemblance in low words, as of a mighty marvel, and a proof not less of the power of the painter than of his deep love for her whom he depicted so surpassingly well. But at length, as the labor drew nearer to its conclusion, there were admitted none into the turret; for the painter had grown wild with the ardor of his work, and turned his eyes[w] from the canvass rarely, even to regard the countenance of his wife. And he *would* not see that the tints which he spread upon the canvass were drawn from the cheeks of her who sat[x] beside him. And when many weeks had passed, and but little remained to do, save one brush upon the mouth and one tint upon the eye, the spirit of the lady again flickered up as the flame within the socket of the lamp. And then the brush was given, and then the tint was placed; and, for one moment, the painter stood entranced before

---

u   pourtray *(A, B)*   w   visage *(A)*
v   ghastily *(A)*   x   sate *(A, B)*

the work which he had wrought; but in the next, while he yet[y] gazed, he grew tremulous and very pallid, and aghast, and crying with a loud voice, 'This is indeed *Life* itself!' turned[z] suddenly [a]to regard his beloved: — *She was dead!"* [a]

NOTES

Title: In the first version, the title "Life in Death" may be from Coleridge's "Ancient Mariner." See "Berenicë," n. 11.

Motto: The epigraph of the first version means "He is alive and would speak did he not observe the rule of silence." St. Bruno (1040?–1101) was the founder of the Carthusian order, which requires silence of its members except at certain specified times. Poe included the quotation in "Pinakidia," number 111 (*SLM*, August 1836, p. 579), with the comment "Malherbe has taken the hint in his epigram upon a picture of St. Catherine," but Malherbe's verses (*Poésies*, number lxxviii) have little relation to the quoted sentence. A similar remark — on seeing Houdon's statue of St. Bruno for the Carthusian church in Rome — was quoted in a memoir of the sculptor read before the Academy of Beaux-Arts (Paris) in 1829 by its permanent secretary: "Elle [the statue] parleroit, disoit le pape Clément XIV, si la règle de son ordre ne lui prescrivoit pas le silence" (A. C. Quatremère de Quincy, *Recueil de notices historiques...*, Paris 1834, p. 393). The remark has been repeated in a number of French and English accounts of Houdon, but Poe's Italian source has not been found. The quotation was used as a motto for "Life in Death," apparently to illustrate the idea of a "speaking image" (the narrator in "The Spectacles" exclaims, "Ah, this is indeed the speaking image of my beloved!"), but because it was only superficially pertinent to the tale it was discarded in the revision.

1. Compare "The Coliseum," line 9: "...grandeur, gloom and glory," and see also "Eleonora" at n. 16.

2. The scene of terrifying experiences with forces of evil described in Ann Ward Radcliffe's novel *The Mysteries of Udolpho* (1794) was an ancient castle in the Apennines. One of the horrors glimpsed by the heroine in chapter 26 was a recumbent form she took for the victim of a murder — a figure which in chapter 55 turned out to be of wax. (Everyman edition)

3. Pedro is also the name of a character in "The Bargain Lost."

4. For other references to the galvanic battery, mentioned here in the first version, see "A Decided Loss," "Some Words With a Mummy," and "The Premature Burial."

5. Although the picture Poe had in mind was by Robert Sully, most readers must have thought of his more famous uncle, Thomas Sully (1783–1872), whose work Robert's resembled. Compare "Philosophy of Furniture" at n. 14.

---

y   he yet/yet he *(A)*
z   turned himself *(A)*
a...a   round to his beloved — *who*

was dead. The painter then added —
'But is this indeed Death?' " *(A)*

6. Houris (see the variant here), the black-eyed women of the Mahometan paradise, are referred to also in "Israfel" and "Ligeia."

Initial paragraph of The Oval Portrait *(A)*

My fever had been excessive and of long duration. All the remedies attainable in this wild Appennine region had been exhausted to no purpose. My valet and sole attendant in the lonely chateau, was too nervous and too grossly unskilful to venture upon letting blood — of which indeed I had already lost too much in the affray with the banditti. Neither could I safely permit him to leave me in search of assistance. At length I bethought me of a little pacquet of opium which lay with my tobacco in the hookahcase; for at Constantinople I had acquired the habit of smoking the weed with the drug. Pedro handed me the case. I sought and found the narcotic. But when about to cut off a portion I felt the necessity of hesitation. In smoking it was a matter of little importance *how much* was employed. Usually, I had half filled the bowl of the hookah with opium and tobacco cut and mingled intimately, half and half. Sometimes when I had used the whole of this mixture I experienced no very peculiar effects; at other times I would not have smoked the pipe more than two-thirds out, when symptoms of mental derangement, which were even alarming, warned me to desist. But the effect proceeded with an easy gradation which deprived the indulgence of all danger. Here, however, the case was different. I had never *swallowed* opium before. Laudanum and morphine I had occasionally used, and about *them*

should have had no reason to hesitate. But the solid drug I had never seen employed. Pedro knew no more respecting the proper quantity to be taken, than myself — and thus, in the sad emergency, I was left altogether to conjecture. Still I felt no especial uneasiness; for I resolved to proceed *by degrees.* I would take a *very* small dose in the first instance. Should this prove impotent, I would repeat it; and so on, until I should find an abatement of the fever, or obtain that sleep which was so pressingly requisite, and with which my reeling senses had not been blessed for now more than a week. No doubt it was this very reeling of my senses — it was the dull delirium which already oppressed me — that prevented me from perceiving the incoherence of my reason — which blinded me to the folly of defining any thing as either large or small where I had no preconceived standard of comparison. I had not, at the moment, the faintest idea that what I conceived to be an exceedingly small dose of solid opium might, in fact, be an excessively large one. On the contrary I well remember that I judged confidently of the quantity to be taken by reference to the entire quantity of the lump in possession. The portion which, in conclusion, I swallowed, and swallowed without fear, was no doubt a very small proportion *of the piece which I held in my hand.*

THE MASQUE OF THE RED DEATH

This masterpiece is unsurpassed, perhaps unequaled, among Poe's very short stories. The author made few revisions, but they show supreme artistry. Critics have differed widely in interpreting the tale,* but I see in it a clear moral that one cannot run away from responsibility.

The plot involves the supernatural, but the chief incidents are historical. During the epidemic of cholera at Paris in 1832, people were determined to make what might be a short life a merry one, and many balls were given. The following description comes from the sixteenth letter of "Pencillings by the Way" of N. P. Willis:

> At a masque ball at the *Théatre des Varietés* ... at the celebration of the *Mi-Careme,* or half-lent ... were some two thousand people ... in fancy dresses ... and one man, immensely tall, dressed as a personification of the *Cholera* itself, with skeleton armor, bloodshot eyes, and other horrible appurtenances of a walking pestilence.

This was first printed in the *New-York Mirror,* June 2, 1832, and there can be little doubt that Poe was familiar with it. In his eighteenth letter Willis observed that there had been "two cases within the palace-walls." † Since the letters of Willis were so well known in Poe's day, it is needless to seek other sources for the terrifying costume.

Poe's setting for his tale recalls that of Boccaccio's *Decameron,* where the narrators are members of a group of people who retire to a remote castle to avoid the plague.‡ Prince Prospero's name is Italian, and Poe had another Italian source. In *Graham's Magazine* for September 1841, he had reviewed Thomas Campbell's *Life of Petrarch,* and presumably saw there a grim story of a nobleman named Barnabo, who during a plague shut himself up in his castle and set a sentinel to ring a bell if anyone approached. Yet a party entered unannounced, and Barnabo, finding the sentry dead, fled

---

* See, for example, the papers listed in J. P. Roppolo's "Meaning and 'The Masque of the Red Death' " in *Tulane Studies in English,* vol. 13, for 1963. [See also, for both interpretation and suggestion of sources, Robert Regan's essay cited in n. 19 on "William Wilson."]

† See *The Prose Works* of N. P. Willis (1845), pp. 24 and 30. Poe had used the horrendous costumes of masqueraders in "King Pest," written in 1834 or 1835. An account of the ball in the Paris *Constitutional,* March 31, 1832, was cited by Eugène Sue. See C. P. Cambiare, *Influence of ... Poe in France* (1927), p. 282.

‡ Killis Campbell, *Mind of Poe,* p. 171, picks up a suggestion of W. D. Armes in the *Transactions of the American Philological Association* (1907) that Poe's source was in William Harrison Ainsworth's *Old St. Paul's.* This turns out to be merely an account of a London grocer who, during the Great Plague of 1665, stocks his house with supplies and keeps his family at home. Poe disliked Ainsworth, never mentioned that book of his, and must not be supposed wholly unacquainted with so important a work as the *Decameron.*

to the forest where, it was reported, he too died. In his review, Poe cites as inappropriately humorous Campbell's sentence, "This was a dance of the king of terrors over the earth, and a very rapid one."§

Poe also may have read of the clock at Strasbourg Cathedral, where, shortly before the stroke of the clock, a figure representing Death emerged from the center and sounded the full hour, while at the quarter and half hours the statue of Christ came out, repelling the destroyer.*

The Red Death is imaginary; its name parallels the medieval Black Death of 1348–1349, and the "blue Plague" of Shelley's *Revolt of Islam,* X, xx–xxvi,† but it also reminds one a little of the first plague of the Egyptians described in Exodus.

Other analogues have been pointed out which are more remote, or unlikely to have been known to Poe. There is a legend of a ghostly skeleton dancing at the wedding feast of Alexander III of Scotland, at Jedburgh Castle in 1285.‡ Masquerades gave an advantage to assassins. King Gustav III of Sweden was killed at a masqued ball in 1792 — the basis of Verdi's opera *Un Ballo in Maschera* (1859). The eleventh chapter of J. K. B. Eichendorff's *Ahnung und Gegenwart* (1815) is "Die Maskenball," but I think it most improbable that Poe "may have perused" § that German romance.

§ The direct quotation is from Thomas Campbell's *Life of Petrarch* (Philadelphia, 1841), p. 211. J. B. Reece, discussing this source in *Modern Language Notes,* February 1953, points out that Campbell offers a motive for revelry during the epidemic in "the general persuasion that sadness accelerated the infection of the malady, and that pleasant amusements were the surest defense against it." Reece comments, " 'Poetic' justice, for which Poe had respect, is much better served in the story by the omission of any reference to the motive which Campbell attributes to the pleasure seekers, as is the over-all tone of horror which Poe wanted to achieve."

* I use Wilhelm Ruland, *Legends of the Rhine* (Cologne, 1906), pp. 63, 64, but the clock is famous.

† Gunnar Bjurman, *Edgar Allan Poe* (Lund, 1916), p. 203.

‡ John H. Ingram tells this in *Haunted Homes of Great Britain* (Second Series, 1884), p. 184, but gives his source as Thomas Heywood's *Hierarchy of the Blessed Angels* (1635).

§ See Franz Karl Mohr in *Modern Language Quarterly,* March 1949, and Haldeen Braddy, *Glorious Incense,* p. 44. Poe never mentioned Eichendorff, and could read little German. For other suggestions see C. K. Holsapple in University of Texas *Studies in English,* July 8, 1938; Richard Cary in *Nineteenth Century Fiction,* June 1962; and Gerald E. Gerber in *American Literature,* March 1965. [B. R. Pollin, in *Studies in Short Fiction,* Fall 1968, and in *Discoveries in Poe,* pp. 80–90, adds further suggestions.]

TALES, 1841–1842

Poe presumably composed "The Masque of the Red Death" about March 1842.

TEXTS

(A) Graham's Magazine for May 1842 (20:257–259); *(B) Broadway Journal,* July 19, 1845 (2:17–19); *(C) Works* (1850), I, 339–345. PHANTASY-PIECES, title only.

Griswold's text *(C)* is chosen. It shows one verbal change from *(B)* and corrects a misprint.

Reprints

The Baltimore Saturday Visiter, April 30, 1842, "Selected from *Graham's Magazine* for May"; *The Literary Souvenir* (Lowell, Mass.), June 4, 1842, from *Graham's Magazine.*

THE MASQUE OF THE RED DEATH. [C]

The "Red Death" had long devastated the country. No pestilence had ever been[a] so fatal, or so hideous. Blood was its Avatar[b] and its seal — the redness and the horror of blood.[1] There were sharp pains, and sudden dizziness, and then profuse bleeding[c] at the pores, with dissolution. The scarlet stains upon the body and especially upon the face of the victim, were the pest ban which shut him out from the aid and from the sympathy of his fellow-men. And the whole seizure, progress and termination of the disease, were the incidents of half an hour.

But the Prince Prospero was happy and dauntless and sagacious.[2] When his dominions were half depopulated, he summoned to his presence a thousand hale and light-hearted friends from among the knights and dames of his court, and with these retired to the deep seclusion of one of his castellated abbeys. This was an extensive and magnificent structure, the creation of the prince's own eccentric yet august taste. A strong and lofty wall girdled it in. This wall had gates of iron. The courtiers, having entered, brought

---

Title: The Mask of the Red Death. A Fantasy. *(A);* The Mask of the Red Death. (PHANTASY-PIECES)
a   ever been/been ever *(A)*

b   Avator *(A, B, C) misprint, corrected editorially*
c   bleedings *(A)*

furnaces and massy hammers and welded the bolts. They resolved to leave means neither of ingress or egress to the sudden impulses of despair[d] or of frenzy from within. The abbey was amply provisioned. With such precautions the courtiers might bid defiance to contagion. The external world could take care of itself. In the meantime it was folly to grieve,[e] or to think. The prince had provided all the appliances of pleasure. There were buffoons, there were improvisatori, there were ballet-dancers, there were musicians,[f] there was Beauty, there was wine. All these and security were within. Without was the "Red Death."

It was toward[g] the close of the fifth or sixth month of his seclusion, and while the pestilence raged most furiously abroad, that the Prince Prospero entertained his thousand friends at a masked ball of the most unusual magnificence.

It was a voluptuous scene, that masquerade. But first let me tell of the rooms in which it was held. There were seven — an imperial suite. In many palaces, however, such suites form a long and straight vista, while the folding doors slide back nearly to the walls on either hand, so that the view of the whole extent is scarcely impeded. Here the case was very different; as might have been expected from the duke's love of the *bizarre*. The apartments were so irregularly disposed that the vision embraced but little more than one at a time. There was a sharp turn at every twenty or thirty yards, and at each turn a novel effect. To the right and left, in the middle of each wall, a tall and narrow Gothic window looked out upon a closed corridor which pursued the windings of the suite. These windows were of stained glass whose color varied in accordance with the prevailing hue of the decorations of the chamber into which it opened. That at the eastern extremity was hung, for example,[h] in blue — and vividly blue were its windows. The second chamber was purple in its ornaments and tapestries, and here the panes were purple. The third was green throughout, and so were the casements. The fourth was furnished and lighted[i]

---

d   despair from without *(A)*
e   grfeve, *(B) misprint*
f   musicians, there were cards, *(A)*
g   towards *(A)*

h   examample, *(B) misprint;* example *(C) comma added from A, B*
i   litten *(A)*

with orange — the fifth with white — the sixth with violet. The seventh apartment was closely shrouded in black velvet tapestries that hung all over the ceiling and down the walls, falling in heavy folds upon a carpet of the same material and hue. But in this chamber only, the color of the windows failed to correspond with the decorations. The panes here were scarlet — a deep blood color. Now in no one of the seven apartments was there any lamp or candelabrum, amid the profusion of golden ornaments that lay scattered to and fro or depended from the roof. There was no light of any kind emanating from lamp or candle within the suite of chambers. But in the corridors that followed the suite, there stood, opposite to each window, a heavy tripod, bearing a brazier of fire[j] that projected its rays through the tinted glass and so glaringly illumined the room. And thus were produced a multitude of gaudy and fantastic appearances. But in the western or black chamber the effect of the fire-light that streamed upon the dark hangings through the blood-tinted panes, was ghastly in the extreme, and produced so wild a look upon the countenances of those who entered, that there were few of the company bold enough to set foot within its precincts at all.[3]

It was in this apartment, also, that there stood against the western wall, a gigantic clock of ebony. Its pendulum swung to and fro with a dull, heavy, monotonous clang; and when the[k] minute-hand made the circuit of the face, and the hour was to be stricken, there came[l] from the brazen lungs of the clock a sound which was clear and loud and deep and exceedingly musical, but of so peculiar a note and emphasis that, at each lapse of an hour, the musicians of[m] the orchestra were constrained to pause, momentarily,[n] in their performance, to harken to the sound; and thus the waltzers perforce ceased their evolutions;[4] and there was a brief disconcert of the whole gay company; and, while the chimes of the clock yet rang, it was observed that the giddiest grew pale, and[o] the more aged and sedate passed their hands over their brows as if

---

j   fire, (C) comma deleted to follow A,
B
k   its (A)
l   came forth (A)

m   in (A)
n   momently, (A)
o   and that (A)

in confused revery or meditation. But when the echoes had fully ceased, a light laughter at once pervaded the assembly; the musicians looked at each other and smiled as if at their own nervousness and folly, and made whispering vows, each to the other, that the next chiming of the clock should produce in them no similar emotion; and then, after the lapse of sixty minutes, (which embrace three thousand and six hundred seconds of the Time that flies,)[5] there came yet another chiming of the clock, and then[p] were the same disconcert and tremulousness and meditation as before.

But, in spite of these things, it was a gay and magnificent revel. The tastes of the duke were peculiar. He had a fine eye for colors and effects. He disregarded the *decora* of mere fashion.[6] His plans were bold and fiery, and his conceptions glowed with barbaric lustre. There are some who would have thought him mad. His followers felt that he was not. It was necessary to hear and see and touch him to be *sure* that he was not.

He had directed, in great part, the moveable embellishments of the seven chambers, upon occasion of this great *fête;*[q] and it was his own guiding taste which had given character to the[r] masqueraders. Be sure they were grotesque. There were much glare and glitter and piquancy and phantasm — much of what has been since seen in "Hernani."[7] There were arabesque figures with unsuited limbs and appointments. There were delirious fancies such as the madman fashions. There were[s] much of the beautiful, much of the wanton, much of the *bizarre,* something of the terrible, and not a little of that which might have excited disgust.[8] To and fro in the seven chambers there stalked, in fact, a multitude of dreams.[9] And these — the dreams — writhed in and about, taking hue from the rooms, and causing the wild music of the orchestra to seem as the echo of their steps. And, anon, there strikes the ebony clock which stands in the hall of the velvet. And then, for a moment,[t] all is still, and all is silent save the voice of the clock. The dreams are stiff-frozen as they stand. But the echoes of the chime die away — they have endured but an instant — and a light, half-subdued

---

p   then there *(A)*
q   *fete; (B) accent broken; (C) accent omitted, corrected from A*
r   the costumes of the *(A)*
s   was *(A, B)*
t   for a moment,/momently, *(A)*

laughter floats after them as they depart. And now again the music swells, and the dreams live, and writhe to and fro more merrily than ever, taking hue from the many tinted windows through which stream the rays from the tripods. But to the chamber which lies most westwardly of the seven, there are now none of the maskers who venture; for the night is waning away; and there flows a ruddier light through the blood-colored panes; and the blackness of the sable drapery appals; and to him whose foot falls upon the sable carpet, there comes from the near clock of ebony a muffled peal more solemnly[u] emphatic than any which reaches *their* ears who indulge in the more remote gaieties of the other apartments.

But these other apartments were densely crowded, and in them beat feverishly the heart of life. And the revel went whirlingly on, until at length [v]there commenced the sounding of midnight[v] upon[w] the clock. And then the music ceased, as I have told; and the evolutions of the waltzers were quieted; and there was an uneasy cessation of all things as before. But now there were twelve strokes to be sounded by the bell of the clock; and thus it happened, perhaps,[x] that more of thought crept, with more of time, into the meditations of the thoughtful among those who revelled. And thus, too,[y] it happened, perhaps, that before the last echoes of the last chime had utterly sunk into silence, there were many individuals in the crowd who had found leisure to become aware of the presence of a masked figure which had arrested the attention of no single individual before. And the rumor of this new presence having spread itself whisperingly around, there arose at length from the whole company a buzz, or murmur, expressive of[z] disapprobation and surprise — then, finally, of terror, of horror, and of disgust.

In an assembly of phantasms such as I have painted, it may well be supposed that no ordinary appearance could have excited such sensation. In truth the masquerade license of the night was nearly

---

u   solemly *(B) misprint*
v . . . v was sounded the twelfth hour *(A)*
w   upou *(B) misprint*

x   perhaps *(C) comma added from A, B*
y   thus, too,/thus, again, *(A);* thus too, *(C) comma added from B*
z   expressive at first *(A)*

unlimited; but the figure in question had out-Heroded Herod,[10] and gone beyond the bounds of even the prince's indefinite decorum. There are chords in the hearts of the most reckless which cannot be touched without emotion. Even with the utterly lost, to whom life and death are equally jests, there are[a] matters of which no jest can be[b] made. The whole company, indeed, seemed now deeply to feel that in the costume and bearing of the stranger neither wit nor propriety existed. The figure was tall and gaunt, and shrouded from head to foot in the habiliments of the grave. The mask which concealed the visage was made so nearly to resemble the countenance of a stiffened corpse that the closest scrutiny must have had difficulty in detecting the cheat. And yet all this might have been endured, if not approved, by the mad revellers around. But the mummer had gone so far as to assume the type of the Red Death. His vesture was dabbled in *blood* — and his broad brow, with all the features of the face, was besprinkled with the scarlet horror.

When the eyes of[c] Prince Prospero fell upon this spectral image (which with a slow and solemn movement, as if more fully to sustain its *role,*[d] stalked[e] to and fro among the waltzers)[11] he was seen to be convulsed, in the first moment with a strong shudder either of terror or distaste; but, in the next, his brow reddened with rage.

"Who dares?" he demanded hoarsely of the [f]courtiers who stood near[f] him — "who dares [g]insult us with this blasphemous mockery?[g] [h]Seize him and unmask him[h] — that we may know whom we have to hang[i] at sunrise, from the battlements!"[j]

It was in the eastern or blue chamber in which stood the Prince Prospero as he uttered these words. They rang throughout the seven rooms loudly and clearly — for the prince was a bold and robust man, and the music had became hushed at the waving of his hand.

---

a *are (A)*
b be properly *(A)*
c of the *(A)*
d rôle *(A);* rôle, *(B)*
e stalkod *(B) misprint*
f...f group that stood around *(A)*
g...g thus to make mockery of our

woes? *(A)*
h...h Uncase the varlet *(A)*
i hang tomorrow *(A)*
j battlements. Will no one stir at my bidding? — stop and strip him, I say, of those reddened vestures of sacrilege!" *(A)*

It was in the blue room where stood the prince, with a group of pale courtiers by his side. At first, as he spoke, there was a slight rushing movement of this group in the direction of the intruder, who[k] at the moment was also near at hand, and now, with deliberate and stately step, made closer approach to the speaker. But from a certain nameless awe with which the mad assumptions of the mummer had inspired the whole party, there were found none who put forth hand to seize him; so that, unimpeded, he passed within a yard of the prince's person; and, while the vast assembly, as if with one impulse, shrank from the centres of the rooms to the walls, he made his way uninterruptedly, but with the same solemn and measured step which had distinguished him from the first, through the blue chamber to the purple — through the purple to the green — through the green to the orange — through this again to the white — and even thence to the violet, ere a decided movement had been made to arrest him. It was then, however, that the Prince Prospero, maddening with rage and the shame of his own momentary cowardice, rushed hurriedly through the six chambers, while none followed him on account of a deadly terror that had seized upon all. He bore aloft a drawn dagger, and had approached, in rapid impetuosity, to within three or four feet of the retreating figure, when the latter, having attained the extremity of the velvet apartment, turned suddenly[1] and confronted his pursuer. There was a sharp cry — and the dagger dropped gleaming upon the sable carpet, upon which, instantly afterwards, fell prostrate in death the Prince Prospero. Then, summoning the wild courage of despair, a throng of the revellers at once threw themselves into the black apartment, and, seizing the mummer, whose tall figure stood erect and motionless within the shadow of the ebony clock, gasped in unutterable horror at finding the grave cerements and corpselike mask which they handled with so violent a rudeness, untenanted by any tangible form.

And now was acknowledged the presence of the Red Death. He had come like a thief in the night.[12] And one by one dropped the revellers in the blood-bedewed halls of their revel, and died

---

k   who, (C) comma deleted to follow A   l   suddenly round (A)
and B

each in the despairing posture of his fall. And the life of the ebony clock went out with that of the last of the gay. And the flames of the tripods expired. And Darkness and Decay and the Red Death held illimitable dominion over all.[13]

NOTES

Title: Masque has a double meaning.

1.   Compare Exodus 7:19–21, "Take thy rod, and stretch out thine hand upon the waters of Egypt . . . that they may become blood . . . and all the waters that were in the river were turned to blood . . . and there was blood throughout all the land of Egypt." Virginia Poe had burst a blood vessel in singing during January 1842, and even this may have influenced her husband's description, as William Bittner, *Poe* (1962), p. 177, thinks. One of my students had a great-grandparent who saw Mrs. Clemm take Virginia into the Fordham cottage after blood had gushed from her mouth.

2.   Prince Prospero, like his namesake in *The Tempest,* fled from the world, but ironically Poe's prince ceased to prosper.

3.   There is little doubt that the rooms have poetic meanings; many readers find that the possibility of seeing little more than one room at a time symbolizes man's inability to see the future, or recapture the past. The colors seem to be significant. My student Emily Crandall observed that the absence of yellow is notable. Blue is the color of morning and beginnings, black of night and endings. The rest seem different to different readers. Professor Walter Blair, in *Modern Philology,* May 1944, argued for the seven ages of man, and thought the last room like a coffin. My students have also seen the seven days of the week, the seven deadly sins, and even seven parts of a day. Note also that blue and red are the poles of a compass – the beginning and the end.

4.   The waltz was still considered somewhat risqué in 1842, but Poe himself probably danced it with Mary Andre Phelps. See Woodberry *Life* (1909), II, 272, citing her reminiscences.

5.   The simple enumeration ot the seconds in an hour is supremely effective here.

6.   Prospero shares his contempt for fashionable *decora* as well as his interest in richness of decoration with the hero of "The Assignation."

7.   *Hernani* (1830) is a play by Victor Hugo, on which Verdi later based an opera. It was much discussed and quite evidently made an impression on Poe. See *Politian* and my note (Mabbott I, 297). [The details of Poe's use of *Hernani* as a source are worked out by B. Pollin in his *Discoveries in Poe* (1971), chapter I.]

8.   N. P. Willis, in the seventeenth letter of "Pencillings by the Way" – see his *Prose Works* (1845), p. 28 – describes several Parisian fancy balls (both with

and without masks), each full of a variety of costumes, ranging from the graceful and beautiful to the grotesque and absurd.

9. Compare *The Tempest,* IV, i, 156, "We are such stuff as dreams are made on."

10. To "out-Herod Herod," from *Hamlet,* III, ii. 16, is a favorite phrase with Poe, also used in "Metzengerstein" and "William Wilson."

11. Compare *Politian,* VII, 55, "A spectral figure, solemn, and slow, and noiseless."

12. The phrase "like a thief in the night" may be found in Sir Thomas Browne's *Religio Medici,* Part I, section 46. Compare I Thessalonians, 5:2.

13. The rhymes in the last sentence are, of course, intentional. In the last line, comparison has been made to Pope's verse "And universal darkness buries all." It certainly may have contributed to the power and finality of Poe's conclusion. See Harry Levin, *The Power of Blackness* (1958), p. 150, where he says, "The closing note, echoed from the pseudo-Miltonic last line of Pope's *Dunciad,* predicates a reduction of cosmos to chaos: 'And darkness and Decay and the Red Death held illimitable dominion over all.' "

THE PIT AND THE PENDULUM

If popularity be a test of merit, "The Pit and the Pendulum" must rank high among its author's works. Admirers of Poe's art may complain that the action is not quite completely unified; some gentler readers dislike the cruelty involved as excessive. It can only be said that it is really an account of a series of hairbreadth escapes, and fascinates people as did old-fashioned melodramas. Woodberry (*Life,* 1909, I, 343, 382) called it a work of no striking orginality, but great originality lies in the collection and combination of a series of not wholly incredible experiences for the hero. As in "A Descent into the Maelström," most of the features of the story have been traced to specific, scattered sources; it is Poe's craftsmanship in weaving them together that has created an unforgettable tale.

In "How to Write a Blackwood Article" Poe had sardonically described methods of composing contributions to the Edinburgh magazine. In "A Predicament" he produced a burlesque of the stories the magazine printed. He had already in "King Pest" done a wild parody on the British magazinists. Now, it seems, he decided to do a straight story in the Blackwood manner, but to make the copy better than the model. In this he succeeded, for "The Pit and the Pendulum" has outlived for general readers all the once famous *Tales from Blackwood*. The central idea is that the fear of the unknown exceeds the fear of anything known.

Poe's method was one demanded by the chosen genre. He sought and combined with modifications stories in the Blackwood manner — that is, sensational accounts of terrible experiences usually told in the first person. For details he drew not only from *Blackwood's* but from other British and American periodicals* and from an American novel, and he used some factual material. He must have expected many of his readers to know what he was doing, for some of the sources were stories that had wide circulation at the time, although their popularity has now faded. Even a reviewer of the first volumes of the *Works* pointed out Poe's "plagiarism" early in 1850; and Griswold, in his "Memoir," first published in Volume III, referred to the matter later in the same year.†

Poe's plot may have been suggested by a paragraph in Thomas Dick's *Philosophy of Religion* (1825), IV, iv:

On the entry of the French into Toledo during the late Peninsular War, General Lasalle visited the palace of the Inquisition. The great number of instruments of torture, especially the instruments to stretch the limbs, and the drop-

* For a recent study of Poe's use of British periodicals, see Michael Allen's *Poe and the British Magazine Tradition* (1969).

† See Lewis Gaylord Clark's review of the first two volumes of Poe's *Works* in the *Knickerbocker*, February 1850, and Griswold's "Memoir," p. xlviii. Notable articles on the sources of Poe's tale include a discussion by Margaret Alterton in her *Origins of Poe's Critical Theory* (1925), p. 27, where she mentions two stories in *Blackwood's;* a discussion by David Lee Clark of Poe's indebtedness to Charles Brockden Brown in *Modern Language Notes*, June 1929; and Miss Alterton's illuminating supplementary piece in the same periodical, June 1933, demonstrating Poe's use of material suggested by or derived from Juan Antonio Llorente's history of the Spanish Inquisition. In my notes below I mention specific sources found for certain passages in the text, omitting notice of suggestions superseded by better ones. [David Hirsch, in *Mississippi Quarterly*, 1969–70 (23:35–43), makes a good case for including another *Blackwood's* tale among Poe's sources: "Singular Recovery from Death," December 1821. Burton Pollin, in *Discoveries in Poe*, pp. 18–20, suggests Poe's indebtedness to Victor Hugo's *Notre Dame*.]

baths, which cause a lingering death, excited horror, even in the minds of soldiers hardened in the field of battle.‡

Poe knew Dick's work — he had drawn upon Dick's *Christian Philosopher* in connection with "The Conversation of Eiros and Charmion." The Inquisition material that supplied the framework for the present tale, however, as well as some unifying threads and one of its most outstanding features, he found — as Miss Alterton pointed out in 1933 — in the history of the Inquisition by Juan Antonio Llorente (1756–1823) or in magazine articles and reviews based upon it.§

Poe's story was finished by the summer of 1842, and its title named in the page of "Contents" for PHANTASY-PIECES, but crossed out.

‡ I have seen the information about General Lasalle's visit to the palace of the Inquisition used as a filler in newspapers, such as the *Portsmouth* (New Hampshire) *Journal*, June 2, 1832, p. 1, col. 4, which says, in a short article headed "Spanish Inquisition": "When Gen. Lasalle entered Toledo he immediately visited the palace of the Inquisition. . ."; and goes on to describe the instruments of torture.

§ After the French invasion of Spain in 1808, Joseph Bonaparte suppressed the Inquisition and appointed Llorente to take charge of its archives and write its history. His *Anales de la Inquisicion de España* (2 vols., Madrid) appeared in 1812. When the French were driven out and the Inquisition was restored by Ferdinand VII, Llorente took refuge in Paris, where a translation by A. Pellier of his work was published as *Histoire critique de l'Inquisition de l'Espagne, depuis . . . son établissement jusqu' au règne de Ferdinand VII* (4 vols., 1817–18). *Historia critica de la Inquisicion de España* (10 vols., Madrid, 1822) was issued after the second suppression of the Inquisition (1820), and *Histoire abrégée de l'Inquisition d'Espagne . . . par L[éonard] Gallois* (3rd ed., Paris, 1824), preceded by a note on the life and writings of Llorente, appeared the year after his death. In 1826 two one-volume editions in English appeared: *The History of the Inquisition of Spain from the time of its establishment to the reign of Ferdinand VII . . . abridged and translated from the original works of D. Jean Antoine Llorente* (London: G. B. Whittaker), and *History of the Spanish Inquisition abridged from the original work of M. Llorente, late secretary of that institution, by Leonard Gallois: Translated by an American* (New York: G. C. Morgan). In 1843 a reprint of the London edition was issued in Philadelphia. Poe may have seen one of the versions of Llorente's work, but it is more likely that he drew upon the two articles cited by Margaret Alterton: (1) "The Inquisition of Spain, with Anecdotes of Some of Its More Illustrious Victims," by James Browne, in *Blackwood's Magazine,* July and August 1826, which surveys earlier writings on the Inquisition and gives special attention to Llorente, quoting from a French edition, and (2) a review of the one-volume English edition of 1826 in the *British Critic,* January 1827, reprinted in the Philadelphia *Museum of Foreign Literature and Science* for April of that year.

THE PIT AND THE PENDULUM

TEXTS

(A) The Gift: a Christmas and New Year's Present, MDCCCXLIII (1842), pages 133–151; *(B) Broadway Journal,* May 17, 1845 (1:307–311); *(C) Works* (1850), I, 310–324.

Griswold's text *(C)* is followed; it shows a few auctorial corrections, the most important of which changed "vibrations" to "oscillations," although this laudable change was neglected in the succeeding paragraphs.

We follow the printing of the motto in "Pinakidia" *(SLM,* August 1836), which has the comma after *fuit,* and the circumflex over the second *a* in *patriâ,* both missing in texts *B* and *C.*

THE PIT AND THE PENDULUM [C]

Impia tortorum longas hic turba furores
Sanguinis innocui, non satiata, aluit.
Sospite nunc patriâ, fracto nunc funeris antro,
Mors ubi dira fuit, vita salusque patent.

[Quatrain composed for the gates of a market to be erected upon the site of the Jacobin Club House at Paris.]

I was sick — sick unto death[1] with that long agony; and when they at length unbound me, and I was permitted to sit, I felt that my senses were leaving me. The sentence — the dread sentence of death — was the last of distinct accentuation which reached my ears. After that, the sound of the inquisitorial voices seemed merged in one dreamy indeterminate hum. It conveyed to my soul the idea of *revolution* — perhaps from its association in fancy with the burr of a mill-wheel.[2] This only for a brief period; for presently I heard no more. Yet, for a while, I saw; but with how terrible an exaggeration! I saw the lips of the black-robed judges. They appeared to me white — whiter than the sheet upon which I trace these words — and thin even to grotesqueness; thin with the intensity of their expression of firmness — of immoveable resolution — of stern contempt of human torture. I saw that the decrees of what to me was Fate, were still issuing from those lips. I saw them writhe with a deadly locution.[3] I saw them fashion the syllables of my name; and I shuddered because no sound succeeded. I saw, too, for a few moments of delirious horror, the soft and nearly

---

Motto: This first appears in B

imperceptible waving of the sable draperies which enwrapped the walls of the apartment.[4] And then my vision fell upon the seven tall candles upon the table.[5] At first they wore the aspect of charity, and seemed white slender angels who would save me; but then, all at once, there came a most deadly nausea over my spirit, and I felt every fibre in my frame thrill as if I had touched the wire of a galvanic battery,[6] while the angel forms became meaningless spectres, with heads of flame, and I saw that from them there would be no help. And then there stole into my fancy, like a rich musical note, the thought of what sweet rest there must be in the grave. The thought came gently and stealthily, and it seemed long before it attained full appreciation; but just as my spirit came at length properly to feel and entertain it, the figures of the judges vanished, as if magically, from before me; the tall candles sank into nothingness; their flames went out utterly; the blackness of darkness supervened;[7] all sensations[a] appeared swallowed up in a[b] mad rushing descent[8] as of the soul into Hades. Then silence, and stillness, and night were the universe.

I had swooned; but still[c] will not say that all of consciousness was lost. What of it there remained I will not attempt to define, or even to describe; yet all was not lost. In the deepest slumber — no! In delirium — no! In a swoon — no! In death — no! even in the grave all *is not* lost. Else there is no immortality for man. Arousing from the most profound of slumbers, we break the gossamer web of *some* dream. Yet in a second afterward,[d] (so frail may that web have been) we remember not that we have dreamed.[9] In the return to life from the swoon there are two stages; first, that of the sense of mental or spiritual; secondly, that of the sense of physical, existence. It seems probable that if, upon reaching the second stage, we could recall the impressions of the first, we should find these impressions eloquent in memories of the gulf beyond. And that gulf is — what? How at least shall we distinguish its shadows from those of the tomb? But if the impressions of what I have termed the first stage, are not, at will, recalled, yet, after long interval, do they not come unbidden, while we marvel whence they

---

a   sensation *(A)*
b   that *(A)*
c   *Omitted (A)*
d   afterwards, *(A)*

come? He who has never[e] swooned[f] is not he who finds strange palaces and wildly familiar faces in coals that glow; is not he who beholds floating in mid-air the sad visions that the many may not view; is not he who ponders over[g] the perfume of some novel flower — is not he whose brain grows bewildered with the[h] meaning of some musical cadence which has never before arrested his attention.[10]

Amid frequent and thoughtful endeavors to remember; amid earnest struggles to regather some token of the state of seeming nothingness into which my soul had lapsed, there have been moments when I have dreamed of success; there have been brief, very brief periods when I have conjured up remembrances which the lucid reason of a later epoch assures me could have had reference only to that condition of seeming[i] unconsciousness. These shadows of memory tell, indistinctly, of tall figures that lifted and bore me in silence down — down — still down[11] — till a hideous dizziness oppressed me at the mere idea of the interminableness of the descent. They tell also of a vague horror at my heart on account of that heart's unnatural stillness. Then comes a sense of sudden motionlessness throughout all things; as if those who bore me (a ghastly train!) had outrun, in their descent, the limits of the limitless, and paused from the wearisomeness of their toil. After this I call to mind flatness and dampness; and then all is *madness* — the madness of a memory which busies itself among forbidden things.

Very suddenly there came back to my soul motion and sound — the tumultuous motion of the heart, and, in my ears, the sound of its beating. Then a pause in which all is blank. Then again sound, and motion, and touch — a tingling sensation pervading my frame. Then the mere consciousness of existence, without thought — a condition which lasted long. Then, very suddenly, *thought,* and shuddering terror, and earnest endeavor to comprehend[j] my true state. Then a strong desire to lapse into insensibility. Then a rushing revival of soul and a successful effort to

---

e   *Omitted (B) misprint*
f   swooned, *(B, C) comma deleted to follow A*
g   ever *(B) misprint*

h   the intense *(A)*
i   what men term *(A)*
j   realize *(A)*

move. And now a full memory of the trial, of the judges,[k] of the sable draperies, of the sentence, of the sickness, of the swoon. Then entire forgetfulness of all that followed; of all that a later day and much earnestness of endeavor have enabled me vaguely to recall.

So far, I had not opened my eyes. I felt that I lay upon my back, unbound. I reached out my hand, and it fell heavily upon something damp and hard. There I suffered it to remain for many minutes, while I strove to imagine where and *what* I could be. I longed, yet dared not to employ my vision. I dreaded the first glance at objects around me.[1] It was not that I feared to look upon things horrible, but that I grew aghast lest there should be *nothing* to see. At length, with a wild desperation at heart, I quickly unclosed my eyes. My worst thoughts, then, were confirmed. The blackness of[m] eternal night encompassed me. I struggled[n] for breath. The intensity of the darkness seemed to oppress and stifle me. The atmosphere was intolerably close. I still lay quietly, and made effort to exercise my reason. I brought to mind the inquisitorial proceedings, and attempted from that point to deduce my real condition. The sentence had passed; and it appeared to me that a very long interval of time had since elapsed. Yet not for a moment did I suppose myself actually dead.[12] Such a supposition, notwithstanding what we read in fiction, is altogether inconsistent with real existence; — but where and in what state was I? The condemned to death, I knew, perished usually at the *autos-da-fé*,[o] and one of these had been held on the very night of the day of my trial.[13] Had I been remanded to my dungeon, to await the next sacrifice, which would not take place for many months? This I at once saw could not be. Victims had been in immediate demand. Moreover, my dungeon, as well as all the condemned cells at Toledo, had stone floors, and light was not altogether excluded.

A fearful idea now suddenly drove the blood in torrents upon my heart, and for a brief period, I once more relapsed into insensibility. Upon recovering, I at once started to my feet, trembling convulsively in every[p] fibre. I thrust my arms wildly above and

---

k   judges, of the tall candles, *(A)*
l   around me./around. *(A)*
m   of the *(A)*
n   gasped *(A)*

o   *auto-da-fes, (A, B, C) corrected*
editorially
p   ever *(C) misprint, corrected from A,*
B

around me in all directions. I felt nothing; yet dreaded to move a step, lest I should be impeded by the walls of a^q *tomb*. Perspiration burst from every pore, and stood in cold big beads upon my forehead. The agony of ^{q'}suspense grew, at length,^{q'} intolerable, and I cautiously moved forward, with my arms extended, and my eyes straining from their sockets, in the hope of catching some faint ray of light. I proceeded for many paces; but still all was blackness and vacancy. I breathed more freely. It seemed evident that mine was not, at least, the most hideous of fates.[14]

And now, as I still continued to step cautiously onward, there came thronging upon my recollection a thousand vague rumors of the horrors of^r Toledo.[15] Of the dungeons there had been strange things narrated — fables I had always deemed them — but yet strange, and too ghastly to repeat, save in a whisper. Was I left to perish of starvation in this subterranean^s world of darkness; or what fate, perhaps even more fearful, awaited me? That the result would be death, and a death of more than customary bitterness, I knew too well the character of my judges to doubt. The mode and the hour were all that occupied or distracted me.

My outstretched hands at length encountered some solid obstruction. It was a wall, seemingly of stone masonry — very smooth, slimy, and cold. I followed it up;[16] stepping with all the careful distrust with which certain antique narratives had inspired me. This process, however, afforded me no means of ascertaining the dimensions of my dungeon; as I might make its circuit, and return to the point whence I set out, without being aware of the fact; so perfectly uniform seemed the wall. I therefore sought the knife which had been in my pocket, when led into the inquisitorial chamber; but it was gone; my clothes had been exchanged for a wrapper of coarse serge. I had thought of forcing the blade in some minute crevice of the masonry, so as to identify my point of departure. The difficulty, nevertheless, was but trivial; although, in the disorder of my fancy, it seemed at first insuperable. I tore a part of the hem from the robe and placed the fragment at full length, and

q   *a (A)*
q'...q' suspense, grew at length *(B, C) corrected from A*
r   at *(A)*
s   subterrene *(A)*

·6 8 5·

at right angles to the wall. In groping my way around the prison, I could not fail to encounter this rag upon completing the circuit. So, at least, I thought: but I had not counted upon the extent of the dungeon, or upon my own weakness. The ground was moist and slippery. I staggered onward[t] for "some time,"[u] when I stumbled and fell. My excessive fatigue induced me to remain prostrate; and sleep soon overtook me as I lay.

Upon awaking, and stretching forth an arm, I found beside me a loaf and a pitcher with water. I was too much exhausted to reflect upon this circumstance, but ate and drank with avidity. Shortly afterward,[v] I resumed my tour around the prison, and with much toil, came at last upon the fragment of the[w] serge. Up to the period when I fell, I had counted fifty-two paces, and, upon resuming my walk, I had counted forty-eight more — when I arrived at the rag. There were in all, then, a hundred paces; and, admitting two paces to the yard, I presumed the dungeon to be fifty yards in circuit. I had met, however, with many angles in the wall, and thus I could form no guess at the shape of the vault; for vault I could not help supposing it to be.

I had little object — certainly no hope — in these researches; but a vague curiosity prompted me to continue them. Quitting the wall, I resolved to cross the area of the enclosure. At first, I proceeded with extreme caution, for the floor, although seemingly of solid material, was treacherous with slime. At length, however, I took courage, and did not hesitate to step firmly — endeavoring to cross in as direct a line as possible. I had advanced some ten or twelve paces in this manner, when the remnant of the torn hem of my robe became entangled between my legs. I stepped on it, and fell violently on my face.

In the confusion attending my fall, I did not immediately apprehend a somewhat startling circumstance, which yet, in a few seconds afterward,[x] and while I still lay prostrate, arrested my attention. It was this: my chin rested upon the floor of the prison, but my lips, and the upper portion of my head, although seemingly

---

t onwards (A)
u . . . u perhaps half an hour, (A)
v afterwards, (A)

w *Omitted* (A)
x afterwards, (A)

at a less elevation than the chin, touched nothing. At the same time, my forehead seemed bathed in a clammy vapor, and the peculiar smell of decayed fungus arose to my nostrils. I put forward my arm, and shuddered to find that I had fallen at the very brink of a circular pit, whose extent, of couse, I had no means of ascertaining at the moment. Groping about the masonry just below the margin, I succeeded in dislodging a small fragment, and let it fall into the abyss. For ʸmany secondsʸ I hearkened to its reverberations as it dashed against the sides of the chasm in its descent: at length, there was a sullen plunge into water, succeeded by loud echoes. At the same moment, there came a sound resembling the quick opening, and as rapid closing of a door overhead, while a faint gleam of light flashed suddenly through the gloom, and as suddenly faded away.

Iᶻ saw clearly the doom which had been prepared for me, and congratulated myself upon the timely accident by which I had escaped. Another stepᵃ before my fall, and the world had seen me no more. And the death just avoidedᵃ' was of that very character which I had regarded as fabulous and frivolous in the tales respecting the Inquisition. To the victims of itsᵇ tyranny, there was the choice of death with its direst physical agonies, or death with its most hideous moral horrors. I had been reserved for the latter. By long suffering my nerves had been unstrung, until I trembled at the sound of my own voice, and had become in every respect a fitting subject for the species of torture which awaited me.

Shaking in every limb, I groped my way back to the wall — resolving there to perish rather than risk the terrors of the wells, of which my imagination now pictured many in various positions about the dungeon. In other conditions of mind, I might have had courage to end my misery at once, by a plunge into one of these abysses; but now I was the veriest of cowards. Neither could I forget what I had read of these pits — that the *sudden* extinction of life formed no part of their most horrible plan.

Agitation of spirit kept me awake for many long hours; but at

---

y . . . y   nearly a minute *(A)*   a'   avoided, *(B, C) corrected from A*
z   I now *(A)*   b   *Omitted (A)*
a   Another step/A step farther *(A)*

length I again slumbered. Upon arousing, I found by my side, as before, a loaf and a pitcher of water. A burning thirst consumed me, and I emptied the vessel at a draught. It must have been drugged — for scarcely had I drunk,[c] before I became irresistibly drowsy. A deep sleep fell upon me — a sleep like that of death. How long it [d]lasted, of course I[d] know not; but when, once again, I unclosed my eyes, the objects around me were visible. By a wild, sulphurous lustre, the origin of which I could not at first determine, I was enabled to see the extent and aspect of the prison.

In its size I had been greatly mistaken. The whole circuit of its walls did not exceed twenty-five yards. For some minutes this fact occasioned me a world of vain trouble; vain indeed — for what could be of less importance, under the terrible circumstances which environed me, than the mere dimensions[e] of my dungeon? But my soul took a wild interest in trifles,[17] and I busied myself in endeavors to account for the error I had committed in my measurement. The truth at length flashed upon me. In my first attempt at exploration, I had counted fifty-two paces, up to the period when I fell: I must then have been within a pace or two of the fragment of serge; in fact, I had nearly performed the circuit of the vault. I then slept — and, upon awaking, I must have returned upon my steps — thus supposing the circuit nearly double what it actually was. My confusion of mind prevented me from observing that I began my tour with the wall to the left, and ended it with the wall to the right.

I had been deceived, too, in respect to the shape of the enclosure. In feeling my way, I had found many angles, and thus deduced an idea of great irregularity; so potent is the effect of total darkness upon one[f] arousing from lethargy or sleep! The angles were simply those of a few slight depressions, or niches, at odd intervals. The general shape of the prison was square. What I had taken for masonry[f'] seemed now to be iron, or some other metal, in huge plates, whose sutures or joints occasioned the depressions.[g]

---

c drank, (A)
d...d lasted I, of course, (A)
e dimension (A)
f our (A)

f' masonry, (C) corrected from A, B
g depression. (B, C) misprint, corrected to follow A

The entire surface of this metallic enclosure was rudely daubed in all the hideous and repulsive devices to which the charnel superstition of the monks has given rise. The figures of fiends in aspects of menace, with skeleton forms, and other more really fearful images, overspread and disfigured the walls. I observed that the outlines of these monstrosities were sufficiently distinct, but that the colors seemed faded and blurred, as if from the effects of a damp atmosphere.[18] I now noticed the floor, too, which was of stone. In the centre yawned the circular pit from whose jaws I had escaped; but it was the only one in the dungeon.

All this I saw indistinctly and by much effort — for my personal condition had been greatly changed during slumber. I now lay upon my back, and at full length, on a species of low framework of wood. To this I was securely bound by a long strap resembling a surcingle. It passed in many convolutions about my limbs and body, leaving at liberty only my head, and my left arm to such extent, that I could, by dint of much exertion, supply myself with food from an earthen dish which lay by my side on the floor. I saw, to my horror, that the pitcher ʰhad been removed. I say,ʰ to my horror — for I was consumed with intolerable thirst. This thirst it appeared to be the design of my persecutors to stimulate — for the food in the dish was meat pungently seasoned.

Looking upward,ⁱ I surveyed the ceiling of my prison. It was some thirty or forty feet overhead, and constructed much as the side walls. In one of its panels a very singular figure riveted my whole attention. It was the painted figure of Time as he is commonly represented, save that, in lieu of a scythe, he held what, at a casual glance, I supposed to be the pictured image of a huge pendulum, such as we see on antique clocks. There was something, however, in the appearance of this machine which caused me to regard it more attentively. While I gazed directly upward at it, (for its position was immediately over my own,) I fancied that I saw it in motion. In an instant afterwardʲ the fancy was confirmed. Its sweep was brief, and of course slow. I watched it for some minutes, somewhat in fear, but more in wonder. Wearied at length

h...h was absent: *(A)*   j afterwards *(A)*
i upwards, *(A)*

with observing its dull movement, I turned my eyes upon the other objects in the cell.

A slight noise attracted my notice, and, looking to the floor, I saw several enormous rats traversing it. They had issued from the well, which lay just within view to my right. Even then, while I gazed, they came up in troops, hurriedly, with ravenous eyes, allured by the scent of the meat. From this it required much effort and attention to scare them away.[19]

It might have been half an hour, perhaps even an hour, (for I could take but imperfect note of time,) before I again cast my eyes upward. What I then saw[k] confounded and amazed me. The sweep of the pendulum had increased in extent by nearly a yard. As a natural consequence, its velocity was also much greater. But what mainly disturbed me[l] was the idea that it had perceptibly *descended*. I now observed — with what horror it is needless to say — that its nether extremity was formed of a crescent of glittering steel, about a foot in length from horn to horn; the horns upward, and the under edge evidently as keen as that of a razor. Like a razor also, it seemed massy and heavy, tapering from the edge into a solid and broad structure above. It was appended to a weighty rod of brass, and the whole *hissed* as it swung through the air.[20]

I could no longer doubt the doom prepared for me by monkish ingenuity in torture. My cognizance of the pit had become known to the inquisitorial agents — the[m] *pit,* whose horrors had been destined for so bold a recusant[21] as myself — *the pit,* typical of hell, and regarded by rumor as the Ultima Thule[22] of all their punishments. The plunge into this pit I had avoided by the merest of [n]accidents, and[n] I knew that surprise, or entrapment[o] into torment, formed an important portion of all the grotesquerie of these dungeon deaths. Having failed to fall, it was no part of the demon plan to hurl me into the abyss; and thus (there being no alternative) a different and a milder destruction awaited me. Milder! I half smiled in my agony as I thought of such application of such a term.

---

k saw, (C) comma deleted to follow A, B
l me, (C) comma deleted to follow A, B
m the (A)
n...n accidents. (A)
o *entrapment* (A)

THE PIT AND THE PENDULUM

What boots it to tell of the long, long hours of horror more than mortal, during which I counted the rushing oscillations[p] of the steel![23] Inch by inch — line by line — with a descent only appreciable at intervals that seemed ages — down and still down it came! Days passed — it might have been that many days passed — ere it swept so closely over me as to fan me with its acrid breath. The odor of the sharp steel forced itself into my nostrils. I prayed — I wearied heaven with my[q] prayer for its more speedy descent. I grew frantically mad, and struggled to force myself upward[r] against the sweep of the fearful scimitar. And then I fell suddenly calm, and lay smiling at the glittering death, as a child at some rare bauble.

There was another[s] interval of utter insensibility; it was brief; for, upon again lapsing into life, there had been no perceptible descent in the pendulum. But it might[t] have been long — for I knew there were demons who took note of my swoon, and who could have arrested the vibration at pleasure. Upon my recovery, too, I felt very — oh, inexpressibly — sick and weak, as if through long inanition. Even amid[u] the agonies of that period, the human nature [v]craved food.[v] With painful effort I outstretched my left arm as far as my bonds permitted, and took possession of the small remnant which had been spared me by the rats. As I put a portion of it within my lips, there rushed to my mind a half-formed thought of joy — of hope. Yet what business had *I* with hope? It was, as I say, a half-formed thought — man has many such, which are never completed. I felt that it was of joy — of hope; but I felt also that it had perished in its formation. In vain I struggled to perfect[w] — to regain[x] it. Long suffering had nearly annihilated all my ordinary powers of mind. I was an imbecile — an idiot.

The vibration of the pendulum was at right angles to my length. I saw that the crescent was designed to cross the region of the heart. It would fray the serge of my robe — it would return and repeat its operations[y] — again — and again. Notwithstanding

---

p   vibrations *(A, B)*
q   *Omitted (A)*
r   upwards *(A)*
s   an *(A)*
t   *might (A)*

u   amid all *(A)*
v . . . v   *craved food. (A)*
w   realize *(A)*
x   reain *(B) misprint*
y   operation *(A)*

its terrifically wide sweep, (some thirty feet or more,) and the hissing vigor of its descent, sufficient to sunder these very walls of iron, still the fraying of[z] my robe would be all that, for several minutes, it would accomplish. And at this thought I paused. I dared not go farther than this reflection. I dwelt upon it with a pertinacity of attention — as if, in so dwelling, I could arrest *here* the descent of the steel. I forced myself to ponder upon the sound[a] of the crescent as it should pass across the garment — upon the peculiar thrilling sensation which the friction of cloth produces on[b] the nerves. I pondered upon all this frivolity until my teeth were on edge.

Down — steadily down it crept.[c] I took a frenzied pleasure in contrasting its downward with its lateral velocity. To the right — to the left — far and wide — with the shriek[d] of a damned spirit! to my heart, with the stealthy pace of the tiger. I alternately laughed and howled, as the one or the other idea grew predominant.

Down — certainly, relentlessly down! It vibrated within three inches of my bosom! I struggled violently — furiously — to free my left arm. This was free only from the elbow to the hand. I could reach the latter, from the platter beside me, to my mouth, with great effort, but no farther. Could I have broken the fastenings above the elbow, I would have seized and attempted to arrest the pendulum. I might as well have attempted to arrest an avalanche!

Down — still unceasingly — still inevitably down! I gasped and struggled at each vibration. I shrunk convulsively at its every sweep. My eyes followed its outward or upward whirls with the eagerness of the most unmeaning despair; they closed themselves spasmodically at the descent, although death would have been a relief, oh, how unspeakable! Still I[e] quivered in every nerve to think how slight a sinking[f] of the machinery would precipitate that keen, glistening axe upon my bosom. It was *hope*[g] that prompted the nerve to quiver — the frame to shrink. It was *hope*[h] — the hope

---

z of the serge of *(A)*
a *sound (A)*
b in *(A)*
c *crept. (A)*
d shriek and the plunge *(A)*

e Still I/I still *(A)*
f sinking or slipping *(A)*
g hope *(A)*
h hope *(A)*

that triumphs on the rack — that whispers to the death-condemned even in the dungeons of the Inquisition.

I saw that some ten or twelve vibrations would bring the steel in actual contact with my robe — and with this observation there suddenly came over my spirit all the keen, collected calmness of despair.[i] For the first time during many hours — or perhaps days — I *thought*. It now[j] occurred to me, that the bandage, or surcingle, which enveloped me, was *unique*.[24] I was tied by no separate cord.[k] The first stroke of the razor-like crescent athwart any portion of the band, would so detach it that it might be unwound from my person by means of my left hand. But how fearful, in that case, the proximity of the steel! The result of the slightest struggle, how deadly! Was it likely, moreover, that the minions of the torturer had not foreseen and provided for this possibility? Was it probable that the bandage crossed my bosom [l]in the track[l] of the pendulum? Dreading to find my faint, and, as it seemed, my last hope frustrated, I so far elevated my head as to obtain a distinct view of my breast. The surcingle enveloped my limbs and body close in all directions — *save in the path of the destroying crescent*.

Scarcely had I dropped my head back into[m] its original position, when there flashed upon my mind what I cannot better describe than as the [n]unformed half[n] of that idea of deliverance to which I have previously alluded, and of which a moiety only floated indeterminately through my brain when I raised food[o] to my burning lips. The whole thought was now present — feeble, scarcely sane, scarcely definite — but still entire. I proceeded at once, with the nervous energy of despair, to attempt its execution.

For many hours the immediate vicinity of the low framework upon which I lay, had been literally swarming with rats. They were wild, bold, ravenous — their red eyes glaring upon me as if they waited but for motionlessness on my part to make me their prey. "To what food," I thought, "have they been accustomed in the well?"

---

i *despair. (A)*
j now at once *(A)*
k cords. *(A)*
l...l *in the track (A)*

m in *(A)*
n...n *unformed half (A)*
o *food (A)*

They had devoured, in spite of all my efforts to prevent them, all but a small remnant of the contents of the dish. I had fallen into an habitual see-saw, or wave of the hand about the platter; and, at length, the unconscious uniformity of the movement deprived it of effect. In their voracity, the vermin frequently fastened their sharp fangs in my fingers. With the particles of the oily and spicy viand which now remained, I thoroughly rubbed the bandage^p wherever I could reach it; then, raising my hand from the floor, I lay breathlessly still.

At first, the ravenous animals were startled and terrified at the change — at the cessation of movement. They shrank alarmedly back; many sought the well. But this was only for a moment. I had not counted in vain upon their voracity. Observing that I remained without motion, one or two of the boldest leaped upon the frame-work,^{q} and smelt at the surcingle. This seemed the signal for a general rush. Forth from the well they hurried in fresh troops. They clung to the wood — they overran it, and leaped^r in hundreds upon my person. The measured movement of the pendulum disturbed them not at all. Avoiding its strokes, they busied themselves with the anointed bandage. They pressed — they swarmed upon me in ever accumulating heaps. They writhed upon my throat; their cold lips sought my own;^{25} I was half stifled by their thronging pressure; disgust,^{s} for which the world has no name, swelled my bosom, and chilled, with a heavy^t clamminess, my heart. Yet one minute, and I felt that the struggle would be over. Plainly I perceived the loosening of the bandage. I knew that in more than one place it must be already severed. With a more than human resolution I lay *still*.

Nor had I erred in my calculations — nor had I endured in vain. I at length felt that I was *free*. The surcingle hung in ribands from my body. But the stroke of the pendulum already pressed upon my bosom. It had divided the serge of the robe. It had cut through the linen beneath. Twice again it swung, and a sharp sense of pain shot through every nerve. But the moment of escape had arrived. At a wave of my hand my deliverers hurried

---

p bundage *(B) misprint*
q fame-work, *(C) misprint, corrected*
from A, B

r leapt *(A)*
s a disgust, *(A)*
t deadly *(A)*

tumultuously away. With a steady movement — cautious, sidelong, shrinking, and slow — I slid from the embrace of the bandage and beyond the reach[u] of the scimitar. For the moment, at least, *I was free.*

Free! — and in the grasp of the Inquisition! I had scarcely stepped from my wooden bed of horror upon the stone floor of the prison, when the motion of the hellish machine ceased, and I beheld it drawn up, by some invisible force, through the ceiling. This was a lesson which I took desperately to heart. My every motion was undoubtedly watched. Free! — I had but escaped death in one form of agony, to be delivered unto worse than death in some other. With that thought I rolled my eyes nervously around on the barriers of iron that hemmed me in. Something unusual — some change which, at first, I could not appreciate distinctly — it was obvious, had taken place in the apartment. For many minutes of a dreamy and trembling abstraction, I busied myself in vain, unconnected conjecture. During this period, I became aware, for the first time, of the origin of the sulphurous[v] light which illumined[w] the cell. It proceeded from a fissure, about half an inch in width, extending entirely around the prison at the base of the walls, which thus appeared, and were completely separated from the floor. I endeavored, but of course in vain, to look through the aperture.

As I arose[x] from the attempt, the[y] mystery of the alteration in the chamber broke at once upon my understanding. I have observed that, although the outlines of the figures upon the walls were sufficiently distinct, yet the colors seemed blurred and indefinite. These colors had now assumed, and were momentarily assuming, a startling and most intense brilliancy, that gave to the spectral and fiendish[z] portraitures an aspect that might have thrilled ever firmer nerves than my own. Demon eyes, of a wild and ghastly vivacity, glared upon me in a thousand directions, where none had been visible before, and gleamed with the lurid lustre of a fire that I could not force my[a] imagination to regard as unreal.

---

u sweep *(A)*
v sulphureous *(A)*
w illuminated *(A)*
x rose *(A)*

y fhe *(B) misprint*
z fiendship *(B) misprint*
a my diseased *(A)*

Unreal! — Even while I breathed[b] there came to my nostrils the breath of the vapor of heated iron![26] A suffocating odor pervaded the prison! A deeper glow settled each moment in the eyes that glared at my agonies! A richer tint of crimson diffused itself over the pictured horrors of blood. I panted! I gasped for breath! There could be no doubt of the design of my tormentors — oh! most unrelenting! oh! most demoniac of men! I shrank from the glowing metal to the centre of the cell. Amid the thought of the fiery destruction that impended, the idea of the coolness of the well came over my soul like balm. I rushed to its deadly brink. I threw my straining vision below. The glare from the enkindled roof illumined its inmost recesses. Yet, for a wild moment, did my spirit refuse to comprehend the meaning of what I saw. At length it forced — it wrestled its way into my soul — it burned itself in upon my shuddering reason. Oh! for a voice to speak! — oh! horror! — oh! any horror but this! With a shriek, I rushed from the margin, and buried my face in my hands — weeping bitterly.

The heat rapidly increased, and once again I looked up, shuddering as with a fit of the ague. There had been a second change in the cell — and now the change was obviously in the *form*.[27] As before, it was in vain that I at first endeavored to appreciate or understand what was taking place. But not long was I left in doubt. The Inquisitorial vengeance had been hurried by my twofold escape, and there was to be no more dallying with the King of Terrors. The room had been square. I saw that two of its iron angles were now acute — two, consequently, obtuse. The fearful difference quickly increased with a low rumbling or moaning sound. In an instant the apartment had shifted its form into that of a lozenge. But the alteration stopped not here — I neither hoped nor desired it to stop. I could have clasped the red walls to my bosom as a garment of eternal peace. "Death," I said, "any death but that of the pit!" Fool! might I not have[c] known that *into the pit* it was the object of the burning iron to urge me? Could I resist its glow? or if even that, could I withstand its pressure? And now, flatter and flatter grew the lozenge, with a rapidity that left me no time for contemplation. Its centre, and of course, its greatest width,

b   gazed (A)   c   not have/have not (B)

THE PIT AND THE PENDULUM

came just over the yawning gulf. I shrank back — but the closing walls pressed me resistlessly onward.ᵈ At length for my seared and writhing body there was no longer an inch of foothold on the firm floor of the prison. I struggled no more, but the agony of my soul found vent in one loud, long, and final scream of despair. I felt that I tottered upon the brink — I averted my eyes —

ᵉThere was a discordant hum of human voices! There was a loud blast as of many trumpets!ᵉ There was a harsh grating as of a thousand thunders! The fiery walls rushed back! An outstretched arm caught my own as I fell, fainting, into the abyss. It was that of General Lasalle. ᶠThe French army had entered Toledo.²⁸ The Inquisition was in the hands of its enemies.ᶠ

NOTES

Motto: The motto appears in "Pinakidia," no. 145 (*SLM,* August 1836, p. 581). It may be translated: "Here the wicked mob, unappeased, long cherished a hatred of innocent blood. Now that the fatherland is saved, and the cave of death demolished; where grim death has been, life and health appear." Charles Baudelaire says, in a footnote to his translation of the tale, that the Marché St. Honoré, erected on the site of the Jacobin Club, never had either gates or an inscription (*Nouvelles Histoires extraordinaires,* 1857).

1. Compare *Politian,* VI, 29: "I am sick, sick, sick, even unto death," and see also Isaiah 38:1, "sick unto death."

2. Compare "MS. Found in a Bottle," paragraph 5: "As I placed my foot upon the upper step of the companion-ladder I was startled with a loud humming noise, like that occasioned by the rapid revolution of a mill-wheel."

3. Writing lips appear also in "Berenicë" and "The Facts in the Case of M. Valdemar."

4. Compare the draped walls of the bridal chamber in "Ligeia," and also the following description of the torture chamber where a victim faced the Inquisitor: "This was a large apartment under ground, vaulted, hung round with black cloth, and dimly lighted by candles placed in candlesticks fastened to the wall. At one end, there was an inclosed place, like a closet, where the Inquisitor in attendance and the notary sat at a table; so that the place seemed . . . the very mansion of death, everything being calculated to inspire terror" (*Blackwood's Magazine,* July 1826, p. 81, cited in the fourth footnote to the introduction, above). Margaret Alterton quoted this passage in 1933. The substance is ascribed in the *Blackwood's* article to the account of Isaac Orobio, a Jew, as recorded by the Dutch theologian and historian Philip van Limborch (1633–1712).

5. Poe's seven candles may reflect the "seven golden candlesticks" of Revelation 1:12. Compare also the "flames of the seven lamps," in "Shadow."

---

d onwards. (A)
e . . . e There . . . trumpets! There . . . voices! (A)

f . . . f The . . . enemies! The . . . Toledo! (A)

6. The simile of the galvanic battery is canceled from "MS. Found in a Bottle" and "The Oval Portrait." The galvanic battery, in "The Buried Alive," *Blackwood's,* October 1821, was instrumental in the revival of the narrator. See also "Some Words with a Mummy."

7. Compare Jude, verse 13: "wandering stars, to whom is reserved the blackness of darkness forever." Poe also refers to "the blackness of darkness" in chapter 21 of *The Narrative of Arthur Gordon Pym.*

8. Compare "mad, rushing, horrible sound" in "The Conversation of Eiros and Charmion," at note 1.

9. See "Marginalia," number 150 (*Graham's,* March 1846, p. 117), for an elaborate discussion of visions that appear just *before* slumber.

10. Compare this passage to a description of what may be called partial self-hypnotism in "Berenicë," at note 6.

11. Compare "Fairyland," line 15, "Comes down — still down — and down"; and especially "A Predicament," where the heroine says of the hand of the great clock, "Down, down, down it came, closer and yet closer."

12. In contrast, Ugo in *Politian,* X, thinks he is dead, as did a character in an early version of "Loss of Breath." George III was finally recognized to be insane when he talked of having attended his own funeral.

13. The Spanish phrase means acts of faith, but came to be used for public burning of heretics or Jews.

14. For similar gruesome passages on people who think themselves buried alive, see early versions of "Loss of Breath"; *Arthur Gordon Pym,* chapter 21; and "The Premature Burial."

15. Toledo was a center of the activities of the Inquisition.

16. Some sensations and experiences described in the next few pages resemble some recounted in chapter 16 of Charles Brockden Brown's *Edgar Huntly.* See David Lee Clark's article (1929), cited above. Poe planned and perhaps began a study of Brown's novels; in "American Novel Writing" (*Pittsburgh Literary Examiner,* August 1839), he said, "In our next article under this head we shall comment upon the novels of Charles Brockden Brown."

17. His "wild interest in trifles" combined with coherent thinking under stress leads to a solution for the narrator as in "A Descent into the Maelström" (at note 16) and — as pointed out by Clark — in Brown's *Edgar Huntly.* For comment on the basic, undying curiosity, see "The Power of Words" at note 2.

18. For the pictures, compare Charles Robert Maturin, *Melmoth the Wanderer* (1820), chapter 6: "I started up with horror ... on perceiving myself surrounded by demons, who, clothed in fire were breathing forth clouds of it around me ... what I touched was cold ... and I comprehended that these were hideous figures scrawled in phosphorus to terrify me." See the Bison edition (1961), ed. William F. Axton, p. 118. Poe mentioned *Melmoth* as if he was familiar with it in his "Letter to B——" (*SLM,* July 1836) and in his review of Henry Cockton's *Stanley Thorne* in *Graham's* for January 1842. The "fearful

images" recall also the draperies of the bedchamber in "Ligeia," where the arabesque figures changed from "the appearance of simple monstrosities" to "an endless succession of ghastly forms" as one advanced.

19. A versification of the legend that Archbishop Hatto II of Mainz was eaten by mice in the tower he had built as a refuge from them appeared in the *Knickerbocker Magazine,* November 1837, p. 403 (Alterton, 1933). Poe may also have known Southey's verses, "God's Judgement on a Wicked Bishop."

20. The pendulum came from the passage below, a note appended to the preface (pp. xix–xx) of Llorente's *History of the Inquisition* (London, 1826). Poe probably found it in the review of the book in the *British Critic,* January 1827 (p. 129), where it was quoted in full, or in the reprinted review in the Philadelphia *Museum,* April 1827, p. 333. The passage, quoted in part by Alterton in 1933, is here reproduced from the book:

The following fact shews that the inquisitors of our own days do not fall below the standard of those who followed the fanatic Torquemada. * * * * was present when the Inquisition was thrown open, in 1820, by the orders of the Cortes of Madrid. Twenty-one prisoners were found in it, not one of whom knew the name of the city in which he was: some had been confined three years, some a longer period, and not one knew perfectly the nature of the crime of which he was accused.

One of these prisoners had been condemned, and was to have suffered on the following day. His punishment was to be death by the *Pendulum.* The method of thus destroying the victim is as follows: — the condemned is fastened in a groove, upon a table, on his back; suspended above him is a Pendulum, the edge of which is sharp, and it is so constructed as to become longer with every movement. The wretch sees this implement of destruction swinging to and fro above him, and every moment the keen edge approaching nearer and nearer: at length it cuts the skin of his nose, and gradually cuts on, until life is extinct. It may be doubted if the holy office in its mercy ever invented a more humane and rapid method of exterminating heresy, or ensuring confiscation. This, let it be remembered, was a punishment of the Secret Tribunal, A.D. 1820 ! ! !

21. A recusant is properly one who falls back into a heresy once recanted. Poe apparently thought it meant one who refused to obey.

22. The remotest part of the known world, in Vergil's *Georgics,* I, 30, hence indicating an extreme limit. Poe used the phrase in a sense close to the original in his poem "Dream-Land," lines 5–8:

> I have reached these lands but newly
> From an ultimate dim Thule —
> From a wild weird clime that lieth, sublime,
> Out of Space — out of Time.

23. Margaret Alterton in 1925 mentioned "The Man in the Bell" as probably Poe's source for some of the thoughts and sensations described in the next few pages, quoting the narrator:

"Every moment I saw the bell sweep within an inch of my face ... To look at the object," he said, "was bitter as death," but he could not prevent his eyes from following it instinctively as it swung. "The bell pealing above and opening its jaws with a hideous clamor," seemed at one time "a ravening monster raging to devour" him. "In the vast cavern of the bell hideous faces appeared, and glared down on me with terrifying frowns, or with grinning mockery, still more appalling. At last the devil himself, accoutred, as in the common description of the evil spirit, with hoof, horn, and tail, and eyes of infernal lustre, made his appearance ... "

The story, in *Blackwood's,* November 1821, signed Thomas Mann, a pseudonym of William Maginn, is reprinted in his *The Odoherty Papers* (1855). Poe mentioned the piece in a letter to Thomas W. White, April 30, 1835, and in "How to Write a Blackwood Article." Maginn's tale was also a source for "The Devil in the Belfry."

24. Poe uses the word in a sense now termed obsolete by the *OED*: formed or consisting of a single thing — in this case, all in one piece.

25. Professor R. C. Blackmur cited the cold lips of the rats as a bold and unexpected touch, in *The Fall of the House of Usher and Other Tales* (1960), p. 378.

26. For the heating of the room, compare "The Involuntary Experimentalist" in *Blackwood's* for October 1837, a story of a man working on the interior of a boiler which begins to be heated by people unaware of the workman inside it. This is one of the stories mentioned in "How to Write a Blackwood Article."

27. The room that decreases in size is from "The Iron Shroud" by William Mudford, first printed in *Blackwood's* for August 1830 and reprinted in many places. This is the "plagiarized" source immediately recognized by Lewis Gaylord Clark and Griswold — see introduction above — but they called it "Vivenzio, or Italian Vengeance." The name of the protagonist is Vivenzio. Mudford's room is made of blocks that are removed a few at a time. The room in Poe's story is constructed on a different plan.

28. General Antoine-Chevalier-Louis Colbert, Comte de Lasalle, entered Toledo during the Peninsular War in 1808. Poe reviewed W. F. Napier's book on that war in *Graham's* for November 1841, but probably had in mind the passage from Thomas Dick quoted above.

THE LANDSCAPE GARDEN

"The Landscape Garden" is the first of Poe's prose stories of pure beauty, with no tinge of sadness or of humor. Earlier he had tended to disparage the "quietists," but now he showed that he could emulate them if he liked. Later in his life he expanded the piece into "The Domain of Arnheim" and several of his editors — notably Ingram, like Stedman and Woodberry — have chosen, with some justification, to omit the earlier form; Harrison followed Griswold in collecting it as a separate entity.

THE LANDSCAPE GARDEN

Critics have tended to comment only on the elaborated version of the tale, yet since Poe said in a letter to Helen Whitman on October 18, 1848 that the later form had much of his soul in it, we must remember that "The Landscape Garden" has that too. There is a slight nostalgic element no doubt. As a boy the poet had known the home of John Allan's partner, Charles Ellis, with its beautiful garden, and Poe called the wealthy young hero of his tale Ellison.

But Poe had in mind a large estate when he wrote his tale, and revealed both his sources in the story itself. The immensely wealthy protagonist, as acknowledged in Poe's footnote, comes from an account by Prince Hermann Pückler-Muskau in his *Tour in England, Ireland, and France* (Philadelphia, 1833). The second source Poe quoted directly in the tenth paragraph of his story without saying whence he took it, but it has been found in an unsigned article, "American Landscape Gardening," reviewing Andrew J. Downing's notable book* in the New York magazine *Arcturus,* June 1841. Poe's continued interest in the subject is reflected in his remark in his lecture of 1848 on "The Poetic Principle," where he said: "The Poetic sentiment, of course, may develop itself in various modes — in Painting, in Sculpture, in Architecture, in the Dance, very especially in Music — and very peculiarly, and with a wide field, in the composition of the Landscape Garden."

Poe's tale was probably written soon after he gave up his editorship of *Graham's Magazine* in the spring of 1842. It was completed by July 18, 1842 when it was offered to J. and H. G. Langley, publishers of the *Democratic Review,* for that magazine, "in the event of Mr. [John L.] O'Sullivan's liking" it. The editor named did not buy it. He may have been influenced by the recent publication, in the December 1841 number, of an unsigned but full and appreciative review of Downing's book in an article entitled "Landscape Gardening and Rural Architecture." †

* *A Treatise on the Theory and Practice of Landscape Gardening, Adapted to North America, with a View to the Improvement of Country Residences,* etc. (New York and London, 1841).

† This was pointed out by John Ward Ostrom in publishing Poe's letter in *American Literature,* March 1957.

TALES, 1841–1842

Poe's story appeared first in Snowden's *Ladies' Companion* for October 1842 — not entirely to Poe's satisfaction, as the first and second paragraphs from his letter of October 3, 1842 to one of the editors, Robert Hamilton, make clear:

My dear Hamilton,

    I see that you have my Landscape-Garden in your last number — but, oh Jupiter! the typographical blunders. Have you been sick, or what is the matter?

    I wrote you, some time since, saying that if, upon perusal of the "Mystery of Marie Rogêt," you found anything not precisely suited to your pages, I would gladly re-purchase it, but, should you conclude to retain it, for God's sake contrive to send me the proofs; or, at all events read them yourself. Such errors as occur in the "Landscape-Garden" would completely *ruin* a tale such as "Marie Rogêt."‡

TEXTS

    (A) Snowden's *Ladies' Companion* for October 1842 (17:324–327); *(B) Broadway Journal*, September 20, 1845 (2:161–164); *(C) Works* (1856), IV, 336–345.

    Griswold's text *(C)* is followed without emendation. Although Poe does not mention it particularly in his letter to Hamilton, the punctuation of this story is faulty. This is true of all texts. Poe made corrections for the later version. Three incorrectly placed commas in the first paragraph, for example, were eliminated in the corresponding paragraph of "The Domain of Arnheim," for which we have his manuscript.

THE LANDSCAPE GARDEN. [*C*]

The garden like a lady fair was cut,
  That lay as if she slumbered in delight,
And to the open skies her eyes did shut;
  The azure fields of heaven were 'sembled right
In a large round set with the flow'rs of light:
The flowers de luce and the round sparks of dew
That hung upon their azure leaves, did show
Like twinkling stars that sparkle in the ev'ning blue.

GILES FLETCHER

No more remarkable man ever lived than my friend, the young Ellison.[1] He was remarkable in the entire and continuous profusion of good gifts ever lavished upon him by fortune. From his

---

‡ Quoted by permission from p. 55 of *A Descriptive Catalog of Edgar Allan Poe Manuscripts in The Humanities Research Center Library, The University of Texas at Austin.* © 1973 by Joseph J. Moldenhauer.

Title: The Landscape-Garden *(A)*

cradle to his grave, a gale of the blandest prosperity bore him along. Nor do I use the word Prosperity in its mere worldly or external sense. I mean it as synonymous with happiness. The person of whom I speak, seemed born for the purpose of foreshadowing the wild doctrines of Turgot, Price, Priestley,[a] and Condorcet[b] — of exemplifying, by individual instance, what has been deemed the mere chimera of the perfectionists.[2] In the brief existence of Ellison, I fancy that I have seen refuted the dogma — that in man's physical and spiritual[c] nature, lies some hidden principle, the antagonist of Bliss. An intimate and anxious examination of his career, has taught me to understand that, in general, from the violation of a few simple laws of Humanity, arises the Wretchedness[d] of mankind; that, as a species, we have in our possession the as yet unwrought elements of Content; and that, even now, in the present blindness and darkness of all idea on the great question of the Social Condition, it is not impossible that Man, the individual, under certain unusual and highly fortuitous conditions, may be happy.

With opinions such as these was my young friend fully imbued; and thus is it especially worthy of observation that the uninterrupted enjoyment which distinguished his life was in great part the result of preconcert. It is, indeed, evident, that with less of the instinctive philosophy which, now and then, stands so well in the stead of experience, Mr. Ellison would have found himself precipitated, by the very extraordinary successes[e] of his life, into the common vortex of Unhappiness which yawns for those of pre-eminent endowments.[3] But it is by no means my present object to pen an essay on Happiness. The ideas of my friend may be summed up in a few words. He admitted but four unvarying laws, or rather elementary principles, of Bliss. That which he considered chief, was (strange to say!) the simple and purely physical one of free exercise in the open air. "The health," he said, "attainable by other means than this is scarcely worth the name." He pointed to the tillers of the earth — the only people who, as a class, are prover-

---

a   Priestly (A, B, C)   d   Wickedness (A)
b   Condorcêit (A)   e   success (A)
c   andspiritual (B) misprint

· 7 0 3 ·

bially more happy than others — and then he instanced the high ecstasies[f] of the fox-hunter. His second principle was the love of woman. His third was the contempt of ambition. His fourth was an object of unceasing[g] pursuit; and he held that, other things being equal, the extent of happiness was proportioned to the spirituality of this object.[4]

I have said that Ellison was remarkable in the continuous profusion of good gifts lavished upon him by Fortune. In personal grace and beauty he exceeded all men. His intellect was of that order to which the attainment of knowledge is less a labor than a necessity and an intuition. His family was one of the most illustrious of the empire. His bride was the loveliest and most devoted of women. His possessions had been always ample; but, upon the attainment of his one and twentieth year, it was discovered that one of those extraordinary freaks of Fate had been played in his behalf, which startle the whole social world amid which they occur, and seldom fail radically to alter the entire moral constitution of those who are their objects. It appears[h] that about one hundred years prior to Mr. Ellison's attainment of his majority, there had died, in a remote province, one Mr. Seabright Ellison. This[i] gentleman had amassed a princely fortune, and, having no very immediate connections, conceived the whim of suffering his wealth to accumulate for a century after his decease. Minutely and sagaciously directing the various modes of investment, he bequeathed the aggregate amount to the nearest of blood, bearing the name Ellison, who should be alive at the end of the hundred years. Many futile attempts had been made to set aside this singular bequest; their *ex post facto* character rendered them abortive; but the attention of a jealous government was aroused, and a decree finally obtained, forbidding all similar accumulations. This act did not prevent young Ellison, upon his twenty-first birth-day, from entering into possession, as the heir of his ancestor Seabright, of a fortune of *four hundred and fifty millions of dollars.** [5]

---

* An incident similar in outline to the one here imagined, occurred, not very long ago, in England. The name of the fortunate heir (who still lives,) is Thelluson. I

f ecstacies (C) *misprint*   h appeared (A)
g unnecessary (A)   i Tnis (B) *misprint*

THE LANDSCAPE GARDEN

When it had become definitely known that such was the enormous wealth inherited, there were, of course, many speculations as to the mode of its disposal. The gigantic magnitude and the immediately available nature of the sum, dazzled and bewildered all who thought upon the topic. The possessor of any *appreciable* amount of money might have been imagined to perform any one of a thousand things. With riches merely surpassing those of any citizen, it would[1] have been easy to suppose him engaging to supreme excess in the fashionable extravagances of his time; or busying himself with political intrigues, or aiming at ministerial power; or purchasing increase of nobility; or devising gorgeous architectural piles; or collecting large[m] specimens of Virtu;[n] [6] or playing the munificent patron of Letters and Art; or endowing and bestowing his name upon extensive institutions of charity. But, for the inconceivable wealth in the actual possession of the young heir, these objects and all ordinary objects were felt to be inadequate. Recourse was had to figures; and figures but sufficed to confound. It was seen, that even at three per cent., the annual income of the inheritance amounted to no less than thirteen millions and five hundred thousand dollars; which was one million and one hundred and twenty-five thousand per month; or thirty-six thousand, nine hundred and eighty-six per day; or one thousand five hundred and forty-one per hour; or six and twenty dollars for every minute that flew. Thus, the usual track of supposition was thoroughly broken up. Men knew not what to imagine. There were some who even conceived that Mr. Ellison would divest himself forthwith of at least two-thirds of his fortune as of utterly superfluous opulence; enriching whole troops of his relatives by division of his superabundance.

I was not surprised, however, to perceive that he had long

---

first saw an account of this matter in the "Tour" of Prince Puckler Muskau. He makes the sum received ninety millions of pounds, and observes, with much force, that "in the contemplation of so vast a sum, and of the services[j] to which it might be applied, there is something even of the sublime." To suit the views of this article, I have followed the Prince's statement — a grossly[k] exaggerated one, no doubt.

j   purposes *(A)*
k   a grossly/an *(A)*
l   woul *(B) misprint*
m   rare *(A)*
n   Virtû; *(A)*

made up his mind upon a topic which had occasioned so much of discussion to his friends. Nor was I greatly astonished at the nature of his decision. In the widest and noblest[o] sense, he was a poet. He comprehended, moreover, the true character, the august aims, the supreme majesty and dignity of the poetic [p]sentiment. The proper gratification of the sentiment he[p] instinctively felt to lie in the *creation of novel forms of Beauty*. Some peculiarities, either in his early education, or in the nature of his intellect, had tinged with what is termed materialism the whole cast of his ethical speculations; and it was this bias, perhaps, which imperceptibly led him to perceive that the most advantageous, if not the sole legitimate field for the exercise of the poetic sentiment, was to be found in the creation of novel moods[q] of purely *physical* loveliness. Thus it happened that he became neither musician nor poet; if we use this latter term in its every-day acceptation. Or it might have been that he became neither the one nor the other, in pursuance of an idea of his which I have already mentioned — the idea, that in the contempt of ambition lay one of the essential principles of happiness on earth. Is it not, indeed, possible that while a *high* order of genius is necessarily ambitious, the *highest* is invariably *above* that which is termed ambition? And may it not thus happen that many far greater than Milton, have contentedly remained "mute and inglorious?" [7] I believe that the world has never yet seen, and that, unless through some series of accidents goading the noblest order of mind into distasteful exertion, the world will *never* behold that full extent of triumphant execution, in the richer productions of Art, of which the human nature is absolutely capable.

Mr. Ellison became neither musician nor poet; although no man lived more profoundly enamored both of Music and the Muse. Under other circumstances than those which invested him, it is not impossible that he would have become a painter. The field of sculpture, although in its nature rigidly poetical,[r] was too limited in its extent and in its consequences, to have occupied, at any time, much of his attention. And I have now mentioned *all* the provinces in which even the most liberal understanding of the

---

o nobelest *(B) misprint*
p . . . p sentiment he *(A)*
q modes *(A)*
r physical, *(A)*

poetic sentiment has declared this sentiment capable of expatiating. I mean the most liberal public or recognized conception of the idea involved in the phrase "poetic sentiment." But Mr. Ellison imagined that the richest, and altogether the most natural and most suitable province, had been blindly neglected. No definition had spoken of the *Landscape-Gardener,*[s] as of the poet; yet my friend could not fail to perceive that the creation of the Landscape-Garden[t] offered to the true muse the most magnificent of opportunities. Here was, indeed, the fairest field for the display of invention, or imagination, in the endless combining of forms of novel Beauty; the elements which should enter into combination being, at all times, and by a vast superiority, the most glorious which the earth could afford. In the multiform of the tree, and in the multicolor of the flower, he recognized the most direct and the most energetic efforts[u] of Nature at physical loveliness.[v] And in the direction or concentration of this effort, or, still more properly, in its adaptation to the eyes which were to behold it upon earth, he perceived that he should be employing the best means — laboring to the greatest advantage — in the fulfilment of his destiny as Poet.

"Its adaptation to the eyes which were to behold it upon earth." In his explanation of this phraseology, Mr. Ellison did much towards solving what has always seemed to me an enigma. I mean the fact (which none but the ignorant dispute), that no such combinations of scenery exist in Nature as the painter of genius has[w] in his power to produce. No such Paradises are to be found in reality as have glowed upon the canvass of Claude.[x] [8] In the most enchanting of natural landscapes, there will always be found a defect or an excess — many excesses and defects. While the component parts may exceed, individually, the highest skill of the artist, the arrangement of the parts will always be susceptible of improvement. In short, no position can be attained, from which an artistical eye, looking steadily, will not find matter of offence, in what is technically termed the *composition* of a natural landscape. And yet how unintelligible is this! In all other matters we

---

s   *Landscape-Gardner, (A)*
t   Landscape-Gardner *(A)*
u   effort *(A)*

v   Beauty. *(A)*
w   has it *(A)*
x   Claude, or Poussin or Stanfield. *(A)*

are justly instructed to regard Nature as supreme. With her details we shrink from competition. Who shall presume to imitate the colors of the tulip, or to improve the proportions of the lily of the valley? The criticism which says, of sculpture or of portraiture, that "Nature is to be exalted rather than imitated," is in error. No pictorial[y] or sculptural combinations of *points* of human loveliness, do more than approach the living and breathing human beauty as it gladdens our daily path. Byron, who often erred, erred not in saying,

> I've seen more living beauty, ripe and real,
> Than all the nonsense of their stone ideal.[9]

In landscape alone is the principle of the critic true; and, having felt its truth here, it is but the headlong spirit of generalization which has induced him to pronounce it true throughout *all* the domains of Art. Having, I say, *felt* its truth here. For the feeling is no affectation or chimera. The mathematics afford no more absolute demonstrations, than the *sentiment* of his Art yields to the artist. He not only believes, but positively *knows*, that such and such apparently arbitrary arrangements of matter, or form, constitute, and alone constitute, the true Beauty. Yet his reasons have not yet been matured into expression. It remains for a more profound analysis than the world has yet seen, fully[z] to investigate and express them. Nevertheless is he confirmed in his instinctive opinions, by the concurrence of all his compeers. Let a composition be defective; let an emendation be wrought in its mere arrangement of form; let this emendation be submitted to every artist in the world; by each will its necessity be admitted. And even far more than this; in remedy of the defective composition, each insulated member of the fraternity will *suggest* the identical emendation.

I repeat that in landscape arrangements, or collocations alone, is the *physical* Nature susceptible of "exaltation,"[a] and that, therefore, her susceptibility of improvement at this one point, was a mystery which, hitherto I had been unable to solve. It was Mr.

---

y   pictural *(A)*   a   exultation," *(A)*
z   *Omitted (A)*

Ellison who first suggested the idea that what we regarded as improvement or exaltation of the natural beauty, was really such, as respected only the mortal or human *point of view;* that each alteration or disturbance of the primitive scenery might possibly effect a blemish in the picture, if we could suppose this picture viewed *at large* from some remote point in the heavens. "It is[b] easily understood," says[c] Mr. Ellison, "that what might improve a closely scrutinized detail, might, at the same time, injure a[d] general and more distantly-observed effect." He spoke upon this topic with warmth: regarding not so much its immediate or obvious importance, (which is little,) as the character of the conclusions to which it might lead, or of the collateral propositions which it might serve to corroborate or sustain. There *might be* a class of beings, human once, but now to humanity invisible, for whose scrutiny, and for whose refined appreciation of the beautiful, more especially than for our own, had been set in order by God the great landscape-garden of *the whole earth.*

In the course of our discussion, my young friend took occasion to quote some passages from a writer who has been supposed to have well treated this theme.[10]

"There are, properly," he writes, "but two styles of landscape-gardening, the natural and the artificial. One seeks to recall the original beauty of the country, by adapting its means to the surrounding scenery; cultivating trees in harmony with the hills or plain of the neighboring land; detecting and bringing into practice those nice relations of size, proportion, and color which, hid from the common observer, are revealed everywhere to the experienced student of nature. The result of the natural style of gardening, is seen rather in the absence of all defects and incongruities — in the prevalence of a beautiful harmony and order, than in the creation of any special wonders or miracles. The artificial style has as many varieties as there are different tastes to gratify. It has a certain general relation to the various styles of building. There are the stately avenues and retirements of Versailles; Italian terraces; and a various mixed old English style,

---

b   was *(A)*   d   in *(A)*
c   said *(A)*

which bears some relation to the domestic Gothic or English Eliza-
bethan architecture. Whatever may be said against the abuses of
the artificial landscape-gardening, a mixture of pure art in a garden scene, adds to it a great beauty. This is partly pleasing to the
eye, by the show of order and design, and partly moral. A terrace,
with an old moss-covered balustrade, calls up at once to the eye,
the fair forms that have passed there in other days. The slightest
exhibition of art is an evidence of care and human interest."

"From what I have already observed," said Mr. Ellison, "you
will understand that I reject the idea, here expressed, of 'recalling
the original beauty of the country.' The original beauty is never
so great as that which may be introduced. Of course, much depends
upon the selection of a spot with *capabilities*.[11] What is said in respect to the 'detecting and bringing into practice those nice relations of size, proportion, and color,' is a mere vagueness of speech,
which may mean much, or little, or nothing, and which guides in
no degree. That the true 'result of the natural style of gardening is
seen rather in the absence of all defects and incongruities, than
in the creation of any special wonders or miracles,' is a proposition
better suited to the grovelling apprehension of the herd, than to
the fervid dreams of the man of genius. The merit suggested is, at
best,[e] negative, and appertains to that hobbling criticism which,
in letters, would elevate Addison into apotheosis. In truth, while
that merit which consists in the mere avoiding demerit, appeals
directly to the understanding, and can thus be foreshadowed in
Rule, the loftier merit, which breathes and flames in invention or
creation, can be apprehended solely in its results. Rule applies but
to the excellences of avoidance — to the virtues which deny or refrain. Beyond these the critical art can but suggest. We may be instructed to build an Odyssey, but it is in vain that we are told *how*
to conceive a 'Tempest,' an 'Inferno,' a 'Prometheus Bound,' a
'Nightingale,' such as that of Keats, or the 'Sensitive Plant' of
Shelley.[12] But, the thing done, the wonder accomplished, and the
capacity for apprehension becomes universal. The sophists of the
negative school, who through inability to create, have scoffed at
creation, are now found the loudest in applause. What, in its

---

e   least, *(A)*

chrysalis condition of principle, affronted their demure reason, never fails, in its maturity of accomplishment, to extort admiration from their instinct of the beautiful or of the sublime.

"Our author's observations on the artificial style of gardening," continued Mr. Ellison, "are[f] less objectionable. 'A mixture of pure art in a garden scene, adds to it a great beauty.' This is just; and the reference to the sense of human interest is equally so. I repeat that the principle here expressed, is incontrovertible; but there *may be* something even beyond it. There may be an object in full keeping with the principle suggested — an object unattainable by the means ordinarily in possession of mankind, yet which, if attained, would lend a charm to the landscape-garden immeasurably surpassing that which a merely *human* interest could bestow. The true poet possessed of very unusual pecuniary resources, might possibly, while retaining the necessary idea of *art* or *interest* or *culture,* so imbue his designs at once with extent and novelty of Beauty, as to convey the sentiment of *spiritual* interference. It will be seen that, in bringing about such result, he secures all the advantages of *interest* or *design,* while relieving his work of all the harshness and technicality of Art. In the most rugged of wildernesses — in the most savage of the scenes of pure Nature — there is apparent the *art* of a Creator; yet is *this* art apparent only to reflection; in no respect has it the obvious force of a feeling. Now, if we imagine this sense of the Almighty Design to be *harmonized* in a measurable degree; if we suppose a landscape whose combined *strangeness,*[13] vastness, definitiveness, and magnificence, shall inspire the idea of culture, or care, or superintendence, on the part of intelligences superior yet akin to humanity — then the sentiment of *interest* is preserved, while the Art is made to assume the air of an intermediate or secondary Nature — a Nature which is not God, nor an emanation of God, but which still is Nature, in the sense that it is the handiwork of the angels that hover between man and God."[14]

It was in devoting his gigantic wealth to the practical embodiment of a vision such as this — in the free exercise in the open air, which resulted from personal direction of his plans — in the con-

f   are little *(A)*

tinuous and unceasing *object* which these plans afforded — in the high spirituality of the object itself — in the contempt of ambition which it enabled him more to feel than to affect[g] — and, lastly, it was in the companionship and sympathy of a devoted wife, that Ellison thought to find, *and found,* an exemption from the ordinary cares of Humanity, with a far greater amount of positive happiness than ever glowed in the rapt day-dreams of De Staël.[h] [15]

NOTES

Motto: The stanza is the forty-second of "Christ's Victorie on Earth" (1610), by Giles Fletcher the younger (1588?–1623). The lines quoted are in the selection from Fletcher in Samuel Carter Hall's *Book of Gems* (1836), p. 153. Poe reviewed Hall's book in the *Southern Literary Messenger* for August 1836. The same stanza is one of four quoted in the article "American Landscape Gardening," *Arcturus,* June 1841, p. 37.

1. Ellison is an obvious modification of Thellusson — see Poe's footnote — probably influenced by the name of John Allan's partner, Charles Ellis.

2. These authors are named by a "human perfectibility man" in "Lionizing," and are called writers of "eloquent madness" in Poe's review of Alexander Dimitry's *Lecture on the Study of History, applied to the Progress of Civilization,* in *Burton's,* July 1839. They are Anne-Robert-Jacques Turgot, French philosopher and statesman; Richard Price, an English preacher; Joseph Priestley, English liberal and chemist, who came to America; and Marie-Jean Caritat, Marquis de Condorcet, mathematician and philosopher.

3. See "Marginalia," number 247 (*SLM,* June 1849, p. 337), on a "*very* far superior" mind as a handicap to its possessor.

4. Poe's principles, or conditions, for happiness sound very like the ideals of a Southern aristocratic gentleman, with the exception perhaps of the dedication implied in having an "object of unceasing pursuit." On contempt of ambition, see his letter to J. R. Lowell, July 2, 1844; but Poe on other occasions admitted his inability to despise fame; see his assertion, "to be excelled where there exists a sense of the power to excel is unendurable" ("Marginalia," Number 187, *Graham's,* December 1846, p. 313), and Woodberry, *Life,* II, 437, quoting Mrs. Gove Nichols, "Reminiscences of Edgar Poe," *Sixpenny Magazine,* February 1863.

5. Poe, as he states in his note, follows the *Tour* (chapter 22). The will of Peter Thellusson (1737–1797) was declared valid by Baron Loughborough in 1799, but in 1800 an Act of Parliament (39–40 George III, c. 98) prohibited similar trusts in the future. At the time of settlement, by decision of the House of Lords, the accumulated sum was found to be far less than the estimated nine-

---

g effect *(A)*
h Stäel. *(A, B);* Stäel. *(C)*

teen (not ninety) million pounds. For a description of the will and an account of the settlement see, respectively, *Annual Register,* chronicle section, for 1797 (pp. 148–149) and for 1859, chronicle: law cases, pp. 333–340. See also the article "Thellusson Act" in *Chambers's Encyclopedia* (1872).

6. The hero of "The Assignation," in collecting pictures for his apartment, showed "little deference to the opinions of Virtu."

7. With the two preceding sentences compare "Marginalia," number 187 (cited in n. 4 above): "Indeed I cannot help thinking that the *greatest* intellects (since these most clearly perceive the laughable absurdity of human ambition) remain contentedly 'mute and inglorious.' " See Gray's *Elegy* for "mute inglorious" Miltons.

8. The artist is Claude Lorrain (Gelée), French landscape painter of the seventeenth century. In the earliest version of the story Poe also named another French landscapist, Nicolas Poussin (1594–1665), and the British William Clarkson Stanfield (1793–1867). The last was also mentioned in "Philosophy of Furniture."

9. The lines are slightly misquoted from Byron's *Don Juan,* II, cxviii, 7–8. "I've seen much finer women, ripe and real," is Byron's line 7.

10. The long quotation following is from *Arcturus,* June 1841, p. 36.

11. "Capability Brown" (Lancelot Brown, 1716–1783), English landscape gardener and architect, nicknamed for his habit of appraising the "capabilities" of territories he was engaged to improve, is mentioned in the *Arcturus* review on p. 39.

12. The disparagement of the *Odyssey* is in keeping with Poe's dislike of all epics. For a longer list of pieces he thought wholly poetical, see his review "Drake-Halleck" (*SLM,* April 1836). One wonders if Poe would have been so enthusiastic about Aeschylus, had he tried to read the original.

13. Poe often insists that beauty must have "some strangeness in its proportion." See "Ligeia" at note 4.

14. Compare the "Mystery of Marie Rogêt," near the end, where Poe said: "That Nature and its God are two, no man who thinks, will deny. That the latter, creating the former, can, at will, control or modify it, is also unquestionable."

15. Anne Louise Germaine Necker (1766–1817), daughter of the great French minister of finance, best known as Madame de Staël, celebrated writer and outstanding theorist of European Romanticism, was named by Poe along with other writers on human perfectibility in the story and review referred to in note 2 above.

University of Illinois Press
1325 South Oak Street
Champaign, IL 61820-6903
WWW.PRESS.UILLINOIS.EDU